# THE HISTORY OF
# THE DUKE OF WELLINGTON'S REGIMENT
# (WEST RIDING)

## 1702 – 1992

© The Duke of Wellington's Regiment (West Riding)
Maps originated by Major A C S Savory and drawn for reproduction by Mr Ken Wingad of Oerlikon Logistics Limited.

ISBN 0 9521552 0 6

Typeset by Highlight Type Bureau Ltd, Shipley
Printed by Amadeus Press Ltd, Huddersfield

# THE HISTORY OF
# THE DUKE OF WELLINGTON'S REGIMENT
# (WEST RIDING)

# 1702 – 1992

*J M Brereton and A C S Savory*

The Duke of Wellington's Regiment (West Riding)
Wellesley Park
Halifax
1993

Brigadier His Grace The Duke of Wellington KG LVO OBE MC BA DL
Colonel-in-Chief The Duke of Wellington's Regiment (West Riding)

# FOREWORD

*by*

Brigadier His Grace The Duke of Wellington
KG LVO OBE MC BA DL

STRATFIELD SAYE HOUSE
BASINGSTOKE
HAMPSHIRE RG27 0AS

BASINGSTOKE (0256) 882218

In 1974 Her Majesty The Queen appointed me Colonel-in-Chief of the Duke of Wellington's Regiment (West Riding), thus reinforcing the strong link that existed between Arthur Wellesley, 1st Duke of Wellington, and the 33rd Regiment. Two hundred years ago, in April 1793, he joined the 33rd as a major. He remained closely associated with it for the next twenty years, first as its commanding officer and later as colonel.

I take great pride in the fact that I am still closely linked with my ancestor's Regiment and that I am the only Colonel-in-Chief in the British Army who is not a member of the Royal Family.

The Duke of Wellington's Regiment (West Riding) was formed in 1881 with the amalgamation of the 33rd (or Duke of Wellington's) Regiment, which had been raised in 1702, and the 76th Regiment, raised in 1787. Notwithstanding the many changes that have taken place in the army since then, the Regiment retains its title and with it its reputation for unobtrusive excellence.

This new history records the long and distinguished services the Regiment has given to the country in many parts of the world. It makes stimulating reading and will, I am sure, be of great interest not only to members of the Regiment but also to the general reader.

Colonel-in-Chief

# CONTENTS

Foreword by Brigadier His Grace The Duke of Wellington KG LVO OBE MC BA DL (v)
Contents (vi)
List of maps (vii)
Campaigns, battles and battle honours (viii)
Introduction (ix)
Acknowledgements (x)

| CHAPTER | | INCLUDES | |
|---|---|---|---|
| 1. | 1702 | The Raising of the 33rd Regiment | 1 |
| 2. | 1702-1714 | The War of the Spanish Succession | 12 |
| 3. | 1715-1748 | The War of the Austrian Succession | 25 |
| 4 | 1749-1763 | The Seven Years War | 39 |
| 5. | 1764-1792 | The American War of Independence | 54 |
| 6. | 1787-1800 | The Raising of the 76th Regiment and the 3rd Mysore War | 76 |
| 7. | 1793-1813 | Arthur Wellesley and the 33rd Regiment | 90 |
| 8. | 1801-1807 | Gerard Lake and the 76th Regiment | 110 |
| 9. | 1808-1814 | The 76th in Spain, Walcheren and North America | 126 |
| 10. | 1812-1853 | The Waterloo Campaign | 138 |
| 11. | 1854-1856 | The Crimean War | 159 |
| 12. | 1857-1881 | The Indian Mutiny and the Abyssinia Campaign | 179 |
| 13. | 1815-1881 | "Pax Britannica". The 76th Regiment from 1815-1881 | 196 |
| 14. | 1881-1899 | Amalgamation: The Duke of Wellington's Regiment | 201 |
| 15. | 1899-1913 | The Boer War | 214 |
| 16. | 1913-1918 | The First World War | 232 |
| 17. | 1919-1939 | Between the Wars | 262 |
| 18. | 1939-1947 | The Second World War | 279 |
| 19. | 1948-1970 | Rationalisation, Reductions and Reorganisations | 323 |
| 20. | 1951-1955 | The Korean War | 328 |
| 21. | 1956-1970 | The End of the Empire | 340 |
| 22. | 1970-1992 | Keeping the Peace and Training for War. | 350 |
| 23. | | Epilogue | 364 |

**APPENDICES**
1.  The Colours 365
2.  Succession of Colonels of the Regiment 374
3.  Succession of Lieutenant Colonels 389
4.  The Victoria Cross and George Cross 393
5.  Militia, Volunteer, Territorial and Cadet Forces 402
6.  Music of the Regiment 412
7.  Three Previous Regiments numbered 76 418
8.  Rugby in the Regiment 421
9.  Regimental Chapels, Museum, Journal and Alliances 427
10. The Old Comrades 430

**BIBLIOGRAPHY** 433
**INDEX** 436

# LIST OF MAPS

| | | |
|---|---|---|
| 1. | Netherlands 1702 – 1703 | 13 |
| 2. | Spain and Portugal 1704 – 1710 | 19 |
| 3. | Netherlands 1742 – 1748 | 32 |
| 4. | Battle of Dettingen 27 June 1743 | 29 |
| 5. | Operations against the French coast 1758 | 42 |
| 6. | Western Germany 1760 – 1763 | 46 |
| 7. | Campaigns in New Jersey and Pennsylvania 1776 – 1779 | 62 |
| 8. | Campaigns in the Carolinas 1780 – 1781 | 66 |
| 9. | Battle of Guilford Court House 15 March 1781 | 68 |
| 10. | Mysore 1791 and 1792 | 85 |
| 11. | Netherlands 1794 – 1795 | 92 |
| 12. | Seringapatam 4 May 1799 | 100 |
| 13. | The war against the Mahrattas in Hindoostan 1803 – 1805 | 116 |
| 14. | Aligarh 4 September 1803 | 112 |
| 15. | Walcheren campaign 1809 | 129 |
| 16. | Northern Spain, Corunna 1809 and Nive 1813 | 132 |
| 17. | The American war 1812 – 1814 | 135 |
| 18. | Ligny and Quatre Bras 16 – 18 June 1815 | 146 |
| 19. | Battle of Waterloo 18 June 1815 | 150 |
| 20. | The Crimean war 1854 – 1856 | 161 |
| 21. | Battle of the Alma 20 September 1854 | 164 |
| 22. | Indian Mutiny 1857 – 1859 | 180 |
| 23. | Abyssinia Expedition 1867 – 1868 | 183 |
| 24. | The Boer War 1899 – 1902 | 215 |
| 25. | The relief of Kimberley 15 February 1900 | 217 |
| 26. | Battle of Paardeberg 18 – 27 February 1900 | 220 |
| 27. | Western Front 1914 – 1918 | 234 |
| 28. | Gallipoli campaign 1915 | 256 |
| 29. | Italian campaign 1918 | 259 |
| 30. | North West India: 3rd Afghan war 1919. Loe Agra and Mohmand 1935 | 263 |
| 31. | North West Europe 1940 and 1944 – 1945 | 285 |
| 32. | North Africa 1943 | 292 |
| 33. | Italy 1944 | 297 |
| 34. | Burma 1942 | 308 |
| 25. | Burma 1944 | 313 |
| 36. | Korean war 1950-1953 | 330 |
| 37. | Cyprus 1957, 1967 and 1975 | 341 |
| 38. | Northern Ireland 1957–1989 | 351 |
| 39. | The Regimental area | 403 |

# CAMPAIGNS, BATTLES AND BATTLE HONOURS
*Names in capital letters are battle honours and are emblazoned on the Regimental Colour.*

*War of Spanish Succession (1702-1713):* Venloo, Ruremonde, Liège, Huy, Valencia de Alcantara, Alcantara, Almanza, Saragossa, Brihuega.
*War of Austrian Succession (1742-1748):* DETTINGEN, Fontenoy, Rocoux, Lauffeld,
*Seven Years war (1756-1763):* St Malo, St Cast, Warburg, Kloster Kamp, Vellinghausen, Wilhelmsthal.
*War of American Independence (1775-1783):* Brooklyn Heights, White Plains, Fort Washington, Brandywine, Germantown, Freehold, Verplanks, Charleston, Camden, Guilford Court House, Yorktown.
*3rd Mysore war (1789-1792):* Bangalore, Arikera, Seringapatam, MYSORE
*Netherlands campaign (1793-1795):* Bostkel, Geldermalsen
*West Indies (1794-1796):*
*4th Mysore war (1799):* Mallavelly, SERINGAPATAM
*1st and 2nd Mahratta wars (1803-1806):* ALLY GHUR, DELHI 1803, LESWAREE, DEIG, Bhurtpore
*Peninsular war (1808-1814):* CORUNNA, Nivelle, NIVE, PENINSULAR
*Walcheren campaign (1809)*
*Mauritius and Ile de Bourbon (1810)*
*2nd American war (1812-1814):* Plattsburg
*Holland (1813-1814):* Merxem, Bergen-op-Zoom
*Waterloo campaign (1815):* Quatre Bras, WATERLOO
*Crimean war (1854-1856):* ALMA, INKERMAN, SEVASTAPOL
*Indian Mutiny (1857-1858)*
*Abyssinia campaign (1867-1868):* Magdala, ABYSSINIA
*Rhodesia (1893 and 1896):* Matabeleland (1893): Mashonaland (1896)
*Boer war (1899-1902):* RELIEF OF KIMBERLEY, PAARDEBERG, Rhenoster Kop, SOUTH AFRICA 1900-02
*The First World war (1914-1918):* Of the following 72 battle honours the ten shown in capital letters are emblazoned on the Queen's Colour:
MONS, Le Cateau, Retreat from Mons, MARNE 1914, 18, Aisne 1914, La Bassee 1914, YPRES 1914, 15, 17, Nonne Bosschen, HILL 60, Gravenstafel, St Julien, Aubers, SOMME 1916, 18, Albert 1916, 18, Bazentin, Delville Wood, Pozieres, Flers-Courcelette, Morval Thiepval, Le Transloy, Ancre Heights, ARRAS 1917, 18, Scarpe 1917, 18, Arleux, Bullecourt, Messines 1917, 18, Langemarck 1917, Menin Road, Polygon Wood, Broodseinde, Poelcappelle, Passchendaele, CAMBRAI 1917, 18, St Quentin, Ancre 1918, LYS, Estaires, Hazebrouck, Bailleul, Kemmel, Bethune, Scherpenberg, Tardenois, Amiens, Bapaume 1918, Drocourt-Queant, Hindenburg Line, Havrincourt, Epehy, Canal du Nord, Selle, Valenciennes, Sambre, France and Flanders 1914-18, PIAVE, Vittorio Veneto, Italy 1917-18, Suvla, LANDING AT SUVLA, Scimitar Hill, Gallipoli 1915, Egypt 1916
*3rd Afghan war (1919):* Spin Baldak, AFGHANISTAN 1919
*North west frontier of India (1935):* Loe Agra, Mohmand
*The Second World war (1939-1945):* Of the following 23 battle honours the ten shown in capital letters are emblazoned on the Queen's Colour.
DUNKIRK 1940, ST VALERY-EN-CAUX, Tilly sur Seulles, Odon, FONTENY LE PESNIL, NORTH WEST EUROPE 1940, 44-45, Banana Ridge, Medjez Plain, Gueriat el Atach Ridge, DJEBEL BOU AOUKAZ 1943, Tunis, North Africa 1943, ANZIO, Campoleone, Rome, MONTE CECO, Italy 1943-45, SITTANG 1942, Paungde, Kohima, CHINDITS 1944, BURMA 1942-44
*Korean war (1950-1953):* THE HOOK 1953, KOREA 1952-53
*Cyprus (1956-1957)*

# INTRODUCTION

*by*

## Brigadier W R Mundell OBE
## Colonel of the Regiment

This new history of the Regiment was conceived in 1987 when the then Colonel of the Regiment, General Sir Charles Huxtable KCB CBE, on the advice of the Regimental Council, decided that it was time to produce a comprehensive history of the Regiment. Of the four previous histories only one, that covering the period 1919-1952, was still in print. The overseeing of the production of the history was delegated to a sub-committee of the Council, consisting of Major General D E Isles CB OBE DL (Colonel of the Regiment from 1975-1982), Lieutenant Colonel W Robins OBE (Regimental Secretary) and Major A C S Savory MBE (Editor of the Iron Duke). Major John Brereton wrote the text, which was then added to and edited by Major Tony Savory, taking full advantage of his extensive knowledge of the Regiment's history.

The Regiment, while operating very much in the present, has before it constant reminders of its past in the form of battle honours emblazoned on the colours and drums and in items of dress such as cap and collar badges. All these distinctions have been hard won, but if they are not to be anything more than meaningless mementos of days long gone by it is vital that members of the Regiment should be aware of how and when they were gained. This new history not only fulfils that role, but also emphasises the Regiment's long and enduring links with the West Riding of Yorkshire. I have no hesitation in commending it to all who have served, are serving and will serve in the Regiment in the future. I am confident they will read it with enjoyment and justifiable pride.

I am greatly indebted to the authors for producing this excellent and comprehensive history of the Dukes.

W R Mundell

# ACKNOWLEDGEMENTS

The authors and the publishers wish to thank the following for giving their permission to reproduce copyright illustrations.


The Director, National Army Museum, London. Pages 14, 21, 30, 48, 61, 71, 97, 102, 130, 149, 166 and 187.
Imperial War Museum, London. Pages 239, 253, 280, 282, 295, 296, 319 (lower), 335 and 337.
The British Museum. Page 79.
National Portrait Gallery, London. Page 17.
Anne S K Brown Military Collection, Brown University, Rhode Island, USA. Page 94.
Mr Stuart Barr. Page 240.
Stamp Publicity (Worthing) Ltd. Page 8.
Fotomas Index Library. (Worthing). Page 35.

CHAPTER 1

# The Raising of the 33rd Regiment

*"It was an act of criminal imbecility, the most mischievous work of the most mischievous Parliament that ever sat at Westminster"*, wrote Sir John Fortescue, historian of the British Army, castigating the drastic reduction of the army after the Treaty of Ryswick in 1697. This treaty, concluded by King William III, saw Louis XIV and his Catholic allies curbed in their ambitions for a Catholic-dominated Europe. King William, anticipating a call for a reduction in the strength of the army, disbanded ten regiments. But it was not enough for those who raised the old populist cry of *no standing army*. In December 1697, on the motion of Robert Harley, the House of Commons resolved that all forces raised since 1680 should be disbanded. The House thereby wreaked more destruction on the army than had been wrought by King William's enemies. However, one year later, after heated debate, the establishment was agreed at the inadequate figure of 7,000 horse and foot for England, 12,000 for Ireland and some 6,000 in Scotland. Furthermore, the House also declined to renew the Mutiny Act, with the result that the officers had no means of enforcing discipline. King William was so deeply chagrined that he was only with difficulty dissuaded from abdicating.

The peace of Ryswick proved a fragile one. The treaty between William III of England and Louis XIV of France had provided that on the death of the Habsburg King of Spain, Charles II, his possessions should pass to the Archduke Charles of Austria. But when Charles died in 1700, William and his Protestant allies were dismayed to find that the monarch had willed all his dominions to the young grandson of Louis XIV, Philip of Anjou. In direct contravention of the treaty terms, Louis lost no time in accepting his grandson as King Philip V of Spain, thereby uniting the two countries into a formidable Catholic empire and completely upsetting the balance of power in Europe. He was confident that the war-weary Dutch and English would no longer seek to defy him.

All this was gall enough to the English, but insult was added to injury when the deposed King James II died in exile at St Germains in 1701. Louis now proclaimed his son, James Francis Edward (The Old Pretender) as James III, rightful King of England. That was more than William and his Parliament could stomach, and although actual hostilities did not commence until May 1702 (when William was dead), the War of the Spanish Succession was set in train.

With war again inevitable, Parliament hastily set about making good the damage it had inflicted on the army after Ryswick: existing units were augmented and, between June 1701 and March 1702, fifteen new regiments were created, nine of them classed as foot, the remainder as marines.

As was the custom, the honour (and expense) of raising a regiment was delegated by the King to *"trustie and well-beloved"* members of the aristocracy or the landed gentry whose loyalty (and purses) could be relied upon.

And so on 12 February 1702, George Hastings, 8th Earl of Huntingdon, was granted a commission as colonel, and in March was commanded as follows:

> ANNE R. [a]
>
> These are to authorise you by Beat of Drumme or otherwise, to raise Voluntiers for a regiment of Foot under your command, which is to consist of twelve Companys of two Serjeants, Three Corporals, Two Drummers and Fifty-nine private soldiers, with the addition of one Serjeant more to the Company of Grenadiers. And as you shall raise the said Voluntiers you are to give notice thereof to Our Commissary General of the Musters, in order that they may be mustered according to our directions in that behalf. And when the whole number of non-commission officers and soldiers shall be fully or near completed, they are to march to our city of Gloucester, appointed for the rendezvous of the said regiment. And you are to order such person or persons as you think fit to receive Arms for our said regiment out of the Stores of our Ordnance. And all Magistrates, Justices of the Peace, Constables and other of our Officers, whom it may concern, are to be assisting to you in providing Quarters and otherwise as there shall be occasion.
>
> Given at Our Court of St James' this 14th day of March 1702 in the first year of Our Reign.
>
> To our Trustie and Well-beloved The Earl of Huntingdon, Coll. of One of Our Regiments of Foot

It is not possible to be precise about the recruiting area of the Earl of Huntingdon's

---

[a] King William had died on 8 March after a riding accident.

Regiment, but apart from the fact that Gloucester was the location of the first muster, and therefore might be classified as the birthplace of the Regiment, it seems likely that most of the soldiers came from Gloucestershire and adjacent counties.

In the absence of complete muster rolls for the period, there is little to go on as regards the rank-and-file, but a detailed list of the officers is preserved in the Public Record Office.

**A List of Officers in the Ea: of Huntingdons Regiment of Foot, dated the 10th of March 1701/2, Except the Field Officers Commissions that were signed by the late King the 12th of Feby before.**

| **Captains** | **Lieutenants** | **Ensigns** |
|---|---|---|
| Geo: Ea: of Huntingdon | Capt Lt Jos. Dolling | Richd. Cooke |
| Lt Coll Robt Duncanson | Oliver Wheeler | Hump: Brown |
| Majr. John Rose | Thurston Haddock | Theo: Nicholls |
| Abra. Delivron | Tho: Collom | Saml. Hutchison |
| Jno. Harnage | Tho: Wilson | Jno. Powell |
| Giles Erie | Jno. Bland | Ja: Dejoy |
| Hen: Blount | Jno. Bresbin | Tho: Edwards |
| Phil. Honywood | Jno. Hauteclaire | Noah Webb |
| Hen: Killegrew | Rene Deguan | Ja: Mercer |
| Jno. La Tour | Alexr. Mackram | Richd. Stroughill |
| Jno. Van Brook | Jno. Owen | Jno. Harris |

Oliver Harcourt Granadr. (Coy)      Jno. Baraton 1st Lieut
                                    Jno. Grace  2nd Lieut

Staff Officers
Tho: Colom (sic.)   Adjt
Wm. Chiswick        Qr. Mr.

No surgeon or chaplain is shown. They were appointed on 1 May 1702, one Hosea Figuel being the surgeon, and Robert Doiley the chaplain. These functionaries, although quartered with the officers, were not commissioned and were usually appointed by the colonel.

In keeping with 18th century practices, the curious date "..1701/2" was the result of the new style or Gregorian Calendar adopted by most European countries before 1700, there being a difference of eleven days between that and the old style.

The apparently illogical designation of the three field officers (colonel, lieutenant-colonel and major) as captains was due to the contemporary system whereby these officers were theoretically company commanders (or captains) in addition to their other duties. They did very nicely out of this, for not only did they receive pay of rank, but also pay as company commanders, which were actually commanded by 'de facto' captains. He who had the honour of commanding the colonel's company was distinguished by the rank of captain-lieutenant.

The 18th-century colonel was a very different personage from the modern colonel of the Regiment who is very often a retired general officer, his appointment purely honorary. In 1702, and for several decades afterwards, the colonel was the actual commanding officer, responsible for all the duties of clothing, arming, pay and general administration of his command, including the leading of it on active service. The lieutenant colonel was the second-in-command, while the contemporary major had a particular responsibility for drill and worked closely with the adjutant.

The founding-colonel of the Regiment, George Hastings, or Lord Hastings, was born in 1677, eldest son of Theophilus, 7th Earl of Huntingdon, who owned extensive estates around Donington Park near Spalding, Lincolnshire.

Theophilus married twice, George being the son with his first wife who died in 1689. In his younger days George seems to have led a dissolute life. Having "*refused to stay at Eton*", young George was sent down from Oxford for associating with "*disreputable young women*". Having no wish to settle down at home and learn to manage the family estates he would inherit, the lad began to lead a life of indolence (and mounting debts) in London. In 1698, however, he obtained a captaincy in the 1st Foot Guards. Playboy or not, the 21 year old Captain of Guards dutifully served with his Regiment in King William's campaign in Flanders, and when the Duke of Portland was appointed ambassador in Paris, he took Lord George with him on his staff.

In 1701, Theophilus 7th Earl of Huntingdon died and Lord George succeeded as the 8th Earl. Now a wealthy, well-connected member of the aristocracy, it was not surprising that he should be selected as "*Colonel of One of Our Regiments of Foot*", the more so because "*King William thought well of the young man, who was greatly attached to his royal master*". Having inherited his father's estates, he was now well able to bear all the expense of kitting out his command.

Many of the founder members of the Regiment had already seen active service, and some were to become distinguished. Lieutenant Colonel Robert Duncanson, had acquired a questionable reputation for his part in the notorious massacre at

Robert Duncanson, Lieutenant Colonel 1702-1705.
Colonel, February to June 1705

Glencoe. In February 1692 King William directed that the Jacobite MacDonald faction at Glencoe should be brought to heel and it was Duncanson, then attached to the Duke of Argyll's Regiment, who ordered Captain Campbell of that regiment "*to fall upon the rebels and to put all to the sword under 70*". He later served in Flanders with Argyll's Regiment before going on half pay.

There was a useful body of experience among the other officers of the Regiment. Major John Rose had been captain in Colonel Douglas's Regiment and was wounded at the siege of Limerick during King William's Irish campaign. Captain Abraham Delivron was present with Colonel Seymour's Regiment at the siege of Namur (1695). Henry Killigrew had been known to Huntingdon as ensign in his company of 1st Foot Guards. Dolling and Wheeler had seen service in foot regiments, while Bland had been a lieutenant in the Scots Dragoons (later Scots Greys).

Of those who achieved later fame perhaps the most noteworthy was Captain John ("Jno") Van Brook. Born in 1664, the youth was later sent to study architecture in Paris – a task he evidently performed to good effect. He started his military service in 1686. His career in the 33rd was brief. By June 1702, he had been appointed Comptroller of the Board of Works in Whitehall. In 1707, John Van Brook formally changed his name, to become eventually Sir John Vanbrugh, architect of Blenheim Palace and other stately homes, and author of such risqué comedies as "*The Provok'd Wife*" and "*The Relapse*".

Captain Philip Honeywood became General Sir Philip Honeywood and successively Colonel of the 3rd Dragoons (Hussars) and 1st (King's) Dragoon Guards.

So much for the officers. With the rank and file the picture is shadowy and its details merely conjectural. It is, however, reasonably certain that the great majority of the men was a very motley bunch, if not perhaps what Fortescue describes as *the sweepings of the streets*. Almost entirely illiterate, coarse in their habits and foul-mouthed, these early soldiers were far removed from the traditional picture of the British redcoat. Although there would have been a leavening of men (including ex-NCOs perhaps) who had been cast adrift after the wholesale disbandments following the Treaty of Ryswick, most of them must have been raw youths unused to arms and to military discipline. Some may have been attracted by the government levy money, or bounty, which Parliament had recently increased from 40 shillings to three pounds, while the prospect of regular employment and pay was an undoubted inducement to enlist. The daily pay of a private of foot may have been only 8d, but it should be borne in mind that the average earnings of an unskilled labourer in the early 1700s were no more than about five shillings (25p) per week, out of which he had to find all living expenses for himself and any family. A sergeant of foot on 1s 6d per day and a corporal on 1s were theoretically well off.[b] But with numerous stoppages, authorised and unauthorised (depending on the colonel), the rank and file saw only fractions of their entitlements.

Since there was no conscription and sufficient volunteers were not forthcoming to augment the army, Parliament resorted to successive Recruiting Acts. In 1703 imprisoned convicts were authorised to be released if they undertook to enlist in the

---

(b) Rates of pay had been fixed by a Royal Warrant of James II in 1685, and remained unaltered for more than one hundred years. 1 shilling = 5p.

army. In March 1705, the contemporary chronicler, Narcissus Luttrell, recorded that *"about 350 pickpockets, housebreakers etc. .... got to be soldiers in the guards, the better to hide their roguery"*. An earlier Act of 1704 enabled all insolvent debtors in prison to be discharged if they agreed to enlist. The type of recruits willed on the regiments by government is made sadly clear by several historians and contemporary officers. *"Criminals were drafted in wholesale, and the debtors' prisons were emptied into the Army ... the Recruiting Acts were seized upon as a chance to rid the countryside of poachers and suspected persons ...."* A captain of horse in Marlborough's army described some of his latest recruits: *"Such a set of ruffians and imbeciles you never beheld, you may call them canon fodder, but never soldiers"*.

Although there are no contemporary comments on the Earl of Huntingdon's recruits of 1702, or subsequent drafts, there is no reason to believe that they were of superior quality. But the astonishing fact is that these same *ruffians and imbeciles* were soon transformed into the staunch, indomitable redcoats who earned for Marlborough and the British Army glory and renown throughout the Continent of Europe. This must speak volumes for the training and discipline that licked the new regiments into shape.

The binding force was discipline, and discipline was based on punishment. The soldier well knew that if he disobeyed an order, was insolent to his NCO, or was dirtily turned out on parade, he would suffer for it with the harsh penalties then in force. Although the infamous reign of the lash – barbaric flogging with the flesh-searing cat-o'-nine-tails – had not yet defamed the army, some of the punishments inflicted on the errant soldier were horrific. For *uttering blasphemy or profanity* his tongue was seared with a red-hot iron; insubordination or *disgraceful conduct* incurred the gauntlet: he was marched between ranks of his comrades who beat his naked back with stout canes; or he could be set astride the wooden horse – two planks joined lengthwise like an inverted 'v', with roundshot or other weights attached to his feet to ensure maximum pressure on his crutch. An even more fiendish device was the picquet. Here the offender was suspended by his wrists from a post with his bare feet just touching the sharp points of wooden stakes driven into the ground. The strain on his arms could only be relieved by the agony of punctured soles. All these perfectly legitimate means of correction were specified in the current Articles of War, which together with the Mutiny Act formed the basis of military discipline in Queen Anne's day.(c) The ultimate of capital punishment could be inflicted for no fewer than 25 offences, including not only murder, mutiny or cowardice in the face of the enemy, but also some crimes for which the death penalty now seems incredibly severe – such as *offering violence to a superior officer*, robbery and *hindering a Provost Marshal or his deputies in the performance of their duties*.

Thus subjected to a draconian code of discipline, the recruits of the Earl of Huntingdon's Regiment were taught the elements of their profession as soldiers. This was based on drill: drill in handling their muskets and pikes, drill in the complex movements and exercises with which a commander manoeuvred his company or battalion from line to column of route, to deploy into line again, to form square, to advance in column of platoons, and so forth. All this entailed no more than blind,

---

(c) The Articles of War were first promulgated in 1640. The Mutiny Act came into force in 1689 as a result of the mutiny of Colonel Dumbarton's Regiment (later Royal Scots).

automatic obedience to words of command. The prototypes of The Duke of Wellington's Regiment were not expected to display initiative (few of them could have done so, anyway); the era of thinking bayonets was far off.

The Regiment first paraded as such at Our City of Gloucester in March 1702. With 37 officers and twelve companies, it deployed about 830 all ranks. The chief offensive weapon was the musket. Prior to about 1701, all infantry battalions had from two to three companies of pikemen, who were considered the élite. But when Huntingdon's regiment was mustered, the cumbersome 18ft pike (weighing nearly 17lb) had become virtually obsolete, and it is unlikely that the Ordnance Department would have issued any to the new regiments. It so happened that Huntingdon's and others came into existence just in time to be armed with an improved type of firelock. Previously the foot soldier had been burdened with the primitive matchlock musket, weighing almost 13lb and requiring 44 separate motions to prime, load and ram, ignite with the slow match, and *give fire*. The fully-trained musketeer could achieve no more than one round per minute. Between about 1690 and 1703 this antique piece was replaced by the flintlock weapon, known as the William III musket, ancestor of the famous "Brown Bess". This was still heavy, weighing 12lb, but the advantages of the flint over the match were obvious, while another improvement was the introduction of pre-packaged cartridges of greased paper containing both ball and powder. The drill was for the soldier to bite off the top of the cartridge, retaining the ball in his mouth, then empty the powder down the muzzle and spit the ball after it. Using the paper to serve as a wad, he finally rammed down as before. All this resulted in only 26 motions instead of the 44 with the matchlock, and the maximum rate of fire was doubled to give two rounds a minute. Despite these improvements, however, the flintlock was not an accurate weapon, and its effective killing range was no more than about 100 yards. But this mattered little, for in Marlborough's day, and long thereafter, marksmanship was totally unnecessary. With the ranks bravely standing erect within less than a hundred yards of the enemy, all that was demanded was a succession of disciplined *firings* or volleys into the opposing mass. There was a rigid drill for this: a number of platoons would be ordered to deliver the first firing and while they were reloading, the platoons of the second firing would proceed, followed by the "third firing". Captain Robert Parker of the 18th Foot (Royal Irish) described this drill when his Regiment was in action with Marlborough:

> *"Colonel Kane .... having drawn us up and formed our platoons, advanced gently towards them, with the six platoons of our first fire made ready. When we had advanced within a hundred paces of them, they gave us a fire of one of their ranks: whereupon we halted and returned them the fire of our six platoons at once, and immediately made ready the six platoons of our second fire and advanced upon them again. They then gave us the fire of another rank and we returned them a second fire, which made them shrink .... on which we sent our third fire after them and saw them no more".*

While the musketeers of the battalion formed the main fire-power, the grenadier company – usually the 12th – was no less tactically important. Like the former pikemen, the grenadiers were hand-picked soldiers from the line companies, above average height, robust and of proven courage. Apart from setting an example of discipline and coolness in a linear fire-fight, they were expected to lead storming parties (or *forlorn hopes*), hurling their grenades and hacking through obstacles with their hatchets. In addition to grenades, carried in a leather pouch, the grenadier was armed with the musket which, unlike that of the line soldiers, was equipped with a sling so that it could be slung from the shoulder for grenade action. The grenade's fuse was ignited by a length of smouldering slow match wound around the grenadier's wrist.

All rank-and-file, except sergeants, had both bayonets and swords. Originally the former was the so-called 'plug' type, fitting directly into the muzzle so that the musket could not be fired with fixed bayonet. Around 1690 the socket bayonet was introduced, obviating this drawback. Even so, the advantage was dubious with muzzle-loading weapons, for it was almost impossible to reload with the bayonet fixed.

The foot-soldier's sword was shorter (usually about 26 inches) than the officer's and of course with plainer hilt. It was slung in a black leather scabbard from a buff waistbelt, with the bayonet in a frog alongside. Although the sword continued as part of the private soldier's weaponry until the 1760s, none of the contemporary drill and training manuals devote any attention to its use as an offensive weapon. It was probably regarded as a last resort if the man was deprived of his musket in a hand-to-hand encounter. At least there is evidence that it came in handy for chopping firewood in the field.

It is difficult to be precise about the spectacle presented by the Earl of Huntingdon's Regiment drawn up at Gloucester, kitted out in its first uniforms, as there is no contemporary description. Traditionally the British foot-soldier was a *redcoat*, but although red (or scarlet) had become the accepted colour for uniforms when Marlborough was leading his *scarlet caterpillar* on his famous march to the Danube in 1704, there were no sealed patterns at this date, and in 1702 such minutiae as colour, facings and embellishments were left very much to the whims of the colonels – who were entirely

Private sentinel, the Earl of Huntingdon's Regiment, 1702.

responsible for the provision of clothing, through the offices of a civilian agent, or contractor. During William III's reign several regiments, horse and foot, adopted blue out of deference to the King, whose own Dutch troops were thus clad. However, the Earl probably followed the more common preference for red.(d)

It is also reasonable to assume that he adopted the common style of dress then worn by all regiments of foot. This was the long, full-skirted coat reaching to the knees and buttoned up to the neck, round which a plain cravat or neck-cloth was tied. The head-dress was the cocked hat of felt, which is still worn by Chelsea Pensioners. The grenadier company, however, was distinguished by a mitre-shaped cap with no brim. This had been adopted when the musketeers' hat had been uncocked, and the wide brim would have hindered the motions of hurling grenades. Underneath the coat was a stout waistcoat which could be retained when the coat itself was doffed – e.g. for fatigues.

The lower limbs were clad in knee-breeches of coarse cloth (kersey), woollen stockings and square-toed shoes, or straights, so called because they were inter-changeable on either foot. More sensible ankle-boots did not appear until some fifty years later. Apart from the sword belt and cartridge pouch, the only other accoutrement was a canvas knapsack slung by a belt over the left shoulder. This sufficed for spare clothing and necessaries and any odd comforts that could be stuffed in – pipe, tobacco, flint-and-tinder.

A feature of the dress was the coloured lining of the coat, revealed in the turned-up cuffs and turned-back skirts on the march (also in the later lapels). This lining became known, rather illogically, as the *facings* the colour being left to the colonel's preference. But, as with other details, there is no evidence to show what colour the Earl of Huntingdon selected – or when the red facings were adopted.

The officers' dress was basically similar to the men's, though of finer material and embellished with a profusion of white or silver lace. Round his waist the officer wore a silk sash (incongruously termed a scarf). He was further distinguished by the small gorget plate of metal suspended from the neck. There were no badges of rank as such, and the field officer was recognizable from a captain or subaltern only by his greater richness of lace and embroidery. Officers carried no firearms, only their swords and a variety of half-pikes and spontoons according to rank. These latter were really little more than indications of rank rather than offensive weapons. Like the pike, they were cumbersome and impractical in a close-quarter fight, and it was always the sword that was regarded as the officer's true weapon.

The senior non-commissioned officers were the company sergeants (there were no warrant officers then), who were distinguished by the halberds they carried in place of the musket. Whether these were used offensively is not at all clear: probably the sergeant preferred his sword for in-fighting, like the officer.

During the 17th century, all foot regiments had presented a truly colourful appearance on parade, for in addition to gay uniforms each of the twelve companies

---

(d) It is often asserted that the *martial hue* of red was adopted because that was the colour of blood, and thus would serve to mask the gore of wounded soldiers. The true explanation is more mundane: it was found that the red dye used for the material was cheaper and easier to produce than other dyes.

bore its own distinctive flag or colour, the various devices on them being left to the whims of the colonel, which was usually some private badge or part of his coat of arms multiplied according to the seniority of the company. By 1702 regiments carried only two colours – the colonel's and the lieutenant-colonel's, which were later to become the King's (or Queen's) Colour and the Regimental Colour.

As Colonel, the 25-year old Earl of Huntingdon was saddled with responsibilities and authority far exceeding those of a later commanding officer or regimental colonel. Not only was he answerable for the discipline and training of his command (and expected to risk life and limb by leading it in the field), but the expenditure of government funds for equipping and clothing was left entirely to his own devices. The colonel was tacitly expected to make some profit out of all this – by bargaining with suppliers for uniforms and equipment. Some even indulged in nefarious practices such as appropriating some of their soldiers' pay by unauthorised stoppages. Fortescue records several instances of dishonest colonels being cashiered.[e]

The officers were not only gentlemen in every sense of the term, but men of some substance. And indeed they needed to be. For nearly two hundred years, the officer had to pay out considerable sums for his first commission and subsequent steps up the promotion ladder. In 1702, a young gentleman needed to put down £200 for the privilege of serving Queen and country as a humble ensign of foot; a captain paid £1000 for his company; a major aspiring to a lieutenant colonelcy would have to find about £2400. Although both Queen Anne and George I attempted to abolish the purchase system, their efforts were thwarted by the government which regarded the sale of a commission on retirement (to the highest bidder) as a convenient substitute for a pension out of the public purse.

Officers' rates of pay were scarcely sufficient to meet expenses. The rates, which had been laid down by a Royal Warrant of James II in 1685, were:

| | |
|---|---|
| Colonel | 12s per day rank, plus 8s per day as 'captain' of his company. |
| Lieutenant-Colonel | 7s rank, plus 8s for his company |
| Major | 5s, plus 8s as above |
| Captain | 8s |
| Lieutenant | 4s |
| Ensign | 3s |

(1s = 5p)

Out of these sums, officers had to find not only all their uniform and clothing (including replacements), their swords, their messing and any other living expenses, but numerous stoppages and deductions for the pockets of such Whitehall bureaucrats as the Paymaster-General, Commissary-General of Musters, government auditors, even the official who drew up and issued their commissions. In addition, all ranks were required to donate one day's pay annually for the benefit of the Royal Hospital, Chelsea.

---

(e) The Earl of Huntingdon's father (the 7th Earl) had raised the 13th Foot (Somerset Light Infantry) in 1685. In 1688 he was cashiered for dressing his regiment in cast-off clothing.

The Regiment was designated by the name of its colonel, a practice in force throughout the army. It was ranked 33rd in the precedence table which King William III had first established in 1694. A regiment's position in the order of precedence was of importance since at the conclusion of a war it was always the most junior, or highest numbered, regiments that were the first to be disbanded. For that same reason senior officers were commonly promoted from the colonelcy of a high numbered regiment to one with a lower number, thereby securing their income.

On 1 May 1702, the Earl of Huntingdon was commanded to march his Regiment from billets in Gloucester, Tewkesbury and Ross ("on-Wye") to different places around London, there to await embarkation orders to join the Duke of Marlborough's army in the Netherlands.

CHAPTER 2

# The War of the Spanish Succession

*1702 Venloo, Ruremonde, Liège*
*1703 Huy*
*1705 Valencia de Alcantara*
*1706 Alcantara*
*1707 Almanza*
*1710 Saragossa, Brihuega*

On 4 May 1702 the Grand Alliance[a], including England, formally declared war on the France of Louis XIV and his Catholic empire. The resulting conflict, to become known as the War of the Spanish Succession, was to last nearly eleven years and was to see the Duke of Marlborough rise to fame.

In June the 33rd, now quartered around London, was warned for embarkation to join Marlborough's English contingent in the Netherlands. On 8 June an entry in the *State Papers (Domestic)* quotes an order for a convoy to sail immediately for Holland and to take the Earl of Huntingdon's regiment of Foot with them but, according to the *London Gazette*, it was not until 30 June that the convoy with the Earl of Huntingdon's regiment arrived at the Hague.

After disembarking, the 33rd endured a march of some 70 miles to rendezvous with Marlborough's command at Duckenberg near Nijmegen. The Captain General had arrived there on 2 July to open his first major campaign. He had under him 60,000 troops, of whom 12,000 were British, including 14 battalions of foot. His troubles began at once. Not only was he opposed by a roughly equal force of the enemy under the French Marshal Boufflers, but also by his obstructive, hidebound Dutch masters.[b] The States General at the Hague had resented his appointment as commander-in-chief and sent two Dutch deputies with him, whose duty it was to see that he did nothing imprudent. Three times they foiled his efforts to bring Boufflers to battle so that he was obliged to confine his campaigning to the reduction of the French fortresses on the Meuse. It was during these operations that the 33rd underwent its baptism of fire.

The first fortress to be besieged was that at Venloo where the 33rd was in a brigade

---
(a) This second Grand Alliance consisted of England, Holland, Austria and the Protestant states of Germany.
(b) Marlborough's celebrated march to the Danube, culminating in the victory of Blenheim, was achieved only by the ruse of concealing his real objective from the Hague.

commanded by Brigadier Frederick Hamilton, in which there were also the 8th (King's Liverpool), 13th (Somerset LI), 17th (Royal Leicestershire) and 18th (Royal Irish). The operation was commanded by Lieutenant General Lord Cutts, and the actual fortifications of Fort St Michael were stormed on 18 September 1702, after a softening up from the siege artillery. The storming party consisted of the élite grenadier companies of the five regiments in Brigadier Hamilton's brigade, together with a Dutch corps and a detachment of musketeers. The first objective was to form a lodgement on the top of the glacis, and as the grenadiers hurled their grenades and then stormed up with musket and bayonet, they were closely followed by several senior officers, including the Earl of Huntingdon. The covered way was carried sword and bayonet in hand, and after a few ineffectual volleys the enemy fled. Lord Cutts had ordered a relentless pursuit, *let the consequence be what it might*, and the remaining garrison was chased to a ravelin (outwork in a salient), from where a furious storm of musketry accounted for most of the British casualties. But further showers of grenades and a determined rush with the bayonet drove out the enemy. Fort St Michael was captured and the citadel of Venloo capitulated two days later – after an operation which had lasted 18 days. The British casualties were 136 all ranks killed and 161 wounded. There are no figures for the 33rd's losses.

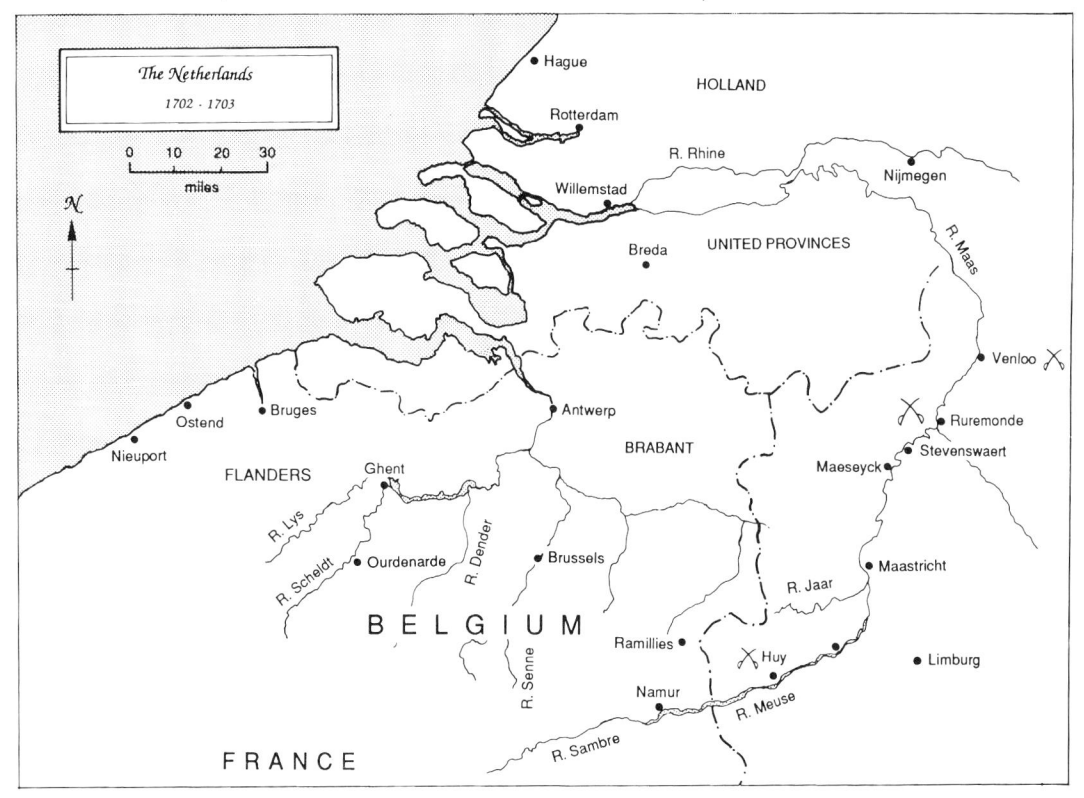

Marlborough's next success was the siege and capture of Ruremonde, some 12 miles south of Venloo, which was taken with the loss of only 60 men. Then followed the investment of the prize of Liège itself, which fell on 23 October "...*With a very inconsiderable loss on our side*", (wrote Captain Parker of the 18th), "*our men gave no quarter for some time so that the greater part of the garrison was cut to pieces*". The British casualties amounted to a total of 534. Although Brigadier Hamilton's brigade played a prominent part at both Ruremonde and Liège, there is no record of particular activities of the 33rd.

The victorious conclusion of Marlborough's first continental campaign, which had resulted in the whole line of the Meuse/Maas passing into the hands of the Allies, brought him the reward of a Dukedom from Queen Anne (and a pension of £5000 a year). But there was little reward for the soldiers who had gained the triumphs with him – only the privations of primitive quarters during the customary close season. Captain Parker relates that "*In a few days after the reduction of Liège, all the British troops were ordered back to Holland....*" And there the 33rd spent the winter, probably billeted around Breda which was the British assembly area for the subsequent operations.

*Siege of Huy, 1703*

The year 1703 saw little gains for the allies, largely owing to the Dutch generals who were occupied with quarrelling among themselves rather than with the French. Having been thwarted in his bold plan of carrying the war into the heart of Brabant, Marlborough could only resign himself to the Dutch mentality of siege warfare. In

*14*

August 1703 Brigadier Hamilton's brigade, which still included the 33rd, took part in the capture of the fortress at Huy on the Meuse. The newspaper *Post-man* reported that the approach march to Huy *"was the most difficult that ever was"*, and that *"heavy rains deluged the ground"* when the army was on the march to Limburg, which was captured in the following month.

By these dates the Regiment had ceased to be the Earl of Huntingdon's. In his entry for 13 February 1703, Narcissus Luttrell wrote *"Tis said the earl of Huntington (sic) will lay down his regiment in order to travel"*. On 2 March he added *"The Lord Huntington's regiment is given to Collonel Leigh"*. It seems odd that a commanding officer should throw up his command while on active service in order to travel, but in the early 18th century an officer was quite at liberty to resign (or sell) his commission whenever the spirit moved him, war or no. On 22 February 1705, at the early age of 28, died the founding Colonel of The Duke of Wellington's Regiment. There is a memorial to him, an ornate tablet, in the church of St James, Piccadilly, erected by his sister.

The second Colonel (or commanding officer) of the 33rd was Colonel Henry Leigh, a curiously shadowy figure. In his *English Army Lists and Commission Registers*, Charles Dalton cites him as Colonel in 1704, but there is no further reference and the index ignores him.

In December 1703 the Imperial contender for the Spanish crown, the Habsburg Archduke Charles of Austria, was received by Queen Anne at Windsor, and a month later it was arranged that the war in Spain should be promoted by the presence of the Archduke himself (or King Charles III as the Grand Alliance termed him), together with a force of British, Dutch and Portuguese. In view of the Archduke's reputation as a rather effete, vacillating youth, unpopular with the Spanish people, utterly ignorant of warfare and with no stomach for hazards, it is difficult to understand what advantage could have accrued from his presence.

The agreement with the Spanish and Portuguese required the despatch of 6,500 troops to the Peninsula, and these it was decided to withdraw from the *"best British regiments in the Low Countries"* (Fortescue). Among the two cavalry regiments and six infantry regiments[c] selected was the 33rd Foot, the only one of the regiments raised in 1702 that had, up to that date, seen service under Marlborough.

The British reinforcements from Holland landed at Lisbon in March 1704, by which time the 33rd had seen yet another change of Colonel (and title). On 11 January 1704 Luttrell noted *"Lieutenant Colonel Donkinson (sic - Duncanson) – has the regiment given him of collonel Lee (sic) deceased"*. How or where Colonel Leigh died is not known. Colonel Robert Duncanson had been the Lieutenant Colonel of the Regiment since the date it was raised.

At the opening of the Peninsula campaign of 1704 the allied force consisted of the 6,500 British troops and 4,000 Dutch, plus unpredictable support from the Portuguese army. In command of the British contingent was the Huguenot, General Meinhardt Schomberg, son of the gallant old Duke who had fought and died for William III at the

---

(c) The others were Harvey's Horse (2DG), Wentworth's Horse (1st Royals) 2nd, 9th, 11th, 13th and 17th Regiments.

Battle of the Boyne. The Dutch commander was Lieutenant General Francois Fagel, another veteran soldier. From the outset, things began to go awry. The Portuguese proved not only sullen and unco-operative, but tamely surrendered three of their frontier fortresses to the advancing French under the renowned Marshal the Duke of Berwick[d]. Furthermore, a clash of personalities arose between the two allied commanders, who, says Fortescue, *"quarrelled so bitterly that they went off, each with his own troops, in two different directions"*. Neither the 33rd nor the rest of the British contingent were given any opportunity to distinguish themselves in this sorry prelude to their campaigning. But elsewhere in Spain there was a boosting of British prestige when in July Admiral Sir George Rooke's fleet besieged and captured Gibraltar.

In July 1704 Schomberg was relieved of his command and replaced by the Earl of Galway, an officer of undoubted generalship and wide experience gained in Flanders and Ireland. Like Schomberg, he also was a Huguenot refugee, bearing the family name of Ruvigny. Thus arose the odd circumstance of the French forces being commanded by an Englishman (Berwick), and the allies by a Frenchman.

Galway's land operations did not get under way until the following year when in May 1705 he captured the fortified city of Valencia de Alcantara on the Portuguese-Spanish frontier[e]. The siege began on 2 May and six days later the storming party went in. Heading it were the grenadiers of the 33rd and 17th, together with some Dutch and Portuguese battalions, who met fierce resistance and were forced to halt and take cover. The Portuguese then preferred discretion to valour, but *"Duncanson's (33rd) advancing most bravely and with Colours flying"*, pushed forward and entered the breach, driving the defenders into the castle. *"..Our men, with sword in hand, would have entered pell-mell, had not the enemy immediately held out the white flag and surrendered at discretion"*. (London Gazette 28 May 1705). Fortescue wrote *"It is somewhat singular that the first regiment which signally distinguished itself in this first Peninsular War was the 33rd (Duke of Wellington's) which covered itself with honour at the storm of Valenza"*. Dalton adds that *"Colonel Robert Duncanson fell mortally wounded at the head of his Regiment (33rd Foot) fighting in the deadly breach"*. No records have survived of other casualties. After the capture of the weak fortresses at Albuquerque and Badajoz the campaign came to an end.

The replacement for Duncanson was to become one of the most distinguished field marshals of the British Army, though at the time of his appointment to the vacancy he was relatively unknown. Colonel George Wade started his service in 1690 as a 17 year old ensign in the Earl of Bath's Regiment (10th, Lincolnshire). By 1702 he was captain commanding the grenadier company, and as such was heavily engaged in Marlborough's sieges – Kaisersworth, Venloo, Ruremonde, Liège, Huy. In October 1703 he was given a brevet lieutenant colonelcy in Colonel Blood's Regiment (later 17th, Leicestershire). In January 1704 Wade was serving with the expeditionary force sent to Portugal. When the Earl of Galway assumed command of the British contingent he was quick to discern

---

(d) The allies' chief adversary throughout the Spanish campaign, the Duke was a natural son of James II, born James Fitzjames.
(e) In the literature there is some confusion over nomenclature. Fortescue wrongly writes "Valenza", which is a totally different city; some accounts have Valencia, while Luttrell refers to "Alcantara".

Wade's potential, promoting him colonel on his staff.

Since Colonel Wade served in this capacity for the remainder of the campaign it is improbable that the 33rd, or Wade's Regiment as it had now become, could have seen much of their titular commander, involved as he was with his demanding staff duties at Galway's Headquarters. The de facto command of the Regiment must have fallen to the lieutenant colonel, probably Philip Honeywood who, it is recorded, was rewarded with the lieutenant colonelcy of his regiment for his conduct during Galway's campaign.

Galway's plans for the 1706 campaign were directed towards the capture of Madrid in conjunction with the Earl of Peterborough, who after landing at Valencia (on the east coast), had taken Barcelona and was marching to join forces. The total strength of Galway's army now amounted to some 19,000 horse and foot of which only 3,000 were British. In addition to the 33rd the latter included Harvey's Horse (2nd Dragoon Guards) and the 2nd (The Queen's), 9th (Norfolk), 17th (Leicestershire), together with Colonel Brudenell's Foot (subsequently disbanded). Owing to a prevalence of dysentery and other enteric afflictions, few regiments were up to strength.

Field Marshal George Wade, Colonel 1705-1717

The advance into Spain commenced with Galway making for the strategic fortress of Alcantara, on the River Tagus.(f) The siege opened on 10 April and after stout resistance the French garrison surrendered four days later. Dalton records that *"the Regiments now known as the 17th and 33rd Foot gained distinction in this siege"*. At home the capture of Alcantara was hailed as a splendid victory, Luttrell noting that *"the garrison of 4,000 foot and 300 horse (all newly cloath'd and arm'd) were made prisoners of war"*. The spoil included 64 guns, 5,000 muskets, huge quantities of ammunition and *"provisions for 15,000 men for 60 days"*. The losses of the 17th and 33rd amounted to 50 killed and wounded, Colonel Wade being among the latter.

Galway continued his advance and place after place fell into his hands. However the reluctant Portuguese, after much persuasion, only agreed to go as far as Almaraz. Meanwhile Berwick continued to retreat until, finding himself in a strong position

---

(f) Not to be confused with Valencia de Alcantara only some 20 miles south.

behind a river, he determined to make a stand. The official despatch says: "*the attack commenced by artillery; the infantry, after wading the river, carried the hostile entrenchments with great spirit and routed Berwick in confusion*". Despite this victory the Portuguese were loath to advance further beyond their frontier. As a compromise Ciudad Rodrigo was besieged and after its capture on 22 May the obdurate Portuguese were persuaded by direct orders from Lisbon to act in concert with Galway. He then continued his daring march. Salamanca fell on 3 June and on the 27th, after a three months' campaign, Madrid was entered, whereupon the Archduke Charles was proclaimed King of Spain. It was a bloodless victory: King Philip was no soldier and had hastily evacuated, having "*burnt and destroyed all the rich hangings, pictures and other things of value which he could not carry away, besides hamstringing the horses to make them unserviceable*", as Luttrell recorded. With the proclamation of Charles III as King the object of the war seemed to have been fulfilled. However, by the time Charles, who was with Peterborough, joined Galway on 6 August the situation had materially changed. First the whole of the country through which Galway had marched rose in revolt against the new King. At the same time the Bourbon forces had been reinforced and were now twice that of the allies. Galway therefore decided to retreat east to Valencia, which he successfully accomplished in September. As Fortescue commented "*so closed the year 1706, memorable for two of the most brilliant, even if in some respects disappointing, campaigns ever fought simultaneously by two English generals*". Another distinguished historian (C T Atkinson) wrote about the same campaign, "*This exploit (Galway's march to Madrid) like Peterborough's success at Barcelona and in Valencia might well be recorded on the Colours of the regiments involved*".

A Council of War was held at the end of 1706 to decide on the campaign strategy for the following year. Peterborough was for coming to grips with Berwick around Madrid, but was over-ruled by the timid Charles, whereupon he betook himself off to Italy, ostensibly to raise a loan for the army, as Fortescue has it. At the same time Charles withdrew the whole of his Spanish troops to Catalonia. In January 1707 Galway was reinforced by some 6,000 men. They had originally been destined to make a landing on the French coast, near Bordeaux, then had been diverted to Cadiz and were finally sent to join Galway after the fleet carrying them had been dispersed by a storm in the Bay of Biscay. But even these reinforcements brought Galway's total strength to no more than 15,000 with which to confront the 24,000 odd of the Duke of Berwick's army. Nevertheless he was not to be deterred by disparity in numbers: boldy, he resolved to march again on Madrid.

Having performed a wide flanking movement north from Valencia, without being able to bring Berwick to a fight, Galway learned in April (1707) that Berwick's main force was advancing towards the small town of Almanza where, said two French deserters, he would be joined by a strong contingent under the Duke of Orleans. Almanza lay some 70 miles north-east of Burgos and just south of the great mountain range of the Cordillera Cantabrica. Though walled like most Spanish towns, it was not fortified. On 25 April the opponents came to grips. Berwick and Orleans were drawn up on level ground just south of the town, infantry in the centre, cavalry on the flanks.

*The War in Spain and Portugal 1704 - 1710*

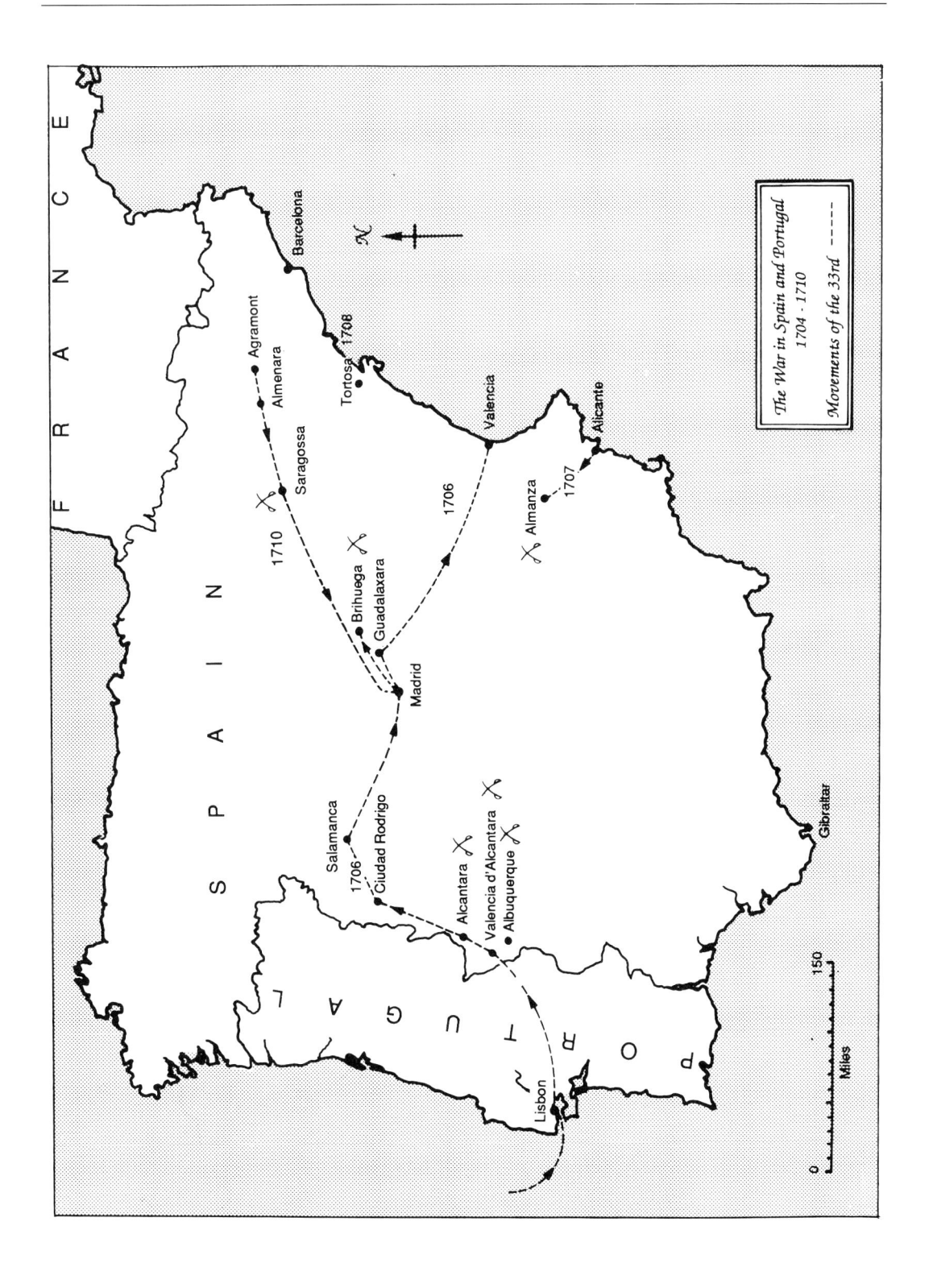

*Movements of the 33rd* - - - - -

However, learning that the Portuguese were to deploy on the right of Galway's line, the French re-deployed their own troops so that the best of them were opposite the English and Dutch. Galway mistook these movements to be the preliminary to a retreat and therefore hastily deployed his own army before it was even in sight of the enemy. Having reluctantly acceded to the Portuguese demand to be given the post of honour on the right flank, he deployed his Dutch in the centre and his British regiments on the left, though (again with some misgivings) some Portuguese cavalry squadrons were interposed between the battalions. The 33rd (458 all ranks) was on the left wing in Wade's brigade of foot with Southwell's (6th Royal Warwickshire), Blood's (17th Royal Leicestershire) and Mountjoy's (subsequently disbanded). Interposed with them were two regiments of dragoons.

Galway opened the action at about 3pm, launching his six British cavalry regiments in a massed charge against Berwick's right wing. They were met by a storm of musketry which emptied many saddles and killed all but one of the commanding officers. Then Berwick's Spanish horse put in a counter charge, driving back the already-mauled British squadrons in some disarray. At this critical moment the 33rd together with Southwell's (6th) opened a murderous fire on the left flank of the Spanish, effectively halting their attack and allowing the British cavalry to rally and charge yet again, so that the enemy horsemen were in their turn sent rearwards in confusion. Now the rest of the British foot fell upon the enemy centre and drove them back upon their second line. Following up, the Guards battalion and Lord Portmore's (2nd Foot) burst through the second line and exultantly pursued the fugitives as far as the walls of Almanza. Thus far, with the British left wing victorious, the successful outcome seemed in little doubt. However, while all this struggle was going on, the Portuguese battalions in their place of honour on the right flank had remained motionless and supine. Berwick thereupon assaulted them with his left wing horse. Not waiting to receive the galloping squadrons, the battalions turned and ran, and Berwick's infantry followed up. The British battalions were now left to bear the brunt. *Then there was the magnificent spectacle of Southwell's and Wade's (6th and 33rd Foot), deserted by the Portuguese cavalry on their flanks, holding their own against nine battalions of the enemy, until supported by Steuart's (9th), Blood's (17th) and Mountjoy's Foot.* (Dalton). But weight of numbers told, and the British lines were overwhelmed. Galway himself was led to the rear with blood streaming from sword cuts to the head. His second-in-command, the Dutch General das Minas, was also desperately wounded.(g) Galway's losses amounted to 4,000 killed and wounded and 3,000 taken prisoner. It seems that the majority of prisoners was taken after the actual battle, when Major General Shrimpton led some 3,000 survivors to a mountain pass where they might have made a stand, but where Shrimpton surrendered to Berwick instead. The British regiments bore the heaviest burden of Galway's losses, but complete casualty lists have not come to light. Dalton's "Almanza Casualty Roll", detailing officers only, shows that the 33rd lost five officers killed (two captains, one lieutenant and two ensigns) and seventeen taken prisoner, only five of those being

---

(g) Dalton: *"One more never-to-be-forgotten sight ... must have have been to see the veteran Das Minas leading a desperate cavalry charge with his mistress riding by his side dressed in a soldier's uniform.."* This brave amazon was killed.

unwounded. As was the gentlemanly custom in those days, officer prisoners could be exchanged or paroled after a few months.

*Almanza, 25 April 1707. General Galway and General das Minas surrender to Duke of Berwick.*

With the appalling total of 7,000 casualties, Almanza was a major reverse, and at home dismay was followed by constant debate in the House, directed not so much at Galway's generalship, but at the government's apparent failure to allow him adequate forces.

After Almanza, Galway (now minus an eye as well as an arm) withdrew his mauled command to a Catalonian base where he endeavoured to recoup and reorganise with stragglers from the battle, some cannibalising of strong regiments to make up the weak, and officer prisoners returned from parole. So successful was he in this task that within five months he was ready to take the field with 14,000 fully equipped troops. But, severely disabled, Galway was now considered unfit to continue in command, and was replaced by the Austrian prince, Field Marshal von Stahremberg, with Lieutenant General James Stanhope commanding the British contingent. The latter's second-in-command was the 33rd's Colonel, now Brigadier General George Wade.

As Stahremberg could do little to oppose the vastly superior forces of Berwick he embarked on an operation to capture the French-held island of Minorca. This successful assault was undertaken by General Stanhope in September 1708, with trifling British losses. The 33rd was not engaged, but its Colonel was. George Wade led the storming party on Fort Philip which captured a redoubt and forced a capitulation. The island of Minorca became a British dependency.

Meanwhile the 33rd remained uncommitted in Catalonia, one of only two regiments to have suffered at Almanza and again being operational. In May 1709 the Lieutenant Colonel, Philip Honeywood, was promoted to the colonelcy of a newly raised regiment. His probable successor was Oliver D'Harcourt – records for this period in the history of the 33rd are incomplete.

In July 1710 Stahremberg, reinforced by 20,000 foot and 5,000 cavalry, took the offensive and on 27th fought a brilliantly successful action at Almenara in which he captured the town and inflicted 1,300 casualties on the enemy for only some 400 of his own. Almenara was chiefly a cavalry combat, but the infantry was active in the pursuit of the defeated enemy. *The London Gazette* of 17 August stated "*our infantry came on with great intrepidity, but though they pursued the enemy two hours in the night, till it was so dark our troops could not distinguish the faces of each other, it was impossible to come up with them*". The 33rd (in company with the 6th Foot) took part in the pursuit, but there is no record that it suffered any casualties.[h]

The French withdrew towards Saragossa where, on 18 August, by rapid marching the allies renewed contact with them. They seem to have run ahead of their supplies and there was nothing to eat that night. However, the following morning, while the two forces exchanged artillery fire, the troops were able to get a meal. The French were posted on a hill and had placed their best troops on their right as the British were opposite. The British cavalry was drawn up with the five infantry battalions (of which only the 6th and 33rd were not later disbanded) interposed between them, as at Almanza. This was apparently on the recommendation of Brigadier Wade. Some of the Portuguese cavalry was dressed in red in order to resemble the British. However the first onset by the French squadrons fairly swept the red coated Portuguese from the field. Carried away by success, the French cavalry pursued wildly and did not draw rein to return to the battle until Stanhope and the interposed infantry had worsted their opponents, the 33rd well to the fore. The total casualties of the allies were 1,660 of which 355 were suffered by the British, mostly by the cavalry. All the enemy's colours and standards were taken as well as 16 pieces of artillery, all their baggage and ammunition and 4,000 prisoners.

Stahremberg, contrary to his better judgement, then marched on Madrid and again attempted to install the Habsburg Archduke Charles as King. But to no avail. The Spanish were still not disposed to accept the interloper. On 16 December 1710, Luttrell observed that "*King Charles has quitted Madrid and Toledo in such haste, and they left behind them 4 cannon, 2 mortars with abundance of ammunition ..... King Philip has come to Madrid, where he was received with great acclamations*". Before leaving Madrid Stanhope was able to recover the colours captured from the British regiments at Almanza, though whether

---

(h) At this period the home authorities, and the Press were more concerned with Marlborough's triumphs at Oudenarde and Malplaquet, and the troops in Spain were virtually a forgotten army.

those of the 33rd were among them is not recorded.

Having again evacuated Madrid, Stahremberg marched eastwards, his force divided into five columns. The British under Stanhope formed the fifth, which acted as rearguard. By 3 December the first four columns under Stahremberg had reached Cifuentes in the Guadalajara region (some 60 miles north-east of Madrid), while Stanhope's British rearguard halted at Brihuega, about twenty miles behind the main body. Lying on the right bank of the Tajuna River, Brihuega was a small town of no importance, walled but unfortified. Although Stanhope had reported a strong body of enemy horse following up his rearguard, Stahremberg was unperturbed, ordering the British to halt for another day while supplies were collected. Next morning Stanhope was astonished to discover not only the French horse, but massed battalions of infantry in position on the heights overlooking the town. The whole, amounting to some 25,000 men, was commanded by the redoubtable Marshal Vendôme who had performed a remarkable forced march of 170 miles in seven days. Stanhope was now hopelessly outnumbered. All he could do was to shut his force within the ancient, decaying walls of Brihuega, where he was within range of the French guns, and even their musketry. By morning of 8 December some 9,000 of Vendôme's infantry had completely surrounded the town, rendering any escape impossible. Nevertheless, ignoring summons to surrender, Stanhope managed to send off an aide to Stahremberg urging relief, and bravely resolved to hold out until this arrived.

But his situation was desperate. At midnight King Philip himself arrived with more horse, foot and guns and the investing force now totalled more than 20,000. To confront this, all Stanhope had were four regiments of horse and dragoons and eight battalions, all weakened by previous casualties and sickness and amounting to no more than some 4,500 all ranks,[i] among which was the 33rd. On 9 December Vendôme's infantry launched its assault and then followed Stanhope's heroic struggle against impossible odds. The French were beaten back again and again, but by 7 o'clock in the evening the British ammunition was practically exhausted. Since there was no sign of Stahremberg's relieving force, Stanhope was loath to sacrifice more lives in hopeless resistance and was forced to surrender. There was such a volume of musketry that the drummers ordered to beat the Parley had to do so three times before they were heard by the enemy. The casualties of the British regiments are not accurately known but the total was about 600. The losses of the enemy were nearly three times as great. Stanhope, in his despatch to Lord Dartmouth, concluded by stating, *"if after this misfortune, I should ever again be entrusted with troops, I never desire to serve with better men"* and Fortescue wrote, *"Never did British troops fight better than at Brihuega"*.

Next day the 3,862 British prisoners-of-war (who included 303 officers) marched out of Brihuega during the course of which the enemy grabbed everything off the soldiers except *"the clothes that was on our backs which were not worth taking"*. Then followed a series of long marches as the prisoners were dispersed to various towns. *"They used us very basely: they run lighted straw in our faces & firebrand and cursing our Queen and us, & we were*

---

(i) Fortescue gives the British strength as 2,500. The figure of 4,500 is taken from: A Royal Dragoon in the Spanish Succession War, Society for Army Historical Research Special Publication No 5.

*forced to run to keep up with our guards*". The food also was atrocious, "*we were treated wors than doggs*". Eventually the troops arrived at their various destinations – the 6th Foot location being Gumiel de Izan. It is not known where the 33rd finished up. There they stayed until the middle of May 1712 when they learnt they were at last to be released, though it was the end of the year before some regiments left Spain.

In a directive dated 28 July 1712 Brigadier Wade was informed by Sir William Wyndham, Secretary-at-War, that the foot regiments of Brigadiers Munsden, Gore and Dalzell "*now prisoners in Spain*" were to be disbanded and the NCOs and men "*shall be incorporated (as soon as released) proportionably into yours and other Regiments of Foot taken prisoners at the same time*". Wade's and the others thus made up were to be regarded as placed on the Irish Establishment(j) from the previous December. In response to Wade's enquiry, a Whitehall official informed him of the number of prisoners "*coming from Spain .. which are to be carried to Ireland*". The total of Wade's own regiment was given as only 117 NCOs and men, so that the numbers killed or died, either of wounds or while in captivity, must have been many times that figure.

The Treaty of Utrecht in April 1713 brought the War of the Spanish Succession to an end. No battle honours were awarded as it did not become practice to do so until 1800. From then on the award of battle honours became more and more frequent, but the wars fought before 1800 remained unrecognised. It was not until 1881 that an attempt was made to remedy the situation. For the War of the Spanish Succession Blenheim, Ramillies, Oudenarde, Malplaquet and Gibraltar all became battle honours for the participating regiments, but for the regiments which had fought in Spain there was nothing.

More than one historian has remarked on this omission. C.T. Atkinson declared "*If any regiment's colours should bear 'Spain and Portugal 1704-1710', the 33rd's should, especially as they have nothing to show for the two campaigns in the Netherlands, 1702 and 1703, under Marlborough*". He also pointed out that the 33rd was the one regiment of the original force of 1704 who served right through to Brihuega. The 33rd Regiment's only reward was disbandment.

The selection of regiments for disbandment was politically motivated. The aim of the ruling clique was the elimination of officers and whole corps who favoured the Protestant succession and so to make way for the Jacobite interest. Prompted by such motives they violated the old rule that the youngest regiments should always be the first to be disbanded. Even such old corps as the 6th Foot were not exempt. Between 1713 and 1714 eight regiments of horse and dragoons and 32 of foot were struck off.

On 25 May 1714 Brigadier General Wade, now on the Irish C-in-C's staff, learned that his regiment was to be *broke*. All the officers were retired on half pay, the soldiers cast adrift with a minimal gratuity of £2. And so, having fought and suffered almost from the year it was raised, the 33rd Regiment of Foot ceased to exist.

---

(j) Regiments were held on the Irish establishment as it allowed more regiments to be raised than Parliament was prepared to pay for, since the Irish establishment was made a charge on the revenue of Ireland.

CHAPTER 3

# The War of the Austrian Succession

*1715 33rd re-raised*
*1719 Expedition to Vigo*
*1743 Dettingen*
*1745 Fontenoy and the '45 Rebellion*
*1746 Roucoux*
*1747 Lauffeld*

On 1 August 1714, Queen Anne died and was succeeded by the Elector of Hanover, the grandson of James I's daughter and now King George I of England. The new monarch (who could not speak a word of English when he ascended the throne) was never thoroughly popular with his subjects. But he was a soldier of wide experience on the Continent, and was quick to recognise that the recent pruning of the armed forces rendered his country unprepared not only against foreign threat, but also for internal unrest.

In the early summer of 1715 alarming intelligence reported that the Jacobites of Scotland were rising in support of whom they regarded as their rightful King, the Stuart Prince James Francis (The Old Pretender), son of the late King James II. The Prince himself was reported to be planning a descent on the Kingdom, with the enthusiastic support of Louis XIV. Thus, in July 1715, King George persuaded Parliament to repair some of the damage it had lately inflicted on the defence forces. Thirteen regiments of dragoons and eight of foot were raised, or re-raised, some of them having been disbanded only the previous year.

One of the re-raised regiments of foot was the 33rd, or General Wade's, and according to Dalton, the date of its rebirth was 25 March 1715 when it was still on the Irish Establishment. Among the thirty officers were many who had only recently been retired on half-pay. One of three more commissioned in June was Ensign William Wade who was a natural son of the general. While there is no record of the other ranks' make-up, it is reasonable to assume that most of them were former soldiers set adrift after the disbandments. By this date, George Wade was Major General of the forces in Ireland (appointed in October 1714) and it is unlikely that his Regiment saw much of him, the actual command, as before, devolving on the Lieutenant Colonel, Thomas Howard [a].

With the Jacobite rebellion in spate, many of the units in Ireland were hastily routed to England and Scotland, among them the 33rd. By December 1715 they seem to have been at Taunton, for on the 29th the Secretary-at-War, William Pulteney, recommended to Wade that he should relieve that town of their presence and quarter them in other adjacent centres.

After the battle of Sheriffmuir in Scotland and the decisive defeat of the Jacobite force at Preston in November, the last embers of "the '15 petered out". The 33rd played no part in the operations.

In March 1717, King George I granted Wade the Colonelcy of Viscount Windsor's Regiment of Horse (3rd Dragoon Guards). He was succeeded by Colonel Henry Hawley who had received his first commission in 1694 as ensign in what became the 19th Foot (The Green Howards). He was then a child of nine! The scandal of "infant commissions" or "nursery officers" persisted until 1711 when the government, at Marlborough's instigation, was persuaded to ban the practice. Hawley, whose harshness made him unpopular, held strong views on most subjects, including marriage. In 1725 he wrote:

> *"I am entirely against officers having wives until they are in a post to be able to keep them from following them about. There never was a subaltern good for anything after he was married and very few captains. I have a notion an honest married man who loves his wife and children can't be so brave on any desperate attaque or in any warm service as another man when he thinks as he goes on that his woman and children must starve".*

Hawley, not surprisingly in the circumstances, never married.[b] Also in 1717 John Archer became the Lieutenant Colonel of the Regiment.

In that same year Britain became involved in a quarrel with Spain over her territorial ambitions (including Gibraltar), and a would-be invasion force – another Armada – was roundly defeated by the Royal Navy. Such aggression prompted British reprisals. In September 1719, the 33rd was one of seven regiments sent to the Isle of Wight in readiness for a landing on the Spanish coast at Corunna. For strategic reasons, the attack was re-routed to the port of Vigo, some 80 miles south, and the expeditionary force sailed on 21 September. However, the assault ended tamely with capitulation of the weakly-held citadel, and if the Regiment (or the others) suffered any casualties, they are not recorded. Having captured large quantities of arms, ammunition and stores, and given the Spanish a bloody nose – the prime objective – the expedition re-embarked for England.

In 1720 a treaty with Spain was ratified, and there followed some twenty years of

---

(a) Because of the defeat at Almanza, the surrender at Brihuega and the Regiment's disbandment in 1714 the succession of lieut colonels between 1706 and 1715 is uncertain. Thomas Howard was listed as a lieut-colonel when captured at Brihuega in 1710.
(b) In 1726 Hawley's illegitimate son, John Toovey, was appointed a lieutenant in the Regiment. He eventually became a major-general.

peace. For seventeen of those years the 33rd's Lieutenant-Colonel was Richard Challoner Cobbe who had succeeded John Archer in 1721. While the long period of peace was uneventful in military terms, the army was far from inactive. At that time the country was in a state of lawlessness. All over England strikes, riots, smuggling and incendiarism flourished. So much so that the Secretary-of-State was obliged to confess to Parliament that it was unsafe for magistrates to do their duty without the aid of the military. Against this disorder the only orderly force was the army, which led to an outcry against its power as a disciplined body to execute the law. There were also political opponents who wished to re-establish the Stuarts on the throne of England who, seeing the army as an obstacle, raised the old cry of *no standing army*. As a result of these pressures the army was once again reduced to a dangerously low level and it was only by hiding a substantial number in Ireland, where the costs were borne by the Irish revenue, that a nucleus of an army was retained. There is no record of the movements and activities of the 33rd during these times. It can be certain however that it was employed in curbing disorder, constantly on the move and periodically in Ireland.

During this period there were no significant alterations in dress or accoutrements, but by 1722, the Ordnance Department was becoming concerned at the proliferation of non-regulation muskets contracted for (at a profit) by some infantry colonels. Accordingly, in July of that year, Horse Guards (later War Office) decreed that "*all Collonells who have any new Arms made shall be obliged to make them according to the said Pattern and proved and viewed by the Proper Officers of the Ordnance*". The said Pattern was the prototype of the musket which, as the famous Brown Bess, remained the British infantryman's principal weapon until the 1830s. There were several modifications of Brown Bess, but all of course were muzzle-loading, with flint-lock ignition. Officially known as Long Land Service, the new weapon had a 46 inch barrel and weighed about 10lb 4oz. Around 1724, the wooden ramrods, prone to breakage, were replaced by steel substitutes.

Soon after the 33rd had received an issue of the Brown Bess prototype, there was another change of Colonel. In March 1730, Colonel Henry Hawley, having "yearned for a dragoon regiment" (Dalton) achieved his desire when he was appointed Colonel of the 13th Dragoons (later Hussars).

Hawley's successor as Colonel of the 33rd was Major General Robert Dalzell (in early records sometimes spelt "Dalziel"). A member of the Scottish family of the Earls of Carnwath and then in his 68th year, Dalzell had a lengthy military career behind him. By 1694, he had become captain in Colonel Gibson's (28th, Gloucestershire), and served with them at Ramillies. In 1709, as colonel, he raised a foot regiment for service in Spain and was captured at Brihuega. His regiment was disbanded in 1712 and there followed staff appointments, as brigadier general (1711) and major general (1727). His Colonelcy of the 33rd was not marked by any campaigning, for after nine years – in 1739 – he exchanged as Colonel of the 38th Foot (Staffordshire). Meanwhile, John Johnson became Colonel and Commanding Officer of the 33rd. He had begun his career as cornet in Major General Harvey's Regiment of Horse (later 2nd Dragoon Guards) in 1706.

In 1740, the Emperor Charles VI of Austria died, leaving his vast Habsburg territories to his daughter, the young Maria Theresa. Eager to pay off old scores France immediately supported the rival claimant to the Imperial throne, the Elector Charles Albert of Bavaria, in which it was joined by King Frederick II of Prussia. Once again the balance of power in western Europe and the security of the Netherlands were being threatened. As a result Britain allied itself with Maria Theresa. At first Britain contributed only monetary support, but in February 1742 King George II ordered the despatch of 16,000 troops to join the Dutch, Hanoverians and Austrians, and the country was committed to the War of the Austrian Succession.

In September 1742, the 33rd and nine other regiments in Ireland were ordered to recruit up to war establishment prior to being posted to Flanders. After sailing to Chester and thence to a Channel port, the 33rd arrived on the Continent in December and by January had joined the army at Mons, commanded by Colonel John Johnson, with Lieutenant Colonel Robert Sampson second-in-command.(c)

Command of the British contingent was given to General John Dalrymple, Earl of Stair, who had distinguished himself in William III's and Marlborough's campaigns. Though now in his 70th year, he was still as active as ever. Since this was the era of winter hibernation for armies in the field, the 33rd and the rest of the troops spent the next few months in primitive billets around Ghent and elsewhere. It was only in early February 1743 that Stair, now commanding the entire allied force, marched east towards Germany.

The early stages of Stair's advance met no serious opposition, but owing to difficulties in securing forage for the cavalry and supplies for the troops, it was not until the end of May that the combined force was able to reach the River Main. Stair now planned to fall on the rear of the French army facing the Austrians. Lacking any of Stair's strategic vision and apprehensive of any manoeuvre that would take the army further from Hanover, George II forbade the plan, ordering Stair to occupy the heights of Mainz in order to command the confluence of the Rhine and Main, between the towns of Aschaffenburg and Hanau. Some eight miles downstream of Aschaffenburg lay the village of Dettingen.

Hearing that a French army under Marshal Noailles lay on the west bank of the Main, Stair planned to attack it even though Noailles had the numerical superiority of 70,000 all arms against his own 40,000. But the British commander was troubled not so much by disparate strengths as by the all-too-familiar bickerings among allied commanders. The Austrian Count d'Arenberg constantly disputed his plans; the Hanoverians were reluctant to take orders from any but their own Elector, King George II. Then the King himself arrived at Hanover and proceeded to confuse his unhappy commander-in-chief with relays of ambiguous orders. Striving to sort all this out, Stair was moved to pen a despatch to Lord Carteret, Foreign Secretary, mildly complaining that *"the importance of giving an army to a person who is trusted is now evident"*. Finally, on 19 June, King George, accompanied by his son, the Duke of Cumberland, appeared in person at Stair's headquarters and took over supreme command.

---

(c) Robert Sampson had succeeded Hugh Viscount Primrose, who commanded the 33rd from 1738-1741.

Meanwhile Noailles had cut the river above the allies, thus preventing them from gaining any supplies from upstream, placed batteries of guns along the west bank of the river to command the road between the allied camp and their base at Hanau and prepared a force under his second-in-command, the Duc de Grammont, with 28,000 horse and foot, to take up position in Dettingen, there to block the allies' progress.

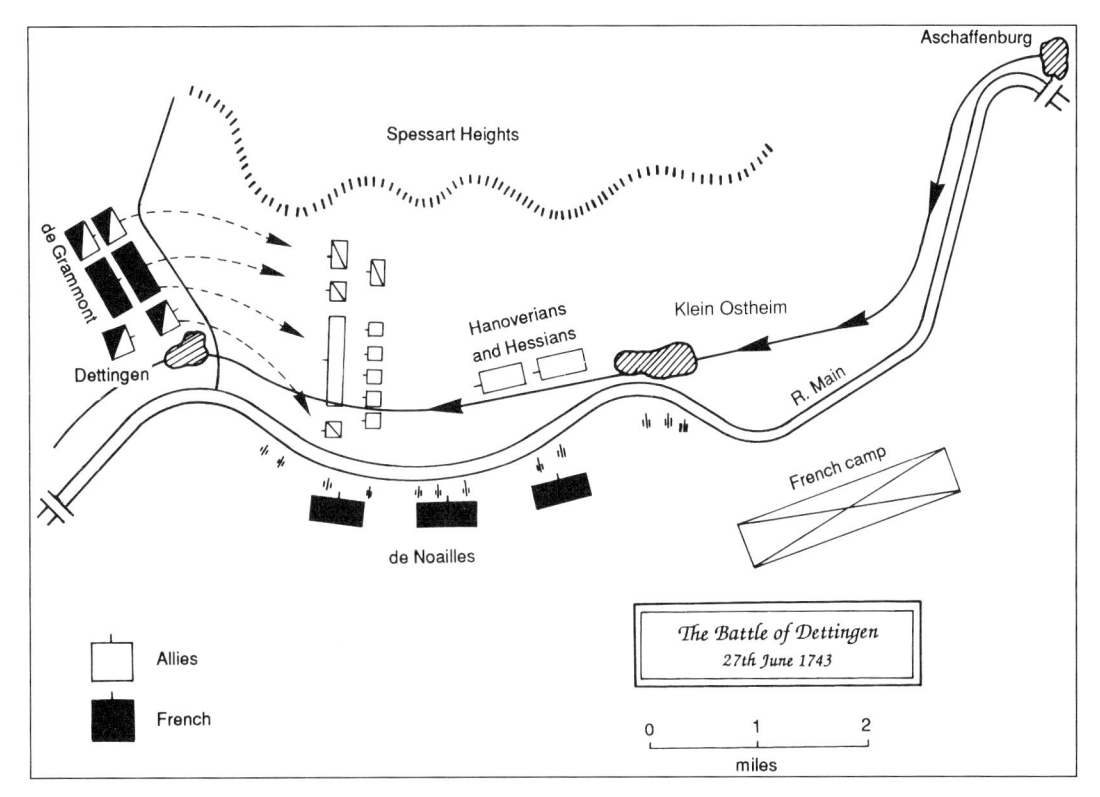

*The Battle of Dettingen, 27th June 1743*

Since his army was short of supplies the King had no choice but to order a retreat on Hanau. By the morning of 27 June, he had marched his heterogeneous command to a position midway between the villages of Klein Ostheim and Dettingen, where the lengthy column of horse, foot and guns found itself in a perilous situation. Its left flank was bounded by swampy ground leading to the steep banks of the river; on the right rose the Spessartwald, a thickly-wooded bluff impenetrable for horse or guns. Though not yet apparent, ahead lay Grammont waiting to smite them before they could deploy. Within cannon-shot across the river stood the main French force with some sixty field guns. As Noailles gleefully commented, he had trapped King George and his army in a *souricière* (mousetrap).

The allied advance began before dawn on 27 June, but it took several hours for the 40,000 troops and their baggage tail to be sorted in some order of march. As soon as they did so, the French guns on the south bank opened fire and inflicted the first casualties. By now, intelligence revealed the threat of Grammont at Dettingen, so that a pitched battle was inevitable. The approach march was a scene of confusion in the constricted terrain. "*The King capered about on horseback in great excitement*" says Fortescue, "*staff officers galloped to and fro*", and so did the youthful Duke of Cumberland, whose orders did not always conform with those of the rest. All this while Noaille's murderous guns were assaulting the mass with their roundshot. At first the British gunners could not reply, for having unaccountably been posted at the rear of the column, their batteries were effectively hindered from advancing to drop into action by the dense mass of horse, foot and baggage wagons in front of them.

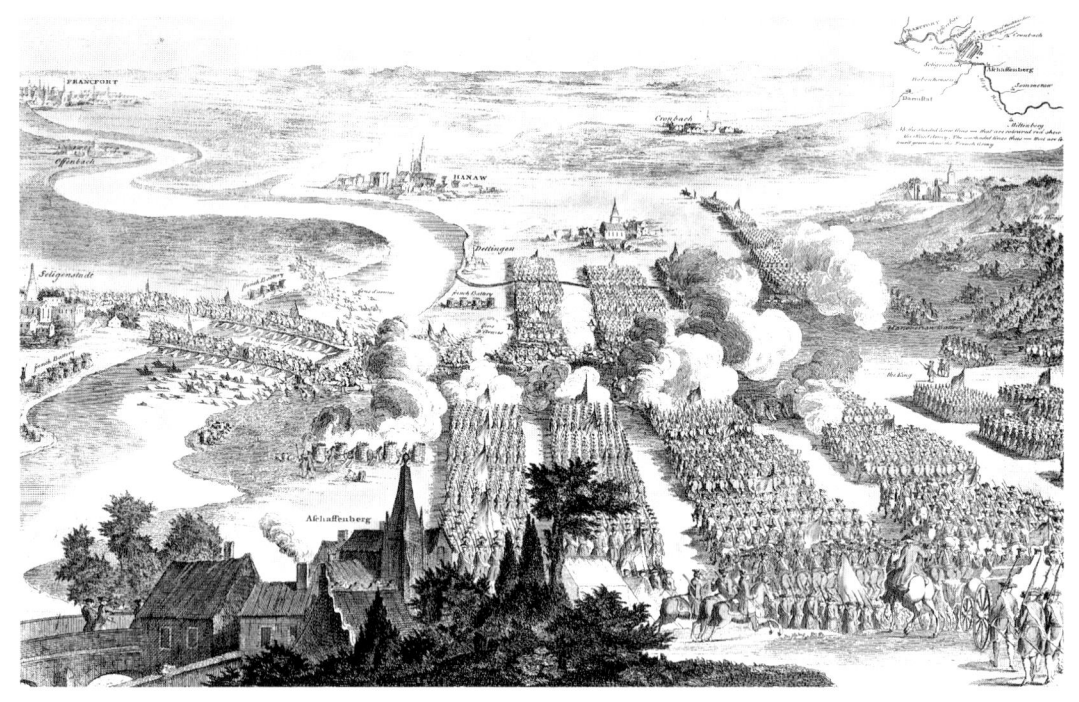

The Battle of Dettingen, 27 June 1743

At length, about midday, the column approached within a mile of Dettingen and began to deploy into a semblance of battle formation. The 33rd Foot was posted on the extreme left of the first line, within some 200 yards of the river. To its right were six battalions of British infantry, then an Austrian brigade, then four regiments of British cavalry. Forming the second line were five battalions of redcoats and six regiments of horse and dragoons. Just before action commenced, Bland's Dragoons (3rd Hussars) and the 11th Foot (Devonshire) were redeployed to protect the 33rd's vulnerable left flank.

Noailles had ordered Grammont to remain on the defensive, behind Dettingen, but the spectacle of his opponents struggling to deploy prompted him to ignore orders, and he rashly advanced to attack. The first assault was led by the élite Maison du Roi (Household Cavalry), who had the post of honour on the right flank, and therefore confronted the 3rd Dragoons and 33rd Foot. This fine body of horsemen proceeded to canter aimlessly to and fro between the two armies *"without a thought except for the fine figure it was cutting"* (Fortescue). Catcalls and a few volleys of musketry from the 33rd and others on the flank curtailed this display, but not before Stair himself had galloped up and bade them desist from such indisciplined conduct. This light relief was followed by a further comedy. King George's conspicuous white charger, startled by the sudden outburst of fire, took the bit between its teeth and bore its royal master to the rear. Dismounting the King swore that it least he could rely on his legs to carry him in the right direction. But entertainment quickly gave way to more serious business.

Emerging from the village of Dettingen, Gramont's first line infantry advanced to within range and opened fire with successive volleys of musketry. The stolid British first line replied with its disciplined platoon fire which felled so many of its opponents that the rest withdrew in some disarray. Then the Maison du Roi, anxious to prove that they were not mere show troops, and supported by the equally élite Gens d'Armes, thundered down towards the British left flank where the 33rd, 21st(Royal Scots Fusiliers) and 23rd(Royal Welch Fusiliers) stood to receive them. Before these could use their muskets, however, a gallant charge by Bland's Dragoons (3rd Hussars) halted the horsemen and for a brief space the fight on the left wing developed into a fierce cavalry mêlée. Though Bland's could muster only two weak squadrons to dispute the nine of the enemy, they charged again and again until they were all but annihilated. Now the infantry bore the brunt of the attack. Says Fortescue: *"The Thirty-Third faced the attack as boldly, never giving way for an inch, and brought men and horses crashing down by their eternal rolling fire"*. Even the bravest horsemen were seldom a match for the disciplined firepower of resolute infantry. But with casualties mounting, the 33rd together with the 21st and 23rd were hard pressed to repel the repeated attacks. Stair ordered six more British cavalry regiments to gallop to their aid from the right wing. These eighteen squadrons crashed into the now weaker force of French Household Cavalry and sent them reeling back with heavy casualties.

Meanwhile the action elsewhere was proving chiefly an infantry fight. Time and again the French battalions advanced only to be driven back by that *"eternal rolling fire"*. After some four hours' struggle, the French infantry, *"who had behaved very unworthily of itself all day"* (Fortescue) could stomach no more and took to its heels. King George now ordered a general advance and the whole of Grammont's routed force was pursued through the village of Dettingen, where the King ordered a halt. The French Duke's impetuosity and disobedience had lost Noailles the battle. Grammont suffered some 4,000 casualties, many of them in the panic-stricken rush to ford the Main, where they perished *by scores, if not hundreds*. The British losses amounted to 265 all ranks killed and 554 wounded, of which total the 33rd had 30 killed and 80 wounded.

As Grammont's survivors fled beyond the river, Stair urged King George to follow up with a vigorous pursuit, but he was over-ruled. Mindful of the uncommitted forces of Noailles, he was not prepared to be caught in another mousetrap. Instead, basking in what he considered his own personal triumph, the King left his victorious soldiers to camp in pouring rain and took himself off to Hanover, thence to London, where he was acclaimed as England's hero and celebrated with a special Dettingen Te Deum hastily composed by his fellow-Hanoverian, Georg Friedrich Händel.

Dettingen was an epic victory[d] and King George II was the last British sovereign to command his troops in battle. Although the King was accorded all the honour due to a victorious general, the victory was owed not so much to his own generalship as to Noailles's lack of it. While battle raged within earshot across the river, the Marshal and his 20,000-odd fresh troops had sat immobile and uncommitted, and on Grammont's retreat, he withdrew likewise. He may have set a mousetrap for King George, but he failed to spring it properly.

---

(d) The Battle Honour **Dettingen** was eventually approved in 1882.

After Dettingen, French aggression was temporarily curbed and a period of stalemate followed. In December 1743 the Earl of Stair resigned his command, to be replaced by the 33rd's former Colonel, George Wade, now of field marshal's rank. But he was not to see any further serious fighting on the Continent. His old regiment and the rest of the British contingent spent the usual winter recess in quarters around Maastricht, and the following year the battalions endured fruitless marching and countermarching, without any encounters in force. Like his predecessor, Wade was bedevilled by quarrelling and dispute, not only among his allied commanders but from his masters at Westminster. At length, in February 1745, he threw up his post and returned home *"sick in body and distressed in mind"* (Fortescue). The King now appointed his 25-year old son, the Duke of Cumberland, as Commander-in-Chief in Flanders. As proved at Dettingen, the Duke's spirit was unquestioned, but his generalship had yet to be tried.

In April 1745 the Duke reviewed the British troops (including the 33rd) in camp outside Brussels, where they had come to rest after the previous year's peregrinations. The weary months of inaction were over and Cumberland was about to lead his force of British, Dutch, Germans and Austrians to confrontation at Fontenoy.

By now the French had recovered from the humiliation of Dettingen, and with some 80,000 troops under Marshal Saxe were eager to retrieve their prestige. Aware that the Allies also intended to take the offensive, Saxe forestalled them by investing the strategic fortress of Tournai, held by the Dutch. This, the key to western Flanders, lay in the veritable "cockpit of Europe" which already had seen much bloody fighting. Northwards was the field of Oudenarde, southwards were Cambrai and Mons, to the west lay Waterloo and Ramillies. Some five miles south of Tournai was the hamlet of Fontenoy.

On 29 April, Cumberland, having been apprised of the threat to Tournai, marched his force for its relief, and by 9 May had approached to within a mile or so of Fontenoy. His total strength numbered about 47,000 all arms, of which 16,900 were British. Saxe meanwhile had moved to meet him with some 60,000 troops (he had left 21,000 to press the siege of Tournai) and the clash came on 11 May.

The 33rd, commanded by Lieutenant Colonel Henry Clements, who had assumed the appointment in September 1744, was brigaded with the 19th (Green Howards) and 25th (KOSB) on the extreme right of the allied first line. Saxe had taken up a commanding position on a ridge south of Fontenoy, his flanks protected by the thick forest of Barri and the Redoubt d'Eu. Cumberland's plan was for a frontal attack by the right wing infantry while the left wing assaulted the positions between Fontenoy and the Barri forest. There was preliminary cannonading from the French guns, which wrought destruction among the British cavalry massed on the right flank. The British gunners could not reply for their hired civilian drivers had preferred discretion to valour and vanished rearwards, leaving the pieces immobile. Since the d'Eu Redoubt could bring enfilade fire on the British line as it advanced up the ridge, Cumberland ordered Brigadier Ingoldsby, 1st Foot Guards, to lead a special task force of four battalions (12th (Suffolk), 13th (Somerset), 42nd (Black Watch) and a Hanoverian) to assault and capture it *"at the point of the bayonet"*. Ingoldsby moved off at 6.00am but, perplexed by his orders or disinclined to hazard himself, he soon halted to confer with his subordinate commanders, and seek further instruction from Cumberland. Despite repeated urgings from the latter, the Brigadier remained where he was and never resumed his advance. This officer's vacillations contributed to the defeat of the allies. Meanwhile, after the British cavalry had been mauled by the French guns, Cumberland ordered his Dutch contingent in the centre to advance directly on Fontenoy. They were smitten by devastating cross-fire and driven back, their cavalry thundering in panic through the British lines, *"crying out that all was lost"*. So far the 33rd and its right-flank infantry comrades had been uncommitted, suffering only some "overs" from the French guns. But they were soon to display their prowess. Undeterred by the failures, Cumberland bravely placed himself at the head of the British infantry and ordered a general advance.

> *"Forward tramped the ranks of scarlet, silent and stately as if on parade. Full half a mile of ground was to be traversed before they could close with the invisible enemy that awaited them and the way was marked by the red flashes and clouds of white smoke that leaped from Fontenoy and the Redoubt d'Eu on either flank. The shot plunged fiercely and more fiercely into the serried ranks as they advanced into that murderous cross-fire, the perfect order was never lossed, the stately step was never hurried .... Silent and inexorable, the scarlet lines strode on .... the proud battalions strewing the sward behind them with scarlet, like some mass of red blossom that floats down a lazy stream and sheds its petals as it goes".* (Fortescue)

On gaining the high ground in front of Fontenoy, *"the ranks of scarlet"* came face to face with the French infantry deployed to receive them, little more than a hundred yards away. There now followed an incident about which there are conflicting accounts. Leading a company of the 1st Foot Guards (Grenadiers) was Lieutenant Colonel Lord Charles Hay, who had been a captain in the 33rd, and was to become their Colonel. According to the contemporary French writer, Voltaire, Hay stepped forward from the ranks and, raising his hat, cried *"Messieurs les Gardes Francaises, tirez les premiers"*. *(Gentlemen of the French Guards, fire first)*. To which the equally courteous reply was *"Mais non, monsieur, nous ne tirons jamais les premiers"*. *(But no, Sir, we never fire first)*. Fortescue, however, prefers a different version. Lord Hay, *"flask in hand"*, drinks a toast to the enemy and then utters the taunt: *"I hope, gentlemen, that you are going to wait for us today and not swim the Scheldt as you swam the Main at Dettingen"*. Just before the French replied with a volley, an English guardsman was heard to mutter, with the British soldier's never-failing sense of humour, *"for what we are about to receive, may the Lord make us truly thankful"*. Whoever did in fact fire first, it was the murderous volley of musketry from the ten battalions of redcoats (the 33rd among them) that shattered the French line and drove the survivors back in disorder. Now again advancing in perfect order, the battalions swept aside further faint-hearted opposition to find themselves triumphant in

*The battle of Fontenoy, 9 May 1745. The French, in the foreground, face the British infantry*

the centre of the enemy position. They might well have imagined that the battle was won. Saxe, however, now brought up eight fresh battalions and smote the British right flank with them. The attack was repulsed, but caught in a severe cross-fire, the redcoats were forced to retire to the Barri Wood – Fontenoy ridge, where they were assaulted by Saxe's cavalry. Formed in a single large square, they beat off charge after charge, inflicting heavy casualties on men and horses. Had the twenty-six squadrons of British horse and dragoons been allowed to gallop in a counter-attack at this juncture, the day could still have been won. But throughout the fight they were sitting on their horses, chafing and uncommitted, for no orders reached them. Their gallant 78-year old commander, General Sir James Campbell, had been carried off the field dying of a wound; the impetuous young Cumberland had so far forgotten his Commander-in-Chief's responsibilities as to involve himself in the infantry attack, and was now where no general should have been, immured in the middle of their square, thus losing control of all but what went on in his immediate vicinity.

By 1.30pm, defeat had become inevitable. The Dutch attack on Fontenoy itself had failed. French guns at close range were mauling the British infantry, Saxe threw in his infantry reserve against the British right flank, while the Maison du Roi charged the broken left flank to complete its destruction.

Cumberland could only concede the day, and order a withdrawal. This was carried out with remarkable discipline, as the British remnants of *"the heroic battalions retired, facing about in succession every hundred yards, as steadily and proudly as they had advanced"* (Fortescue). Even Voltaire paid tribute to the steadiness of the British withdrawal: *"Les anglais .... quittèrent le champ de bataille sans tumulte, sans confusion, et furent vaincu avec honneur". The English left the field of battle without tumult, without confusion and......with honour.*

Cumberland's shattered forces camped for the night under the fortress of Ath, some fifteen miles along the road to Brussels, where they counted their losses. These were severe indeed: some 6,300 killed and wounded, most of the latter being left by Cumberland to the tender mercies of the French who treated them with uncustomary lack of chivalry. The 33rd's casualties included 5 officers killed, among whom was its Commanding Officer, Lieutenant Colonel Henry Clements – an outstanding officer, and 13 wounded. The other rank casualties, killed, wounded and missing, amounted to 189. The death of Colonel Clements saw Major George Mure (or Muir) promoted to lieutenant colonel to fill the vacancy. He is listed among the wounded, but evidently his wound was not serious.

The battle of Fontenoy may have been a defeat, but it gained great lustre for the stolid British infantryman. A correspondent to *The Gentleman's Magazine* of June 1745 declared: *"Where has English history a nobler account of the strength and bravery of the common soldiers than that of our Foot in this engagement, who though under miserable disadvantages of the horse not being come up to support them, and after having stood for more than three hours the continual fire of these terrible batteries, could drive the French, though in superior numbers, from the lines ... When and where have any single men more eminently signalised themselves than in this very action?"* Fortescue's verdict was: *"As an example of the prowess of British infantry, Fontenoy stands almost without a parallel in is history".*

Despite all this well-earned praise, none of the regiments who fought at Fontenoy has ever been awarded a Battle Honour. It was the rule that defeats should not be so honoured, no matter what gallantry was displayed.

However the Duke of Cumberland had no praise for the Colonel of the 33rd. On 9th July 1745 he wrote to the Secretary of State :

> *"....you are sensible how much it is for the good of the service to get rid of useless, worn out officers, I desire your advice which way you think it best to get the King's consent for two worn out colonels who are of no use to us. One is Major General Johnson, and the other Sowl, who is now in a madhouse..."*

However the request did not commend itself to the King and Johnson continued to be Colonel of the 33rd for another eight years.

The British setback at Fontenoy encouraged Prince Charles Edward (the Young Pretender) to make a bid for the restoration of his Stuart line on the throne of England. In July 1745 he landed with supporters in Scotland, and the '45 rebellion began. Since much of the internal security forces in England had been denuded by the war on the Continent, the Government hastily recalled ten of the best regiments from

Cumberland's army. On 9 September Cumberland, having named the ten regiments he had selected, which included the 33rd, not withstanding his poor opinion of its Colonel, wrote to Lord Harrington, the Secretary of State:

> "I can assure his Majesty that last Fryday I had the satisfaction to see the whole army under arms, and can with the greatest truth say that the battalions were equally fine and in good order; but I can say if there were any prefference to be given, it was to these ten, which I have pick'd out for that very reason".

On 24 September, *The Gentleman's Magazine* noted that "*yesterday were landed at Gravesend and Blackwall from Flanders the three battalions belonging to His Majesty's regiments of foot guards together with ye seven regiments of foot..*"

For the next two months the 33rd was encamped in and around London. However in late November it marched north to join the Duke of Cumberland at Stafford, where it arrived on 4 December. There it was placed in Brigadier Bligh's brigade, along with the 21st (Royal Scots Fusiliers), 25th (KOSB) and 32nd (DCLI). From Stafford Cumberland moved to Lichfield. By this time Prince Charles Edward and his army had reached Derby. Cumberland would have hastened there at once "*had the troops been as able as they seemed willing*", but they . . .

> "had scarcely halted six hours in ten days, had been without victuals for twenty four hours, and been exposed to the coldest nights I ever felt without shelter".

Derby was, however, the limit of the Young Pretender's advance as he was persuaded to consent to a retreat back to Scotland. Subsequently Bligh's brigade served in Lancashire and Cheshire but does not appear to have moved further north. Meanwhile all the regiments from Flanders had been authorised two additional companies, those for the 33rd being raised at Newcastle. These two companies were moved to Scotland and were initially stationed at Glasgow before being moved to Fort William, where fierce fighting took place when the rebels demanded its surrender. They were driven off with heavy loss.

With the Young Pretender's defeat at Culloden on 27 April 1746, the rebellion was quelled. The whole business had been a French-inspired diversion, and recognised to be such as was made clear from the shout of the troops to Cumberland after the battle: "*Now, Billy, for Flanders!*"

The Regiment embarked on 21 June and in July 1746 it and six others disembarked at Willemstadt on the Dutch coast and marched to join the allied army, now commanded by the veteran General Sir John Ligonier.

The first clash came on 11 October at the village of Roucoux near Liège where the allies' old enemy of Fontenoy, Marshal Saxe, deployed some 120,000 horse and foot to do battle with the allies' 80,000. The 33rd in company with the 8th (King's), 19th (Green Howard's) and 43rd (Oxford LI) endured repeated attacks by French brigades of infantry, beating them off with their volleys of musketry, while elsewhere Ligonier's

Dutch battalions behaved with equal staunchness. After a furious contest in which the outlying villages of Liers and Varoux were captured, lost, then recaptured, the weight of numbers told and Ligonier was forced to break off and withdraw across the Meuse, covered by his British cavalry. The total allied losses amounted to some 5,000 men, the British contingent losing 350 killed and wounded. Although heavily engaged throughout the day, the 33rd was fortunate in the surprisingly light loss of only five killed and two wounded. After Roucoux, operations ceased for the usual winter recess and both armies went into quarters where Lieutenant Colonel Mure was succeeded by James Lockhart. (He became Sir James Lockart-Ross Bt.)

In March 1747, the Duke of Cumberland once more arrived on the scene, taking over supreme command from Ligonier who was given command of the allied cavalry. By the end of June, Cumberland, determined to challenge Saxe, had encamped by the village of Lauffeld, a few miles south of Maastricht, while Saxe himself had approached after a forced march of fifty miles in two days. On the morning of 2 July, the French attacked with waves of infantry, concentrating their fury on Lauffeld itself, where stood the 33rd, two other British and two Hessian battalions. The fight raged back and forth for several hours, the 33rd and its comrades being driven into the straggling village, only to advance again and send the French back in their turn. Reinforced by two brigades, the enemy once more attacked when Cumberland brought up the whole of his infantry who sent the French rearwards in some confusion. The battle of Lauffeld might have been an allied victory but for the Dutch cavalry who performed its customary manoeuvre of galloping in the wrong direction. Ordered to charge the fleeing French, they were assaulted by musketry, turned tail and thundered regardless through the ranks of the British infantry, creating havoc. It was Fontenoy once again. Taking advantage of the confusion, the enemy hurled an overwhelming attack on Lauffeld and all that Cumberland could do to save further carnage was to order the drummers to beat a Chamade (retreat) and withdraw to Maastricht. During this the British cavalry, led by Sir John Ligonier, performed prodigies of valour, charging through the French ranks and allowing the infantry to retire unmolested. The 33rd, who had had heavy officer casualties, was led from the field by Captain Sir Ralph Gore Bt (created Earl of Ross in 1772), despite the fact that he had lost a hand during the battle. The following day he was thanked at the head of the Regiment for his conduct by the Duke of Cumberland.

The battle of Lauffeld could be accounted a victory for Saxe, but it was a Pyrrhic one. He lost some 10,000 of his best troops, the allies suffering about 6,000 all ranks killed and wounded. According to Lee,[e] the 33rd's casualties were twelve officers killed, ten wounded and 64 other ranks wounded or missing. The number of other ranks killed is not recorded. The Regiment saw no actions of consequence after Lauffeld. Both allies and French were weary with campaigns that seemed to bring no decisive advantage, and in October 1748 peace was signed at Aix-La-Chapelle.

---

(e) *History of the 33rd Foot.* Albert Lee. Jarrold & Sons. 1922

CHAPTER 4

# The Seven Years War

*1756 Raising of 2nd/33rd*
*1758 St Malo and St Cast*
*1760 Warburg, Kloster Kamp*
*1761 Kassel, Vellinghausen*
*1762 Wilhelmsthal*

The end of hostilities in 1748 did not see immediate home posting for all the British troops. In the spring of 1749, the 33rd, having wintered in Brabant, was routed to the Mediterranean island of Minorca (Menorca). Since its capture from the French the previous year, Minorca had come to be regarded by Britain as important strategically as Gibraltar, demanding an infantry garrison to supplement the fortress guns. The Regiment spent the next four years there while the French refrained from any attempt at recapture.

In 1753 the 33rd was posted home to be quartered at Reading where it was reviewed by the Duke of Cumberland. In November of that year Lieutenant General John Johnson died in London, and was succeeded by Colonel Lord Charles Hay – he who saluted the French guards at Fontenoy. Son of the Marquis of Tweeddale, Hay had been gazetted ensign in the 2nd Foot Guards (Coldstream) in 1722. Becoming captain in the 33rd in 1727, he moved up to the 1st Foot Guards in 1743, with the army rank of lieutenant colonel, and continued to serve with that regiment until appointed Colonel of the 33rd. Soon after this change, the 33rd was routed north to Edinburgh.

At that time, the programme of opening up the Highlands with the network of "Wade" roads was still in progress, and no sooner had the Regiment marched into Edinburgh than five companies were sent off to the bleak passes of the Grampians, where they were employed as navvies with pick and shovel. The completion of their labours was commemorated by the erection of an inscribed stone by the roadside at a site known as the Well of the Lecht. This is still in existence, being cared for by the Royal Commission on Ancient and Historical Monuments of Scotland.

The plaque bears the rudely cut (and whimsically spelt) inscription:-

A...D 1754
FIVE . COMPANIES
T E . 33D REGIMENT

RIGHT. HONLE . LORD
CHAS . HAY . COLONEL
MADE . T H . ROAD . FROM
HERE . TO . T H
SPEY

*The Well of the Lecht*

The fifteen mile stretch of road between Cock Bridge and Tomintoul now forms part of the A939 between Ballater and Grantown-on-Spey.

When Lord Charles Hay assumed the Colonelcy in 1753 he was not able to continue the practice of designating the Regiment by his own name. On 1 July 1751, King George II had signed a Royal Warrant which expressly prohibited the use of colonels' names in regimental titles; instead, all regiments were to be known simply by their numbers or ranking in the order of precedence. Four years earlier, in 1747, a regulation had directed that (for the first time) regiments' numbers were to be displayed on the Colours. But it was only with the 1751 Warrant that these numbers were formally adopted as titles.

The innovation was a very practical and long overdue step. In future, no matter how often colonel succeeded colonel, the regiment's title remained unchanged, which surely simplified records and administration. The 1751 Warrant laid down mandatory details of dress, appointments and colours. The 33rd conformed to the rest of the line infantry's dress: scarlet knee-length coat with lapels and white lace, red knee-breeches, black gaiters and ankle boots, the headdress being the cocked hat or tricorne of the Marlborough period. The facings were red (or "scarlet", as later described). There is no record of when such facings were first adopted. [a]

The treaty of Aix-la-Chapelle, signed in 1748, had concluded the war of Austrian Succession. However outside Europe the British and French continued their struggle for colonial power with undiminished vigour, particularly in North America and India. The dividing line between nominal peace with hostilities and open war was crossed in May 1756 when the French, under Marshal Richelieu, attacked and captured Minorca. As soon as the news reached England the British government declared war on France.

---

(a) The earliest reference to the red facings of the 33rd is dated 1742, when water coloured illustrations were made for King George II of the uniforms of nearly every regiment then existing.

In October the inclusion of William Pitt in a newly formed Cabinet resulted in a new spirit and vigour being awakened in the country. The principal aim of Pitt's strategy was to overthrow the French in America. Elsewhere he intended to use seapower to lop off French interests, trade and territory in India, the West Indies and Africa, while subsidising Hanover and Prussia in order to prevent the French from sending reinforcements overseas.

Once more the government was forced to make amends for the reductions and disbandments it had demanded after Aix-la-Chapelle. In January 1757, ten new regiments of foot were raised, numbered 50th to 59th, and in the same month, fifteen of the already existing regiments were ordered to raise second battalions. The 33rd, then stationed at Blandford, was one of the fifteen. Where its second battalion was raised and how it was recruited is not known. Major Peter Daulhat of the 33rd was appointed to command. The 2nd/33rd had only a very brief existence as such before being divorced from the Regiment. In 1758 an order was issued directing all the 2nd battalions to be designated *regiments* in their own right "*to take rank from the time of their raising in the same manner as if they had immediately formed into regiments*". And so, after only two years, the 2nd/33rd was transformed into the 72nd Regiment of Foot [b]. Command was given to Charles Lennox, 3rd Duke of Richmond, who had been commanding the 1st/33rd since June 1756, the vacancy in the 33rd being taken up by the Duke's younger brother, Lord George Lennox.[c]

At the beginning of May 1758, the 33rd moved from Blandford to the Isle of Wight, then the customary concentration area for task forces. The current task was a raid on the French coast at St Malo. Four infantry brigades were detailed, the 33rd being in the 3rd Brigade, together with the 23rd (Royal Welch Fusiliers) and 68th (late 2nd RWF and subsequently Durham Light Infantry). The force was commanded by the young Lieutenant General Charles Spencer, 2nd Duke of Marlborough, who had neither the character nor the military prowess of his illustrious forebear.

The landing at Cancale Bay was effected without opposition on 5 May, and while the main force advanced inland to attack the walled town of St Malo, the 33rd and its brigade were held back to secure the beachhead by digging entrenchments. The attack was a failure. When the storming parties reached the town walls, their scaling ladders proved too short, so no storming was possible. Meanwhile the French had been alerted, and were advancing in such superior numbers that Marlborough thought it prudent to withdraw. However, before re-embarking, his men managed to burn most of the shipping in the harbour. The force then made for Le Havre, but as the French were obviously well prepared, no landing was attempted. Cherbourg was the next objective, and yet again there was failure. Before the main force could be disembarked, a gale intervened and this, together with now depleted supplies, obliged Marlborough to abandon further attempts and make for home at Portsmouth, which was reached on 1 July. The entire enterprise had cost the task force no lives, but neither had it achieved

---

(b) The regiment was disbanded at the end of the war. Later other regiments were given the number 72. The last, raised in 1778, becoming The Seaforth Highlanders.
(c) Lord George was another example of the "nursery officers" scandal. An ensigncy was purchased for him when he was 13. He was 20 when he acquired command of the 33rd.

*Operations against the French Coast 1758*

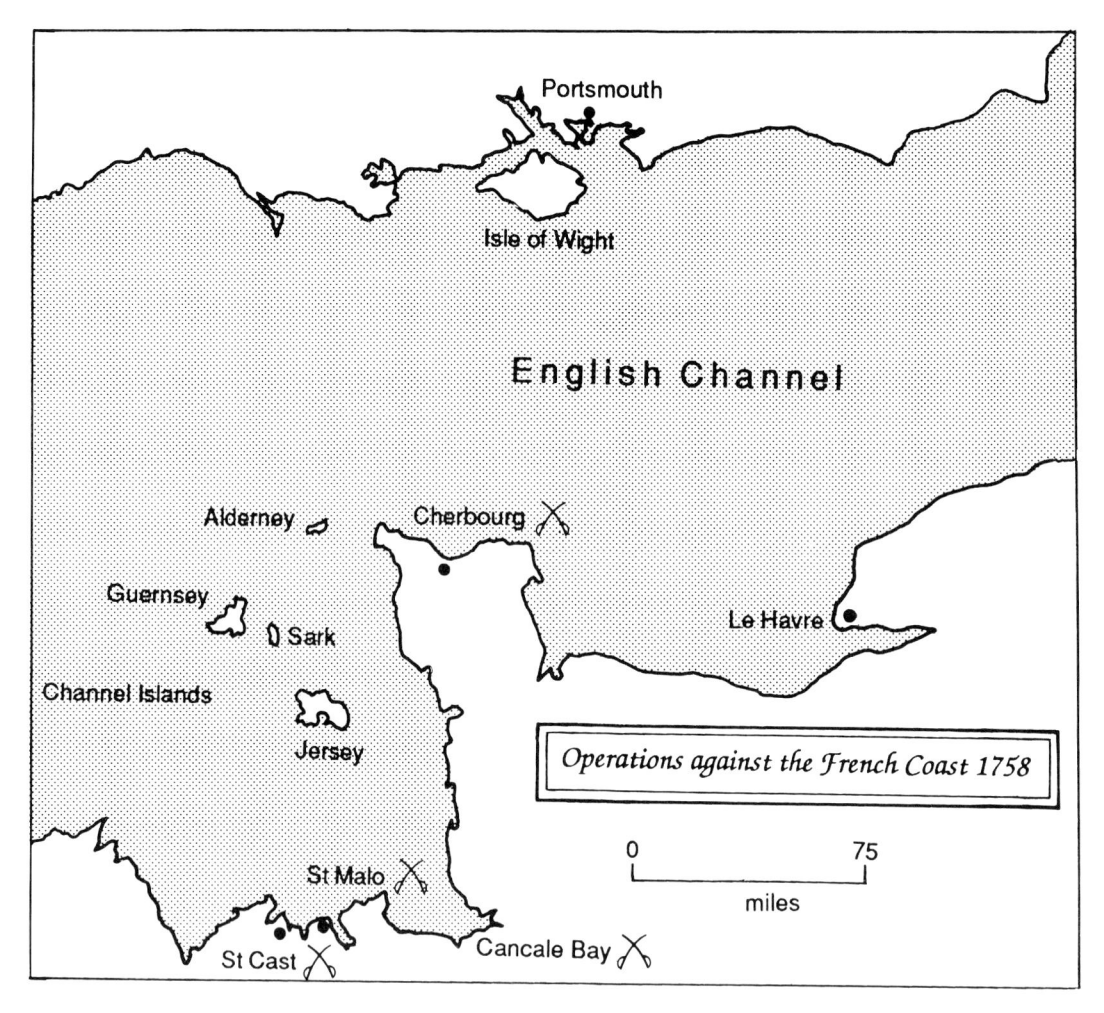

anything except the destruction of a few ships.

After exactly a month back on the Isle of Wight, the 33rd was committed to yet another descent on the French coast. Despite the previous setback, Pitt was determined that the enemy's morale should suffer by a successful attack on Cherbourg, and by late July another task force had been assembled. All that was wanting was a suitable commander. By now both the young Marlborough and Lord George Sackville (who had been his second-in-command) were weary of these unrewarding attempts and had engineered appointments in the more potentially fruitful field of Germany. What followed is described by the contemporary author and MP, Horace Walpole, in one of his letters:

> "You know of course that Lord George Sackville refused to go a-bucaneering again, as he calls it; that my friend Lord Ancram who

*loves a drain of anything from glory to brandy, is out of order; that just as Lord Panmure was going to take command, he missed an eye; and that at last they have routed out an old General Bligh, from the horse armoury in Ireland ….."*

While Lieutenant General Thomas Bligh could well be described as "old" at 74, and for many years had been rusticating in titular command of the cavalry in Ireland ("horse armoury"), he was a veteran of continental campaigning in which he had displayed great personal courage if also small powers of command. The expedition set sail on 1 August with the 33rd and the 72nd among the nine battalions of infantry. The grenadier companies of the battalions were withdrawn and formed into a separate grenadier battalion under the command of Major Peter Daulhat of the 33rd. This was a relatively new practice that had first been advocated during the war of the Austrian Succession but had then been forbidden by the King, as an undesirable Austrian innovation. The effect of forming the companies into a separate battalion was to give the force commander an élite body under his direct control.

The fleet arrived off Cherbourg on 7 August and next morning an assault force was made up of the three Guards battalions and the grenadier battalion. Put ashore in the bay of St. Marais, six miles from Cherbourg, the force successfully drove off some 3,000 French infantry and established a secure beachhead, thus allowing the main body to land on the following day and advance on Cherbourg itself. Threatened on the landward side where there were no defences, the garrison tamely surrendered without a fight. The raiders now proceeded to wreak destruction in the harbour: 30 ships were set on fire, quays were demolished by explosives. The booty captured and taken on board the fleet included 200 guns and mortars and a number of French colours.

Re-embarking for further exploits along the coast, General Bligh and his troops could well congratulate themselves on a splendid operation. For all the damage they had inflicted, they had lost only about 20 men. But fate and the weather now intervened. Having been blown off course almost back to the English coast, the transports and men-o'-war eventually dropped anchor in the Bay of St. Lunaire, a few miles east of St. Malo, where the troops disembarked, apparently without opposition. The intention was another attempt on St Malo from the landward side, but plans were upset by the steadily worsening weather. Admiral Howe informed Bligh that the fleet must leave its dangerous anchorage at St. Lunaire and make for the sheltered bay of St. Cast, some fifteen miles to the west. Only here would it be possible to re-embark the troops. So the attack was called off, and as the fleet made sail for shelter, Bligh and his troops were left to find their own way overland to St. Cast. The first obstacle was the estuary of the river Equernon, which Bligh proposed to cross at 6.00am the following day. But no one had troubled to find out that this was the hour of high tide, so that the troops could only sit around until 3.00pm when they waded across up to their waists in water and under a brisk fire from French guerillas and soldiers. By the third day (10 September), Bligh had arrived within reach of the St. Cast beaches, having en route brushed aside some opposition and taken a few prisoners. From the latter came alarming rumours of some 10,000 French advancing from the Brest direction with the obvious intent of cutting off the raiders. Speedy evacuation was now paramount and Bligh managed to send word to Admiral Howe, anchored in the bay, that the soldiers would embark on the following morning. This they might have done unmolested if the veteran general and his staff had been more alive to the danger, and stolen silently away. Instead, at 3.00am on the 11th, his drummers roused all within earshot with the reverberations of the *Assembly* "*... to give the French all the information that they desired*", (Fortescue). As if on peacetime manoeuvres, the force then moved off in a single column "*so to consume the longest possible time on the march*", and it was not until 9.00am that the beaches were reached and embarkation could commence. Two hours later the enemy appeared in force. As the soldiers struggled through the surf for the boats, many were shot or drowned. The rearguard of Guards and grenadier companies commanded by General Drury valiantly fought off repeated attacks but, suffering casualties, and ammunition failing, the survivors could only rush for the boats. By the time embarkation was completed, General Bligh had lost 750 all ranks killed or wounded.

On 18 September the fleet made into Cowes, and the troops went into camp at Newport (I O W). There are no records of the 33rd's casualties (nor of the 72nd's) in this humiliating end to Pitt's designs on the French coast. Captain Dansey Collins (33rd) wrote to his wife on 21 September, informing her that Lieutenant Drummond was killed, and Lieutenant Price, together with 62 men of the grenadier company were "*killed or taken*". Also killed was Captain Thomas Edmonstone, commanding the grenadier company.

For the following two years the Regiment remained inactive in the Isle of Wight "*for the internal security of the Kingdom*". In the European theatre the allied force of British, Hanoverians and Prussians was under the supreme command of Prince Ferdinand of Brunswick[d], whose principal aim was to fulfil Pitt's strategy of containing the maximum number of French troops within the European theatre. To assist him in his task Pitt had sent him, in 1758, six regiments of cavalry and six battalions of infantry. In August 1759 he had been instrumental in gaining a magnificent victory at Minden. This might have been a still greater one but for the negligence of the commander of the British contingent, Lord George Sackville, for which he was subsequently tried by court martial.[e] He was replaced by Lieutenant General John Manners, Marquis of Granby.

The defeat of the French at Minden was followed by the customary winter recess, profitably utilised by both sides to recoup losses. In the autumn of 1759 Pitt persuaded Parliament to approve the raising of additional units, six of cavalry and eleven of infantry. As a result of this and the great naval victory at Quiberon Bay, which removed the threat of a French invasion, he was able to despatch five more regiments of cavalry and seven of infantry to join the allied army with Ferdinand in May and June 1760. Known as "the Glorious Reinforcement", this included the 33rd, commanded by

---

(d) The Prince was the brother in law of King Frederick of Prussia and an experienced Prussian general.
(e) Despite repeated orders, he sat idle with his cavalry, leaving the infantry to retrieve the day. On his court martial he was dismissed the service as "*unfit to serve His Majesty.....*" But later, as Lord Germaine, he became Secretary of State for the Colonies.

Lieutenant Colonel Lord George Lennox.

But before the 33rd confronted the enemy, it underwent a change of colonelcy in somewhat curious circumstances. Lord Charles Hay had been Colonel since 1753, though it is improbable that the Regiment saw much of him after March 1757. On this date, he was promoted major general and given command of a force sent to Halifax, Nova Scotia, where Lieutenant General the Earl of Loudoun (C-in-C of British troops in North America) was ostensibly preparing for an attack on the French at Louisberg. These preparations took an interminable time, so long that, apparently unable, or unwilling, to commit himself to a definite course of action, the earl was recalled to England. Such indecision had provoked Lord Charles Hay into uttering some indiscreet criticism of his superior officer: *"The General was keeping the courage of His Majesty's troops at bay"* said he *"and expending the nation's wealth in making sham sieges and planting cabbages when he should have been fighting"*. However justified, such criticism could not go unnoticed, and in January 1760, Lord Charles was summoned home to face a court martial. The proceedings dragged on from 12 February to 4 March, the accused presenting *"a very good soldierly defence"*, as observed by Dr Johnson who was a friend of Hay's. Before the findings could be made public they had to be submitted to the King for approval, but two months elapsed without a hint of the royal decision. In the meantime Major General Lord Charles Hay, Colonel of the 33rd Foot, had died on 1 May 1760 aged 66.

His successor, appointed on 5 May, was Major General John Griffin Griffin, son of William Whitwell of Oundle, Northamptonshire. He assumed the name of Griffin in 1749, his mother's family name. John Griffin, now aged 41, had served with the 3rd Foot Guards since 1744, and had fought in the war of the Austrian Succession. At this period it had become rare for a colonel to concern himself with the actual command of his regiment. This was left to the lieutenant colonel, now the *de facto* commanding officer.

The 33rd sailed from Gravesend on 15 May 1760 and disembarked at Bremen a week later. Together with the 5th (Northumberland Fusiliers) and 11th Foot (Devonshire), it marched to join Ferdinand's reserve at Wabern, near Fritzlar, which it reached on 17 June. The allied army under Prince Ferdinand could now deploy some 80,000 horse, foot and guns to confront Marshal Broglie's roughly equal French army.

The 33rd was in a brigade consisting of the 11th (Devonshire), 23rd (RWF) and 51st (KOYLI), commanded by its Colonel, Major General John Griffin Griffin who, however, was shortly succeeded by Major General Brudnell, Colonel of the 51st. As was by now customary, the seven grenadier companies of the infantry battalions were detached from their parents and formed into a separate grenadier battalion, command being given to Major Peter Daulhat of the 33rd (f).

On 23 June, following a move forward by the French, Ferdinand ordered nine British battalions (including the 33rd) to join his forward troops near the River Ohm. The rest of the army followed the next day. However the troops had scarcely arrived at

---

(f) It formed part of a special brigade under Lieut Colonel Beckwith, (20th, Lancashire Fusiliers). The other battalions were a battalion of grenadiers under Major Maxwell, (20th Foot) and the 87th and 88th Highlanders.

*Western Germany 1760 - 1763*

the Ohm before a withdrawal was decided upon with the result that they found themselves toiling back over the roads they had just covered. This was a foretaste of what was to follow; two years of marching, counter marching and camping in wild country, often in appalling weather with little chance of distinguishing themselves in battle.

Further forced marches followed when an attempt was made to relieve the Hereditary Prince (g) at Korbach, but the relieving troops arrived too late to prevent his crushing defeat. Ferdinand next decided to make a raid on the French lines of communication in the course of which, on 16 July 1760, a single, newly-raised regiment of British cavalry, the 15th Light Dragoons, charged six French infantry battalions, slaying or capturing some 1,600 of them.

---

(g) The Hereditary Prince of Brunswick was a nephew of Prince Ferdinand.

In the face of continued French pressure Ferdinand reluctantly decided upon a further withdrawal so as to protect his main base at Kassel. Broglie, observing these movements and anxious to get to the Diemel river before Ferdinand, ordered the Chevalier du Muy to occupy a position at Warburg. By 30 July a French force of some 20,000 all arms had taken up a strong position along a ridge on the left bank of the Diemel. Their right flank extended almost to the walls of Warburg, then left towards the village of Ossendorf. The Hereditary Prince, with 14,000 British and Hanoverians, was encamped at Liebenau, about seven miles east of Warburg, while Ferdinand with the main force had halted 15 miles south of Liebenau. Having personally reconnoitred the enemy position, the Hereditary Prince resolved on a bold plan. Two columns would execute a wide flanking movement around the north of the French position and then fall upon their left flank near Ossendorf, while the main force under Ferdinand himself would advance simultaneously on the right wing around Warburg. Ferdinand, having ridden ahead of his command, approved the plan, and the attack was to go in soon after first light on the 31st.

This plan demanded close co-ordination between the two movements, especially as one was fifteen miles short of the start line and with the Diemel to cross. Ferdinand's main body began the approach march at 9.00pm on the 30th. However his infantry not only suffered delays in crossing the Diemel the following morning but also had to make its way forward over marshy land and through standing corn, As a result the Hereditary Prince's two columns had arrived in position for attack hours before the main body could come up.

By 1.30pm, hard marching had brought both columns round to the left rear of du Muy's position, between the hamlets of Ossendorf and Menne, where they deployed into battle formation. Just behind the ridge held by the French was another similar feature, the Heinberg, and this was the first objective. It was occupied, without opposition, by two grenadier battalions under Major Maxwell (20th Foot) and Major Daulhat (33rd). They were joined by some Hanoverian grenadiers and the 87th and 88th Highlanders, led by Colonel Beckwith, and by the Hereditary Prince in person. On the latter's orders, battle was opened by fire on the French rear from the two regimental guns dragged up the height.[h] Thus provoked, and realising the threat to his left flank, du Muy immediately launched two infantry brigades against the Prince's position, and a fierce struggle ensued. Daulhat's grenadiers were overwhelmed and forced back on to Maxwell's in the rear, where the two battalions bravely rallied, and now supported by the Hanoverian grenadiers, stormed forward once more. Meanwhile the other flanking column (the left) had deployed and was assaulting the depleted enemy's left flank. Then the Royals and 7th Dragoons galloped up and made repeated charges against the broken enemy ranks.

His left wing now in utter disarray, du Muy could only order a withdrawal across the Diemel with the intention of making a stand on another tactical feature. But this plan was thwarted by the Marquis of Granby and his British cavalry. Riding hard ahead of

---

(h) At this period each infantry battalion was allotted two light 3-pounder guns for close support.

Lieutenant General John Manners, Marquis of Granby, with a sick soldier. Because of his care of his soldiers he was beloved by them. Hence the large number of public houses that bear his name.

Ferdinand's main body of infantry, the ten cavalry regiments came on the field in time to deploy with fourteen squadrons in their first line, eight in the second, and crashed into the French just as they were preparing to withdraw [i]. As they struggled across the river, they were pursued by grape and roundshot from the British field gunners who had displayed unprecedented mobility in bringing up their pieces.

The battle of Warburg cost the French some 7,000 casualties in killed, wounded and prisoners, while they also lost twelve field guns. The total casualties of the allies amounted to 1,237. General Savory [j] details casualties by regiments, but he does not mention the 33rd. It was doubtless trudging the 18-odd miles from Calden with Ferdinand's main body arriving too late to see action. However, Savory records that Daulhat's grenadiers lost 173 all ranks. The grenadier company of the 33rd had 5 men killed and 33 wounded. Immediately after the battle Major Peter Daulhat was rewarded with command of the 51st Regiment. Command of his grenadier battalion was given to Lieutenant Colonel Lord George Lennox, who continued, however, to be in nominal command of the 33rd.

Warburg was granted as a battle honour to the twelve cavalry regiments who took part. Although the infantry bore the brunt of the initial fighting, no infantry regiment

---

(i) It was then that Granby at the head of his own regiment, the Blues, lost first his hat, then his wig, and so galloped 'bald headed' for the enemy.
(j) *His Britannic Majesty's Army in Germany during the Seven Years War.* Lieutenant General Sir R A Savory. OUP 1966.

was granted the honour.[k]

Despite the victory at Warburg, Kassel fell the following day. Its possession by the French became a key factor in the strategy of both sides for the next two years. Ferdinand, planning ahead, noted that the Lower Rhine was denuded of French troops. The opportunity therefore presented itself of capturing Wesel and using it as a base for future operations. To draw Broglie's attention away from the Lower Rhine a raid against the enemy's communications was planned. In the small hours of 6 September, the Hereditary Prince carried out a brilliantly successful night raid on the French fortified post of Zierenberg (between Warburg and Kassel), during which the garrison was surprised and attacked with bayonet only, losing 120 killed and wounded and 400 captured. The 33rd was not involved in this affair, but its Colonel, Major General John Griffin, led the main raiding party of 20th Foot, some grenadiers and Highlanders. He was accidentally bayonetted by one of his own men in the darkness and confusion, but the wound was not serious.

Zierenberg, though a morale booster, was a minor part of the operations, but in October came a major confrontation at Kloster Kamp on the left bank of the Rhine. This was an insignificant village, taking its name from a former convent (Kloster) and lying some nine miles south west of the strategic fortress of Wesel, on the opposite bank, which guarded one of the main river crossings. But the bridge was destroyed, and the pontoons ordered up from Holland were delayed, so that a direct assault proved impossible, and the Hereditary Prince was resigned to preparing a formal siege. While his troops were labouring to dig entrenchments and redoubts, the French were creating a diversion. By 14 October, their commander in the field, the Marquis de Castries, had moved up a force of some 7,000 horse and foot to take position along a line threatening the allies' rear, in the area of Kloster Kamp. However the day before a boat bridge had at last been established and, learning of this threat, the Prince at once decided to dispel it by attack. At 7,500 men his strength was a little more than the enemy's. With his force was Major General Brudnell's brigade, which included the 33rd, together with five Hessian battalions, all under Lieutenant General Howard. The grenadier company of the 33rd was with Lord George Lennox's grenadier battalion.

Bearing in mind the success of the bayonet-only night raid at Zierenberg, the Prince launched his attack at midnight on 15/16 October. The main column comprised the 20th (Lancashire Fusiliers), 23rd (RWF) and 25th Foot (KOSB) under Major General John Griffin, with 150 Highlanders and Lennox's and Maxwell's grenadiers under Beckwith. Two Hanoverian and two Hessian battalions completed the assault force. The battalion companies of the 33rd were held in reserve, together with those of the 11th (Devonshire), 51st (KOYLI) and five Hessian battalions.

At first all went according to plan. The bold night attack (highly unorthodox for that period) again caught the French by surprise. Indeed, had it not been for the sacrificial bravery of one officer, the outcome might well have been different. At about 4.00am, the stealthily advancing British ("*no firing*") ran into a French outpost,

---

(k) This was because only their grenadier companies were present. To be eligible for an award the headquarters and at least half of a regiment had to be present.

bayonetted the soldiers and captured their officer. But instead of allowing himself to be hustled quietly to the rear, this noble fellow yelled at the top of his voice *"A moi! A moi Auvergne! Voila les ennemis!"* *(To me! To me Auvergne! The enemy is here!)* Then he fell, pierced by half a dozen bayonets.[1] All the element of surprise was now lost. Alerted by the Auvergne regiment, Castries ordered a general stand-to at alarm posts, and the advancing line of British infantry was met by fire. There was no faltering, however, and having over-run the outposts and forward defences, the Highlanders and the rest swept on at the double through farmyards, orchards and coppices, yelling and cheering as they went. In such conditions the attack became fragmented, units losing all cohesion and control. Thus, when Castries brought up a reserve brigade with its regimental guns, and smote the British right in a fierce counter attack, the disintegrated line was in no fit state to withstand it. What followed can only be described as a shameful rout, with officers, including the Hereditary Prince himself, vainly striving to restore some control. At one point, the Prince's horse was shot under him, and, falling heavily, he lay temporarily stunned. He was dragged under cover by Lord George Lennox. Also struggling to re-form his brigade was General John Griffin who was so severely wounded that he had to be evacuated to England after the battle. Had Castries chosen to follow up with a vigorous pursuit he might well have destroyed the allied army and captured (or slain) its commander. But unaccountably he did no such thing, and the mauled attackers were allowed to regain cohesion behind the line of reserves who had pushed forward too late to play any part in the fight.

Although Kloster Kamp was a somewhat ignoble defeat, it cost the French some 3,120 casualties, to the allies' 1,600. The battalion companies of the 33rd with General Howard's reserve did not come into action and thus suffered no loss, but Lennox's grenadiers, in the thick of the attack, lost 132 all ranks. The heaviest sufferer was Griffin's brigade which lost a total of 1,050 all ranks. Largely due to sickness the British brigades, which had started the campaign below strength, were now so weak that they had to be sent to Münster on garrison duty to recover. The 33rd was only 120 strong and the other regiments were in a similar state.

Ferdinand's plan of campaign for 1761 was to launch an attack on Kassel. His intention was to surprise the French by commencing his campaign during the winter months when hard frost would facilitate the movement of his troops and supplies. On 9 February he set his plan in motion when he ordered his troops to concentrate at various places on the River Diemel. His main force was in the centre. Two British infantry regiments (the 33rd and 51st) were allocated to the troops under command of the Hereditary Prince on the right flank. On 11 February the advance started. Serving in the 33rd was Ensign William Collins who described events in a letter to his mother.

*"The 11th we march to the heights of Stadbergen where we stood for 4*
*hours for the Army to come up, it snowing the whole time very fast ...*

---

[1] This officer was later identified as the Chevalier d'Assas, captain in the Regiment d'Auvergne. A memorial to him stands in his home town of Le Vigan, near Montpelier.

*We march all that day, at Night we came within a mile and a half of Cantonements where we lay for 3 hours in the Snow without a bit of Fire .... I did not get any sleep that night, or under cover before 12o'clock..... The next morning we marched about 9o'clock came to the Heights of Fritslar (sic) where we had our first camp in the beginning of the last campaign....* (The Hereditary Prince summoned the town to surrender, but this being refused, an assault was planned). *We march and Attack'd the Town, Our Regt. was at ye Head of the Column and marched under the town into a Hollow Way, by that means we were cover'd from the Enemy's fire. We had one man killed and 2 wounded that Day.... Our Regt. lay all Night before ye Town though ther was Frost and Snow on the Ground. The next day we took the Town. Our Regt. took possession of it ..... I mind nothing, thank God I am as well and in great spirits as ever, if I get a blanket and Ration of Straw it make an excellent Bed for me ...."* (m)

Matters proceeded well and the investment of Kassel was ordered while the French endeavoured to recover from their surprise. However at this point the weather broke and the frost on which Ferdinand had relied so strongly started to thaw. The roads *"became excessive deep, by which means the artillery had a great deal of difficulty to keep up, and the infantry marched up to their knees in dirt and mud"*. The French, meanwhile, had begun to take offensive action and in the process inflicted some defeats on Ferdinand's troops. On 23 March he started to withdraw and on the 31st re-crossed the Diemel.

A major cause of the lack of success of the campaign was a breakdown of the commissariat from which the British troops seem to have suffered most. The British generals were not logistically minded. Winter conditions, great exertions and insufficient food brought on sickness. The hospitals were filled and the medical staff was too small to deal with all the sick. One result of these shortcomings was the appointment of General Howard as Intendant General to co-ordinate the whole administration of the army.

By 1 June, however, the allied army had recuperated and reinforcements were at last reaching the British contingent. The French meanwhile had formed two separate armies. Prince de Soubise commanded that of the lower Rhine; de Broglie the army of the Main. Soubise was to open the campaign, which he did by crossing the Lower Rhine early in June, and by the 29th Ferdinand and Soubise were facing each other. Ferdinand then took the bold decision to march round Soubise's northern flank by night, and attack him in the rear. However no attack was possible as the ground was found to be water logged. Ferdinand then followed Soubise eastwards until the latter met up with

---

(m) He was the son of Captain Dansey Collins (33rd), who was also serving with the Regiment in Germany. William had come to Germany as a volunteer and been appointed ensign as the result of his mother's entreaties. *"I am told"*, wrote Viscount Barrington (the Secretary of State for War) to Granby, *"there is a vacancy of Lieutenant or Ensign in the 33rd Regiment, and that a young man of sixteen, son of Captn Collins of that corps, now actually carrys(sic) arms in it. If you had seen his mother, who is one of the handsomest women I have ever beheld, and does not seem above twenty herself, you would not have been to able to refuse writing at her request such a letter as I now write...Do not let Mrs Collins reputation suffer by unjust suspicion. I never saw her but for one minute in my life, and probably shall never see her again".*

Broglie when Ferdinand took up a defensive position near Vellinghausen. The 33rd was brigaded, as before, with the 11th, 23rd and 51st, now under the command of Major General Lord Cavendish. The French commenced their attack in the afternoon of 15 July and the fighting continued into the night, much of it at short distance between the opposing infantry. There was a further French attack the following morning until Ferdinand, noticing some confusion among the French, ordered a general assault. The French were caught on the point of withdrawal and were forced into full retreat. Despite their overwhelming superiority in strength, the French had been defeated with the loss of some 6,000 men, while the allies' casualties did not exceed 1,600. Writing to his mother on 4 September, William Collins said nothing about the action itself, but informed her that *"Poor Mr Ward of our Regt. is dead of the Wound he received in his ancle the 16th of July at the Battle of Tillinghausen (sic.) after having his leg cut off"*. Ward was one of Collins' fellow ensigns. According to Lee, the only other regimental casualties were one sergeant and six other ranks wounded.

At the battle of Vellinghausen the French had been beaten by an army half their size and their loss in morale seems to have been in proportion. For the rest of the war they avoided battle.

The next three months were spent marching and counter marching. Ensign Henry Benjamin of the 33rd recorded an itinerary of 329 miles between 29 July and 8 November 1761[n]. After the usual winter close season of 1761-62 there was little activity until Ferdinand, discovering that the French were concentrating their armies in the area of Kassel, decided to launch an attack on them. On the 24 June 1762, the main body of 70,000 French under the Marquis de Castries was in position just north of the small town of Wilhelmsthal, between Warburg and Kassel. Prince Ferdinand and the Allies, some 50,000 strong, opened the action with two columns attacking the French left while the Prince personally led a direct attack on the centre. With him was all the British infantry. Co-ordination of the two-pronged attack was skilfully executed: no sooner had the French centre been assaulted by Ferdinand than the two other columns fell upon their left wing. Near panic followed as the French retired in confusion before the dual assault, in spite of the gallant stand of the Comte de Stainville and his grenadiers, who were practically annihilated. Ferdinand pursued the fugitives south of Wilhelmsthal and then stopped. His 50,000 had driven off 70,000 and inflicted 3,000 casualties for the loss of some 500 of his own. As Fortescue observes, *"the French were not a little shamefaced and discouraged"* by this defeat.

Captain Dansey Collins wrote to his wife on the following day:

> *"I have the Pleasure to acquaint you that Yesterday we attacked the whole French Army and drove them before us for 7, 8 or 10 Miles or perhaps more. Their loss is very considerable ours I believe not very great, but yr News papers will clear that up....Miss Cock o Colchester whom I believe you remember, had a brother killed in front of our*

---

(n) Henry Benjamin had been appointed ensign in the 33rd on 24 March 1761. Prior to that he was probably a volunteer. A year later he purchased a lieutenancy in the 11th Foot (Devonshire).

> *Regiment. If we had one Man killed that is all, but not I think in the Battln but our Grenadiers I hear have suffered greatly I should have been glad if your Son had been present on so Glorious an Occasion but his Duty obliges him to continue at Bremen".*

There followed more marching, counter marching and ponderous manoeuvring for position but no notable engagements, as far as the 33rd was concerned. Eventually, on 15 November 1762, an Armistice was signed, following which the British troops moved to the area of Münster and Osnabrück. In February the following year the Treaty of Paris was ratified and the war came to an end. (o)

The British contingent was the backbone of the army in Germany and its exploits caused Pitt to declare in the House of Commons on 13 November 1761: *"America has been conquered in Germany, where Prince Ferdinand's victories have shattered the whole military power of that great Military monarchy, France".*

---

(o) Among the officers who served with the 33rd during the war in Germany was Captain James Webster, a cousin of James Boswell. In his diary for 20 December 1762 Boswell recorded *"I went and sat awhile with Captain James Webster. He told me that the fatigues of a German campaign are almost incredible. That he was fourteen nights running without being under cover, and often had scarcely any victuals...."*

CHAPTER 5

# The American War of Independence

*1776 Brooklyn Heights, White Plains, Fort Washington*
*1777 Brandywine, Germantown*
*1778 Freehold*
*1779 Verplants*
*1780 Charleston, Camden*
*1781 Guilford Court House, Yorktown*
*1782 33rd (or 1st Yorkshire West Riding) Regiment*

At the conclusion of The Seven Years war in 1763 Britain had become a dominant power over much of the world. Her flag flew throughout North America and the West Indies, around the Mediterranean and in the eastern and southern reaches of the Indian peninsular. For most of the British Army the next decade or so held only undemanding peacetime duties.

Having arrived home from Germany in the summer of 1763 the 33rd spent an uneventful year of garrison duty at Colchester and Ipswich, before being posted to Minorca. During this period its strength was brought up to twenty officers and 706 other ranks. Minorca had been captured from the Spanish in 1708, during the war of Spanish Succession, but was lost to the French in 1756 at the beginning of the Seven Years war. As a result of his failure to defeat the French fleet Admiral Byng was court martialled and sentenced to be shot, *"pour encourager les autres"*, as Voltaire said. At the conclusion of the War, under the terms of the Treaty of Paris, Minorca was restored to the British. Six infantry battalions were allocated to garrison the island. They were quartered at Mahon, Fort San Filipe and Ciudadela, on the western extremity of the island, and the regiments seem to have been rotated between them. The quarters at San Filipe were particularly bad and in 1767 a board of officers, convened by order of the Governor, reported that the soldiers' barracks were *"neither wind or water tight.. and were past repairing"* and that *"some of the officers quarters are not fit for officers to live in......"* The board, which included Lieutenant Colonel Hildebrand Oakes, commanding the 33rd [a], and

---

[a] Lieutenant Colonel Hildebrand Oakes had succeeded Lieutenant Colonel Lord George Lennox in command of the 33rd in April 1762

Major John Gore (33rd), the Fort Major, recommended that new barracks should be built. But no action was taken on the ground of expense.

At that time the 33rd was quartered around the town of Ciudadela and it was there that Lieutenant William Collins, who had been on half pay, rejoined the Regiment from England. During his two years on the island his letters contain not a single reference to any military duty or training. Instead he regaled his parents with tittle-tattle about brother officers and his own leisurely lifestyle. *"I am in a Corps remarkable for genteelness, sobriety and amity ... I suppose there is not a more friendly Corps in the army which Colonel Oakes has been the means of making ..."* Major John Gore and his wife dispensed lavish hospitality: *"Major Gore keeps an exceeding good House, every Thing of the best of this Island, I believe as good as the Governor's; keeps a great deal of Company and very frequent Card Nights which Mrs Gore is very fond of. She seems to be a gay expensive woman ..."* To add to the amenities, the officers and civilian gentlemen clubbed together to form an amateur theatrical group: *"the Actors are any Gentlemen or Ladies that chose it"*. Later, when the Regiment was moved to Fort San Filipe, he was on detached duty and able to live in his own comfortable quarter some distance from the mess. His description of his normal routine reads more like that of a gentleman of leisure than a serving junior officer:

> *"I spend the Morning in my Quarter in dishabille (sic.) sitting in a Banian (loose house coat) and Trousers, and read, write, draw or Net, just what happens to be my favourite at the time ... about 3 o'clock I take my Dinner ... I generally drink a Pint of Wine which costs me about a Penny. After Dinner I put on a clean Shirt, dress and powder my Hair and walk up into Town to hear the News and somebody or other generally picks me up so that I seldom find my way to my Fort again till between 11 and 12 o'clock. I have not supped above 5 times at my own Expense since we have been at St Philips ... I can't be easy or show my Face without a clean Shirt and Powder in my Hair and clean white stockings for we Military Gentlemen are very dressy in these Days .... "*

While in Minorca, in March 1766, Brigadier General Lord Charles Cornwallis had succeeded General Sir John Griffin Griffin [b] as Colonel of the Regiment. Born in 1738 as Lord Charles Brome (eldest son of Earl Cornwallis of Brome Hall, Suffolk, whom he succeeded as 2nd Earl in 1762), the young nobleman began his military career in the 1st Foot Guards at the age of eighteen. Five years later, he was lieutenant colonel commanding the 12th Foot (Suffolk), with whom he saw active service in Germany during the Seven Years war.

The Regiment returned from Minorca in 1769 and was billeted around Salisbury. In June 1769 it was warned to march to Hounslow for a grand review of the troops by the King. On 12 June, William Collins informed his father that *"Lord Cornwallis and Lord*

---

(b) Later Field Marshal and 4th Lord Howard de Walden.

*Ancram came down to the Regiment on Thursday last, they live in our Mess and will stay with us'till after The Review ... Lord Cornwallis has a great deal to do now to get us ready to shew before the King and all Morning, we have nothing but the Art of War going on one way or another".* For the occasion of the royal review at Hounslow, the Regiment was kitted out with new articles of dress and equipment. This was in part the result of new Dress Regulations issued in 1768, though the King had stated that the plainer the uniforms were, the better he would be pleased. In a letter to his father Lieutenant Collins bewailed the additional expense: *"We have been all put to the same Expense as young Gentlemen that have just joined the Regiment, since we came here* (Salisbury) *we have had new Hats and Silver Hilted Swords besides our Regimentals which we expect down from the Taylor every day, and when we are reviewed by the King we must have new Sashes and Gorgets ... We are all run over head in Debt. It is next to impossible to live on ones Pay here".*

In 1772 the Regiment was moved to Gloucester and then, one year later, to Plymouth. Since about 1720 it had become the rule for all regiments to be reported on annually in order to assess their fitness for service. In 1769, the Regiment was reported to be *"in an excellent state of training"*. By 1772, it had become *"One of the finest Regiments in His Majesty's Service"*. While at Plymouth, in March 1774, the Regiment was inspected by Major General William Howe, a highly respected officer of wide experience. His subsequent report confirms the continued excellent state of the Regiment.

The officers were *"a good corps ... exceedingly expert at their duty. Properly armed. Saluted well"*. The colonel, Lord Cornwallis, was aged 35; the lieutenant colonel, Hildebrand Oakes, was 43, the major, James Webster, 33. The total of 30 officers included 22 English, 5 Scottish and 3 Irish.

There were 385 other ranks on the strength, of whom 319 were English, 8 Scottish, 57 Irish, with "1 Foreigner". The NCOs were of *"Good Appearance. Attentive and expert at their Duty..."* The Drummers and Fifers *"beat and play well"*. Altogether the men were *"a very fine corps very young"*.

After complimentary remarks on the marching, manual exercises, clothing, arms and accoutrements (and noting that there were "no complaints"), General Howe gave his summing up:

> *"General Observations. Fit for Immediate service ... The men are well dressed. Remarkably upright strictly silent under Arms. The files are always very open. The Battalion is exceedingly rapid in all movements, which for the most part are performed on the run, the same good front being nevertheless preserved without heeding any assistance from the Officers to dress the Battalion on the Halt ... The men are so perfectly attentive, steady and well acquainted with their respective places in the Rank and File in the Battalion that the C.O. calling upon a file or single man by the number in which they stand in their respective Companies to fire, the Battalion previously made ready, the order is obeyed without the least hesitation.*

*The Regiment made a most formidable charge running upwards 200 yards in the best order and fired a volley as soon as halted ... An exceedingly fine company of Light Infantry. The officers and men well trained and perfectly acquainted with their duty. It was posted on the left of the Battalion for the manual exercises and firing the Grenadiers remaining on the right. The Light Company has a bugle horn to give signals.*

*The Regiment has nine musicians enlisted as soldiers.*

*The Officers have a Sutler, eat together and live in friendship".*

Finally the general gave it as his opinion that the discipline of the Regiment was *"far superior to any other Corps within my observation"*. Shortly after the inspection Lieutenant Colonel James Webster succeeded Lieutenant Colonel Hildebrand Oakes in command of the 33rd [c].

Later in 1774, the 33rd was posted to Dublin, and while there, Sergeant Lamb of the 9th (Norfolk) was sent to the Regiment to be instructed in the new light infantry manoeuvres. Like all the infantry the 33rd now deployed a second "flank" [d] company in addition to the grenadiers. This was the light company (added in 1771) who were supposed to be men of "superior intelligence", able to display some degree of initiative in skirmishing, patrolling and "scouting" or reconnaissance tasks. For those reasons they were smaller in stature than the grenadiers. In 1775 the average height of the grenadiers in the 33rd was 5' 10½" whereas there was no man taller than 5' 7" in the light company. In the 33rd, command of the light company was given to the erstwhile William Collins who had now changed his surname to Dansey.[e] Sergeant Lamb's impressions, like those of the general officers who had carried out the annual inspections, were also highly complimentary to the 33rd.

### HEREFORDSHIRE.

ANY able-bodied young Man, between the age of 17 and 22, and not under five feet six inches high, ſtreight and well made, who is fired with ambition, has a roving diſpoſition, and whoſe ſpirit ſoars above the dull ſameneſs of ſtaying at home, having courage, inclination, and freedom, to serve *His Majeſty King* GEORGE *the Third*, in His MAJESTY's Thirty-third Regiment of Foot, whereof The Right Honorable CHARLES Earl Cornwallis is Colonel, and in the company under the command of Capt. WILLIAM DANSEY, of Brinſop near Hereford, or Captain THOMAS GORGES, of Eye near Leominſter, now quartered in the city of Dublin, in the kingdom of Ireland, ſhall meet with the greateſt encouragement from Capt. DANSEY of Brinſop, or at Eye aforeſaid, and enter into preſent pay and good quarters, as alſo immediately receive new cloathing.

It is deſired, that none will apply who cannot have an honeſt character, as thoſe Men only will be taken who promiſe to be a credit to their officers, and an honor to their country.

A recruiting poster for the 33rd Regiment c. 1774.

---

(c) Hildebrand Oakes: The elder of his two sons, also named Hildebrand, served with the 33rd during the American War of Independence. He eventually became Lieutenant General Sir Hildebrand Oakes 1st Bart.
(d) So called because when a regiment formed in line the grenadier company took position on the right flank and the light company on the left.
(e) Collins/Dansey. His grandmother had been born Dansey. When the Dansey male line ceased the Collins family had, in 1768, taken the Dansey name.

*"I am bound to record here that I felt a certain shamefacedness, on visiting the barracks of The Thirty-Third Regiment, who were commanded by the young Earl of Cornwallis, to compare their high state of appointment and the steadiness of their discipline with the slovenly and relaxed bearing of most of our own companies. One can always correctly judge a regiment's capacities by the behaviour of its sentries ...I have seen men go on duty in the Ninth dead drunk and scarcely able to stand. But with The Thirty-Third the sentry was always alert and alive in attention; when on duty he was all eye, all ear. Even in the sentry-box, which he never entered unless in a downpour of rain, he was forbidden to keep the palm of his hand carelessly on the muzzle of his loaded firelock; for this was considered as dangerous an attitude as it was awkward. During the two hours that he remained on his post the sentry continued in constant motion and could not walk less than seven miles in that time. The Thirty-Third thus set a standard of soldier-like duty which made me secretly dissatisfied with The Ninth and which I have never seen equalled since but by a single other regiment which was brigaded with The Thirty-Third under the same Lord Cornwallis in the later campaigns of the American War. I resolved at least to bring the men who were under my immediate command into a state of discipline for which I should have no cause to blush".*

The training of the 33rd was not confined to the parade ground and it became noted for its unconventional displays of professionalism. Thus in 1774 (after moving to Kinsale) it staged an ambitious exercise during which, with the 20th Foot as enemy, it landed in the harbour and attacked the defences, only to be driven back by the "fire" of the fortress guns.

Meanwhile, more serious events had been unfolding in America. For some years past an undignified wrangle had been going on as to the American contribution towards the cost of the last war, which had been largely waged for their benefit. They declined to contribute voluntarily, so taxes, trivial in amount but none the less contrary to the principle of *"no taxation without representation"*, were imposed by the British government. That on tea was the chief grievance, and at the end of 1773 a party of Boston citizens boarded three ships and threw their cargoes of taxed tea overboard. Events soon took a more serious turn, with armed uprising and overt opposition to British rule. In a bloody confrontation at Bunker's Hill near Boston, in June 1775, a British force suffered 1,150 casualties. A month later the "rebel" colonial, George Washington (whose family hailed from Northamptonshire), was appointed commander-in-chief of the *"Continental Army"* – that is, the Continent of North America.

With full-scale hostilities now inevitable in the American colonies, the Government was forced to augment the pitifully weak garrison across the Atlantic. The first

## THE AMERICAN WAR OF INDEPENDENCE

reinforcements were ordered out in January 1775. In October eight infantry battalions on the Irish establishment were warned for service. In deference to the Irish executive this was reduced to six.

At the special request of Lord Cornwallis, who had been appointed in command of the force, the 33rd was added as a replacement for one of the other regiments. The regiments were to recruit up to an establishment of 672 rank and file, or twelve companies of 56 effectives each. In the event, when the six regiments were finally despatched from Cork in February 1776, they did not muster as many as 3,000 men. They then had to face the rigours of the Atlantic crossing – herded in cramped holds or troop-decks (usually battened down because of seas and weather) they were afflicted with sea-sickness and the resultant stench combined with that of the primitive "heads".[f] Rations were the usual naval variety: "hard tack", or ship's biscuit (often containing weevils), and salted beef or pork, normally served up in a boiled hash.

The American War of Independence, or "American Revolution", was one of the least positive episodes in British military history. The soldiers and their officers fought bravely, but in the utterly unfamiliar conditions of thick forest and swamp – not the type of terrain favourable to the stereotyped linear manoeuvring and rigid formations for which they had been trained. The Secretary-at-War was Lord Germaine, who as Lord George Sackville had covered himself with dishonour at Minden. He proceeded to confuse his commanders in the field with contradictory depatches – *"His blindness to facts, his deafness to wise counsel...his appalling ignorance of the elements of war"* wrote Fortescue, all led to the ultimate disaster at Yorktown. The Commander-in-Chief in America was General Sir William Howe, the same officer who had given the Regiment such a glowing inspection report two years earlier.

The force commanded by Lord Cornwallis landed at Cape Fear, North Carolina, in May 1776, having taken three months to cross the Atlantic. His task was to join up with General Clinton and give support to the southern loyalists, but by the time he had arrived these had been beaten and dispersed by the Americans. Clinton was loath to leave without doing something, and believing that Charleston might provide a base for future operations, he decided to capture the port. In June the force re-embarked and sailed south. But the attack, on 28 June, went disastrously wrong. The plan was for the troops to wade ashore, covered by the ships' guns, and carry the fortress of Moultrie by storm; but it was discovered too late that the shoals were too deep for wading and no landing was possible. Instead the soldiers remained inactive on board, while the heavy guns of the fort pounded their ships whose lighter armament was no match for them. Severely mauled, the squadron could only withdraw, having lost one ship and some 200 seamen and soldiers killed and wounded. This was the 33rd's unhappy baptism of fire in the war, though there were no casualties. The first of these occurred a few days later in Captain Dansey's light company, as he described in his letter of 6 July. After lamenting *"Our Failure of Success on the 28th of last month"* he goes on to relate how one of his sentries was stalked at night by three rebels who crept up and shot him through the

---
(f) Ship's latrines, so called because in the days of sail they were located in the bows.

wrist before running off – *"such cowardly Scoundrels have we to deal with"* bewailed Dansey, incensed at this ignoble method of warfare. However, although he feared that the man would lose his hand, he recovered on board the hospital ship. *"He is the first man wounded in our Regiment, and my Company"* Dansey wrote, adding that the private, Wilcox by name, was one of his Herefordshire recruits who had behaved very well.

After lingering for three weeks longer in the hope of achieving his aim, General Clinton's force sailed north to join General Howe on Staten Island, just south of New York, where it arrived on 1 August. Here the command, totalling some 25,000 troops, was organised in seven brigades and a reserve under Lord Cornwallis which consisted of the 33rd, the 42nd Highlanders and four battalions of grenadier companies. Howe's plan was to capture New York and with it command of the Hudson. On 22 August the British landed on Long Island. Cornwallis's troops immediately pushed three miles inland but then Howe spent four days reconnoitering before deciding how he was going to attack the Americans who were established in entrenched positions on Brooklyn Heights. The attack began at day break on the 27th and by mid-day the Americans had been routed with some 2,000 men killed, wounded or captured and the loss of 32 guns and quantities of ammunition. Howe's losses were less than 400. The losses of the 33rd, which was heavily engaged, are not known. In his despatch Sir William Howe reported:

> *"The Grenadiers and the 33rd regiment being in front of the column, soon approached within musket-shot of the enemy's lines at Brooklyn, from whence these Battalions, without regarding the fire of Cannon and Small arms upon them, pursued numbers of the rebels that were retiring from the Heights so close to their principal Redoubt, and with such eagerness to attack it by storm that it required repeated orders to prevail upon them to desist from the attempt. Had they been permitted to go on, it is my opinion that they would have carried the Redoubt ... but I would not risk the loss that might have been sustained and ordered them back to a Hollow Way in front of the works, out of reach of Musketry".*

On 30 August, Captain Dansey wrote to his fiancée of *"the Glorious Victory obtain'd over the Rebels"*. He led his light company *"into the very thick of them and had a most miraculous Escape. In about three minuits (sic.) I had three men kill'd & six wounded out of thirty. Mr Cotton my Lieutenant got a graze upon the Shoulder. We were well supported by three Companies or there would not have remain'd a man to tell the Story."*

Two days after his defeat at Brooklyn, Washington decided to evacuate Long Island, which he achieved with great skill. This left the way open for Howe to invade Manhattan (the island on which New York is situated). The attack, which took place on 15 September and was led by Cornwallis, whose 4,000 troops included the 33rd, was immediately successful. That same evening the British forces took possession of New York. The American losses were small but the loss of New York was a severe blow to their morale.

Several weeks passed while the cautious Howe prepared his next move. On 12

British troops enter New York, 15 September 1776

October he sent Cornwallis with his 4,000 troops up the East River with a view to attacking Washington from the rear. Washington thereupon re-deployed his troops, withdrawing all of them from Manhattan, except those at Fort Washington at the northern most end of the island. Howe followed Cornwallis with his main body and the two armies met at White Plains, about 20 miles north of New York. After an inconclusive engagement Washington withdrew. His instinct was now to evacuate Fort Washington but his generals prevailed upon him not to do so as they deemed it impregnable. The British launched their assault on 16 November, the 33rd being with the Guards, grenadiers and light infantry (Howe's best troops) in one of the attacking columns. Despite stubborn resistance by the Americans the Fort was obliged to surrender. The Americans had about 3,300 killed, wounded and prisoners. The British loss was 458 killed and wounded. In Fortescue's words *"It was a pretty little action....neatly executed... Howe at his best was no contemptible commander"*. Following the fall of Fort Washington Cornwallis took a flying column of 4,500, including the 33rd, to attack Fort Lee. Marching with great swiftness he would have captured the Fort and its garrison had not a deserter betrayed his movements as a result of which the garrison was able to escape. By the end of November Cornwallis' troops were worn out and half starved and it was time to settle into cantonments for the winter.

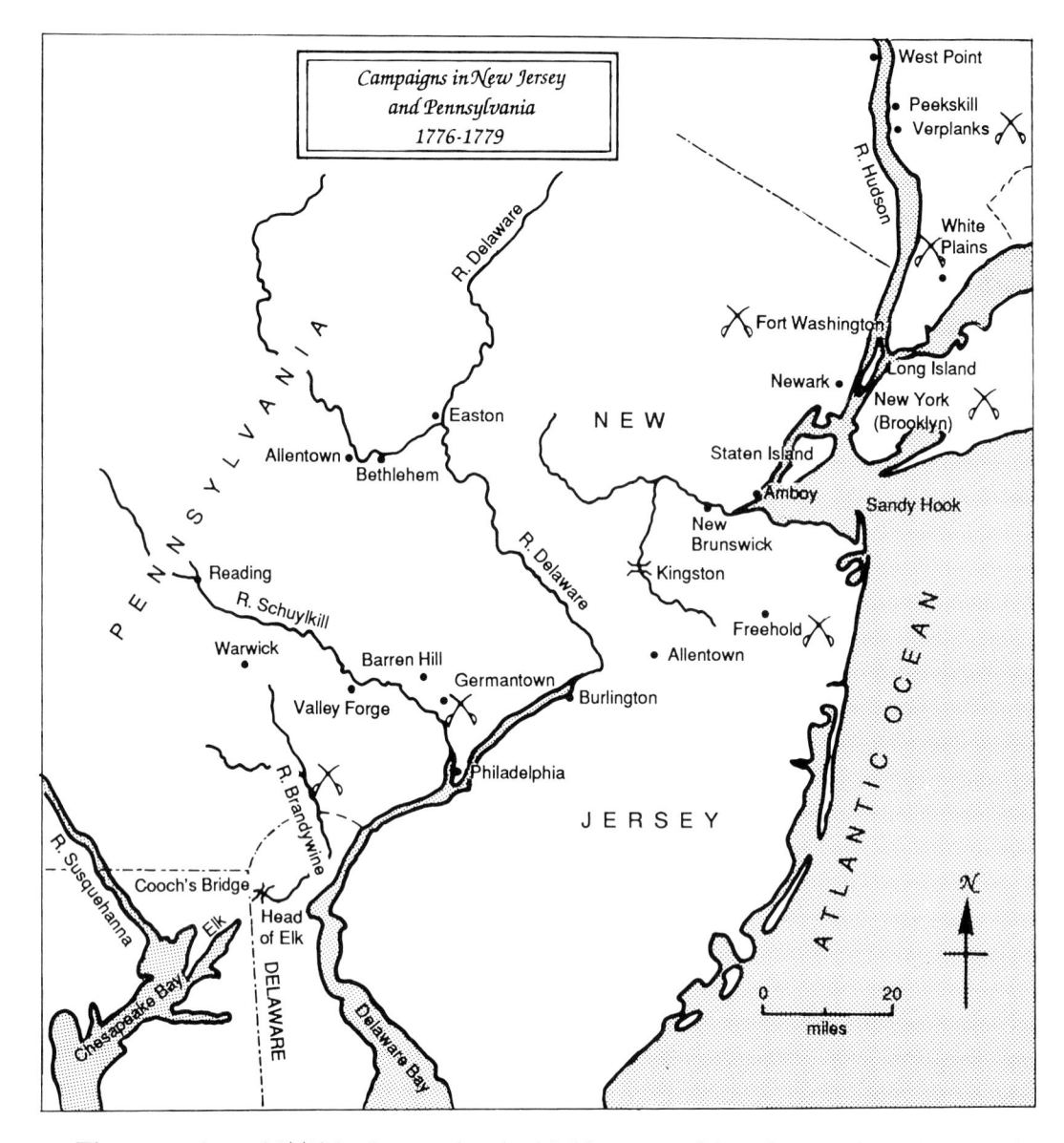

*Campaigns in New Jersey and Pennsylvania 1776-1779*

The campaign of 1776 had proved to be highly successful and many Americans took the oath of loyalty to the King as a result. However before long they were to be captured in arms against the British, still with their certificates of loyalty in their pockets.

General Howe's plan of campaign for 1777 was to capture Philadelphia, then the American capital, where there was said to be strong support for the loyalist cause. However, he was not helped by Lord Germaine who not only failed to send him the reinforcements he had requested but also directed that General Burgoyne was to launch an attack from Canada in order to join up with Howe in New York. He expressed the hope that Howe would get back from Philadelphia in time to assist Burgoyne in his task.

In the meantime Washington made a number of successful attacks on Howe's outposts with consequent improvement in the morale of the American troops.

Howe left Staten Island on 23 July and eight days later was off Delaware Bay, where he intended to land. However when the navy pointed out the severe difficulties of doing so he decided to proceed to Chesapeake Bay. Because of a combination of foul weather and a lack of wind, the 350 mile journey took 24 days. This allowed ample time for intelligence of the move to reach General Washington and for him to take appropriate counter-measures. Thus, having disembarked at Chesapeake Bay in August to advance northwards to Philadelphia, Howe found his progress blocked. The clash came at Brandywine Creek on 11 September (1777). The 33rd in the 4th Brigade [g], along with 37th(Royal Hampshire), 46th (DCLI) and 64th (North Staffordshire) regiments, was part of a flanking column under Cornwallis. The Americans facing him were in strength and posted in a strong position. However they were unable to resist the British advance. The soldiers fought *"muzzle to muzzle in such a manner that General Conway, who has seen much service, says he never saw so close and severe a fight"*. The outcome of the battle was a victory for the British. The Americans lost 300 killed, 600 wounded and 400 prisoners. It was only because Cornwallis and the column under General Knyphausen were prevented by darkness from joining up that they escaped a far worse defeat. Howe's casualties amounted only to 570-odd killed and wounded. The 33rd escaped lightly: three officers wounded, one soldier killed and twelve wounded.[h]

From Brandywine Howe moved towards Philadelphia, in the process occupying Germantown, about five miles to the north. On 25 September Philadelphia was entered without a fight. Believing it was only lightly defended, Washington decided to launch a surprise attack on Germantown. However, Howe had full information of his intention and was ready for him. Following a night march Washington attacked on 4 October in dense fog. The rock on which the American attack foundered was the defence of Chew House by Colonel Musgrave[i] and the 40th Foot (Prince of Wales Volunteers (South Lancashire)). After two and a half hours the rebels were once more defeated, with the loss of 673 killed and wounded and 400 prisoners, Howe's force losing 517. The casualties in the 33rd were surprisingly light, at four killed and 13 wounded. The light company was reported to have suffered severely, but there are no details.

Howe's next task was to open up navigation of the Delaware in order to ease supply for the army. This was achieved early in November, after which the troops retired to winter quarters in Philadelphia. Before that Howe, disenchanted by the lack of the reinforcements he considered essential to fight his campaigns, had written to Germaine resigning his command.

(g) Fortescue shows the 33rd in the 3rd Brigade, which was kept in reserve. However Howe's dispatch makes it clear the Regiment was in the 4th Brigade.
(h) One of the wounded was Captain Dansey, who in a letter of 17 October described how, just before the battle of Brandywine, his company captured the drums, a colour and arms belonging to a "Rebel Colonel" of the Delaware Militia, and he hoped to take the colour home with him. This he did in due course, and for nearly 150 years the trophy remained at the family home in Herefordshire. In 1927 the colour and Dansey's letters were put up for auction at Sothebys. The lot was knocked down to the Historical Society of Delaware for £850, a small fortune at that date and in excess of what the Regiment could afford. In 1950 the Society presented the Regiment with copies of the letters.
(i) Thomas Musgrave was later, in 1787, to raise the 76th Regiment.

Meanwhile, on 17 October General Burgoyne had been utterly defeated by the Americans at Saratoga. It was a momentous event, one result of which was the decision of the French government to sign a treaty (on 6 February 1778) with the Americans to uphold their independence.

By this time Dansey (and no doubt other officers) was paying more regard to personal comforts in the field – no longer satisfied with a bale of straw for bedding, as in Germany. Having acquired a horse, he had been *"contriving what things to carry on him that will be most comfortable and convenient and not overload him"* (undated letter, spring 1778). His first thought was shelter, and to this end he designed and constructed a tent which was *"admired by every Body for its convenience, Elegance and Lightness"*. Made of calico with a central pole and 28 pegs, it could sleep four persons and could be pitched or struck in five minutes. In a later letter, the proud inventor revealed that his design was *"copied by all that can get my Instructions for the making of it ... and if I can get my invention patronised by some Great Man I shall mortalise (sic) my Name by the simplicity and Use of it, for they are called Danseys now, not Tents"*.

In May 1778 General Sir William Howe was replaced by General Sir Henry Clinton – an unwelcome move. Howe, for all his indolence, always retained an immense popularity with the men whom in the previous three years he had led to victory in six battles and for whose welfare he had always been genuinely concerned. Clinton was a brave soldier, but of questionable generalship and with a propensity to quarrel with subordinates, especially Cornwallis.

Soon after Clinton took over he was ordered by Germaine in London to withdraw to New York – a seemingly pointless manoeuvre. Having sent off his sick and wounded by sea, Clinton with 15.000 men (j) crossed the Delaware and started his march northwards on 18 June. Almost immediately a storm arose and it rained incessantly for fourteen hours. Ammunition and food were ruined and the sultry heat that followed was almost intolerable. The Americans meanwhile laid waste to the land ahead of Clinton. On 28 June, at Freehold (k), Washington made a determined effort to stop Clinton's advance, his intention being to cut off Clinton's rearguard with a superior force. He might have succeeded but for the ineptitude of one of his generals. As it was, the battle ended with both sides exhausted from the heat, *"the most sultry day which had ever been endured since mankind learned to read the thermometer"*, and with about 350 casualties and some 50 heat stroke cases each. The 33rd was engaged during the day but its casualties are not recorded. Clinton's withdrawal was completed by sea from Sandy Hook. On 5 July he arrived at New York.

Ten days later a new enemy entered the field with the arrival of French naval squadrons and troops to support the Americans. To combat this threat, Admiral Howe called for soldiers to act as marines, and so in July 1778 Captain Dansey and his company found themselves in this unfamiliar role, on board HMS The Experiment. But they saw no action, for a violent storm dispersed the two fleets before they could close,

---

(j) 600 men, mostly Germans from the large Hessian contingent, had deserted because, says Fortescue, *"they had contracted attachments of one description or another to the town of Philadelphia"*.

(k) Also sometimes referred to as Monmouth Court House.

and by August all the temporary marines had reverted to their infantry role ashore.(m)

During 1779 Clinton could do little, having had 10,000 men detached by order of Germaine for operations in the South and in the West Indies. Washington, for his part, was content to contain the British on New York Island. To this end and to improve his east/west communications he constructed strong works on both banks of the River Hudson at Verplanks, on the eastern bank, and Stoney Point on the opposite side. Clinton determined to make a rush for the forts and capture them before Washington could come to their aid. The 33rd formed part of the force assigned to this task, which was successfully achieved in May 1779. The 33rd and 71st were left to garrison Verplanks, under the command of Lieutenant Colonel Webster, while the 17th formed the garrison at Stoney Point. In July a swift and undetected attack by the Americans led to the re-capture of Stoney Point with the loss to the British of 500 men taken prisoner. However their attempt also to capture Verplanks was beaten off by Webster.

During 1778 Germaine had conceived the idea of opening up a new front against the Americans in the southern states, which were supposedly highly loyalist. The idea proved successful and as a result Georgia was entirely cleared of the rebels by the end of 1779. Encouraged by this success it was decided to stand on the defensive in New York while a force was sent to subdue Carolina. Accordingly, on 26 December 1779, Clinton set sail with 7,600 men, including the 33rd, six other British battalions, some light infantry and grenadiers and six battalions of Hessians.

The first objective was the important base at Charleston in South Carolina. The investment started in April 1780 when Lieutenant Colonel Webster and his 33rd Regiment, together with the 64th (South Staffords) and some cavalry, were given the task of cutting the American lines of communications. This they did with such good effect that the American force was completely cut off and the siege of Charleston begun. Assaulted from both land and sea, the garrison surrendered on 13 May and 5,600 soldiers and 1,000 seamen became prisoners of war. British losses were no more than 265 killed and wounded, to which the 33rd contributed only one man killed and two wounded. Later, in his despatch, the Commander-in-Chief, General Clinton, paid tribute to the 33rd: *"I have especially to express my obligation to Lieutenant Colonel Webster, and the Corps which acted under him"*.

After consolidating in Charleston, Clinton sent off three columns into the interior. One of these, consisting of the 23rd, 33rd, 71st (Frasers) Highlanders and the Volunteers of Ireland (composed of deserters from the American army) was directed to Camden where a base was established. At the same time the recruitment of loyalists to serve alongside the regulars was put in train. After completion of these arrangements General Clinton returned to New York with a portion of his army, leaving Cornwallis with 4,000 troops to pacify the rest of the South.

Early in August it became apparent that the victor of Saratoga, General Gates, was planning to attack Camden, which intelligence sent Cornwallis riding hard from Charleston to take over command. Covering the hundred-odd miles in four days, he arrived in Camden on the 14th, and at once conformed to the old maxim, *"the best*

---

(m) However, Fortescue records that there was a brisk fight between two British and two French ships in which the light company of the 23rd (RWF) on board HMS Isis bore a distinguished part.

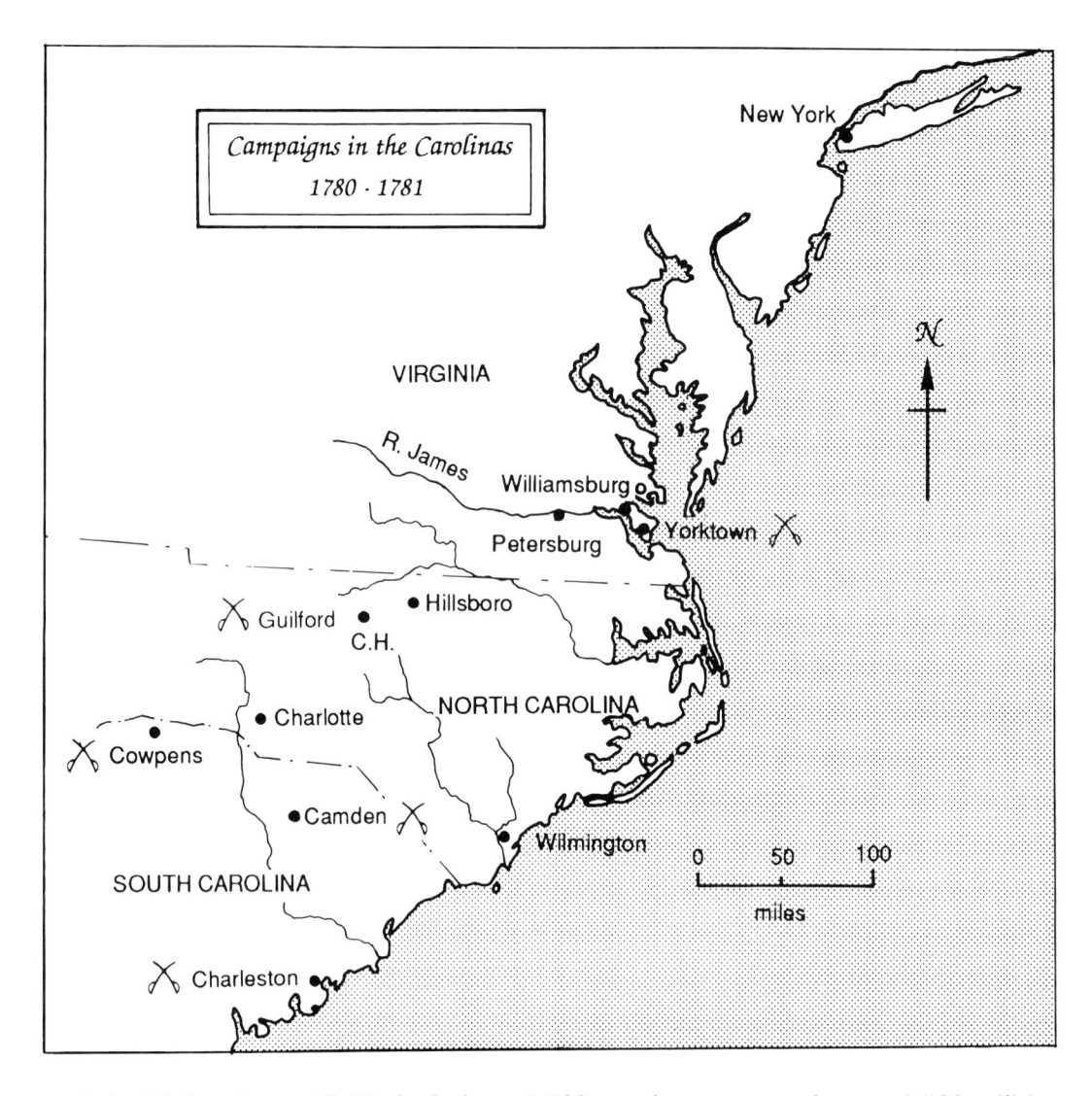

*method of defence is attack"*. He had about 1,500 regular troops and some 1,500 militia. Gates deployed roughly the same number of regulars but more than three times as many militia.

Marching north from Camden on the night of 15 August, Cornwallis hoped to fall upon an unsuspecting enemy in camp. But, by what Fortescue terms *"a ludicrous coincidence"*, Gates had moved off at exactly the same hour, heading south. The opponents came face to face at 2am – and halted to await first light. Came the morning, the Americans advanced to find the British were already deployed in line. The right brigade, under Colonel Webster, consisted of the 23rd, 33rd and three companies of light infantry. Lord Rawdon commanded the left brigade. The attack by the American militia on the British right flank was easily repulsed. Then, with Webster at their head, the 23rd and 33rd, after firing one volley, charged the Americans. The militia, who had never before seen such an enemy, fell back in disorder and then, scarcely firing a single round, burst through their reserve brigade and headed north. Webster disdained to pursue them, but instead wheeled his brigade to join Rawdon in the attack on the American regulars. These put up a stout fight but then they also, led by their general, broke and fled. When Gates finally drew rein 150 miles from the battle he found himself without an army. Rarely had there been a victory more complete or a defeat more total. In less than an hour Cornwallis had shattered the only American army in the south. It had lost 1,000 killed and wounded, more than 1,000 prisoners, the whole of its baggage and stores and seven guns. The British losses were 324 all ranks killed and wounded. The 33rd went into action with 13 officers and 223 other ranks. Its casualties were one officer and 17 other ranks killed and five officers (including Webster) and 76 other ranks wounded – a total of 99. The battle at Camden showed, not for the first time, that the British had nothing to learn from the Americans in the art of woodland fighting. Dansey, in a letter to his mother, had written:

> *"There's no people in the world that can shoot Black Duck better than they can; but the ducks carry no Firelocks and Bayonetts (sic). It is astonishing to think how the leaders of this Rebellion have made the poor ignorant People believe that because they are brought up to Gunning, as they call it, they must beat everything, but now they are convinced that being a good Marksman is only a trifling requisite for a soldier, indeed I myself saw them beat as Marksmen, at Frogneck. I was engaged....for upwards seven hours at their favourite Distance about 200 yards......We killed an Officer of them besides Several Men and had not one of ours wounded....which shows that a good soldier with a good Firelock was beyond a Rifleman with all his skill".*

Cornwallis was now determined to subdue North Carolina, but owing to difficulties in obtaining transport he was not able to move until 18 September. His first objective was Hillsboro, which he planned to turn into his main base. While he was marching north a column of loyalist militia, under Major Ferguson, was scouring the country to raise more loyalist soldiers. In the course of these operations Ferguson had an engagement with the Americans in which his force was badly defeated, with 300 casualties and 600 taken prisoner. As a result of this event Cornwallis withdrew to South Carolina and winter quarters at Winnsborough, west of Camden.

During the winter, the Secretary-at-War, Lord Germaine, *"always crooked and purblind and dazzled by the success of Cornwallis at Camden"*, gave orders that Cornwallis was to have a virtually independent command and that his operations were to have priority over those of Clinton, his superior. On 7 January 1781, without a word of his intentions to his commander-in-chief, Cornwallis set off northwards with 3,200 men, which included 2,000 recently sent to him by Clinton. His force included the 33rd with a strength of 328 effectives. On the American side, the bungling Gates had been replaced by the brave and skilful Major General Nathaniel Greene, the most able of Washington's commanders. Although his regular troops did not exceed 3,000, he could count on many times that number of guerillas, while as Cornwallis was only too well aware, the populace of North Carolina was fiercely hostile to the British.

Greene divided his force into two and Cornwallis was forced to follow suit. One party, under Tarleton, was soundly beaten by General Morgan at Cowpens. Although a setback for Cornwallis it did not long delay him and he pushed forward in drenching rain to try and catch Greene and Morgan. Greene fell back rapidly and a day and night chase continued through North Carolina until Greene crossed into Virginia. In the middle of March he re-crossed into North Carolina and took up a position at Guilford

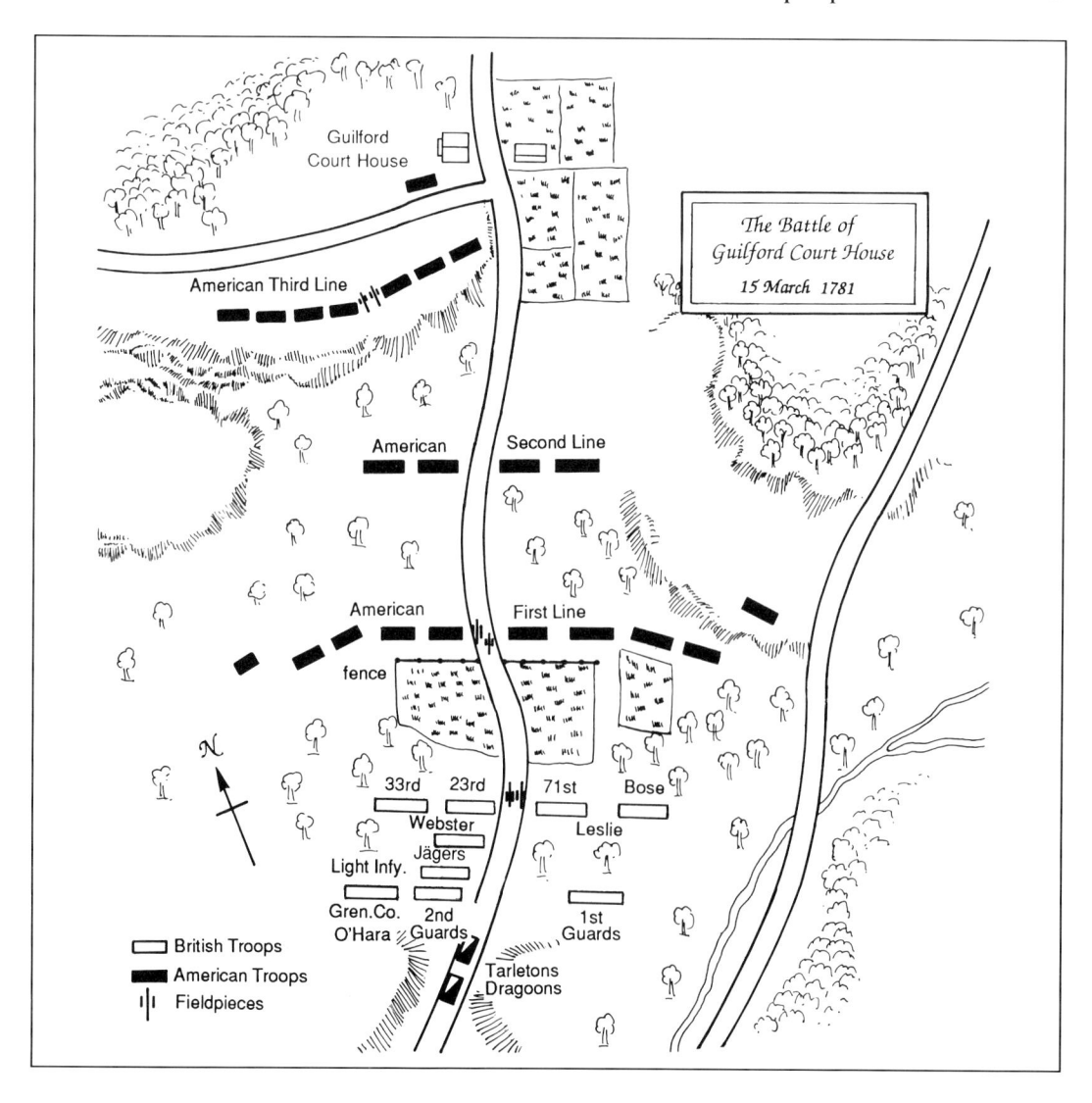

Court House. Greene's force consisted of about 4,300 men. Cornwallis, who lay about twelve miles away, only had about 1,900 men but was determined to give battle. Greene deployed his force in three lines. His first, manned by militia, was placed behind a fence about 500 yards from a defile through which Cornwallis would be obliged to approach. His second was about three hundred yards behind the first. Greene placed his third and principal line, consisting of the cream of his force, about 500 yards behind the second, but at an angle to the road which ran through his position.

At dawn on the 15th, without pausing to give his men breakfast, Cornwallis started for Guilford which he reached at mid-day. The left of his line was commanded by Lieutenant Colonel Webster, who had the 23rd (RWF) and 33rd, with the grenadiers and the 2nd Battalion Guards in support. At half past one the battle began with the thin red line of British infantry marching forward as if on parade. The Americans fired a volley but the line continued to advance until within musket shot when they delivered their own volley. Then, at Colonel Webster's command, they charged forward, only to come to a halt fifty yards from the fence because, said Sergeant Lamb of the 23rd, it was perceived that the Americans' *"whole force had their arms presented and resting on the rail fence...they were taking aim with nice precision"*. Urged on by Webster his troops resumed their advance on which the militia turned and fled. Without waiting to finish off the second line Webster next led his weary troops against Greene's third line. The battle swung to and fro. An attack by American cavalry was only broken up when Cornwallis ordered his artillery to fire grape shot, which in the process inflicted terrible destruction on the Guards. Eventually the Americans fell back, Greene considering his object done, having severely crippled his enemy. Cornwallis could claim a victory, but it had cost him dear. The Royal Artillery commander, Major General Phillips, described the battle of Guilford as *"the sort of victory that ruins an army"*. The British casualties were 93 killed and 439 wounded – over a quarter of the force. The 33rd had 11 killed and 63 wounded from a strength of about 300. Its greatest loss was that of its Lieutenant Colonel who died a fortnight later. It was acknowledged that James Webster's *"skill as a commander and his bravery as a soldier was scarcely equalled among his contempories"*. According to Sergeant Lamb, Cornwallis, on hearing of Webster's death exclaimed *"I have lost my scabbard"*. Starting half starved on a march of twelve miles the British troops had attacked a well posted enemy who had outnumbered them two to one and driven them from the field. In Fortescue's words *"Never, perhaps has the prowess of the British soldier been seen to greater advantage than in this obstinate and bloody battle"*. There were no immediate rewards for these extraordinary accomplishments, only more hardships. There was no food, nor was there any shelter from the torrential rain that fell that night. Nearly fifty of the wounded expired before the morning.

Cornwallis, having first buried his dead and scoured the country-side for food, withdrew unmolested to Wilmington, on the estuary of the River Fear, where he arrived on 7 April after a trying march of 150 miles. Before his army could recover its strength, Greene marched on South Carolina. This time, however, Cornwallis did not join Greene in an exhausting game of cat and mouse. Cornwallis had learnt that there were less expensive ways to deal with rebel armies. He would counter Greene's threat by striking at his base of supply, the state of Virginia. Virginia was ripe for invasion in 1781. Like other Americans, her people were weary after six years of war. He also decided to cease putting any trust in the loyalists, who, time and again, had changed sides as the fortunes of war had fluctuated. On 25 April he began his march northwards with his command of 1,600 men, which included a Guards battalion, the 23rd, 33rd and 71st Highlanders. In just over three weeks he arrived at Petersburg, a distance of roughly 300 miles. There he was joined by a force under command of Benedict Arnold which was augmented, a few days later, by a welcome reinforcement of 1,700 from New York (including the 17th (Leicestershire) and 43rd (Oxfordshire LI), which brought Cornwallis' strength to 6,481, though more than 1,600 of these were sick.

For the next three months Cornwallis kept his army constantly on the move, conducting his operations on both banks of the James River. By seizing many of the fine horses available from the stables of the wealthy Virginians he was able not only to mount his hussars and dragoons on fresh horses but also to put some 700 infantry on horseback. As a result Lafayette, who commanded the American troops, had to keep at least twenty miles from the British. *"The British have so many dragoons"* Lafayette informed the Governor of Virginia, *"that it becomes impossible to stop or reconnoitre their movements"*. Besides taking their horses, Cornwallis also liberated many black slaves, so that by the middle of June 12,000 of them were with his army. *"Every officer had four to six horses and three or four Negroes"* wrote a Hessian officer. Cornwallis' actions were steadily bringing Virginia to its knees and the people were beginning to consider making peace. Fortunately for them events elsewhere intervened.

On 26 June Cornwallis was at Williamsburg where he received orders from Clinton to establish a defensive position either there or at Yorktown and to send back every man he could spare to New York where Clinton was expecting to be attacked by Washington. A later letter from Clinton countermanded the previous order and instead pressed Cornwallis to establish a defensive base at Yorktown for the protection of the British cruisers, which by now was a matter of some importance in view of the anticipated arrival of a French fleet under Admiral de Grasse.

After a brisk fight with a detachment of Lafayette's force at Williamsburg, where the French were repulsed with the loss of men and guns, Cornwallis had by 22 August concentrated his army at Yorktown. Well protected on the north by the bluffs overlooking the York River, the site needed only entrenchments and redoubts on the other three sides to make a secure base, and the troops were immediately set to work digging and constructing lines of defence. A defended post was also established at Gloucester on the other side of the river. The total force of British, Germans and provincials, amounted to about 7,000 all ranks. The 33rd, together with the 17th (Leicesters), 23rd (RWF) and 71st (Frasers) Highlanders, was in a brigade commanded by Lieutenant Colonel John Yorke[n], who had taken over command of the 33rd following the death of James Webster. The Regiment mustered only 231 effectives and

---

(n) Lieutenant Colonel John Yorke had been appointed ensign in the 33rd in 1761. In 1778 he was appointed to command the 22nd Foot (Cheshire).

Yorktown, 19 October 1781. The British surrender their arms to General Washington

the other three regiments were at similar strengths. Less than twenty miles away at Williamsburg, Lafayette and 5,000 French lay awaiting the arrival of Washington's army, and had he chosen, Cornwallis might well have inflicted another defeat on them. But he too was awaiting reinforcements, confidently expected by sea. A message from Clinton revealed that Admiral Digby with 5,000 troops and 26 ships of the line should arrive by 5 October. However, unbeknown to Clinton, a large French fleet, under de Grasse, was established in Chesapeake Bay and command of the sea by the British could no longer be assumed. Meanwhile Washington was marching. On 14 September, he arrived at Lafayette's Williamsburg headquarters, and by the 26th, all his troops had marched in, bringing the investing force to some 16,000 men with a powerful train of artillery. Unless the expected reinforcements actually arrived, Cornwallis was in a desperate position. Outnumbered by more than two to one (and sickness, including smallpox and malaria, constantly depleting his strength) and with supplies running short, he could hardly endure a lengthy siege, while a withdrawal through the enemy lines would entail inevitable slaughter.

On 28 September the Americans and French (now under the command of Rochambeau) arrived before Yorktown. Cornwallis thereupon deliberately advanced outside his line of defence in the hope of tempting his opponents to do battle in the open. But they had no stomach for a fight in the field with a general of Cornwallis' reputation, despite their superior numbers. Then followed a heavy artillery bombardment, while the building of parallels was pressed ahead. By 9 October, the French and Americans on the eastern flank had advanced their line so that their batteries' range had closed to no more than 300 yards. On the 14th, the last of British redoubts on the other flank were captured in a night attack. By now, most of the earthenwork defences were destroyed or crumbling under the ceaseless pounding of the French guns, to which Cornwallis had no effective reply, for his own few guns had been put out of action after expending all their ammunition. Daily the garrison had been expecting the cheering spectacle of Clinton's relieving force making into harbour, but no ships came. Meanwhile, rations were almost exhausted, and so was small arms ammunition. Many of the soldiers who were still effective were so debilitated by lack of adequate food and sleep that they could scarcely handle their muskets.

On 16 October, Cornwallis took a desperate decision. All the baggage and non-essentials would be abandoned in Yorktown and a small detachment would be left with the sick and wounded to make such terms as they could with Washington, while the remainder would endeavour to steal away in small parties across the river to Gloucester Point (about 1,000 yards of water). One party of the 23rd and light infantry actually managed to cross, but a violent storm prevented the rest from making the attempt. Washington got wind of the scheme and next morning posted men and guns to cover the crossing, so that withdrawal was now impossible.

Abandoning all hopes of relief, Cornwallis had to face the bitter truth. With stores exhausted, his troops almost incapacitated, further resistance was not only useless but would bring more suffering. On 17 October, nearly three weeks since the siege had begun, he sent a flag of truce to Washington, proposing a cease-fire and discussion of terms of capitulation. And so, on 19 October 1781 the garrison of Yorktown formally surrendered[o]. By a cruel irony, on that very day, the captives beheld Clinton's fleet with 7,000 men bearing up the estuary. Too late, the ships went about and sailed back to New York.

Next morning, the British and German troops still fit to do so, (2,000 men were in hospital), marched out of Yorktown between the ranks of Washington's and Rochambeau's victors, while the British bands played the old English tune, *"The World Turned Upside Down"*. There is some doubt about the exact number of prisoners. Fortescue records 6,360, but adds that a return by the cavalry commander, Major Banastre Tarleton, shows 7,247. The battle casualties during the siege were 500 killed and wounded. Those of the American and French totalled some 400.

Although the American War of Independence was not formally concluded until the Peace Treaty of 1783, the surrender of Yorktown virtually put an end to military operations, and there was no more fighting of consequence. It was sad that it should have fallen to the lot of that brave soldier and Colonel of the 33rd to suffer the humiliation that lost Britain her American colonies. But his reputation was in no way diminished. The disaster of Yorktown was more properly attributed to Lord Germaine, Secretary-at-War, with his bungling and controversial attempts to direct the war from

---

(o) Cornwallis, pleading illness, remained in his quarters and his second-in-command, General O'Hara led the British surrender. Cornwallis was granted parole and returned to England taking with him, it is said, the colours of the 33rd Regiment.

33rd soldier, 1742
*(By permission of Prince Consort's Army Library)*

A captain of the 33rd Regiment, c 1825

33rd (or 1st Yorkshire West Riding) Regiment, 1792

A recruiting sergeant of the 33rd (c 1814) who, in addition to the normal coloured ribbons on his hat, also has a havercake on his sword. This practice led to the Regiment being known as the "Havercake Lads"

Battle of the Alma, 20 September 1854
*(By permission of the Director, National Army Museum)*

Incident in the Crimea.
Private Patrick McGuire, 33rd Regiment, achieves his escape from two Russians who had taken him prisoner

The Duke of Wellington's (West Riding Regiment), India 1905-1920

Storming of Magdala, 13 April 1868
The 33rd, in khaki uniforms, scramble up the ridge to the side of the unblown gate to the fort
*(By permission of the Director, National Army Museum)*

Whitehall. At all events, King George III and his government saw no cause to disgrace Cornwallis. On arrival in England he was almost immediately offered the posts of Governor-General and Commander-in-Chief in India, which he declined as he was still on parole. To his officers and soldiers he was, to quote one of them, *"Deservedly the favourite of every person of every rank under his command"*. And his enemies held him in high respect. *"Lord Cornwallis's abilities are to me more frightening than his superiority of forces....to speak plain English I am devilish afraid of him"* – thus wrote Lafayette.

The 33rd Regiment now temporarily ceased to exist as a cohesive, effective unit. The prisoners of Yorktown were dispersed throughout Virginia, Maryland and Pennsylvania, but where those of the 33rd found themselves is not known. Lee hazards that they probably went to Lancaster (Pennsylvania). However, not all the Regiment had suffered at Yorktown. Some British details had been left at the Charleston base, those of the 33rd being under command of Major William Dansey. According to Atkinson, their strength was then 69 all ranks.

Writing on 27 March to Lieutenant Colonel Yorke, who was on parole in England, Dansey gives him some not too agreeable details of the situation at Charleston. Here, he said, was *"a broken Army of all manner of Corps, of which Debris of Lord Cornwallis's Army are the most respectable, amounting to about 300 wounded men and Recruits that never joined. We are all much hurt at the seeming indifference at home concerning the Fall at York Town. Great Britain will not see such an Officer (Cornwallis) nor Such an Army again soon"*. With Dansey from the 33rd were four lieutenants, but whether these had not been captured at Yorktown or had been released on parole is not clear. Regrettably, two of them, Wynyard and Gore *"proceeded so far in improper and irregular behaviour that I was obliged first to reprimand them at the head of the Regiment and afterwards on another offence to go to the Extremity and put them in Arrest"*. Why is not revealed.

At the end of December 1782, the remaining troops at Charleston (or James Island) were moved to Kingsbridge near New York. Colonel Yorke still being on parole in England, Major Dansey had command of the 33rd's remnants. Exactly what these consisted of is not known, but in his letter to Cornwallis on 13 March 1783, Dansey draws attention to the grenadier company (not present at Yorktown) who *"have been Conspicuous for their good Behaviour as for everything else and Captn Cornwallis has done them great justice ..."* (the captain was a distant relative of Lord Cornwallis).

The first explicit statement of strength occurs in Dansey's letter of 28 May 1783, written from Kingsbridge. Present and effective were 14 officers, 30 sergeants, 22 drummers and 399 other ranks. But where all these came from is problematical. Drafts from England? Released prisoners? Rejoined stragglers? On 22 August, Dansey informs his mother from New York, that he now has command of five regiments: 33rd, 38th (South Staffordshire), 71st, King's Americans and a flank battalion, all totalling 59 officers and 1,630 other ranks. In the same letter, he reveals that the 33rd was to be posted to Nova Scotia, and in fact the move took place in October 1783. Apart from one of 30 August to Colonel Yorke there are no more letters from Major William Dansey.[p]

---

(p) In July 1790, he purchased his lieutenant colonel's "Parchment" and assumed command of the 49th (Hertfordshire) Regiment, in which appointment he died four years later. One of his sons, Lieutenant Colonel G H Dansey, commanded the 76th Regiment in 1839.

In July 1785, the Regiment moved north to Sydney, Cape Breton, to become the first troops to occupy the new barracks built there the previous year. Later that year occurred a most mysterious event. On 15 October Captain John Sherbrooke and Lieutenant George Wynyard had gone to Wynyard's quarters after dinner to do some studying. Both men were silently concentrating on their work, when Sherbrooke happened to look up and there, by the door, stood a thin, tall youth dressed in light indoor clothes. (Because of the cold both Sherbrooke and Wynyard wore furs and wraps). As soon as Wynyard also saw the unexpected presence of the stranger he became very agitated. *"I have heard of a man being as pale as death"*, Sherbrooke is quoted as saying, *"but I never saw a living face assume the appearance of a corpse, except Wynyard's at that moment"*. The figure slowly withdrew into an adjoining room, looking at Wynyard with melancholy affection. Then Wynyard muttered *"My God! My brother"*. Both officers made a note of the day and hour of the occurrence. The winter being long it was not until spring that a ship arrived with letters from England. Among them was one for Sherbrooke the first line of which read *"Dear John, break to your friend Wynyard the death of his favourite brother"*. He had, in fact, died on the day and at the very hour the two friends had noted.(q)

At last, after ten years in North America, the Regiment was routed home in 1786, to be posted to Taunton. Meanwhile, there had been a significant amendment to its title.

The philosophy of associating infantry (but not cavalry) regiments with individual counties to encourage recruiting had been first suggested by the Duke of Cumberland as early as 1760, to be revived by Sir George Howard in the House in November 1780. The idea was taken up, and on 13 May 1782, the Deputy Adjutant General, Colonel A Williamson, was instructed by the Commander-in-Chief to write to the agents of all those infantry regiments who, like the 33rd, were neither "royal" nor bore any "distinctions" of title, other than a number. They were to inform General Conway whether they had *"any particular connexion (sic) or Attachment to a particular County, or any reason to wish for bearing the name of any particular County, and if so to name the County"*. A total of 54 regiments (or their Agents) were circulated. Some proved lukewarm, some obstructive, some did not even bother to reply. But the 33rd's Colonel welcomed the scheme, and on 1 July, Lord Cornwallis wrote as follows to the DAG:

> *"Sir,*
> *I am to desire that you will please to inform General Conway that the 33rd Regt. of Infantry has always recruited in the West Riding of Yorkshire, and has a very good interest & the general good will of the people, in that part of the Country:- I should therefore wish not only to be permitted to recruit in that county, but that my Regt. may bear the name of the 33rd or West Yorkshire Regt. If that district is thought too extensive to give a name to one regt. only, I should desire to have my regt. called the 1st West Yorkshire; and am fully sure that no older*

---

(q) Sherbrooke became General Sir John Sherbrooke and succeeded Wellington as Colonel of the 33rd. Wynyard became a major general and was killed at the battle of Salamanca in 1812.

> *Regt. can claim so long and intimate connection with the West Riding of Yorkshire.*
>
> > *I am, Sir,*
> > *Your Most Obedt.*
> > *& Most Humble Servant*
> > *(sgd) CORNWALLIS"*

*Col. Williamson D.A.G.*

On 31 August (1782), Lord Cornwallis learnt that the King had approved the new title:

"33rd (or the 1st Yorkshire West Riding) Regiment of Foot"

The DAG's circular to all regiments granting "County" titles went on to stress that it was *"His Majesty's further pleasure that you shall in all things conform to that idea* (i.e. the county connection) *and endeavour by all means in your power to cultivate and improve that connection, so as to create a mutual Attachment between the County and the Regiment, which may at all times be useful towards recruiting the Regiment".*

Additional recruits were soon needed. Under the special Recruiting Acts of 1778 and 1779, great numbers of men had been enlisted for three years service. Following the ratification of peace in 1783 all soldiers who had been engaged for this term were at liberty to take their discharge. With only a few exceptions most of them did so, leaving many regiments with no more than a handful of privates. Recruiting parties were despatched in all directions, but few recruits were available and such as were secured, by fair means or foul, soon deserted. In 1787 the Regiment was routed to Windsor Castle, to do duty as "King's Guard". From 1789 to 1792 it was stationed in Devon and Cornwall. The army was so stretched at this period, often having to find men to man naval ships, that for a time the 33rd was the only regiment in the south of England.

The Regiment's reputation for excellence continued so that it became known as The Pattern.[r] In 1788 the Inspecting General reported, *"The Regiment appears founded up on the same system as in the Last War... likely to retain its usual discipline".* The following year the Regiment was inspected at Plymouth when it was concluded that *"..to report them fit for Service without adding they are adequate for any military service whatsoever, would be too indifferent a representation of their gallant and warlike Deportment".* The author of the book[s] from which these and the earlier quotations are taken, gave it as his opinion that, *"the 33rd was unquestionably the best trained regiment in the British Army during the last three decades of our period"*

Meanwhile there was trouble in Ireland where the Whiteboys, so called because they wore white cockades in their hats, were carrying out an audacious campaign of insurgency, breaking into gaols and releasing the prisoners, burning houses and intercepting provisions. The call for extra troops in Ireland was imperative, and the 33rd was sent to Dublin in 1792.

---

(r) *"Soon after (1787) I was appointed to a Lieutenancy in the 33rd, at that time denominated the Pattern or Lord Cornwallis's Corps"* Stations Gentlemen by James Gatliff).

(s) *Fit for Service: The Training of the British Army 1715-1795.* J A Houlding. OUP 1981.

CHAPTER 6

# The Raising of the 76th Regiment and the Third Mysore War

*1787, 76th Regiment raised*
*1791, Bangalore, Arikera, Seringapatam*

With the end of the American War of Independence Britain paused to draw breath after nearly a century of struggle against the military and naval might of France. Campaigns in both the old and new worlds had brought her substantial territorial possessions in the Caribbean, North America and the East Indies, but only at considerable cost in financial and human terms. With peace, economy and retrenchment became the keynote, even though tension between the European powers remained high. The regiments that had fought in the late war were disbanded or reduced. Trained and battle hardened soldiers were discharged, the lucky few to steady civilian employment, but most to a precarious life on the borders of penury and starvation. In the autumn of 1787, however, the possibility of renewed hostilities with France persuaded the ministry of the younger Pitt that steps must be taken to make the army equal to the challenges it faced. Although a colony had been lost in America the remainder of Britain's overseas possessions had still to be garrisoned.

Of special concern was India. During the first half of the 18th century Britain's chief adversary there had been the French with their possessions in Madras and along the Coromandel coast, all protected by disciplined troops under such energetic leaders as Dumas and Dupleix who were intent on extending their territories. But in 1761 Sir Eyre Coote inflicted decisive defeat on the French at Pondicherry and two years later the treaty following the Seven Years war saw their power in India finally dissipated.

One of the Indian potentates who had connived with the French against the British was the Muslim ruler, or Sultan, of the Hindu state of Mysore, Hyder Ali, who had no mind to be overlorded by anyone. His overt hostility led to the First Mysore War of 1767-69. This was concluded by a treaty which was broken by Hyder Ali the following year, resulting in the Second Mysore War, which ended in 1783 with the death of the Sultan and yet another treaty with his son, Tipu Sultan.(a) This proved as impermanent as the others.

Tipu was even more xenophobic than his father in his attitude towards the British. In 1787 he hoped to gain support from Louis XV in Versailles, but no aid was forthcoming. Nevertheless, intelligence of Tipu's move aroused alarm in Whitehall. At that date there were only five British (or *King's*) infantry regiments to back up the Honorable East India Company's (H.E.I.C) forces. Although the directors of the company agreed with Pitt that the renewed tension with France warranted an increase in the military establishment of the sub-continent, they were loath to meet the expense of maintaining additional British regiments and would have preferred raising some further regiments of their own. Notwithstanding the company's objections, it was decided to raise four new British regiments.

On 22 October 1787 the Secretary at War, Sir George Yonge, wrote to Lieutenant General Lord Cornwallis, Governor-General and Commander-in Chief in the East Indies, as follows:

> W.O. 22nd October 1787
>
> My Lord
> I have the honor to acqt. your Lordship that His Majesty has been pleased to order that four Regt. of Infantry shall be forthwith raised for H.M.'s service in India and H.M. has appointed M. General Archd. Campbell, & Colonels Robert Abercrombie, Musgrave & Marsh to be Colonels of the said Regts. Each Regt. is to consist of eight Battn. Companies, one Company of Grendrs. & one of Lt. Infantry, together with an additional Company, which is to remain at home for the purpose of recruiting ........ I am to add that it has been ordered that these Regts. shall be actually raised and approved after being reviewed by the 25th of December next.
>
> I have &c
> (Sd.) Geo. Yonge

The Royal Warrant for their raising was sent to all four colonels on 12 October 1787:

> GEORGE R.
> Whereas We have thought fit to order a Regt. of Foot to be forwith raised under your Command, which is to consist of ten Companies, with 3 Sergts, 4 Corpls, 2 Drumrs & 71 private Men in each, with two Fifers to the Grenadier Compy and one Compy, of 8 Sergts, 8 Corpls, 4 Drumrs & 30 private Men with the usual Comd. Officers, these are to authorize you by Beat of

---

(a) In much of the literature the name is anglicised to "Tippu" or "Tipoo" with the honorific "Sahib" added. Similarly "Hyder" is an anglicisation of the more correct "Haidar".

Drum or otherwise to raise so many Men in any County or part of our Kingdom of Great Britain as shall be wanted to complete the said Regt. to the above mentioned numbers. And all above Given the 12th Octobr. 1787 in the 27th Year of Our Reign.

By H.M.'s Command

(Sd.)   Geo. Yonge

The additional *one Compy* was the recruiting company which in effect formed the home depot. The total establishment of each regiment was: one colonel, one major, seven captains, twenty two lieutenants, eight ensigns, thirty sergeants, forty corporals, twenty drummers and 710 privates, together with chaplain, surgeon and quarter master. The four new regiments were to be numbered 74th to 77th, Thomas Musgrave's becoming the 76th Foot.[b]

More detailed instructions from the Secretary at War were sent out with the Warrant of 12 October. An important provision was that *"As this Regt. is to be raised with a particular view to serve in the East Indies"*, the East India Company was to be allowed to nominate a proportion of the officers from its own forces. These were to consist of: one major, three captains, eleven lieutenants and four ensigns. Officers appointed in England below field rank were expected to raise a specified number of recruits: thus a captain on half-pay, 30; a lieutenant on full pay, 50; ensign on full pay, 20. For each recruit approved and attested a bounty of three guineas was payable. On 22 October Colonel Musgrave was ordered to establish his headquarters at Chatham Barracks which, a few years earlier, had been established as a recruiting depot.

The Adjutant General was required to submit to the Treasury a detailed estimate of the total annual cost of pay, allowances, clothing, etc. for each regiment. This amounted to £17,209.13s., and the breakdown shows the following rates of pay:

|                     | £   | s  | d    |
|---------------------|-----|----|------|
| Colonel             | 513 | 0  | 7    |
| Lieutenant Colonel  | 292 | 2  | 0    |
| Major               | 257 | 14 | 9    |
| Captain             | 171 | 16 | 6    |
| Lieutenant          | 80  | 3  | 81/2 |
| Ensign              | 63  | 0  | 03/4 |
| Sergeant            | 18  | 6  | 0    |
| Corporal            | 12  | 4  | 0    |
| Drummer             | 12  | 4  | 0    |
| Private             | 9   | 3  | 0    |

Yet another letter from the Secretary at War requested the Master-General of the

---

(b) The regiment was the fourth to bear the number 76. Previous regiments numbered 76 were raised in 1745 at the time of the '45 rebellion, in 1756 for the Seven Years war (disbanded 1763) and in 1777 at the time of the American War of Independence (disbanded in 1784).

Ordnance to provide 788 firelocks, bayonets and cartridge boxes, six sergeants' fuzees, 32 halberts (sic) and 24 drums for each regiment. The only reference to uniforms occurs in a directive of 24 October 1787 from the Deputy Adjutant General, specifying the facings of the four new regiments. The 76th (like its future partner, the 33rd) enjoyed the rare distinction of red facings; the 74th (Highland Light Infantry) wore white, the other two, yellow.

In all instructions it was emphasised that the colonels were to *"use every exertion"* to ensure that their regiments were fully kitted, armed and mustered by 25 December. Most of the other ranks came from Nottinghamshire and Leicestershire, but many recruits were brought south from the Musgrave family estates around Hayton Castle, near Carlisle.

Brevet Colonel Thomas Musgrave had seen some 33 years' service, having been commissioned ensign in the 3rd Buffs in 1754, at the age of seventeen. In 1776 as lieutenant colonel, he commanded the 40th Foot (South Lancashire) in the American War of Independence, greatly distinguishing himself at Germantown. In 1778 he went as Quartermaster-General to the notoriously fever-ridden West Indies where, predictably, he became so stricken that he had to be invalided home. On recovery he returned to North America to serve as the last commander of the British forces in New York.

At the first muster parade, on Christmas Eve 1787, only Musgrave and seven of his officers were shown as present. There could have been another twenty-two shown if their appointments had been approved by the King. But the Secretary at War was on his estate in Devon and could not present the establishment to the King until his return to London in mid-January. All the appointments were then back-dated to 25 December 1787. Among them were three officers who had previously served in the Colonel's old regiment, the 40th Foot, including a Captain Edward Musgrave. He was almost certainly a son of the Colonel. Another newly appointed officer was Lieutenant Hon Arthur Wesley, as the future Duke of Wellington then spelt his name[c]. However his stay in the 76th was shortlived as, having been appointed ADC to the Lord Lieutenant in Dublin, it was essential for him to exchange into a

General Sir Thomas Musgrave Bt.
Colonel of the 76th Regiment, 1787-1812

---

(c) On 30 October 1787 the promotion of Ensign Arthur Wesley from the 73rd to a lieutenancy in the 76th was approved *"on the condition of raising 20 men by 20 December next"*.

regiment that was not about to embark for service in India. His widowed mother, Lady Mornington, came to his rescue and on 23 January 1788 he transferred to the 41st Foot (Welch Regiment).[d]

On 26 March 1788 the 76th Regiment under Colonel Thomas Musgrave embarked at Gravesend for India. The total strength was 25 officers and 673 other ranks.

At that period and for long afterwards there was little rapport or harmony between the officers of the East India Company's regiments and those of the *Royal* or *King's* forces. Not only did the latter enjoy seniority over those in the same rank, but they considered themselves socially superior to the "Sepoy" officers of the Company, who did not purchase their commission, nor did they receive them from the sovereign, but from a body of merchants. In short, the two officer corps had little in common, and no love was lost between them.

Thus on 22 March four days before sailing Colonel Musgrave and the commanding officers of the other three regiments received from the Secretary at War, under the King's name, the following words of caution:

GEORGE R.

You will before embarking call together the Officers of the Regt. under yr Command & recommend to them in a particular manner the avoiding all manner of Disputes they use their utmost Endeavors to live with them in the greatest Harmony, as the contrary behavior will be very displeasing unto Us as well as detrimental to the Service they are jointly to be employed in; the respective Officers of Companies are to recommend the same to the Non Commd. Officers & Soldiers under their Command; the 76th Officers of the East India Company having the same Orders as to their behaviour to Our Land Forces ..... In every thing you will consider the Honor of Our Forces, the Good of Our Service, & the interest of the East India Company. You will accordingly cheerfully concur in all things which the principal Officers of the East India Company shall judge conducive thereto, & for that purpose you will use your utmost Endeavors betwixt Our Land Forces & those of the East India Company. Given &c. 22nd Day of March 1788 in the 28th Year of Our Reign.

The "Orders & Instructions" also included dictates about general discipline and duties on board ship. The men were to be divided into watches, and no officers or soldiers were to be allowed ashore without the authority of the ship's captain, while the officers were charged to ensure that bedding should be aired daily, *for keeping the births (sic) clean & sweet*. Gaming and *Drams of spiritous Liquours* were prohibited.

---

(d) *"I have so much to get done for Arthur, that I am sure it will not be done in time. The King has given him leave to go to Dublin only upon the condition of making an exchange into another regiment....this will cost some money and take time to effect it".*

After a swift and trouble free voyage the five transports carrying the 76th arrived at Madras between 14 and 20 July. The Regiment was posted to the out-station of Poonamallee (Punamali) a few miles north of Madras, where it was joined in September by two companies formed in Calcutta by Captain John Hamilton [e] of the H.E.I.C's army. According to Hayden[f], the men, numbering 301, had been found from volunteers from European regiments around Calcutta.

Apart from the principal forts such as those of St. George at Madras, Fort William at Calcutta, and a few others, there was no proper barrack accommodation, so that the constantly-marching troops had to bivouac as best they could, either in the soaring temperatures of the hot weather or in the drenching downpours and mud of the monsoon season. And all this was performed in the thick red coat attire of home service, complete with constricting stock and cross-belts, tight-fitting trousers and a cocked hat that was as useless in the hot weather as it was in the deluge of the monsoons (which must have rendered it shapeless). No serious attempt was made to provide the British soldier with a more suitable tropical dress until the Indian Mutiny in the middle of the next century. Southern India was notorious for its health hazards. There was no revitalising cold weather as in the north, only constant high temperatures combined with enervating humidity. But more serious than personal discomfort were the endemic afflictions of malaria, dysentery, and that dread scourge, cholera, which could carry off more men than enemy bullets. The medical officers, or "surgeons", were utterly ignorant of these diseases and could offer neither prophylactic nor treatment.

Four years prior to the arrival of the 76th in Madras, in July 1788, Pitt's government had passed the East India Bill which in effect forbade the Company to interfere in native affairs or to take aggressive action except in the case of aggression against itself. Since Lord Cornwallis' arrival as Governor-General and Commander-in-Chief in 1786 the embargo had been faithfully observed, but by 1788 it had become clear that Tipu, *"the Tiger of Mysore"* [g], was once more seeking British prey. In the following year Tipu invaded the friendly state of Travancore, to wreak devastation and mayhem. The inept Governor of Madras who, according to Fortescue *"should have been hanged from the nearest tree"*, did nothing to counter this hostility. Exasperated, Cornwallis resolved to take firm action, judging himself freed from the restriction of the East India Act.

And so when a more energetic Governor, Major General William Medows, arrived in Madras, Cornwallis ordered him to take the field against Tipu. This was in February 1790, and it marks the onset of the the Third Mysore War. The plan of campaign, of which Cornwallis was not greatly enamoured, was for a division of 15,000 troops to concentrate at Trichinopoly and from there to advance northwards, capture Tipu's base at Palgautcherry and then to move further into his territories, while a second column was to protect the right flank. In April that year Thomas Musgrave of the 76th had risen to major general, and was appointed to command Medows' left wing infantry.

---

(e) Captain Hamilton served with the 76th until 1795 when he transferred as lieutenant colonel to command the 81st Foot. He eventually became Lieutenant General Sir John Hamilton, Colonel of the 69th Foot.
(f) *Historical Records 76th "Hindoostan" Regiment. 1787-1881.* F.A. Hayden. 1908.
(g) Tipu had a mania for tigers. Tiger symbols adorned most of his possessions. His army, for instance, had mortars shaped like sitting tigers.

Musgrave's own 76th Regiment was posted to the other column under Colonel Hamilton Maxwell. Numbering some 9,000 all ranks, this comprised two brigades, each of one British and three Bengal Native infantry battalions, together with a reserve of Madras Sepoys. The 76th was the British element of the 2nd Brigade. Because the colonel was commanding the left wing infantry in the other division, the lieutenant colonel, George Harris, was on General Medows' staff as military secretary and the major (Brevet Lieutenant Colonel) Alexander Ross[h] was away as Adjutant-General of the Bengal army in Calcutta, command of the 76th fell to the senior captain, Robert Shaw – another of the officers who had joined the 76th from the 40th Foot.

General Medows' division marched on 26 May 1790, but his transport and commissariat service were so defective it took him twenty days to traverse the first fifty miles to Caroor. By then nearly 1,200 of his troops had fallen sick. After further ponderous manoeuvring against Tipu's forces he succeeded in capturing several of his bases, including Palgautcherry. But it was not until September that Maxwell's division, with the 76th, was able to move from the concentration area at Arnee in the Carnatic. In November Maxwell joined up with Medows, bringing the total King's and H.E.I.C. forces to some 20,000 men, *"the finest army hitherto sent into the field by the British in India"*. The year 1790 closed without any decisive actions, and by the following January, Medows was back in Madras. During the whole of this period the 76th had not fired a shot in anger. Cornwallis now took over personal command of the field army. His first objective was Tipu's fortress of Bangalore which, when captured, would form the base for an attack on Seringapatam (now Sriranga Patnam) where lay the *Tiger's* palace and headquarters. The march began on 5 February 1791 and by a cunning feint Cornwallis succeeded in reaching the environs of Bangalore *"without any let, check or impediment"* as Medows recorded.

By now the Colonel of the 76th, Major-General Thomas Musgrave, had been appointed Adjutant-General of the British troops in Bengal and Madras, and was thus effectively divorced from his Regiment. He had acquired the reputation of being somewhat self-opinionated and argumentative, and on 4 February Cornwallis thought fit to send him a despatch with a few words of caution. *"I need hardly add, how earnestly I wish that you may live on the most friendly terms with the Government of Fort St. George; ......It is also encumbent upon you to acquiesce without anger or murmur in their opinion, when it happens to differ from your own"*.

It is remarkable that the march of Cornwallis' army of some 20,000 men, guns and baggage train over about 250 miles of jungle, unmade roads and across the mountain barrier of the southern Ghats should have been accomplished within four weeks. Then, and for more than a century, an army in the field was encumbered by its enormous "tail" of baggage transport, not to mention the battering train of heavy 18 and 24 pounder siege guns. In southern India the common draught animal was the slow plodding bullock, or Indian buffalo, harnessed to primitive two-wheeled carts. In all, some 26,000 of these beasts accompanied Cornwallis, in addition to 64 elephants

---

(h) Alexander Ross had been ADC to Cornwallis in America, during the War of Independence. He eventually became a general and Colonel of the 89th Foot and later of the 59th Foot

employed to drag and push the siege guns; the first time the British used elephants for this purpose.

Like most large southern Indian towns, Bangalore consisted of a stone-built fortress with its adjacent township or pettah, itself defended by entrenchments and redoubts. When Cornwallis arrived on 5 March, Tipu had garrisoned the fort with 8,000 men, with another 9,000 protecting the pettah. Confident that these were adequate to repel any attack he had withdrawn his main force six miles westwards. A lesser general than Cornwallis might have hesitated to attack a strongly-held position with a superior enemy reserve ready to intervene, but with no covering force available to deal with it. But Cornwallis was undeterred.

At dawn on 7 March he launched the 36th Foot (2nd Worcestershire) and a battalion of Bengal sepoys against the defences of the pettah. The defenders were driven back to the walls of the fort and more than half the town was soon in British hands. But Tipu then sent up a reinforcement of some 6,000 men with orders to re-take the town. There followed a fierce contest in which the 36th, 76th and two sepoy battalions cleared the narrow streets with the bayonet. *"Gathering impetus from this success, they then drove the enemy from quarter to quarter, until they fairly swept them out of the town with the loss of over two thousand killed and wounded"*.

The fort was still holding out however, and Cornwallis brought up his siege guns to batter breaches in the walls. On the moonlit night of 21 March a storming party of flank companies from the 36th, 52nd (Oxfordshire LI), 71st (1st HLI), 74th (2nd HLI), 76th and Madras Europeans (a total of twelve companies) rushed a breach, and, gaining the parapet, swept into the defenders with the bayonet. They were quickly followed by the battalion companies, and after furious hand-to-hand combat the garrison's survivors fled. The victors had the grim task of burying more than 1,000 enemy dead.

Although the 76th was heavily engaged in both assaults, on the pettah and the fort, its casualties were extraordinarily light – eight soldiers killed and one officer and 45 other ranks wounded, the officer being Captain David Markham.

Having secured Bangalore for his base, Cornwallis now prepared for his attempt on Seringapatam. Before this could be put into effect he was anxious to join forces with those of his Indian ally, the Nizam of Hyderabad, and with an army marching from Bombay under General Robert Abercromby. But as ill-luck would have it, this initial design on Seringapatam went sadly awry. First, Cornwallis was beset with commissariat problems, not only in shortage of rations and forage, but in serious mortality among the transport bullocks which had died off in their hundreds. Accordingly, all officers were ordered to give up their private animals for the general good. One can only wonder what they did with all the baggage comforts, including wine[i], then considered necessary. Then there was the problem of transport for the sick and wounded. On 2 July, Cornwallis complained to Sir Charles Oakeley, Governor of Madras, about the lack of doolis and native dooli-bearers. It was *"hardly credible"*, he wrote, that successive generals *"could have seen their wretched soldiers, either with a broken bone or a violent fever,*

---

(i) Not long after the capture of Bangalore, Cornwallis was writing (July 1791) to his brother, the Bishop of Lichfield and Coventry, desiring him to arrange for the despatch of *"fifteen chests of claret"*

*sqeezed into a blanket carried by two of their comrades"*. So grave was the transport problem in fact that local women and boys were hired to carry ammunition for the guns. One rupee was paid for an 18pdr roundshot, and half as much again for a 24pdr.

The junction with the Nizam's forces was achieved in April, but these were to prove more a liability than an asset. Abercromby had now advanced to Periapatam, south-west of Seringapatam, and Cornwallis pushed on to link up with him. By 4 May he had reached Arikera, about nine miles east of Seringapatam, but it proved impossible to ford the swollen river Cavery to reach Abercromby, and the commander-in-chief resigned himself to marching west of Seringapatam where there was a passable ford. Meanwhile, Tipu had moved to take up a strong position just east of Seringapatam, his right flank secured by the river, his front extending along a rocky ridge at the foot of which ran a swampy nullah. A frontal attack was out of the question. Cornwallis therefore planned an outflanking movement at night, to come upon Tipu's unsuspecting left rear. The force detailed comprised the same six British battalions who had already tasted victory at Bangalore – the 76th being one – plus the 19th Light Dragoons, some Madras cavalry and 12 native battalions. Squadrons of the Nizam of Hyderabad's cavalry were to follow up after dawn.

Cornwallis was a commander who would ensure that the smallest detail of his plan was understood and faithfully carried out, but even he could not discipline the elements. Just before the force moved off in the inky darkness of near midnight on 14 May, a fearful thunderstorm burst over the countryside, causing many of the transport bullocks to panic and the native guides to lose direction, or to panic likewise. After no more than four or five miles the ordered column had disintegrated into chaos. There was nothing for it but to await the coming of first light. The storm had roused the enemy, and by the time the advance was resumed Tipu had been warned of the threat to his rear, enabling him to make fresh dispositions. There followed fierce fighting for the ridge, which was stormed by the six British battalions who drove off the Mysoreans with severe casualties. But pursuit was effectively hindered by the Nizam's cavalry which blocked the advance and enabled Tipu's army to make good its withdrawal to the safety of Seringapatam.

Although Cornwallis' plans had been largely thwarted by the elements, the battle of Arikera could be claimed as a victory.(j) Tipu lost about 2,000 men, Cornwallis only some 500. Again, as at Bangalore, the 76th's casualties were surprisingly light: one officer (Lieutenant Edward Brooke) and two other ranks killed, one officer (Lieutenant Charles Griffiths) and 18 other ranks wounded.

But the goal of Seringapatam and subjugation of Tipu Sultan was not yet to be, and in July 1791 Cornwallis retired to Bangalore, having failed to join up with Abercromby. On 8 September he was moved to pen an oddly despondent letter to his friend the Rev B Grisdale at home. *"God knows where our war will end. I hope and trust it will be soon, or it will end me; I do not mean that I am sick, I have stood the burning sun and cold as well as the youngest of them, but I am plagued, and tormented, and wearied to death"*.

---

(j) The action was fought nearer Seringapatam than Arikera, but the latter place-name has always been preferred.

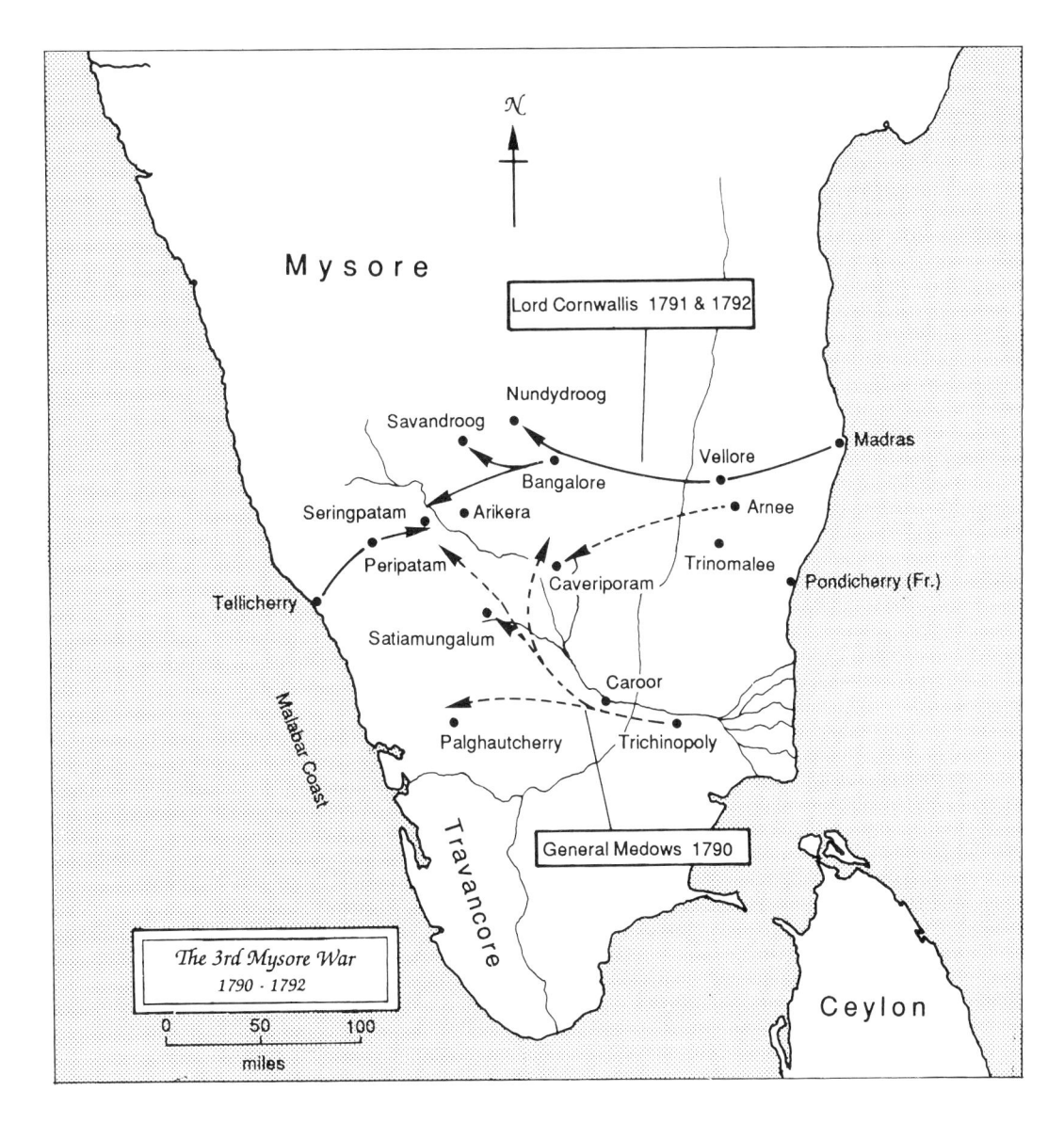

# THE RAISING OF THE 76th REGIMENT AND THE THIRD MYSORE WAR

However, after the capture of several hill forts or "droogs" which had menaced communications (k) Cornwallis was able to try once more for the prize of Seringapatam. This fortress and its adjacent township lay on an island roughly three miles long, formed by diverging branches of the Cavery river. The extensive fort itself stood in the extreme western angle of the island, while a chain of fortifications extended to the eastern angle. On the north bank of the river lay a vast defended expanse bounded by a thick hedge of bamboo and thorn and enclosing six redoubts erected on natural hillocks. In this area

---

(k) The most formidable of these was Savandroog known locally as *the Hill of Death*. It was successfully stormed (with the help of the 76th) on 21 December 1791. Incredibly there was only one British casualty, a private soldier wounded.

85

lay the bulk of Tipu's infantry and cavalry, numbering about 50,000 men besides irregular levies, and 300 field pieces. By 5 February Cornwallis had halted within six miles of the northern defences, and on the following day he laid his plans. The fact that he could deploy no more than 8,700 men to confront the vastly superior enemy was of little consequence now that at last he had brought the *Tiger* to bay. Once more, a night operation was decided upon and the assault force was split into three wings or columns. The 76th, still commanded by Captain Robert Shaw and mustering about 690 all ranks, was posted with the 36th and two sepoy battalions to the right wing commanded by General Medows. Their task was to sweep round the enemy's left flank, penetrate the defences and then join forces with the centre wing commanded by Cornwallis himself. The latter had cautioned Medows not to attempt an attack on Tipu's strong left-flank redoubt. The left division (Colonel Hamilton Maxwell) was to force Tipu's right wing position and then cross to the island. Since surprise was the chief element of the plan, no artillery accompanied the force, and it was not until a couple of hours before zero hour, at 6pm, that officers were briefed.

By what Cornwallis described as *"one of those accidents to which all operations in the night must be liable"*, Medows' column strayed too far to the flank and ran straight into the forbidden redoubt, which the advance guard impetuously attacked before it could be called off. Thus committed, the column became embroiled in a fierce, protracted fight which delayed further advance. The story is taken up by the anonymous author of a History of the 76th "Hindoostan" Regiment:–

> *"On approaching the redoubt a heavy fire of grape and musketry was opened on the leading division....... when a few companies of the 36th Regiment were instantly formed and attacked some of the enemy's troops..... While the flank companies of that Regiment and the 76th Regiment rushed forward to the redoubt and drove the enemy from the covered way....... The enemy however brought a gun to bear upon the traverse and with it and their musketry did such terrible execution that it was judged expedient to cease the British fire and lead the men to the charge. The Mysoreans perceiving this movement loaded the cannon with grape; and reserving their fire until the assailants were advancing, opened upon them a most destructive volley..... They were however prevented from taking advantage of this by the exertions of Captain (James) Gage who with the 76th Grenadiers had mounted a banquette to the right of the gorge from which he kept up a brisk fire into the redoubt..... the 36th under Captain Burne leapt upon the parapet at the hill of the gorge; and all rushing forward with the most daring intrepidity, struck the enemy with such dismay that many of them attempted to escape by leaping through the embrasures into the ditch. After a murderous conflict in which four hundred of the Mysoreans with their commandant were slain, this formidable position*

*remained in the possession of the British who had eleven officers and eighty men killed and wounded. Of the 76th Regiment, Lieutenant Jones was killed, and Captain Markham, Lieutenants Robertson, Philpot and Shaw, one Sergeant, and seven rank and file were wounded".*

Medows' column had been so delayed by the redoubt fight that it completely lost touch with the centre column under Cornwallis and spent the rest of the night vainly seeking it, eventually coming to rest on the extreme left wing without firing another shot. By dawn, however, the two columns were able to make contact, and a few hours later the British made a lodgement on the island of Seringapatam, while the rest of the force was in position around the defended area on the north bank of the river. At daybreak on the 8th it was found that the enemy had abandoned its defended camp to the north of the Cavery and evacuated the whole of the island except the fort, where Tipu himself had taken refuge. His losses were severe: more than 20,000 killed, wounded and missing.

Next day the ever-treacherous Sultan released some of his English captives with the message that he was prepared to open negotiations. At the same time he sent a troop of his light horse with orders to enter the British lines under the guise of the allied Nizam's cavalry, seek out the commander-in-chief and slay him. Both missions failed.

Seringapatam 25 February 1792. The hostages: two of Tipu's sons are presented to Lord Cornwallis

Cornwallis was not yet prepared to negotiate with the fort still in enemy hands, and the murder squad failed to reach the commander-in-chief's headquarters tent and was driven off by alert sentries.

The investment of Seringapatam fort dragged on until March, during which period the 76th lost one soldier killed and four wounded, one of whom later died. Conceding defeat (but only temporarily) Tipu agreed to a Peace Treaty on 19 March 1792, though he had no intention of observing all the terms. One of these was the surrender of two of his three sons as hostages.

This first capture of Seringapatam marked the end of the Third Mysore War and was hailed as a victory. It seemed that the *Tiger of Mysore* had finally been muzzled. Nearly half his territories were to be ceded to the British and an indemnity of several thousands of rupees was to be paid. All this for the loss of some 535 all ranks of British and H.E.I.C. troops.

As a reward for his services, in August 1792, Charles Lord Cornwallis (still Colonel of the 33rd Regiment) was created Marquis, the first and last of that title. For the 76th there was the award of the battle honour **Mysore** – though not until 1889.

In 1792 the 76th was ordered to join the Bengal army at Fort William, Calcutta. In 1794 George Harris, who was still nominally in command of the Regiment, returned from England where he had been on two years leave. That same year he was promoted a major general in the army. Two years later he was appointed commander-in-chief of the Madras army and at the end of 1797 he was succeeded in command of the 76th by Lieutenant Colonel the Hon William Monson. However, Monson was at that time returning to England with his regiment (52nd Foot) and did not learn of his appointment until arriving at Cape Town in June 1798. Being in poor health he continued his journey and did not return to India until 1799. In the meantime the Regiment's de facto commanding officer was its second Lieutenant Colonel, Michael Symes. Because there was no permanent organisation larger than a regiment, the outbreak of a war meant that the senior officers in a regiment were usually required either to take command of newly created formations or to fill staff appointments. The experience of the 76th during the 3rd Mysore War, during which it was commanded by a captain, was not untypical. In 1793 it was decided to rectify the shortcomings of the system by authorising an increase in establishments of a second lieutenant colonel and a second major when a regiment was on active service. However the appointments do not appear to have been implemented in India until October 1795. Alexander Ross was the first to fill the appointment of second lieutenant colonel in the 76th. He was succeeded by Michael Symes in 1797 when Ross became Colonel of the 89th Regiment.

Lieutenant Colonel the Hon. William Monson, who now assumed command of the 76th Regiment, had obtained an ensigncy in the 52nd Foot (later Oxfordshire Light Infantry) in 1780 and had commanded the light company of the Regiment in the attack on Seringapatam in 1792.

The 76th Regiment remained in Calcutta until 1800, apart from a brief posting to Dinapore, 300 miles up the Ganges. During this period the East India Company became concerned at the activities of French warships and privateers. The Company therefore decided to equip four of its East Indiamen as fighting units to protect its shipping. As the squadron was to cruise as warships the ships' complements were augmented by soldiers. Detachments of the Bengal artillery were to work the guns and men from the 76th were to act as marines. In January 1794 three of the ships, (Britannia, Nonsuch and William Pitt), under command of Charles Mitchell, had a successful encounter with two French privateers. On board Britannia was a detachment of 34 men of the 76th, commanded by Captain-Lieutenant James Robertson. It can be assumed that the other two ships had detachments from the Regiment as well.

During the Regiment's campaigning against Tipu Sultan, battle casualties had been relatively light, but as usual, sickness struck severely. The actual losses from this cause are not recorded, but it is significant that in November 1798 four drafts totalling 145 men were received from England, while in the following month no fewer than 425 rank-and-file volunteered to join the Regiment from the 36th Regiment, when that regiment was ordered to return to England. These reinforcement brought the other ranks' strength to 873, which seems to show that previously it had fallen as low as 203.

In 1800 the 76th moved to Cawnpore, where Lieutenant Colonel Monson joined and took over command.

CHAPTER 7

# Arthur Wellesley and the 33rd Regiment

*1793 Wesley joins*
*33rd Flank companies to the West Indies*
*1794 Bostkel, Geldermalsen*
*1799 Mallavelly, Seringapatam*
*1810 Flank companies, Ile de Bourbon and Mauritius*

On 21 September 1792, following King Louis XVI's detention by the revolutionaries, France declared itself a republic. The attitude of the British government was initially one of neutrality while at the same time trying to influence the French not to attack Holland with whom Britain had a defensive treaty. However on 21 January 1793 King Louis was executed. Alarm spread throughout Europe and in Britain the Prime Minister, William Pitt, ordered the French ambassador home. On 1 February 1793 France declared war against Britain and Holland.

Also in 1793 Captain the Hon Arthur Wesley (as the future Duke of Wellington's name was then spelt), with financial assistance from his elder brother, the Earl of Mornington, purchased his majority from Major Ralph Gore of the 33rd. Five months later, in September, again with help from his brother, he purchased the lieutenant colonelcy from John Yorke. He was then aged 24. He had advanced from ensign to lieutenant colonel in six years and served in seven different regiments. Such progress was by no means uncommon in an age when advancement was by purchase.[a]

Arthur Wesley had been born in May 1769 at the family home of Dungan Castle, Co Meath. After three unhappy years at Eton he was sent to France to the fashionable Academie Royale d'Equitation at Angers, where sons of the nobility and gentry from both sides of the Channel were instructed not only in horsemanship and swordsmanship but also in the humanities. Most of the pupils were destined for a military career. His mother, Lady Mornington, had decided that the army was the only refuge for her awkward son, averring that *he was food for powder and nothing more.*

---

(a) Ensign (1787) 73rd; lieutenant (1787) 76th, 41st and 12th Light Dragoons; captain (1791) 58th and 18th Light Dragoons; major (1793) 33rd.

Two months after Wesley had assumed command the flank companies of the 33rd, along with those of all the other regiments then serving in Ireland, were sent to the West Indies as part of a force under General Sir Charles Grey. Pitt had decided that as France was on the verge of bankruptcy he would hasten the process by capturing the country's wealth producing sugar plantations, where the negro slaves were already in revolt. Grey, ably assisted by Sir John Jervis who commanded the fleet, soon captured Martinique, St Lucia and Guadeloupe. However, their forces then began to suffer the ravages of the endemic diseases of the fever ridden islands. In October 1974, as a result of sickness and mortality, the troops on Guadeloupe were obliged to surrender. Among them were the two flank companies of the 33rd. The MS Digest of Services of the 33rd Regiment states that the companies *"were totally destroyed"*.[b]

Arthur Wesley (later Wellesley) Lieutenant Colonel of the 33rd, 1793-1802

In addition to the ravages of the climate, Grey was also plagued by the maladministration of the Secretary of State for War [c], Henry Dundas. Time and again Grey's requests for reinforcement and clothing and necessaries for his men were ignored. As early as July 1794 he wrote *"You seem totally to have forgotten us"*.

Perhaps one of the worst aspects of the campaign was the way in which 24 regiments were denuded of their flank companies, which consisted of their finest soldiers. They made a superb body of troops, but it *"practically destroyed for some years the efficiency of the battalions from which they had been drawn"*.

Meanwhile, in 1794, the Regiment, less the unfortunate flank companies, had moved to Cork where Major John Coape Sherbrooke assumed the newly authorised appointment of second lieutenant colonel. It was not to remain there long.

In Europe, where Britain's allies were the Austrians and Prussians in addition to the Dutch, Pitt's aim was to maintain the integrity of the Netherlands and thereby deny the use of their ports to the French. However the Dutch army was poorly led and organised and in order to put some backbone into it he sent three battalions of Guards, under Major General Gerard Lake[d], to Holland soon after the outbreak of war in 1793. In

---

(b) In the papers of the 1st Duke of Wellington, in Southampton University, is a return giving the names of 60 men of the grenadier company who died in the West Indies.
(c) The appointment was created in 1794. The Secretary at War then became responsible for political matters.
(d) The Guards were seen off on their way to embark at Greenwich by an enthusiastic crowd. The head of the column arrived in good order but the rear had been so well entertained that its members collapsed dead drunk and had to be brought on in carts.

March he sent a further brigade. The whole of the British force, which included four cavalry regiments, was under the command of the young Frederick Duke of York. He also had contingents of Hanoverians and Hessians who were paid for by Britain. The Allies had some outstanding successes on the French/Belgian[e] border, until the French army was increased to twice that of the Allies. Further complications occurred in May 1794 when the Austrians decided to withdraw most of their forces from the Netherlands in order to make troops available to operate in Poland.

In June 1794 the news that Ostend was in danger prompted the incompetent Dundas to unwonted action. Twelve battalions under the able and much respected Major General Lord Moira[f] were ordered to Holland from the Isle of Wight and three from Ireland: the 8th (King's), 33rd and 44th (Essex). By the end of June all had arrived at Ostend where the infantry was organised into seven brigades, the three regiments from Ireland forming the 2nd Brigade. This was probably the brigade which was given to Arthur Wesley who, when Moira marched away to join the allied army, was left as rearguard, *"to settle matters at Ostend* (the French were getting near) *and then come*

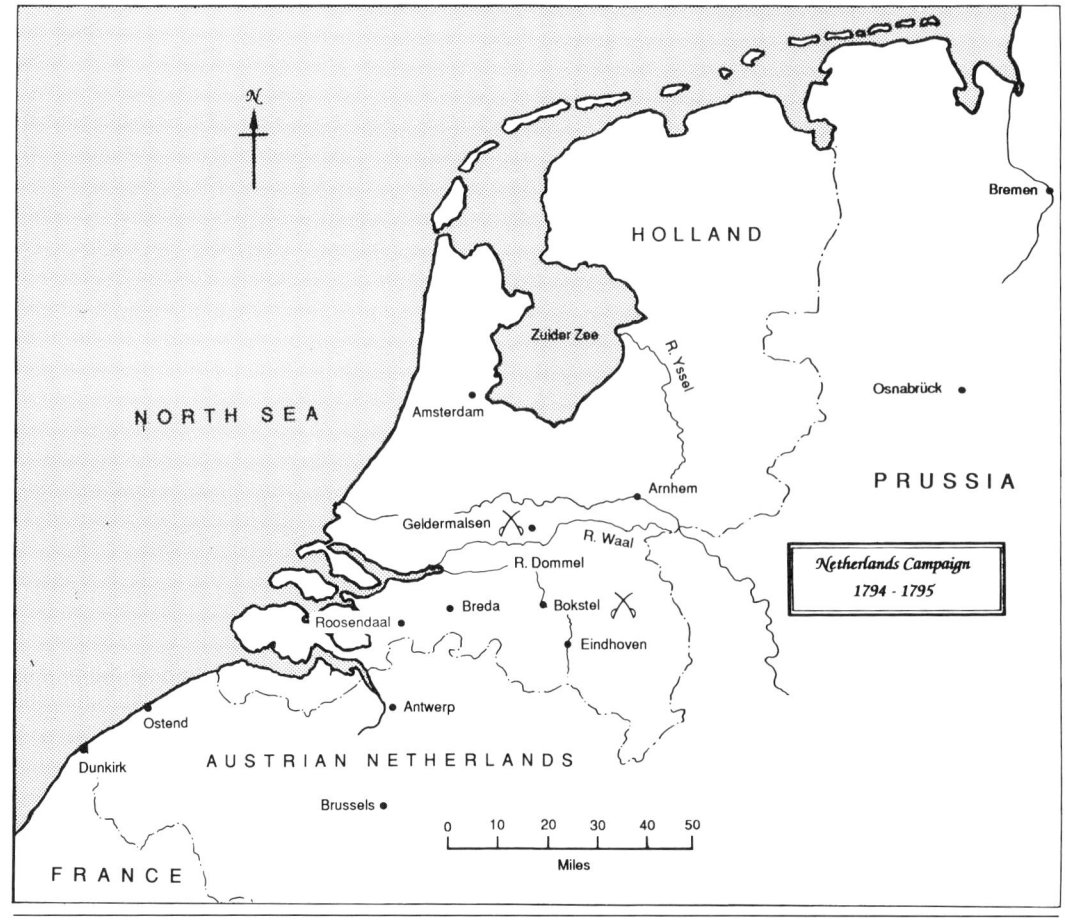

---

(e) Or Austrian Netherlands as Belgium was then called.
(f) He was Lord Rawdon when he served in the Carolinas under Cornwallis. Became 1st Marquess of Hastings.

*on as quick as I could".* Ostend was promptly evacuated, and preferring a short sea voyage to a long march, he re-embarked his men, put them ashore at Antwerp and reached the Duke of York before the leading files of Moira's force.

Further withdrawals became necessary and by the end of July the Duke of York was at Roosendaal, near Breda. His force, which now numbered some 32,000, excluding Hanoverians and Hessians, was however of indifferent quality. This was partly due to peacetime neglect, but was also due to the scandalous traffic in commissions whereby ignorant young men with no interest in their duty were placed in command of untrained, ill equipped and hastily raised recruits.

By September the army had retreated to a position along the River Dommel between Eindhoven and Hertogenbosch, and on the 15th of the month a skirmish occurred at Bostkel (Boxtel), memorable for the stout conduct of the 33rd. On 14 September a strong French force captured the town and with it some 1,500 of the Hessian garrison. On the following day the Duke ordered Lieutenant General Abercromby to recover the town. The task was given to the Guards Brigade and the 3rd Brigade, 12th (Suffolk), 33rd, 42nd (Black Watch) and 44th (Essex), under the command of Arthur Wesley. Abercromby advanced boldly enough but, encountering unexpectedly superior opposition, he judged it prudent to withdraw. Then followed some disorder as the retreating infantry became mixed up with the cavalry squadrons. Seeing this, the French cavalry deployed for a charge and the situation became critical. It was resolved by the 33rd, commanded by Lieutenant Colonel John Sherbrooke :

> *"When he (Sherbrooke) had obtained the rank of Lt-Col., he served under the Duke of York in Flanders, and during this unfortunate and memorable retreat, the 33rd was appointed to cover it... Two regiments of French Cavalry were seen coming down with the intention of charging the 33rd ... Col. Sherbrooke faced his Regt to the rear and gave the word 33rd 'Steady'. In this awful crisis not a man moved, but with determined fortitude they awaited the attack. When the first French Regt. was within 50 yards the command was given to 'Fire!' – the steady coolness of the men gave it full effect... men and horses were precipitated to the ground – those who were neither unhorsed nor wounded, halted and attempted to retreat, but before they had gained a very short distance a second volley completed the work of destruction and the whole Regt. lay stretched on the ground. The second Regt witnessing the dreadful over-throw faced about and were seen no more. This brilliant action Sir John (Sherbrooke) always declared was more satisfactory to him, and he took more pride in it, than any affair in which he was ever engaged".*(g)

Undoubtedly the 33rd saved the day, enabling the rest of the force to withdraw

---
(g) This account was apparently dictated to his daughter-in-law in 1830, the year of Sherbrooke's death. Most accounts are based on that given in W H Maxwell's 'Life of Wellington',(1849), which states Wesley commanded the 33rd at Bosktel. That is clearly incorrect.

*Two soldiers of the 33rd and a light dragoon in Holland in 1795*

unmolested. On 19 September Wesley wrote to his elder brother, the Earl of Mornington, saying that General Abercromby had called on him to convey the Duke of York's thanks, and his own, *"to the 33rd for their good conduct on the 15th"*. The Regiment's casualties in this engagement were incredibly minimal: one sergeant and one private missing.

The Duke of York and the Prussians continued their withdrawal, pausing on successive river lines. By the end of October they were on the north bank of the Waal. When the river froze at the end of December the French crossed it and captured a position at Geldermalsen held by the Dutch, who by then were more concerned to come to terms with the French than defending their own country. The French were driven back but on 5 January 1795 they crossed the river again, only to be repulsed, with some loss by the 33rd, 42nd(Black Watch) and 78th(Seaforths). Writing of this time Arthur Wesley complained *"I was on the Waal from October to January and during all that time I only saw once one General from headquarters"*. In another letter he wrote *"We turn out once, sometimes twice every night; the officers and men are harassed to death...I have not had my clothes off my back for a long time"*.

The winter of 1794 - 1795 was the coldest within living memory, and as the miserable soldiers continued the demoralising retreat they were afflicted not only by pursuing French cavalry but by blizzards and perpetual arctic temperatures, which short rations and ragged clothing did nothing to ameliorate. In January 1795 the cold was so intense that the hands and feet of some men were frozen to such a degree as to drop off at the wrists and ankles.

> *"Far as the eye could reach over the whitened plain were scattered gun limbers, waggons full of baggage, stores, or sick men . . . Besides them lay the horses dead; around them scores and hundreds of soldiers, dead; . . . there a group of British and Germans round an empty rum cask; here forty Enlishmen huddled about a plundered wagon . . . one and all frozen dead".* (Fortescue)

At last, in March 1795, the Cabinet called a halt to the disastrous campaign and ordered transports to Bremen for the evacuation of the British remnants. The 33rd embarked for England on 13 April 1795. During the ten months it had been campaigning on the Continent only six men had been killed by enemy action. Two hundred, however, had died from disease and other causes and another 192 were left behind sick in hospital. But at least, the Netherlands campaign had been instructive to Wesley. He later wrote: *"Why – I learnt what one ought not to do, and that is always something"*. After arriving in England the 33rd went into camp at Warley to recruit and refit. Recruiting parties were certainly sent to Yorkshire where, since 1794, the Regiment had had a recruiting company at Halifax. It was about this time that the 33rd acquired the nickname of the *"Havercake Lads"* on account of the recruiting sergeants carrying a havercake (a West Riding form of the oatcake) on the points of their swords.[h]

Meanwhile Arthur Wesley had resumed his post as ADC in Dublin Castle, and the representation of his Irish constituency in Parliament. Indeed, he now seems to have set his sights on politics rather than military glory, and among other attempts at string-pulling he put in bids for the appointment of Secretary-at-War for Ireland, or failing that, *"something in the Revenue or Treasury Boards"*. The new governor general was not responsive and he therefore resumed his military career.

Early in 1795 the government realised that conditions in the West Indies required a major expedition. In October the officer selected to command the expedition, Sir

---

(h) *Haver*, the Dutch word for oats, is usually used in conjunction with another, hence haversack.

Ralph Abercromby, was instructed to sail his force to Barbados where he was to deal with the situation in St Lucia and Guadeloupe before embarking on further operations. Twenty five infantry regiments were placed under his command, one of which was the 33rd. Because of the lack of essential equipment and contrary weather, the force, totalling some 18,000 men, was unable to leave Portsmouth until 16 November. Almost immediately it ran into a hurricane and the ships were forced to take shelter in Portland and other ports along the south coast. However 12,000 of the force were in a condition to re-start immediately and they set to sea again on 3 December, only to run into another gale. The 33rd was not among them. Instead it was sent to Lymington to recuperate. It remained until February 1796 when the authorities decreed that the East rather than the West Indies was to be the 33rd's theatre of operations. In April 1796 the Regiment left England and on reaching Cape Town, which had been taken from the Dutch the previous year to prevent the colony from falling into the hands of the French, it disembarked. There it was joined by Arthur Wesley who was sick at the time the Regiment left England but had followed it in a fast frigate. He was by now a colonel, having been appointed to that rank in May 1796. After an inexplicable delay at the Cape, the Regiment finally arrived at Calcutta on 17 February 1797.

Calcutta was the headquarters of the Governor-General of India and the hub of both military and society alike. It afforded ample opportunity for Arthur and his officers to indulge in the frequent banquets, balls, wining and dining in the numerous gentlemen's seats and the gambling sessions that were characteristic of headquarter life. One young officer of the 33rd, Captain Amos Norcott,(i) lost in excess of £500 the first time he gambled. Arthur Wesley paid his debt, making him promise never to gamble again. William Hickey who, after a dissolute and profligate youth, had made a successful career at the Calcutta bar, was a regular guest of the 33rd. He reported that they *"lived inimitably well, always sending their guests away with a liberal quantity of the best claret"*. At one drinking party thrown by the 33rd he found himself competing with *"eight as strong-headed fellows as could be found in Hindoostan"* which ended at 2.00am with *"the jovial crew"* being carried to bed insensible: *"....A more severe debauch I never was engaged in any part of the world"*. Another session followed on the King's birthday, 4 June 1797, when Hickey, Wesley, General St. Leger (founder of the Doncaster horse-race) and other notables consumed vast quantities of champagne, hock, claret and madeira, followed by *"several choice songs from junior members of the 33rd, and to crown it all a solo rendering of The British Grenadiers by the General himself"*. At breakfast next morning the revellers complained of *"slight sickness"*.

Such activities ceased when Spain rashly entered the war on the French side. Britain thereupon decided to appropriate the Spanish colonies in the Pacific. A small force of some 7,000 men, which included the 33rd, was assembled to capture Manila and set sail in August 1797. Colonel Wesley insisted on having responsibility for the health of his men, against the claims of the naval surgeons. Whereupon he drew up a code of thirty-six *"Regimental Orders on Board Ship"* which left nothing in the matter of health,

---

(i) In 1802 he transferred to the 95th Regiment. He later became Major General Sir Amos Norcott.

cleanliness, exercise and discipline to the unaided imagination of the troops. However the force only got as far as Penang when apprehension that Tipu, the *"Tiger of Mysore"*, might seize the opportunity to launch an attack, led to its recall.

In April 1798 Lord Mornington, Arthur's elder brother, became Governor General of India. He was at the same time raised to the English peerage as Baron Wellesley. Shortly afterwards Arthur Wesley changed his name to Wellesley.

In September the 33rd Regiment left Calcutta for Fort St. George at Madras. The voyage came near to disaster when Wellesley's transport struck a reef and would have foundered but for the exertions of soldiers and crew in refloating it. Then the whole Regiment, including Wellesley, went down with *"the flux"* caused by foul drinking water. Wellesley blamed this on the ship's captain whom he reported to the Adjutant-General in Calcutta, complaining that the dysentery had carried off *"fifteen of my best men"*.

The move to Madras was to enable the 33rd to join a force assembling for another campaign against Tipu Sultan, who was yet again intriguing with the French. The Governor General informed Lieutenant General George Harris (late of the 76th Regiment), who had been selected to command the field force, of the imminent arrival of the 33rd:

General Lord George Harris of Mysore & Seringapatam

> *"There can be no objection to the public mention of your expectation of the 33rd Regiment. I should even be glad that the news reached Tipu, as it would convince him I am in earnest.. "*

The Regiment disembarked at the end of September and was forthwith involved in the preparations for the campaign. Colonel Wellesley, following the death of the previous commander in a duel with one of his subordinates, was given command of the Nizam of Hyderabad's contingent. This consisted of *".....six excellent battalions of the Company's sepoys, four rapscallion battalions of the Nizam's, which, however, behaved well, and really about 10,000 (which they called 25,000) cavalry of all nations, some good and some bad....."* At Wellesley's insistence the 33rd joined the contingent. However the larger command that now rested on his shoulders and the amount of work it entailed meant that, much to his regret, he had less time to devote to it.

> *"There is nothing about which I am personally so much interested as the proper equipment of the 33rd and knowing perfectly well that if they were not provided with good lascars and good carriage for their tents, not only they would themselves be very uncomfortable during the campaign, but that they would be unable to render all the service which would be expected from them......This was promised; and if I had been in Fort St George with the 33rd, I believe I may safely assert that it would now be as well equipped ...as any regiment in the service. It is hard upon them that they should suffer because I am employed on other duty...."*

As John Sherbrooke was required to command a brigade, command of the Regiment devolved on Major John Shee, an Irish officer with an explosive temper, between whom and Wellesley no love was lost.

As in 1792, the British objective was once more the capture of Tipu's fortress of Seringapatam and the demolition of the *"Tiger's"* Mysore empire. Lord Mornington gave the order to invade Mysore on 3 February 1799. At one time he had thought of himself taking the field. Fortunately he asked his brother's advice, who replied bluntly:

> *"...all I can say upon the subject is, that if I were in General Harris's situation, and you joined the army, I would quit it".*

Having concentrated at Vellore, General Harris' army of some 37,000 men marched on 11 February 1799, while another force under Lieutenant General James Stuart advanced from Bombay. Harris' army moved in a vast parallelogram with the two sides seven miles long and the front and rear two miles wide. Within this space were crowded 120,000 bullocks needed for baggage and grain, together with a rabble of followers belonging to individuals, as was the luxurious fashion of Indian campaigns. A captain in the 33rd recorded a personal entourage of fourteen servants.

Shortly after the march began Wellesley had occasion to send a message to Major Shee on the subject of some men of the 33rd straying from the line of march, some without arms. Shee hotly resented what he regarded as interference in his command and wrote to Wellesley to say so. Wellesley may have been Irish too, but his reply was coldly restrained. Having explained the circumstances which had given rise to his message, he went on:

> *"I conceive that I have a right and that it is my duty, to interfere in any matter of detail in which the 33rd are concerned; and that being the case, it was my duty to send to you when I thought something had escaped your notice.*
> *This is not the first time that I have had occasion to observe, that, under the forms of private correspondence, you have written me letters upon public duty, couched in terms to which I have not been*

> *accustomed....it is necessary that I should inform you, that the next letter of that kind that I receive I shall send to the Commander-in-Chief, and leave it for him to give such answer to it as he may think fit..... Of this you may be certain, that however my attention may be engaged by other objects, whenever I find it necessary I shall interfere in everything that concerns the 33rd. I have written more than I intended: and in hopes that I shall hear no more of it".*

Not in the least chastened, Shee retorted that he would be only too glad to submit himself to a court martial. This unhappy affair seems to have been patched up, but only temporarily.

Despite these domestic squabbles the 33rd was soon to distinguish itself. By 26 March Harris' force had reached Malvalli (Mallavelly) some 14 miles south of Bangalore, and on the following day was heavily attacked by 20,000 of Tipu's horse and foot. Wellesley's contingent and his 33rd were on the British left, upon which fell the brunt of the attack. Serving with the Regiment was Captain Charles MacGrigor who described the action in his diary:

> *"March 27th. Marched at 5 o'clock this morning about twelve miles to Mallavilly where, about 1 o'clock, we came up with Tippoo, who had pushed his army on some heights on our front. After forming on the left of the army, the 33rd Regiment with the five battalions under Colonel Wellesley were ordered to move forward by eschelon (sic) of battalions from the centre, 33rd in advance. The enemy were at this time marching very regularly down in front of us, at about 300 yards they commenced a heavy fire of musketry but with little effect, we all this time were ordered to charge and set off as fast as we could, at about 10 yards we halted and fired, but their cavalry seeing us not well formed tried to come round our flanks and were repulsed with great loss, our cavalry under General Floyd, who were formed in our rear....moved briskly on, did a great deal of execution, about 500 of enemy were killed and left wounded; 33rd had six men slightly wounded; a most fatiguing day".*

What this somewhat breathless account does not make clear is, as Fortescue records, that the 33rd on its own actually repulsed some 10,000 of Tipu's infantry supported by cavalry. No wonder that next day *"we received the thanks of the Commander-in-Chief, who expressed himself particularly pleased with the conduct of the 33rd Regiment and Colonel Wellesley"*. MacGrigor's figure of 500 enemy casualties was an under estimate. According to Fortescue the actual figure was 1,000 killed and wounded, Harris' force losing less than 70 all ranks. Having driven back Tipu's protective screen around Seringapatam, Harris was able to advance within two miles of that fortress by 5 April. Then followed an

**Seringapatam 4th May 1799**

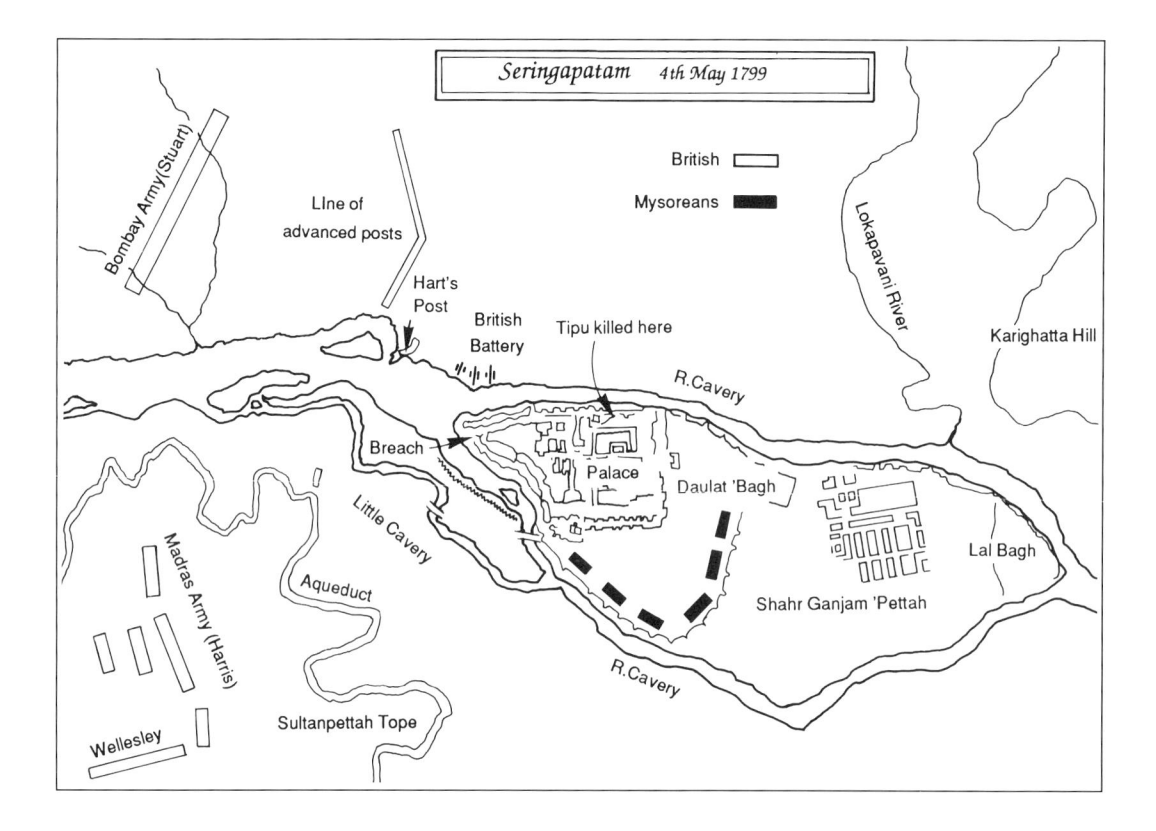

*(Map showing positions of Bombay Army (Stuart), Line of advanced posts, Hart's Post, British Battery, Tipu killed here, Breach, Palace, Daulat 'Bagh, Lal Bagh, Shahr Ganjam 'Pettah, Madras Army (Harris), Wellesley, Sultanpettah Tope, Aqueduct, Little Cavery, R. Cavery, Lokapavani River, Karighatta Hill)*

action that was less creditable for the future Duke of Wellington. Among the numerous enemy outposts was one known as the Sultanpettah tope (or thicket), held by a strong garrison. Wellesley and his 33rd, together with the 12th (Suffolk), were ordered to take this by a night attack. As so often with such operations, this one went awry. In the pitch darkness the troops lost direction, were fragmented, and, assaulted by murderous fire, were forced to withdraw.

> "We lost our way going into the wood and being under a tremendous fire... for nearly an hour we were obliged to withdraw the party from the tope or Wood, out of five companies of 33rd that went in about 12 were killed and missing and 40 wounded. Lieut Fitzgerald was killed, Lts. Campell and O'Hara wounded.... Colonel Wellesley was slightly wounded.....After waiting till nearly daybreak we were ordered home by Colonel Shaw [of the 12th], we again lost our way in going back to the camp". (Captain MacGrigor.)

Nine of the grenadiers of the 33rd, who led the attack, were taken prisoner. According to Captain John Chetwood of the 33rd, they were later put to death because

*The 33rd in the assault on Seringapatam, 4 May 1799*

they *"refused to work on artillery while pointed towards brother soldiers"*. The method of their death was gruesome. They either had a nail driven into their skull or their necks wrung by the Tiger's "strong men". This information reached the army on 27 April and no doubt accounted for the ferocity of the fighting when Seringapatam was stormed eight days later.

The lesson of this unhappy episode was not lost on Wellesley. He wrote to his brother, Lord Mornington,: *"I have come to a determination; when in my power, never to suffer an attack to be made by night upon an enemy who is....strongly posted, and whose posts have not been reconnoitred by daylight"*. His failure was made good the following day when he led another attack on the tope which succeeded in driving back the enemy without loss to himself.

By 17 April all the outlying defences of Seringapatam had been captured or abandoned by Tipu's men. Junction had been made with General Stuart's Bombay army and the siege began. With the enemy and Tipu himself effectively penned within the fortress, the next two weeks were spent in preparations for the assault: trenches and parallels were dug, siege guns dragged into position, scaling ladders fashioned out of bamboo. By 3 May the battering of Harris' 24-pounders had smashed a practicable breach in the fortress's north-western wall, and as his supplies were now dangerously low, he resolved on an assault the following morning. Wellesley was hopeful that he should command, but Harris gave that honour to Major General David Baird who had old scores to settle, having spent nearly four years as a captive of Tipu's father, Hyder Ali. Wellesley had to be content with command of the reserve, mostly H.E.I.C. sepoys.

The assault force comprised two columns. The left, under Lieutenant Colonel Dunlop, including the 12th (Suffolk) and 33rd Foot, was to attack the north-western rampart. The right column, directed to the southern ramparts, was led by Colonel John

*Seringapatam. The finding of Tipu's body.*

Sherbrooke and consisted of the 73rd and 74th Highlanders (1st and 2nd HLI), and flank companies from other units. With both its senior officers otherwise employed, command of the 33rd again fell to Major John Shee. His battalion numbered 20 officers and 462 other ranks. Judging, correctly, that his oriental enemy would not expect an attack in the searing heat of midday, General Harris launched his storming parties at 1.00pm on 4 May. The two columns had no difficulty in crossing the almost dry bed of the southern branch of the Cavery river, and within six minutes had driven back the surprised garrison around the breaches. *"In two hours the place was completely carried"*, wrote Captain MacGrigor, and there was terrible slaughter as those Mysoreans who did not escape over the other branch of the river were ruthlessly bayonetted. *"At least 9,000 of the enemy were killed"* (MacGrigor – Fortescue says 10,000).... *"the slaughter was immense all over the Fort; in some passages the dead were five and six deep, laying on one another....."* By 4.00pm the British flag was flying over the Tiger's lair of **Seringapatam**, and the 33rd had earned its second battle honour.(j)

The total British casualties in the siege were given by Fortescue as 203 all ranks killed, 667 wounded and 22 missing. The 33rd escaped with six other ranks killed and 28 wounded.

At first it was believed that Tipu himself had escaped or had taken refuge in some hidden recess of his palace, but then one of his retainers said he had seen him slain at the northern gateway. The discovery of the body was described by Captain John Knox, commanding the 33rd's light company:

> *"Genl. Baird gave orders for a Body of Troops to move with all expedition to that Gate and the 33rd being on the spot were ordered there.... the Guides led us to the Gate which we found filled with Dead and Dying heaped one over the other. Genl.Baird ordered the Regt. to Pile their Arms and look for Tippoo who it was now imagined must have died of his wounds or made his Escape.... The Light Infantry [i.e. 33rd's Light Company] were then ordered into the Gate by Lt. Col. Shee who commanded the Regt. and a search was immediately commenced.... After a tedious search the people came to a Body at which our Guides looked very attentively and said must be disengaged from the Dead Bodys which lay over it.... on examination it was found to be Tippoo himself.... At first Lt. Col. Wallace [12th], and others suggested that life might still Remain... but upon his being examined by Mr. Trevor, surgeon of the 33rd and a surgeon who had accompanied Genl. Baird, it was found he was quite cold and not the least particle of life remained".*

Lieutenant Knox went on to describe the conveyance of the body to the Palace by men of the 33rd's light company, who were *"not a little vexed at being made Palanquin Boys"*. Next day, on Baird's orders, Tipu's remains were buried with military ceremony beside those of his father, Hyder Ali, in the Lalbagh garden outside the Palace, where a mausoleum still stands The funeral party was found from the flank companies of the 12th and 33rd Regiments, commanded by Lieutenant Goodlad (33rd).

The victorious conclusion of the 4th Mysore War brought its rewards to generals and soldiers alike. The total prize money amounted to the then enormous sum of nearly £1 million, which was distributed according to rank. General Harris received £150,000, Colonel Wellesley £4,000 (which helped to settle his mounting debts). Private soldiers got £7, sepoys £5. Besides his share of £4,000, Colonel John Sherbrooke was singled out for particular praise by General Baird. Writing to General Harris the day after the assault, he claimed *".... I know no Man so justly entitled to praise as Colonel Sherbrooke, to whose exertions I feel myself much indebted for the success of the attack"*. Among the trophies

---

(j) Not granted until 1818.

acquired by Sherbrooke were Tipu's own helmet and two of his swords, which are now preserved in the Regimental museum at Halifax. The most famous trophy of all, however, was Tipu's life-size mechanical model of a tiger devouring a British soldier. This was presented by Wellesley to brother Richard at Fort William, who passed it on to the East India Company's Court of Directors, for display in its museum.(k)

Since 1798 the Colonel of the 33rd, Lord Cornwallis, had been serving in Ireland as Viceroy and Commander-in-Chief. As soon as the news of Seringapatam reached him he wrote as follows to Wellesley:

*Dublin Castle.*
*21st Septr, 1799.*

Dear Sir,

*It has given me the greatest satisfaction to observe the distinguished share which you and Colonel Sherbrooke and the 33rd Regiment have had in the late glorious war against Tippoo Sultan, which reflects so much honour on our Councils and our Arms.... I request that you will accept my sincere congratulations on this happy occasion, and that you will likewise convey them to Colonel Sherbrooke, and to the Officers and Soldiers of the Regiment, and assure the latter that I am happy to find the same spirit exists in the Corps which I have so often witnessed when I had the honour to command them in the Field.*

*I am with great regards,*
*Dear Sir, your most obedient*
*and faithful Servant*
   *(Sd) CORNWALLIS*

Two days after the victory Colonel Wellesley was appointed Governor of Seringapatam and was immediately confronted with the onerous and distasteful tasks of hanging and flogging to put a stop to looting, and disposing of the hundreds of malodorous corpses. As for the 33rd one of its final tasks in the war was to send out some men to shoot six or seven of Tipu's tigers, which were dangerously roaming around.

In July 1799 Wellesley was given command of all the forces in Mysore. His duties were demanding, but it was not all work without play. A Captain Elers of the 12th Foot, a member of his staff, recorded that *"Colonel Wellesley had at that time a very susceptible heart, particularly towards, I am sorry to say, married ladies and his pointed attention to this lady (Mrs F...) gave offence, not to her husband but to the aide-de-camp* (Captain F R West, 33rd Regiment), *who considered it highly criminal and indecorous..."*

The 33rd meanwhile, according to Elizabeth Longford, *"under Shee's erratic*

---

(k) After the abolition of the H.E.I.C. in 1858 the tiger was transferred to the Victoria and Albert Museum.

*surveillance had become a nightmare of drunkeness and brawling"*. Matters came to a head in May 1801 when Lieutenant Goodlad (the same who commanded Tipu's funeral party) was placed under arrest by Shee *"for taking Utley out shooting with him, contrary to orders"*. Who Utley was, or why this should have contravened orders, is not revealed. However, on Wellesley's intervention, Goodlad was released from arrest and assumed command of the grenadier company. Then followed an incident in the garrison mess when no doubt in their cups, Goodlad or Shee, or both, uttered unseemly remarks (*"Something passed which neither party was ever willing to explain"*). Shee now demanded that Goodlad should be exchanged into another regiment. Once more Wellesley over-ruled Shee and Goodlad was reprieved. But the hot-tempered Shee, furious at the continued encroachment on his authority, took drastic action by sending in his papers for resignation of his commission. Wellesley gladly accepted and forwarded them to the Deputy Adjutant-General. Then it seems that Shee had second thoughts and sought to withdraw his application. Wellesley refused. The problem was resolved by Shee's deteriorating health. He was sent home on leave and finally allowed to sell out in 1802.

That same year Arthur Wellesley, on promotion to major general, gave up his command of the 33rd. Of his time in command of the 33rd he wrote:

> *"I have commanded them now for nearly ten years, during nine of which I have scarcely been away from them and I have always found them to be the quietest and best behaved body of men in the army".*

The behaviour of the 33rd had already been noted by General Harris, who gave it as his opinion that,

> *"The regiment of Colonel Wellesley is a model regiment:– for equipment, for courage, for discipline, for good conduct. It is above all praise."* [l]

Cornwallis wished to have John Sherbrooke as his successor, but poor health, which had obliged him to return to England in 1800, ruled him out. Sherbrooke proposed that instead Arthur Gore[m] of the 78th Highlanders should fill the vacancy. Cornwallis concurred, writing to Sherbrooke: *"It gives me much concern that I must at last lose you as my Lieut-Colonel. You may rest assured that I will use my endeavours to obtain the succession for Arthur Gore, who I would be exceedingly glad to serve, not only in conformity with your wishes, but likewise on its own account and that of his Family"*. Wellesley, far away in India, was meanwhile pressing the claims of Major Walter Elliot, but without success. On confirmation of Gore's appointment he secured Elliot the command of the 80th. Despite his other responsibilities Arthur Wellesley never ceased to maintain a lively interest in the 33rd, using his influence to secure advancement for deserving officers, or expressing disapproval where this seemed justified. In a later age Wellesley might have

---

(l) Wellington. C Latham-Browne (1888).
(m) Lieutenant Colonel Arthur Gore was another member of the family which provided eleven officers to the Regiment between 1766 and 1895 (and one to the 76th). He had been in Sherbrooke's column at the storming of Seringapatam.

been accused of racial prejudice: although respecting the fighting qualities of Indian troops, he would have none but white-skinned "sahibs" in the 33rd. When in 1801 it was proposed to accept two Anglo-Indians *"as black as my hat"* as officers he objected to the commander-in-chief that though they might be intrinsically as good as the others, the 33rd *"was not a Sepoy Regiment"*.

The destruction of Tipu's power in Mysore now brought the British face to face with the Mahrattas. The Mahrattas were a loose confederation of five Indian princes who occupied an area of 970 by 900 miles and lived by pillaging and plundering their neighbours. Of particular alarm to the British was the fact that they were now being led and trained by Frenchmen. By August 1803 war was inevitable. Two principal armies were formed: the northern under General Gerard Lake and the southern under Arthur Wellesley. The latter earnestly wished that his own regiment, to which he was much attached, should join his force. However *"The 33rd could not join me. I should have lost the campaign if I had attempted to have drawn troops from General Campbell's division"*. It therefore remained with the reserve which, for strategic reasons, was kept some 200 miles in the rear of Wellesley's army. As a result it took no part in his famous victory at Assaye on 23 September 1803 which was, he wrote, *"the bloodiest for the numbers that I ever saw"*. After the peace treaty in 1804 the 33rd joined the Indian garrison of Vellore, where the sons of the late Tipu Sultan were held captive. That same year Wellesley had a knighthood of the Order of the Bath conferred on him.

On receiving news of Sir Arthur Wellesley's departure for England, early in 1805, Lieutenant Colonel Arthur Gore wrote a fulsome valedictory to his chief, stressing *"the very friendly and paternal attention you have paid to the Corps, while it had the honour of being under your immediate command, as well as of the unremitting manner in which you have continued your vigilance for its welfare since you have removed to a higher station"*.

Wellesley's reply paid generous tribute to others who had raised the Regiment's prestige:

> *"To Lieut-Colonel Arthur Gore*
> *Commanding H.M.'s 33rd Regiment*
>
> *Sir,*
> *I have had the pleasure of receiving your letter of 28 February. Nearly twelve years have elapsed since His Majesty was pleased to appoint me Lieut-Colonel of the 33rd Regiment, and in the whole course of that period I have been either in the exercise of the command of the regiment, or in constant communication with the actual commanding officer, and I have every reason to be satisfied with their conduct.*
> *It has been my uniform object to maintain the system of discipline, subordination, and interior economy, which I found established in the regiment by the Marquis Cornwallis, our Colonel.... and by the support and assistance I have uniformly received from Colonel Sherbrooke, Lieut-Colonel Elliott, and yourself, and the officers of the regiment, my duties as Lieut-Colonel have always been a pleasing occupation.*

> *It is most gratifying to me to receive this mark of approbation....from officers with whose conduct I have so much reason to be pleased, and with whom I have been so long and intimately acquainted. I beg that you will assure them that I shall never forget their services, and that I shall always be happy to forward their views.*
>
> *I have only to reccomend (sic)them to adhere to the system of discipline, subordination and interior economy which they have found established in the regiment, and above all, to cherish and encourage among themselves the spirit of gentlemen and soldiers.*
>
> *With the most anxious wishes for the prosperity of yourself and the 33rd Regiment,*
>
> *I have the honor to be, Sir,*
>
> *Your most obedient humble Servant,*
>
> *(Sd) ARTHUR WELLESLEY"*

*Fort St. George*
*March 2nd, 1805.*

On 5 October 1805 General Marquis Cornwallis who, in March 1803, had reluctantly accepted the post of Governor General and Commander-in-Chief in India, died at Ghazipur (in the Province of Benares), aged 67. He had been Colonel of the Regiment for 39 years. After his death the officers of the 33rd clubbed together to provide an ornamental silver vase, the "Cornwallis Cup", one of the most handsome pieces of silver in the officers mess. On 30 January 1806 Major General Sir Arthur Wellesley KB was appointed as his successor.

In 1805 the 33rd moved to Hyderabad where it remained for the next four years. On departure to Bangalore the Resident wrote to the Governor General, Lord Minto, commending the behaviour of the 33rd:

> *"..great jealousy and fear were felt at this court at the prospect of so large a body of European soldiers being stationed in the immediate vicinity of the capital; it was of much importance therefore...that the conduct of the regiment first stationed near Hyderabad should be such as to dispel the jealousies and fears of the Court...*
>
> *I am happy to assure your Lordship that these desirable objects have been obtained by the deportment and behaviour of HMs 33rd Regiment, whose conduct for a period of four years has uniformly calculated to inspire the inhabitants of these territories with perfect confidence, and with the most favourable opinion of the discipline, regularity and subordination of British soldiers".*

In 1810 the Regiment's two flank companies were involved in an almost forgotten operation in the Indian Ocean. The island of Mauritius (or Ile de France as it was then known), and its outlying islets formed the base for French men-o'-war and privateers which were wreaking havoc among British merchant shipping en route to and from India, and even carrying out raids on the Indian coast. Lord Minto was determined to put an end to all this piracy, and in June 1810 he ordered an expeditionary force to bring the French in Mauritius to heel. A force under command of Colonel Henry Keating (n), consisting of the 69th (Welch), 86th (Royal Irish Rifles) and the flank companies of the 12th and 33rd, quickly captured the outlying island of Ile de Bourbon. With the arrival of 10,000 reinforcements from India under command of General Sir John Abercromby an attack on Mauritius was launched. The first landing was effected on 29 November and heavy fighting followed until the fortress Port Louis was invested. The French commander then sent a flag of truce and on 2 December 1810 the whole of Mauritius was secured for the East India Company. Abercromby's casualties were 167 killed and wounded, among which were 3 killed and 13 wounded of the 33rd. One of those killed was Lieutenant Colonel James Campbell. In his despatch to the Governor General, Sir John Abercromby wrote:

> *"The European flank battalions forming the advance guard under Lieutenant Colonel Campbell (o) of the 33rd Regiment.. charged the enemy with the greatest spirit and compelled him to retire with the loss of his guns, and many killed and wounded. This advantage was gained by the fall of Lieut-Colonel Campbell, a most excellent and valuable officer".*

In 1811 the 33rd moved to Madras as a preliminary to a return to England the following year. In July 1812, after an absence of 17 years, the Regiment landed at Gravesend and from there moved to Hull.

Meanwhile Sir Arthur Wellesley had been offered the Colonelcy of a regiment with two battalions, which would have been to his pecuniary advantage if he had accepted, however he declined:-

> *Viseu*
> "To: Lieut Colonel Torrens  *January 30 1810*
> Military Secretary
>
> *I shall esteem it a great favour if you will tell Sir D Dundas that I am very much obliged to him, but I have no wish to be removed from the 33rd Regiment, of which I was Major, and Lieutenant-Colonel and then Colonel. I must say, however, that my friend, the late Secretary at War, made it the least profitable of all the regiments of the army, and, I believe, a losing concern, having reduced the establishment at once from 1,200 to 800, when it consisted of above 750 men; and I had to pay*

---

(n) Keating was appointed ensign in the 33rd in 1793. He later transferred to the 56th Regiment (Essex). In 1845, by then Lieutenant General Sir Henry Keating, he became Colonel of the 33rd.
(o) Lieutenant Colonel J Campbell had been appointed second lieutenant colonel in 1807. Arthur Wellesley held him in high esteem.

*the freight of the clothing to the East Indies, and its carriage to Hyderabad, about 500 miles from Madras. With all this I have a reputation of having a good thing in a regiment in the East Indies !"*

However on 1 January 1813, at the personal insistence of the Prince Regent, Wellesley who was by then General the Marquess Wellington, relinquished the Colonelcy of the 33rd for that of the Royal Horse Guards. On 2 February he wrote to Colonel Arthur Gore, commanding his old regiment:

*"My Dear Colonel,*

*Before you receive this letter you will have heard that H R H The Prince Regent has been pleased to appoint me to be Colonel of the Royal Horse Guards, an honour entirely unexpected by me...*

*Although highly gratified by the honour which has been conferred on me, as well as the manner in which it has been conferred, I cannot avoid to feel regret at one of its circumstance, viz; that I should be separated from the 33rd Regiment to which I have belonged with so much satisfaction for more than twenty years. I beg that you will take the opportunity of informing the regiment of the sentiments with which I quit them, and that though no longer belonging to them, I shall ever feel an anxiety for their interest and honour and shall hear whatever conduces to the latter with the most lively satisfaction.*

*Ever, my dear Colonel.*
*Yours most sincerely*
*WELLINGTON"*

CHAPTER 8

# Gerard Lake
# and the 76th Regiment

*1803 Ally Ghur, Delhi, Leswarree*
*1804 Deig*
*1805 Bhurtpore*
*1806 "Hindoostan"*
*1807 "Elephant" badge*

Difficulties with the Nawab of Oudh, which had been the cause of the move of the 76th from Calcutta to Cawnpore, were settled by treaty in 1801. Part of the Nawab's territory was ceded to the H.E.I.C. but only a year later the treaty was repudiated by some of the large landowners. One of their forts was at Sassnee and in December a force was sent to capture it. The assault having failed, the newly arrived Commander-in-Chief, Lieutenant General Gerard Lake, hurried there with five companies of the 76th, a native cavalry and a native infantry regiment. In February 1803 the fort was captured and in March the detachment of the 76th returned to Cawnpore.

Following the breakdown of the Treaty of Amiens in May 1803 the war against France was resumed. As this was likely to stimulate the Mahratta into hostilities, the Governor General, Lord Wellesley,(a) decided it was time to break up their confederacy. Two armies were formed, one in the south (Deccan) under Arthur Wellesley and the other in the north (Hindoostan) under Gerard Lake. The principal threat in Hindoostan came from a French officer, Perron, who commanded the Mahratta infantry and exercised wide powers under Scindia, the most powerful of the Mahratta princes. Lake's task was to annex his territories in the north and deliver the Mughal Emperor of India from Scindia's clutches. He therefore determined to destroy Perron's army in the field, to break his influence, and in the process induce him to change sides.

On 7 August Lake left Cawnpore for Karouge, on the Ganges, where his army assembled. It consisted of nine cavalry regiments, three of them British, and fourteen battalions of foot, of which only the 76th Regiment was British with a strength of 24 officers and 780 other ranks. The total force amounted to 15,000 which was

---

(a) Lord Mornington had been created a marquess in the Irish peerage in 1799.

The siege of Sassnee, January/February 1803. Painted by Lieutenant F W St. Aubin, 76th Regiment

accompanied by about ten times that number of followers and about the same proportion of bullocks. This was due, in part, to the necessity for the army to be self contained in the face of the Mahratta policy of scorched earth. But comfort was not neglected. The personal attendants of officers were about ten to each subaltern, rising to thirty for a field officer and so on in proportion.

By 28 August Lake had advanced within striking distance of his first objective, the fortress of Aligarh[b], held by 4,000 Mahrattas under Perron. Its environs were protected by another 11,000 horse and foot. However, after a screen of Mahratta cavalry had been driven off by the British light dragoons and their galloper guns (*the skirmish of Koil*) Perron withdrew the bulk of his force, leaving the fort to be defended by another Frenchman, Colonel Pedron. At first Lake endeavoured to avoid bloodshed by negotiating for Pedron's surrender who, hoping to gain time for improving his defences, prevaricated. Lake had no mind to undertake a lengthy siege, and so on 3 September he resolved to take the place by storm. The decision was a bold one for the fortress was very strong and, being surrounded by an immense wet ditch which could only be passed by a single gateway, was deemed impregnable. Its weak point was the lack of a drawbridge. Lieutenant Colonel Monson of the 76th was chosen to lead the

---

(b) In many accounts anglicised to Ally Ghur and appears thus in the battle honours of the Regiment.

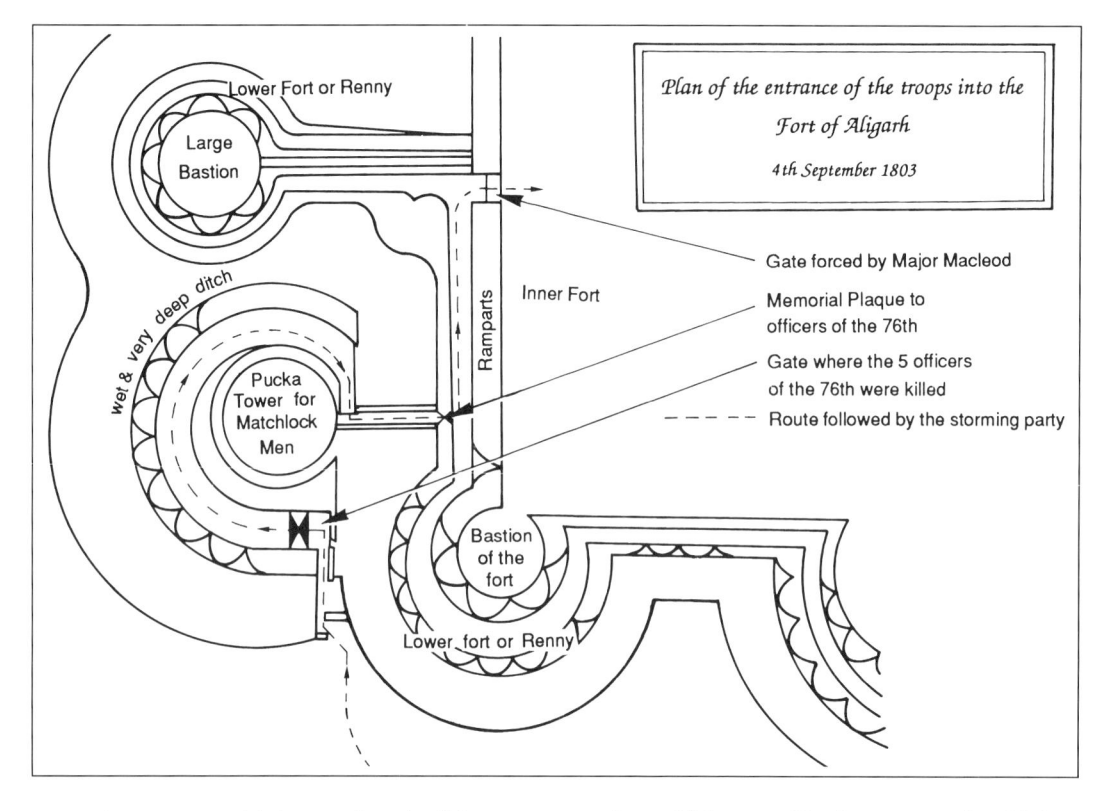

**Plan of the entrance of the troops into the Fort of Aligarh**
*4th September 1803*

- Gate forced by Major Macleod
- Memorial Plaque to officers of the 76th
- Gate where the 5 officers of the 76th were killed
- - - - Route followed by the storming party

Labels on plan: Lower Fort or Renny; Large Bastion; wet & very deep ditch; Pucka Tower for Matchlock Men; Inner Fort; Ramparts; Bastion of the fort; Lower fort or Renny.

storming party, which consisted of four companies of his own Regiment, under Major William Macleod, and four companies of a native battalion with another native battalion in support.

The attack went in at first light (about 4.30am) on 4 September when the storming party rushed the gate. Some guns guarding the entrance were overrun and Monson tried to enter on the heels of the fleeing gunners. However the gate was shut and the stormers were met by a destructive fire. A six-pounder was hurried up to force the gate, but without success. A twelve-pounder was then brought forward. In the twenty minutes it took before the gate could be destroyed the storming party remained helpless under deadly fire. The adjutant of the 76th and all four officers of the grenadier company were killed outright. Once through the gate the stormers, having pursued their way round a circular tower and crossed the causeway which connected the tower to the main fortress, came to another gate. The twelve pounder was again brought up but the gate proved too strong to be broken down. However, Major Macleod managed to gain access through a wicket and led his men into the fort itself where the now demoralised garrison preferred discretion to valour and fled, many of them being drowned as they tried to escape by leaping into the surrounding ditch. Within an hour all resistance had crumbled, and Scindia's fortress of Aligarh had fallen. The storming party was then allowed three hours to plunder, as was then the custom. The enemy losses totalled about

2,000, while 281 guns and most of Perron's military stores were captured. Lake's casualties amounted to 55 all ranks killed and 205 wounded. The 76th lost five officers and 19 other ranks killed, four and 59 wounded. Among the wounded officers were Colonel Monson and Major Macleod.

The capture of Aligarh was a signal victory, bringing a laudatory despatch to Lake from the Governor-General in Council at Fort William, in which *"the bravery, discipline and steadiness of the men of His Majesty's 76th Regiment"* received well-merited praise, as did Colonel Monson and Major Macleod. Arthur Wellesley, on learning of the capture of the fort wrote: *"I think General Lake's capture of Ally Ghur is one of the most extraordinary feats that I have heard of in this country"*. Lake himself confessed that he had never spent a more anxious time than during the long hour of the attack. Such was the moral effect of Aligarh's capture on General Perron that a few days later he surrendered himself to Lake.

The Commander-in-Chief, having first established Aligarh as his advanced base and equipped it with a drawbridge, now set out for Delhi. On 11 September a march of eighteen miles brought him in sight of the city. His troops came into camp at 11.00am much fatigued, but

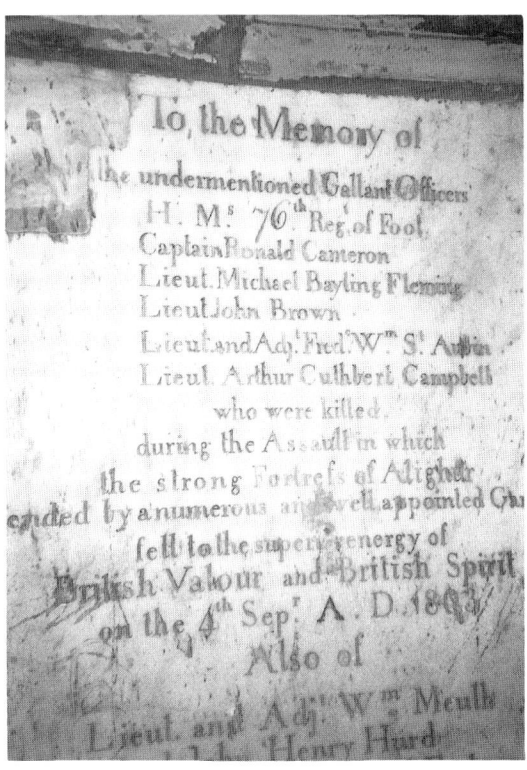

Aligarh fort. The memorial to the officers killed in the attack on 4 September 1803

hardly had the tents been pitched than the Mahratta army appeared. On the plain between Lake's position and the river Jumna that bounded the eastern walls of the Red Fort lay a force of some 19,000 Mahratta horse and foot, commanded by another of Scindia's French generals, Louis Bourquain. Depleted by the Aligarh casualties and men left behind to garrison that fortress, Lake could deploy no more than about 4,500 all arms: three cavalry regiments (two of them native) seven native infantry battalions and, as at Aligarh, just one British regiment – the 76th. Since both Colonel Monson and Major Macleod were still ineffective from wounds, Captain William Boyes was in command.

Outnumbered by more than four-to-one, Lake could not hazard a direct attack, but instead resorted to a cunning stratagem. He ordered his cavalry to advance while the whole of the infantry deployed into line under cover of a low rise, leaving intervals for the cavalry to withdraw through. Having approached within musket-shot of the enemy, the three cavalry regiments turned about and slowly retired according to plan. The Mahratta hordes fell for the ruse and, leaving their defences, poured after their "fleeing" foe. They were brought up sharp on breasting the rise to behold a solid line of 4,000 infantry, the "defeated" cavalry re-forming behind them. Lake then placed himself at the head of the 76th, on the right flank, and ordered the whole line to advance. Under a galling fire of roundshot and grape, the line of infantry marched steadily forward, the men of the 76th keeping their muskets on their shoulders despite the concentration of the Mahratta guns. Then, when they were within a hundred yards of the enemy, the infantry halted and discharged a devastating volley of musketry into the mass of men in front of them. Completely taken aback, the Mahrattas hesitated, and seizing the moment, the 76th and their Indian comrades charged in with the bayonet. There followed a rout. Those of the enemy not bayonetted or shot were assaulted by the cavalry, and all of them were driven back to the Jumna river where many were drowned as they attempted to cross. The action came to an end at seven in the evening by which time Lake's troops had been on their feet for sixteen hours, for the most part under a burning sun. Mahratta casualties were estimated at 3,000 killed and wounded. Sixty-eight guns were captured, together with huge amounts of Scindia's accumulated treasure. Lake lost 461 killed and wounded of which 138, including one officer, were from the 76th.

After the battle General Lake established his camp close to the Jumna opposite Delhi. On 14 September he entered Delhi where Louis Bourquain surrendered to him. At the same time the Emperor Shah Alam was granted British protection. If Aligarh had been a significant victory, Delhi was even more so, for the ancient Mughal capital of Hindoostan (since 1771 Scindia's "jewel in the crown") and all the Mahratta territory to the north as far as the Punjab were now secured for the East India Company.

On 1 October 1803, the Governor-General of India at Fort William issued a special General Order granting honorary colours to the regiments that had been present at Aligarh and Delhi:

> "........*The conduct of Captain Boyce (sic.) and of His Majesty's 76th Regiment is noticed with the warmest applause by the Governor-General in Council; the high reputation established by that respectable Corps in various sources of difficulty and danger in India appeared in the battle of Delhi with a degree of lustre which has never been exceeded..... His Excellency in Council signifies his most distinguished approbation of the firmness and intrepidity of the officers and men of the native infantry, who, with His Majesty's 76th Regiment, at the point of the bayonet, forced an enemy, considerably superior in numbers, from a powerful and well served artillery, and opened the way for the successful charge of the cavalry.......*
>
> *In testimony of the peculiar honour acquired by the army under the personal command of His Excellency General Lake, the Governor-*

*General in Council is pleased to order that honorary Colours, with a device properly suited to commemorate the reduction of the fortress of Ally Ghur on the 4th, and the victory obtained at Delhi on the 11th September, be presented to the Corps of Cavalry and infantry (European and native) respectively employed on these occasions............*

*The honorary Colours granted by these orders to His Majesty's 27th Regiment of Dragoons and to the 76th Foot are to be used by those Corps while they shall continue in India, or until His Majesty's most gracious pleasure be signified through His Excellency the Commander-in-Chief.*

*(Sd) L. Hook*
*Secretary to the Government*
*Military Department "*

Thus in 1803 the 76th's Honorary Colours were not unique. But in subsequent years the other regiments that had also been granted them were, for one reason or another, disbanded.

Lake's next task was the capture of Agra which lay 120 miles south of Delhi, on the Jumna, its garrison posing a threat to communications between Delhi and Cawnpore. After a ten-day march the British-Indian force arrived before the city on 4 October and overcoming the outlying defences of the fort with his native infantry, the general sent a summons to surrender. In command of the 5,000 strong garrison were two of Scindia's co-opted English officers, Hessing and Sutherland, who were inclined to accept terms, but their Mahratta officers and men were not, and the summons was ignored. Lake therefore prepared for a siege, and the next week was spent in digging entrenchments and moving up the battering train of heavy guns. On 17 October the guns opened on the bastions and walls of the fort, inflicting serious damage. Practicable breaches would inevitably have followed had not the two Englishmen managed to persuade their troops to lay down their arms and accept surrender. Next day the garrison was allowed to march out, to be replaced by Lake's infantry, so that the 76th Regiment became the first British unit to occupy the great Fort of Agra. The capture of the fortress, the key to Hindoostan, produced a profound impression on the natives; and Lake, when he saw its formidable strength from within, felt thankful that no storm had been necessary. Although Lake lost 228 killed and wounded (including nine British officers) among his native battalions, these all occurred in the initial attack. The 76th, awaiting the assault by storm that never came, suffered not a single casualty. The spoil included 176 guns and a treasure chest of rupees worth £240,000.

With Agra secured, General Lake could now concentrate efforts on Scindia's force of some 9,000 horse and foot reported to be moving north-west of Agra. Being *"not disposed to allow them to wander at large about Hindoostan"* (Fortescue), on 27 October he set off to give battle, taking the three British light cavalry regiments, five of native cavalry, the 76th (under command of Major Macleod, in the absence of Colonel

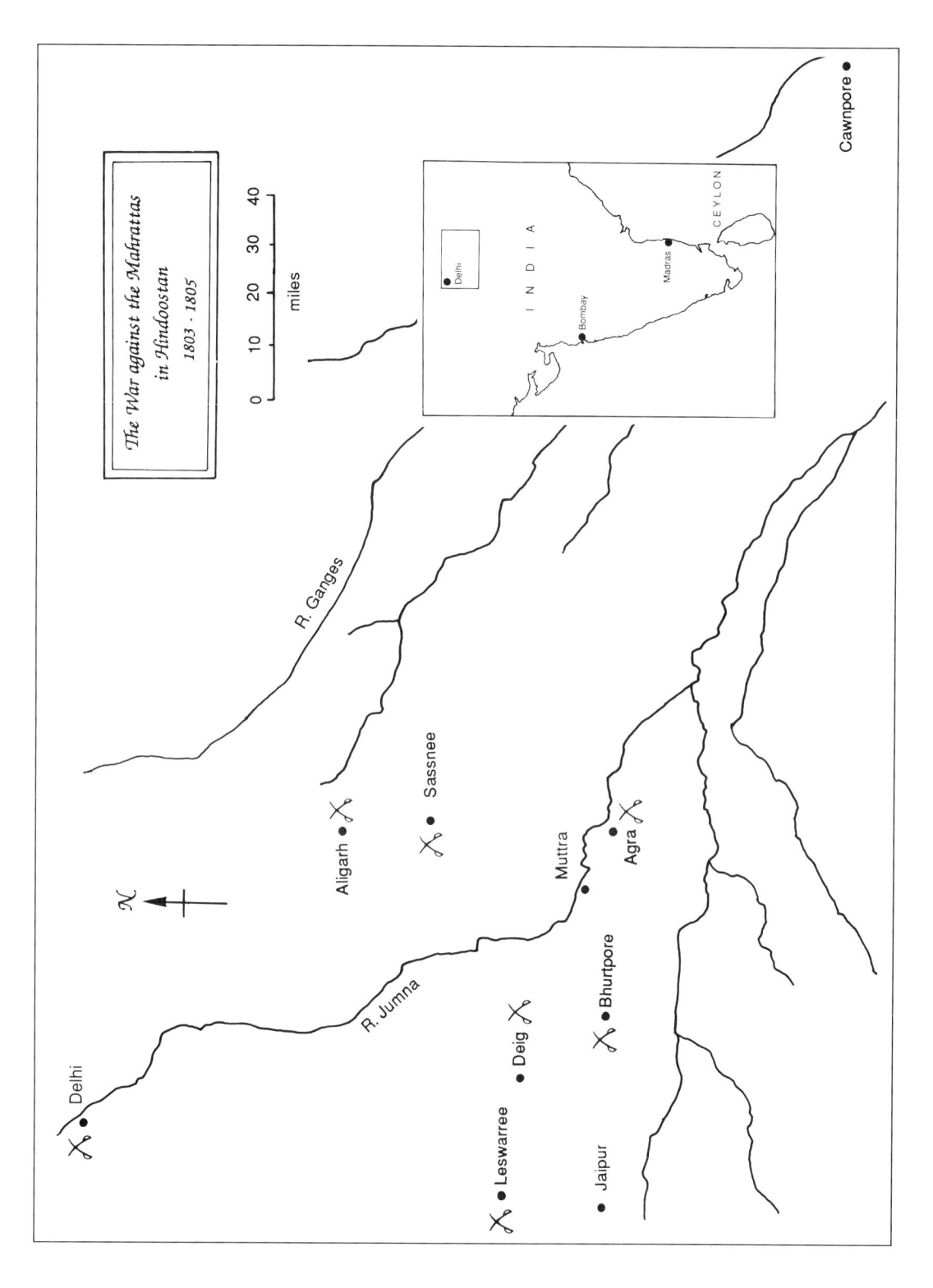

*The War against the Mahrattas in Hindoostan*
*1803 - 1805*

Monson who was commanding a brigade) and seven native infantry regiments. On 31 October, after exhausting forced marches, he sighted the enemy near the village of Leswarree (Laswari), some 90 miles south of Delhi.

Intent upon overtaking them, Lake started that same night with the whole of his cavalry, hoping to keep the enemy engaged until the infantry should come up. Next morning he made contact and immediately launched the cavalry upon the Mahratta hordes who seemed to be retiring. But in fact they were merely redeploying, and having re-formed, inflicted heavy casualties on the British and native horsemen, with their brigade commander, Colonel Vandeleur, being fatally wounded. After further gallant but ineffectual charges, Lake was forced to withdraw the mauled cavalry to await the arrival of the infantry. At 11.00am the 76th and four native battalions arrived. Since 3.00am they had marched 25 miles and were much fatigued.(c) They were allowed an hour's halt for breakfast, during which time the Mahratta commander, Rao Abaji, sent a message proposing to surrender all his guns if Lake would grant certain terms. This the general agreed to do, but the interval was employed by Abaji in improving his dispositions, and as the stipulated hour passed without any further word from the enemy, Lake decided to attack. The 76th, in the lead, and a battalion and a half of sepoys reached their appointed positions, but the remainder of the infantry was held up. As a result the 76th and the sepoys had to wait inactive under heavy and well directed fire. Lake, seeing that the troops could not endure such a trial for long, ordered them to advance. They immediately came under a murderous salvo from every gun in their front, while at the same time a body of cavalry bore down upon their left flank. With perfect steadiness the 76th levelled its muskets and drove back the horsemen, but then these rallied with the obvious intention of delivering a second charge. At this critical moment the 29th Light Dragoons galloped up, to be hailed with cheers from the 76th, and not choosing to cross swords with British cavalry, the Mahratta horse reined in to gallop rearwards. In those brave days a commander-in-chief did not consider himself exempt from leading his troops in person. At the head of the 76th, General Lake had his horse shot under him, his son and ADC being severely wounded by his side. Pressing on with their general, the 76th and the native infantry, by now increased to three battalions, drove back the Mahratta sepoys on to their own guns, whose detachments fled, leaving the pieces to be captured. The remainder of the infantry came up to attack the Mahratta's second line who contested every inch of the ground.(d) But at length they were forced back and then the 29th Light Dragoons and the other cavalry fell upon the disorganised enemy to complete the rout. *"So ended the long agony of this most fateful and bloody fray, as fierce a fight as was fought by mortal man"* (Fortescue).

The battle of Leswarree cost Scindia's force all but 2,000 of his 9,000 men (the 2,000 were made prisoners), besides all his guns and vast amounts of treasure and munitions. It marked the end of the Mahratta empire. But it was a costly victory. Lake suffered the loss of 13 officers and 159 men killed and 29 officers and 623 men wounded of which

---

(c) Lake's cavalry had ridden 42 miles in 24 hours. The infantry (including the 76th) had marched 65 miles in 48 hours.
(d) *"The enemy fought like devils, or rather heroes. I never was in so severe a business in my life"* (Lake).

the greatest number were in the 76th who lost 43 killed, including two officers and four officers and 166 other ranks wounded.

In his despatch to the Governor-General, Lake singled out the 76th Regiment, *"this handful of heroes"*, for special notice. *"It would be a violation of my feelings were I to close my despatch without bearing testimony to the gallant conduct of Major Macleod and Captain Robertson of His Majesty's 76th Regiment, and of every officer and soldier of that inestimable corps in the attack of the village of Leswarree"*. In his General Orders of 4 November, the Commander-in-Chief again singled out the Regiment, stating that he *"beheld with admiration the heroic behaviour of the 76th Regiment, whose gallantry must ever leave a lasting impression of gratitude in his mind"*. Summing up the battle Fortescue gave his opinion that, *"the conduct of the 76th ranks with the very highest that has ever been recorded in the British army"*.

In a little over two months Lake and his army, which, because of the need to detach troops for line of communication duties, at no time had exceeded 8,000 men, had destroyed thirty one of Scindia's European trained battalions, captured the strong fortress of Aligarh, entered the imperial city of Delhi as conqueror, taken Agra, captured 426 pieces of cannon and defeated the enemy in four pitched battles, the last being one of the most decisive ever fought in India.

On 17 December Scindia sued for peace and on the 30th a treaty was ratified. It seemed that the fighting was at an end and the army retired to Agra.

However, almost immediately a new menace appeared in the person of Jaswant Rao Holkar, the only Mahratta chieftain still unconquered or unconciliated. Contemptuously dismissing all attempts at negotiation, Holkar proceeded to plunder and ravage, and in March 1804 invaded the territories of Britain's ally, the Rajah of Jaipur. On 16 April Lord Wellesley ordered General Lake to take to the field once more. The next few months were spent in exhausting marches in great heat in pursuit of Holkar's elusive and highly mobile detachments. By the end of May the effects of the excessively hot weather (55°C in the shade) was the cause of many deaths among the troops – a single march of eighteen miles cost the lives of 30 British soldiers and 250 sepoys. Lake therefore decided to withdraw his army to Cawnpore, except for a force under

Leswaree, 1 November 1803
General Lord Gerard Lake and his son

command of Colonel Monson, who was ordered to destroy Holkar's forces around Jaipur. By 16 June Monson had arrived at Kotah, 120 miles south of Jaipur, where he expected to be joined by another detachment under General Murray, marching from Baroda. But attacked by superior forces, Murray failed to press his advance and withdrew, leaving Monson on his own. He had with him five-and-a-half native battalions, and some irregular cavalry, totalling about 6,000 men, with twenty guns. To the disturbing news of Murray's withdrawal was added the even more serious intelligence that Holkar was approaching with his entire army and all his artillery. Somewhat unkindly, Fortescue remarks *"like Murray, he had not the nerve of Wellesley and Lake"*, and not risking a major confrontation with such disparate numbers, Monson also resigned himself to withdrawal.

There now followed what can only be described as a disastrous retreat. Constantly harassed by Holkar's horse, foot and guns, his troops on dwindling rations, Monson abandoned all his artillery and baggage, and having struggled for seven weeks over 270 miles, he and his survivors reached Agra on 31 August. Besides his guns he had lost 21 British officers (of the native infantry) and more than half of his sepoys. In all justice it must be said that Colonel Monson's retreat was not without its creditable moments. Time and again he bravely fought off assaults by the Mahrattas, and on one occasion charged their batteries to capture guns.

Monson blamed Murray for his failure to join forces; the latter retorted with a similar criticism of Monson's withdrawal. But Lord Wellesley and Lake were forgiving. *"Whatever the result of his [Monson's] misfortunes to my own fame"*, wrote the former, *"I will endeavour to shield his character from obloquy, nor will I attempt the mean purpose of sacrificing his reputation to save mine"*. General Lake was even more generous: *"....All blame ought to fall on me for detaching the force on the first instance .......all censure for that measure must be attributed to me and to me alone...."*

The consequences of Monson's disaster were not slow to show themselves. The Jats, lately allies, threatened to seize the newly acquired territory in Hindoostan and, more dangerously, the Raja of Bhurtpore was discovered to be conspiring with Holkar to drive the British from India. In response to these threats Lake[e] left Cawnpore on 3 September 1804 and concentrated his army at Agra. From there he set off for Delhi, which was being besieged by Holkar. However by the time he arrived Colonel Ochterlony had beaten off the attackers and the 76th Regiment again encamped, beneath the walls of the Red Fort, for a short-lived stay.

Holkar, having failed at Delhi, sent his infantry to Deig (Dig) while he himself embarked on a plundering expedition with his cavalry. Lake thereupon split his force in two. With the greater part of his cavalry he set off in pursuit of Holkar. The remainder of his army, under Major General Fraser, was despatched to watch Deig. By 11 November Fraser had reached Deig, about ten miles north of the great fortress at Bhurtpore (Bharatpur), where he encountered a force of some 14,000 Mahratta infantry with 160 guns and a strong body of cavalry. To oppose this Fraser could muster

---

(e) On 1 September 1804 he was created Baron Lake of Delhi and Leswarree and Aston Clinton. He had a grenadier of the 76th as one of the supporters on his coat of arms.

no more than 5,760 all ranks, among whom were the 76th and the 1st Bengal European Regiment. The rest of the infantry was all sepoy regiments. Although there was a strong fort at Deig, the enemy was drawn up in the plain outside, its flanks protected on the right by an extensive lake, or "tank", on the left by an equally extensive area of swamp. To the right of the tank stretched a ridge of low hills. Regardless of his enemy's overwhelming superiority, Fraser did not hesitate to plan an attack. His first line was formed by the 76th and two native battalions, all commanded by Colonel Monson, the second by the Bengal Europeans and two more native battalions. The cavalry was detached to watch the enemy horsemen on the left flank.

The attack went in at three o'clock on the morning of 13 November. Led by Fraser himself, the 76th advanced straight upon the line of guns to its front, coming under murderous fire of roundshot, grape and cannister. Undaunted, it swept upon the gunners with the bayonet, took the position and continued to the enemy's second line. At this juncture, one of Fraser's legs was severed by a roundshot, compelling him to be carried to the rear after handing over his command to Colonel Monson, the next senior. With his own Regiment followed by the two native battalions, Monson smashed through the second line, and *"from thence this intrepid band pressed on for two full miles capturing battery after battery till they fairly drove the mass of fugitives against the walls of the fortress, where hundreds perished in the swamp....."* In the meantime a battery of British guns had been overrun and captured by a body of Mahratta cavalry who turned the guns upon their owners. Detached as escort to this battery were Captain Henry Norford and 28 men of the 76th. This young officer promptly led a counter-attack with his puny force, drove off the interlopers and recaptured the guns. But sadly, Norford was killed. By noon the Mahrattas had conceded defeat: they had lost some 2,000 killed and 87 guns captured, the latter including fourteen which Monson had abandoned during his previous retreat to Agra. The British-Indian casualties totalled 168 killed and 462 wounded. The 76th Regiment suffered one officer (Norford) and 31 other ranks killed, two officers and 131 other ranks wounded. General Fraser, who later died from his wound, felt it *"impossible to express his high sense of obligation to the whole of the troops under his command.... particularly to His Majesty's 76th Regiment, who have on this occasion, as on every former one, done honor to themselves and their country"*. On learning of the action, General Lake felt it had been a *"very near business. The personal courage of Monson alone saved it"*.

However Monson's next action, which was to withdraw towards Agra in order to obtain supplies, was not at all well received by the commander-in-chief, who considered it both foolhardy and unnecessary. *"It grieves me"*, he wrote, *"to see a man I esteem, after gaining credit in this way, throw it away immediately in such a manner"*. Lake resolved to go to Deig, where most of Holkar's infantry had taken refuge in the fort. On 28 November he joined Monson at Muttra. Deig was reached on 2 December but the siege of the fort could not start until the arrival of the siege cannon on the 10th. By 23 December a practicable breach had been made and the assault took place that night. The storming party consisted of the flank companies of the 22nd (Cheshire), 76th and 101st (Royal

Munsters), under command of Lieutenant Colonel Kenneth MacRae of the 76th. By 2.00am 24 December all of the fort had been taken, except for the citadel. The following night the enemy evacuated it, leaving behind them Holkar's remaining artillery. British losses were slight, amounting to 43 killed and 184 wounded. Of these the 76th had five other ranks killed and one officer and 18 others wounded.

Well up with the forward troops, as they entered the fort, were the prize agents[f]. Their task was to search for treasure before it could be plundered. It was a lucrative appointment as the prize agents received 5 per cent on all sales and 3 per cent on cash.

The capture of Deig cleared the way for Lake's advance to the main objective, Bhurtpore, before the tremendous walls of which he encamped on 2 January 1805. Known as "the Bulwark of Hindustan" the fortress was one of the largest and strongest in India, its ramparts encompassing an area of more than four miles in circumference and towering 50 feet above a wide, deep ditch which, on Lake's approach, had been flooded to present a hazardous obstacle. Rajah Jaswant Singh's Jat garrison had been reinforced by Holkar's Mahrattas, and now numbered some 50,000, with about 60 guns, both heavy and light.

Lake's native infantry was stiffened by four European regiments. In addition to the 76th, these were the 22nd (Cheshire), 75th (Gordon Highlanders) and the Bengal Europeans. The total British-Indian force amounted to no more than 7,800, while the artillery was pitifully weak with only six 18 pounders and eight mortars. To do battle with an enemy nearly seven times his strength in the most formidable stronghold he had yet encountered was a daunting prospect for Lake. But, as ever, he was undeterred by any disparity in numbers.

The first assault was launched on 9 January with three columns directed to a breach in the south-west angle of the fort. The centre column, in the lead, comprised all the flank companies of the 22nd, 75th, 76th and Bengal Europeans, who met not only devastating fire from guns and muskets, but unreconnoitred obstacles in the ground over which they advanced. After a heroic struggle, all three columns were repulsed with the loss of 456 killed and wounded, among which were 30 of the 76th's flank companies. Those of the wounded who had to be left behind were brutally slaughtered.

On 18 January a reinforcement of three native infantry battalions and 100 Europeans arrived from Agra, and on the 21st a second assault was attempted. The storming party was chosen from the 75th (120 men), 76th (150), Bengal Europeans (100) and the 50 that remained of the 22nd's flank companies – a total of 420 all ranks, commanded by Lieutenant Colonel Kenneth MacRae of the 76th. Again there was disaster. A pontoon constructed to cross the flooded ditch proved too short. Efforts to extend it with scaling ladders merely capsized it and sent it floating uselessly away. A few brave men managed to swim across the ditch and mount the breach, but the heavy close range fire to which the troops were continuously subjected and the consequent inability to get more men across the ditch, obliged MacRae to order a withdrawal. At this juncture another column under Colonel Simpson came up, and with the remnants

---

(f) At Deig there were six prize agents, representing headquarters, the artillery, the King's cavalry, the King's infantry (Captain Boyes of the 76th), the native cavalry and the native infantry.

of the storming party attempted to force a gate. But this proved impracticable and the whole force withdrew. This second assault cost Lake 601 killed and wounded. Of the 76th's total of 150 in the storming party, two officers and 14 other ranks were killed and four officers and 61 wounded. Once again many wounded had to be left to the mercy of the enemy who having mutilated and murdered them then displayed their uniforms on the ramparts.

Still undeterred by these reverses, Lake refused to give up the siege, although his troubles were compounded by marauding Mahrattas' attacks on supply columns marching to replenish his dwindling resources. On 11 February, however, there was a welcome reinforcement by the 65th (York and Lancaster) and 86th (Royal Irish Rifles) Regiments, five battalions of Bombay sepoys and some native cavalry, which did much to recoup his losses, though he was still woefully short of siege guns.

The third assault took place on 20 February, and proved even more costly than the previous two. A new breach had been made and approach trenches dug to shelter the storming party almost to the edge of the ditch. Most of the European soldiers, who *"had covered themselves with glory during the past weeks"* (Fortescue), formed the left column under Colonel Don. However when the storming party got into the trenches it found them occupied by a wildly intoxicated enemy. The British losses were severe and because of the enemy's fire the wounded and dying had to be left where they lay, their groans and writhings throwing gloom and discouragement over the men of the 75th, 76th and Bengal Europeans, who formed the storming party. So when they were ordered forward, they refused, and no amount of exhortation and example by their officers induced them to face what they considered a hopeless, suicidal task. As Lieutenant John Pester of the native infantry recorded in his diary, they said *"they would not go to be slaughtered"*.(g) At length, in desperation, Don led two battalions of sepoys towards the ditch and started to attack one of the fort's bastions. Thus shamed the survivors of the storming party followed suit, but to no avail. Struggling up the bastion, they met a storm of fire and missiles of all sorts, including primitive incendiary devices. Once again the assault had to be called off. The casualties amounted to nearly 900, of which 62 were recorded by the 76th.

Next morning General Lake paraded the European regiments whose men had staged the "sit-down" and gave them a haranguing in terms which left no doubt about his *"disapprobation and disgust"* (h). But he was willing to give them a chance to retrieve their honour and called for volunteers for another assault. Every man promptly stepped forward.

This fourth attack went in at 3.30pm on 21 February. The storming party was picked from the fit men of the 76th, the flank companies of the 22nd, 65th, 86th and Bengal Europeans, together with three battalions of native infantry, the whole commanded by Colonel Monson of the 76th. The forlorn hope, or spearhead, was led by another 76th officer, Lieutenant Charles Templeton. This time the focus of attack

---

(g) Pester fought throughout the Mahratta campaigns, including Bhurtpore. His diary, edited by J A Devenish, was published as "War and Sport in India 1802 - 1806".

(h) These are Pester's words. According to Fortescue Lake spoke *"rather in sorrow than anger"*. However Pester was present.

was one of the towers that had been partly destroyed by Lake's 24-pounders, leaving a gap in its base, which raised hopes that the upper portion would fall by its own weight. On reaching this objective the attackers found that the almost vertical wall of mud brick was impossible to scale. Under a hail of missiles and gunfire from the neighbouring bastion, some valiant soldiers desperately strove to clamber up by driving their bayonets into the earthwork to form makeshift ladders, and a few actually made the top of the rampart. One of these was Lieutenant Templeton who was immediately felled as he gained the summit. The hopeless struggle went on for two hours, when Monson, acknowledging the impossible, ordered a retirement. And so, as in all previous attempts, the assault was a failure, while the casualties were the heaviest of all. A total of 987 officers and soldiers had fallen, among them being 133 of the 76th.

The four attempts on Bhurtpore had cost the Regiment a total of seventeen officers and 289 other ranks killed and wounded, while the casualties of the whole force amounted to 2,940 officers and men. All this to no avail. The great fortress remained as inviolate as ever. But even now Lake refused to admit defeat. Calling a temporary halt to the siege, he withdrew his army to camp a few miles to the north, there to await supplies and reinforcements while the men were set busy making fascines. Fortunately, a second siege of Bhurtpore proved unnecessary, for in March Rajah Jaswant Singh opened negotiations and on 10 April a treaty was signed.(i) The following month the army broke up and was dispersed to various camps in and around Agra, the 76th being sent to Fatehpur Sikri. By this time the Regiment had acquired the nickname of the "Immortals" because its veterans seemed to be bullet proof.

In August, on learning that the Regiment was shortly to proceed to Calcutta prior to return to England, Lieutenant Colonel William Monson wrote to Lord Lake expressing the Regiment's sincere regret at no longer serving under his command and gratefully acknowledging *"the paternal solicitude your Lordship has so uniformly bestowed ..and which has so materially contributed to our interest and advancement"*. In reply Lord Lake, having referred to the *"many arduous situations we have been in together"*, wrote *"I must ever feel in a high degree indebted to the singular exertions of the 76th Regiment for that success which has on so many occasions crowned our exertions"*. He concluded, *"You will continue to possess my most affectionate regard and attachment"*.

As was customary for a regiment posted home, a call was made for volunteers for transfer to other units remaining in India, and no fewer than 386 men of the 76th elected to transfer to the 75th (Gordon Highlanders) and the Bengal European Regiment. On arrival at Calcutta in December 1805 another 92 men volunteered for the H.E.I.C.'s European foot. Thus when the final Indian muster was taken on 1 February 1806, the Regiment could produce only 161 rank-and-file (officers seldom chose to transfer and their strength stood at the usual 25). It might seem puzzling that so many soldiers evidently preferred to endure all the hazards and hardships of Indian service rather than return safely to their homeland. But there were compensations. First, discipline though never lax, was less rigid than in an English garrison, and there

---

(i) When Bhurtpore was finally stormed and taken by Lord Combermere in 1826 his army consisted of eighteen battalions, eight cavalry regiments, six troops of horse artillery and 165 siege guns. The casualties were 505 all ranks.

was less parade-ground drill or "square bashing". Then there were higher rates of pay and prize money. Not least among inducements was relief from most of the onerous chores and fatigues that were the lot of the rank-and-file at home. These were undertaken by the numerous low-caste native menials, while, when in barracks or cantonments, even the humble private could employ a servant (bearer) to clean his kit.

On 16 February 1806 the depleted 76th embarked in several transports and after an eventful voyage during which shots were exchanged with French frigates, arrived at Long Reach on 10 July. Marching to Dartford and having recruited up to strength, the Regiment settled into billets at Lincoln.

Colonel William Monson was still in command, and as a result of his urging, in October 1806 the directors of the Honorable East India Company submitted to the King that in acknowledgement of the 76th's distinguished services in Hindoostan the Regiment might be permitted to bear that name on its colours and appointments as an honorary badge. King George III signified his approval on 22 October, and from that date the Regiment became known as the 76th (Hindoostan) Regiment – though this was never an official title.

Meanwhile, Lord Lake had been true to his word in vowing never to forget his *"most meritorious Corps"*. On 7 February, 1807, the following notification appeared in The *London Gazette*.

The Hon William Monson.
Lieutenant Colonel 76th Regiment, 1797-1808

*"In consequence of the earnest recommendation of General Lord Lake, Commanding-in-Chief of His Majesty's Forces in India, His Majesty has been pleased to signify his most gracious pleasure that, in addition to the permission recently granted to the 76th Regiment for placing the word Hindoostan on its Colours and appointments, as an honorary badge, the Regiment shall be allowed to place the Elephant on its Colours and appointments, inscribing the word Hindoostan around it, as a distinguished testimony of its good conduct and exemplary valour during the period of its services in India".*

In July 1807 the 76th was posted to Jersey. In December Lieutenant Colonel William Monson died at his home in Bath. He was only 47 years old.

General Lord Lake left India in February 1807. In October he was created Viscount. He died in London on 20 February 1808, in his 64th year. Gerard Lake was a great field commander whom all ranks loved and under whose leadership they performed outstanding feats of marching and fighting. However, he was impetuous and inclined to rough and ready methods and Bhurtpore stands as an example of these two failings. Fortescue expressed the opinion that the 76th should bear Lake's crest upon its colours since it was *"the fighting battalion of one of Britain's greatest fighting generals"*. A view shared by Lake when he said *"Bring me my boots and the 76th Regiment of Foot and I am ready to go anywhere"*.

CHAPTER 9

# The 76th Regiment in Spain, Walcheren and North America

*1809 Corunna*
*1809 Walcheren*
*1813 Nivelle, Nive*
*1814 Plattsburg*

On 27 January 1808, while stationed in Jersey, the 76th was presented with new colours by the Governor, Lieutenant General Sir George Don, on behalf of the Honourable East India Company. In addition to the "Elephant" and the word "Hindoostan", which had been duly authorised by the King, both the King's and Regimental Colours bore the names and dates of the battles of Ally Ghur, Delhi, Agra and Leswarree.[a] As, at that time, the emblazoning of battle honours (on the Regimental Colour only) was a rarity, the new colours of the 76th were uniquely distinguished.

In May 1808 the Regiment returned to England, and was posted to Colchester for what proved only a brief stay. In November 1807 a French army had marched into Spain and Portugal on the pretext that these countries had failed to seize British shipping as ordained by Napoleon, who then placed his brother, Joseph, on the Spanish throne. The Spanish and Portuguese took up arms in protest, but being no match for the French troops, they appealed to the British government for help, which sent Sir Arthur Wellesley with an expeditionary force in response. Landing in Portugal in July 1808 this force was followed by Sir John Moore who brought reinforcements and, being the senior, assumed command. After stiff fighting he was ordered to await further reinforcements before making renewed attempts to eject the French. In September a force of some 18,000 all arms was despatched to Corunna under General Sir David Baird. Among the 14 infantry battalions was the 76th, commanded by Lieutenant Colonel Michael Symes, and brigaded with the 51st(KOYLI) and 2/59th(East

---

(a) For some reason Deig was not included on the colours. It was not until 1886 that the battles (including Deig, but excluding Agra) were officially approved as battle honours. Ally Ghur, Delhi 1803 and Deig are now unique to the Regiment. Leswarree is shared with The Queen's Royal Irish Hussars.

Lancashire) under Major General James Leith. The Regiment embarked with the rest of the force at Falmouth on 9 October and arrived at Corunna on the 13th. The plan was for Baird to move south-east towards Salamanca and to join forces there with Moore coming up from Ciudad Rodrigo. The combined army was then to advance on Madrid. By 13 November Baird was at Astorga. Following the defeat of one of the Spanish armies Baird was then ordered to withdraw to Vigo, the preferred port for re-embarkation should this prove necessary. However having learnt that the Spaniards were still determined to resist the French, Baird and his troops were once again directed to Astorga. In late December Napoleon himself entered Spain with some 200,000 men and soon dispersed the Spanish armies. Moore, with no more than 38,000 men could not risk a pitched battle. He had no option but to withdraw, which he did through Zamora before joining up with Baird near Benavente[b] on 20 December. And so on 23 December began the dreadful retreat to Corunna. Between that haven and Moore's position lay about 180 miles of some of the wildest country in all Spain with the 6,000ft mountains of Galicia presenting a formidable obstacle.

The march would have been arduous enough in summer, but now snow, ice and perpetual sub-zero temperatures added to the miseries, while the thrusting French cavalry was constantly harrying rearguard and stragglers. On one two-day march of 48 miles the 76th alone lost 45 men, nearly all from exhaustion and exposure. As several diarists recorded, it was distressingly common to discover men – and women and children of the baggage train – lying as frozen corpses after a night's halt, while even the cavalry horses were decimated. Under such conditions morale and discipline suffered, especially among the infantry, and there were disgraceful instances of pillage and plundering in search of food, fuel and drink.

During the whole sorry retreat there was one redeeming action, when at Benavente on 28 December Lord George Paget's rearguard of Hussars and Light Dragoons drove off a superior force of French cavalry and captured its general. At Lugo on 6 January 1809 Moore halted his army and prepared to give battle. Despite the wet and dreadful cold the effect on discipline was instantaneous. For two days the troops bivouacked on an icy ridge without shelter and with scarcely any food. On the third day, as the enemy made no sign of attacking and the last provisions were exhausted, the retreat was resumed during a terrrible night of sleet and hail.

On the 12 January the remnants of Moore's army staggered into Corunna ragged, shoeless and starving. On the evening of the 14th the transports entered the harbour and by the 16th the sick, the dismounted cavalry, all the artillery except 8 guns, and the non-combatants had been put on board. Everything was ready to withdraw the fighting men that night. However, at two o'clock the French launched a determined attack. By five o'clock they had been repulsed at all points. In this battle Leith's brigade was posted in the rear of the centre of the British defensive position. However, only the 59th was heavily engaged. The 76th had one killed and six wounded in the total British losses of about 900, which were the same as the French. During the fighting General Sir John

---

(b) Leith's brigade, having been in the van in the withdrawal to Vigo, was still at Villa Franca between Astorga and Corunna. The flank companies of the 76th were, however, forward at Benavente.

Moore received a mortal wound. He was buried on the 17th as the army was embarking on the transports which were to take them back to England. *"Not a drum was heard, not a funeral note / As his corpse to the rampart we hurried"* (Charles Wolfe). But his campaign had not been a failure. By drawing the French away to the north-west Moore had given the Spaniards in the south a chance to rally.

During the whole campaign the Regiment lost 170 men killed, wounded and died of exposure. Among the latter was their Commanding Officer, Lieutenant Colonel Michael Symes (c). Most of the thirty-three regiments which bear the battle honour Corunna had this granted before 1881. As for the 76th, it seems successive colonels and/or commanding officers failed to put forward a claim, and it was only after the Regiment had become the 2nd Battalion The Duke of Wellington's that the omission was rectified. In December 1906 the then commanding officer, Lieutenant Colonel F M H Marshall, made a reasoned application to the Army Council for submission to the King. The result was Army Order 51 of February 1908, authorising the distinction **Corunna** to be borne on the Regiment's Colours.

*************************

Having been shipped home at the end of January 1809, the 76th returned to its previous base of Colchester, where Lieutenant Colonel Meyrick Shawe assumed command. In April the Regiment was moved to Ipswich. At about this same time it was proposed to send a force to capture the island of Walcheren (d) and thus deny the French the use of the port at Flushing. However, initially it was not possible to raise sufficient troops as the men who had fought at Corunna were still in poor health and not yet re-clothed or re-equipped. But the Admiralty, which was responsible for the protection of England, continued to press for an attack on Walcheren and in June 1809 the Secretary for War, Lord Castlereagh, issued orders for an expedition to be launched. The aim was to capture or destroy the French ships at Flushing and Antwerp, the destruction of the arsenals and dockyards and, if possible, rendering the Scheldt unfit for navigation by men-of-war. It was also anticipated that the expedition would keep French troops in Holland and thereby prevent them from joining Napoleon's army, which was then attacking Austria.

The most powerful force ever to leave England was assembled, comprising 40,000 all arms and 238 vessels of all classes, from 100-gun ships of the line to frigates and sloops, besides transports. Command of the land forces was given to Lieutenant General the Earl of Chatham, that of the Fleet to Rear Admiral Sir Richard Strachan. Both seem questionable choices: the former's notorious dilatoriness had earned him the sobriquet "the late Lord Chatham", while the Admiral was described as *"very irregular in his hours aboard ship, and of greater zeal than ability"*.

The 76th Regiment, (835 all ranks) was brigaded with the 2nd (Queen's Royal West Surrey) and 2/84th(York and Lancaster), in the 3rd Division, commanded by

---

(c) *"He"* (Lieutenant Colonel Symes) *"was a gentleman whose civil and military qualities were equally conspicuous; and in all the private relations of life he was universally esteemed"*. (Life of Sir David Baird).
(d) Walcheren is no longer an island. Dykes and reclamation have connected it with neighbouring Zeeland.

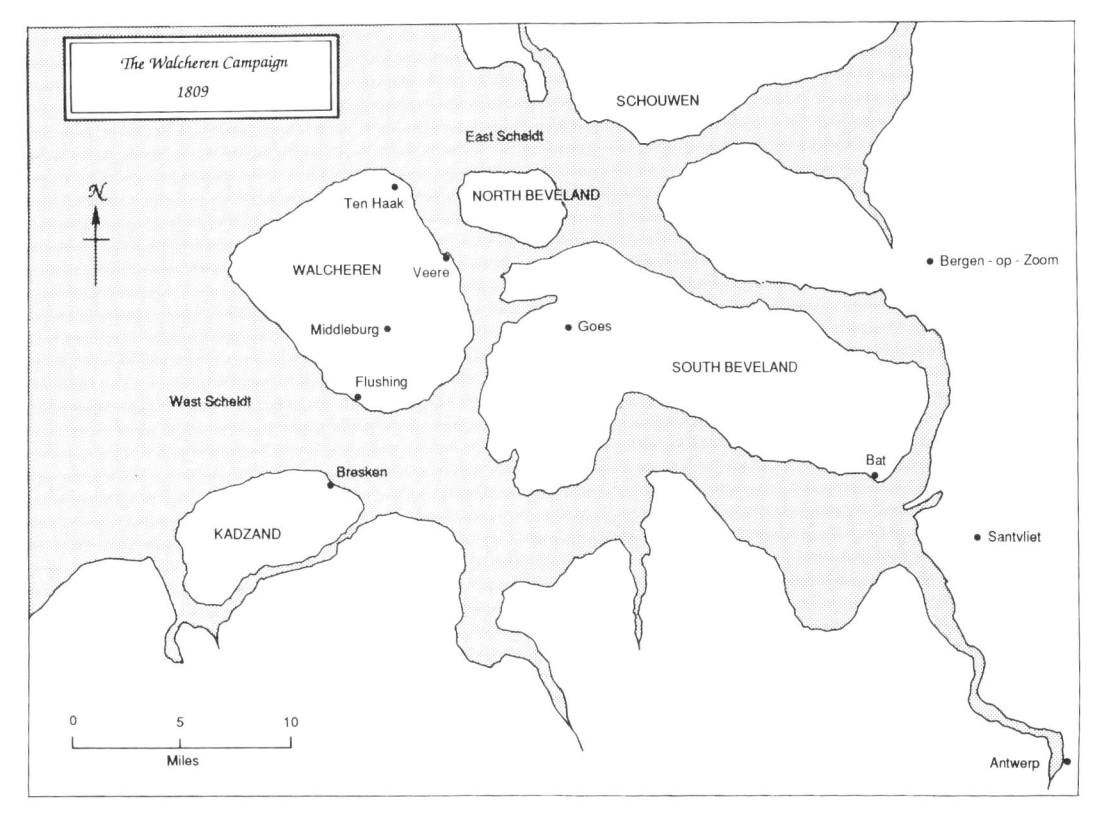

Lieutenant General Thomas Grosvenor. On 28 July the force set sail, arriving off the coast of Walcheren on the evening of the 29th. The plan was for the major part of the force to move up the East Scheldt and advance on Antwerp while the remainder besieged Flushing. An essential preliminary to the siege was the capture of the island of Kadzand, thus clearing the West Scheldt. However, delays due to bad weather gave the French time to reinforce the island to the point where it became impractical to launch an assault. Meanwhile troops had been landing at Ten Haak in preparation for the siege of Flushing. Grosvenor's division, which included the 76th, was to have taken the island of Schouwen, but finding it undefended, was re-directed to Veere, where it commenced disembarking on 1 August. Its new task was to join the right centre of the force encircling Flushing. On 10 August the French opened the sea dykes, flooding the surrounding land, much to the discomfort of the British troops who often had to spend hours up to their knees in water. By 13 August the siege guns were in position and they, together with naval guns, began their bombardment. Flushing surrendered on 16 August, too late to capture the French fleet which had already escaped up the Scheldt estuary to Antwerp. During this affair Chatham lost 738 killed and wounded. Two men killed were the 76th's only losses from enemy action. The French losses exceeded 7,000 including 5,800 taken prisoner.

Two divisions, one being Grosvenor's, were then sent forward to an advance

The Walcheren campaign, 1809. Entrance to the Scheldt

anchorage off Santvliet, ten miles from Antwerp. On 30 August they were on their way down river again when the whole expedition was called off. Apart from the fact that the enemy had greatly reinforced Antwerp, an epidemic described as *Walcheren fever* [e] had started to afflict the troops, causing alarming reductions in fighting strength – so much so, that already by 28 August about 4,000 officers and men were ineffective. The timing of the expedition could not have been worse, for *Walcheren fever* regularly broke out in mid August – a fact well known to Napoleon, (but not, apparently, to the planners in London) who said *"We must oppose the English with nothing but fever which will soon devour them all. In a month the English will be obliged to take to their ships"*.

On 7 September, Chatham (constantly at loggerheads with Strachan), leaving a garrison of 19,000 in Walcheren, withdrew to England. The troops still in Walcheren suffered severely. By 1 October 1,000 had died and 9,000 were sick. On 24 November the 76th had 107 men in hospital at Middelburg, who were suffering from Walcheren fever, besides 539 others invalided to England. The island was finally evacuated on 23 December, the 76th being among the last British regiments to leave.

Apart from the tame reduction (and evacuation) of Flushing and causing considerable alarm in Paris, the Walcheren expedition had achieved nothing. By the time the regiments returned to England they had become virtual skeletons. Fortescue puts the total losses as 106 killed in action, 4,000 died from disease and 11,500 in hospital at the date of the final evacuation. A manuscript record of the 76th's services, compiled by Captain John Mackenzie Kennedy in 1831, gives a complete list of the Regiment's Walcheren casualties:–

|  |  |
|---|---|
| Killed in action: | 1 drummer, 2 privates |
| Died on service: | 1 officer (Lieut R Parker). |
|  | 57 other ranks |
| Died after evacuation: | 34 other ranks |

The 76th returned to Ipswich where Major John Wardlaw from the 64th Foot (North Staffordshire) succeeded Lieut Colonel Shawe in command of the Regiment in May 1810. After recruiting, the 76th was posted to the Irish Establishment later in the year.

On 31 December, 1812, the Regiment's founding father and Colonel, General Sir Thomas Musgrave, died. He had held the appointment since the raising of the Regiment in 1787. In his Will he bequeathed an annual sum of £10, for the benefit of the Regimental school. This was a rare and far-sighted gesture, for at that date little attention was paid to the education of the soldier or his family, and it was not in fact until 1844 that regimental schools became obligatory throughout the army. On 2 January 1813, the Colonelcy was assumed by Lieutenant General Sir George Prevost. Governor-General of Lower Canada.

************************

---

(e) The fever took two forms, malaria and typhoid. The latter seems to have become epidemic.

In April 1809 Sir Arthur Wellesley[f] had again assumed command of the British troops in the Peninsula. By the middle of 1813 he had driven the French out of Spain and was pressing them back to the mountain barrier of the Pyrenees and the very frontier with France. In June 1813 the 76th was ordered out to Spain. After disembarking at Passages near San Sebastian on 16 July, it became one of the regiments in Major General Lord Aylmer's brigade which initially consisted of the 76th, 84th (2nd York and Lancaster) and 85th (KSLI). Its strength was 32 officers and 625 other ranks, a large proportion of whom were young soldiers recruited after the Walcheren disaster. On 25 July there was an unsuccessful attack on San Sebastian. It finally fell on 31 August, followed by a shocking orgy of looting, arson and debauchery as the city was sacked. On 1 September Aylmer's brigade was sent into the city to help restore order.

Although now opposed by Napoleon's distinguished Marshal Soult, Wellington continued to press forward and by early September had harried his enemy across the Bidassoa river into France. The next river obstacle was the Nivelle, where for the preceding three months Soult had been fortifying a defensive position. On 10 November Wellington launched his attack with his centre and right. Aylmer's brigade was on the left flank with the troops who were to hold the French right. Within a few hours the French had been driven from their positions with a loss of 4,265 men. Most of the British casualties were in the centre and right. The 76th had one man wounded. The left flank had played a significant part in the victory by keeping 25,000 French from the main battle.

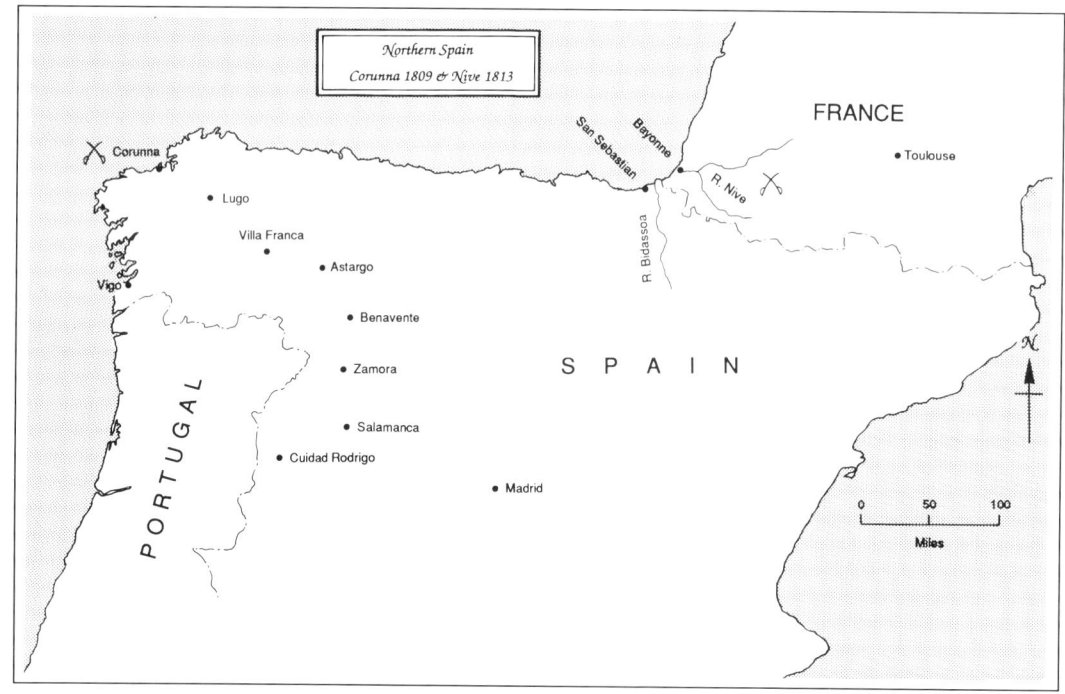

*Northern Spain  
Corunna 1809 & Nive 1813*

(f) Sir Arthur was created Baron Douro of Wellesley and Viscount Wellington of Talavera in 1809, Earl of Wellington in 1812 and, later that year, following his victory at Salamanca, a Viscount. In 1813 he was promoted to field-marshal.

The next objective was Bayonne, but heavy rain made the roads impassable and on 16 November the army was ordered into cantonments. Before Bayonne could be approached the River Nive had to be crossed. Operations started on 9 December and by the end of the day half the army was across the Nive. Soult saw a chance to launch a counter attack. The battle lasted a further four days before victory could be claimed. As at the Nivelle, the 76th was on the left flank, nearest the sea, and although it was engaged in the fighting, it suffered only one drummer killed and fifteen other ranks wounded.

A spell of inaction followed except for skirmishes between opposing detachments and pickets, and it was not until 27 February 1814 that Wellington was able to inflict another defeat on Soult at the battle of Orthes, in which the 76th was in the reserve. Soult retreated towards Toulouse where, on 10 April, he was again defeated. Meanwhile, on 6 April, Napoleon had finally submitted to the allies and had abdicated. This news did not reach Wellington until 12 April. He immediately informed Soult who presumably informed the Governor of Bayonne. Be that as it may, on 14 April the garrison made a gallant sortie which resulted in heavy casualties on both sides. Fortunately for the 76th it had been withdrawn from the outposts two days earlier and thus escaped this useless and final engagement of the Peninsular War. On 18 April a suspension of arms was agreed.

On 28 April Napoleon was exiled to the island of Elba and on 30 May the Treaty of Paris brought a formal end to hostilities. The 76th (Hindoostan) Regiment had played its part in this victorious culmination of the Peninsular War, but there are no records of its total cost in casualties from enemy bullets or sickness. It had, however, earned two more battle honours: **Nive** and **Peninsular**. And its services were acknowledged by Major General Lord Aylmer, its brigade commander who, on leaving for home in May 1814, issued a farewell order in which he praised *"the excellent state of discipline and interior arrangements established in the 37th, 76th and 85th regiments [which] reflect the greatest credit upon the commanding officers of these regiments"*.

*************************

In July 1812, taking advantage of Britain's preoccupation in the Peninsula, the American Congress with its eyes on Canada, and using the practice of the Royal Navy searching American ships for deserters as the pretext, had declared war. The Americans were confident of an easy victory. *"The acquisition of Canada this year"*, wrote Jefferson, the American President, *"as far as the neighbourhood of Quebec, will be a mere matter of marching"*. The British Commander-in-Chief and Governor of Lower Canada (g) was Lieutenant General Sir George Prevost. Pitifully short of troops, he was cautious in deploying them. Brigadier Isaac Brock, the more aggressively minded Governor General of Upper Canada, had some successes. But even after two years of fighting the Americans had achieved little.

---
(g) Canada, at that period, was divided into two provinces; Lower Canada with the seat of government at Montreal; and Upper Canada, which covered the whole of the country to the north and west of Ottawa, with the seat at Toronto.

Then, with the Peninsular war at an end, it became possible to send Prevost[h] 16,000 reinforcements from battle-hardened regiments. And so on 14 June 1814, the 76th was ordered to embark at Bordeaux. Still commanded by Lieutenant Colonel John Wardlaw, the Regiment numbered 31 officers and 609 other ranks. The convoy took more than two months to complete the voyage to the St. Lawrence River, where the Regiment disembarked at different ports towards the end of August and concentrated at Chambly.

General Prevost resolved on an advance across the American frontier to New York. Between that city and his base at Montreal lay the vast 120-mile-long waters of Lake Champlain, command of which was essential for the protection of his lines of communication. The two naval forces were about equal but a British vessel had just been launched which was stronger than any of the American ships and the Navy was confident that there was nothing to fear in the event of a naval action. Accordingly the advance began on 31 August, the 76th marching from Chambly as an element of Major General Robinson's brigade. The whole column, amounting to three brigades, was commanded by Lieutenant General Sir Francis Rottenburg. The first objective was the capture of Plattsburg, a small town with a harbour on the western shores of Lake Champlain, some 60 miles south of Montreal and about half that distance inside American territory. Apart from minor skirmishing with enemy patrols, which the British troops brushed aside, the eight-day march to Plattsburg, which was reached on 6 September, was unopposed. The Americans were strongly entrenched across the River Saranac to the south, or far side, of the town, but they could have soon been swept aside if Prevost had been a more forceful general and had attacked at once. Instead he decided to wait for the navy which, however, was delayed as some of the ships still had to be fitted out. It was not until 11 September that he ordered General Rottenburg to attack. This necessitated a wide flanking movement, which was carried out by the light company of the 76th together with those of the other eleven battalions. There was some difficulty in fording the swollen, waist-deep Saranac river under fire, but the advance was bravely pressed forward and would almost certainly have prevailed had not the astonished troops heard their buglers sounding the Retire all along the line. Describing this unhappy outcome, Captain Mackenzie Kennedy of the 76th, wrote :

> *"At the moment when the hearts of the regiment beat high with glorious expectations, an order was issued for the retreat of the army. The men, unwilling to believe their ears, treated with indignation such of their comrades as announced that the sound they heard was the retreat. Mortification and disappointment pervaded the ranks when the order was repeated; and the troops withdrew under feelings of annoyance which they took no pains to conceal".*

The light companies of the 76th and the others were well in advance of the main body when the "Retire" was sounded, and the order reached them too late. They were

---

(h) In February 1814 Prevost had been appointed Colonel of his old Regiment, the 16th (Bedfordshire). He was succeeded as Colonel of the 76th by Lieutenant General Christopher Chowne.

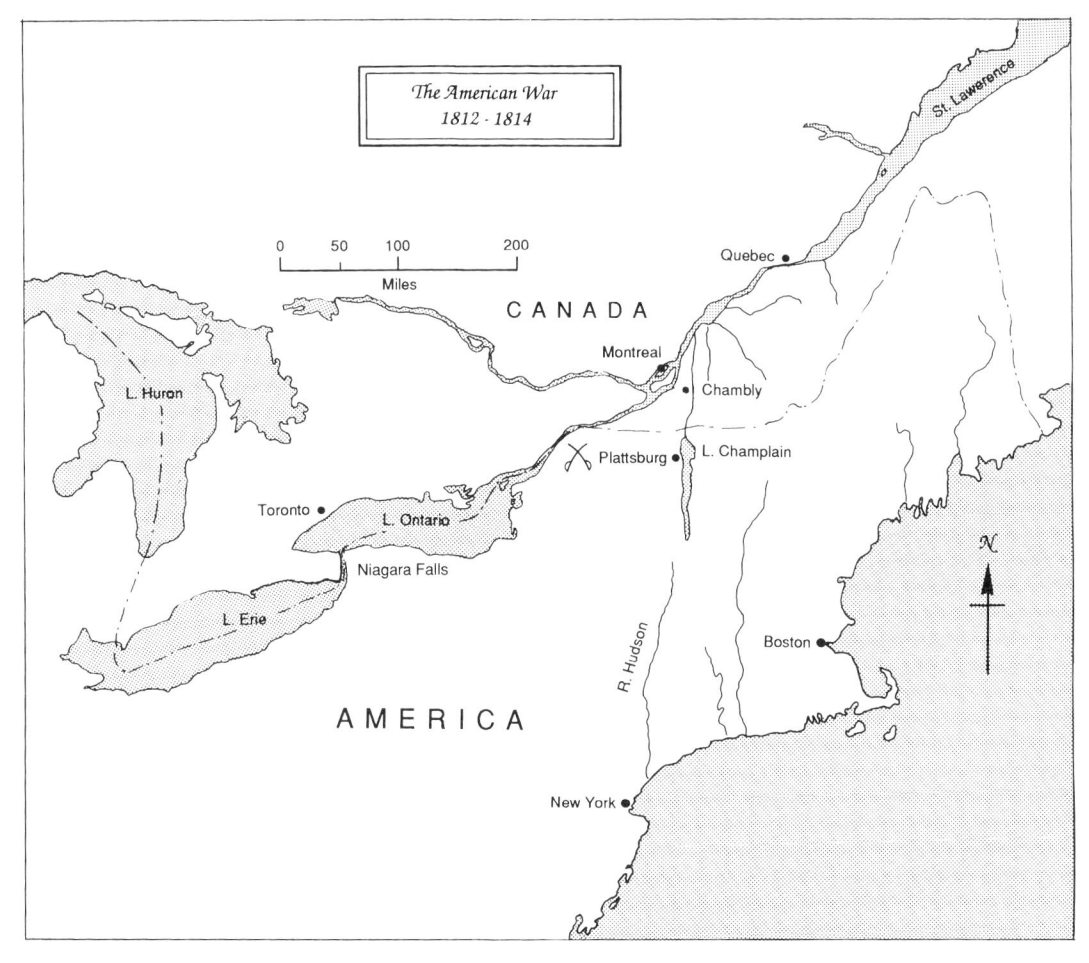

surrounded and cut off by overwhelming numbers of American militia and when at length they surrendered, they were captured. Captain John Purchas, commanding the 76th's light company, was killed in the act of waving a flag of truce – his white waistcoat – while three other officers and 31 other ranks of the company were made prisoners.

The sudden order to retire was given because the British naval force, after two and a quarter hours of incessant fighting, had been totally defeated. And without naval support any military advantage would have been worthless. In the circumstance Prevost had no option but to withdraw. But such was the troops' "annoyance" that, as Kennedy records, some 500 soldiers threw down their arms and deserted to the Americans. However he adds, *"to the honour of the 76th Regiment not a man forsook its ranks"*. Its actual battle casualties were low: one man killed and three wounded.

The navy was furious with Prevost and raised such an outcry that he was recalled to be tried by court-martial. The gist of the charge against him was that he had hurried the fleet into battle before it was ready. In the opinion of Fortescue the affair was principally due to the failure of the naval and military commanders to grasp the limits of each others' capabilities. Prevost died before he could stand trial.

In October the Regiment was withdrawn to cantonments across the Canadian frontier, and saw no more action in the war. But there had been significant British victories elsewhere. On 24 August Major General Robert Ross had defeated the Americans at Bladensburg and on that evening entered Washington and set the Capitol ablaze. On Christmas Eve of 1814 the Americans sued for peace and with the Treaty of Ghent "the War of 1812" was formally concluded.

************************

The period sometimes called "the Age of Wellington" brought sundry changes of dress and accoutrements. In 1811 the line infantryman's stovepipe shako was replaced by a lighter pattern with a small peak, and a plume and cockade on the left side. To protect the felt material in foul weather a black oilskin cover was issued, and this was usually worn in the field. This headdress become known as the Waterloo shako, since it was the regulation pattern for the British infantry at that battle. Officers had continued to wear the clumsy, impractical bicorne hat even after their men had adopted the first shako, but in 1812 they too were issued (on purchase) with the Waterloo shako. While the other ranks' red coatee remained little changed until after 1815, the officers' was now double-breasted and could be worn in alternative fashions: the front could be buttoned over, displaying silver lace, or the top lapels could be buttoned back to reveal the facings. Since the latter were red for the 33rd and 76th, colour contrast was lacking. In full dress, white breeches and knee-length long black gaiters continued in wear, but for field service, overalls were substituted. Originally they were worn over the rest, hence overalls, but by 1809 they became the only nether garments. White was the regulation colour until, during the Peninsular War, Wellington introduced the more practical shade of grey, or blue-grey. The infantry soldier's accoutrements comprised a knapsack of black lacquered canvas, or sometimes hide, canvas haversack and wooden waterbottle slung from the right shoulder, metal mess tin strapped to the top of the knapsack, and black leather cartridge box suspended from the left shoulder. In bad weather the soldier could don his heavy serge greatcoat which at other times was carried rolled and secured to the top of the knapsack, thus adding to the constrictive effect of his cross-belts. While the officer enjoyed the privilege of baggage mules or carts, the common soldier had to stow away everything he possessed, including spare boots, clothing and necessaries, in knapsack and haversack. With arms and ammunition, the total load on his back was seldom less than 60lb. This Field Service Marching Order was virtually the same as Full Dress Order and except for some changes in materials, remained practically unaltered until after the Crimea War.

The famous Brown Bess flintlock musket (officially, Tower Musket), had been introduced between 1727 and 1730. It was the British infantryman's sole firearm throughout the Napoleonic wars, and with minor modifications continued as such until ousted by the percussion musket in the 1830s. Thus with a service life of more than a century, Brown Bess was the longest-serving weapon of the British Army. Officers had relinquished their spontoons in 1786 and were now armed only with the sword, which was the pattern introduced for line infantry in 1796. It had a straight 32in blade with brass knuckle-bow hilt, and was carried in a black leather scabbard with gilt mounts.

The now familiar chevrons as NCOs' badges of rank were ordered into wear in 1803-04: sergeant-majors wore four, sergeants three, corporals two (the rank of lance-corporal did not then exist), and all were worn only on the right arm. Apart from their finery of dress, officers were distinguished principally by their epaulettes. Field officers wore two, a colonel's displaying embroidered crowns and stars, a lieutenant colonel's crowns, and a major's stars. Captains and below had only a single, unembellished, epaulette, on the right shoulder.

In 1808 came a change that must have been heartily welcomed by all ranks: the abolition of the absurd, time-consuming coiffure of greased and powdered hair and the queue.[i] The soldier was now permitted a natural hair style, provided the locks did not fall below the top of the collar.

New rates of pay for all ranks had been laid down in 1798, when the infantry private received an increase from 8p to 1s per day, at which rate it remained to the end of the 19th century.

---

(i) In his memoirs, John Shipp, who enlisted into the 22nd Regiment (Cheshires) in 1795, described the process of having his hair "tied". Candle grease was applied to his hair and then "a large pad filled with sand is poked into the back of the head, round which the hair is gathered tight and tied with a leather thong". Shipp, as a corporal, led three "forlorn hopes" against Bhurtpore for which he was gazetted ensign in the 65th. Later he was promoted a lieutenant in the 76th Regiment.

CHAPTER 10

# The Waterloo Campaign

*1814 Bergen-op-Zoom*
*1815 Quatre Bras*
*1815 Waterloo*
*1853 The Duke of Wellington's Regiment*

On returning from India in July 1812 the 33rd (or 1st Yorkshire West Riding) Regiment proceeded to Hull where the Regimental depot had been established for some years. In January 1813 it was informed that Wellington's successor as Colonel of the Regiment was to be General Sir John Sherbrooke and in February came orders for a "march route" south to Windsor, where the Regiment was to carry out "King's Duty" – that is, mounting guards and providing escorts at the Royal residence of Windsor Castle.

The preceding year had witnessed Napoleon's disastrous retreat from Moscow. But neither this nor his subsequent defeat at Leipzig deterred him from carrying on the conflict in the Peninsula, while in the Netherlands his occupying forces still posed a threat. To counteract this and to present the emperor with a diversionary problem, Britain and her allies resolved to mount a joint operation to eject the French from their northern theatre. And so in July 1813 the 33rd left Windsor for a march to Harwich where the British contingent was assembling for embarkation. The force amounted to about 6,000 infantry, with one cavalry regiment of the King's German Legion, commanded by Major General Thomas Graham, veteran of the Peninsula.

But the entire force did not sail at once. On 10 July the 33rd with a contingent of 3,000 men under Major General Samuel Gibbs embarked at Harwich, and after a lengthy voyage around Denmark arrived at the Baltic port of Stralsund on 14 August. The plan was for Gibbs to co-operate with Crown Prince Bernadotte's Swedish contingent, but by now the French had evacuated this part of northern Germany and the only co-operation required was for a labour force to assist in repairing defences.

Since 1802 the Regiment had been commanded by Lieutenant Colonel Arthur Gore. However, in September 1813 Gore was promoted brigadier general and given a brigade under Graham. His successor in command of the 33rd was Lieutenant Colonel

William Elphinstone, late of the 15th Light Dragoons.

On 2 November the seemingly pointless manoeuvring of Gibbs's contingent came to an end when all embarked at Rostock. The transports sailed back across the North Sea to anchor off Great Yarmouth on the 29th, only some 50 miles from where they had set off at Harwich four months previously. Here, the 33rd's Digest of Services records, the women, heavy baggage &tc were landed, but the troops were kept confined on board, after more than three weeks at sea. At length (without women and baggage) the contingent set sail once more on 13 December, and disembarked at Willemstad in Holland on the 17th.

The French had evacuated Willemstad only a few days previously, to retire to Breda and Bergen-op-Zoom, but they still had a strong garrison in Antwerp. Sir Thomas Graham with the remainder of the British force also disembarked near Willemstad on 17 December and prepared to co-operate with the Russian contingent under Benckendorff and the Prussians under Bülow. Then followed some inconclusive manoeuvring, marred largely by Bülow's disregard of plans, until on 13 January the young soldiers of the 33rd underwent their baptism of fire. This was at the village of Merxem, about four miles from Antwerp. The attack was led by the 2/78th (Seaforths) and 95th (Rifle Brigade) with 2/25th (KOSB) and 33rd in support, and the village was carried at the point of the bayonet, sending the enemy survivors fleeing to the greater safety of Antwerp. In his despatch, Graham praised the conduct of the assault troops, including *"the 33rd Regiment under Lieut-Colonel Elphinstone"*. He stated that *"no veterans ever behaved better than these men, who then met the enemy for the first time and whose discipline and gallantry reflect equal credit upon themselves and their officers"*. [a] British casualties were light, the 33rd escaping without any.

After an unsuccessful attempt on Antwerp, in early March attention was focused on Bergen-op-Zoom. On the eastern Scheldt estuary, this strongly-garrisoned fortress had always been of great strategic significance, forming a link on the line of fortifications between Antwerp and Flushing and a sort of bridgehead between the sea at Zeeland and the Brabant hinterland. Graham had earlier envisaged an attack, but considering it too hazardous, had deferred. Now, however, the Secretary of State for War, Earl Bathurst, intimated that the British contingent would shortly need to be withdrawn to reinforce the troops in North America, and so circumstances dictated that if Bergen-op-Zoom was to be taken, there must be no more delay. The fortress, garrisoned by some 2,700 French with heavy guns, was protected by broad, deep moats, high masonry walls and numerous bastions, and Graham had previously thought it impregnable. The only hope of success lay in a surprise attack by night, and with great secrecy the assault force was moved up during the evening of 8 March. Under Major General Cooke, the 3,950-odd troops were deployed in four columns. The 33rd was in the left centre column with the 55th (Border) and 2/69th (Welch), all under Lieutenant Colonel Charles Morice of the latter regiment. It was intended that the attack by this column was to be the principal one. Graham's plans had been well laid and the French had no knowledge of

---

(a) The force as a whole was of a very poor quality, including many boys and old men. Many of the regiments were recently raised second battalions.

the impending attack which was due to start at 10.30pm.

However, almost immediately the plans began to go awry. A column under Colonel Henry had been directed to carry out a feint on the right. But not only did he attack an hour earlier than planned, thereby alerting the French, but he also disregarded his orders by committing his troops to a full-scale attack. The other columns, hearing the firing, came into action. Colonel Morice's, with the 33rd bearing the brunt of the fighting, attacked the Breda Gate where they met a destructive fire of grapeshot and musketry as they attempted to climb over the pallisades. In the course of doing so Colonel Morice was wounded. Scarcely had Colonel Elphinstone taken over than he too was wounded. According to Lieutenant William Thain of the 33rd: *"Major Muttlebury was the next senior officer, but he having no orders and not knowing of whom to get any, ordered the whole to retire"*. In a short while the column was back at its starting point.

At about one o'clock on the morning of the 9th the column was ordered round to the left where the Guards, together with part of Brigadier Gore's column had staunchly fought their way to the central square of the town. For two hours a furious combat ensued in the constricted area. At length, weight of enemy numbers told, and when Gore, Colonel Clifton (1st Guards) and several other officers and men were killed, the remnants were forced to flee back to a bastion. According to Thain the 33rd took no part having been ordered to wait and lie down in the snow. This was presumably because good progress had been made elsewhere and when the firing died down some time after one o'clock Graham was told that the place was in his possession. However the French launched a counter attack and drove the British towards the Water Gate which was held by the 1st (Royals) who, unfortunately, were commanded by Lieutenant Colonel Muller, a most incompetent officer. He immediately asked for reinforcements and the 33rd was despatched to help him. When the French brought up their field guns Muller, without warning Major Parkinson, who was now commanding the 33rd, capitulated and in excess of 500 of the Royals were taken prisoner. The 33rd declined to share their fate and returned to the main force, having only 50 taken prisoner. During this withdrawal the Regiment had to wade through several streams with water up to their shoulders. It eventually arrived back at Calmpthout, the British base, at 5 o'clock in the evening.

Major Edward Parkinson subsequently wrote a report of the Regiment's actions:

*Calmpthout, 11th March, 1814.*

"Sir,

*As it is possible that opinions may be formed prejudicial to the troops employed in the late affair against Bergen-op-Zoom, I feel it a duty I owe to the gallantry and good conduct of the 33rd Regiment to state the following particulars for the information of his Excellency the Commander of the Forces.*

*Upon Lieutenant-Colonel Elphinstone being wounded at the first attack on the night of the 8th instant, I succeeded to the command of the regiment. This attack having failed, the regiment retired and formed in column on the Wouw Road in the rear of the 69th. Shortly afterwards I received orders from Major Muttlebury, commanding 69th Regiment, to move on in his rear, and was informed that we were destined to support the Guards, who made a lodgement on the works of the place. We accordingly marched and got into the place between 1 and 2am of the 9th. At this time, from the loss we had sustained in the first attack, our actual strength was under 300 men. About 4 o'clock I was ordered by Major-General Cooke to proceed with the regiment to the Lower Water Gate, then in possession of the Royal Regiment, and to place myself under the command of Lieutenant-Colonel Muller, the commanding officer. This order was immediately obeyed, and we remained in a very exposed situation from that time, the 1st Royals having occupied the passage of the bridge and the bridge itself, at the Water Gate. About 9 o'clock General Cooke came to our position, and we discovered the enemy in pursuit of a party of the 91st, which had been cut off. General Cooke ordered the 33rd to advance to their relief. This was immediately done, but as there was a wide, deep, and impracticable ditch between us and the enemy, the situation of the 91st became endangered by our fire, which it was impossible altogether to prevent. We were accordingly withdrawn, and resumed our former position.*

*The enemy's fire from this moment increased upon us. I observed he was approaching the Water Gate along the ramparts: but, supposed the gate and bridge to be occupied by the Royals (General Cooke and Colonel Muller having gone there only a short time before), I felt secure on that point, and continued to defend our front, until I discovered the enemy getting round our right flank towards our rear, and likewise busily getting guns to bear on us from the ramparts.*

*I then sent to Colonel Muller to inform him of these particulars and request his orders, when to my astonishment it was reported to me that he had withdrawn through the gate and not a man of the Royals was to be seen! My next object was to effect a junction with the Guards, if possible, and with this in view, I retired to the rampart, where I could see what I considered to be their post, but as there was no appearance whatever of our troops towards that point, and the enemy collecting in considerable force on our right, there was no doubt left in my mind that the Guards had also retired.*

*Thus situated, with the regiment reduced to little more than 200 men, and attacked by a very superior force with cannon and musketry on front and flanks, deprived of any point of communication or support, and without orders, I considered my duty was to make every possible effect to save the remnant of the regiment and colours from falling into the hands of the enemy, and immediately took the resolution of retiring over the works and ditch of the place to the river and inundation, trusting to the ice for a passage along that face of the works towards the point where we first entered. This has been fortunately accomplished, and not without loss, it is true, both in killed and drowned, but without suffering a single prisoner to be taken that was not previously wounded.*

*E. Parkinson.*

*P.S. – Since writing the above, it has been ascertained that a portion of those men who were covering the retreat of the regiment were cut off. The loss of the regiment amounts, therefore, to fifty, including the wounded, and one officer who was also wounded".*

The reference to *"prejudicial"* opinions may be related to an alleged incident recounted by Fortescue, in which he asserts that in the initial phase *"Morice's men were seized at the critical moment with one of those panics to which the best of troops are subject during a night attack, turned about before a shot had been fired at them, and fled in all directions...."* This slur on the 33rd and their comrades of the 55th and 69th is not borne out by contemporary accounts. There is no mention of a "panic" in General Cooke's report to Graham, nor in the latter's despatch, nor in the diaries of Lieutenant Thomas Austin who, serving in the 35th, could not be suspected of bias towards the 33rd and the others.

But it must be conceded that the Bergen-op-Zoom assault was an abject failure. The troops fought gallantly, but were thwarted by their own senior commanders' bungling and disregard of orders. Only General Graham emerged with credit. The British had lost more than 2,550 men, of whom nearly 400 were killed, 500 wounded and some 1,600 captured. The 33rd's casualties were one officer and 28 other ranks killed, 11 officers and 58 other ranks wounded and two officers and 56 captured. The officer killed was Brigadier General Arthur Gore, who is commemorated by a monument in St. Paul's Cathedral, and another erected by the officers of the 33rd at Goresbridge, Co Kilkenny, where he was born. The French casualties totalled no more than 500.

After their defeat at Bergen-op-Zoom the 33rd and the rest of Graham's force set about recouping their losses and preparing to besiege Antwerp. Happily circumstances rendered any fresh campaign unnecessary. Napoleon abdicated on 6 April and was conveyed to the island of Elba on 28 April. On 5 May Antwerp was occupied without a fight. Then on 30 May came the Treaty of Paris and the official cessation of all hostilities.

Graham's troops remained in Belgium where they were joined by the King's German Legion and 15,000 Hanoverian militia. In August the whole force was placed under the command of the Prince of Orange with the task of maintaining the provisions of the Treaty of Paris, pending the final settlement of Europe by the Congress of Vienna.

This uneventful period saw the 33rd marching from cantonment to cantonment with little other than generals' inspections to concern them. Lieutenant Colonel Elphinstone was still absent, recovering from his wounds, and for the whole of this span the Regiment was led by Major Edward Parkinson. On more than one occasion inspection reports paid tribute to his command. Thus, while at Courtray, in January 1815 the Regiment was reviewed by Lieutenant General Sir Henry Clinton, Inspector-General of Infantry, who summed up his report by stating *"I consider this Battalion to be in the most advanced state of any in the Army"*. In March of the same year Major General Sir John Vandeleur was the inspecting officer and his report was equally complimentary, remarking on the *"very high state of discipline, high order of appointments, and precision in moving"*.

While the 33rd was in cantonments at Menin in early March 1815, there came alarming news of Napoleon's escape from Elba. Having landed in France on 1 March, he was welcomed by wildly enthusiastic members of his old army and on the 20th made a triumphal entry into Paris, whence King Louis had fled. In response the four allies – Great Britain, Russia, Austria and Prussia – agreed that each put an army of 150,000 into the field with the aim of overwhelming Napoleon by sheer weight of numbers.

The strategy was for the Anglo-Belgian-Dutch forces commanded by the Duke of Wellington[b] and the Prussian forces under Marshal Blücher to invade France from the north, while the Russians and Austrians were to attack across the middle and lower Rhine.

Napoleon with the Armée du Nord, numbering 125,000 men, decided that he would deal with his enemies piecemeal and since Wellington and Blücher were the most menacing, being nearest to Paris, he would attack them first. His plan was to strike at the point where the two armies joined and thus force them back on their respective lines of communication. With this in mind he decided to advance on the axis of the Charleroi-Brussels road. By 14 June his army was concentrated in the area of Maubeuge, about 40 miles south west of Brussels. The 33rd was by then at Soignes in the 5th British Brigade under Major General Sir Colin Halkett, together with

A soldier of the 33rd, 1815

---

(b) He had been created a Duke on 3 May 1814

the second battalions of the 30th (East Lancashire), 69th (Welch) and 73rd (Black Watch). Now recovered from his Bergen-op-Zoom wounds, Lieutenant Colonel William Elphinstone had re-assumed command of the 33rd from Major Parkinson,[c] his second-in-command. The Regiment's strength was 38 officers and 535 other ranks. The 5th Brigade was an element of the 3rd Division, (Lieutenant General Sir Charles Alten) which in turn was part of the 1st Corps, commanded by Prince William of Orange.

Before dawn on 15 June Napoleon began his advance into Belgium and by the middle of the morning had driven the Prussians, whose main army was concentrating at Ligny, out of Charleroi. On hearing this, Wellington ordered his troops to be ready to march at a moment's notice, being uncertain, at this stage, whether he was facing a feint or Napoleon's main force. That evening Wellington and many of his officers were attending a grand ball given by the Duchess of Richmond, interrupted in the small hours of the 16th by trumpets, bugles and drums sounding and beating the "General Assembly". A messenger had arrived with the news that the French had advanced up to the vital cross roads at Quatre Bras. The 5th Brigade, with other troops, was immediately ordered to march the 20 odd miles from Soignies. Meanwhile the out-numbered Belgians, Dutch and Hanoverians at Quatre Bras were being hard pressed by a French corps commanded by Marshal Ney. As the regiments sent forward by Wellington came hurrying up to reinforce the position they were deployed piecemeal as they arrived. For much of the day Wellington's force was inferior to Ney's. He was able to conceal his weakness because of the custom of the local farmers to grow their corn six feet high.

It was not until 4pm on the 16th that the 33rd reached Quatre Bras where it was greeted by the noise of battle. Lieutenant William Thain, who had been appointed adjutant in May, described the initial action of the Regiment.

> "........We again advanced and at half past 5 o'clock we were in the field of action when the Hanoverian part of the division immediately left us, and the British Brigade advanced into line in column of companies at quarter distance. We were placed in this order in rear of the line and permitted to lay down in the corn but were soon ordered to stand up for the enemy were making an attempt to turn our right by a wood [Bois de Bossu] upon which it was approached. We gave them a most beautiful volley [d] and charged but they ran faster than our troops (already fatigued) could do, and we consequently did not touch them with the bayonet".

---

(c) Edward Parkinson left the 33rd in 1817 and was placed on the halfpay list of the 11th Foot. He became a lieutenant general in 1854. From 1852 until his death in 1858 he was Colonel of the 93rd (Sutherland Highlanders).

(d) The devastating effect of "a most beautiful volley" from British infantry has been described by several French generals. Thus, Marshal Bugeaud describing a French infantry attack: *"As the column moved forward some men hoisted their shakos on their musket, the quick step became a run; the ranks began to be mixed up; the men's agitation became tumultuous; many soldiers began to fire as they ran. And all the while the red English line, still silent and motionless, even when we were only 300 yards away, seemed to take no notice of the storm that was about to break on it...At this moment of painful expectation the English line would make a quarter turn - the muskets were going up to the 'ready'. An indefinable sensation nailed to the spot many of our men, who halted and began to open a wavering fire. The enemy's return, a volley of simultaneous precision and deadly effect, crashed upon us like a thunderbolt. Decimated by it we reeled together...Then three formidable Hurrahs terminated the long silence of our adversaries. With the third they were down upon us, pressing us into a disorderly retreat..."*

Very shortly the Brigade was assaulted by a more resolute force. Commanding Ney's cavalry was the thrusting General Kellerman, now at the head of squadrons of steel-clad cuirassiers, and seeing his enemy in the act of redeploying, he thundered down upon them. Having already perceived this new threat, Colonel Elphinstone promptly formed square, and daunted by this classic infantry defence, Kellerman wheeled his squadrons to attack a more promising target offered by the 69th Foot. Like Elphinstone, Colonel Morice of the 69th also intended to form square, and was in the act of doing so when disaster intervened in the person of the excitable young Prince of Orange. Galloping up to Morice he forcefully ordered him to deploy back into line.(e) While his better judgement dictated otherwise, Morice could hardly disobey a direct order from his Corps Commander, and so as the hapless battalion was struggling to re-form, Kellerman's cuirassiers were seen galloping through the corn. Orders or no orders, Morice now used his own initiative and once more began to form square. But it was too late. Only two companies had managed to form when the torrent of horsemen crashed upon them. The two unformed companies were ridden down and virtually destroyed; the other two were forced to flee for refuge in the squares of the 42nd(Black Watch) and 44th(Essex), who beat off the charges.

The 69th being for a time non-effective and the 73rd having withdrawn into a thicket on sighting the cavalry approaching, two French batteries opened fire with deadly effect on the 33rd. After enduring this for a short time Elphinstone deployed the Regiment and was in the process of assisting a Brunswick battalion when the cry rose that the cavalry was again approaching. Fortescue states the 33rd then *"rushed into the wood and dispersed"*. However, according to the account of Private Hemingway (33rd), the Regiment tried to form square *"but all in vain as the cannon shot from the enemy broke down our square faster than we could form it.....had it not been for a wood on our right... every man would have been cut to pieces"* (f) Among the killed during this engagement was yet another of the Gore family, the young Lieutenant Arthur Gore. His death was described by Lieutenant Hope Pattison: *"Two French batteries, which had stealthily advanced at point blank range, opened fire simultaneously on our helpless square, cutting down men like hay before the scythe of the mower. At this juncture Lt. Arthur Gore, of the Grenadier Company, who was standing close by me (an exceedingly handsome young man) was hit by a cannon ball and his brains bespattered the shakos of the officers near him"*.(g)

With the intervention of 4,000 men of the Guards Brigade, Ney was forced to concede the day and by nightfall the fight for Quatre Bras was over. The Allies had lost some 4,700 killed and wounded, Ney 4,300. The 33rd's casualties amounted to three officers and 13 other ranks killed, seven officers and 64 wounded, with nine missing. Napoleon's main attack on 16 June was against Blücher's army at Ligny, where it was in the course of concentrating. At the end of the day the Prussians, who had 16,000 casualties as against 12,000 of the French, were obliged to withdraw. It was not until the following morning (17th) that Wellington learned of Blücher's defeat and subsequent

---

(e) However another account states it was an officer of the 69th who was responsible for delay in forming a square. ("The Years of the Sword" : Elizabeth Longford: footnote page 431).
(f) Published in the British Library Journal. 1980
(g) 'Recollections of Waterloo'. Published privately. 1871

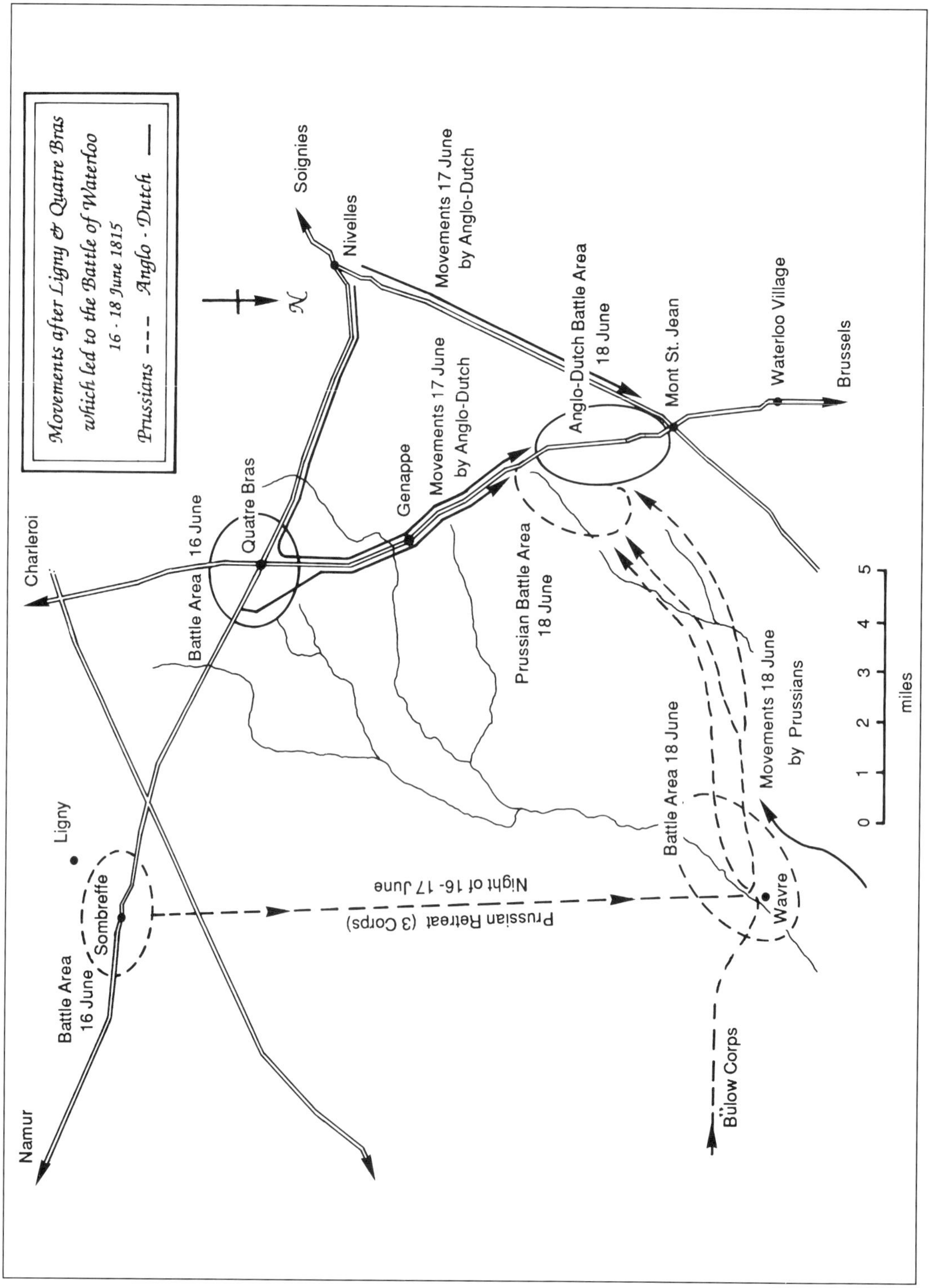
Movements after Ligny & Quatre Bras which led to the Battle of Waterloo
16 - 18 June 1815
Prussians - - -
Anglo - Dutch —
N
Soignies
Nivelles
Movements 17 June by Anglo-Dutch
Anglo-Dutch Battle Area 18 June
Mont St. Jean
Waterloo Village
Brussels
Charleroi
Battle Area 16 June
Quatre Bras
Genappe
Movements 17 June by Anglo-Dutch
Prussian Battle Area 18 June
0 1 2 3 4 5
miles
Movements 18 June by Prussians
Battle Area 18 June
Wavre
Ligny
Sombreffe
Battle Area 16 June
Night of 16 - 17 June
Prussian Retreat (3 Corps)
Namur
Bülow Corps

withdrawal. *"Old Blücher has had a damned good licking and gone back to Wavre, eighteen miles. As he has gone back, we must go too"*, said Wellington as he gave the orders to withdraw towards Brussels, where together with Blücher he would form a defensive line for that city. This previously reconnoitred position, some 15 miles south of Brussels, lay along a stretch of high ground at Mont St. Jean, just north of which was an insignificant village named Waterloo.

The withdrawal on 17 June was a copybook operation, with the British cavalry under Lord Uxbridge keeping the pursuing French horsemen at a respectful distance, and some smart fire-and-movement action by his horse gunners. Only at Genappe was there a slight check with a cavalry mêlée in the narrow street, when Ney's Polish lancers were met and repulsed by squadrons of the Life Guards.

While the infantry was not called upon in the withdrawal, it and the rest were assaulted by the elements. In the afternoon a violent thunderstorm burst upon them, the deluge continuing until well into the night, so that horse and foot had to flounder along flooded roads or through quagmires of surrounding fields. By the time the 33rd had covered the ten miles to Mont St. Jean all were soaked to the skin. And thus, with only cold rations (fire-kindling was virtually impossible), they lay on the muddy ground to await the dawn. After a miserable night Wellington's forces were drawn into line of battle. They totalled 67,660 men and 156 field guns and howitzers, but only some 25,000 of the troops were British, the rest being Belgian, Dutch and German. As the battalions and squadrons manoeuvred into position along the Mont St. Jean ridge they now and then espied across the low valley to their front similar masses of troops manoeuvring in like formation. The Emperor was deploying his superior army of 71,940 men and 246 guns. In an area of no more than three square miles some 140,000 soldiers with 30,000 horses and 400 guns were now assembled. Wellington's position, two lines deep, extended for nearly three miles along the high ground, with the two advanced outposts of the Hougoumont chateau and La Haye Sainte covering his right centre.

By 9 am on that 18 June the 33rd Regiment had taken up position with the 5th Brigade in the right centre, just south of an unpaved road running between Hougoumont and La Haye Sainte. The four regiments were formed in two lines. In the first were the 30th and the 73rd in contiguous columns of companies. The second consisted of the 33rd and 69th in the same formation. For more than two hours there were no signs of hostilities, but at least the mist-dispelling sun did something to dry out their rain-soaked clothing, while some belated rations were brought up. At about 11.15am this peaceful spell was rudely shattered by the thunder of Napoleon's guns, prelude to his first infantry attack. This was concentrated on Wellington's centre and particularly Hougoumont. The 5th Brigade, ordered to lie down below the reverse slope of the ridge, suffered little, as most of the round-shot plunged harmlessly onto the sodden ground instead of bouncing through the ranks. However, the 33rd did not escape entirely.

*"When in this prostrate position, it so happened that Lieutenant Pagan, Captain Trevor and Lieutenant Hart were lying on the ground close to one another....I was standing up, much interested in what was going on, when a missile, supposed to be the fracture of a shell hit Hart so severely on the shoulder as to cause instant death and passing over Trevor, scooped out one of Pagan's ears. He got up staggering and bleeding profusely, when I, with other assistance, placed him on a bearer to carry him to the rear. The men thus employed had hardly left the centre of the square when a cannon ball hit one of them and carried off his leg......"* (Lieutenant Hope Pattison)

The assault on Hougoumont, which was supposed to be little more than a feint, eventually dragged in the best part of two French divisions which were held by just one of Wellington's brigades. Napoleon now decided to launch D'Erlon's magnificent corps of 16,000 men towards Mont St Jean. The attack commenced at about 1 pm and the advancing Frenchmen made an inspiring and intimidating sight as they marched forward in dense phalanxes, up to 200 files wide and twenty-four deep. They swept past and isolated the garrison at La Haye Sainte and pushed on up the crest where they were met by a counter attack by Picton's division. However it looked as if the sheer numbers of D'Erlon's corps would prevail until a charge by the Union and Household brigades of heavy cavalry reduced them to a flying rabble. D'Erlon had been defeated but at a heavy cost: 4,300 British, Dutch and Belgian infantry and 2,500 cavalry dead.

Meanwhile Blücher, who had hoped to join Wellington at noon, was driving his Prussians forward along the road from Wavre. The conditions were appalling and the men were weary from long marches and weak from lack of food. So when they encountered a very steep slope it seemed hopeless even to attempt to drag up the guns, which were axle deep in mud. But the redoubtable Blücher was determined and would hear of no difficulties. *"I have promised Wellington"* he told his men. *"You would not have me break my word".* His strong will and fiery energy stimulated his men to extreme effort.

If Napoleon could capture La Haye Sainte he could hardly fail to break Wellington's centre. The task was given to Ney and his 4,500 prestigious cuirassiers, dragoons and Polish lancers. At about 3.30pm, before the mass advanced, the enemy field guns opened up with renewed fury in a softening-up attempt. As the artillery fire slackened it became clear that Ney's attack was imminent. *"Prepare to receive cavalry"* was the order and Wellington's infantry formed into squares. Soon the 33rd beheld the first wave of horsemen galloping up the slope. Within the squares the front ranks knelt, the butt end of their muskets resting on the ground, their bayonets fixed and forming a ring of steel, the second crouching, also with bayonets fixed, and the third and fourth standing ready to fire. Not until the close-packed leading squadrons were within thirty yards was the order to fire given. The storm of heavy musket-balls smashed into cuirasse and horse-flesh, bringing mount and man crashing down just beyond bayonet-reach of the kneeling front ranks. Survivors who managed to infiltrate the intervals between squares

The battle of Waterloo, 18 June 1815

were smitten by fire from the flank and rear ranks, and within a few minutes the remnants were straggling back down the slope, pursued by grape and cannister from the supporting gunners whose batteries were positioned between the squares. Adding the weight of their nine-pounders, the detachments did terrible execution on the advancing horsemen until the latter were almost upon them when, as ordered, they took refuge within the squares, to dash back to their pieces as soon as the attack was repulsed and inflict further slaughter on the retreating foe.

During the two hours of this phase of the battle the 33rd and its comrades fought off four successive charges, each one leaving dreadful heaps of dead and dying men and horses in front of their squares. *"You could not but admire the undaunted valour of those horsemen"* wrote Captain Mercer whose horse gunner troop was almost destroyed. He likened the attacks to *"waves beating against rocks"*, and the simile was apt, for each wave was shattered upon the impregnable "rocks" of the squares. Shock action by thundering squadrons with the sword was held to be the true role of heavy cavalry, but several decades were to pass before it was accepted that even the most valiant horseman could not ride down staunch bodies of formed infantry. Nevertheless, Ney's gallant squadrons continued their suicidal action. Some of the British squares beat back no fewer than twenty-seven separate attacks. During the pauses between attacks the French guns plied the positions with round-shot, causing further casualties to the long-suffering squares, within which it was now impossible for a man to move a yard without stepping on a wounded comrade, or upon the bodies of the dead. During a slight lull in the fighting Wellington galloped up to Halkett to ascertain how things stood with him and his Brigade.

> *"My Lord, we are dreadfully cut up; can you not relieve us for a little while?"*
> *"Impossible!"*
> *"Very well my Lord, we'll stand until the last man falls".*

By six o'clock the French cavalry conceded defeat having achieved nothing and been destroyed as a fighting force. Blücher meantime had been drawing closer and closer. He had captured Plancenoit and although it was swiftly re-taken by the French, it soon changed hands once again.

Napoleon, aware of these developments and realising that time was running out, ordered Ney to attack again with infantry. Fresh divisions were hurled against the weary squares, which instantly formed line and swept the new attackers away with their deadly musketry. But in the process of this attack the French managed to capture La Haye Sainte when the troops there, who had defended so well for so long, finally ran out of ammunition. This was a serious loss as it was the key to Wellington's centre and only sixty yards from his first line.

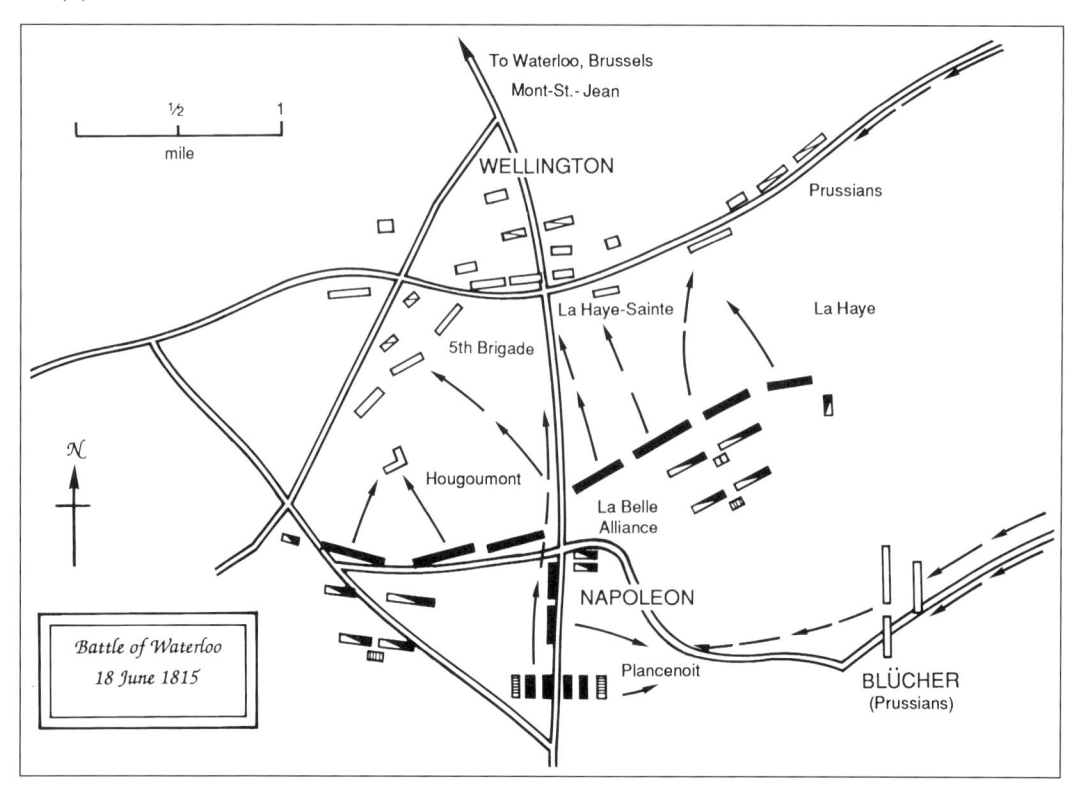

*Battle of Waterloo 18 June 1815*

The battle was now at a critical point. The hands of Wellington's watch had crawled to six-thirty. As he looked at it yet again someone said they heard him say, *"I wish it was night or the Prussians would come"*. So far Napoleon had not deployed a single soldier of his Imperial Guard. Now, at around 7pm he ordered them to advance together with everything else he had left, a total of 15,000 men. The columns advanced on Wellington's position in echelon, the leading one closing in on the 5th Brigade. Halkett prepared to meet them by ordering the 33rd and 69th (now, due to heavy losses, united into a single battalion) into line with the 30th and 73rd. Then, taking the regimental colour of the 33rd from the dying hands of Lieutenant Cameron and resting the pole in his stirrup, he moved forward in order to protect the flank of Maitland's brigade on his right, on which the second French column was advancing. As he got to within a hundred yards of the French his Brigade was met by a withering fire of grape shot. The casualties were heavy, Halkett among them. His place as brigade commander was taken over by the next senior officer, Lieutenant Colonel Elphinstone, who handed over command of the 33rd to Captain Charles Knight.

Meanwhile Maitland's brigade of Guards was lying down behind the crest of the hill, in order to shelter from the French artillery. Wellington had positioned himself behind the brigade and when the French infantry reached the crest of the hill, he called: *"Stand up Guards"* and to their commander *"Now, Maitland, now's your chance"*. The Guards gave a devastating volley and then charged. The French broke. As this happened the third French column was caught in flank by the fire of the 52nd and rolled back on the fourth column (the reserve of two battalions). With Blücher now in action on his left, Wellington waved his cocked hat for the general advance and the whole allied line swept forward. But not all moved forward:

> *"... the 33rd and 69th did not get beyond Hougoumont. Having suffered severely at Quatre Bras, they had been united to form one battalion...and on the 18th had come in for more than their fair share of fighting. When the Imperial Guard made the last grand attack..a withering fire (even when united it formed but a weak battalion), was poured in....confusion ensued but the efforts of the brave Colonel Muttlebury of the 69th rallied the men and they gallantly kept their ground. But physical power has its limits, and the same men who had rallied at a trying and critical time were wholly unable to move forward and take part in the pusuit of the enemy. I found the poor fellows, bivouacked under the treees of Hougoumont, preparing to bury the bodies of their fallen comrades".*[i]

Smitten on his right flank by Blücher's Prussians, his Guard in full retreat before exultant British cavalry and cheering infantry, Napoleon made a last desperate attempt to stem the rout with the reserve of his élite Old Guard but in vain. These too were

---

(i) "Notes and Reminisences of a Staff Officer relating to Waterloo and St Helena" by Lieutenant Colonel Basil Jackson. He married a daughter of Lieutenant Colonel Muttlebury.

swept back and the Emperor was forced to flee the field, while Wellington and Blücher greeted each other near their opponent's erstwhile headquarters of La Belle Alliance.

It was now nearly 9pm, and just light enough to reveal the dreadful carnage of the day-long struggle. Scattered over the field lay some 15,000 dead and wounded of Wellington's army, 7,000 of Blücher's and 25,000 French, all intermingled with the mutilated bodies of six or seven thousand horses. The losses of the 33rd were four officers and 32 other ranks killed, eight and 92 wounded and 48 men listed as missing.(j) The Regiment's total casualties between 16 and 18 June amounted to 277, including 57 missing, from a strength of 561 when it entered the field at Quatre Bras.

Wellington may have been the Iron Duke, but he was not devoid of feelings. On the evening of the battle, as the casualty lists were brought to him, he was overcome with emotion and wept. *"Next to a battle lost"* he told Lady Shelley, *"the greatest misery is a battle gained"*.

Seldom given to lavish praise, he could nevertheless give credit where credit was due. *"Our loss is immense"*, he wrote, *"particularly in that best of all Instruments, British Infantry. I never saw the Infantry behave so well"*. Marshal Blücher and the Prussian army also received fulsome praise, the successful result *"of the arduous day"* being due to the *"cordial and timely assistance I received from them"*. And then there was his own contribution. Reflecting on the battle on the following day he said to his friend Mr Creevey, *"My God! I don't think it would have been done if I had not been there"*.

On 1 July the victorious troops entered Paris. Two weeks later Napoleon left French soil for the last time and on 7 August was exiled to St Helena. For the victors there were honours. In July 1815 the battle honour **Waterloo** was granted. Then, at the instance of Wellington himself, a silver "Waterloo Medal" was struck for issue to every officer and soldier present on the field.(k) This was the first such medal to be granted to all ranks since that bestowed by Cromwell on his Parliamentary soldiers who won the battle of Dunbar in 1650. In addition every man who had served at Waterloo was given two years seniority. Perhaps more welcome was the prize money, ranging from £433 2s 4d for a field officer down to £2 11s 4d for a private soldier. In September 1815 the Prince Regent extended the Order of the Bath to include Companionship for officers distinguished at Waterloo, and among the first to be appointed was Lieutenant Colonel William Keith Elphinstone.

As for the Duke himself, honours were showered upon him. They included, for instance, the field marshal's batons of no less than six countries, in addition to that of Britain. The grateful government also gave him £600,000 and presented him with Stratfield Saye House in Hampshire, at a further cost of £263,000.

The 33rd remained in cantonments near Paris until December 1815. On the 23rd it embarked at Calais and on arrival in England was sent to join its depot at Hull. The next six years saw it employed on uneventful garrison duties throughout the length and breadth of the Kingdom, from Glasgow to Guernsey, finally coming to rest at Dublin in

---

(j) The names of all the officers who were present on 16 and 18 June and all the soldiers who were killed are given in "The History of the 33rd Regiment" by Albert Lee, Appendix 'E'.
(k) The medal was granted to all troops who took part in the campaign, even if they were not present at Waterloo. In the 33rd Lieutenant Colonel Elphinstone applied a more strict rule and only awarded it to those who stood in the square at Quatre Bras or Waterloo. 69 medals were returned for such reasons as *"Batman not in action"*.

1821. During those years it was inspected by seven different generals, each of whom commented most favourably on its appearance, discipline, cleanliness and good conduct as well as the excellent system of interior economy In May 1821 Lieutenant Colonel Elphinstone, CB,[l] departed to take command of the 16th Light Dragoons (Lancers). He was succeeded by Lieutenant Colonel Samuel Moffat of the 1st Ceylon Regiment.

The 33rd's next tour of overseas service came in 1822 when the Regiment was posted to Jamaica. For decades the West Indies had been notorious as *"the graveyard of British soldiers"*, with malaria, yellow fever, dysentery and other endemic diseases carrying off thousands. And on arrival in camp near Kingston it seemed that the 33rd was to suffer its share of the toll. Within two months the "Last Post" was sounded over the graves of three officers and 49 other ranks. On moving to a more salubrious camp, the sick list fell immediately, but this was only a temporary respite. A melancholy entry in the Digest of Services reveals that during the ten years' tour in Jamaica no fewer than eleven officers and 560 NCOs and men succumbed to sickness. Apart from some minor disturbances among rebellious negroes, quickly suppressed, this span saw no action of consequence.

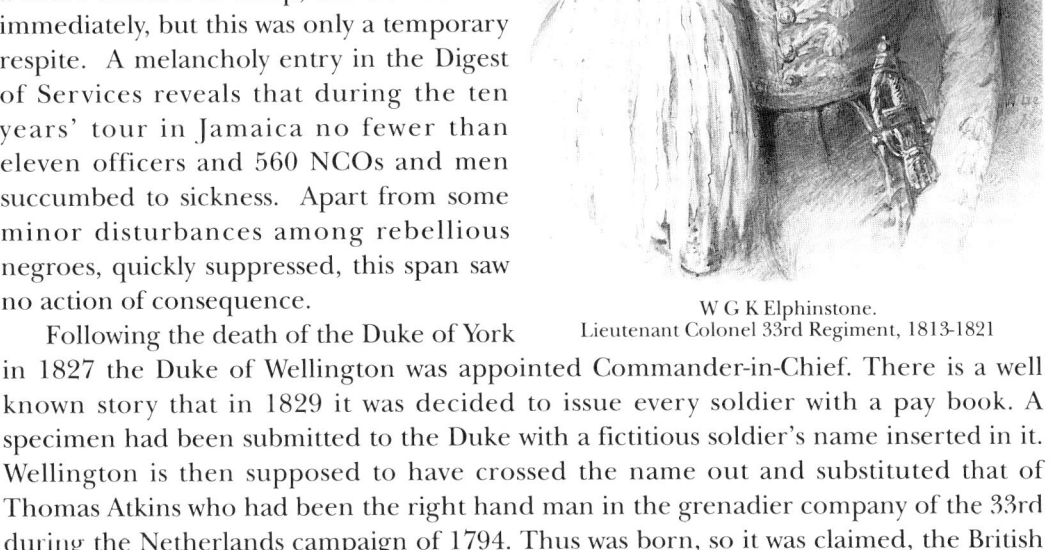

W G K Elphinstone.
Lieutenant Colonel 33rd Regiment, 1813-1821

Following the death of the Duke of York in 1827 the Duke of Wellington was appointed Commander-in-Chief. There is a well known story that in 1829 it was decided to issue every soldier with a pay book. A specimen had been submitted to the Duke with a fictitious soldier's name inserted in it. Wellington is then supposed to have crossed the name out and substituted that of Thomas Atkins who had been the right hand man in the grenadier company of the 33rd during the Netherlands campaign of 1794. Thus was born, so it was claimed, the British "Tommy". However, the story does not stand up to a close examination as far as the 33rd was concerned.[m]

In March 1830 news was received of the death of General Sir John Coape Sherbrooke GCB, Colonel of the Regiment since 1813. His successor, General Lord

---

(l) Elphinstone's career ended ingloriously when as a major general he commanded the British force that occupied Kabul during the First Afghan War of 1839 - 42. Aged 60, in failing health and crippled by gout, he was singularly unfitted for such a task. He died in Kabul in January 1842. His force was decimated as it withdrew from Afghanistan.
(m) Thomas Atkins, as a specimen name, was first used in a War Office circular dated 31 August 1815. In 1794 the grenadier company of the 33rd was in the West Indies.

Charles Henry Somerset, served only a brief spell before death claimed him too. Appointed on 22 February 1830, he died (aged 75) just a year later. The next, longer-lived incumbent was General Sir Charles Wale KCB, who succeeded on 25 February 1831. The Regiment had also had a change of command. In May 1830 Lieutenant Colonel Moffat was injured in an accident and was posted home. After temporary command had been assumed by Major J M Harty, in September Major Charles Knight, who had led the Regiment in the final phase of Waterloo, purchased his Lieutenant Colonelcy and took over from Harty.

Posted home to Portsmouth in March 1832, the 33rd numbered only twelve officers and 240 rank-and-file. Besides leaving 571 of its number in their graves, it had lost 142 men who had surprisingly volunteered to continue in the "graveyard" by transferring to the 22nd(Cheshire) and 84th(York and Lancaster) regiments.

In July the Regiment was moved to Weedon in Northamptonshire where, in November, the recently appointed Colonel, General Sir Charles Wale, visited his Regiment to present new Colours. In October 1836 the Regiment, by then in Ireland, embarked at Cork for its first tour of garrison duty at Gibraltar. With Lieutenant Colonel Knight still in command, it now numbered twenty-five officers and 520 other ranks (plus 31 women and 70 children.)

In addition to providing guards of honour for visiting dignitaries, the Regiment itself was given a temporary infusion of royal blood. In October 1838 the nineteen-year old Prince George, son of the 1st Duke of Cambridge and a cousin of the Queen, was given a brevet-colonelcy in the army and was sent out to Gibraltar to learn the elements of his profession. He was attached to the 33rd *"for the purpose of perfecting himself in Drill and making himself acquainted with all points connected with Regimental Duty."* (Digest). During his seven-months' tour with the Regiment he first did duty as a company subaltern, then as major, and finally commanded the Battalion on drill parades and field days.

While in Gibraltar the 33rd continued to maintain its high standards. Captain H W Bunbury, writing to his parents in January 1841 after a ball given by the Governor said: *"..the ladies declare that they (the officers) are the best dressed best looking and most gentlemenlike people here"*. He went on *"I hope the Regiment will keep up its good name, but I fear that four years in the West Indies will make a woeful change"*.

In February 1841 the 33rd left Gibraltar for another posting to the fever-ridden islands of the West Indies. Within a few months of landing at Barbados inevitable sickness had taken its toll, and among the first to be smitten was Lieutenant Colonel Charles Knight. In early July a medical board recommended his home posting on sick leave, but while awaiting ship *"the Colonel sinking under the encroachment of his disease, expired on the 21st July and was buried with Military Honors the same day.... the Governor and all his Staff being present at the Funeral"*. Almost immediately following his death the changes Captain Bunbury had feared began to materialise. In March of the following year he wrote: *"The 33rd is sadly changed since I joined them at Gibraltar.....with poor Knight we seem to have lost the good system which kept us in such beautiful order"*. The commanding officers who followed Knight did nothing to improve matters. Major J M Harty, having purchased the lieutenant colonelcy, decided not to proceed to the West Indies and within the year was succeeded by Richard Westmore of whom Bunbury wrote *".. my poor Regiment is all at sixes and sevens and I fear that when our Lieutenant Colonel comes out.. it will not mend matters at all; on the contrary he is so much disliked that the Regiment is likely to be even more divided than it is now".* Fortunately he did not last long and was in turn succeeded, early in 1843, by George Whannel. He was, sadly, not much of an improvement; *"He will do nothing"*, wrote Bunbury, *"but puts off all business with some excuse or other".*

Added to these internal problems was the effect of the climate. By December 1843 the Regiment had lost six officers and 156 NCOs and men, all to yellow fever and malaria. Relief came in November 1843, when the Regiment was posted north to the less malignant ambience of Halifax, Nova Scotia, where its forebears had served some 60 years previously. Finally, after twelve years overseas, the 33rd came home in 1848, to be routed to Edinburgh. That same year command was assumed by Lieutenant Colonel F R Blake *"a most popular and excellent officer".*

As early as 1842 there was a feeling in the Regiment that it should be associated in some way with the great Duke who had spent so much of his early service with the 33rd and had been its most illustrious colonel. In that year Lieutenant Colonel J M Harty, during his brief period in command, wrote to the Duke suggesting that the Regiment might be honoured with his name as a title. The reply was :-

"November 6, 1842.

*Field Marshal the Duke of Wellington presents his compliments to Lieut.Colonel Harty.*
*He has always felt the greatest interest in the honour and welfare of the 33rd Regiment and he is much flattered by the desire of its officers to record that he was for some time its commanding officer and Colonel.*
*But he begs that they will observe that the honour solicited is of an unusual description, and will be posthumous and permanent.*
*The Duke must beg leave to decline to be a party of the solicitation of such an honour, to be conferred not upon the 33rd Regiment alone, but in the greatest degree upon an individual, and that individual himself. He hopes therefore that the Officers of the 33rd Regiment will excuse him for declining to make known their wishes to the general commanding the Army in chief, and for suggesting that they should submit their desire through some other channel".*

Another ten years elapsed before the subject was raised once more. Field Marshal Sir Arthur Wellesley, 1st Duke of Wellington KG, GCB, GCH, died at Walmer Castle on 14 September 1852, aged 83. The whole nation was plunged into mourning, and he was buried with solemn pomp and ceremony on 18 November in St. Paul's Cathedral. He was followed to the grave by detachments of every regiment in the army and by the whole of his two regiments, the 33rd and the Rifle Brigade. Based at Manchester the Regiment had travelled by special train to London two days previously. Also present was the 33rd's Colonel, Lieutenant General Henry D'Oyly, who had succeeded Lieutenant General Sir Henry Keating in 1847 . (n)

Soon after the obsequies Lieutenant Colonel Blake wrote as follows to the Colonel of the Regiment:

> "Danesbury
> Welwyn, Herts.
> 22nd November, 1852.
>
> My Dear General,
>
> Now that the last honours have been fired to the Great Duke, I cannot refrain from expressing the universal feeling of gratification and pride expressed by the 33rd Regiment having been specially selected to assist in rendering the last tribute in respect of his memory.
>
> If Her Majesty were graciously pleased to permit the 33rd Regiment to be called The Duke of Wellington's Own Regiment and to bear his name on their Colours and appointments, it would be an honour most thoroughly appreciated by every individual in the Corps. It would moreover do away with the ignorant prejudice against the red facings which certainly considerably checks the success of our recruiting parties. At the same time we should be very sorry that any change should be made in the facings as they were worn by the Great Duke himself who belonged to the Regiment for 20 years and therefore we shall feel a particular pride in continuing them.
>
> From the letter now in your possession written by the Duke in reply to a similar proposal made to himself it is clear he would have been gratified by the regiment being permitted to bear his name, although he justly considered he could not personally move in the matter. May I therefore hope that you will interest yourself in forwarding the request and in bringing it under the notice of the General Officer Commanding in Chief with a view to its being submitted to Her Majesty's consideration.
>
> Believe me, my dear General,
> Ever sincerely yours,
>
> F. R. Blake."

General D'Oyly thereupon approached the Commander-in-Chief. Unfortunately, neither regimental nor public archives can produce any of the correspondence which

---

(n) He had succeeded General Wale as Colonel of the 33rd in 1845.

must have ensued between general and Duke, or Horse Guards, but the outcome was duly circulated and recorded on the 38th anniversary of the battle of Waterloo.

> "*Horse Guards*
> *18th June 1853*
>
> *Her Majesty has been graciously pleased to command that the 33rd Regiment of Foot shall, henceforward, bear the name of "The 33rd (or The Duke of Wellington's) Regiment", which honorable distinction will be inscribed on the Colours of the Regiment.*
> *By Command*
>
> *G. Brown*
> *Adjutant General*
>
> *P.S. It is requested that the Gazette notification may bear the above date."*

On 5 August, the Adjutant-General informed General D'Oyly that Her Majesty had been further graciously pleased *"to approve of the 33rd Regt. bearing on the Regimental Colour and appointments the Crest and Motto of the late Duke of Wellington"*. Since this letter refers to an earlier one from D'Oyly, it seems likely that he himself had requested the distinction, but his letter cannot be traced.

Having secured the long-sought-after honour, General D'Oyly did not leave it at that, but petitioned to have his 33rd further distinguished as a Royal Regiment. How he reconciled this for a regiment named after a commoner is unclear, for again his correspondence is lacking. But the foreseeable reply is extant.

> "*Horse Guards*
> *7th April 1855*
>
> *Sir,*
> *I have the honor, by direction of the General Commanding in Chief, to intimate to you, that Her Majesty considers that the title of Royal, in respect to the 33rd would be incompatible with its present designation of The Duke of Wellington's Regiment, but that there will be not objection to your recommendation that some distinctive colour may be adopted for the facings of the Regiment.*
> *I have &c*
> *G.A. Wetherall AG*
>
> *General D'Oyly*
> *Colonel of the 33rd Duke of Wellington's Regt."*

There is no knowing what D'Oyly was proposing to do about the facings. But if his plea for "Royal" title had been successful, these would almost certainly have been changed to blue, to conform with those of all the Royal regiments. Happily, he let well alone, and the red facings,[o] continued unaltered even though, as Lieutenant Colonel Blake had mentioned in his letter, they were the cause of *"ignorant prejudice"*. This arose because the red facings on a red jacket made it look as if the Regiment had no facings at all. Ignorant men in other regiments would taunt the men of the 33rd that they had been deprived of their facings as a punishment. The Duke, in one of his conversations with Lord Stanhope, said it was *"inconceivable"* how often he had been called upon to *"allay quarrels and arrest fights arising from this petty cause"*.

---

(0) Prior to 1874 the facings of both the 33rd and 76th were always described as red. Thereafter they were described as scarlet.

# CHAPTER 11

# The Crimean War

*1854 Alma, Inkerman*
*1855 Sebastapol*

In August 1853 the 33rd moved from Manchester to Dublin. There, on 28 February 1854, it was presented with a new stand of Colours on which were emblazoned its new distinctions of the name of the Duke of Wellington, his crest and motto. The presentation was made by Lieutenant General Sir Henry D'Oyley, the Colonel of the Regiment. In the opinion of Sir William Fraser, who was present, the Colonel's address left something to be desired: *"... the poor old gentleman could find nothing better to say than that 'the Duke was always a sober man'. I am not sure he did not add that the Duke did not smoke.... I believe he managed to say that where those Colours were brave hearts would be gathered, which he probably read in a book"*. On the day following the presentation the Regiment began embarkation for the East where war had broken out between Russia and Turkey.

Following the defeat of Napoleon, Russia under Tsar Nicholas I had become the most dictatorial and the most feared state in Europe. His description of Turkey as the *sick man of Europe* whose property on his decease would require suitable division, aroused deep suspicion. Nicholas followed this up by demanding a protectorate over all Orthodox Christians in the Sultan's territories. This being refused, he invaded Turkish territory north of the Danube. On 30 November 1853 the Russian fleet based on Sebastopol attacked and destroyed a Turkish squadron in the Black Sea. The threat to Constantinople and a desire to divert Russian attention from India and Afghanistan drove Britain into the arms of the French. Napoleon III of France (nephew of the first Emperor) was no lover of the nation that had humbled French power at Waterloo, but, equally fearful of the Tsar's designs, particularly in the Mediterranean, he could foresee that the only hope of scotching the Russian menace lay in an alliance with his former enemy. All attempts at negotiation having failed, Britain and France declared war on Russia on 28 March 1854. Their aim was the capture of Sebastopol in the Crimea and the destruction of the Russian Black Sea fleet. But the Crimea was no place for long campaigning. Hot and waterless in summer, it was bitterly cold and exposed in winter. Everything depended on the speedy capture of Sebastopol, which would provide shelter for the troops and, above all, a good harbour.

The British "Eastern Expedition", as it was termed, comprised some 27,000 all arms in five infantry divisions and one of cavalry. Selected as Commander-in-Chief was Field Marshal Lord Raglan. As Lord Fitzroy Somerset, he had served under Wellington at Waterloo, when he lost an arm, but since then he had been confined to a desk at Whitehall, and at 66 years of age he was neither physically nor mentally the ideal for a supreme command in the field.[a] The choice of the two cavalry commanders was even more curious. It was well known that Lieutenant General the Earl of Lucan, commanding the Division, and his insubordinate subordinate, the Earl of Cardigan of the Light Brigade, although brothers-in-law, were sworn enemies, while neither had led so much as a troop in action.[b] Command of the élite 1st Infantry Division (Guards and Highlanders) was given to the 35-year-old Duke of Cambridge, the same who had learned his elementary drill and duties with the 33rd at Gibraltar, sixteen years earlier. Though brave and enthusiastic, his only experience of action had been when he deployed his 17th Lancers against some Chartist rioters in Leeds in 1848. However of the five divisional commanders he was the only one under the age of 60.

The troops destined for the expedition initially gathered at Malta, (where the correspondent of *The Times* carefully chronicled the arrival of each regiment, adding very often an exact account of its strength for the edification of the British public and the benefit of the Russians). On 10 April 1854 the 33rd and the 41st (Welch) left Malta for Constantinople where, on landing, they found themselves not only the vanguard of the army, but also the first British troops who had been seen in the Turkish capital since King Richard 'Coeur de Lion' had led his crusaders on their march to Jerusalem six centuries earlier.

The 33rd was sent to Scutari, opposite Constantinople. Following the arrival of Lord Raglan in May it was augmented to a strength of 1,535 all ranks organised into 12 companies, of which eight formed the Regiment on active service. The other four became the depot companies and were located at Malta. Lord Raglan also set about organising the regiments into brigades and divisions. Commanded by Lieutenant Colonel F R Blake, the 33rd was allotted to the 1st Brigade of the Light Division under Lieutenant General Sir George Brown, KCB. The divisional order of battle was:

| | | |
|---|---|---|
| 1st Brigade: | Brigadier General Richard Airey [c] | |
| | 7th | (Royal Fusiliers) |
| | 23rd | (Royal Welch Fusiliers) |
| | 33rd | (The Duke of Wellington's Regiment) |
| 2nd Brigade | Brigadier General George Buller | |
| | 19th | (Green Howards) |
| | 77th | (East Middlesex) |
| | 88th | (Connaught Rangers) |

(a) He was selected because he was the only senior staff officer under the age of 70. Still living in his brave old days with Wellington, he frequently caused embarrassment at GHQ by referring to the enemy as 'the French'.
(b) *"We all agree that two greater muffs than Lucan and Cardigan could not be. We call Lucan the cautious ass and Cardigan the dangerous ass". Letter from Major Forrest 4 DG. May 1854.* ( National Army Museum.)
(c) In September 1854 Airey was appointed Quarter Master General and command of the 1st Brigade was assumed by Major General Codrington.

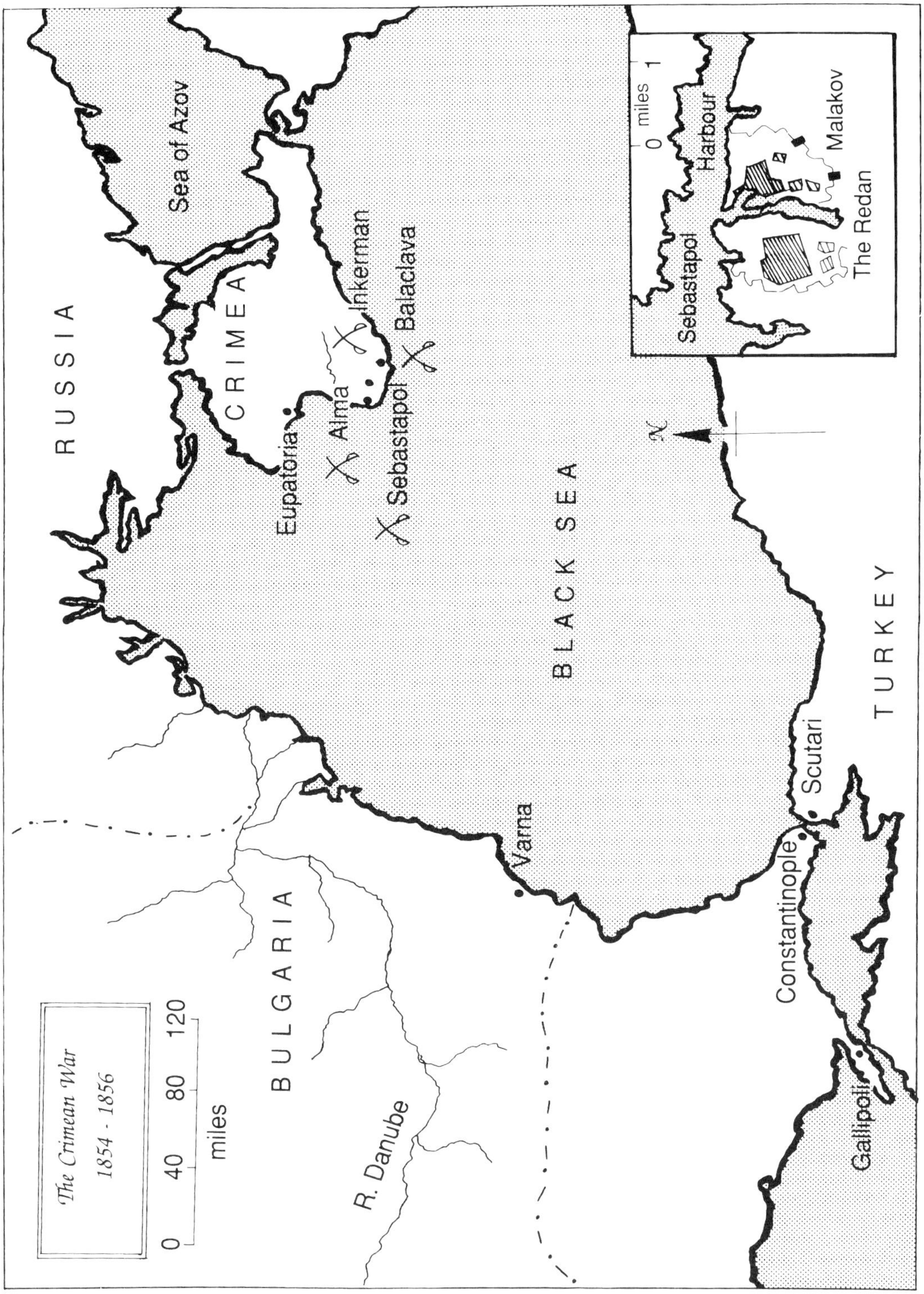
The Crimean War
1854 - 1856
0 40 80 120
miles
RUSSIA
Sea of Azov
CRIMEA
Eupatoria
Alma
Inkerman
Sebastapol
Balaclava
BLACK SEA
N
BULGARIA
R. Danube
Varna
TURKEY
Constantinople
Scutari
Gallipoli
0 miles 1
Sebastapol
Harbour
Malakov
The Redan

Almost 40 years had passed since the British Army had fought its last full-scale European campaign. In those years at times as much as three quarters of its total strength were in garrisons abroad, partly to keep it out of sight of Parliament, which begrudged its cost, and partly owing to the necessity of having troops always available in danger areas since reinforcements took so long to arrive. The result was that the army was still a collection of units, less experienced, less organised and worse provided than it had been at the close of the Napoleonic war. Nor had there been any significant change in dress and equipment. The soldier still marched and fought in unpractical panoply more suited to the ceremonial parade ground than the field of battle. For the infantryman this was the tight-fitting red coatee with constricting cross-belts, blue or grey trousers and the top-heavy "Albert" shako which gave little protection from sun or rain. But at least there was an entirely practical change in his weapon. In 1851 the first rifled musket was introduced, to be well proven in the Crimea. This was officially known as the Rifle-Musket Minié, named after a French captain who had developed it. It was more accurate up to longer ranges than its smoothbore predecessors being sighted up to 1,000 yards, though in practice fire was seldom opened above half that range. Measuring 4ft 6ins overall and weighing nearly 10lb, the Minié was cumbersome, and still a muzzle-loading weapon. The difficulty of ramming the ball down the rifled bore restricted the maximum rate of fire to only two rounds per minute – less than that of the smooth-bore, and this was its only drawback. Thus accoutred and armed, the 33rd was committed to its first serious campaigning since Waterloo.

But there were casualties before it even sighted an enemy. In June the combined British and French forces, the latter consisting of 30,000 men under the command of Marshal St. Arnaud, were concentrated around the Bulgarian port of Varna on the Black Sea, expecting to confront the Russians in the Danube basin. This proved unnecessary as the Turks had been quite capable of dealing with the Russians on their own, and forcing them back across the Danube. However during the nearly three months the expeditionary force was in Bulgaria it was afflicted by a dreadful epidemic of cholera, the result of inadequate sanitary arrangements. Within six weeks the British had buried 600 sufferers, the French 750; the Coldstream Guards lost 82 with more than 150 on the sick list, while the 5th Dragoon Guards were so smitten down that they had to be temporarily amalgamated with the 4th. Dysentry and typhoid also took their toll. The number of fatalities among the 33rd is not known.

One of several soldiers to record their Crimean experiences was Private James Dempsey of the 33rd, who wrote a lengthy letter to his parents from the camp at Devna, (near Varna) on 20 July. Although in a PS he mentions *"a great number of dead"*, he does not specify any of the 33rd's. But he found plenty of other tribulations to grumble at. Presumably to banish idleness and keep the men fit, General Brown ordered field days twice a week, while *"his Brigadier General Aarie (sic) is shure to have 2-3 more for his private practice.....*

> *"The evening before, we would get the order for the following day cook our beef overnight (God forgive me for calling it beef) strike tents at 3 or*

*4 o'clock in the morning, keep working until 7 when we ought to breakfast according to order, but God help the half of us, there's none for some..... and them that's more fortunate to have a small portion of Black Eck (bread), they have neither tea or coffee, milk, or even as much as a good drink of Spring water, but is forced to wet their food with stagnant water that is lying in our canteens all night. We then march out for several miles.... under a scorching sun. Perhaps we may get back by 1 or 2 o'clock, pitch our tents and sit on the sand (for grass there is none) to some buffalo beef without salt or pepper or even the smell of soup.... then they keep us on fatigue duty until tattoo.... We have to go at least one English mile to the top of one of these mountains in the heat of the sun for wood and carry it like donkeys on our back. It is not only for cooking the wood is brought, but to build stables for horses, summer houses for officers besides several things that's too numerous to mention, all to keep us employed".*

Apart from infrequent issues of tea, coffee was the chief beverage supplied. But this was provided in the form of unground beans, which could only be converted into a potable coffee by laborious grinding between two stones and roasting on a spade over camp fires. However, grouse as he might, Private Dempsey was of stolid British infantryman stock. *"The only thing we want is to have a shy with the enemy. If we do we will let them know the kind of metal the English soldier is made of...... I am very proud of my position, as I hope to be one of the number that will muzzle the Russian Bear and revenge the wrongs of the weak on the tyrant's head".*

Imbued with this spirit, Dempsey and his 33rd were soon to have their "shy". By September Lord Raglan and his French counterpart, Marshal St.Arnaud, had formulated their joint plan of operations, the objective being the capture of Sebastapol. After landing on the Crimean peninsula in Kalamita Bay ("Calamity" to the soldiers), the two armies, together with a Turkish contingent, would advance the forty-odd miles south to the environs of Sebastopol, while the British fleet was to establish a base at the harbour of Balaclava. The four French divisions and the Turks would follow the coast, the four British marching on the inland flank. The total allied force amounted to some 64,000 all arms (27,000 British, 30,000 French and 7,000 Turks). There was no reliable intelligence of the Russians' strength: estimates varied wildly, between 45,000 and 70,000, but British naval sources put it as high as 140,000.

Having suffered a stormy passage across the Black Sea, the 33rd and the rest of Raglan's divisions disembarked at Eupatoria on 14 September. Whereas the French, a little to the north, were efficiently organised and equipped, the British force was not. It alighted on the shore of the Crimea without transport, ambulances, litters, or food. Owing to their experiences in Bulgaria most of the men were in a debilitated state. For that reason they had been ordered to leave their packs behind on their ships and bundle up what "necessaries" they could in their blankets (one per man). And so, unlike the French, they had no bivouac tents with them.

Surprisingly, the landing was quite unopposed: apart from a Cossack patrol glimpsed on the heights above the bay, there was no sign of the enemy. But that evening a ferocious storm broke over the bay and heavy rain pelted down all night, against which neither officer nor man had any defence other than sodden greatcoats and blankets. The 33rd's divisional commander, Sir George Brown, took refuge under an ammunition limber, while the Duke of Cambridge huddled under a gun-carriage.

The advance south began on 19 September, when searing sun replaced rain and the troops now suffered from thirst and their unpractical "Field Service Marching Order" with blankets slung around their shoulders. They made a magnificent sight in scarlet, white, blue, green and gold, with bearskins, bands and feathered bonnets – but no forward patrols and only the scantiest provision against flank attack. After some 20 miles Lord Cardigan's advanced cavalry screen observed a large mass of Russian cavalry on the high ground across a valley. The glory-seeking Lord was preparing to lead his Light Brigade on them when he was over-ruled by his divisional commander, Lord Lucan, in the first of several disputes between the two. After some desultory firing from opposing horse artillery, both bodies withdrew, Cardigan's troopers to jibes from the weary infantrymen who had now come trudging up with Lord Raglan himself.

Untroubled by what might lie behind those enemy squadrons, Raglan was happy with his day's exertions and without bothering to send out any patrols, he ordered a halt for the night. As the men lay on the ground around their camp fires they could see similar fires twinkling on a distant ridge to their front.

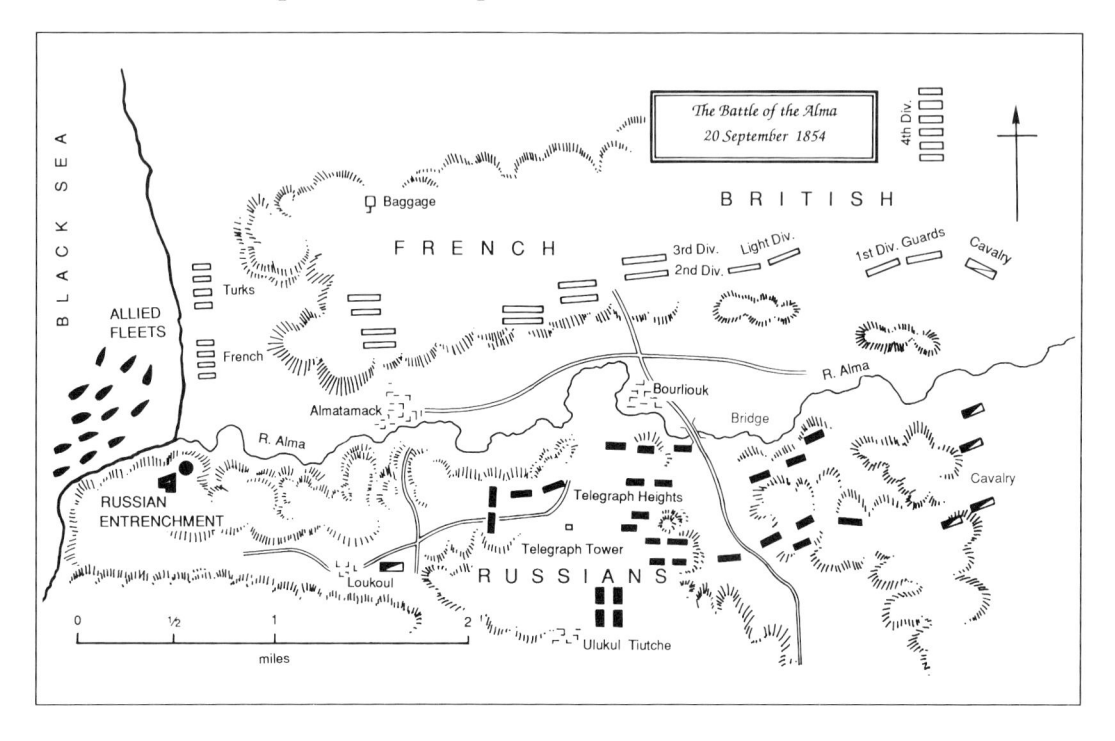

The Russian commander, Prince Mentschikov, had cunningly refrained from offering battle so far, instead drawing his enemy on to what he considered an impregnable position on the River Alma, and while Raglan and St. Arnaud passed a peaceful night, he was busy issuing orders to his army of 37,000 men and 96 guns.

The morning of 20 September dawned bright and sunny, and at 6am the British and French were on the march towards the first major battle of the campaign. With their superior numbers and 126 guns, the joint commanders could be reasonably confident of sweeping away any opposition – of which nothing of consequence had yet been seen. With the usual ponderous evolutions to deploy into divisional and brigade columns of march, it was not until nearly mid-day that the two armies came within sight of their opponents. If not impregnable, Prince Mentschikov's position was certainly formidable. On the other side of the swift-flowing and waist-deep Alma river rose a steep, rocky ridge nearly 500ft high and extending for some six miles from his seaward flank. So confident was the Prince that no enemy could scale these heights under fire that only here and there, at vulnerable points, had he bothered to dig entrenchments. His battalions of infantry, with batteries between them, were deployed all along the heights, while on his extreme right 7,000 cavalry were poised ready to swoop down on routed attackers.

The allied plan was for the French to attack on their seaward, or right, flank, the British to be launched against the centre and left. Soon after one o'clock the advance was ordered and the entire host moved forward, the British being led by the Light and 2nd Divisions, which by now had deployed into line. The 33rd was the centre battalion of the 1st Brigade, with the 7th and 23rd on its flanks.[d] To their left was the 2nd Brigade and on their right was the 2nd Division. They marched forward as if on a parade ground, constantly checking their dressing until the roughness of the ground made this impossible. After struggling through the enclosed vineyards and clambering over stone walls they reached the precipitous banks of the river, to behold on the heights opposite not only massed infantry and guns but, according to Captain A B Wallis of the 33rd,

> "...what looked like a grandstand at a racecourse. This was packed full of ladies and gentlemen who had come out from Sebastopol to see the 'Red Soldiers' driven into the sea; for the Russian commander had said that he could hold his position for three weeks against all the armies Europe could bring against him".

The Russian guns now opened up with plunging roundshot which felled nine men of the 33rd. These are generally acknowledged to have been the first British casualties of the battle. Under this fire men had to ford the river, in places up to waist-deep. No sooner had the Light Division crossed than the 1st Brigade was ordered up the hill and the 33rd, being the centre regiment, had to direct the advance into the teeth of the

---

d) It was the practice, when a brigade was formed in line, for the lowest numbered regiment to form on the right, the next senior on the left and the highest numbered in the centre.

*The battle of the Alma, 30 September 1854*

Russian guns. Meanwhile the 2nd Division, on the right of the British line, had been held up at a blazing village – fired by the enemy – so that the Light was unsupported. Captain Wallis's account continued.....

> *"When we got over the parapet and showed ourselves properly the Russians let us have it. However, we gave as much as we took, and drove them out of the trenches..... When we got past the second trench we found a line of Russians four thick. We halted and kept blazing away at each other; we could see the Russians dropping in every direction.... being four deep each of our bullets went through two men... Colonel Blake now ordered our Colours to be uncased.... General Sir George Brown, who commanded the Light Division, now came up to see how we were getting on, and when he saw no sign of the Russians shifting, he gave the order to Colonel Blake to fire a volley and charge. We charged, the 7th and 23rd following us up: we charged and cheered and cheered, and the Russians turned and retired. When we got to the ground they had left we could hardly get over the pile of dead and wounded Russians.... The 33rd were determined to get to the top, and we kept advancing though it was getting hotter every yard we went up.*

> *The officer carrying the Queen's Colour of the 7th got shot and the regiment never saw it, for one of the 33rd picked it up and [later] gave it back to them: Colonel Blake made him a sergeant for it. When we came within forty yards of the guns and entrenchments.... we came to the charge. The Russians took to their heels, and when we took the guns Captain Donovan, of the Grenadier Company of the 33rd Regiment, wrote his name on it (sic) with the point of his sword. To the left there was a little covered way. A private of the 33rd spotted this and saw three heads and bayonets pointing over and at him. One he shot, another he bayonetted and the third he knocked down with the butt of his rifle. Then he got over into the battery, where were two horses attached to a gun: this he brought away. Sir George Brown saw him, and took him to Colonel Blake with instructions that he was to be made a sergeant and to serve as such whilst he was in the regiment, and never to be reduced."*

The Light Division had been so mauled and was now so disordered it could not resist a Russian counter-attack and was driven back. The supporting 1st Division, hesitantly led by the Duke of Cambridge, was too far back to consolidate the Light Division's success. Trying to assist, the Scots Guards attacked prematurely and also had to fall back. But then the Grenadiers and Coldstream, advancing in perfect order, drove the Russians back, while the Highland Brigade completed the overthrow of the Russian right. After an initial setback, the French had also carried their objectives and by 4pm the battle was over.

It was a notable victory brought about almost entirely by the indomitable courage of the British infantry. In just three hours it had swept the Russians from their formidable position. However it had cost the allies dear – a total of 3,326 all ranks killed and wounded, of whom 1,983 were British. The casualties in the 33rd were particularly severe. The Colour party alone suffered one officer killed and four wounded, while no fewer than ten sergeants were either killed or wounded [e]. The companies were of course even more depleted. Some idea of the losses is given in a melancholy letter from Colour Sergeant George Spence to his brother and his sister while convalescing from his own wound at the Scutari hospital.

> *"I will write you a few names of the wounded ...(sic) Checkley lost a leg, G Lee dead, C Byrne dead, Feather dead... Hancock legs off... Worthington through both legs, and Left cut of (sic) but he died in the Passage. Mr Montague shot Dead, Mr Wallace Leg. Those officers was wounded at the Colours. Major Gough wounded, the Ball entered his Left Hip and came out at his Ribs... I am given to understand that our Regiment lost 390 killed and wounded....."*

---

(e) The Alma was the last occasion Colours were carried in a European pitched battle. By this time more accurate fire had made the Colour party an impossibly conspicuous target.

Colour Sergent Spence may have been told that the 33rd suffered 390 killed and wounded, but this was an overestimate. The *London Gazette* of 8 October, 1854 put the losses of the 33rd at 239, which gained it the sad distinction of suffering more casualties than any other British regiment engaged. The *Gazette* also revealed that in the 33rd's 1st Brigade the 7th (Royal Fusiliers) lost 220, the 23rd (Royal Welch Fusiliers) 203, while in the 2nd Brigade the 19th (Green Howards) lost 220. In no other British regiment did the casualties exceed 200. Among those wounded was Lieut Colonel F R Blake about whom the following was published in a newspaper (probably *The Times*) at that time:

> *"The gallant commander of this brave regiment, Lt Col Frederick Rodolph Blake (brother of Mr F W Blake, one of the directors of the Bank of England), was wounded in the wrist and from what we have heard...both the gallant colonel and his brave horse were worthy upholders of the ancient renown of this celebrated Corps. It appears the 33rd crossed the river in deep water up to their armpits under a shower of balls and were first to reach the opposite bank.... Colonel Blake rode down so steep a pitch that his horse went in head foremost and was completely under water for some seconds. The Colonel never dismounted all day, though other mounted officers of his regiment were obliged to do so from their horses being wounded or unsteady. Colonel Blake's horse continued with one ball in his jaw and one in his side and a contusion from grape in his chest, besides these one ball was lodged in the saddle, another in the holster where the pistol stopped it, and a sixth ball hit the Colonel on the left wrist....but was not of any importance."*

The Russian losses, at some 4,600, were even more severe than those of the allies. In part this was due to their inability to manoeuvre their men other than in solid formations, one result of which was, in the words of Captain Wallis *"each of our bullets went through two men"*. Their losses would probably have been even greater had it not been for the over-cautious Lord Raglan. Throughout the battle, Lord Lucan's Cavalry Division of 1,000-odd eager horsemen was kept inactive, chafing in reserve. When the Russians were finally sent fleeing, that was surely the moment to unleash them and complete the rout. But to the undisguised fury of Lucan and Cardigan, Raglan peremptorily forbade any pursuit, so that Prince Mentschikov was allowed to withdraw the remnants of his army unmolested to the safety of Sebastopol.

However Mentschikov had so little faith in the ability of Sebastopol to resist capture that he retired from it with his army, leaving a skeleton garrison of sailors and militia. The allies, completely unaware that the town was theirs for the taking, pondered what to do. Lord Raglan was eager to advance and assault the northern forts of Sebastopol. This was in accordance with the spirit of the campaign, the object of which was to seize the place by a sudden stroke. But the ineffectual St. Arnaud refused to move, alleging, in excuse, the fatigue of his troops. Eventually they decided to outflank it and establish their bases in the south, in the area of Balaclava cove. Mentschikov at once decided to re-enter Sebastopol and immediately to set about improving its defences. In this task he was brilliantly helped by a young Russian engineer of genius, Colonel Todleben.

Because of the need to get the wounded and sick away to the ships the Allies did not resume their march until 23 September. For the 33rd, and the rest of the infantry, the advance was unopposed, though there was a cavalry skirmish when Lord Lucan's horsemen lost their way and bumped into Mentschikov's then retreating baggage train (there were no reliable maps of the terrain, and the troops had to navigate by primitive compass bearings.)

On 26 September Balaclava was occupied after only token resistance. Marshal St. Arnaud having resigned, command of the French forces was assumed by General Canrobert and his and Lord Raglan's first task was to decide on the location of their respective bases. On the advice of the navy Lord Raglan opted for Balaclava – a great and far reaching blunder. Not only was the harbour very small, but there was also a severe lack of space on shore to receive the stores from the ships.

Preparations now began for what proved the year-long siege of Sebastopol. This opened on 17 October with *the most tremendous conflict of artillery which up to that time the earth had ever witnessed*. It continued intermittently for nearly a week, with little impression on the Russian defences. The British guns succeeded in silencing their enemy counterparts in the Malakov Tower, but to the astonishment of the besiegers, the Russians restored all the damage within one night, and elsewhere the duel was indecisive. All this while the 33rd and the Light Division were deployed on the plateau facing the Inkerman Heights, ready to assault demoralised defenders with the bayonet. No such assault was possible, and the infantry merely had to endure the enemy's cannonading. The 33rd was fortunate in losing only one sergeant and seven privates wounded.

It was during this initial phase that an incident occurred which has been dubbed that of "the failed VC". The earliest account appeared in a letter written by Colonel the Hon. Somerset Gough Calthorpe, a staff officer on Raglan's H.Q.

*"23 October 1854*

*You hear every day of heroic acts of bravery by the soldiers: one I call to mind. A few days ago a private of the 33rd (Duke of Wellington's Regiment) was surprised and made prisoner by two Russian soldiers when an advanced Sentry. One of these worthies took possession of his musket and the other his pouch and marched him between them towards Sebastopol. The Englishman kept a wary watch and when he fancied his captors off their guard sprang on the one who had his musket, seized it and shot dead the other who carried the pouch as well as his own arms and accoutrements. Meanwhile the Russian from whom our fellow had taken his own musket... fired, missed and finally had his brains knocked out by the butt end of the English-man's musket; after which the man coolly proceeded to take off the Russian accoutrements etc., with which he returned laden to the post where he had been surprised, fired at by the Russian sentries, and cheered by our own pickets."*

Private Patrick McGuire enjoyed remarkable acclaim at the time. Hearing of his exploit, Lord Raglan ordered him an immediate gratuity of £5; the *"Illustrated London News"* published an account of the incident and coloured prints appeared depicting the event. In December 1854 a Royal Warrant instituted the award of the Distinguished Conduct Medal for gallantry in the field – the first such decoration to be granted to other ranks – and McGuire was among the first in the 33rd to be so decorated (in March 1855). Meanwhile, the French had awarded him the Médaille Militaire, one of only nine gained by the Regiment in the entire war.

At the instigation of Queen Victoria herself, the supreme award For Valour was authorised by Royal Warrant on 29 January 1856, by which date the war was almost over, but recommendations were allowed to be retrospective back to June 1854. Lieutenant Colonel Johnstone, then commanding the 33rd, considered that McGuire was worthy, and submitted his name which was duly forwarded to the Queen for approval. Her Majesty declined, on "moral" grounds that can only be described as tortuous. In the published correspondence of Lord Panmure, Secretary of State for War, appears the following letter to the Commander-in-Chief dated 17 February 1857, referring to recommendations for the Victoria Cross.

*"There is only one case which the Queen thinks had better be omitted, viz: Pte P. Macguire (sic) of the 33rd. His deed, although publicly praised and rewarded by Lord Raglan, was one of very doubtful morality, and if pointed out by the Sovereign as praiseworthy, may lead to the cruel and inhumane practice of never making prisoners but always putting to death those who may be overpowered for fear of their rising over captors."*

And so, with such strange reasoning, Private McGuire's name was deleted from the recommendations.(f)

A short while after the McGuire incident the Russians decided it was time for them to take the initiative and resolved to destroy the base at Balaclava. Their attack on 25 October by a mass of cavalry was repulsed by the memorable stand of the 93rd Highlanders – the "Thin Red Line". As the Russians withdrew the Heavy Brigade of cavalry hastened them on their way. That was followed by the spectacular but costly charge of Lord Cardigan and his Light Brigade against the Russian batteries. However although Balaclava had been saved the Russians were still in a position to continue to harass the communications between it and the allied camp, near Sebastopol.

---

(f) A generous total of 82 VCs were awarded, the highest number for any campaign until the Great War.

The long eastern flank of the allies facing Sebastapol was held by the 2nd Division, supported by the 1st Brigade of the Light Division, which included the 33rd, and the Guards Brigade. On the morning of the day following Balaclava the Russians launched an attack against the 2nd Division with a force of six battalions amounting to about 5,000 men. They advanced, as was their custom, in densely packed columns, for the Russian army was trained and equipped not so much to fight as to present an awesome spectacle. However, the Russians did not press home their attack and withdrew into Sebastopol, having suffered heavy casualties from the devastating fire of the Miniés. Coming, as it did, the day after the disaster to the Light Cavalry Brigade, 'Little Inkerman', as it came to be called, gave a fillip to the whole Crimean army.

In fact the Russian attack on 26 October had been no more than a reconnaissance in force for a major attack against the 2nd Division, near Inkerman. The attack was launched at 5am on 5 November when the Russians approached the British lines in two columns of 20,000 each. Under cover of darkness and in thick fog they advanced unobserved almost to the 2nd Division's positions. The first intimation the 33rd had of their presence was a rattle of musketry on its brigade's flank and the driving in of the outlying pickets. It was then discovered that a mass of enemy infantry was scaling the heights to their front. Sir George Brown immediately deployed his Light Division to meet this attack, with the 1st Brigade – 7th, 23rd and 33rd – occupying the left-flank slopes and protecting the redoubt known as the Lancaster Battery. Meanwhile, now thoroughly awake to the threat, the other divisions were likewise deployed all over the ridges and the fight began in earnest. In the face of furious musketry and grapeshot the Russians everywhere pressed their assaults with no regard for mounting casualties. They were in considerably greater numbers and because of the unexpectedness of the engagement Raglan had no means of setting his troops in order. As a result Inkerman has rightly been termed "the soldiers' battle". It was fought not by divisions and brigades, but by companies, detachments and small groups of men who, as they reached the battle, piled in with rifle and bayonet wherever danger threatened. No tactical brilliance marked the grim struggle, only the dogged and unyielding tenacity of the old long-service infantrymen, highlighted by the initiative of junior ranks. Once again their linear formations proved to be far superior to the massed formations of the Russians who were forced to withdraw after a battle lasting nearly eight hours. Their losses amounted to 4,976 killed and some 10,100 wounded. The total British casualties amounted to 2,640 killed and wounded, while the French lost 1,465. In terms of the total casualties of both sides it was the most costly battle since Waterloo.

The specific actions of the 33rd are nowhere recorded, despite the fact that it had one officer and ten other ranks killed and two officers and 52 other ranks wounded.

With the advent of the most bitter Crimean winter for more than a century a period of stalemate set in, the Russians penned within their Sebastopol defences, the allies exposed to the elements on the surrounding heights, and neither side committed to any offensive action other than constant artillery duels and occasional sorties. Meanwhile the British soldiers were suffering (as so often before) not from enemy action, but from gross maladministration. The despatches of William Russell, the first war correspondent,[g] to *The Times*, shocked the public by revealing that the British "Army of the East" had apparently been sent out with no proper regard for logistics. Lord Raglan himself admitted that his medical department was "broken down" (many of the conscripted surgeons were unqualified), while the commissariat was in such a shambles that it had no transport to bring up supplies the seven-odd miles from Balaclava, so that weary infantrymen and half-starved cavalry horses had to be impressed – as they were for the evacuation of the sick. The men had no suitable clothing for a Crimean winter, only their greatcoats permanently soaked by gales of rain, sleet and snow, while their flimsy tents were constantly flattened by those same gales. Soon after Inkerman – on 14 November – a violent hurricane smote the Balaclava base, destroying store-sheds and their contents, sinking transport shipping and inflicting further chaos to an already chaotic situation. Among the stores lost in just one of the ships were thousands of desperately needed coats, blankets and boots. *"You can hardly conceive of the misery of our position"*, wrote a cavalry subaltern, *"First, mud up to our knees and pelting rain day and night. Then blizzards of snow and freezing wind which no amount of extra clothing could keep out – but of course we haven't any. Our tents are blown down as often as we re-erect them, and as for eatables we have to make do with sickening lumps of salt pork and coffee beans, but it is seldom we can render the latter consumable for it is almost impossible to get wood for fires"*. Thus afflicted by the elements, and mismanagement, Lord Raglan's army suffered more from privation than from any enemy annoyance.

By the end of December the death rate had mounted to more than one hundred per day, while in the overcrowded hospital at Scutari Florence Nightingale and her nurses were struggling to tend some 8,000 sick and dying. One of the widespread causes of sickness among the men was scurvy. In December 1854 20,000lb of lime juice, "equal to 634,000 rations", arrived at Balaclava, but due to the incredible ineptitude of the supply and transport service it was not until February next that the first issues were made. Nor was there an issue of fresh vegetables to the men in the trenches. However in December a ship from Varna docked at Balaclava, *"the decks piled up with cabbages"*. But since the bill of lading had omitted to specify the recipient, the commissariat refused to accept them and so the whole consignment was flung overboard. In the circumstances it is not surprising that scurvy was so prevalent.

The wretched cavalry horses suffered as much as the men. Completely exposed in open lines, without adequate forage, they succumbed in their hundreds. It was a common sight to see starving animals gnawing their neighbours' manes and tails. Lord Lucan complained to Raglan that his Cavalry Division was now virtually "useless" as a fighting force: it had lost nearly 1,000 horses out of its original strength of 2,216.

On the night of 20 December there was a surprise sortie from Sebastopol on the heights around the 33rd's brigade position, but this was beaten off with the loss to the Regiment of two men killed, four wounded and two missing. During this skirmish a "stoning match" occurred when a section of the 33rd found itself confronting a dozen

---

(g) Also present during the war was Roger Fenton, the first war photographer.

An incident in Crimea. A party of ten men of the 33rd encounter a dozen Russians.
Both sides having expended all their ammunition, they resort to throwing stones at each other.

or so Russians. Both parties had run out of ammunition and *"....looked at one another with great astonishment, both expecting a volley; at length an impatient 33rd man took up a large stone and flung it in the midst of the Russians; the example was followed on both sides, and the original spectacle of a stone-throwing match now offered itself; until the English, getting tired of the work, charged the Russians with the bayonet which the latter, with very good judgment, declined"*.

On 15 December the Queen ordered that a special Crimea medal should be awarded to all her soldiers who had fought at the Alma and Inkerman. This boost to morale was not entirely effective since most of her soldiers would have preferred a general issue of some warm clothing and supplies. However, in January 1855 such issues materialised in the shape of a second blanket for each soldier, a woollen jersey, flannel drawers, socks and a winter coat. In addition, a number of prefabricated wooden huts were sent up.

The sufferings of the 33rd during that terrible winter are not recorded, but the Digest of Services reported that *"the Regiment was considerably reduced by sickness brought on by the severity of the weather and constant and arduous duty in the trenches"*. Among eight officers evacuated to the Scutari hospital was Lieutenant Colonel Blake.[h]

In March 1855 Major John Johnstone who had been invalided home the previous

---

(h) Lieutenant Colonel Blake died at his home at Welwyn in August 1855, at the early age of 47.

June, returned to duty and, promoted lieutenant colonel, took over command. By this time reinforcements from the 33rd's campaign base at Malta had brought the strength to thirty-eight officers and 1,076 other ranks.

Now that the deadly winter had given way to a mild spring, hostilities started up again. On the night of 22 March a force of some 8,000 Russians stole out of Sebastopol and fell upon the French trenches. Supported by Sir George Brown's Light Division, (with the 33rd), the French drove off their attackers after some furious hand-to-hand encounters. Acting as ADC to Lieutenant Colonel Richard Kelly of the 34th, temporarily in command of a British brigade, was the youthful adjutant of the 33rd, Hans Marsh. During one of the mêlées Colonel Kelly and his next senior, Major Gordon, RE, were both wounded and taken prisoner. Without a moment's hesitation, Lieutenant Marsh took command and ejected the enemy from a redoubt they had entered, thereby saving the guns from capture.[i]

Shortly afterwards, on 19 April, there was another example of initiative when, during a British attack on the Sebastopol Redan, Brevet Lieutenant Colonel G V Mundy of the 33rd took over command from the mortally-wounded Colonel Egerton of the

A group of officers of the 33rd, Lieutenant Colonel G V Mundy is seated in the centre.

---

(i) Three months later Hans Marsh was shot in the head during a Russian sortie. In his despatch Lord Raglan stated: *Among the killed I lament to announce the loss of Lieutenant H Marsh 33rd Regiment...This young officer had served throughout the campaign, and was distinguished for his gallantry and devotion to the service....*

77th and led his force to victory. In the action the 77th lost 45 all ranks, but the 33rd was singularly fortunate in losing only three other ranks wounded.

One of the most formidable outworks of the Sebastopol defences was the eastern redoubt known as the Great Redan, strongly defended by infantry and guns, and its capture was essential before any assault on Sebastopol itself could be contemplated. Following a successful assault on the outworks, dubbed the Quarries, in which the 33rd was heavily engaged, the attempt on the Redan was planned for 18 June (anniversary of the Battle of Waterloo). Again it was to be a combined British-French operation, the former to attack the Redan itself while the latter were to carry the nearby Malakov redoubt. Raglan had ordered a three-hour preliminary artillery bombardment on the Redan, but the precipitate French launched their attack ahead of timing, to be severely mauled, and seeing this, Raglan ordered his British force to advance before his guns could complete their softening-up.

The storming party of the Light Division comprised detachments of the 7th, 23rd and 33rd, to which a company of the 34th was added at the last minute. The attack went in at first light on the 18th, and proved a disaster. Fully alerted by the ineffectual artillery overture, and heartened by their repulse of the French, the Russians were ready to do likewise with the British, and their storm of grapeshot and musketry devastated the attackers struggling up the slope to the glacis, broken by shell-holes, trenches and old gravel-pits. One of the 33rd's officers, who had joined from home only the previous day, was Captain Basil Fanshawe, and his subsequent letter to his parents forms the only eyewitness account of the Regiment's sufferings:

> *"We had to cross, on leaving the trenches, 150 yards of open ground, exposed to a very heavy fire of grape-shot from the enemy.... Our loss, I regret to say, was very considerable, having had 50 men killed and wounded. Lieut-Colonel Johnstone has lost his left arm, Mundy is hit in the leg with a bullet, Bennett I am sorry to say is killed; Quayle shot in the elbow and arm. Wickham is so hit in the foot that he is likely to be disabled for some time to come.... I have had a bruise on the shoulder which has made it stiff.... The loss our Division has sustained is frightful. The Rifle Brigade [2nd Brigade] are almost annihilated! Out of 130 men 35 only survive. The 23rd nearly cease to exist!..."*

Owing to the broken terrain in the initial advance, the formed companies and platoons disintegrated into scattered, disordered parties, easily shot down, *"....their line was quite broken the moment they came out of the trenches. The well aimed fire of the Russians on our men increased the want of order and unsteadiness caused by their mode of advance"*. (Fanshawe).

As the British and French withdrew the Russians, as was their habit, continued to fire on the wounded men endeavouring to return to their lines, and ignored for some hours the white flag of truce so that the killed and wounded could be recovered. The disastrous outcome of the assault was almost entirely due to the impetuous behaviour of

*175*

General Pélissier, the commander of the French forces. Their losses in killed and wounded amounted to 3,551. The shattered British battalions suffered 22 officers and 247 men killed, 78 officers and 1,207 wounded. Of those the 33rd lost two officers and 21 men killed, three officers and 46 men wounded, a heavy toll for only a detachment of the Regiment. One of the two officers killed was Lieutenant Langford Heyland and a gallant attempt to recover him (supposed wounded) was made by a private soldier of the Regiment.

> *"Richard Worrell, a soldier of the 33rd Regiment, having heard that Lieutenant Heyland had not returned with the regiment, but was supposed to be lying wounded on the scene of action.... was heard to say 'I will go and seek him and bring him back if he lives, or die with him if he has been killed'..... This noble-hearted man (notwithstanding the continued fire from Sebastopol) determined on returning to the spot where he and the young officer had stood side by side that morning for the last time on earth. He braved death and met it, for his body, pierced with wounds was found close to that of Lieutenant Langford Heyland, so nearly had he reached him."*

In his despatch after the battle, Lord Raglan mentioned the distinguished conduct of Lieutenant Colonel John Douglas Johnstone of the 33rd. As Captain Fanshawe related, he "lost his left arm": in fact, the arm was mangled by grapeshot and had to be amputated after his evacuation to Scutari. Command was now assumed by Brevet Lieutenant Colonel T B Gough, only recently returned from sick leave after his wound at the Alma.

The Russians next launched an attack. Unfortunately for them the British had received information that they were to be attacked on or about 26 June. The Light Division was moved into the forward trenches, the 33rd with the 1st Brigade, which had now been increased to five battalions with the addition of the 34th (Borders) and 2nd/95th. The expected attack began at 11.30pm. As the Russians advanced flares were fired. Then *"Our two front ranks gave them a deadly point blank volley and at once stepped back, for we stood six deep in the trench waiting for them. The next two ranks moved up and gave them another... The deadly fire was too much for them and they broke....We chased them right up to the Redan and then returned to our trenches"*. (Sergeant Timothy Gowing, 7th Foot). The enemy dead lay in columns, in places four or five deep. Once again the Miniés had done some fearful work.

Infirm since the outset of the campaign, Lord Raglan succumbed to his exertions (and "Crimean fever") on 28 June, and with due ceremony his body was escorted to Balaclava for shipment home and private burial at Badminton. He was succeeded as Commander-in-Chief by General James Simpson. For the next three months the siege of Sebastopol dragged on with little but furious artillery duels. In these the British had the advantage of far superior artillery, which was nullified to some extent by the

Russians constantly replacing their battered units. In the meantime great improvements had been made in the administration of the army, including the construction of a light railway line from Balaclava to the British forward area.

In early September another attempt was made to carry the fortress by storm. After three days of bombardment by British and French guns, the assault was launched on 8 September, the French attacking the Little Redan and the Malakov, the British again committed to the Great Redan. General Simpson declared that *"the Second and Light Divisions should have the honour of the assault, from the circumstances of their having defended the batteries and approaches against the Redan for so many months...."* This was a blunder, although made with laudable intentions, since both divisions had suffered cruelly and had been filled up with raw recruits. Furthermore, while the French force numbered some 40,000 men, Simpson inexplicably entrusted the "honour" to no more than 4,000. Among them was a detachment of 300 officers and men of the 33rd, under Colonel Gough, with equal numbers of the 7th and 23rd Fusiliers. Having bravely fought their way to the parapets, where they doggedly held on for an hour, suffering heavy casualties, they were overwhelmed by the superior opposition and forced to withdraw. Now, however, the French had carried the Malakov, and this so demoralised the Russian Commander, that he conceded that Sebastopol was no longer defensible. By evening the British were astonished to find the Redan evacuated, and next morning there were no occupants in the smoking debris of Sebastopol but the corpses of 8,000 Russians and 5,000 British and French. In this final assault the British alone lost 158 officers and 2,026 other ranks killed and wounded. The 33rd's casualties amounted to two officers and 19 men killed, four and 52 wounded. The dead included Lieutenant Colonel T B Gough who was severely wounded and died ten days later.[j]

The capture of Sebastopol marked the virtual end of the war. The Russians continued to occupy the inland heights, but with their main base gone and their fleet dispersed, they had no stomach for further offensives and the winter of 1855-56 passed with nothing but occasional skirmishes, while elsewhere overtures for peace were set in motion. These resulted in an armistice in February, and on 30 March 1856 the Crimean War was formally concluded with the Treaty of Paris.

For the 33rd it had been the most costly campaign in its history, but not all the appalling casualties were caused by enemy action. The Digest of Services reveals that between landing in Bulgaria in May 1854 and the final operations of 1855-56, no fewer than 357 all ranks perished from cholera or other diseases, while 587 were killed, died of wounds or from sickness contracted in the field. Two hundred and ninety three men were invalided home during the war, of whom 115 were discharged as unfit for further service.

On 17 May, 1856 the depleted Regiment sailed for home under the command of the second lieutenant colonel, George Mundy, and disembarked at Portsmouth on 21 June. Here it was met by Lieutenant Colonel Johnstone who, despite the loss of an arm at the Redan, was now fit enough to resume command. [k]

---

(j) T B Gough had purchased his ensigncy in the 33rd in 1827. He was a nephew of Field Marshal Viscount Gough of Sikh wars fame. A memorial to him is in Londonderry Cathedral.
(k) See page 178

Mr William Russell of *The Times*, who had done so much to publicise the inefficiencies of the army, wrote a series of articles about the regiments that had served in the Crimea. On 26 June 1856 the following appeared in *The Times*.

> *"Of the 33rd Regiment, or as is its delight and honour to be called The Duke of Wellington's Regiment, it can fairly be said that no regiment has more largely shared in the losses, the sufferings and hard work of the expedition from first to last. At the Alma the 33rd was in the centre of the right brigade of the Light Division and went up the hill in the teeth of the half moon battery..."*

The Crimean War gained for the Regiment the three battle honours **Alma**, **Inkerman** and **Sevastopol**.[l] Lieutenant Colonel John Douglas Johnstone was appointed CB, while 17 NCOs and privates received the newly-instituted Distinguished Conduct Medal.

In spite of the bungling prosecution of the war by the government and senior officers, the army had, together with its French and Turkish allies, achieved what it had been sent to do – the halting of Russian expansionism in the Near East. It had also, by its sacrifices and heroism, hastened the long needed overhaul of an outdated military system.

---

(k). It is not recorded whether the Colonel of the Regiment, Field Marshal Sir Charles Yorke, who had succeeded General D'Oyley in September 1855, was also present. He was the son of Lieutenant Colonel John Yorke who had commanded the 33rd at Yorktown.
(l) The usual English spelling is 'Sebastopol'. However in Russian a 'b' is pronounced 'v', thus the battle honour version is phonetically correct.

CHAPTER 12

# The Indian Mutiny and the Abyssinia Campaign

*1857 Indian Mutiny*
*1867 Abyssinia*
*1868 Magdala*
*1872 The 33rd and 76th are linked*

Following its return from the Crimea, the 33rd or 'Duke's Own', as it was then commonly called, proceeded to Aldershot. However, it was only there for two months, during which it was inspected by the Queen, before being sent to Dublin. Shortly after arrival it received a draft of 344 rank and file from the depot companies at Fermoy. There is evidence to suggest that most, if not all of them, were Irishmen. The stay in Dublin was also of short duration. Early in 1857 the Regiment was ordered to Mauritius where it arrived on 5 May 1857. The voyage had lasted three months during which the food had, for the most part, consisted of biscuits with salt pork and beef on alternate days.

May was a fateful month for the British in India. For some time the sowars and sepoys of "John Company" (East India Company) had, for a number of reasons, been unsettled. Then early in 1857 the Enfield rifle had been introduced, which necessitated the use of greased cartridges. The end of a cartridge had to be bitten in order to empty the powder down the barrel. Owing to an incredible error the grease was made from a mixture of pig and cow fat. The pig was forbidden to Muslims and the cow was sacred to Hindus. A rumour quickly grew that the British intended to make the sepoys 'unclean', so that they would all be forced to become Christians. On 10 May Indian troops at Meerut broke into open mutiny, and within a week the whole Bengal Army was in revolt, with the *Shaitan ki Hawa* (Devil's wind) sweeping through the land from Calcutta to Delhi.

Away in Mauritius the 33rd felt no reverberations other than alarming letters and newspaper reports. But the situation had become so grave that Lord Canning, Governor General of India, demanded reinforcements of "Royal" (i.e. British regular) infantry from wherever they could be spared, and on 20 July the Regiment received

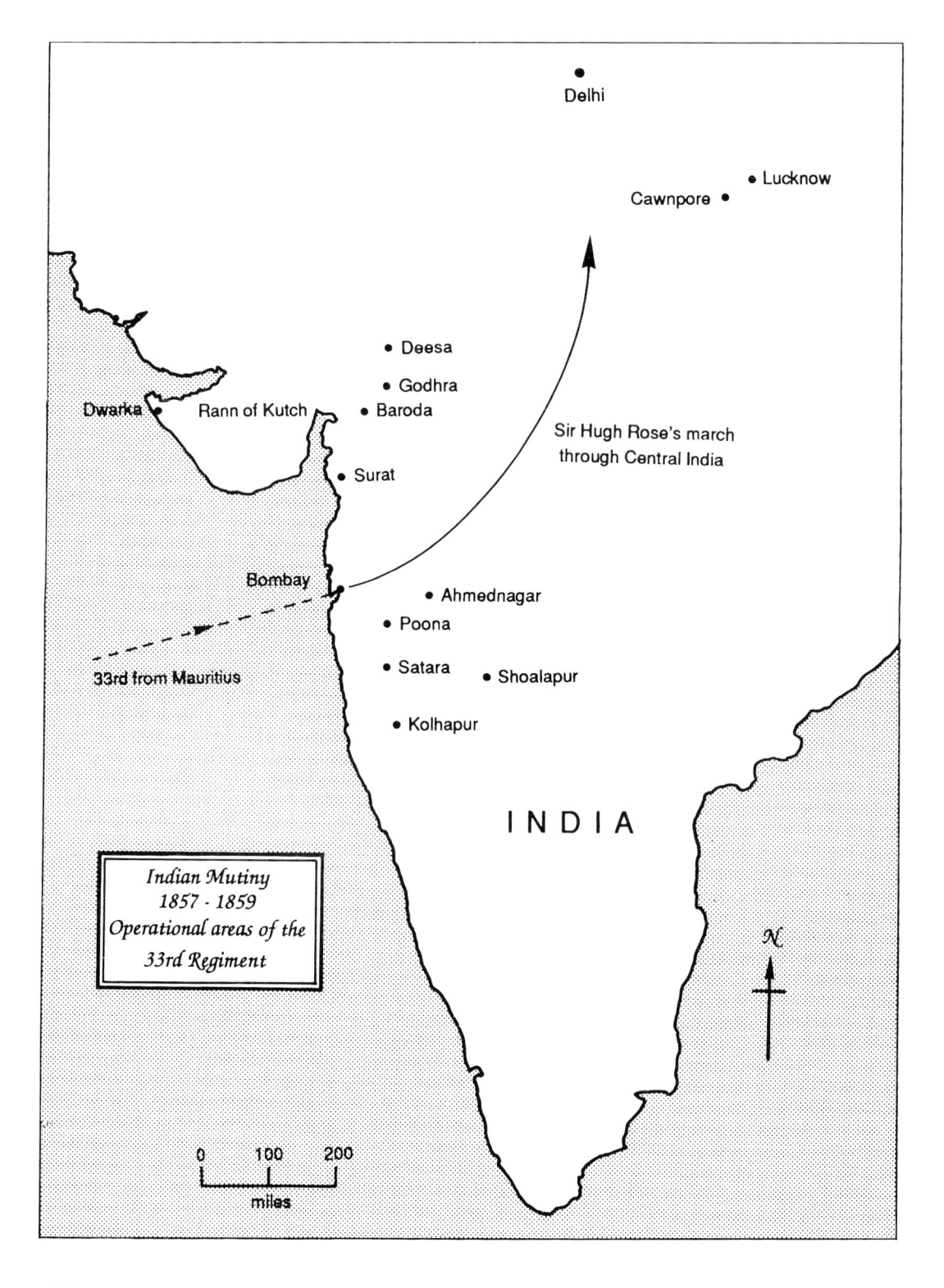

*Indian Mutiny
1857 - 1859
Operational areas of the
33rd Regiment*

orders to embark for Bombay. Eight companies, with RHQ, arrived there on 7 August, having left two companies in Mauritius awaiting replacement by the 4th Regiment from England. Duly relieved, these two followed on 28 August and the 33rd was now at full strength with 37 officers and 1,087 other ranks. In command was Lieutenant Colonel J D Johnstone. The arrival of the Regiment in Bombay was greeted with relief by the Europeans, many of whom already had their belongings on board ships.

One of the matters for consideration was whether to keep the 33rd in hand for emergencies, or break it up into detachments. The latter course having been decided, the headquarters of the Regiment moved to Poona while the companies became widely dispersed in fragmented detachments, mostly to the south of Bombay, in such places as Sotara, Sholapur and Kolhapur. Because of this dispersion there are few records of the Regiment's actions during the mutiny.

On 1 November 1858, even before the mutiny had been fully quelled, the East India Company was dissolved, the government of India being vested in the Crown and the Governor General, Lord Canning, becoming the first Viceroy.

In December 1858 there was an outbreak of mutiny in Kolhapur which resulted in most of the 33rd being temporarily sent there. According to the reminiscences of Colour Sergeant John McGrath, who served in the light company throughout the campaigning, retribution for the mutineers was savage and swift:

> *"There was ugly work done during that time. Several mutineers were blown away from the guns. The artilleryman ....was assisted by others but he fired the gun... Indeed you might call him the public hangman or blowman. He used to get a glass of grog for each one".*

At the end of December the 33rd, now under the command of Lieutenant Colonel J E Collings, was moved to the north of Bombay. Headquarters was located at Deesa but, as before, the companies were often widely dispersed. Two of the companies, under Major Quayle, accompanied Sir Hugh Rose's field force in his thousand mile pursuit of the rebel leader Tantia Topi through Central India.

While the Regiment saw nothing like the bloody engagements which took place at Delhi, Lucknow and Cawnpore, it was nonetheless frequently involved in arduous campaigning. In September 1859, for instance, a strong body of rebels had gathered at Dwarka.

> *"We had it pretty quiet in Deesa for a short time until a wing (or half battalion) was ordered to a place called Dwarka, not far from the Rann of Kutch. I was one of this number. We made a start in September and reached there in October, the distance being 500 miles which we did in 30 days exactly. Getting to this place was very difficult, the month of September being the close of the monsoon season, the country we had to travel over being flat. Scarcely a day passed without our wading through water 3 or 4 times during our days or rather nights march.*

*This had to be done with boots on, and my readers can imagine what an unpleasant thing it is to walk or march in wet socks and boots, and this happening once (very often) every hour.... the company I belonged to were 8 days without taking boots off."*

(Colour Sergeant McGrath)

During its time at Deesa the Regiment buried eight officers and 57 other ranks, all smitten down with cholera.

By the end of 1859 order had been restored throughout India. Before it had been dissolved the East India Company had, in August 1858, authorised the grant of a medal for services during the Indian Mutiny. However no member of the 33rd was able to claim it, on the grounds that it had not campaigned as a regiment. Nor was it able to claim the battle honour "Central India", for the same reason. Considering all the hardships it had undergone it is not surprising that members of the Regiment felt that they had been less than fairly treated.

In 1858 orders had been issued for the two flank companies to be abolished. However implementation of the order in India seems to have been delayed, as it was not until May 1861 that the 33rd lost its grenadier company and light company. Later in that year the Regiment was moved to Bombay where it remained for two years before being sent to Poona in February 1863. In April of that year Lieutenant General W N Hutchinson was appointed Colonel of the Regiment. It was while stationed at Poona that the second lieutenant colonel, E W Donovan [a] exchanged into the 100th Foot[b] with Lieutenant Colonel A R Dunn VC. Alexander Dunn, while serving with the 11th Hussars, had taken part in the charge of the Light Brigade at Balaclava, following which he was awarded the VC on the general vote of the survivors.[c] In 1855 he sold out, taking with him Mrs Douglas, the wife of his commanding officer, and retired to Canada where his father was Receiver General. Three years later he joined the newly raised 100th Foot. In 1861 he purchased the lieutenant colonelcy for £10,000, but after three years, under some pressure – there were rumours of his excessive gambling – exchanged into the 33rd. At about the same time Ensign W A Wynter joined the Regiment. He later recorded his views on Dunn. *He was a handsome man, 6 feet 2 inches tall and thirty years of age, a kind, good natured dandy, a bad commanding officer and not a good example to young officers... he was very popular but nearly destroyed the Regiment.* Despite these shortcomings he was promoted colonel shortly after joining the Regiment and thereby became the youngest colonel in the army.

\*\*\*\*\*\*\*\*\*\*\*\*\*\*\*\*\*\*\*\*\*\*\*\*

In 1864 events in Abyssinia were causing concern at Westminster. The native ruler was the self-appointed "King" Theodore who was at first on friendly terms with, and

---

[a] Lieutenant Colonel Donovan later became a general and Colonel of the 15th Regiment (East Yorkshire).
[b] Raised as the Royal Canadians. In 1881 it became 1st Battalion Leinster Regiment. The Regiment was disbanded in 1922.
[c] This practice was not uncommon in the Crimean war and Indian mutiny.

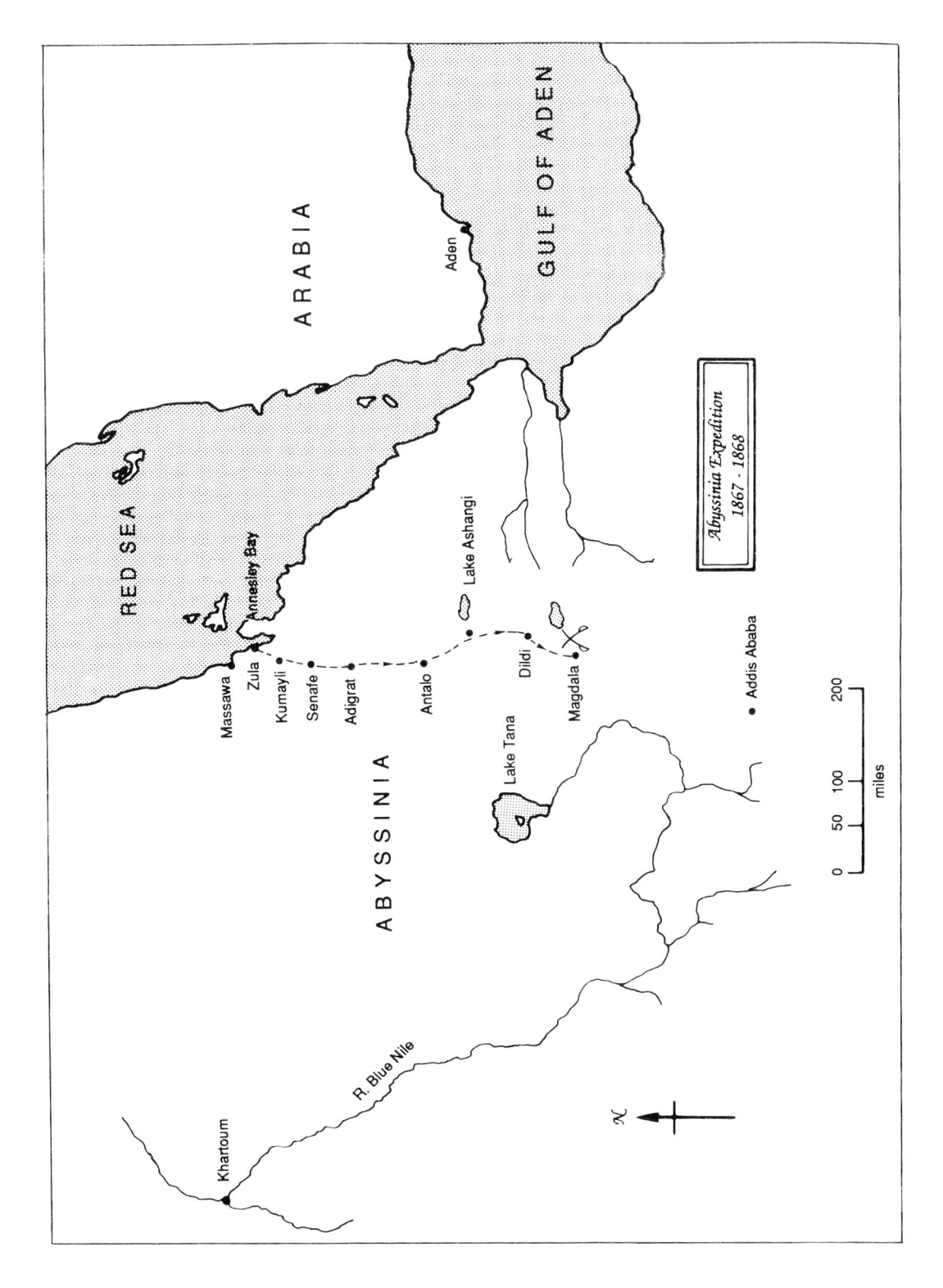

*Abyssinia Expedition 1867 - 1868*

anxious to secure aid from, Britain. With this objective he sent a British consul, Captain Cameron, to England, carrying a personal letter to the Foreign Secretary. The letter was ignored: Earl Russell was not minded to become involved with a petty Abyssinian dictator. Cameron was sent back to the consular post at Massawa without any reply, but assuming this had been delivered by other means, he visited the Magdala palace, to find the King so angered by the apparent contempt displayed by the British Government that he and his entourage were immediately cast into prison. The despotic ruler had already imprisoned sundry missionaries and others of various nationalities.

In March 1866 a British envoy was despatched to intercede with Theodore for the release of all prisoners. He seemed to have achieved his objective when all were released and on their way to the coast. But the unpredictable King changed his mind: the party was seized, brought back to Magdala and clapped in irons, together with Cameron. These were the days of gunboat (or bayonet) diplomacy, and after Theodore had emulated the previous "contempt" of the Foreign Secretary by ignoring demands for the release of the captives, the British Government resorted to force.

And so, in October 1867 the 33rd (which had moved to Karachi at the end of 1866) found itself committed to one of the numerous Victorian "small wars" – the Abyssinian Campaign. Commanded by Lieutenant General Sir Robert Napier, the Abyssinian field force totalled some 12,000 British and Indian troops. Apart from batteries of Royal Artillery, the British element initially consisted of a wing (two squadrons) of the 3rd Dragoon Guards, the 4th (King's Own) and the 33rd Regiments. Later the force was joined by the 26th (Cameronians) and 45th (Sherwood Foresters), although the former did not arrive in Abyssinia until the campaign was nearly over. The 33rd was in the 1st Brigade commanded by Brigadier General J E Collings. As a result of this appointment Colonel Alexander Dunn VC assumed command of the Regiment, which at that time consisted of a high proportion of Irishmen. So much so that H M Stanley (later the discoverer of Dr Livingstone), who accompanied the expedition as the correspondent of the *New York Herald*, frequently described the 33rd as the *"Irish Regiment"*.

Sailing from Karachi on 21 November, the Regiment's transports arrived at Annesley Bay, on the Red Sea coast, on 4 December, but because of the chaos prevailing on shore it was not until 7 December that the first two companies were disembarked. Not the least cause of the chaos was the fact that thousands of mules had been sent to Abyssinia from Egypt and other Middle East countries before proper arrangements had been made to look after them. The first task of the 33rd was therefore to create some order out of the chaos. Ensign John Barton of the 33rd, in a letter to his mother, described what that involved:

> *"I have been out all this morning since daylight catching mules, it is desperate hard work. I should think I ran about five miles already today. They turn the wretched brutes loose as soon as they land and as the mule drivers are busy taking things up country they are left to die of hunger or thirst.... However things are much better since our*

*detachment landed...we feed and water them every day (but) have to send an officer and 50 men armed with long whips to keep them from trampling one another to death."*

The condensed sea water had to be piped ashore from a warship, then carried in chaguls (canvas bags) to be emptied into makeshift wooden troughs, many of which were destroyed by the thirst-crazed animals. Order was eventually restored and on Christmas Day 1867 the 33rd's officers in their tented mess at the base camp at Zula partook of a dinner of local chicken and *"a plum pudding made from pounded ships' biscuits".* (Wynter).

Since this was the Indian cold weather season, all ranks were attired in what Ensign Wynter described as *Waterloo-red full dress tunics and khaki drill trousers.* However, before operations began, the thick serge was replaced by more practical khaki drill. The headdress was the white-cloth-covered cork helmet or topi, which, introduced by Lord Wolseley after the Indian Mutiny, was ever afterwards (down to the Second World War) known as the Wolseley topi (or topee). If uniforms had changed little since Wellington's day, there was a significant improvement in weaponry: the soldiers were now armed with the Snider rifle. Issued only the previous year, this was the first breech-loading rifle to be supplied to British troops. and with it the trained soldier's rate of fire was increased from two to ten rounds per minute. The Abyssinian campaign was its debut in action. As in the Crimea, officers (still encumbered with swords) carried their own preference of "pistols, revolving" of Colt, Smith & Wesson, Adams and other manufacturers.

Sir Robert Napier's objective was the capture of King Theodore's fortress-capital of Magdala and the release of all his prisoners. Poised on a craggy plateau nearly 10,000 feet above sea level, Magdala lay some 390 miles from the Red Sea coast, a daunting wilderness of barren mountain, steep valleys and rock-bound tracks climbing over 7,000 feet passes. The task had to be completed with speed as campaigning was restricted to the dry season, that is to say between January and June. By early January 1868, when Sir Robert Napier arrived, important progress had been made. One pier had been completed in Annesley Bay, a water condenser had been established on shore and equipment had arrived for the construction of a light railway from Zula to Kumayli, at the foot of the uplands. Sir Robert's arrival gave added impetus to these exertions while the organised mule trains from India, which followed shortly after him, brought some much needed efficiency to the transport system. Eventually there were some 12,000 muleteers with the force.

An advanced base camp had been established at Senafe, 60-odd miles from the coast, where the 33rd arrived on 12 January. Here the force halted for three weeks while the commander-in-chief organised rations and supplies for what he estimated would be an advance of 30 marches to Magdala. But there was no rest for some of the troops. Within three days two companies of the 33rd were ordered forward to Gunguna (twelve miles) to prepare the road – in other words to act as navvies with pick and shovel, clearing the track of rock and boulder and scree.

It was just at the end of this three-week halt at Senafe that a mysterious tragedy occurred in the 33rd. For 25 January the Digest of Services has a single terse entry: *Colonel Dunn, V.C. died.* Always ready to seize opportunities for sport, most officers took their sporting guns with them in the field, as did Colonel Dunn. In the evening of 25 January he and the regimental surgeon, James Sinclair, set off in search of game, each accompanied by an Indian hospital orderly to carry any bag. The two men soon separated, and shortly afterwards Sinclair heard a shot. Within minutes the colonel's orderly came panting up, *"Sahib, Sahib! Colonel Sahib is dead!"* Sinclair ran back with him to where Dunn was indeed lying dead, his body riddled with shot from both barrels of the gun which lay by his side. Next morning a Regimental Court of Inquiry was convened whose findings were:

> *"The Court, having considered all the evidence before it, is of the opinion that the death of Colonel Dunn was purely accidental, caused by his own rifle (sic) exploding while he was in the act of using his brandy flask, when sitting on a stone, out shooting."*

Apparently, none of the evidence was preserved: the only witness was of course the Indian orderly. This seemed to be the end of the sad affair, but there were some who harboured ugly doubts and suspicions, among them Ensign Wynter. *"But how did Dunn die?"* he later wrote. *"He had no reason to shoot himself, he was 32 years old (sic he was 34), a full colonel and next for a brigade"*. An immensely wealthy man, Dunn had bequeathed his entire estate to Mrs. Douglas, his mistress, but before embarking to Abyssinia he made a second Will, leaving the greater part of his money to his sister. The witnesses to this Will were a Captain Lacy of the Regiment (*"Unfit to command a corporal's guard"*, commented Wynter) and one Private Hastie who had been Dunn's servant for many years. For his services, Hastie was presented with a cheque for £300 – a small fortune for a soldier at that date. After his death Dunn's kit was thoroughly gone over and it was discovered that not only had his second Will disappeared, but also a number of valuable gold rings were missing. The sorry story eventually ended with lengthy legal proceedings at home, when both Mrs. Douglas and Dunn's sister were awarded shares of the estate.

But the true cause of Dunn's death was never established for it is difficult to imagine how a man well used to handling firearms could accidentally discharge both barrels of a gun into his body. He was buried at Senafe[d]. With the death of Colonel Dunn command of the 33rd devolved on Major Arthur Cooper, who had transferred to the 33rd from the 27th in 1861. Wynter remarks of this officer: *"He had always had staff appointments. He was quite unknown to the officers and men and seldom spoke to anyone"*. Ensign Barton went further and wrote that if Cooper continued in command he would leave the Regiment.[e] Clearly he was not an inspiring leader.

By 2 March Napier had reached Antalo, half way to Magdala. With the help of two

---

(d) Five others are buried in the same plot, including Quartermaster Vyse, 33rd, who died at Senafe on 22 May 1868.
(e) Major A S Cooper succeeded Colonel Collings in command of the 33rd in 1868. Ensign Barton lasted out until 1871, when he resigned from the army.

The advance to Magdala. The Chetta ravine

elephants he had with him a battery of Armstrong guns plus half of the 33rd, two Indian cavalry regiments and one Indian infantry battalion, altogether about 2,000 men. This advanced body reached Ashangi on 18 March by which date one half was employed as an armed working party and the other half as an armed transport corps – for it had been found a great economy to place every mule in charge of an armed fighting man. From Ashangi the road south became increasingly precipitous and more than one mule, with its load, was lost when it slipped down to destruction.

On 22 March Napier made preparations for the final advance to Magdala by a drastic reduction in baggage and tentage and forbidding the use of private baggage animals. The 15 mile march to Dildi on 24 March *"was terrible"* (Fortescue). By sunset the transport train had scarcely covered half the distance. The rear of the column was then afflicted with a terrible storm so that by the time they had groped their way into camp they were drenched to the skin. They then had to bivouac in a sea of mud. This was too much for some men of the 33rd who vented their feelings by cursing, swearing and abusing everything relating to the expedition – and mentioning names. Sir Robert Napier, on hearing of this, took prompt action and immediately called forward the 4th Regiment to take over the lead. As a result the 33rd now found itself in the 2nd Brigade under command of Sir Charles Staveley. The Regiment does not appear to have been unduly put out by the commander-in-chief's displeasure, for a few days later it announced its arrival by marching into camp to the tune "Slap bang, here we are again".

By 31 March over half the force of 11,000 men, after five months of incessant effort, had been assembled within striking distance of Magdala. Extremes of temperature were now added to their other hardships, with daytime temperatures in excess of 40°C falling to below freezing at night. They were also having to operate at heights of over 10,000 feet interspersed with deep valleys, with the result that the difference between one camp and the next was often several thousand feet. Ensign Barton described what it was like, *".... heavy rain every night, nothing but our thin Indian serge clothing, one day's rations in eight days, water so putrid that one only drank it in desperation.... no wood to make a fire however cold the night..and not a bush or even a big stone to shelter behind".*

The Talanta plain, some 12 miles from Magdala, was reached on 5 April but there was then a delay of four days waiting for supplies. While at Talanta the force was strengthened by the arrival of six companies of the 45th Regiment and the Armstrong battery, which had a terrible struggle getting there despite the best efforts of the elephants that carried the guns.

Though King Theodore's intelligence had alerted him to the approaching threat, he apparently felt secure in his Magdala fortress, and apart from denying supplies to the advancing force by burning villages and destroying cattle, he had so far offered no opposition. But on 10 April he decided to give battle, with disastrous results. In his despatch to London, General Napier reported:

> *"Yesterday morning (we) descended three thousand nine hundred feet to Bashilo River and approached Magdala with First Brigade to*

*reconnoitre it. Theodore opened fire with seven guns from outwork one thousand feet above us, and three thousand five hundred men of garrison made a gallant sortie which was repulsed with a very heavy loss and the enemy driven into Magdala. British loss, twenty wounded...."*

The enemy's casualties were heavy indeed: some 800 killed and 1,500 wounded, among the dead being several of Theodore's senior commanders. In this encounter the fighting fell to the 1st Brigade, the 4th King's Own being the only British infantry engaged. The 33rd with the 2nd Brigade did not come up until the enemy had fled. Sometimes referred to as the battle of the Daw-Wang Ravine, it is recorded as the first occasion on which the new Snider rifle was fired in anger. This reverse so shook the King that on the following day he sent two of his British captives on parole to offer terms. Napier returned a curt reply: unconditional surrender and release of all prisoners. After further attempts at negotiation it became clear that Theodore was not prepared to submit unconditionally, and Napier resolved to take the Magdala citadel by storm.

The assault was launched on the morning of 13 April (Easter Sunday), with a preliminary bombardment by all 18 guns and mortars plus the rocket tubes of the Naval Brigade. Because the 2nd Brigade had by now overtaken the 1st Brigade the 33rd found itself committed to leading the assault, an honour it would not have had if it had stayed in the 1st Brigade. It was supported by a detachment of Madras Sappers and Miners tasked to blow in the citadel's gates. It was a daunting prospect. The force was assembled on a narrow rocky ridge from which the only practicable route to the summit, some 500ft above, lay up a steep boulder-strewn track bounded on one side by a sheer drop, on the other by a perpendicular basalt cliff-face. The track led to one of the citadel's main gateways known as the Koket-bir – a pair of massive timber doors set in a 15ft-long stone archway. On each side of the gateway were defences of thick prickly-thorn hedges strengthened with stakes. Beyond the gateway it was necessary to scramble up a 70ft escarpment covered with thorn bushes and rocks at the top of which was another thorn-and-stake hedge defence. From here another steep boulder-strewn path led to a second fortified gateway, finally giving access to the flat plateau of Magdala, or the *amba*.

On the "Advance" being sounded, the 33rd and Sappers struggled up the lower path and the former used its Sniders to good effect on the defenders of the Koket-bir. Under this cover the leading company with the Sappers managed to approach within assaulting distance of the gateway. At this critical moment occurred what previous historians have described as "an awkward pause": the 33rd discovered that the Sappers had forgotten to bring with them not only their explosives for blowing the gate, but scaling ladders, crowbars and other tools of their trade. The Sappers were sent back to repair their incredible omission. But General Staveley was averse to further delay and ordered the 33rd to continue the assault as best it could. Under heavy fire, the companies bypassed the unblown gate, scrambled up the ridge to their right and reached the second prickly-hedge defence, which was discovered to be on top of a sheer rocky ledge some eight feet high.

Now occurred a sequence of events which resulted in the first VCs to be awarded to the Regiment. Private Bergin, a very tall man, stabbed a gap in the hedge with his bayonet; Drummer Magner then clambered on Bergin's shoulders, heaved himself through the gap and on to the ledge and turning, dragged Bergin up after him, with the help of Ensign Connor and Corporal Murphy, shoving from below. While Bergin kept up a steady fire with his Snider on the Koket-bir gate, Magner helped others of the 33rd to gain the ledge. All this while the defenders were firing back, but miraculously none of the storming party was hit. Fearing an imminent attack with the bayonet, the enemy withdrew through the gate and Bergin, Magner and the rest rushed it before it could be slammed shut. The party then scrambled up the escarpment to the second gate, which was likewise gained and the 33rd stood triumphant on the Magdala plateau, with the Regimental Colour, borne by Ensign Wynter, flying on the defences.[f] Just inside the second gate lay the body of King Theodore who, true to his word, had not surrendered, but had shot himself with the revolver that had been presented to him by Queen Victoria. With his death all opposition petered out and Magdala was in British hands. He left one typical legacy. As he did not wish the British to release his 300 odd native prisoners (which included women and children), he had their hands and feet cut off before having them forced over a precipice to their death.

The five-and-a-half months' Abyssinian campaign and the capture of Magdala were rigorous enough, but battle casualties were astonishingly minimal: in the whole expeditionary force not one officer or soldier was killed, while the wounded amounted to two officers and 27 other ranks, five of them 33rd soldiers.

Orders about looting had been very strict, records Wynter. Anything not taken at the point of the bayonet had to be handed over to the prize master. Such was the fate of King Theodore's silver drum, looted by Bandsman Thomas Dunn of the 33rd. His son, who became director of music of the Royal Horse Guards, recorded his father's account of the affair:

> *"After the storming of the stockade by the regiment, B Company, led by Lieut. Connor advanced to the Palace. My Father, together with other bandsmen.... attached themselves to this company, and on the Palace being taken, evidently went out to enrich themselves. They eventually got into the "Throne Room" and there, the Silver Drum, hidden under a pile of rugs, was found by my father... During the night he got the drum out of the Palace and took it to where the Band was billeted. It was covered with great-coats and my father and Sandy Martin slept one on either side of it. The following day, the drum having been missed by the palace authorities, the Regiment was visited by the Batty*

---

(f) This was the last occasion the 33rd carried its Colours into action.

*Officer, and all articles looted had to be produced. My father paraded with the silver drum and the Batty Officer instantly ordered it to be returned. The Bandsmen appealed to the Colonel of our Regiment, saying they wished to keep it for use in the Band. He then referred the case to Sir Robert Napier, afterwards Lord Napier of Magdala, who decided that the drum be cut into three pieces, one portion to go to the 4th King's (their title in those days), the second to the 3rd Dragoon Guards, and the third to our Regiment. Our Commanding Officer claimed the centre piece... as it had been captured by a man of his Regiment."* (g)

On 19 April, having first blown up the fortress at Magdala, Napier commenced the return march. Two marches later, after crossing the Bashilo river, a grand review took place, after which Napier held an auction of all the loot which had been collected centrally. The money thus raised was distributed among the troops. It was at this auction that Captain Sandys Wason of the 33rd acquired King Theodore's splendid throne cloth, 10ft long and 6ft wide, richly worked with gold thread on blue and scarlet velvet. In due course it was presented to the Regiment by his grandson, Mr. Rigby Wason.

The retirement back to the coast was even more trying than the advance. The men, overworked, insufficiently fed and deprived of all stimulants for five weeks past, reacting to the great strain, began to break down. Frequent rain storms added to their other trials. It was only when Dildi was reached, ten marches from Magdala, that they came into the comfort of the tents and clothing that had been left there. And so the troops wended their weary way back.

At last, on 31 May 1868, the 33rd embarked for home, arriving at Portsmouth on 21 June. All the ships in the harbour were dressed and manned, while on shore bands played "Home Sweet Home" and "See the Conquering Hero Comes". There were large crowds in the streets who chaffed the soldiers on the ragged condition of their clothing. Thus ended the Abyssinia campaign, one of the most remarkable expeditions in the 19th century. For the part it had played the Regiment was awarded the battle honour **Abyssinia**. On 28 July, *The London Gazette* announced the awards of the Victoria Cross to Drummer Michael Magner and Private James Bergin *for their conspicuous gallantry in the assault of Magdala.*

While stationed at Portsmouth the strength of the Regiment was reduced from the Indian to the Home Establishment of 36 officers and 672 other ranks in ten companies. In October 1868 Colonel J E Collings relinquished command to retire on half-pay. For his services as brigade commander in Abyssinia he was appointed Companion of the Order of the Bath.(h) Major A S Cooper was promoted lieutenant colonel without purchase and assumed command. The next seven years saw the Regiment performing routine garrison duties at Aldershot, Colchester, and sundry stations in Ireland before

---

(g) The drum has been twice reassembled. Firstly in 1926 and again in 1952.
(h) Although retired and on half pay he eventually became General Collins. Under the then promotion system an officer, once he had reached the rank of lieutenant colonel, could become a general, if he lived long enough, with no obligation for any further service.

King Theodore's drum. It was divided between 4th King's Own Royal Regiment (left section), the 33rd (centre section) and 3rd Dragoon Guards (right section).

being warned for another spell of Indian service in 1875. The Regiment, then stationed at Fermoy, was ordered to be brought up to a strength of 31 officers and 889 NCOs and men. However, it was so far below strength that it was thrown open to volunteers from other regiments and 263 men were obtained in this manner. The Regiment, under command of Lieutenant Colonel T B Fanshawe, who had served with it during the Crimean war, embarked for Bombay on 29 October.

On arrival in India the 33rd was posted to Kamptee in the Madras Presidency. In March 1878 Colonel Fanshawe was succeeded by Lieutenant Colonel E F Chadwick. However he only remained long enough to see new colours presented by Major General Mark Walker VC, CB on 3 March 1879, before handing over to Lieutenant Colonel J D Johnstone. Johnstone, the son of the Lieutenant Colonel J D Johnstone who had commanded the 33rd during the Crimean war, was in command for only seven months before returning to England on health grounds. He then exchanged with Lieutenant Colonel F J Castle of the 107th (Royal Sussex), who arrived from England on 30 November 1879 and assumed command. The following month the Regiment was posted to Lucknow.

*********************

The 1870s saw some far-reaching changes in the army as a whole, and in the infantry in particular. In December 1868, Edward Cardwell was appointed Secretary of State for War, and immediately set about introducing the organisational and other reforms which became linked with his name, and which were to mould the Victorian army into a near-resemblance of the force that went to war in 1914. Starting at the top, Cardwell reorganised the Horse Guards into the War Office with three departments, Military, Supply and Finance, all answering to the Secretary of State. This was in 1870 and a year later, in July 1871, came the radical Regulation of the Forces Act which abolished the two-hundred-year-old practice of buying and selling officers' commissions. Henceforth promotion would be by examination and seniority, while all candidates for first commissions in the cavalry and infantry would have to be accepted as cadets at Sandhurst and undergo the regulation course of training (Gunners and Sappers were not affected, since they had never conformed to the purchase system). Such a revolutionary change aroused consternation and dismay among members of the more fashionable and expensive regiments who feared that their messes would now have to admit types who would never have survived the obligatory interviews with colonels or commanding officers. But Cardwell asserted in the House that *"for the first time the Regular Army will become in reality as well as in name, the Queen's Army, instead of belonging to those who have paid for their commissions"*. Punch however, put it rather more acidly: *"Notice to Gallant but Stupid Young Gentlemen. You may purchase your Commissions up to the 31st day of October. After that you will be driven to the cruel necessity of deserving them"*. As it turned out, fears about the characters and morals of non-purchase officers proved groundless. Another result of the Regulation of the Forces Act was the transfer of the

Militia infantry from control of the Lord Lieutenants of their counties direct to the War Office.

The army had two main functions. First there was the Empire to police and defend, which had meant that for many years the greater part of the army had been stationed overseas. Thus in 1868 out of 141 line battalions only 47 were at home. The army's second task was the security of Britain, but with so many battalions overseas it had become increasingly ill prepared for that commitment. All Cardwell's reforms were designed to fashion an army capable of fulfilling its dual function.

In 1872 he introduced the Localisation Scheme of linked battalions. At this date none of the regular infantry battalions had any permanent, static depot. When a battalion was posted overseas it left one or two companies at home to act as temporary depot and to provide drafts as necessary. Although some regiments had been given territorial titles as long ago as 1782 in order to assist recruiting, few of them had established firm associations with such territories, and did not always recruit therein.

All this was changed by the Localisation Scheme. In future, pairs of battalions (except those numbered 1 to 25, who already had two battalions) would be linked or brigaded together with a common, static depot which would train recruits for both. The home-based battalion would supply reinforcements for its partner overseas. There was an almost paranoid opposition to the Scheme and in particular its linking together of units with no common regimental interests. Two such were the 33rd and 76th Regiments who learned that they were to be "linked" with a common depot at Halifax, West Riding of Yorkshire. As far as the 33rd was concerned, the choice of Halifax (i) for the depot was a happy one, for although the title "West Riding" (j) had disappeared on its becoming The Duke of Wellington's Regiment, recruiting was still carried out in that part of Yorkshire. The new depot was to be known as No. 9 Brigade Depot and besides companies of the 33rd and 76th, it would also include a detachment of the 6th West Yorkshire Militia, which later became the 3rd Militia Battalion of the Dukes.

As there was no accommodation for troops in Halifax, an entire complex of purpose-built barracks had to be erected. But before this project got under way, an unforeseen hitch occurred. In Victorian days the soldier was not generally popular among the public, who tended to regard him, if not brutal and licentious, at least undesirable in its midst, given to drunkenness and brawling and a great threat to daughters. This was the attitude of many of the citizens of Halifax. However there was an equally active faction that welcomed the idea and their petition was handed over to Mr Cardwell on 24 March, two days before that of the "antis". Their deputation presented a "memorial" to Mr. Cardwell and the Commander-in-Chief, signed by 4,664 townspeople, respectfully urging that *"the selection of Halifax as a military centre is contrary to the wishes of the inhabitants, and such centres should not be established in prosperous industrial districts, in as much as they offer strong inducements to irregularity and neglect of work and tend generally to demoralisation and immorality".*

---

(i) It was originally proposed to locate the Depot at Bradford.
(j) However the title was far from forgotten. It was inscribed on the both the Crimea and Abyssinia memorials. In 1870 a formal application had been made to the War office for the words "West Riding" to be included in the title of the Regiment, but it was turned down.

Neither Secretary of State nor Commander-in-Chief were swayed by the objections, and on 1 April Colonel Ackroyd, MP for Halifax, was informed by the War Office that the project would go ahead. The site selected for the barracks was a piece of then open ground at Highroad Well on the outskirts of the town. Building commenced almost immediately but it was not until the summer of 1877 – after four years' work – that the barracks were ready for occupation. The complex consisted of two stone-built double-storey blocks containing the men's barrack rooms, various administrative and stores buildings, officers' mess, hospital and married quarters block. At the entrance gate stood an imposing stone keep where ammunition was stored. On 30 August, 1877 the *Halifax Guardian* reported that *a detachment of the 33rd and 76th Regiments arrived in Halifax by special train from Aldershot. They were met at the railway station by the band of the 6th West Yorkshire Militia and marched to Highroad Well.* The detachment consisted of two companies of both Regiments, commanded by Major Caldecott of the 33rd, and a month later they were joined by the headquarters of the 6th West Yorkshire Militia. The Depot was soon fulfilling its function. In 1879 the Digest of Services noted that three officers and 203 soldiers enlisted for the 76th Regiment were drafted to join the 33rd in India.

The home-based British infantry was now armed with the Martini-Henry rifle which had replaced the Snider in 1874. The new weapon, of .45in calibre, was lighter than its predecessor at 8lb 10oz, and with its improved breech mechanism gave the trained soldier a rate of fire of 12 rounds per minute.

The Cardwell reforms brought another innovation which was welcomed by many soldiers. Hitherto, a man had enlisted for twelve years with the Colours, after which he was discharged unconditionally (with a meagre pension). With the passing of Cardwell's Army Enlistment Act in 1870, the soldier could sign on for a short-service engagement of six years with the Colours and six on reserve. This measure provided, for the first time, a fully-trained body of reservists available in the event of general mobilisation. If he so wished, and was of good character, the six-year soldier was permitted to re-engage for further periods, up to a maximum of twenty-one years. The short-service scheme was not without its drawbacks and critics, however. An alarming percentage of men opted for the reserve after their six-year term, so that regiments were bereft of experienced, fully-trained soldiers who might have become useful NCOs or WOs.

CHAPTER 13

# "Pax Britannica" The 76th Regiment from 1815 - 1881

Peace had been concluded with America at the end of 1814. Almost immediately 190 NCOs and men of the 76th, who were time expired, were discharged. As a result of the reduced state of the Regiment it was ordered home. However, the escape of Napoleon from Elba re-opened the war in Europe and in consequence only the strongest regiments based on Canada were now required to return. The 76th therefore continued on the American establishment. The following year it was moved to Quebec, preparatory to return to England, but the order was again countermanded. It remained in Quebec until June 1818 when it moved to Kingston. In June 1819 it was sent to Quebec for embarkation but once again the order was cancelled. For the next seven years it wandered uneventfully between the Canadian cantonments at Quebec, Kingston, Fort George (on the Niagara frontier) and Montreal. At last, in 1827, the 76th's fourteen years' spell of foreign service came to an end when it sailed from Quebec, to be posted to the Irish Establishment.

Shortly after arriving at Fermoy in September 1827, the Regiment lost Brevet Colonel John Wardlaw who retired on half pay. He had commanded for seventeen years, *"..... a period replete with honour to himself and satisfaction to the corps"*. He was succeeded by Lieutenant Colonel William Maberley from the 96th Foot (later 2nd Manchester).

In 1828 the Regiment was inspected by Sir George Bingham who reported that the Colours of the Regiment, which had been presented by the East India Company in 1808, were no longer fit for service. An application was made for new Colours which, upon arrival, were found to be of the then regulation pattern. Although the new Colours carried the badge of the 'Elephant' and the word 'Hindoostan', the words Ally Ghur, Delhi, Leswaree and Agra were conspicuous by their absence. *"Under these circumstances"*, wrote Lieutenant Colonel Maberley in a letter to the East India Company, *"we find ourselves placed in the distressing alternative of either receiving these new Colours and abandoning the memorial of former good conduct, or of obtruding ourselves on the liberality of your Honourable Company, and petitioning for a renewal of the mark of approbation before conferred on us, as the only method of retaining a distinction to which we always look with pride and satisfaction....."*

The East India Company replied sympathetically and stated the directors would not object to the expense of new Colours, of the old pattern, *provided they are assured of His Majesty's sanction.* Colonel Maberley thereupon wrote to the Adjutant General, requesting that his application be placed before His Majesty for authority for the 76th to receive the Colours. This must have been forthcoming, for on 21 May the Secretary to the Court of Directors of the East India Company wrote:

> *"East India House,*
> *21st May, 1829*
>
> *Sir,*
>
> *Having laid before the Court of Directors of the East India Company your letters of the 5th ultimo and 13th instant .... I am commanded to state in reply that the Court of Directors retain an undiminished sense of the gallant services of the Corps whilst employed in India, and that it will afford them great satisfaction to renew the expression of those sentiments by presenting the 76th Regiment with a new set of Colours according to your request.*
>
> *Instructions have accordingly been given for carrying the Court's intentions into effect.*
> *Colonel. Maberley, M.P.*
> *H.M.'s 76th Regiment."*

After further correspondence the new Colours were made up and forwarded to the Regiment at Dublin, where on 3 July 1830 they were formally handed over by Lieutenant Colonel Maberley on behalf of the East India Company. It is from this date and in this manner that the 76th came to possess two stands of colours.

Soldiering in Ireland seems to have been uneventful for the 76th. However it still maintained high standards. In May 1833 Lord Anglesey, Lord Lieutenant of Ireland, wrote to Lord Melbourne, Home Secretary, telling him that in case of emergency he could spare one cavalry regiment and four infantry battalions. He added his opinion of each of the regiments, including the 76th, *"The 76th – an excellent regiment, – now in Kerry ...It is for early foreign service".*

In January 1834, the 76th left Ireland for the West Indies, disembarking at St. Lucia in the Windward Islands. Lieutenant Colonel Maberley had retired in 1832. In the next seven years the Regiment had six commanding officers. Such a high turnover was not uncommon when service in the West Indies threatened. In 1838 the 76th was sent to Demarara where before long yellow fever took its toll. Lieutenant Colonel G H Dansey (a son of William Dansey, 33rd Regiment.), five other officers, and 102 other ranks, besides eight women and twelve children were carried off. From Demarara the Regiment went to Nova Scotia via Barbados, (where Lieutenant Colonel Joseph Clarke

76th Regiment in Dublin, 1858. The Sergeant Major (four stripes),
the Drum Major (wearing a bearskin) and a group of sergeants.

assumed command) and Bermuda. By October 1842 the Regiment was back in Ireland. In 1843 Lieutenant General Sir Robert Arbuthnot succeeded General Sir Peregrine Maitland as Colonel of the Regiment.

In February 1845 the 76th, then stationed at Manchester, received orders to augment its strength from 873 rank-and-file to 1,200. By the end of March energetic recruiting parties throughout Lancashire had signed up 396 men, bringing the total to 1,296. It also brought a congratulatory letter to Lieutenant Colonel Joseph Clarke from the Adjutant General, passing on the Commander-in-Chief's (Duke of Wellington) *"sense of the extraordinary zeal and activity manifested by Colonel Clarke and the officers and non-commissioned officers ....whereby the number of 400 men had been recruited in an unprecedently short time, and a great benefit had thus been conferred upon the Public Service"*. After being dispersed between Manchester, Stockport and Wigan (with one company in the Isle of Man), in May 1846 the Regiment sailed from Liverpool to Glasgow, and the next two years were spent in sundry stations north of the border from Edinburgh to Aberdeen.

These were troubled times. The Corn Law riots throughout the country saw the troops, scattered about the Kingdom for just such a contingency, called out on that distasteful duty "in aid of the Civil Power". In February 1847 two companies of the 76th under Captain Gordon were summoned to Wick where discontents were attempting to

Christmas Day in the barracks of the 76th, 1858

prevent shipment of grain. On being ordered by the Sheriff to open fire on the mob, they did so. Evidently complying with regulations to employ "minimum force", they only wounded two rioters. Later the Commissioners of Supply and magistrates of the county of Caithness expressed their thanks to Gordon for *"the able, firm and temperate manner in which he had acted under trying circumstances"*. These distasteful duties did not, however, endear the army to the population as a whole and it was not until police forces (first established in London in 1829) took them over that the army's popularity started to improve.

While in Edinburgh, in September 1847 the Regiment underwent a reorganisation when, following orders from the Adjutant-General, it was split into two battalions. Of the existing twelve companies, six, with Colonel Clarke and his RHQ, were to be known as the 1st Battalion, the other six to form a 2nd Battalion under the second lieutenant colonel. But this second battalion had only a very brief existence, and was in fact designated the Reserve Battalion. In March 1848 the whole Regiment was posted to the Island of Corfu where the two battalions were united.

The next thirty one years up to 1881, when the 76th was formally linked with the 33rd Regiment, proved an uneventful period of garrison duties, mostly overseas. During this period the Regiment was stationed in:

| | |
|---|---|
| Malta | (1850-53) |
| Canada | (1853-57) |
| Ireland | (1857-64) |
| India | (1864-68) |
| Burma | (1868-71) |
| India | (1871-76) |
| England | (1876-79) |
| Ireland | (1879-81) |

In August 1857 the Regiment lost its Commanding Officer for seventeen years, Brevet-Colonel Joseph Clarke, who at the age of 64 retired on half-pay. Colonel Clarke had served with the 76th for the remarkable span of 47 years, having joined as ensign in 1810, rising to command in 1839. In 1868, by then a major general, he became Colonel of the Regiment, the only colonel of the 76th to have spent the whole of his service with the Regiment.

There are several remarkable aspects of this period in the history of the 76th Regiment, which lasted for 66 years:

– Although there were one major (the Crimean) and numerous colonial wars, the 76th took no part in any of them. In fact, the record suggests that the only shots fired in anger by the men of the 76th were those few directed at civilians in Wick in 1847.

– Nineteen years were spent in Ireland but only three in England. This despite the fact that for much of the period its chief recruiting areas seem to have been in the south of England.

– The Regiment served in six different countries – in Canada three times and in India twice.

– Two thirds of the period was spent overseas. This was the normal pattern. It was to help solve this particular problem of military service that Cardwell introduced his Localisation Scheme of linked battalions.

The regulation Colours of the 1st Battalion and the Honorary Colours

General Charles Cornwallis, 1st Marquis Cornwallis, KG, Colonel of the 33rd Regiment, 1766-1805
*(By permission of National Portrait Gallery)*

Field Marshal Sir Arthur Wellesley, 1st Duke of Wellington, KG, GCB, GCH
Colonel of the 33rd Regiment, 1806-1812
*(By permission of National Portrait Gallery)*

Waterloo, 18 June 1815
A British square is attacked by French cavalry
*(By permission of the Director, National Army Museum)*

Waterloo, 18 June 1815
The 33rd (or 1st Yorkshire West Riding) Regiment charging the Chasseurs à Pieds

CHAPTER 14

# Amalgamation: The Duke of Wellington's Regiment

In 1874, as a result of a swing in the political pendulum, Edward Cardwell lost his office as Secretary of State for War. The new government did not have army reform high on its agenda but did appoint a committee to enquire into the workings of the Localisation Scheme. In its report this recommended the unlinking of battalions. However, there soon was yet another change of government which resulted in Hugh Childers becoming Secretary of State for War. Not only did he reject the recommendations of the committee but he also decided that the main defect of Cardwell's reforms was that they did not go far enough.

The result was General Order No. 41 of 1 May, 1881, issued by the Duke of Cambridge, Commander-in-Chief. At that date there were 141 separate regiments of the line, each with its almost autonomous individuality and jealously preserved customs, traditions, insignia and dress distinctions. Except for those regiments numbered 1 to 25 which already had two battalions, and the KRRC and Rifle Brigade, each with four, they were to be reorganised – amalgamated – into single territorial regiments, each with two regular battalions and two militia battalions.

General Order 41 (Army Organisation) came into effect from 1 July 1881 and the relevant extracts from it are:

> II **Organisation:** The Infantry of the Line and Militia will in future be organised in Territorial Regiments, each of four battalions for England, Scotland and Wales, and of five battalions for Ireland; the 1st and 2nd of these being Line battalions, and the remainder Militia. These regiments will bear a territorial designation corresponding to the localities with which they are connected; and the words Regimental District will in future be used in place of Sub-District hitherto employed.
>
> VIII **Honours and Distinctions.** All distinctions, mottoes,

badges or devices appearing hitherto in the Army List, or on the Colours, as borne by either of the Line battalions of a Territorial Regiment, will in future be borne by both those battalions. Battalions which have not hitherto borne a special device, will adopt a national badge, as follows:

| | |
|---|---|
| English Regiments | ............ A Rose |
| Scotch Regiments | ............ A Thistle |
| Irish Regiments | ............ A Shamrock |
| Welsh Regiments | ............ A Dragon |

The facings and the Officers' Lace of Territorial Regiments will be the same for all regiments belonging to the same country (Royal and Rifle regiments excepted) and will be as follows:

| | Facings | Pattern of Lace |
|---|---|---|
| English and Welsh Regiments | White | Rose |
| Scotch | Yellow | Thistle |
| Irish | Green | Shamrock |

XIV The accompanying Tables (see appendix) show the precedence, composition, title and uniforms of the new Territorial Regiments.

Extract from the appendix

| Precedence | Title | Composition | Headquarters | Uniform & Facings | Pattern of lace |
|---|---|---|---|---|---|
| 33 | The Halifax Regiment (Duke of Wellington's) | 1st Bn. 33rd Foot<br>2nd Bn. 76th Foot<br>3rd Bn. 1/6th West Yorks Militia<br>4th Bn. 2/6th West Yorks Militia | Halifax | Scarlet White | Rose |

Neither the 33rd nor 76th gave a whole-hearted welcome to these changes: the 33rd resented the subjugation of its "Duke of Wellington's" title to a mere parenthesis, while as far as can be ascertained the Regiment had not been consulted about "The Halifax" designation. As for the 76th, all vestiges of its former existence had disappeared. The rare red facings of both Regiments had also gone, replaced by the obligatory white for an English regiment. All, including the twenty-five unamalgamated regiments, had their numerical titles substituted by a territorial title. The 76th had some of its pride restored when the new collar badges displayed the Elephant device of the "Hindoostan" Regiment.

The "Halifax" title lasted no longer than a couple of months. As a result of representations by those regiments concerned with the unsuitablity of the titles they had been given, a revised Appendix to General Order 41 was issued on 30 June 1881, showing new titles. The Halifax Regiment had now become The Duke of Wellington's (West Riding Regiment). Though commonly called the Dukes, its official abbreviated title was the West Riding Regiment or WRR.[a]

During all this reorganisation the 33rd was remote in Lucknow, and as the 76th was nearer the scene in Ireland, its Commanding Officer, Lieutenant Colonel J M D Allardice, was deputed to represent both Regiments. The story of how he secured the change from "The Halifax Regiment" was later recounted by his widow:

> *"Just before the Territorial names were to be published, the Brigade Major of the Curragh, a cavalry officer who had never been in Yorkshire, came to Colonel Allardice and said: "I do not know how you will like it, but you are going to be called The Halifax Regiment. What have you got to do with Canada?" The brigade major had mistaken the Yorkshire town for the Canadian one! The fact that the Regiment's Territorial title was to be a Yorkshire one had been settled long before, the only difficulty was what its actual title was to be. There was the old nick-name of the 33rd "the Havercake Lads", which connected it with Sowerby Bridge, an outlying village of Halifax at that time, so that the proposed title was, apart from the confusion with the Nova Scotia town, quite a suitable one. Colonel Allardice, who was commanding the 76th Regiment, therefore took leave and went over to England and saw the Duke of Cambridge who was then the Commander-in-Chief, and told him the story of the mistake the brigade major at the Curragh had made.... The Duke was most understanding in the matter and eventually said: "I cannot call you the 'West Yorks', because that has gone to the 14th, and they are an older Regiment. Will you be called the 'West Riding"? It was essentially a Yorkshire title and Colonel Allardice accepted the offer, and so the title which the Regiment has borne since that day was settled".*

Now joined together in military matrimony, the 33rd and 76th (or 1st and 2nd Battalions of the Dukes) accepted their fate in a spirit of co-operation. The Colonels of the two Regiments, General William Hutchinson and General Frederick George, shared the appointment of colonel until 1886 when the latter was appointed Colonel of the Cheshire Regiment.

One of the aims Cardwell had pursued was the creation of a trained reserve which

---

(a) In 1920 the title of the Regiment was changed to The Duke of Wellington's Regiment (West Riding).

he considered vital for the country's needs. In 1883, therefore, an Army Order was issued to the effect that the 4th, 6th and 9th Yorkshire (West Riding) Volunteer Corps would in future be designated 1st, 2nd and 3rd Volunteer Battalions of The Duke of Wellington's Regiment. In 1890 another change in the organisation of the Regiment came about when the 3rd and 4th Militia Battalions were amalgamated to form a single battalion - the 3rd

In 1881 a committee was convened, under General Sir Archibald Alison, to clarify the situation regarding battle honours consequent upon the amalgamation of infantry regiments. It came to the conclusion: *"The names of such victories only should be retained as either in themselves or by their results have left a mark on history which rendered their names familiar, not only to the British Army, but also to every educated gentleman".*

The report threw up some glaring omissions, such as Blenheim, Ramilles, Oudenarde, Malplaquet, Quebec and Dettingen, all of which were notified as battle honours in 1882. In more general terms the committee recommended the principles that only victories should be commemorated and that in order to qualify the headquarters and at least half the regiment must have been present. Since the award of battle honours is an inexact science many anomalies remained, despite the committee's efforts to rationalise.

************************

The Depot rifle team, 1883

In 1882 the 1st Battalion, under the command of Lieutenant Colonel F J Castle, moved north from Lucknow to Nowshera, some 30 miles east of Peshawar in what was then the North-West Frontier Province. While elsewhere on the frontier were the usual clashes with the turbulent Pathan tribesmen, the Battalion's tour was free of incident or casualty. The hill station for Nowshera was at Cherat, an outpost perched on a rugged mountain range nearly 4,000ft above the Peshawar plain, and here the married families took refuge from the fierce hot-weather months. Detachments of two companies, changed every two months, also did tours up here, and in July 1884 Headquarters Company left an abiding memorial of the Regiment's presence. This was (and is) the laboriously carved badge of the 33rd, high on a rock face above the East End Barracks. Later it was joined by the 76th's badge and those of other regiments. In 1984 the badges were reported to be still in good shape, being cared for by the Pakistan Army.

In early 1885 the 1st Battalion, now under command of Lieutenant Colonel W Bally, a veteran of the Crimea, marched some 80 miles down country to Rawalpindi, the "Aldershot" of the Punjab. On 31 March there was a state visit by the newly proclaimed Amir of Afghanistan, Abdur Rahman Khan, who was accompanied by an entourage of 10,000 tribesmen. To impress them with the might of the British Empire the Battalion was ordered to provide a guard of honour of one officer and 100 of the tallest men it had available. The guard paraded with not a single man less than 6 feet in height. The Commander-in-Chief in India, who was present, stated it was the most magnificent body of men he had ever seen. The reason why the Battalion had so many tall men at that time was a reflection of the efforts of the OC Depot at Halifax, Colonel Richard Freer. He had no compunction in enlisting suitable tall men into the Regiment, even if their first choice might have been some other regiment or corps. He was widely known throughout the army in England as *"that damned old body snatcher Freer"*.

There was more ceremonial two years later when at Rawalpindi on 30 November 1887, the Battalion, under command of Lieutenant Colonel D C de Wend, was reviewed by the Viceroy (The Marquess of Duffferin), accompanied by the Commander-in-Chief (Duke of Cambridge). In December 1887, the Battalion was on the march again, to the Mian Mir cantonment at Lahore. On leaving the Rawalpindi command the Battalion was given an autographed portrait of the Duke of Cambridge as a memento of the days when he was learning his military duties with the 33rd at Gibraltar in 1838.

The Indian tour came to an end in November 1888 when the Battalion received a posting to Aden at the tip of Arabia. Before leaving, NCO's and men not time-expired were allowed to transfer to other regiments remaining in India, and a total of 135 did so.

The year's tour of garrison duty in Aden was broken by a visit, in October 1889, by Prince Albert (Prince of Wales), on his way to a tour of India, followed in November by a similar ceremonial when the Duke of Connaught, Commander-in-Chief of the Bombay Army, came ashore to inspect the Battalion. *"H.R.H. expressed himself greatly satisfied with the smart soldierlike appearance of the troops, their steadiness at drill, and turn-out on Guard"*. (Digest of Services).

On 29 November, the Battalion embarked for England. On arrival at Portsmouth it was posted to York. There, on 26 September 1890, it was inspected by the Duke of Cambridge, the Commander-in-Chief. On the conclusion of the inspection he addressed the Battalion:

> *"Colonel de Wend, officers non-commissioned officers and men I have pleasing remembrances of the old 33rd Regiment, than which a better never existed in the old campaigns. I am very glad to see the men turn out so smartly and so well; and they are probably as good as ever they were. The only part about which I regret is that their numerical strength is so small. In 1838 it was the first regiment I had the honour to do duty with in Gibraltar, and I sincerely hope that if it ever falls to my lot to inspect the Battalion again, I shall find it considerably increased in numbers".*

In 1891 the Battalion moved to Bradford with companies detached at Tynemouth and Lichfield. Two years later it moved to Dover from where, commanded by Lieutenant Colonel C Conor, it was sent to Malta in September 1895. The following year command of the Battalion was taken over by Lieutenant Colonel G E Lloyd DSO, who had served with the South Wales Borderers and KOYLI in sundry North-West Frontier campaigns, in the Second Afghan War of 1878 - 1879, and with Kitchener in Egypt and the Sudan. In September 1898 the Battalion left Malta. Bidding the Battalion farewell the local paper gave as its opinion that *"...As an all round smart corps the 1st West Ridings (sic) would be very hard to beat".*

On arrival in England the Battalion was stationed at Dover. While there it was once again inspected by the Duke of Cambridge. He was so impressed with the steadiness of the marching of the troops that he pressed forward on his horse to see better down the ranks and exclaimed: *"They're as good as the Guards – as good as the Guards".* In December 1899 it underwent the annual inspection by Major General L Rundle, GOC South Eastern District, whose report was highly complimentary: *"This is a very fine regiment and will do credit anywhere. They have a great idea of themselves – which is well deserved... They are one of the best behaved battalions I have ever come across, and this I attribute to Colonel Lloyd and the system in the regiment"*

\*\*\*\*\*\*\*\*\*\*\*\*\*\*\*\*\*\*\*\*\*\*\*

In 1885 the 2nd Battalion, which had been stationed in Ireland since 1879, was sent to Aldershot. Both the regulation Colours and the Honorary Colours needed to be replaced. The latter, in particular, were after 56 years service in such a poor state that they could not be unfurled or even uncased, for fear of serious damage. On 1 February 1886, Lieutenant Colonel T T Hodges wrote to the India Office, requesting that the Colours be repaired and thus remain an intact gift from the East India Company. On 30 March the Military Secretary at the India office informed Colonel Hodges that the

The 2nd Battalion at Halifax, Nova Scotia, 1889

Earl of Kimberley *"has much pleasure in acceding to your request.... and availing himself of the opportunity thus afforded of renewing the cordial relations which existed in former times between the Home Government of India and the distinguished Regiment now represented by the battalion under your command"*.

Accordingly, the Colours were despatched to the India Store Department in Lambeth, with the request that original embroidery should be retained as far as possible and mounted on new silk. However, on inspection by the professional restorers it was found that this proved impossible since the embroidery was too far deteriorated. On 19 June Colonel Hodges was emboldened to *"beg a still greater favour, and request that since it is more or less impossible for the Colours now in possession to be well repaired, the Secretary of State for India, as representing the East India Company, should be pleased to recommend that the favour of 1829 should be renewed in 1886 and a new stand presented"*. This request met with success and by 1887 the new Colours were ready for issue, by which time the Battalion was overseas in Bermuda. The Colours were despatched there in July 1887 and taken into use shortly afterwards. On 2 May of the following year there was a ceremonial parade when the new stand of Regulation Colours was presented by the Governor of Bermuda, Lieutenant General T C Gallway.

The Battalion, under command of Lieutenant Colonel E G Fenn, had been posted

*A mounted infantryman of the 2nd Battalion in South Africa, 1893*

to Bermuda in 1886, and dispersed among the islands. This came to an end in September 1888, when there was a move to Halifax in Nova Scotia and another change in commanding officer (Lieutenant Colonel E Nesbit). The Battalion was based in what had become known as Wellington Barracks. After three years in Halifax the Battalion returned to the West Indies, this time to Barbados. In 1893 it was posted to South Africa, going into camp at Wynberg, near Cape Town.(b)

In that year the Matabele tribes of what became Southern Rhodesia were in revolt against the British South Africa Company, and a force of Bechuanaland Border Police, stiffened by British troops, was sent to subdue them. The troops comprised two officers and 50 men of the Dukes and a similar detachment of The Black Watch, together with a troop of the Cape Mounted Rifles. The combined Dukes and Highlanders contingent formed another mounted infantry troop, horsed and equipped by the Chartered Company.

By the time the mounted infantry had reached Matabeleland, the main body of police had defeated the rebel chieftain and the back of the rebellion was broken. Thus neither Dukes nor Black Watch saw any fighting, but were employed on extensive patrols to round up cattle, search kraals for dissidents, and escort prisoners. How both battalions managed to find 50 horsemen each at such short notice is not revealed, but this was certainly the first time that men of the West Riding Regiment found themselves in the saddle on active service. It was also the first time that the men of the 76th/2nd Battalion had seen any form of active service since 1812.

In September 1894 the Battalion, under Lieutenant Colonel C W Gore,(c) was posted up country to Pietermaritzburg, the capital of Natal. Here it was rejoined by B Company under Major P T Rivett-Carnac, who had been on the island of St. Helena since the Battalion left Barbados.

There was pressure in the Transvaal from the British and European immigrants (Uitlanders) for the granting of citizen rights which Krüger, the President of the Transvaal, resisted. Late in 1895, taking advantage of the troubled situation in the

---

(b) It is said that Wynberg was selected as the site for a military camp by Colonel Arthur Wesley during the 33rd's short stay there in 1796, while en route to India.
(c) Yet another member of the family which had provided officers to the Regiment since 1707. He joined the 76th in 1869. He was the last of the family to serve in the Regiment.

Lieutenant Colonel C W Gore, 2nd Battalion, and a Colour party in uniforms worn during the period of white facings, 1881-1905.

north, the British South Africa Company's representative in Rhodesia, Dr Leander Starr Jameson, had carried out a raid into Boer territory in an attempt to oust Paul Krüger's government. This "Jameson Raid" (which precipitated the Boer War) ended in abject failure, with Jameson captured, handed over to the British, and sent for trial in London. On 16 March 1896, the Digest of Services recorded :

> " *A party of 100 NCO's and men under Major Rivett-Carnac ....proceeded to Charlestown on 14 January 1896, to take over Doctor Jameson's prisoners from the representatives of The South African Republic. Major Carnac, Lieut Smith and 45 men returned on the 16th, the remainder remained behind and conducted the prisoners to Durban and embarked the officers and Dr Jameson on the hired transport S.S. "Victoria..."*

In June 1896 the natives of Mashonaland rebelled, and, operating over a large area, murdered more than 120 white settlers. In response to a telegram sent by the British South Africa Company, a force of mounted infantry was sent to Salisbury. They were reinforced by about 100 men of the York and Lancaster Regiment and 13 officers and 320 other ranks of the Dukes. The latter were formed into one mounted infantry company and two rifle companies. It was difficult country of bush and scrub-covered kopjes or low hills, which afforded excellent cover and hideouts for the Mashona tribesmen.  These never risked a confrontation in force, and the operations were essentially a campaign of attrition, denying the enemy life support by capturing his herds and grain stores, destroying kraals, and generally harassing him by constant patrolling. Then the force took the kraal of the biggest chief in Mashonaland by surprise and captured it, inflicting some 200 casualties for the loss of three killed and four wounded. By the end of November, after considerable manoeuvering around the countryside, the rebel chieftain was dead and his people scattered. One month later the Mashonaland Field Force was broken up. The total casualties were 7 killed and 18 wounded. Despite the fact that more than half the Battalion was engaged in this bush warfare there are few details of its activities. The only known casualties were Captain F H A Swanson, who succumbed to fever, and Lieutenant N Fraser who was wounded.

The British South Africa Company was given permission to issue a medal to all those who had taken part in the campaigns in Matabeleland in 1893 and Mashonaland in 1896. The medal was the first issued by a private company since the days of the East India Company. In addition Lieutenant Norman Fraser received a DSO *"for conspicuous gallantry when wounded in the Matoppo Hills"* and Major Rivett-Carnac was granted a

2nd Battalion Rugby XV, Maritzburgh, 1895

brevet lieutenant-colonelcy.

During the 1890s there were two changes in the appointment of Colonel of the Regiment. General George Erskine, who served with the 33rd in the Crimea, was Colonel from 1895 to 1897. He was succeeded by General Sir Hugh Rowlands who had also fought in the Crimea, where he was awarded the VC while serving with the 41st Regiment (Welch).

In July 1897 command of the Battalion was assumed by Lieutenant Colonel H E Belfield of the Royal Munster Fusiliers. In September a detached company at Eshow, Zululand, rejoined the Battalion at Pietermaritzburg – *"the whole Regiment being now together for the first time since it left England in 1886"* (Digest). Three months later the Battalion embarked at Durban and sailed to India. After two years in Bangalore it was sent to Rangoon, arriving on 17 October 1899. Following the outbreak of the Boer war Lieutenant Colonel Belfield was promoted colonel and appointed to Headquarters at the Cape. He was succeeded by Lieutenant Colonel S J Trench.

***********************

This period saw the last appearance of the time-honoured red coat on the battlefield. It is usually claimed that this distinction belonged to the 19th (Green Howards) 49th (Royal Berkshire) and 50th (Royal West Kent), who wore their red serge tunics at the battle of Ginnis in the Sudan, in December 1885. Another claimant for this distinction is 1st Royal Scots, who it is stated, wore "colonial type red serge" during operations in Zululand in 1888.

By this date khaki drill had been officially introduced for wear in India, but the red coat was still worn for ceromonial parades, as it was at home. Since 1881 there had been attempts to introduce a more practical service dress than the traditional red, In 1884 the 1st Dorsetshire Regiment at Aldershot was issued with a grey tweed tunic resembling the then fashionable Norfolk jacket, and baggy ankle length trousers. This did not catch on, either with the Regiment or with military society. A local newspaper likened the Battalion to *"a gathering of gamekeepers rather than the Queen's soldiers"*.

It was not until 1899 that the British Army finally abandoned its red coats for khaki service dress. The Boer War became the first "all khaki" campaign. The first issues were of tropical khaki drill, but a year later a similar serge dress was issued for winter wear. Army Order No. 10 of 1902 marked the final demise of the red coat for active service. Entitled *"Introduction of a Service Dress (Regular Forces and Militia)"* it decreed that while a full or ceremonial uniform would be retained for ceremonial, the universal service dress would be worn at home and abroad for all other purposes.

The War Office, and others, had also been debating the problem of how best the infantryman was to carry his load upon his back. In 1871 a completely new pattern of equipment had been issued. This was known as the valise equipment, the valise itself (or pack as it was later known) being slung low down across the man's buttocks, where it bounced up and down at the double. On top of it was strapped the mess tin, and above that the folded greatcoat. To get at his mess tin the soldier had to dismantle the whole edifice. During the next decade various modifications were introduced (the valise was moved a little higher up the back), until in 1888 yet another new pattern gained approval (by the War Office, if not by the soldier). Named after the two infantry colonels, who had devised it, the Slade-Wallace equipment did little credit to them, for it was scarcely an improvement on its predecessors. The valise of stiff black leather was now perched high across the man's shoulders, rendering the whole set top-heavy, while the folded greatcoat was strapped to the back of his waist. But despite much criticism, this pattern remained in use until after the Boer War. In Field Service Marching Order the equipment included (besides the valise) haversack, water-bottle, mess tin and two ammunition pouches. In the valise were packed: emergency ration, grease pot, towel and soap, clothes brush, cap comforter, spare shirt, spare trousers, spare drawers, spare socks, holdall complete, pocket notebook, spare boot-laces. With his rifle, bayonet, entrenching tool and ninety rounds of ammunition, the total load was between 45 and 50lb. In Battle Order, however, the valise was discarded.

If the soldier's equipment left much to be desired, there was a significant improvement in his weapon. After much experiment, the Lee-Metford rifle replaced the Martini-Henry in 1888. This was the first bolt-action magazine rifle, and the first with the calibre of .303in. As always, there was delay between acceptance and complete issue, and the Duke of Wellington's Digests of Services show that the 1st Battalion did not receive its until 1892, while the 2nd Battalion's was even later, in 1894. The following year saw minor modifications, including a ten-round magazine in place of the eight-round, and as the weapon was now manufactured at the government small arms factory in Enfield, it was renamed the Lee-Enfield. With it the trained soldier could fire off fifteen aimed rounds per minute.

An even more potent addition to the infantry's firepower emerged in 1891 with the introduction of the Maxim automatic machine gun. Since the 1880's the British Army had been armed with a variety of machine guns, such as the Gatling and the Nordenfelt, but these multi-barrelled and cumbersome contrivances had to be cranked by hand, and were thus not really automatic nor very reliable in service. Put simply, the American-born Hiram Maxim's invention utilized the kinetic energy of the recoil to eject the spent case, reload and fire again, all by maintaining pressure on the firing thumb-piece. This was the first truly automatic machine gun, and with its unprecedented rate of fire of 600 rounds per minute it so impressed the die-hard old Duke of Cambridge (C-in-C since 1856) that he willingly agreed to its adoption by the army. Thus around 1898-1899 each infantry battalion was armed with two Maxim guns, which, horse-drawn on wheeled carriages with limbers, were more resemblant of miniature field guns. There is no record of when the Dukes' battalions received these weapons.[d]

The Sam Browne Belt is one of the distinguishing features of the British (and other) officer's service dress, with its single shoulder strap over the right shoulder. General Sir Sam Browne, who won a VC and lost an arm in the Indian Mutiny, devised this belt in 1850 to balance the weight of the sword on the left and the pistol on the right. Thus the

---

(d) Maxim's gun company was taken over by Vickers-Armstrong Company, and the weapon became the more familiar Vickers Machine Gun, which remained in service until 1963.

original Sam Browne had two shoulder straps. This was approved for officers of all arms in 1899 and is described and illustrated in the *Dress Regulations* of 1900. It was only during the First World War, when officers finally discarded their useless swords, that the second shoulder strap became superfluous.

In 1794 the private soldier's daily rate of pay was raised from 8d to 1s(5p), before stoppages. One hundred years later this was increased by just two pence to 1s 2d(6p). Out of this sum there were stoppages for such items as tailors' and bootmakers' bills, laundry, hair cutting, repairs to dress and accoutrements, and that age-old penalty "barrack damages". However, the Royal Pay Warrant of 1893 directed that after all stoppages had been deducted *"a residue of at least 1d a day shall be left to the soldier"*. A corporal received 1s 8d (9p) a day, a sergeant 2s 4d (12p) and the RSM 5s (25p). When examined in the light of relative monetary values, these rates were not ungenerous. It has been calculated that in 1899 the average *weekly* wage of an unskilled labourer in London was 29s 2d (146p). Nearly half the working class families in York were existing on a total income of 30s (150p) or less per week. Out of these sums a man had to meet his entire living costs, including any medical expenses, while unlike the soldier, he had no guarantee of regular employment or job security. The great majority of soldiers was drawn from the unskilled labouring classes, and with all living expenses found (including free medical attention), permanent employment and prospect of promotion up to warrant officer (or even lieutenant-quartermaster), they were indisputably better off than their civilian counterparts.

The practice of buying and selling officers' commissions had been abolished in 1871, but twenty-odd years later there was no change in their class structure. Except for the very rare officer promoted from the ranks, most were from the public school class, with moneyed parents. In 1891 statistics from the Royal Military College Sandhurst showed that out of 373 officer cadets, 237 had entered from leading public schools: 34 came from universities, and the remainder from *"Private Schools and Tutors"*. Wellington College, long associated with The Duke of Wellington's Regiment, exceeded all the other public schools with 37 entries (Eton followed with 29, while Harrow lagged behind with 16).

Personal (or parents') means were still essential for any young gentleman aspiring to become an officer. On being commissioned second lieutenant from Sandhurst, the infantry subaltern received 5s 3d (26p) a day. He found he had to pay for all his numerous orders of dress (including full dress and mess kit), his Wilkinson sword, his revolver, his mess bills, the obligatory band subscription, and other contingencies. Obviously, all this was impossible on his pay. If he survived three years as a "one-pipper" and was favourably reported on by his commanding officer, he could receive his second pip as full lieutenant with a pay rise to 6s 6d ($32^1/_2$p). Climbing up the promotion ladder (with examination passes), his successive rates (in 1893) were thus: captain, 11s 7d (56p); major, 13s 7d (68p); lieutenant colonel, 18s (90p). After that, pay rates were regulated by staff appointments as well as rank. As brigadier-general commanding an infantry brigade he could expect £1,500 a year; as major-general of a division, £1,700. In the unlikely event of his achieving the supreme appointment of Commander-in-Chief, he could enjoy a salary of £4,500 a year, plus expenses and other fringe benefits.

CHAPTER 15

# The Boer War

*1900 Relief of Kimberley, Paardeberg, Rhenoster Kop*
*1908 Formation of Territorial Force*

Following the discovery of gold in the Transvaal in 1886, the great influx of foreigners, mainly British, had so threatened Boer supremacy that the Republic's President, Paul Krüger, wary of British intentions, had determined to curb the influence of these "Uitlanders" (foreigners) by denying them the vote and other rights, despite the fact that they paid most of the taxes. The ill-fated Jameson raid in 1896 did nothing to improve relations between the Boers and the "Uitlanders". Having secured an alliance with the sister Boer Republic of the Orange Free State, Krüger began to build up his military strength.

In June 1899 the British High Commissioner in South Africa met Krüger in a last attempt to obtain some representation for the Uitlanders, but without success. Because of the deteriorating situation the British Government decided to reinforce the weak British garrison in South Africa. This was the pretext for which Krüger had been waiting. On 9 October 1899 he issued an ultimatum demanding the withdrawal of all British troops from the frontiers, the evacuation of all British troops landed since 1 June 1899, and the immediate recall of all reinforcements on the high seas. Hostilities began on 11 October when the ultimatum expired.

The Boers had evolved a system of warfare admirably suited to the South African conditions. It was based on the principle of inflicting as much loss as possible on opponents while running as little risk as possible of suffering retaliation. The fact that practically all of them were mounted on the hardy ponies they had ridden since boyhood meant that they could move around quickly in attack or retreat.

The British, for their part, were quite unprepared for the war they were about to undertake. For half a century Britain had fought small wars against ill-armed tribesmen. To transport and supply his men in desert or jungle was the chief problem of a British general. The British soldiers were seldom as good marksmen as the Boers, nor were they as skilled at fieldcraft. Most important of all, they had vastly fewer mounted men. Field days in which the troops were formed into four waves, firing volleys by numbers, were hardly ideal preparation for coming events. In all the circumstances it is not surprising

# THE BOER WAR

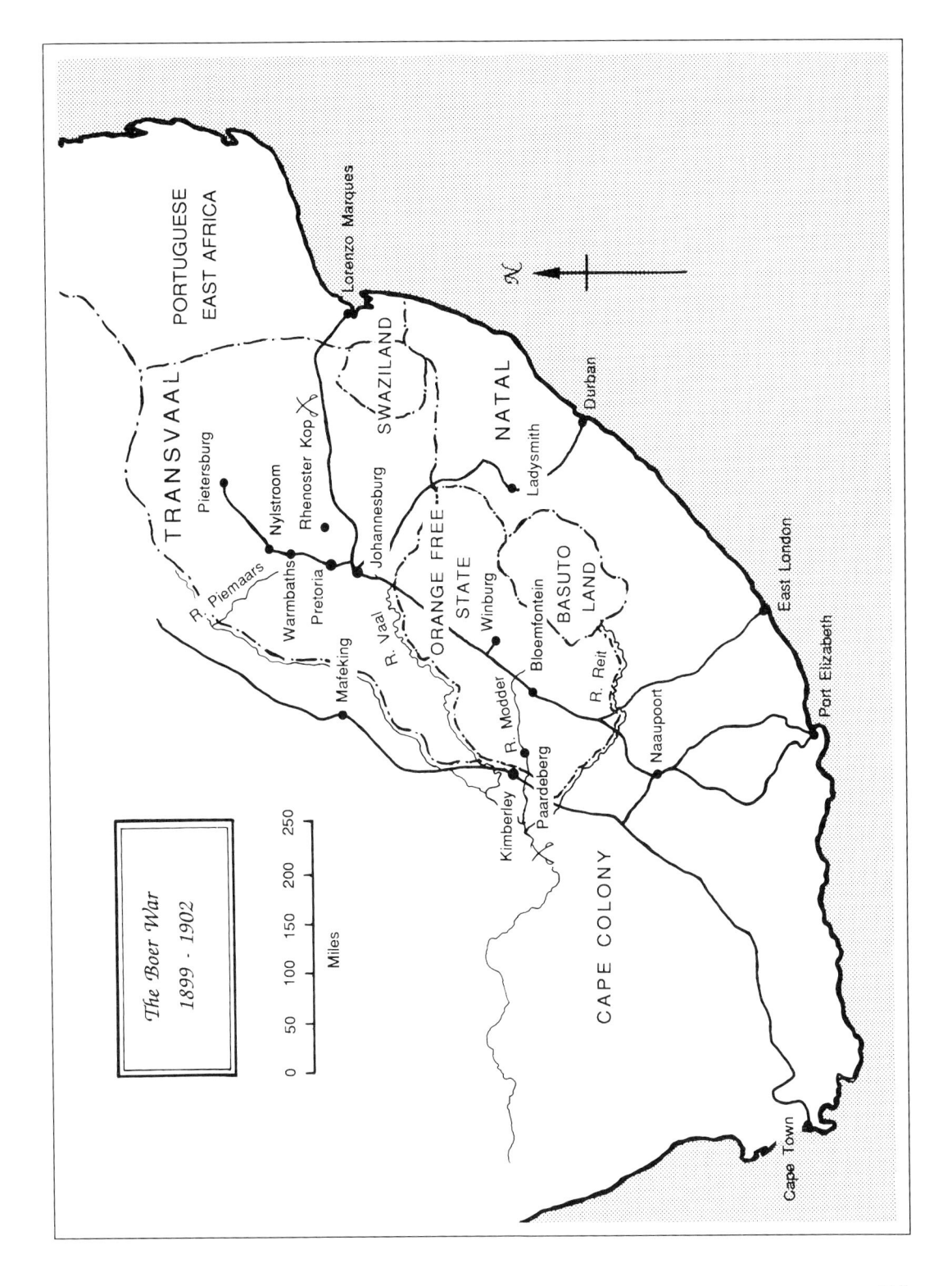

that they suffered a series of humiliating defeats in the opening months of the war and particularly in their attempts to relieve Kimberley and Ladysmith, both besieged by the Boers, and to drive the Boers from Cape Colony. All three defeats occurred during the period 9 - 15 December, which became known as "Black Week".

The events of Black Week awoke Britain to the fact that she was faced with a major war in South Africa. The Government reacted by appointing Lord Roberts Commander-in-Chief, with Kitchener his Chief of Staff, the militia was embodied and thousands of yeomanry and volunteers offered their services overseas. Among the regular units destined for South Africa as reinforcements was the 1st Battalion of The Duke of Wellington's (or West Riding Regiment), then stationed at Aldershot. On 2 December Colonel Lloyd received orders to mobilise. Mustering 1,013 all ranks, the Battalion embarked on the 29th and arrived at Cape Town on 20 January 1900 from where it was routed by train some 400 miles north to Naaupoort. There it joined 13 Brigade (Major General C E Knox) (a) of 6th Infantry Division under Lieutenant General T Kelly-Kenny.

In January 1900 the 3rd (Militia) Battalion of the Dukes had been embodied as part of the plan to relieve the regular units that had been sent to South Africa. It went to Ireland, but having volunteered for service abroad was posted to South Africa where it arrived on 24 March. The Battalion under command of Lieutenant Colonel A K Wylie and with a strength of 27 officers and 488 other ranks, was then employed in Cape Colony, mainly guarding Boer prisoners of war.

On 2 February 6 Division moved forward to the Modder river. When it arrived the hills to the north, occupied by Boers under Piet Cronje, were being shelled. However this activity ceased on the 4th – as it was a Sunday.(b) By the 9th the whole of Roberts' force, amounting to 37,000 men, organised into one cavalry and four infantry divisions and a brigade of mounted infantry, had been secretly assembled at the Modder River.

To reduce his dependence on the railway system for his supplies, Roberts had set Kitchener to organise a vast supply train based on animal transport. He had also taken a leaf out of the Boer book by building up his mounted infantry. As early as December 1899 certain infantry battalions had been ordered to raise companies of mounted infantry. Accordingly, while still at Aldershot, the 1st Battalion of the Dukes formed a company of 137 all ranks under Captain A F Wallis, which joined companies from the Buffs, Gloucesters and Oxford Light Infantry, to become 1 Mounted Infantry Battalion commanded by Major Everleigh of the latter Regiment. Even regiments serving in the east were called upon. In January 1900 the 2nd Battalion of the Dukes, at Rangoon, sent a company of five officers and 103 other ranks, under Captain J A C Gibbs, to join what was known as the Burma Mounted Infantry Regiment, drawn from the four infantry battalions then stationed in that country.(c)

Roberts planned to postpone the relief of Kimberley, besieged by Cronje, until after the capture of Bloemfontein, the capital of the Orange Free State. However, imperious demands from Cecil Rhodes for the prior relief of Kimberley, where he was located,

---

(a) Also in 13 Brigade were: 2nd Buffs, 2nd Gloucesters and 1st Oxford LI.
(b) Not for nothing was the war named *"The last of the gentlemen's wars"*.
(c) The other battalions were: 2nd Staffs, 2nd Essex and 2nd DLI.

**Relief of Kimberley
15 February 1900**

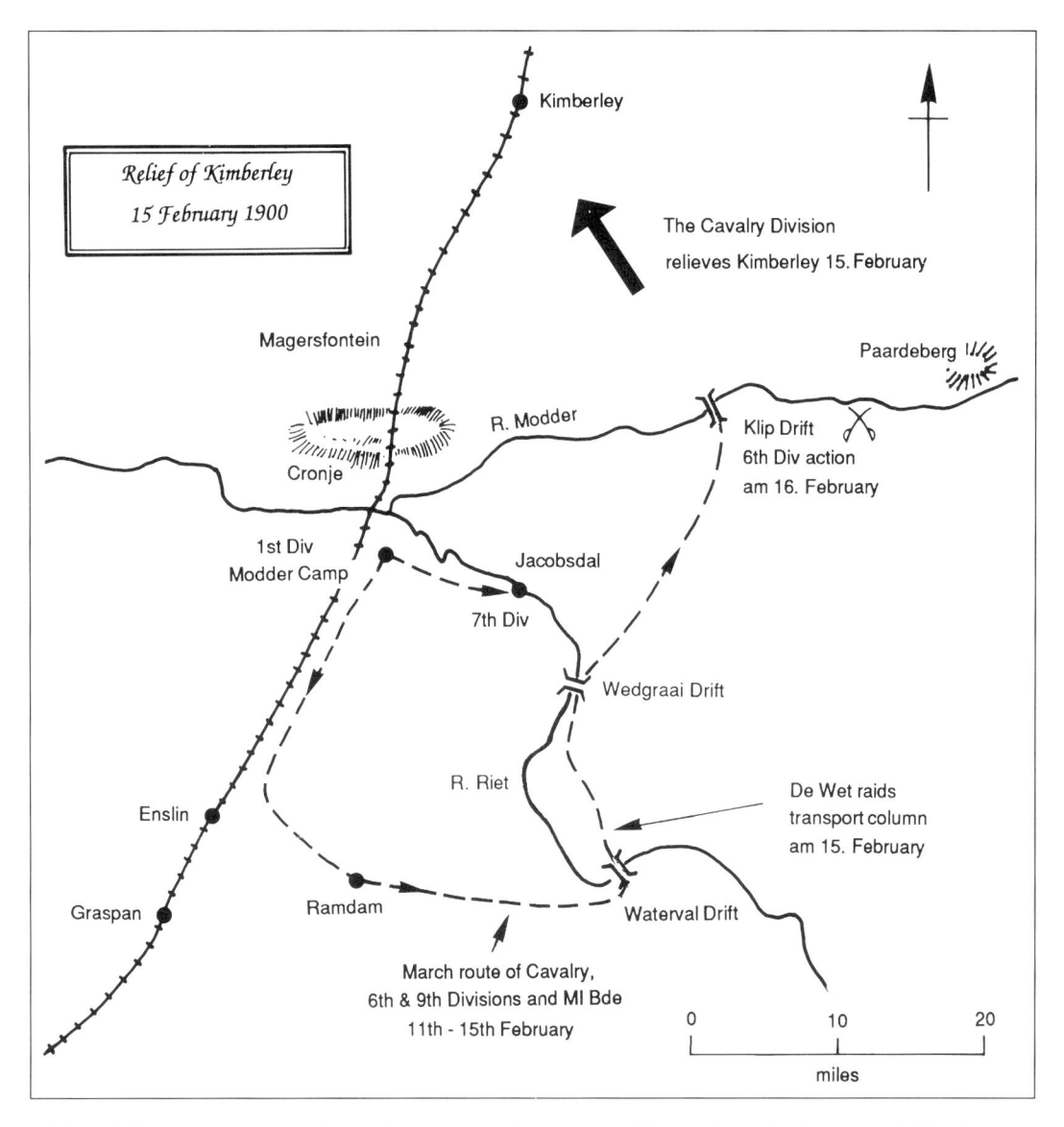

*Map showing the Relief of Kimberley, 15 February 1900, with locations including Kimberley, Magersfontein, Paardeberg, Klip Drift, Modder Camp, Jacobsdal, Wedgraai Drift, Waterval Drift, Ramdam, Enslin, and Graspan, and the march route of the Cavalry, 6th & 9th Divisions and MI Bde from 11th–15th February.*

obliged Roberts to alter his plan to an advance on Bloemfontein by way of Kimberley. This began on 11 February. Leaving two infantry divisions to watch Cronje, Roberts despatched the cavalry division under Lieutenant General French on a wide flanking march with orders to relieve Kimberley at all costs, while the 6th and 9th Divisions followed in his wake. French advanced with great speed and entered Kimberley on the 15th by which date the 6th Division had reached Klip Drift on the Modder River. This otherwise successful advance was only marred by a Boer commando under de Wet which destroyed a large part of the supply column. As a result the force had to be placed on reduced rations.

By now Cronje realised he was being outflanked and began to withdraw along the line of the Modder River towards Bloemfontein. The GOC 6 Division decided to attack him as his force crossed the divisional front, the task being given to 13 Brigade. The initial attack, on the morning of the 16th was made by the Buffs and Oxford LI. Later in the day they were joined by the Dukes and the Gloucesters who drove the Boers from two kopjes. However, the Boers had achieved their purpose in protecting Cronje's flank as he continued to move eastwards. This action brought the first battle casualties for the Dukes: one NCO was killed, two officers and 27 other ranks were wounded. It also brought the Regiment the battle honour **Relief of Kimberley**.

The quarry was now Piet Cronje's army. It was his intention to cross the Modder by Vendutie Drift and join up with De Wet. He might have done had he been prepared to sacrifice his wagons, but they were the private property of the Boers who accompanied him. By 17 February Cronje with some 5,000 men had reached the Modder just east of Paardeberg, and realising that he would have to do battle, took up a strong position on the bluffs overlooking the river, where his men dug themselves in. At this critical juncture Lord Roberts was laid low by a severe bout of fever and temporarily vested command in Major General Kitchener, his Chief of Staff. This was an unhappy development: not only was Kitchener junior to the divisional commanders, who were lieutenant generals, but his overbearing, arrogant manner made him less than popular

The 1st Battalion crossing Modder river, February 1900

Officers at the Modder river

with superior and subordinate alike: increasingly he had been behaving as though he were the Commander-in-Chief himself. Furthermore, he had no body of staff to issue plans and orders, while those orders he issued verbally were uttered in an excitable manner, and were often contradictory.

By nightfall on the 17th the main British force had reached a position on the south bank of the Modder, almost opposite Cronje's defences at Vendutie Drift. The 6th Division, with 1 DWR, had marched all day from Klip Drift, while the 9th Division had covered more than thirty miles in twenty-four hours. General Kelly-Kenny, senior commander on the spot, was averse to committing the troops to an all-out costly attack on Cronje's formidable position, but favoured an investment, starving and shelling him into submission. In this he was supported by the GOC 9th Division. But such a low-key form of offensive did not suit the aggressive Kitchener, who (junior or no) demanded an immediate assault. In theory, his plan was simple: Kelly-Kenny's 13th Brigade was to put in a frontal attack across the river at Vendutie Drift; the two brigades of 9th Division were to storm across upstream, and the 18th Brigade (6th Division) was to attack downstream, or from the east. Kitchener also demanded that General French's cavalry should gallop in from the north, but both men and horses had become so done up after their exertions around Kimberley that they were relegated to a long-stop role of

*Battle of Paardeberg 18 - 27 February 1900*

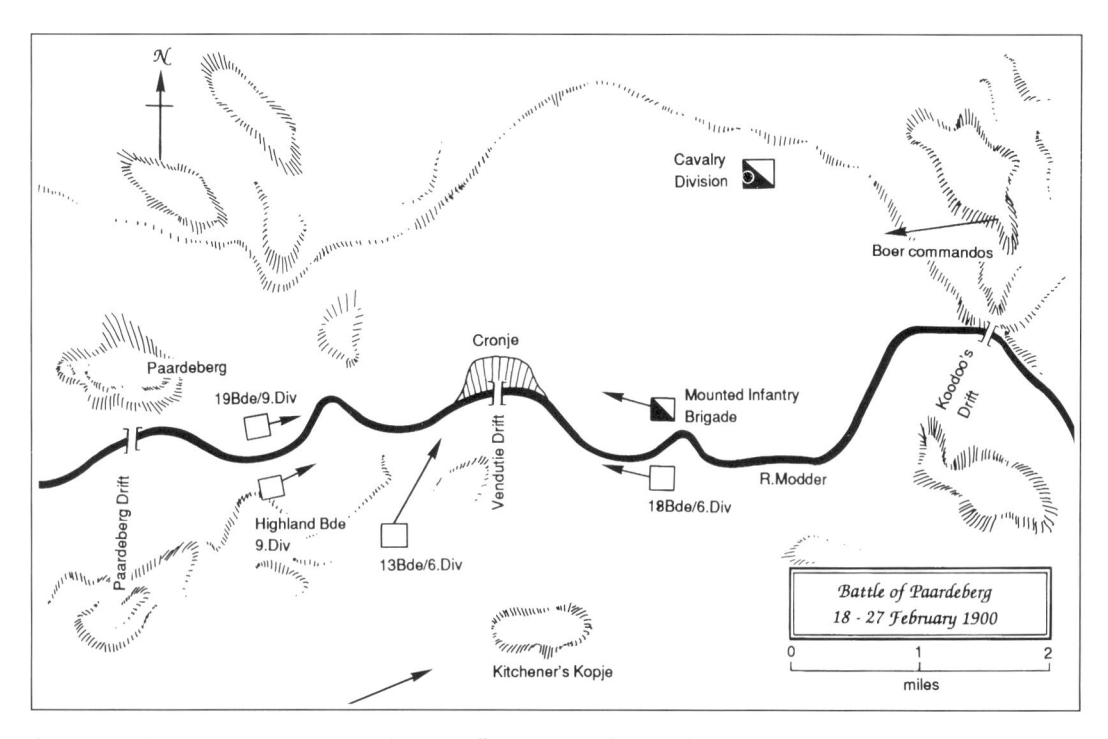

intercepting anyone attempting to flee from Cronje's position. With such a three-pronged master-plan, Kitchener was confident of victory. Perhaps if he had not been Kitchener (or "K of chaos" as he was dubbed by some), the plan might have succeeded. The attack was launched without any detailed briefings of senior officers. He did not even meet the two divisional commanders beforehand and with subsequent conflicting orders the operations became confused and uncoordinated. General Smith-Dorrien, leading the 19th Brigade on the left of the 6th Division, was merely told to get his men across the river as best he could: *"I could get neither detailed instructions nor information from anyone"*.

The 13th Brigade advanced about 8am, first crossing nearly two miles of open ground before approaching the river. A vivid account of the events that followed has been given by Second Lieutenant (later Lieutenant Colonel) M V Le P Trench,

> *"Soon after the advance began my skipper Major de Gex (O.C G - Company) was wounded ....I was now left in command of the Company, a 2/Lieutenant with under three months' service. We moved forward by short rushes, keeping as far as possible the correct distance from the two companies in front of us.... There was nothing to be seen of the enemy, as they were hidden by the trees lining the banks of the Modder River which ran across our front. On the far side one could see the wagons of Cronje's laager with our lyddite shells bursting among*

*them sending up clouds of yellow and greenish smoke. A constant stream of bullets with occasional pom-pom shells* (d) *was coming from the river and casualties were occurring pretty frequently, [the Gloucesters and East Kents on the right flank suffered heavily and were pinned down, but 1 DWR and Oxford L.I. kept going] It was a most trying time as we were unable to return the enemy's fire with our own troops in front of us. A hot sun beat on our backs and we had burning sand to lie on with no cover whatever. We had had no breakfast or proper rest, and had a raging thirst with no water in our bottles.*

*As we were nearing the river I with some of the Company got to some rocks which appeared to give some cover, but it was a death trap as the Boers had concentrated their fire on such an obvious landmark. The bullets seemed to be coming from all directions, hitting the rocks and making such a din that I was first dazed by it and did not notice that our front line had disappeared. As soon as I realised that they had reached the trees, I made a dash across with as many men as I could signal to. That was a terrifying few minutes, as in addition to the rifle fire, shrapnel began bursting between us and the trees, ploughing up the sand like a hailstorm* [This was from French's Horse Artillery, overshooting their target from north of Cronje's position].... *On getting to the bank, after filling our bottles, I came upon the Colonel and Tyndall (the Adjutant.) and a number of officers and men of various regiments. The Colonel told me to collect as many of our men as I could and, leading us, he worked along the river bank to see if there was any place we could cross, but with the Boers hidden on the opposite bank it was impossible. Many men going down to drink were now getting hit and the Colonel had to stop more going*(e). *Capt. Greenwood was hit in this way and, we discovered later, lay near the water's edge all day.... The Colonel assembled us in a pit which had apparently been occupied by the Boers previously. There we had to sit under cover from sniping.... Then a new trouble began as some regiment began to advance over the ground we had come by and were firing almost into us, so that we were caught between two fires. Col. Lloyd got up and waved his flag and also his helmet and rifle, but it had no effect. A highlander volunteered to go out and stop them, but he never came back and must have been hit. So the Colonel and Tyndall went out and eventually got in touch with them. Col. Lloyd bore a charmed life, his 6ft 2ins or more made him a good target, but he continually walked about calmly in the open throughout and was never hit.*

*When darkness came on the firing ceased and we went out to collect*

---

(d) The pom-pom, so called because of the pumping noise it made when fired, was a Vickers-Maxim automatic gun firing 1lb shells at 300 per minute.
(e) According to Corporal Major, ".. we knew the enemy would have to be removed before we could obtain water, which we were mad to get and therefore the men became reckless and literally threw away their lives".

*the wounded and carry them to our pit where Anderson the MO [Capt. RAMC] attended to them. Poor Siordet [Lieutenant F J Siordet] was brought in shot through the stomach in great pain, continually asking for water. His Colour/Sgt. Throupe and I sat with him for some time and did what little we could, but he died in the early hours of the morning. I fell asleep from fatigue very early on and missed a small ration of bully beef and biscuits which had been sent down to us. We had had nothing to eat since 4pm the day before....*

*Before light next morning, Monday, February 19, we started to entrench with a few shovels that had been collected. There was very little firing, and soon that ceased altogether and an order came for us to retire to our previous position.... a party being left to bury the dead and carry the wounded. We were not fired on at all going back; the reason we discovered later was that Cronje was asking for an armistice to bury his dead."*

The other attacks Kitchener had ordered proved to be no more successful than that of 13 Brigade so that by the evening the fighting ended with no advantage gained. However, Kitchener remained optimistic and reported to Roberts that he hoped for something more definite on the following day.

Among the bitter wrangles between Kitchener and Kelly-Kenny had been the matter of how to defend the kopje immediately to the south of the Modder river – "Kitchener's kopje". It was on this vital kopje, stripped of troops on Kitchener's orders, that de Wet with 500 commandos launched an attack shortly before sunset. The handful of irregulars who had been left to defend the kopje surrendered with hardly a fight.

By Monday 19 February, Lord Roberts had recovered sufficiently to reassume command from Kitchener. The British casualties had been heavy and despite reinforcement by General Tucker's 7th Division and Kitchener's taunts, the other two divisional commanders were firmly opposed to another attack. Although the artillery bombardment continued, by Wednesday Roberts was seriously considering a withdrawal. Fortunately he did not have to make the decision. For three days Kitchener had been trying to sweep de Wet off the kopje. Then de Wet, realising that there was no hope of linking up with Cronje, abandoned it. Cronje was now completely penned in, and with continual artillery bombardment, dwindling rations and ammunition and mounting casualties, the end seemed inevitable.

On 23 February the Dukes were sent across the river to dig entrenchments, in case Cronje should make a desperate effort to break out. At first light on the 27th Captain Edward Houghton was in charge of a working party when *"..... a corporal came to me and said that a white flag was flying from the corner of the laager nearest the river and also on the inland corner.... All firing ceased and I sent a message to Col. Lloyd saying that white flags were flying from the Boer laager. He and other officers went forward to the laager and many of the Boers came out to meet them".*

After enduring nine days of investment, Piet Cronje had surrendered and the battle of Paardeberg was over.  Although none of Kitchener's aggressive plans had been carried to fruition, this was the first major setback for the Boers who lost 4,250 men, the great majority being prisoners, while the capture of General Cronje himself was a severe blow to their morale.  British casualties amounted to 300 all ranks killed and some 900 wounded – nearly all during the first day's attacks.  The 1st Battalion had Lieutenant F J Siordet and 22 other ranks killed, and Captain F J de Gex and H D E Greenwood and 104 other ranks wounded, the heaviest casualties of any battalion engaged.  **Paardeberg** was later awarded as a battle honour.

While 1 DWR had been engaged at Paardeberg, its Mounted Infantry Company saw a brisk little action near Arundel in Cape Colony.  On 24 February the company was making a reconnaissance towards a Boer outpost named Plowman's Farm when it came under heavy fire from some 500 commandos.  Lance Corporal Blackman fell wounded and lay exposed within 400 yards of the enemy.  Heedless of Mauser bullets kicking up dust all round, Sergeant James Firth immediately dismounted and, running forward, carried Blackman to safety.  Later in the day Second Lieutenant J H B Wilson was likewise wounded in open ground, and once more Sergeant Firth braved hot fire to bring him in.  On this occasion Firth did not escape unscathed, being shot through nose and eye.  He was awarded the Victoria Cross for his bravery, the first to be gained by the Regiment since the Abyssinia campaign thirty-two years earlier.  During the Plowman's Farm action the commander of the Mounted Infantry Company, Captain Wallis, was killed, while Second Lieutenant Wilson and eleven other ranks (including Sergeant Firth) were wounded.

Lord Roberts could now press on for the capture of Bloemfontein.  The advance began on 7 March, when French's cavalry bumped the Boers at Poplar Grove and narrowly missed capturing President Krüger himself.  Three days later there was a more serious clash around Driefontein, some 40 miles from Bloemfontein.  The enemy, 6,000 strong under De la Rey and De Wet, was entrenched on a cluster of kopjes, well supported by artillery and pom-poms.  The Buffs, Gloucesters, Essex and Welch were committed to a bold frontal attack on the main kopje, where, after losing heavily, they drove off the Boers at bayonet point.  The Dukes had been employed as escort to the baggage convoy and, as the Digest of Services recorded, only *"F and G Companies were slightly engaged, but there were no casualties in the Battalion".*

With the Boers' reverse at Driefontein, the way was finally open for the advance to Bloemfontein. So low had enemy morale become after its two successive defeats that no opposition was encountered, while the city itself was evacuated on 13 March. Thus on the following day Lord Roberts achieved his goal by entering the capital of the Orange Free State without firing a shot.

For the Dukes and their 13th Brigade comrades the approach march and formal entry were scarcely the triumphal progress that might have been expected.

*"The 7th and 9th Divisions moved off during the morning [March 13th] and we were supposed to be starting at 3pm. but after several*

*changes of orders we eventually got off at 11.45pm. acting as escort to the last portion of the immense convoy which covered about seven miles. Our own transport had gone on ahead, so we had no blankets or greatcoats and as dusk came on it started to rain.... It was a nightmarish night, pitch dark, pouring with rain, and we were strung out in single file alongside the wagons, stumbling into holes or tripping over ant-heaps. After about eight miles of this we were halted and lay down in pools of water so dog-tired that, though drenched to the skin in our thin khaki drill and very cold, we slept on till roused at daylight.*

*Very soon the sun rose and we began to dry out.... About four miles further on we reached Bran Dam Kop, where the rest of the Brigade was assembled, and just as the cooks had started fires to get us some breakfast we had orders to move on again with the whole Division. Colonel Lloyd protested that we had had no food after a gruelling night's march, but the staff officer said that we had to go on and that it was only three miles to the town. Our drum and bugles were got off the transport wagons, now with us, and our buglers practised as we went along, so as to play us into Bloemfontein.*

*After marching over a kopje we came in view of the town, lying in a broad valley. It proved to be a good seven miles by the time we reached it, and we were all very tired and footsore; many of the men's boots were completely worn out, and they had tied their puttees round their feet, while all our uniforms were torn and dirty, some being in rags. At about 1pm. we entered the town, our drums and bugles playing a quickstep, and it was remarkable how everyone made a great effort to step out smartly and keep in fours at correct distances. A number of people lined the route; the Dutch seemed in a minority and the English residents gave us a great reception, many holding out loaves of bread and cups of water to the men with remarks such as Thank God you have come at last...."* (Second Lieutenant M V Le P Trench)

After marching thus through the city, the Dukes went into camp with the whole of the 6th Division, about a mile beyond the outskirts, and remained there to rest and for refitting. Both officers and men were allowed into the city to sample such civilised amenities as hotels, bars and cafés, which they had not seen since leaving Cape Town. But as everywhere else in South Africa, inflation had hit Bloemfontein: Second Lieutenant Trench complained that a whiskey-and-soda cost 2s 6d (12p), a lager 4s (20p), while English tobacco could not be had for less than 10s 6d (52p) per pound. The Boer variety was only 1s 6d (7p), but it was almost unsmokeable.

Roberts had entered Bloemfontein on 14 March. A six weeks' delay now followed owing to a severe epidemic of enteric fever, the need to secure the railway from Bloemfontein southwards to Cape Colony, and the amassing of supplies and reinforcements for the next stage, the capture of Pretoria, the Transvaal capital.

Taking advantage of the lull, the Boers regrouped under Botha and De Wet, who were to prove their most forceful (and to the British, most elusive) leaders during the subsequent guerilla war. On 31 March De Wet ambushed a British column at Sannah's Post, killing and wounding 170 and taking 400 prisoners besides seven guns and 83 wagons. Four days later, at Dewetsdorp, he compelled the surrender of 546 British troops.

By 3 May Roberts was ready to march with an army of 44,000 troops and 120 guns. De Wet was not disposed to risk a stand-up fight against such a force, and the 300 miles of veldt were covered in 34 days with little opposition. Krüger fled his capital on 2 June, and on the 5th Roberts entered Pretoria, again without a shot being fired. Previously, on 16 May, Mafeking had been relieved, and on the 30th Johannesburg had surrendered with its gold mines intact. Now it really seemed that Boer resistance had crumbled. But in fact, the long-drawn-out guerilla war was only just about to begin.

The Dukes had been retained at Bloemfontein as part of the garrison, and it was not until 11 August that they arrived by train at Pretoria, where they joined a mobile column under Major General A H Paget. This included battalions of The King's Own Yorkshire Light Infantry, Wiltshire Regiment and Royal Munster Fusiliers, plus some mounted infantry and guns. In April the Dukes had been joined by a company of three officers and 98 other ranks formed from the 1st, 2nd and 3rd Volunteer Battalions DWR, and on 18 August these experienced their baptism of fire when, with A, B and G Companies they encountered a strong body of commandos at Ouderstepoorte near Pienaar's River. For some three hours the enemy put down constant shellfire, but surprisingly this caused no casualties, and the concentrated rifle fire of the four companies finally drove the Boers off their kopje.

There followed weeks of arduous trekking in pursuit of elusive commandos, searches of Boer farmsteads for lurking guerillas or hidden arms, and capture of the Boers' mainstay of life, their herds of cattle. On 22 September, after a gruelling march of 26 miles, the Battalion, with a mixed force under General Paget, surprised the Boer station of Wagon Drift on Eland's River, capturing 2,500 head of cattle and sheep. It was during September that the Dukes came into possession of President Krüger's saddle in circumstances later related by Colonel B St. J Le Marchant. *"....I was at the out-posts one morning when I saw a man on a pony with a white flag coming towards the post. When he came up to me he said he wished to surrender and that he was President Krüger's servant.... On his pony was a saddle with the Transvaal Coat of Arms on it. He said the saddle and rifle belonged to President Krüger. At the end of the war the saddle was brought home to England and placed in the officers mess".*(f)

During this period companies were detached on independent missions, but by 28 November the 1st Battalion was concentrated under Paget at Haartesbeestfontein on the Wilge River. Intelligence reported that a force of Boers under General Viljoen was occupying a natural defensive position of kopjes at Rhenoster Kop, a few miles east, and a full-scale attack was planned.

---

(f) In 1939, however, it was decided that its rightful resting place was in the Union of South Africa and it was accordingly offered to the Union Government who display it in the Krüger Museum in Pretoria.

The battle of Rhenoster Kop on 29 November 1900, proved indecisive. The action, which started just after dawn, was later described by Major Francis Marshall:

> "Viljoen had chosen his position well. His men were hidden behind boulders which afforded cover from fire effectively. The ground we had to traverse was undulating grassland, very similar to the Sussex Downs, which afforded cover only in the natural furrows. Colonel Lloyd was in personal command of the Battalion. He decided to lead the first line himself, four Companies, and told me to bring on the second line, three-companies..... C Company was left to protect the camp.... When eventually the first line came into action on the last rise in front of the Boer position, it was 350 yards to the right of the given objective, where Lt. Exham's company had just taken position. I halted the second line, now reduced to two Companies about 80 yards in rear of the first line. About 8.30p.m. Colonel Lloyd came across to me.... he approved my action... After a few minutes' conversation he said he would go and examine Lt. Exham's position over 300 yards away to the left, telling me to carry on meanwhile. I never saw him alive again.... About 9.15a.m. the Adjutant returned alone and reported that Colonel Lloyd was dead.... He said that shortly after the Colonel and he had reached Lt. Exham's company Colonel Lloyd stood up in front of the line and was looking through his binoculars when he was shot and killed on the spot.(g)... As the fight developed I noticed an enfilade fire on our right flank and I brought Lt. Townsend's company to check it and had only just left him when he was shot. He was in the act of signalling his men to lie down when I saw him fall – but the enfilade fire was checked. Lt. Oakes was wounded a few minutes later. The position then was unsatisfactory. There was a big gap between Lt. Exham's company and the rest of the Battalion.... the supporting line was reduced to one company, and there was no reserve. The half battalion of The Munsters was in action to our right, taking orders direct from the General. I was in direct communication through my signallers the whole day with the headquarters staff, but I received no further orders of any sort. Apparently, the General realised that the Battalion was extended beyond its strength and was content so long as it held its ground... The firing throughout the day was incessant on both sides, and the fight was only brought to a close by the fall of night, about 8p.m. The Boers retired during the night".

(g) General Ben Viljoen later gave his account of Colonel Lloyd's death: "...then came their faces, then their breasts; and we fired. The first rank went down like a swathe of grass. But others pressed forward the Colonel leading. We fired again, the Colonel reeled and fell forward, shot through the leg. But almost instantly he was up again, the wounded leg hanging horribly limp and trailing along the ground. He leaped upon a rifle, using it as a crutch, and so forced himself forward in jerks, calling hoarsely to his men, beckoning them angrily on with his arm, and thus limping calmly to the very muzzles of our Mausers. It was splendid, and when he fell for the last time - well we were sorry. Months after, when passing the battlefield, we laid a wreath of flowers on his grave and the card bore the inscription 'In honour of a brave enemy'. It was an act difficult to forget". Asked to name the offficer he replied, "Colonel Lloyd, of the West Riding Regiment".

Besides the Commanding Officer, the Battalion lost five men killed, while Captain Ackworth, Lieutenants Townsend and Oakes and 24 NCOs and men were wounded. The death of Lieutenant Colonel George Evan Lloyd DSO, who was greatly admired by all ranks, was a grievous loss.

Just before he was killed, Colonel Lloyd [h] scribbled a message to Captain Ackworth, telling him to *"hold the enemy for the present as you are now doing...."* Soon after he had been handed the message Ackworth was felled with a bullet in the head. Three days later the blood-stained leaf from the colonel's field message pad was found on the spot where Ackworth had fallen.[i]

It was also on 29 November that the troops in South Africa learned that Field Marshal Lord Roberts had been replaced as C-in-C by his Chief of Staff, Major General Lord Kitchener. Until January of the New Year (1901) the 1st Battalion remained in the area of Rhenoster Kop, with little action of consequence except patrolling and raids on farmsteads.

Lieutenant Colonel G E Lloyd CB, DSO.
Commanded the 1st Battalion, 1896-1900

On 6 January Lieutenant Colonel P T Rivett-Carnac arrived to take over from Major Marshall who had temporarily assumed command on the death of Colonel Lloyd. On the 13th Marshall was involved in a brush with a commando when he was ordered to take a detachment to bring in some released British prisoners who had been abandoned on the veldt by their captors. In the early hours they bumped into a force of some 250 Boers and a sharp fire-fight ensued, during which one of Marshall's men was killed and six were wounded, while Second Lieutenant A S Carlyon and his servant were reported missing, believed prisoners.

Between February 1901 until almost the end of hostilities the Dukes occupied an extended line of blockhouses along some 200 miles of the railway from Pretoria to Pietersburg. These blockhouses of stone and corrugated iron, were sited at intervals of 1,000 yards, with a high wire fence running between them. Normally each was manned by a corporal and six men; a subaltern had command of three blockhouses, a captain ten or twelve, while a battalion was responsible for upwards of 60. Although never constituting an impregnable barrier, the blockhouse lines imposed effective restrictions on the Boers' mobility, besides providing the British with relatively secure lines of communication and supply routes. But for the soldiers confined in these miniature

---
(h) Lieutenant Colonel Lloyd was awarded a posthumous CB. A memorial to him was erected at Rhenoster Kop. In 1963 all those buried there were re-intered at Diamond Hill, near Pretoria.
(i) The last message from Colonel Lloyd was brought home and is now in the Regimental Museum.

fortlets, in stifling daytime heat, freezing nights, with rarely an enemy to shoot at, it was a stultifying existence. During this period Battalion headquarters was located at the station of Warmbaths, which was also the headquarters of the Pretoria District L of C troops. In April 1901 the Battalion was joined by a second company formed from officers and men of the 1st, 2nd and 3rd Volunteer Battalions.

Despite the blockhouses the Boer commandos regularly attacked the railways. On 31 August, for instance, they mined the line near Waterval. As the train, which had an escort of two officers and 45 men of the 1st Battalion, passed over, the mine exploded and the train was completely destroyed. The escort then came under fire from about 200 Boers as a result of which, after having six men killed and 17 wounded, the survivors were forced to surrender. The Boers then looted the train and took away everything of value - including the Battalion's pay.

The 3rd (Militia) Battalion was also employed on blockhouse duties, in its case in Cape Colony. In January 1902 command of the Battalion was taken over by Lieutenant Colonel F A Hayden, who had previously been awarded the DSO for his services with the Battalion. In March the Battalion was warned to prepare for return to England. It sailed from Cape Town on 21 April.

By this time General Botha and the other Boer leaders conceded that it was hopeless to continue the struggle, and after a referendum it was resolved to negotiate for peace. Terms were agreed upon in May and on the 30th of that month the Peace of Vereeniging was signed. It had taken some 500,000 British troops two-and-a-half years to subdue an irregular force of Boer farmers who seldom had more than 25,000 in the field.

The war had cost the British 20,720 lives, while the Boers lost an estimated 4,000 killed. Of the British dead 13,250 officers and men succumbed to disease. According to the Digest of Services, the losses of the 1st Battalion amounted to five officers killed, twelve wounded; 49 other ranks killed and 211 wounded. The volunteer companies attached to the Battalion had ten other ranks killed. The mounted infantry company of the 2nd Battalion lost two officers and two privates killed and the 3rd Battalion had one man killed. These are exclusively battle casualties.

On 1 June, 1902, the men of the Dukes manning the blockhouse line were informed by telephone or signal (helio) that peace had been signed. All were now withdrawn to concentrate with Battalion HQ at Warmbaths. Next day Lieutenant M V Le Poer Trench and ten NCO's and men were selected to represent the Battalion at King Edward VII's Coronation in London, and travelled by train to Cape Town for passage home. It was not until 11 September that the remainder of the Battalion embarked for England, arriving at Southampton on 6 October, with eleven officers and 468 WOs, NCOs and men. From there it was posted to York.

*********************

Largely because of Kitchener's detention of Boer civilians in concentration camps, which had become notorious for poor administration and hygiene and had resulted in the deaths of 28,000 women and children, Britain had become very unpopular, particularly in Europe. At the same time France, Russia and Germany had embarked on a naval arms race with Britain. The Government therefore started to look for allies. Having been rebuffed by the Kaiser in 1901, Britain signed the *entente cordiale* with France in April 1904. Two years later this led to an *entente* with Russia. Germany now felt threatened with encirclement.

In the meantime the army was absorbing the lessons it had learnt during the Boer war. Not the least of these was the absence of a general staff to think and plan for the future, as well as a lack of trained staff officers. Other problems had arisen because there was no permanent organisation larger than a regiment; divisions and brigades having been established on an *ad hoc* basis. In 1904, therefore a general staff was formed with the control of the army vested in the Army Council. The War Office was also reorganised with much of its work decentralised to Commands, which had been established the previous year. There remained the task of organising the army so that it would be ready for any future struggles. This fell to Lord Haldane, the Secretary of State for War. As a result of his reforms all units of the regular army were allocated in peace time to the brigades and divisions with which they were to go to war. They comprised an expeditionary force of six infantry divisions, each consisting of three brigades of four battalions, and a cavalry division.

To provide a second line for the regular army Haldane reorganised the auxiliary forces. The militia was re-modelled as the special reserve with the role of finding drafts for the regular units and the provision of men for certain garrison and lines of communication duties. From 1908 the yeomanry and volunteers were re-shaped as the Territorial Force, liable to serve anywhere in the UK but not abroad unless its members so volunteered. It was organised on identical lines to the regular army into 14 cavalry brigades and 14 infantry divisions. The effect, as far as the Dukes were concerned, was that the 1st, 2nd and 3rd Volunteer Battalions became the 4th, 5th and 6th Battalions TF, to which was added the 7th Battalion formed by dividing the 5th battalion into two. The four battalions were organised into the 2nd West Riding Brigade of the West Riding Division TF.

During this period one other change took place, which was of special significance to the Regiment. By the reforms of 1881 all English regiments had been required to change the previous facings of their uniforms to white. The first regiment that sought permission to change back to its old colour was, perhaps not surprisingly, the Buffs. In August 1890 the change back to buff was approved. Over the next few years other regiments followed with similar requests, and on 24 March 1905 The Duke of Wellington's Regiment was authorised to change its uniform facings back to scarlet. Another uniform change took place in 1912, when the shoulder title "W.Riding Regt" introduced in 1881 was authorised to be changed to "Duke of Wellington's".

************************

The 1st Battalion remained in York until 1905 when it was ordered to India. On 26 October 1905, with Lieutenant Colonel Thorold in command of twenty one officers and

430 other ranks plus 49 wives and 53 children, the Battalion embarked at Southampton and arrived in Calcutta on 3 November. From there it was sent to Lebong in north east India, where it took over a draft of 500 men left behind by the 2nd Battalion which included most of that battalion's rugby XV. (j)

In 1906 the Battalion was moved to Sitapur, near Lucknow. Two years later it was moved to Ambala where Lieutenant Colonel Thorold was succeeded in command by Lieutenant Colonel C V Humphrys. Under him the Battalion achieved a high level of training and was generally reckoned to be the best trained regiment in India. The District Commander, General Pilcher, became so proud of the Battalion that it became known as "Pilcher's Pets". In 1912 Lieutenant-Colonel Humphrys was appointed commandant of the School of Musketry. He was succeeded by Lieutenant Colonel W M Watson. The following year the Battalion moved to Lahore. The hill station, where half the Battalion at a time spent the hot summer months, was at Lower Gharial, near Murree. There, towards the middle of July 1914, rumours began to circulate about the possibility of war in Europe. An officer was detailed to go daily to Murree to read Reuter's telegrams, copy out the news and bring it back. One day the officer returned and announced that there was to be no war. Apparently Paris was placarded with proclamations saying "Order demobilisation". Another officer was sent to check that this important information was correct. He returned to announce that what the proclamation actually said was Ordre de mobilisation. A fortnight later the troops stationed in Murree were ordered to rejoin the rest of the Battalion in Lahore.

****************************

While the 1st Battalion was engaged with the Boers on the veldt, the 2nd Battalion had been serving in Burma, where (in addition to providing the mounted infantry company already mentioned) it had carried out normal garrison duties and training. The tour in Burma was marked by a disaster. In Rangoon in December 1901 the officers' mess caught fire while the Battalion was away on training, and was utterly destroyed together with the whole of the mess plate, many valuable paintings and books and, most tragically, the Regulation and Honorary Colours. Application was immediately made to the Secretary of State for India for the Honorary Colours to be replaced. This was readily agreed and in 1903 they reached the Battalion which was by then in India, having moved there in 1902. Because the Battalion was due to return to England it was decided to postpone the presentation of both stands of Colours until after it had arrived home. After a year at Lebong, followed by another year at Dinapore, the Battalion, now under command of Lieutenant Colonel F M H Marshall, embarked at Calcutta on 26 October 1905 after nineteen years of foreign service.

On returning to England the Battalion was posted to Lichfield. There, on 26 October 1906, the new Colours were presented by the 4th Duke of Wellington. Both stands of colours were consecrated by the Bishop of Lichfield – the only known occasion when the Honorary Colours were consecrated. In 1907 Lieutenant Colonel K E Lean (Royal Warwicks) commanded the Battalion for a few months before being succeeded by Lieutenant Colonel

---

(j) The 2nd Battalion had won the Calcutta Cup, the premier rugby trophy in India in 1903 and 1905. The 1st Battalion emulated that feat by winning the Cup eight years in succession between 1906 and 1913.

F A Hayden DSO in February 1908. Later that year the Battalion moved to Tidworth. The following year the Colonel of the Regiment, General Sir Hugh Rowlands VC,KCB, died. His successor was Lieutenant General Sir Herbert Belfield KCB,DSO.

In 1910 and 1911 it was on duty in London, lining the streets, on the first occasion for the funeral of King Edward VII and on the second for the coronation of King George V. On both all four colours were carried.

In September 1911 the Battalion [k] moved to Dublin and joined 13 Brigade in the 5th Division. The main problem facing the army in Ireland was of a political nature. In March 1914 matters came to a head when the Irish Home Rule bill was being debated in Parliament. Fears grew within the army that it might be drawn into a civil war by military action in Ulster. In that sensitive climate the GOC Irish Command demanded to know within 24 hours whether officers were prepared to take part in operations in Ulster, if ordered. Those officers not prepared to give the undertaking would be dismissed without a pension. As a result of this ultimatum 60 officers of the 3rd Cavalry Brigade, stationed at the Curragh camp, resigned their commissions. Many officers of 5th Division did likewise, though there is no evidence, one way or the other, whether these included officers of the 2nd Battalion. The 'Incident' came to a formal conclusion after the commander 3rd Cavalry Brigade, Brigadier General Hubert Gough, obtained a written guarantee that there would be no military coercion of Ulster. However, the morale of the army continued to be affected by the 'Incident' and its aftermath up to the outbreak of war, four months later.

2nd Battalion, Dublin Castle, 1914. Trooping the Colour

---

(k) Up to 1913 infantry battalions deployed eight companies, lettered A - H. In September of that year the number was reduced to four by amalgamating pairs. Thus A and C companies became A company, B and D became B company and so on.

CHAPTER 16

# The First World War

*1914 Mons, Marne, Ypres*
*1915 Hill 60, Suvla*
*1916 Somme*
*1917 Arras, Cambrai*
*1918 Lys, Piave*

On 28 June 1914 the Archduke Franz Ferdinand, nephew and heir to the Emperor of Austria-Hungary, visited Sarajevo in Bosnia and was assassinated by a young Bosnian Serb. Austria reacted by sending a 48 hour ultimatum to Serbia, requesting submission to ten demands. Serbia responded by ordering mobilisation against Austria even before making an evasive reply. Once Austria had mobilised against Serbia a whole series of treaties and alliances came into force so that by 4 August most of Europe was at war. On one side were Britain, France and Russia and on the other Germany and Austria. As a German journalist wrote, *"Europe stumbled into war as a child walks on thin ice, believing it will bear its weight and finding itself struggling in a torrent"*.

At the outbreak of war the locations of the various battalions of the Regiment were as follows:

- 1st Battalion was at Lahore in India. It was one of eight British infantry battalions which remained in India throughout the war.
- 2nd Battalion was in Dublin in 13 Brigade, 5th Division, II Corps. It sailed for France on 14 August.
- 3rd Battalion (Special Reserve) was mobilised on 8 August and located near Gateshead, guarding the coast and acting as a feeder to the 2nd Battalion.
- 4th, 5th, 6th and 7th Territorial Battalions, forming the 2nd West Riding Infantry Brigade of the West Riding Division, were in camp on the East Coast when war was declared. They returned to their peace stations to

mobilise. After a fortnight at their war stations, Hull, Grimsby and Immingham, they were concentrated at Doncaster for training. On 31 August each was authorised to raise a second battalion.

8th Battalion, the first of the Dukes' Service battalions of the New Armies,[a] was authorised to be raised during August.

Between 1915 and the end of hostilities no fewer than fourteen territorial and service battalions fought in France and Flanders, Gallipoli and Italy. Five of their members gained the Victoria Cross.

The 2nd Battalion, mustering approximately 660 all ranks and commanded by Lieutenant Colonel J A C Gibbs, landed at Le Havre on 16 August where, in pelting rain, officers and men were billeted in warehouses on the quay.

The French had anticipated a German invasion of Belgium,[b] but only to the south of Brussels. With the German right wing entangled in the difficult Ardennes country, they hoped with a sudden counter attack to break the German centre and dislocate the whole plan of attack. In the event the French attack in the centre was repulsed with frightful loss. They also discovered that the German swing through Belgium had a far wider sweep than they had deemed possible. The British Expeditionary Force, *"in every respect incomparably the best trained, best organised and best equipped British army that ever went forth to war"*, consisting of one cavalry and four infantry divisions, found itself on the now exposed allied left flank fighting alone at Mons.

By 22 August 1914, the British II Corps (3rd and 5th Divisions) was established along the line Cond-Mons. 13 Brigade was deployed with 2 KOYLI and 1 Royal West Kents forward, and 2 DWR and 2 KOSB in support. On the following day, in the face of heavy German pressure, the French on the British right were forced to withdraw, and to save the BEF from being isolated, Field Marshal Sir John French had to conform. Orders for the general withdrawal were issued late that night, to start at dawn next day [c]. And so, on 24 August the first phase of the retreat from Mons commenced. It was to prove costly for the Dukes. In the early hours of the 24th the Battalion was holding a front just north of the village of Wasmes. The rest of the 13th Brigade withdrew without difficulty during the morning, but no orders reached Colonel Gibbs, who could only cling to his now perilous position. What followed is described in the official history of the War:

*"By some mishap, the order to retreat did not reach the 2nd Dukes,*

---

(a) Lord Kitchener, the Secretary of State for War, decided for various reasons to raise New Armies rather than rely exclusively on the Territorial Force. New divisions were to be raised in groups of six. The first group, numbered 9 - 14, was raised in August 1914. The early volunteers were among the finest fighting men Britain ever put in the field.
(b) Not withstanding that by a Treaty signed in 1832, Prussia, in common with Britain, France, Austria, and Russia, had guaranteed the neutrality of Belgium.
(c) The Battalion had to leave behind packs and other encumbrances, including drums. One of the drums was taken care of by a Belgian lady who buried it in her garden. There it remained until January 1919 when some members of the Artists Rifles were billeted on her village. The lady then dug it up and gave it to Major R H Goldthorpe, then serving with the Artists Rifles but late of 4 DWR. The drum is now in the Regimental museum.

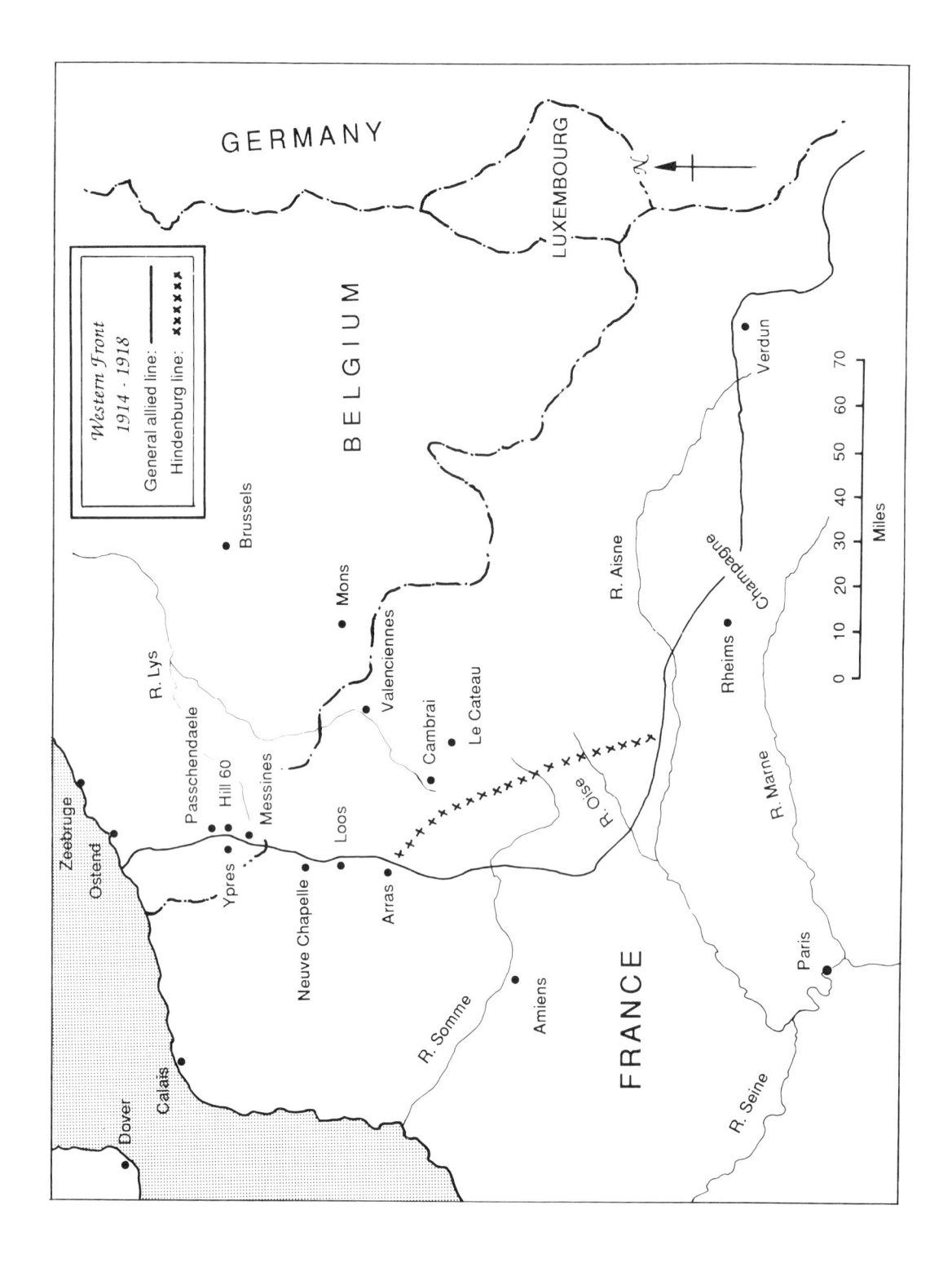

> *which accordingly remained in position, with a battery of the XXVII Brigade R.F.A. close to it. At about 11.30am, exactly the time when the order should have affected the Dukes, the Germans suddenly concentrated very heavy fire on this battery from guns which they had brought up to close range. A sharp fight followed during the next hour and a half, and it was only the rifles of the infantry that saved the British battery. About 1.00pm the Germans debouched in thick skirmishing formation followed by dense masses from the Boussu-Quierain road on the left front of the British battalion, but were greeted by such a rain of bullets from rifles and machine guns at 800 yards, and such a salute from the battery, that they stopped dead. Under cover of this final stroke, the guns limbered up and the battalion withdrew south-west into Dour. The Dukes suffered heavily, their casualties reaching nearly four hundred of all ranks, but they had driven back six battalions".*

The Battalion's actual casualties were three officers killed, four wounded, 33 other ranks killed, 39 wounded (of whom four died), and 244 missing, subsequently reported either killed or prisoners of war. Among the seriously wounded was Colonel Gibbs and command was taken over by Major K A McLeod.[d]

Reaching Le Cateau on 25 August General Smith-Dorrien halted his II Corps for the night. But with von Kluck's 1st Army closely following up, there was little rest. In the battle of Le Cateau the next day, the Dukes were again heavily involved, as Captain H K O'Kelly, having dug in his half company, recorded:

> *".....We stayed there all day under awful shell fire, with our own guns firing right beside us. I saw that day the gunners doing the most extraordinary feats of bravery. I saw one officer with his arm blown off still riding his horse giving orders. Of course he soon fainted from loss of blood...... I also saw batteries blown to pieces, one gun being left intact in one battery.... I saw an artillery major blown high in the air and falling down in pieces. (On being ordered to retire at about 4.00pm, he was stopped by a Staff Officer and told to hold a rear-guard position with some 130 men collected from other regiments). I found that we had a machine gun with us and another very young officer.... I only saw about seven men from our own Regiment, whom I called together and asked to show a bold front and give a good example..... the infantry and cavalry had mostly, except stragglers, passed on, when I saw Germans bringing a big gun down a laneway with twelve horses attached. I got the machine gun on them and shot most of the horses. They brought up another lot and tried to*

---

(d) Major McLeod was only in command for three weeks when he was obliged to enter hospital. Command was then taken over by Captain H C Umfreville.

> *harness them: of these we also shot some and were beginning to enjoy it when a shell burst among us.... this blew up the machine gun and killed seven or eight men, including the young officer. Immediately three other shells burst in our midst, doing frightful havoc..... When we collected together I halted them about thirty yards back in a cave and found eleven men and myself [out of 131 odd]. We sat there until it was dark and then started to try to rejoin our units".*

In the retreat from Mons the mauled Dukes and their comrades of the BEF marched nearly 200 miles in fourteen days, in stifling heat, seldom snatching more than three or four hours' sleep in twenty-four hours.

The sweep of the German right wing through Belgium and northern France was the most tremendous military movement but had within it the seed of eventual failure. The further it advanced the more extended became its lines of communication while for the French, under Joffre, the opposite applied. On 6 September the British and French, now south of the River Marne, faced about and advanced, forcing the Germans to retreat, in good order, to a very strong natural position overlooking the River Aisne. Here the allied advance came to a halt. One move still possible for the allies was to extend their line northwards to the sea. The attempt was made but the odds were in favour of the Germans who had interior lines. As I Corps of the BEF started to advance from Ypres towards Menin it found itself opposed by large and unexpected German forces. On 18 October command of the 2nd Battalion was assumed by Lieutenant Colonel E G Harrison CB,DSO [(e)]. In the opinion of Captain B J Barton, *"He is one of the very few men I have seen devoid of fear....It was popularly supposed that he went every day to Brigade to ask that the Battalion might be allowed to make a charge".*

After moving up from the Béthune area in late October, the Dukes first set eyes on Ypres ("Wipers" to the troops) on 5 November, at which date the fine old city with its historic Cloth Hall was virtually undamaged. Lieutenant Colonel E G Harrison noted in his diary:

> *"Wet drizzly rain and got into billets in an estaminet 5.00pm. Orders came to march to Ypres tomorrow to join I Corps. We were here 15 officers and 800 rank and file* [a draft from the 1st Battalion joined at this time]. *I tried my best to get hold of a photographer...... so as to have an officers' group taken, we also had two officers on the staff to add to our number; unfortunately orders came to move before it could be done. Less than three weeks later we were 2 officers and 380 men".*

The focus of the British salient was Ypres. From 21 October to 21 November the British regulars defied everything the Germans threw at them by their amazing fighting power, discipline and musketry. Throughout the 2nd Battalion was heavily engaged.

---

(e) Colonel Harrison, who was commissioned into the Regiment in 1885, had spent most of his service in East Africa.

On 8 November two companies were ordered to retake a sector captured by the Germans. *"Soon after dark"*, wrote Colonel Harrison, *"Sergeant Taylor reported to me at the dugout with what remained of the two companies. Only half returned, without any officers. Travers killed, Henderson missing and Williamson died at night. Got about 12 prisoners. Total killed, wounded and missing, 3 officers, 87 men"*. In the initial attack when all the officers had been knocked out and the companies driven back, Sergeants E Pogson and A E Taylor rallied the men, resumed the attack and re-occupied the trench. For this fine performance both NCOs were promoted company sergeant major and awarded the DCM.(f)

On 11 November the depleted Battalion fought a day-long action with the Germans only sixty yards away. Although the hastily-dug trench was held, the ferocity of the fight was such that eight officers and nearly 300 men were killed, wounded or missing. By the 16th total casualties had reached fifteen officers and 389 men. The only remaining unwounded officers were Colonel Harrison and two subalterns, one of whom had joined only three days previously. Bitter cold, with rain, sleet and snow did nothing to alleviate the sufferings of the survivors.

Thus ended the first battle of Ypres which was, in the words of the military historian Liddell Hart, *"the supreme memorial to the British regular army"*.

On 20 November the Battalion was withdrawn through the now battered Ypres for essential refitting. *"The French came to relieve us about 11.00pm, after keeping us waiting since 8 o'clock..... We had received orders before leaving to collect all spare rifles and ammunition, and for this purpose I sent patrols to search the woods just around our support and reserve trenches. I could hardly believe it when they brought in 62 rifles and 14,000 rounds of ammunition. (Harrison)"* Captain Barton adds the information that the Battalion was, at that time, attached to another brigade. Two battalions had apparently taken fright and thrown away their arms in panic.

The Battalion again went up the line on 27 November. The misery endured by those in the trenches during that winter of 1914 -15 is well documented. Of course, daily hazards of shelling and machine gunning were the normal lot of front line troops, but to these were added the unspeakable squalor and horrors of daily existence. *"The trenches are perfectly awful"*, wrote Colonel Harrison *"....the men are up to knees in mud and water, and all the reserve dug-outs near Headquarters are full of water, almost impossible to bale out"*. Often the men in the trenches had to stand with water up to their knees and an increasing number of them were incapacitated by what came to be known as trench foot. And that was not all. Dug-outs were infested with rats, many having feasted on unburied dead, while the men, unable to bath or even wash properly, were plagued with lice. Struggling along a flooded trench, a man might stumble over something hidden, soft and yielding: a bloated corpse. Battalion HQ had been established in a farm cottage, but when this was destroyed by shellfire (four men killed, eleven wounded) Harrison took up residence in a potato shed adjoining a pigsty. At least this was dry, but *"it stinks"*.

---

(f) Apart from the VC, the DCM was the only gallantry award for NCOs and soldiers. The MM was not introduced until March 1916.

On 16 December Lieutenant Colonel Harrison went on leave and command of the Battalion was temporarily taken over by the second-in command, Major W E M Tyndall DSO.

With both sides virtually bogged down, the winter saw no major offensive, but there was a constant requirement to carry out raids on enemy trenches, primarily to capture prisoners from whom intelligence about their units' strengths and dispositions might be gleaned.

\*\*\*\*\*\*\*\*\*\*\*\*\*\*\*\*\*\*\*\*\*\*

The failure of the German offensive in Flanders in 1914 led to confidence that the tables might be turned in the spring of 1915. There were now nine regular divisions in France and two Indian divisions. To these were added a number of territorial divisions, including the West Riding Division which arrived in April 1915 (g). However the bulk of the fighting still had to be borne by the regulars. On 10 March the allies launched an attack on Neuve Chapelle which was an effective surprise and the Germans lost heavily in their counter attacks. But the front attacked was too narrow to force a breakthrough. Then, at Ypres, on 22 April the Germans let loose their secret weapon – gas. However they did not exploit their new weapon to the full with the result that though 2nd Ypres was a tactical success for them it was a strategic failure.

March was an uneventful month for the 2nd Battalion. On 5 April, Lieutenant Colonel P A Turner arrived and Major Tyndall reverted to second-in-command. By 10 April the Battalion was in reserve near Ypres preparing for an attack on a feature named Hill 60 – a man-made hump rising no more than 50ft above the otherwise dead-flat plain, some two miles south-east of Ypres. It was actually formed of earth excavated from the adjoining railway cutting. Though in itself an insignificant feature, it afforded the Germans an excellent artillery observation post, as well as complete command over the British positions to the north and north-west. Sir John French, the Commander-in-Chief BEF, had demanded that it should be captured.

On the evening of the 17th, following the detonation of three mines, the hill was attacked from the north by the 1st Royal West Kents and 2nd KOSB who carried it without difficulty. However, during the night there was some desperate fighting as the Germans counter attacked and managed to recapture some of the trenches. On the morning of the 18th the Dukes and 2 KOYLI were ordered forward to relieve the Royal West Kents and KOSB. Later that day the Dukes received orders to attack and dislodge the Germans from the portion of the hill they had regained during the counter attacks made the previous night. The attack went in at 6.00pm, the men charging up the slope with fixed bayonets. There were only some 50 yards of open ground between the attacking troops and the enemy and they suffered very heavily. D Company, which had the furthest distance to cover, lost all its officers (three killed and two wounded) at the start. By dusk the positions had been won and consolidated. Meanwhile, Battalion Headquarters was moving up to the craters when Colonel Turner and Major Tyndall

---

(g) In May 1915 the title was changed to 49 (West Riding)Division, the brigades becoming 146, 147 and 148. The four Dukes battalions were in 147 Brigade.

Hill 60, April-May 1915

were both badly wounded, the latter dying after evacuation. Captain B J Barton, the senior surviving officer, took over temporary command of the Battalion.

The space that had been fought over was only about 250 yards in length and about 200 in depth. Onto that small area the enemy had for hours on end hurled tons of metal and high explosive. Not surprisingly the casualties were heavy. The Dukes' losses amounted to 378 killed and wounded with a further 43 listed as missing believed killed.

On the morning of 19 April 2 DWR and 2 KOYLI were relieved by units of 15 Brigade. The Battalion was withdrawn to billets near Zillebeke for much-needed rest and refitting. It then went into reserve at Hooge, during which period reinforcements of 359 all ranks were received.

On the night of 4/5 May the Dukes were sent forward to relieve the 1st Devons on Hill 60. Some of the trenches taken on 18 April had been re-taken by the Germans, but the crest was still in British hands. The Dukes were determined to hold on to it. At 8.00am the Germans attacked:–

> "..... aided by a favourable wind, the Germans sent over asphyxiating gas (chlorine) with disastrous effects.... Gas had been first employed by the enemy on 22 April at the commencement of the second Battle of

*Ypres, and fully effective counter-measures had not yet been established. We had not received gas masks as yet, only a piece of gauze soaked in a preparation produced by the medical authorities. This solution required renewing after a few minutes, a procedure absolutely impossible in action. On came this terrible stream of death, and before anything could be done, all those occupying the front line were overcome, the majority dying at their posts.... The Battalion suffered over 300 casualties that morning, large numbers dying as a result of this barbarous gas. The writer will never forget the sight of men writhing in agony slowly dying from the asphyxiating effects of the chlorine, nor of the feeling of helplessness at being unable to do anything for them".* (Lieutenant C W G Ince)

On 6 May the Battalion was relieved and withdrawn to billets south of Ypres. All who remained were Captain Barton, CO, Lieutenant Ince, Adjutant, three other officers and about 150 NCOs and men. The Battalion's two battles on Hill 60, on 18 April and 5 May, which had cost it over 700 casualties, is commemorated by the battle honour **Hill 60** [h]. For members of the 2nd Battalion who survived the war it was the one on which they looked back with the greatest pride and sorrow.

On 9 May the British attacked the south west end of Aubers Ridge with the object of assisting French attacks further south. Among the troops who played a part in this battle (albeit a minor one) were those of 147 Brigade (previously 2nd West Riding Brigade), which consisted of 1/4th, 1/5th, 1/6th and 1/7th Battalions of the Regiment. This was the first time the territorials fought as complete divisions.

In effect, the regulars – or such of them as were left – had shot their bolt and it was necessary to wait until Kitchener's New Armies, training in England, would be ready to play their part. During the summer they started to pour into France. By the end of September the British had a total of 37 divisions in France of all kinds. Among them was the 9th Battalion with 17 (Northern) Division and the 10th Battalion with 23 Division, which had arrived in July and August respectively. Other changes at this time included the re-naming of the 2nd/1st West Riding Division, then still in England, as 62 (West Riding) Division. One of its brigades was 186 consisting of the 2/4th, 2/5th, 2/6th and 2/7th Battalions of the Dukes. The 11th Battalion was re-named the 11th (Reserve) Battalion with the task to train and send out drafts to units at the front.

The arrival of new divisions coincided with a change in tactics. In general terms the first year's fighting had involved manoeuvre in the open field, for which the pre-war regulars had been ideally trained. From now on it was to be one of attack and defence of fortified positions. The distinction between regular and non-regular divisions also practically ceased to exist, because of the heavy casualties suffered by the regulars. The last service the pre-war units could render was to hand down their traditions and their example to the units which bore their names and followed in their footsteps.

---

(h) **Hill 60** was awarded to only nine British infantry regiments. viz: The four regiments of 13 Brigade, the four regiments of 15 Brigade and the 9th (Service) Battalion London Regiment.

1/4th battalion, 1915. Officers wearing an early pattern of gas mask

At the end of September 1915, at the urging of the French who were launching an attack further south, the British attacked Loos. Gas was employed on a large scale and Loos was overrun, but due to lack of reinforcements the attack lost momentum and the Germans were able to mount a counter attack. When the battle was called off three weeks later the British losses had amounted to 60,000 men. It was a fatal blow to Sir John French's reputation and he was succeeded as Commander-in-Chief by Sir Douglas Haig.

During the winter months there were constant attacks and counter attacks. One such occured on 19 December when 17th Division was attacked near Ypres. The attack was preceded by a heavy bombardment from the Germans, who also used gas. However by now gas masks were available and as a result there were few casualties. Among the troops involved was the 9th Battalion, commanded by Lieutenant Colonel F A Hayden DSO [i]. As the Battalion moved up to the front through Ypres it was caught in a storm

---

i) The 9th Battalion was in 52 Brigade. One of the other battalions in the Brigade was 12th Battalion Manchester Regiment, commanded by Lieutenant Colonel E G Harrison who had commanded the 2nd Battalion in 1914. Lieutenant Colonel Hayden had commanded the 2nd Battalion 1908-1912.

of bursting shells as a result of which it had three officers and 105 men killed and wounded. But their advance continued and an officer of another regiment, who saw service to the end of the war, wrote: *"Their advance under fire in skirmishing order over the open south of Menin was one of the prettiest movements I have ever seen"*.

*******************

On 21 February 1916 the Germans began their Verdun offensive. Because the French, for reasons of morale, could not abandon Verdun, more and more of their troops were dragged into the battle. By 1 May no fewer than forty French divisions had been drawn in. As the struggle went on it became clear that only a major diversion elsewhere would draw off sufficient German troops to enable the French to hold on to Verdun. The British meanwhile extended their line to the Somme.

Before 1915 had closed the allies had planned a stroke that was confidently expected to end the war. The place was to be the area either side of the River Somme and the time the summer of 1916. However, because of the German attack on Verdun the larger share to be taken by the French dwindled to a British attack with some French assistance. The vast majority of the British troops was the volunteers of 1914. The attack was preceded by a terrific bombardment which lasted seven days. Then, on 1 July, the troops crossed their parapets in a human wave that was expected to sweep all before it. But the German machine gunners were waiting for them. Whole battalions were blotted out. That single day's fighting cost the British 60,000 casualties – the heaviest losses ever recorded for a single day's fighting.

The 2nd Battalion had joined 12 Brigade of the 4th Division earlier in the year. On that first day of July 1916, under the command of Lieutenant Colonel R N Bray, it was in front line trenches near Beaumont Hamel and up to strength with 26 officers and 950 other ranks. The attack of the 4th Division between Beaumont Hamel and Serre, was launched at 5.30am and twelve hours later the Dukes had advanced some 200 yards to occupy German trenches – after losing more than 300 all ranks killed and wounded.

What became termed the Battle of the Somme was really a succession of fierce engagements when both allies and Germans gained little for appalling losses. Thus on 3 September 49 (West Riding) Division fought its first major action in an attack on both sides of the Ancre River. 49 Division was deployed on the south side of the river with two brigades forward. The assaulting troops of 147 Brigade, on the right, were 1/4th and 1/5th Battalions DWR. The 1/6th and 1/7th were in support and reserve respectively. The experiences of the 1/4th were typical of these battles.

At 5.10am on that September morning three companies of the 4th went over the top, into a storm of machine gun fire which immediately felled four officers and several men. Struggling forward, through enemy shrapnel, the depleted companies managed to gain their first objective, the German front line trenches, which had been practically obliterated by the artillery barrage. But they were in a sad state: only four officers were left, most of the senior NCOs were casualties, while D Company had strayed too far to a

*5th Battalion, Thiepval Wood, July 1916*

flank and nothing more was heard of it until later, when twenty survivors reported back. The Germans now launched a fierce counter-attack on both front and flank. At 11.50am, Lieutenant Everitt, now senior officer with A Company, sent a runner to Battalion HQ with the message *"I have only roughly 25 men left, including six from B Coy. Have no bombers. Short of bombs and Lewis gun ammunition. Our artillery firing into our back".*

By 5.00pm it was conceded that the attack had failed, and although the 4th had staunchly fought for nearly twelve hours and gained its first objective it was withdrawn when the 148th Brigade came up in relief. The total casualties for the day were eleven officers and 336 other ranks. Of the officers who went over the top, only two returned, both wounded.

Another example of the type of war then being fought occurred on 28 September when the 2nd Battalion was engaged in the fierce battle for the strongpoint at Morval. This particular action was fought around the village of Lesboeufs, a mile north of Morval, when the four companies thrust back the Germans and occupied their trenches after nearly four hours' fighting, much of it hand-to-hand with bayonet. But, as always, there was a heavy price to pay for success. Five officers (including all company commanders) were killed, two wounded and two missing. Of the other ranks, 43 were killed, 236 wounded, with 54 missing, believed dead.

The 8th, 9th and 10th (Service) Battalions were all engaged on the Somme at one stage or other. The 8th Battalion, in 32 Brigade of 11 Division, which had taken part in the Gallipoli campaign, landed at Marseilles on 5 July and was sent forward from there to the area of Thiepval. On 14 September the Battalion was engaged in an operation to try and take Thiepval Wood. Sergeant Major E Miles described what happened:

> *"Phew! Those three days seemed like an hour's nightmare. We went up on the night of the 14th with three days' rations in our packs, and on our way up we passed field guns wheel to wheel. There must have been thousands of guns there and I think it was that that gave us victory. We lost 200, out of 500, killed and wounded.... The chief praise is due, I think, to one of our companies and a company from the West Yorks who, as we went forward came behind and dug a trench from "Jerry's" front line to our own. How those poor devils worked, while we held on, was marvellous".*

The slaughter on the Somme saw the Dukes gaining the first of five VCs awarded during the war. It was awarded to Second Lieutenant Henry Kelly of the 10th (Service) Battalion, which had been raised at Halifax in September 1914 and went to France in August the following year with the 69th Brigade of the 23rd Division. On 4 October, 1916, the Battalion was embroiled in one of the lesser known Somme fights at Le Sars, during which Kelly won his VC.(j)

Apart from brief spells in reserve the battalions of the Dukes were constantly engaged along the British line, from Beaumont Hamel in the north to Guillemont in the south, earning such costly battle honours as Albert, Pozietes, Morval, and Thiepval. For four and a half months the grim contest raged back and forth along the devastated valley of the Somme, with brigades and battalions of the British 4th Army struggling forward through withering machine gun fire to gain perhaps 50 yards, only to be flung back by counter attack.

The bitter struggle ground to a mud-bound halt in November 1916. Haig claimed a victory, for in one sector his front line had been pushed forward nearly seven miles, but it had cost him some 415,000 casualties. However, more importantly, he had prevented the transfer of German troops to other theatres of war, relieved the pressure on Verdun, and caused a marked reduction in the morale of his enemy. One of the reasons for this was the tank, which Britain had first used on the battlefield on 15 September 1916. The battles of the Somme in 1916 laid the seeds of ultimate victory.

*******************

The winter of 1916-1917 saw no major offensive. But as Lieutenant Colonel A G Horsfall, who had succeeded Lieutenant Colonel Bray in command of the 2nd Battalion, noted in his diary, the winter months brought other afflictions: *"Am mud from head to foot, hair, face, everything. One is just a moving mud clot. One can hardly tell where one's breeches end and boots begin.... I spent two hours digging a man out with my hands, he had been*

---

(j) Another member of the 10th Battalion was J B Priestley (of Bradford) who had enlisted into the 10th as a private in 1914. He was to become a renowned English writer and dramatist.

*in twenty hours and was nearly a gonner. They sniped us all the time, but were damned bad shots, and we got the man out".*

Notwithstanding the respite during the winter 1916-1917 the position of the Germans on the Somme front was steadily growing untenable. Miles to the rear a great fortified system had been constructed, called the Hindenburg Line, and to this the Germans retreated in February and March 1917.

In December 1916 the French Commander-in-Chief, General Joffre, had been succeeded by General Nivelle, who had become a hero in France by winning back much of the ground lost at Verdun. He immediately put forward an ambitious plan to break the German lines by a massed attack and so end the war at a blow. His original plan was to bite off the German Somme salient by a British attack on a broad front either side of Arras, combined with a similar French attack in Champagne. This plan was soon upset by the German withdrawal to the Hindenburg line. Nevertheless it was decided to proceed with the double attack.

On 9 April Haig launched thirteen British and four Canadian divisions on a major offensive in the Arras salient. Known as the Battle of Arras, this, like the Somme, was really a succession of furious individual engagements, fought out north and south of the Scarpe River between 9 April and 23 May.

Still in the 12th Brigade of the 4th Division, the 2nd Battalion was tasked with an attack on Fampoux, east of Arras, and then an advance to the German Green Line, or second defence system. It was snowing hard as the Battalion, nineteen officers and 800-odd other ranks, pressed forward to Fampoux:

> *"We fairly rushed the village, which was a very big one: Luckily for us, the enemy was a bit on the run and it was not until we got to the far end that we had any real fighting; here we had to bomb them out of one or two houses... The Boche made a stand beyond the village, holding a railway embankment on our right, several trenches and a line of houses beyond, with MGs. Trying to advance to the Green Line, we lost about 80 men and 6 officers in two or three minutes. the survivors had to lie flat, any man showing himself the slightest bit being shot to pieces".*

(Lieutenant Colonel Horsfall).

Nevertheless, the Dukes, supported by the King's Own (Royal Lancaster) and the Lancashire Fusiliers, managed to capture some trenches, where they beat off counter-attacks. *"By now"*, wrote Horsfall, *"...apart from casualties, the men were simply dead beat....since 5.15am on the 9th we had practically no rest, had taken part in two attacks and dug in twice and been heavily shelled and fired at by MGs all the time".* At one point, the CO with a company sergeant-major and a Lewis gun were holding a sector by themselves. By 12 April, when the mauled 12th Brigade was withdrawn for regrouping, the 2nd Dukes had lost one officer killed, ten wounded and 185 men killed or wounded. *"Luckily"*, said

Colonel Horsfall, *"we got some top-hole drafts"*. These were soon to suffer in their turn when the Battalion marched back to the front in much the same area. On the night of 3 May there was another attack on the German "Blue Line", in which the Battalion *did magnificently* (Horsfall). *They went bang through with some men of another Brigade and reached the second objective [Blue Line] about 2,000 yards away.* But, swept by machine-gun fire from front and flanks, they had lost heavily. All officers became casualties and the remnants of the Battalion were forced to fall back to their jumping-off trench, where with survivors of the 10 and 12th Brigades - about 100 men in all – they dug in. Colonel Horsfall sent urgent messages for reinforcements, but none was forthcoming until the following day. By then the Battalion could muster no more than 54 effectives. After re-grouping all who remained, the Dukes were formed into two platoons attached to the Lancashire Fusiliers, with whom they put in another, unsuccessful, attack on the Blue Line on 11 May, losing still more. On 13 May they were withdrawn to a rest area. Lieutenant Colonel Horsfall was awarded the DSO for the courage and energy he had shown throughout the operations around Fampoux. Meanwhile the struggle continued until 23 May, when the German line had been pushed back some four miles east of Arras – at the cost of 158,660 British and Canadians killed and wounded.

On 16 April Nivelle's great offensive on the Aisne had been launched. Measured by the number of prisoners taken and guns captured it was a success, but compared with what Nivelle had promised it was a failure. On 15 May he was dismissed.

In France political disappointment with Nivelle's failure communicated itself to the troops and whole divisions were soon in a state of rebellion, not refusing to fight, but declining to make any more costly attacks. It took all the skills of General Pétain, who had succeeded Nivelle, to restore discipline. Meanwhile Haig had no option but to bear the brunt of the struggle almost unsupported by his principal ally.

With the dual aim of denying the German U boats the use of the Belgian ports at Ostende and Zeebrugge and diverting pressure on the French, Haig mounted a major offensive in the Ypres region in early June. This opened on 7 June with the detonation of nineteen enormous mines on the dominating Messines Ridge, which utterly destroyed the German entrenchments and with subsequent artillery barrage left the surviving defenders so demoralised that the whole feature was captured with few casualties. **Messines** is one of the Regiment's battle honours. The 10th Battalion took part in the attack and its history records that the attack was *"brilliantly successful"*. The 8th Battalion was also present below the ridge, but did not take part in the assault.

Consolidating gains, Haig now pressed forward with the objective of clearing the Ypres salient, and with it, northern Belgium. However the whole area was only a few feet above sea level. Constant bombardment had blocked up much of the drainage system with the result that it had become a morass. It was across this swamp that the British army was now required to attack. The offensive was known as the Third Battle of Ypres, but to the soldiers who fought and suffered there – and to the public – it became more familiar as Passchendaele, the name of piles of rubble that had once been a Flemish village. Haig launched his thrust on 31 July. On 11 August the 8th Battalion of the Dukes was in action south of Langemarck (north of Ypres), attacking a strongly held German position. Early in the morning, one of its platoons went over the top, to be met by a storm of machine-gun fire. Among the platoon was Private Arnold Loosemore who was awarded the Victoria Cross for his single handed elimination of a strong party of the enemy.

Meanwhile the 2nd Battalion of the Dukes, still under Lieutenant Colonel Horsfall, had seen little serious action in the Arras sector, apart from daily bombing raids on enemy trenches. As Colonel Horsfall wrote, one of the worries confronting a commanding officer was that of replacing tried and trusted casualties among company officers with raw inexperienced youngsters sent up with reinforcements. *All our best officers seem to have been hit, and then just as one began to despair and wonder how to carry on, a young officer who had been an absolute rotter and good at nothing was suddenly left in command of a company and proved as gallant as any man could be and did most valuable work. It has been the making of him.*

On 20 September 1917 the 2nd Battalion, still with 4th Division, was moved up to the Ypres front, and on 9 October was involved in the fighting around Poelcappelle, a couple of miles west of the ruined Passchendaele. The 12th Brigade went in at 5.20am, with the 2nd Dukes in supporting role. The attack succeeded in gaining the first line of enemy trenches, but as there was a gap between two of the battalions the Dukes were rushed to fill it. Leading the forward company himself, Colonel Horsfall was felled by a bullet through the head and died within minutes. Command was temporarily assumed by the senior surviving officer, Captain J S Browning, who speedily had the Battalion in position. All that day fierce counter attacks were fought off, and after losing heavily the 12th Brigade was withdrawn from the line on the 11th.

The three days had cost the 2nd Dukes 170 all ranks killed, wounded and missing. The death of Lieutenant Colonel Horsfall was a grievous loss. He had joined the Battalion from the 1st Battalion in India just twelve months previously, and had earned the respect of all ranks for his courage and devotion to his men. At the beginning of November, when the Battalion had returned to Arras, command was assumed by Lieutenant Colonel R J A Henniker MC. Meanwhile, the struggle around Passchendaele had continued in all its ferocity. The devastated terrain fought over was even worse than that of the Somme in the previous year. Both British and German heavy artillery had pounded the whole area into a desolation of shell craters, skeleton woods, blasted ruins of villages and farmhouses, while unusually heavy rains had transformed the already soaked ground into a quagmire of mud into which the floundering infantrymen often sank up to their waists. Even with the aid of horses, guns had frequently to be man-handled into position with drag-ropes.

Such were the conditions which confronted 147 Brigade (1/4th, 1/5th, 1/6th and 1/7th Battalions DWR) when on 9 October it went into action on the Belle Vue Spur, an extension of the Passchendaele ridge – the last natural barrier between the British and the low-lying plains of Belgium. Initially the Brigade was in divisional reserve but

5th Battalion, Polygon Wood, 1917

shortly after the battle started it was sent to support 146 Brigade. In the ensuing attack there were many casualties due to intensive machine gun fire and heavy shelling but by the late afternoon the objectives had been achieved. By then every officer and man was covered with mud from head to foot and their clothes soaked. The Brigade was relieved on 11 October, *"thoroughly done up"*, to quote the words of the historian of the 1/4th Battalion, as a result of living in a waste of mud and water, with little shelter and carrying out an attack over the same appalling ground.

On 6 November what had been the village of Passchendaele was captured. This was practically the end of the operations. The Germans in France had been pinned down but it had cost some 245,000 British casualties to do it.

While the Passchendaele slaughter was at its height a staff officer in the newly-formed Tank Corps was mulling over his scheme for a bold tank attack in the Cambrai area. His name was Major John Fuller[m] and like other dedicated tankmen he had been dismayed by the misuse of the new weapon in penny packets during the previous year in the impassable mud and craters of Passchendaele. With the enthusiastic backing of his chief, Brigadier General Elles of the Tank Corps, the plan was put forward to General Sir Julian Byng, commanding 3rd Army in the Cambrai sector, who approved and commended it to Haig. Sir Douglas was receptive, but instead of the original idea

(m) As Major General J F C Fuller CB,CBE,DSO, he became a much respected and prolific writer on military matters.

of a single hit and run raid, he saw the opportunity for a massive full-scale offensive designed to smash through the Hindenburg Line south of Cambrai. All available tanks – 378 – were to be employed in a surprise attack, accompanied by six infantry divisions and supported by two of cavalry and some 1,000 guns.

The Battle of Cambrai opened at 6.20am on 20 November and the initial attack went entirely according to plan, which was to break through the Hindenburg Line and to capture the German strongpoints in the rear at Havrincourt, Graincourt and Bourlon Wood. The massed tanks rolled straight through the German wire and trenches and so demoralised the enemy that the following infantry had little to do but mop up. By nightfall that day the three defence systems of the Hindenburg Line had been penetrated up to nearly five miles along a six-mile front; 6,000 prisoners and several hundred guns and machine guns had been captured. Compared with the appalling casualties on the first day of the Somme and at Passchendaele, the total loss of 4,000 killed and wounded out of the 250,000 all arms seemed a small price to pay. At home the success was hailed as *"the greatest British victory of the war"*, while for the first time church bells were rung in celebration.

Four battalions of the Duke of Wellington's Regiment were engaged at Cambrai. They were: 2/4th, 2/5th, 2/6th and 2/7th, brigaded together as the 186th Infantry Brigade of the 62nd (West Riding) Division. The Brigade was commanded by Brigadier General R B Bradford who had won a VC and an MC in France the previous year. Known as "Boy" Bradford, at the age of twenty-five he was the youngest brigade commander in the British Army.

On the morning of the attack 62 Division, with 185 and 187 Brigades in the lead and preceded by their tanks and a creeping barrage, advanced towards the Brown Line – its first objective. By 10.00am that objective had been achieved. The four Dukes battalions in 186 Brigade had been held in reserve, but were soon ordered forward to consolidate the gains. Although the main enemy defences had been overrun, there were still pockets of stiff resistance which were only overcome by sharp actions, and casualties. On approaching Havrincourt village the 2/5th Battalion met a storm of machine gun fire which killed its Commanding Officer, Lieutenant Colonel T A D Best, together with three other officers and 65 other ranks killed and wounded. But pressing on, the Battalion gained its objective on the Hindenburg support line, having captured 350 prisoners and fifteen machine guns. By nightfall the 62nd Division had overrun the Hindenburg line to a depth of four-and-a-half miles, capturing three villages and some 5,000 prisoners – *"a brilliant achievement"* noted Haig's despatch.

At dusk on the 20th, a company of the 2/6th Dukes with two squadrons of King Edward's Horse (mounted) were pushed forward to capture the village of Anneux, an outpost of the German defences in Bourlon Wood. But horsemen and infantrymen were met by impenetrable wire and withering machine gun fire and forced to withdraw. The next day saw the capture of Anneux by the 62nd Division, in which the four Dukes battalions were heavily involved. By evening they had advanced up to 2,000 yards and were holding a line south of Bourlon Wood. In the two days' fighting 186 Brigade had captured 1,138 prisoners, 34 field guns and 38 machine guns. During the evening of the 21st, the Brigade was withdrawn to positions around Graincourt, being relieved by the West Yorkshiremen of 185 Brigade.

By now the Germans had recovered from their shock of the 20th and reinforcements were being rushed up. The British line on Byng's left flank was completely dominated by the Bourlon Wood ridge, which had to be captured before any further advance was possible. The first attack, by the 40th Division, went in on 23 November and after fierce fighting was successful, all but the far extremity of the wood being occupied. But this was only the beginning of the five-day struggle in that crucial sector. On the 24th the 62nd Division took over from the 40th, and the four Dukes Battalions of 186 Brigade were again committed to action. The objective was now the complete cleaning up of the ridge and the capture of Bourlon village on the northern outskirts.

The attack, on the 27th, met both natural and enemy opposition. In the dense wood and thick undergrowth battalions and companies lost touch with each other, while concentrations of artillery and mortar fire inflicted casualties. The 2/5th Dukes managed to overcome nests of machine guns to occupy the northern edge of the wood by nightfall. The 2/6th lost direction, but pressing ahead it found its way out of the wood and to the outskirts of Bourlon village. Entirely unsupported and having suffered 177 killed and wounded, it was forced to withdraw. Meanwhile the 2/7th, with three companies of the 2/7th West Yorks, gained their objective on the Bourlon village road, but here heavy machine gun fire made further advance impossible. The two battalions had lost twelve officers and some 300 men killed and wounded.

By 29 November 10,500 prisoners had been taken and a large block to the depth of five miles had been bitten out of the Hindenburg Line. The following day the Germans counter-attacked and in places broke through into the original British positions. The battle ended on 7 December by which date much of the ground gained had been lost again, a situation which had not been helped by the lack of British reserves on account of the losses at Passchendaele and the despatch ( in early November) of five divisions to reinforce the Italian front. A great success was followed by a lamentable reverse.

***********************

In January 1918 a reorganisation of brigade establishments, due to a shortage of manpower, resulted in a reduction from four to three battalions. Following this change the 1/5th and 2/5th were amalgamated to form the 5th Battalion, the 2/6th and 8th Battalions were disbanded and the 2/7th was reduced to a training cadre. At about the same time the 2nd Battalion was transferred from the 12th Brigade to the 10th of which the two other battalions were Ist Royal Warwicks and the 2nd Seaforth Highlanders.

On the Eastern Front the Russians had surrendered to the Germans and on 2 March signed the Treaty of Brest-Litovsk. The Germans were thus able to transfer large numbers of troops to the Western Front and so wipe out the superiority in numbers the allies had enjoyed there since 1915. Meanwhile the British Commander-in-Chief faced difficulties from his political master, Prime Minister Lloyd George, who intended to subordinate him to General Pétain. When that failed, he deprived him of his principal ally, "Wully" Robertson, the Chief of the Imperial General Staff. Worse, when Haig demanded 605,000 reinforcements, Lloyd George, with memories of Passchendaele in mind, told him to make do with only 100,000. On the German side, on the other hand, Ludendorff had no such problems. By March he had been able to concentrate 63 infantry divisions with 6,400 guns, poised to strike at Haig's weakest sector between Armentières and the La Basse Canal, held by twelve divisions of Gough's Fifth Army and fourteen of Byng's Third Army. The blow came as a total surprise on 21 March when, preceded by a massive artillery bombardment and spearheaded by newly formed specialist assault troops, the Germans smashed through the British front and by the end of the month had penetrated as far as Amiens, on the River Somme within thirty miles of the Channel coast. The British had suffered 160,000 casualties, and Gough's Fifth Army was virtually annihilated after heroic fighting.

North of Arras, the 2nd Dukes were not seriously involved, but on 23 March the 186th Infantry Brigade, now comprising the 2/4th, 5th and 2/7th battalions, together with the rest of 62nd Division, was transferred to Byng's Third Army and was very actively engaged, for example at the repulse of the German attacks on Bucquoy, 26-28 March, when the 62nd Division lost 2,084 officers and men.

It was now becoming clear that the objective of the German High Command was to drive a wedge between the British and French armies. It was also clear that the allied weakness lay in the lack of a unified command. Accordingly it was agreed that Marshal Foch would be responsible for the general co-ordination of the allied effort and to this America, the first of whose troops had recently been in action, also agreed.

On 9 April, Ludendorff launched another offensive, on the Neuve Chapelle front, in an attempt to push through to the Channel ports. Much of the front was held by Portuguese troops who were swept away by the Germans and by evening sixteen divisions had penetrated five miles and at one point crossed the River Lys. The next day the British counter-attacked heavily and among the troops engaged was the 1/4th Battalion (147 Brigade) who put in an attack on the village of Erquinghem on the River Lys, near Armentières. There was fierce opposition. One company was virtually destroyed and, when withdrawn across the river, the Battalion had lost fifteen officers and 391 other ranks killed, wounded and missing. During the height of the battle Private Arthur Poulter's splendid conduct earned him the VC. His company's casualties were so heavy that the stretcher-bearers could not cope with all the wounded, so on ten separate occasions he braved intense fire to carry in wounded men on his back.

By now British losses since 21 March were approaching 300,000 and the position was desperate. On the 12th the undemonstrative Haig issued his famous "Backs to the Wall" Order of the Day, demanding that every position must be held to the last man *"..... and each one of us must fight on to the end"*. However the Germans continued their attacks on both the Ypres and Amiens fronts and it was not until Foch released some French divisions from his reserve that the tide began to turn. By the end of April Ludendorff's great push against the British had definitely failed. By the end of June the German offensive had petered out and the allies were being reinforced by the long-awaited arrival of the Americans. The final phase of the war was about to begin.

June was very quiet on the 2nd Battalion's front at La Bassée, as was July, but it was enlivened on 18 July by a daring raid to clear the enemy out of the Bois de Pacaut, a thick piece of forest full of infantrymen, machine guns and mortars. The result was very successful: the enemy fled, leaving behind about 40 dead, 29 prisoners and several machine guns – all for the cost of five Dukes killed and 25 wounded. This was but one example of numerous raids carried out by battalions of the Regiment during the period before the final British advance. At midnight on 19/20 June the 1/4th Battalion carried out a four-company raid on German positions at Zillebeke near Ypres. Again, success was achieved. On withdrawing at 1.30am, the companies had inflicted heavy casualties, captured prisoners and machine guns, while out of the 350 who took part, only three were killed and seventeen wounded.

Operating with the reconstituted 186 Brigade of the 62nd Division, the 5th Battalion of the Dukes came in for some tough fighting in the Brigade's attack on the great Forest of Rheims, the dense thickets of which were defended by strongpoints totalling some 1,800 Prussian infantry with numerous machine guns. The 5th Battalion, under Lieutenant Colonel J Walker, was tasked to capture a sector of the forest known as Bois du Petit Champ, and as Wryall's history of the 62nd Division observes, this proved *an extraordinary man-hunt in the depths of the forest*. First to draw the covert was A Company who had scarcely struggled 200 yards through undergrowth when it was met by blasts of machine gun fire. Regardless of casualties the company pressed on with fixed bayonets, to capture the post together with 35 prisoners and six machine guns. D Company now came forward to reinforce the depleted A. After overcoming isolated machine gun nests, the two came up against such fierce fire from a hidden strongpoint that they were forced to halt and form a defensive post. Meanwhile B and C Companies were in trouble on the southern fringe of the wood, meeting heavy fire which felled many of their number and caused a temporary holdup. However, by skilful use of fire and movement and a concerted attack on both flanks, they were able to charge with the bayonet, capturing 50 Germans and eight machine guns. In this southern sector of the wood five more enemy posts were overcome, yielding another 80 prisoners and twenty machine guns. By mid afternoon C Company had pushed on through the wood to reach its objective on the north-western skirts, though it had suffered from those murderous machine gun nests. But no sooner had it begun to dig in when a strong enemy counter-attack burst upon it. Utterly outnumbered, the weak company could only fight a running withdrawal back to the southern fringes, by which time no more than two officers and a dozen or so men remained unwounded. At nightfall the other three companies were reinforced by the 1/5th Devons and were able to consolidate a position along the southern edge of the forest.

As with innumerable other gallant actions in the war, that of the 5th Battalion in the Forest of Rheims is little known. During the single days fighting the Battalion captured

Officers of the Dukes in June 1918

208 prisoners of the élite 53rd Prussian Regiment of Infantry, besides 41 machine guns. The enemy dead and wounded probably greatly exceeded that number. The price paid by the Battalion was five officers and 150 other ranks killed and many more wounded. The 5th Battalion was *"heartily congratulated by Corps, Divisional and Brigade Commanders on their particularly fine fight....."*

On 15 July Ludendorff made a last frenzied effort. The Germans crossed the River Marne and gained some ground, but with enormous loss. This was the last German offensive in the west. On 18 July they were assaulted by the French and forced to withdraw with further heavy losses. The second battle of the Marne was the turning point of the war.

The operations on the Marne, by destroying the Germans' last substantial reserves, opened the way for a deadly British stroke further north. On 8 August the 4th Army broke through the German lines in the old battle ground of the Somme. This surprise offensive, (capturing 21,000 prisoners), was a serious blow to enemy morale, leading Ludendorff to declare that 8 August was *"the black day of the German Army"*. Now, with the 10th Infantry Brigade of the 4th Division, the 2nd Battalion was in action throughout the month, pushing along the Arras-Cambrai road. On the 31st there was a sharp fight over the enemy strongpoint of St. Servin's Farm, near Haucourt, capturing

45 prisoners, nine machine guns and one field gun, for the loss of seventeen all ranks killed and 36 wounded. For his conspicuous bravery during this engagement Second Lieutenant J P Huffam, who had joined the Battalion from the 5th the previous June, was awarded the VC.

The climax of the last great allied offensive came in August and September 1918, when Haig's armies smashed through the Hindenburg Line, to which the Germans had been forced to withdraw, while the French and Americans thrust forward in the Argonne. During this period the 5th Battalion was heavily committed, particularly so during the advance across the Canal du Nord and the capture of Marcoing, during the second battle of Cambrai. On 28 August the Battalion was in action west of the Canal du Nord, when one of several bombing parties on the enemy trenches was led by Private Henry Tandey. As the forward parties seemed to be held up, he took two men, dashed across fire-swept no-man's land, killed several Germans and came back with twenty prisoners. This daring action led to the capture of the German trench, and Tandey was awarded the DCM. On 12 September the Battalion was attacking at Havrincourt and Private Tandey again distinguished himself. Having rescued several wounded men under fire, the next day he led a bombing party into the enemy trenches, when he once more returned with prisoners. This earned him the MM. On 28 September he gave a further display of his outstanding gallantry. An eye witness, Private H Lister, recounted the episode.

> "On 28th September, 1918, during the taking of the crossing over the Canal de St. Quentin at Marcoing, I was No. 1 of the Lewis gun team of my platoon. I witnessed the whole gallantry of Private Tandey throughout the day. Under intensely heavy fire he crawled forward in the village when we were being held up by the enemy MG and found where it was, and then led myself and comrades with the gun into a house from where we were able to bring Lewis gun fire on the MG and knock it out of action. Later when we got to the Crossings (sic) and the bridge was down, Pte Tandey, under the fiercest aimed MG fire went forward and replaced planks over the bad part of the bridge to enable us all to cross without the delay which would otherwise have ensued. On the same evening when we made another attack we were completely surrounded by a huge number of Germans, and we thought the position might be lost, Pte. Tandey, without hesitation, though he was twice wounded very nastily, took the leading part in our bayonet charge on the enemy, to get clear. Though absolutely faint he refused to leave us until we had completely finished our job, collected our prisoners and restored the line".

The bayonet charge led by Tandey consisted only of eight men and resulted in the capture of 37 prisoners. Later the intrepid private, wounds still undressed, led a bombing party which captured twenty more prisoners. Private Henry Tandey's award of the VC was gazetted on 14 December 1918. With the supreme award in addition to the DCM and MM, he became the most decorated private in the First World War.

In that memorable action at Marcoing on 28 September, 1918 the 5th Battalion captured 500 prisoners and twenty-five machine guns. Their casualties totalled five officers and 110 other ranks, killed and wounded.

By 5 October the allies had penetrated the whole of the Hindenburg Line defence system, and with the Germans falling back everywhere, it seemed that the slaughter was nearly over. The German High Command urged peace at any price and made overtures for mediation to the American president, who rebuffed them. However, although the German army's morale was fast collapsing, with some units surrendering without a fight, the final few weeks of the war saw fierce contests. Thus on 24 October the 2nd Battalion was in action near Monchaux, south of Valenciennes. After heavy fighting it captured its objective with 350 prisoners and thirty-one machine guns, while the enemy was forced to withdraw nearly two miles. The Battalion's casualties were eight officers and 209 other ranks killed and wounded.

The final month of the war found the territorial battalions of the Dukes thrusting forward beyond the Hindenburg Line, with several sharp actions to their credit. 147th Infantry Brigade (the 1/4th, 1/6th and 1/7th) advanced with the 49th (West Riding) Division and on 11 October the 7th Battalion was involved in a costly fight to gain a ridge near Villers-en-Cauchies. After a four-hour struggle during which the Battalion was attacked by German tanks, the objective was won, but at a terrible price. Out of the 650 all ranks who had left their trenches in the morning, only some 250 remained. The Brigade's last fight came on 1/2 November with a divisional attack on the southern defences of Valenciennes. This time casualties were not heavy, for the enemy surrendered in droves, showing little stomach for continued resistance. Next afternoon, however, a heavy counter-attack was feared, for the RAF reported masses of troops, guns and transport on the Mons-Valenciennes road. But no attack developed. The columns were moving east, out of the battle area, and the enemy was in full retreat.

Message from 49 (West Riding) Division to 147 Brigade, 11 November 1918

*Gallipoli Campaign 1915*

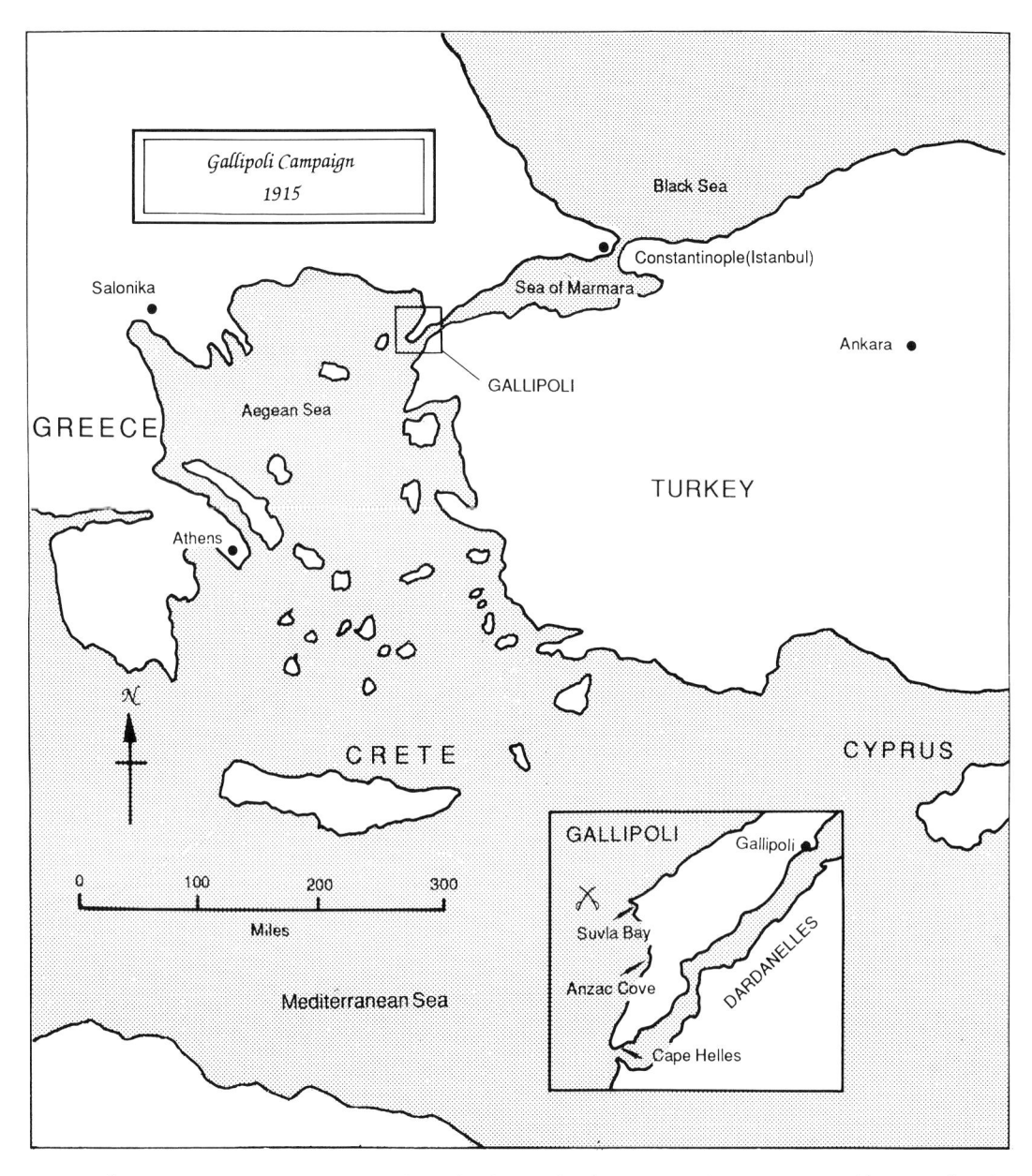

By 7 November the 2nd Battalion had reached Preseau, just twenty miles south of Mons where the British army had seen its first fighting in 1914.

On 8 November the 62 Division with its 186th Brigade (2/4th Hampshires, 2/4th and 5th Dukes), fought its final action at Maubeuge. As elsewhere, German resistance was crumbling. On the previous day the 62nd Divisional HQ had received information that German negotiators were to be allowed safe conduct through another sector of the front. Maubeuge was captured with little loss and, and by 10 November the Dukes were in billets in the village of Sous le Bois, a few miles north of Maubeuge. It was now common knowledge that an Armistice was imminent, and on the eleventh hour of the eleventh month of 1918 Germany accepted unconditional surrender.

***********************

In January 1915 Winston Churchill (First Lord of the Admiralty) and Lord Kitchener had devised a plan to relieve German pressure on the Western Front by a diversionary operation in the Turkish Gallipoli peninsula. The main objectives were the forcing of the Dardanelles straits and the capture of Constantinople, thus removing the Turkish threat to the Suez Canal and Egypt, and at the same time relieving the Russians who were heavily embroiled in the Caucasus. Churchill demanded a purely naval operation, but when this failed – thereby alerting the Turks to what was to follow – it was decided to mount a land attack on the peninsula. General Sir Ian Hamilton was given command of a force consisting of British, Australian, New Zealand (ANZAC) and Indian troops.

The initial landing at Cape Helles and Anzac Cove, on the southern end of the Gallipoli peninsula, was made on 25 April 1915 but despite desperate fighting little impression was made on the Turkish defences and by July there was stalemate. Sir Ian Hamilton therefore planned a new landing which had as its objective the severance of Turkish communications with Constantinople with a view to clearing the way for the fleet to pass through the Dardanelles. In July three divisions of reinforcements began to arrive. All were men of Kitchener's Army without experience of active service. One of the divisions was the 11th (Northern) Division consisting of 32, 33 and 34 Brigades. 8th Battalion DWR, commanded by Lieutenant Colonel H J Johnston DSO, a veteran of the Boer War, was in 32 Brigade. The divisions were formed into IX Corps under command of Lieutenant General Sir Frederick Stopford, who had retired in 1909 and had never held high rank in the field, either in peace or in war.

Sir Ian's plan was to make a feint attack at the southern end of Gallipoli under cover of which IX Corps would be landed at Suvla Bay. It was then to advance inland as rapidly as possible to capture the high ground overlooking the Bay before the Turks could react. On 6 August the landing took place as planned and was virtually unopposed. Advancing inland the 32nd Brigade was sent to the support of the 34th Brigade held up on a Turkish strongpoint named Hill 10. This was covered with gorse, which was set alight by enemy shelling, and for some time confusion reigned as smoke and flames obscured both friend and foe. Seeing this, the Turks launched a counter attack, but this was driven back by the rapid small arms fire of the Yorkshiremen. This was the first time the men of 8 DWR had fired their Lee-Enfields in anger.

General Stopford, well satisfied that he had got his troops safely ashore, made no effort to urge them forward the three miles necessary to drive out what was left of a small Turkish garrison and thereby gain positions on the high ground which were of decisive importance to the whole plan. On the following evening (8th) Sir Ian Hamilton arrived and provided the necessary spur. As a result 32 Brigade was given the task of capturing the vital Anafarte Ridge. It was too late. The Turks had already been reinforced and easily held off the attack. If Stopford had ordered an attack even half an hour earlier it would almost certainly have succeeded. One of those wounded was Lieutenant Colonel Johnston. On being picked up by stretcher-bearers he ordered them to leave him and go to the help of his wounded men. He was never seen again.

By 11 August it was clear that the venture had failed. Major Jack Churchill, writing to his brother Winston, tried to explain what had gone wrong.

> *"We are all trying to understand what on earth happened to these (Suvla) men and why they are showing such extraordinary lack of enterprise. They are not cowards – physically they are as fine a body of men as the regular army. I think it is partly on account of their training. They have never seen a shot fired before. For the year they have been soldiers they have only been taught one thing – Trench warfare...they landed and advanced a mile and thought they had done something wonderful. They had no standard to go by - no other troops to show them what was right".*

The generals were the real culprits and by the end of August Sir Ian Hamilton had replaced General Stopford, the GOC 11 Division and two of the brigade commanders.

On 21 August 32 Brigade was committed to another attempt on Anafarte Ridge. Again it was a failure. By nightfall casualties had been so severe that the attack was called off. One of the 8th Battalion's NCOs was Sergeant (later CSM) E Miles who recorded in his diary on the day following the attack:

> *"As soon as dawn broke we called the roll. What a lot of specimens we looked! There was roughly 250 of us out of a total of about 900. In my company alone we lost seven killed, 43 wounded, the majority of whom died of wounds, I expect, and 23 missing out of a total of 134. We had one officer left in the battalion out of a total of 29".*

The officer was the 18 year old Second Lieutenant R E Edwards who thus became temporary commanding officer. The 32nd Brigade had suffered so severely it was obliged to form a single battalion from the survivors.

By October the High Command was resigned to the fact that the Dardanelles campaign had been a disastrous failure, gaining no advantage and costing some 214,000 casualties. Meanwhile the troops suffered from the intense cold, including deaths from exposure. In Sergeant Miles' words *"..the hardships are our worst enemy now"*. Evacuation took place between December 1915 and February 1916, with such masterly planning and secrecy that no lives were lost. Ironically, the withdrawal was the one really successful operation in the campaign. The 8th Battalion was sent to Egypt to recoup its losses. It remained there in relatively relaxed conditions until being sent to France in June 1916, disembarking at Marseilles on 1 July.

*******************

*Italian Campaign 1918*

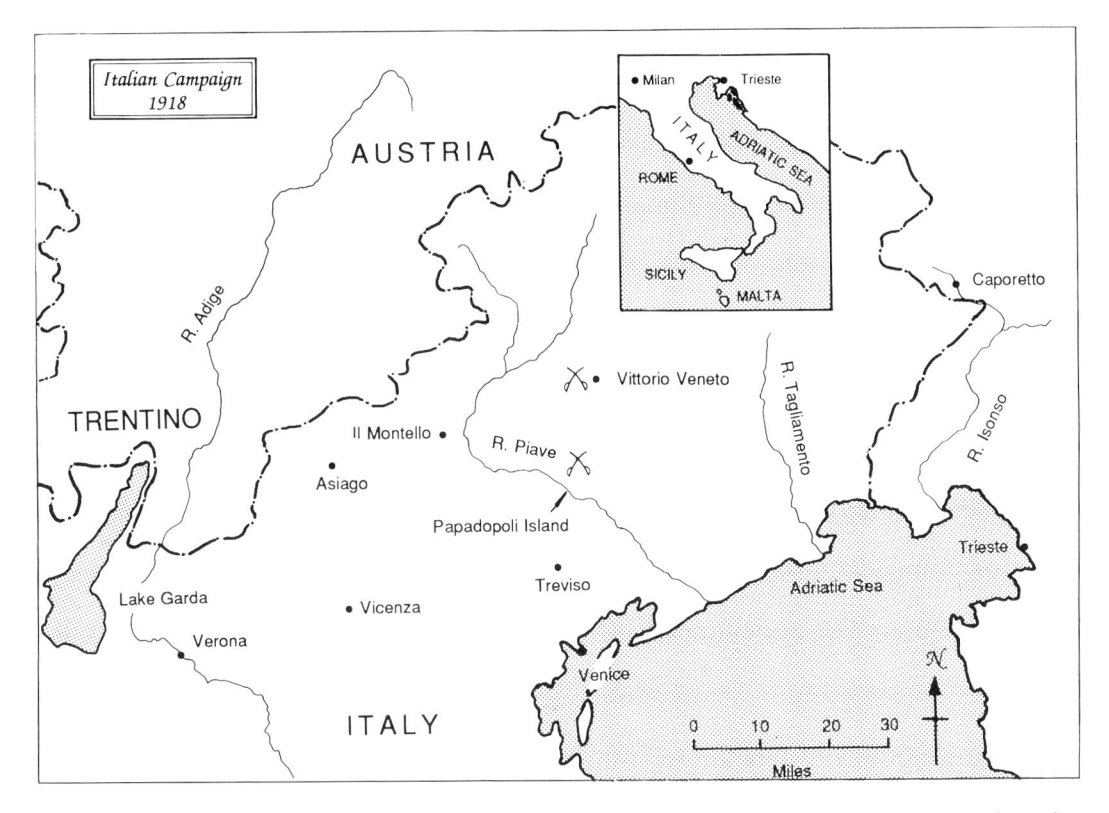

In May 1915 Italy had joined Britain, France and Russia by declaring war on Austria. As a reward she was to get Trentino, Trieste and the Dalmatian coast. The country was, however, very unprepared for war while the salient at Trentino gave Austria a strategic advantage. Italy's one superiority was in numbers – 400,000 first line troops against the 80,000 of Austro-Hungary. In the autumn of 1917 the Germans sent six divisions to help the Austrians and on 24 October attacked at Caporetto. They completely overwhelmed the Italians, who broke and fled. It was not until they abandoned everything east of the Piave that they were able to make a stand. By then they had lost 600,000 men. It was now imperative to support them and in November five British and five French divisions were withdrawn from the Western Front and sent to Italy.

One of the British divisions of the Italian Expeditionary Force was the 23rd, which comprised 68, 69 and 70 Brigades. The 10th Battalion of the Dukes was in 69 Brigade[n]. The Battalion, under command of Lieutenant Colonel F W Lethbridge DSO, entrained for Italy on 9 November and arrived at Mantua on 14 November. The 23rd Division was the first to arrive and was greeted everywhere with great enthusiasm. By early December the Battalion had moved to Il Montello (about 20 miles north west of Venice), where some mountain warfare training was carried out. Two weeks later it was in the front line. Several attempts were made to cross the Piave in order to gain information about the enemy, but the currents were too swift and in the cold conditions the patrols returned

---

[n] The other battalions in the Brigade were: 11th Battalion West Yorks and the 8th and 9th Battalions Yorkshire Regiment (Green Howards).

covered with icicles.

On 15 July 1918 the Austrians attacked along the whole front but were repulsed on the British front. 69 Brigade took no part as it was in reserve. However the 10th Battalion was very much to the fore the following month when a successful raid was made at Cavaletto which resulted in the capture of 55 prisoners. Despite a strong defence put up by the Austrians the Battalion's losses were light.

In October the allies decided to administer a final blow on the Austro-Hungarian army. The plan was to cross the Piave half way up its course and thereby divide the enemy forces. This entailed the capture of Papadopoli island in the Piave, garrisoned by Austrians. On the night 23/24 October it was captured by 7 Division. Two nights later this was joined by 23 Division. The following morning both divisions struggled through the water to the far shore. An officer of the 10th Battalion recorded, *"....the water was much deeper than expected on the battalion front and it was only by linking arms that many men were saved from being washed off their feet. This was done under an Austrian barrage"*. The allies next headed for Vittorio Veneto which was captured on the 29th. The position of the Austrians was now hopeless and an armistice was signed on 3 November by which time the Austrians had lost over half-a-million prisoners. By January 1919 demobilisation was in full swing, but elements of the 10th Battalion remained in Italy until March.

*********************

The total casualties of the British Army during the four years of war have never been exceeded before or since. More than 950,000 men had been killed, a large proportion of these being infantrymen from County regiments. The wounded exceeded two million, while some 190,000 had been taken prisoner. The Regiment's dead were over 8,000.

The Regiment's service was recognised by the award of 72 battle honours. In the past honours had always been emblazoned on the Regimental Colour. However because of the large number granted for service in the war, it was decided that regiments could select up to ten of them to be emblazoned on the King's Colour. The ten selected by the Regiment were: **Mons; Marne 1914, '18; Ypres 1914, '15, '17; Hill 60; Somme 1916, '18; Arras 1917, '18; Cambrai 1917, '18; Lys; Piave 1918** and **Landing at Suvla.**

There was no immediate repatriation for those who had served on the western front, for Britain had to contribute her quota for the occupation forces in Germany. The 2nd Battalion remained on the Rhine until June 1919 when, having been reduced to a cadre of five officers and 60 other ranks, it embarked at Antwerp for England. The Territorial battalions remained in Germany until March 1919 with their 62nd (West Riding) Division – the only Territorial division to join the Army of Occupation.

On 12 May 1923 the Regiment's Memorial Chapel in York Minster was dedicated by the Archbishop of York. Placed in the Chapel was the Roll of Honour Book in which were inscribed the names of the officers and soldiers of all battalions who had lost their lives during the war.

## THE DUKE OF WELLINGTON'S REGIMENT IN THE FIRST WORLD WAR
### Services of individual battalions

| Battalion | Date formed | Date posted overseas | Where employed |
|---|---|---|---|
| 1st | | | India, |
| 2nd | | August 1914 | western front |
| 3rd | | | home service |
| | | | |
| 1/4th (TF) } | | | |
| 1/5th (TF) } | | April 1915 | western front |
| 1/6th (TF) } | | | |
| 1/7th (TF) } | | | |
| | | | |
| 2/4th (TF) } | | | |
| 2/5th (TF) } | August 1914 | January 1917 | western front |
| 2/6th (TF) } | | | |
| 2/7th (TF) } | | | |
| | | | |
| 3/4th (TF) } | | | |
| 3/5th (TF) } | April 1915 | | home service |
| 3/6th (TF) } | | | |
| 3/7th (TF) } | | | |
| | | | |
| 8th (Service) | August 1914 | July 1915 | Gallipoli |
| | | | western front |
| | | | |
| 9th (Service) | September 1914 | July 1915 | western front |
| | | | |
| 10th (Service) | September 1914 | September 1915 | western front |
| | | | Italy |
| | | | |
| 11th (Service) | November 1914 | | home service |
| | | | |
| 12th (Service) | March 1916 | April 1916 | western front |
| | | | labour |
| | | | battalion |
| | | | |
| 13th (Service) | May 1918 | July 1918 | western front |
| | | | garrison |
| | | | battalion |

The battalions employed on home service were mostly engaged in training and drafting.

CHAPTER 17

# Between the Wars

*1919 Afghanistan*
*1935 Loe Agra, Mohmand*

As soon as the war was over the question of demobilisation arose. There were over two million British citizens serving in the army abroad and another 1,600,000 at home. Initially priority was given to those whose occupations were most necessary to the national economy. However, this decision aroused so much discontent that the priority was changed to the older men and those who had served longest abroad. By September 1919 all the war time battalions of the Dukes had been disbanded.[a] And by 1921, despite several small wars and the necessities of imperial policing, the army had been reduced to little more than its pre-war strength of 240,000. Compulsory military service had been abolished and voluntary recruiting for the regular army resumed. The Territorial Force was also re-opened for enlistment and was re-named the Territorial Army.

The British Government under Lloyd George then proceeded to slash the armed forces still further. The "Geddes Axe" [b] cut the army by some 50,000 men. Sixteen cavalry regiments were reduced to eight by amalgamations; five Irish infantry regiments were disbanded; the English regiments with four regular battalions were cut to two each; overseas garrisons were reduced. All this reflected the government's defence planning assumption that there would be no major war for ten years. As a result the army's role once again became what it had been in the late Victorian era: the policing of the Empire.

Having only two regular battalions, the Regiment was not seriously affected by the Geddes Axe, though it had to accept cuts in peace-time strength. It did, however, have a change of title. In 1920 Army Order 509/20 directed that from January 1921 the Regiment's name would be changed from The Duke of Wellington's (West Riding Regiment) – W Rid R for short, to The Duke of Wellington's Regiment (West Riding) or DWR. At that time the 1st Battalion was in Palestine, commanded by Lieutenant Colonel R E Maffett and the 2nd Battalion was near Dublin under the command of Lieutenant Colonel R N Bray CMG,DSO.

\*\*\*\*\*\*\*\*\*\*\*\*\*\*\*\*\*\*\*\*\*\*

---

(a) As a final act the war time battalions were each presented with a King's Colour. Those of the Service battalions were laid up in Halifax Parish Church on 24 July 1920.
(b) Sir Eric Geddes was chairman of a committee appointed by Lloyd George to reduce public expenditure by £86 million.

Throughout the war the situation in India had been relatively quiet, but following the end of hostilities events took a critical turn in April 1919 when agitators in the Indian National Congress Party, aided and abetted by Afghan sympathisers, fomented insurrection with rioting, murder and arson throughout northern India. At Lahore the mob virtually took control of the city until it was dispersed by fire from British patrols and a charge of cavalry. The 1st Battalion of the Dukes was routed to the scene from Quetta, but there are no details of its involvement. On 19 April occurred the deplorable "Amritsar incident" when after the murder of several Europeans and the city being in turmoil, Brigadier General Dyer ordered his Gurkhas to open fire on a political meeting, killing 379 and wounding 1,500.

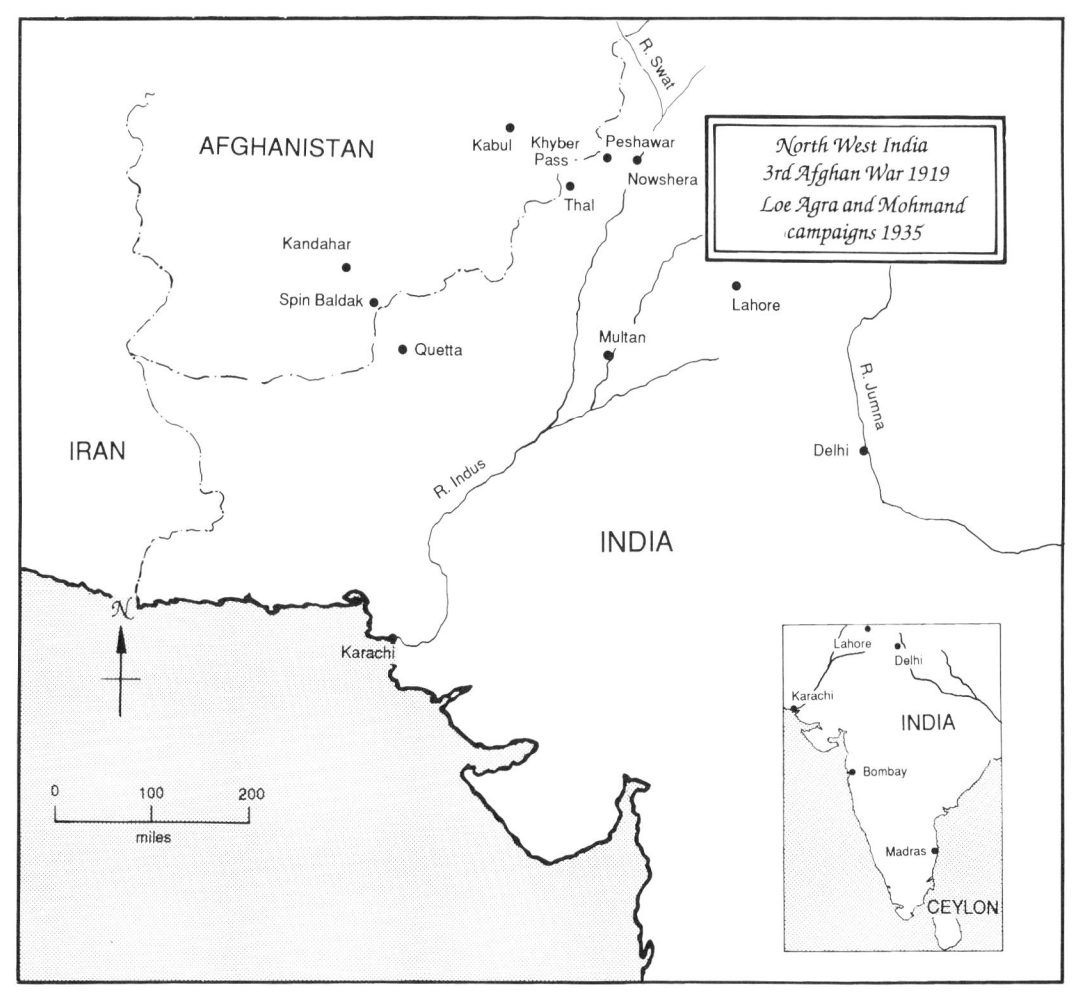

On 20 February 1919 the Emir of Afghanistan had been murdered. His successor was his third son, Amundullah, who, in order to secure the throne, had made lavish boasts to the Afghan army which he could not fulfil. Among them was a promise of Karachi as an Afghan port. In order to extricate himself from his difficulties he

proclaimed a *Jihad*, or holy war. On 8 May a small force of Afghan infantry with guns occupied a village inside British territory at the far western end of the Khyber Pass. This led to the Third Afghan War. The incursion into the Khyber was soon repelled by a British-Gurkha-Sikh field force with mountain gunners and cavalry assembled at Peshawar under Major General Fowler. After some brisk skirmishing the force crossed the frontier and took up position outside the village of Dakka, some eight miles beyond the Khyber.

On 25 May Amanullah's Commander-in-Chief, Nadir Khan, launched an attack some 80 miles south of the Khyber in the Kurram valley of Waziristan, and laid siege to the strategic British fort of Thal, railhead for supplies from Peshawar. The small garrison of Thal, (a few British officers with Gurkha riflemen and Sikh sepoys), beat off Nadir Khan's repeated attacks for five days, until on 1 June a relief column arrived and flung back the attackers. Nadir Khan thereupon withdrew his force across the frontier.

Further south the Afghans had attacked in Baluchistan. On 15 May the 1st Battalion, commanded by Lieutenant Colonel E C Boutflower in the absence of Colonel Maffett, and mustering 18 officers and 450 other ranks, was moved from Lahore to join the 11th Infantry Brigade with two battalions of the 10th Gurkha Rifles at Quetta, the southernmost garrison of the North-West Frontier. Arriving there on 18 May, the Battalion was pushed forward with its brigade to Chaman, a British outpost on the Durand Line, or British-Afghan frontier. So far there had been no trouble in this part of Baluchistan, but just across the frontier was the Afghan fortress of Spin Baldak ("White Spur"), commanding the main route from Kandahar to Quetta, and forming an obstacle to any possible British advance, besides posing a threat to Chaman. Spin Baldak was a formidable-looking mud-brick structure, crowning a long rocky ridge, its 30ft walls pierced with tiers of loopholes and protected by stone towers at intervals. Further defence was provided by three detached towers surrounded by 15ft walls. Field Force HQ at Peshawar ordered that it should be captured.

The attack, in two columns, went in at dawn on 27 May. The right column consisted of the 57th Infantry Brigade, the left being the Dukes' 11th Brigade with the 2/10th Gurkha Rifles and general reserve. Lieutenant Colonel Boutflower was given command of this column, the Battalion being temporarily commanded by Major R H W Owen. When the 57th Brigade was held up by intense fire, the Dukes were ordered up to attack the outlying defences on Tower Hill, which they did with great gallantry, occupying the crest and the towers with minimal loss. Then, after grenade attacks on enemy sangars, they were able to enter the eastern gate of the fort itself, by which time the rest of the force had successfully breached the defences elsewhere. By 1300 hours the Afghan commander had surrendered and Spin Baldak was captured as ordered. For the Dukes it was almost a bloodless victory: only two men were killed and no wounded were recorded. Next day the Battalion and its brigade were withdrawn back to Chaman, to receive a Special Order of the Day from the GOC 4th (Quetta) Division, congratulating the Chaman Force and *"in particular, The Duke of Wellington's Regiment and the 1/22nd Punjabis"*. The latter battalion had been the first to enter the fort.

For the next six weeks the Chaman Force laboured to construct a defence system running for some eight miles along the border beyond Chaman and consisting of a series of stone sangars behind a wire perimeter. Since this work was carried out in the soaring temperatures of the Afghan hot weather – up to about 43°C – the soldiers were sorely tried and afflicted with prickly heat, (c) or heat exhaustion. On 8 August peace was signed and on 13 September the Battalion returned to Quetta. The Duke of Wellington's Regiment (with twelve others) bears the battle honour **Afghanistan 1919** on its colours.

The Battalion now began to post drafts home for demobilisation, so that by October it had been reduced to a cadre of seven officers, three warrant officers and 86 other ranks. In January 1920 the Battalion was posted to Egypt where it was brought up to strength by drafts from home before being sent to Palestine. Four months later, in May 1921, it returned to England – after sixteen years of foreign service.

In the following three years the Battalion, now commanded by Lieutenant Colonel R K Healing, was constantly on the move. From June to October 1921 it was in Tidworth. Then it was sent to the Curragh, near Dublin,(d) before returning to Tidworth in January 1922, following the establishment of the Irish Free State as a self governing dominion. After fifteen months in Tidworth the Battalion was posted to Gibraltar early in 1923.

By the Treaty of Sèvres( 20 August 1920) between the allies and the Ottoman Empire the Greeks were to gain large tracts of Turkey. The Turkish nationalists under Kemal Atatürk were infuriated and progressively drove back the Greeks. By August 1922 the triumphant Turks were poised to cross the Dardanelles and pursue the Greeks into Europe. One of the key positions was Chanak, near Constantinople, which covered the Dardanelles on the Asiatic side and was held by three thousand British infantry, with cavalry and artillery. Lloyd George reacted firmly and reinforcements were swiftly sent from England, Egypt, Malta and Gibraltar. Among them was the 1st Battalion. The Turks were deterred and war was averted. Among the ships of the Royal Navy at Chanak was HMS Iron Duke with whom an affiliation was established which was to last until 1945, when the ship was de-commissioned and scrapped.

On returning to England in October 1923 the Battalion was posted to Gosport. On 30 July 1925 Lieutenant General Sir Herbert Belfield, Colonel of the Regiment, presented new Colours to the Battalion, which was now commanded by Lieutenant Colonel N G Burnand DSO. In May 1926 the Battalion embarked in H T Nevasa for special duty. The move was supposed to be secret, but as the NAAFI stores were labelled Leith, it was obvious that the Battalion was being sent to Scotland in connection with the general strike. On arrival it was stationed at various towns in and around Edinburgh. There was some apprehension as to the reaction of the people to an English regiment being sent to maintain law and order in Scotland, but the six months the Battalion spent across the border passed without incident. On 5 December the Battalion arrived

---

(c) All too familiar to soldiers in India, this was an inflammation of the sweat glands causing an irresistible urge to scratch.
(d) The 2nd Battalion was stationed in Dublin at this time. The only recorded contact between the two battalions was a rugby match, the result of which is not known.

*The cooks of 5 DWR with field kitchen, Ripon, 1928*

back in Gosport by which time command had been assumed by Lieutenant Colonel F H V Wellesley. In 1927 the Battalion moved to Devonport, where it was to spend the next four years, notable mainly for training, in Devon, Cornwall and on Salisbury Plain, and for many successes in the world of sport.

In the army, and the infantry in particular, little had changed in training, dress and arms from its predecessors who had crossed the Channel in 1914. The battalion organisation had settled at a headquarter wing, three rifle companies and the machine gun company with its eight Vickers guns and horse-drawn limbers. The headquarter wing comprised, besides battalion staff, the band and drums, signallers, cooks and orderly room clerks. Emphasis was still on the renowned firepower of the SMLE rifle with its 15 rounds per minute "rapid" and the Vickers medium machine gun. But for LMGs the infantry still had to make do with its unreliable Lewis LMG, which was not superseded until 1938. As in 1914, the soldier performed all his duties, in the field or on the barrack square, clad in service dress: at home, the serge tunic and trousers wound with puttees: in the tropics, khaki drill tunics and shorts, with hose-tops and puttees; though in the Indian hot weather shirt-sleeves order was the norm. In England the peaked cap was the regulation headdress, but in India protection from the sun was afforded by the cork Wolesley topi with puggari bearing a flash in the colour of the regiments' facings.

By 1928 mechanisation began to oust the horse in the cavalry, but in the infantry, horses remained the principal means of transport. The battalion transport included the four-wheeled GS (general service) wagons drawn by two, or sometimes four horses, the drivers mounted on the nearside horse, as in artillery gun-teams. These carried baggage, rations, ammunition and any other loads. Each company had its own company carts, smaller, two wheeled versions of the GS wagon, while there were water carts and a mobile field cooker mounted on a wagon. When on the march, the men's tea and stew could thus be prepared, the cooks trudging behind.

*********************

In June 1919 the 2nd Battalion, under command of Lieutenant Colonel R N Bray CMG, DSO, arrived in England from Germany and was sent to Pembroke Dock. In September the Battalion moved to Sheffield, where efforts were made to re-form as a regular battalion. This had been largely accomplished when, in June 1920, the Battalion was moved to Ireland to be stationed near Dublin. Then followed a difficult period until March 1922, during which guard duties and periodic raids against the Sinn Fein kept the Battalion fully employed. It was twice sent to Belfast to preserve law and order during periods of rioting, and in 1921 crossed to Liverpool as a precautionary measure for strike duty. There was little regret when the Battalion, under the command of Brevet Colonel C L Smith VC, MC,(e) returned to England to be stationed at Aldershot after the establishment of the Irish Free State.(f)

The Battalion was mobilised with the object of moving to Chanak, but this was cancelled and a move to Egypt was ordered instead, whence it sailed on 30 November 1922. It was first stationed at Moascar, then, in January 1924, moved to Cairo and remained there for two years. Under command of Lieutenant Colonel C J Pickering CMG, DSO, it achieved a high state of military efficiency and a splendid run of sporting victories.

The Battalion's next move was to Singapore where it arrived on 3 March 1926. Singapore, with its enervating climate, proved to be a great change from Cairo. The tempo of training was much reduced and there was little competition in the world of sport as the nearest major unit was located 450 miles from Singapore. However a number of highly successful goodwill sporting tours were carried out. The Rugby XV went to Sarawak, Siam, Cochin China, Java and Sumatra, while the Football XI also visited Java and Sumatra.

At the end of 1928 the Battalion left Singapore for India where it was stationed at Ahmednagar. While there, Lieutenant Colonel Pickering completed his long period of command of the Battalion on which he left an indelible mark. He was succeeded by Lieutenant Colonel J C Burnett DSO. The three years spent at Ahmednagar were typical of life in a comparatively small Indian station in peace time. Incidents were few, training up to brigade manoeuvres was the norm, while sporting activities were largely of a local

---

(e) Colonel Smith had been commissioned into the Duke of Cornwall's Light Infantry. He won the VC in 1904 while serving in Somalia.
(f) One result of the army leaving Ireland was the need to find a replacement for the training grounds of the Curragh. Catterick, in Yorkshire, was the place selected.

variety. The stay at Ahmednagar was followed by another three years at Kamptee in Central India, where life followed a similar pattern.

In March 1934 the Battalion, commanded by Lieutenant Colonel M N Cox, MC, and numbering 785 all ranks, was posted to Nowshera in the North-West Frontier Province. A strategic garrison since the 1870s, Nowshera lay some twelve miles east of Peshawar. The Nowshera Brigade was commanded by Brigadier H R L G Alexander CSI,DSO (the future Field Marshal Lord Alexander of Tunis) and included the 3/2nd and 2/15th Punjab Regiments,(g) with a battery of Mountain Artillery. Training in mountain warfare now became a matter of importance.

In India the training pattern was much the same as at home, except that annual camps and manoeuvres were carried out in the cold weather months of December to February. But here, at least for units stationed in the north, there was always the chance of some real soldiering on the North-West Frontier, the brittle peace of which was periodically broken by tribal raids or wholesale risings instigated by anti-British Muslim fanatics, or Mullahs. With its wilderness of harsh mountain ranges intersected by narrow defiles and inhabited by fiercely independent Pathan tribesmen who bore arms from childhood and were adept at guerilla warfare, the Frontier was held to be the finest training ground for British soldiers. It was said that the tribesmen were the best umpires to be found, for they never allowed a mistake to go unpunished. In mountain warfare operations on the Frontier the infantry soldier was lightly clad in Battle Order: pith topi, open-necked angola shirt, KD shorts, hosetops and ankle puttees. The heavy, studded ammunition boots were usually replaced by the footwear of his enemy – stout, rubber-soled sandals or chaplis, while, apart from rifle and bayonet, he carried on his webbing equipment water bottle, haversack and 90 rounds of ammunition. There was an obligatory drill when advancing into tribal territory. On approaching a defile, the head of a column would send out pickets of section, or sometimes platoon strength, to struggle up the rock-bound slopes on each side and occupy commanding vantage points. After their signal "no enemy in sight" (by semaphore or helio) the column continued, and when the rearguard reached the first spot, a red flag was waved to bring the pickets scrambling down. Meanwhile, up front the process was being repeated. In temperatures often exceeding 37°C, all this demanded the utmost in physical fitness.

Fifty-odd miles north of Nowshera lay the Malakand Agency, a region of inaccessible mountain ranges pierced only by mule-tracks and inhabited in scattered villages by the warlike Yusafzai tribe of Pathans. In the heart of this desolation was an area known as the Agra salient in a loop of the Swat river and enclosed by 4,000ft mountains. Since 1907 when a British political agent had penetrated the fastness to the principal village of Loe Agra ("Great Agra") and extracted promises of co-operation, there had been no cause for military intervention. But in 1934 a firebrand Pathan mullah, the Fakir of Alingar, roused the locals into insurrection against the Raj, and a weak force of frontier militia was driven off with casualties. In early February 1935 the Government resolved to take reprisals by imposing a fine on the tribes and establishing a permanent outpost

---

(g) It was normal practice in India for infantry brigades to comprise one British and two Indian (or Gurkha) battalions.

at Loe Agra. The scheme was known as the Loe Agra Operation, and the Nowshera Brigade was detailed to carry it out.

On 19 February the Brigade, less 2/15th Punjabis who had been sent ahead, marched out of Nowshera for Mardan, where it picked up a battalion of The Guides (5/12th Frontier Force Regiment). By 22 February the Brigade column (or "Nowcol") had reached the Malakand Pass, after hot and dusty marches of nearly fifty miles. Here pack-mules took over from the wheeled transport *".... and we said goodbye to our tents and most of the other comforts of life"*.(Major O Price). Next day the Dukes as rearguard debouched into the Swat valley at a point where a mule-track led to Loe Agra. As they marched they heard the mountain gunners in action ahead. A company of 2/4th Gurkhas had attempted to establish pickets on two spurs, but these were so strongly held by the enemy that even with artillery support they were unable to secure the objectives. Two companies of the Guides were pushed up, but after scrambling up the rock-bound slopes and suffering casualties, they too were pinned down, and the situation became serious, for it was essential that the ridges should be captured before dusk to enable further advance next morning. *"But the enemy was in considerable strength, well dug in and covering an almost precipitous glacis, which was further enfiladed from a hill 800 yards to the left. An assault in the prevailing conditions, if unsuccessful, would have entailed serious casualties; and the difficulties of evacuating the wounded in the failing light would have been considerable"*. (Price)

Two companies were ordered up to support the Guides in another attack, which went in at 3.30pm with all the Dukes' Lewis guns and rifles pouring concentrated fire on the enemy position. Just then an RAF plane dropped one bomb on the main enemy sangar, blowing it and its occupants to pieces. The Guides then rushed the position and occupied it without further casualties. When darkness fell the Dukes withdrew to the base camp, just as snow was beginning to fall, and Nowcol's first battle was over. But for nearly eight hours an estimated 400 tribesmen had held up a whole brigade of regular troops. Enemy casualties could not be established, for it was always a matter of honour for them to carry off all dead and wounded.

The final advance to Loe Agra began on 25 February. No opposition was met other than that of the formidable mountainous terrain, with its single-file tracks over 4,000ft passes. The only casualties were fifty of the 1,200-odd mules, which lost their footing and plunged down the khud-side with ammunition and wireless sets. Loe Agra was reached at 11am after a five-hour march to cover less than ten miles. The locals, not withstanding that they had been shooting at the force two days before, dispensed the usual Pathan hospitality of chapattis, boiled eggs and green tea.

The evacuation was completed by 28 February and after retracing their arduous advance march, the Dukes and their Nowcol arrived back at Nowshera on 3 March, the 55 miles being covered in three days. But within two days they were marching back again along the all-too-familiar route to Loe Agra. After the Nowshera Brigade's withdrawal, the Fakir of Alingar seized his opportunity and once more descended on Loe Agra with his lashkar, occupying the levy post without a fight; the militia garrison had fled. And so the whole operation was to be repeated.

This time the advance went without a hitch: the 3/2nd Punjabis drove off an eighty-strong ambush party with heavy casualties, and Loe Agra was reached on 10 March and occupied with no opposition. The next week was spent not in fighting, but in navvying. Between Loe Agra and the southern base camp of Bargholai was a formidable ridge, rising to nearly 5,000ft and necessitating a lengthy detour for supplies between the two. And so the brigadier ordered that a "road" should be built to cut the distance by half. Thus the Dukes laboured with pick and shovel, and within a short time Dukewell Avenue, as it was dubbed, was almost fit for vehicular traffic.

The Battalion was later withdrawn to Kot, and there was little enemy activity until 5 April, when a strong lashkar was reported to be advancing on Loe Agra, a report confirmed by a ferocious attack on a picket of the 3/2nd Punjabis who lost two killed and six wounded. It was now decided to put in a brigade attack to clear the enemy out of the Loe Agra area. This started on 10 April, with the 2nd Dukes supporting the advance of the Guides and Punjabis, while the mountain gunners with their 3.7in howitzers gave covering fire. In the face of this, the lashkar withdrew across the Swat River, leaving the post of Loe Agra to be occupied again. A sweep of the area was carried out the next day, but it was evident that the enemy had dispersed. The second Loe Agra operation was over. The Brigade remained in position for another month, which the Dukes spent patrolling, in reconnaissance and picketing.

By 10 May the Battalion was back at Nowshera, having been almost continuously engaged in frontier warfare for nearly four months. Shortly after returning to Nowshera, Brigadier Alexander carried out the annual inspection. In his report he concluded:

> *"A thoroughly good Battalion all through, with splendid spirit. A very nice type of Yorkshireman who are (sic) keen and very willing workers. By their willingness to help other units at all times, they are very popular with everyone in this Brigade."*

North of Peshawar a strategic road had been constructed, leading up the Gandab valley and through the heart of Mohmand country towards the Nahaki Pass, a distance of some thirty miles. All such attempts to open up inaccessible territory and secure easy access for troops were bitterly resented by the tribesmen who saw them as a threat to their independent way of life and their raiding and ambushing. On 14 August, 1935 it was learned that a lashkar of Mohmands had concentrated on a sector of the road near Dand and was setting about its destruction. Next day the Peshawar Brigade was called out, and on 18 August the Nowshera Brigade was moved up to join it. By 23 August the force had advanced to Dand, the scene of the lashkar's depredations. Meanwhile, the RAF had been busy with bombing sorties (having first dropped warning leaflets) and these had the effect of dispersing the Mohmands to their mountain fastnesses. On reaching Dand at about 1800 hours, a company of the Dukes was ordered to occupy a ridge overlooking the camp site and this it did in the face of heavy rifle fire which wounded four men. The remainder of the Battalion, which was acting as rearguard, did not reach the site until 1050 hours the following day, exhausted after sending up and withdrawing fifteen pickets en route, mostly in darkness. The column had lost nine killed and twenty-one wounded, but the enemy's casualties were reported to be about 60 dead and 40 wounded – many credited to the RAF.

The 2nd Dukes remained at Dand until 8 September, occupied with picketing, reconnaissance patrols and road protection duties. As Lieutenant R K Exham (Adjutant) wrote :

> *"The stay at Dand was without doubt the most trying time that the Battalion experienced throughout the whole operation. The day shade temperature averaged about 104 degrees and as the whole camp was shut in on all sides by high hills, what breezes that blew were never felt. Along one side of the perimeter flowed a sluggish stream which formed a perfect breeding ground for mosquitos, and the several hundred mules which lived inside the perimeter produced swarms of flies which added to the discomforts. All ranks were dosed daily with quinine, but this, as was proved later, did little to prevent malaria. The task of opening the*

Vickers MMG of 2 DWR deployed during the Mohmand campaign 1935

> *road became most monotonous, continuing as it did for sixteen days without a break."*

As in the previous Loe Agra operation, the Dukes had to sweat (literally) with pick and shovel, in addition to all other tasks. Apart from mosquitos, flies and prickly heat, the soldier on the frontier – at least during the hot weather – suffered most from thirst. He carried a pint-sized water bottle, but occasional gulps of the tepid contents were of little help. Only when the picket rejoined the column, a thousand or more feet below, might he encounter pack-mules slung with chaguls, porous canvas bags containing about a gallon of water. Evaporation kept the water almost as cold as if it had come from a refrigerator.

On 8 September the Nowshera Brigade crossed the Karappa Pass, 2,600 feet, and with little resistance camped in the plain. This was an improvement on Dand, for the nights were pleasantly cool and there were hardly any mosquitos. But the Dand pests had already done their work. During the next ten days 192 men of the Dukes had to be evacuated with malaria and the strength of the Battalion was reduced to 310.

The next objective was the forcing of a pass some ten miles beyond the roadhead, which was successfully carried out during the night of 17/18 September. Again, opposition was minimal, for the reported lashkar had melted away, the Pathan being averse to night fighting. The Dukes once more had the task of supplying the pickets and their exertions were mentioned in the force Intelligence Summary of 20 September:

> *"There is one piece of work which merits special notice. The Duke of Wellington's Regiment provided carrying parties for the 5th F.F.R. picquet (Knight's picquet) which was 1,500 feet above the nullah and on a particularly steep hill. They carried barbed wire, entrenching tools, pickets and water pakhals to the top of the hill, and their officers were seen carrying loads on their heads. The work of these carrying parties was beyond all praise."*

Pakhals were large leather water-bags usually borne by mules. Though holding much more than the chaguls, being non-porous they did not keep the contents cool.

Meanwhile, most of the Mohmands had become resigned to submitting to peace terms. On 21 and 22 September representative jirgas assembled at Ghalani and agreed to accept Government terms unconditionally. But although the force's task now seemed to be completed, it was not. Another lashkar, including Afghans from across the border, was reported to be preparing to drive the force back from Wucha Jawar and deny any further road building. The clash came on 28/29 September, with the Peshawar and Nowshera Brigades, reinforced by the 3rd Infantry Brigade from Jhelum, repulsing enemy attacks on the positions around Wucha Jawar. At least 46 of them were killed and 46 wounded, while the force lost 39 killed and 53 wounded. The repulse of this final enemy aggression brought peace.

2 DWR, The Mohmand campaign, 1935. A jirga is held to discuss peace

The force began evacuation on 31 October, and by 5 November the Dukes were back to the relative comforts of their Nowshera quarters, where there was another inspection by Brigadier Alexander who reported:

> *"I have seen a lot of this Battalion in peace and on active operations. A unit proud of its traditions and with a very good moral tone. Keen and efficient in all departments of soldiering. Good at all games without making too much of a fetish at any one sport...... A Battalion always ready to help and pull their weight at anything and anytime, with the consequence that they are immensely popular with the other Indian units in this Brigade."*

The past eight months had seen the Battalion moulded into hardened frontier hands, wearing the green-and-purple ribbon of the Indian General Service Medal with bar "North-West Frontier" 1935.

At the end of 1937 the 2nd Battalion, now under the command of Lieutenant

*2 DWR returning to Nowshera, 1935*

Colonel A F P Christison MC of the Cameron Highlanders, moved to Multan in the Punjab. After less than a year Colonel Christison was selected to command a brigade and was succeeded by Lieutenant Colonel F H Fraser DSO,MC. At the outbreak of war in 1939 the Battalion was still in Multan, preparing to move to Delhi.

***********************

While the campaigns on the North West Frontier of India were largely dependent on soldiers on foot with mule transport, the armies in Europe were undergoing considerable change. For the British army at home the twenties and thirties were difficult periods of reductions, financial neglect and consequent shortages of men and material imposed by the "ten-year rule" and the generally pacifist climate of the country, nurtured by a trust placed in disarmament and the League of Nations. Such money as the government was prepared to spend on defence largely went to the other two services, so the army found itself starved of equipment and since the many overseas commitments required the foreign service battalions to be kept up to strength, those at home dwindled to little more than drafting units. On manoeuvres many weapons had to be represented by flags or rattles, while bodies of troops could be indicated on occasions by lengths of tape held between two men.

In 1933 Adolf Hitler came to power in Germany and embarked on rapid expansion and modernisation of the 100,000 men army which had been allowed to Germany under the Treaty of Versailles. The year before, Britain had at last acquired its first permanent armoured formation, the 1st Tank Brigade. This was followed by the mechanisation of the 2nd Cavalry Brigade whose three regiments exchanged their horses for tanks but only of the lightest kind. The gradual re-armament and modernisation was given a further impetus when Mr Hore-Belisha was made Secretary of State for War in 1937. This was accelerated by the Munich crisis of 1938, when Hore-Belisha was instructed by the Prime Minster, Neville Chamberlain, to make drastic changes. One result was the appointment of younger officers to the Army Council.

Meanwhile, the infantry of the Territorial Army underwent radical reorganisation. Foreseeing the threat of air attack in a future war, in 1936 the War Office had ordered that fourteen TA battalions should be transformed into anti-aircraft units, transferring their allegiance to the Royal Engineers or the Royal Artillery. At that time the TA battalions of the Dukes consisted of the 4th (Halifax), 5th (Huddersfield), 6th (Skipton) and 7th (Milnsbridge) – all forming the 147th (2nd West Riding) Infantry Brigade. The first to suffer divorce from the Regiment was the 5th Battalion, which in December 1936 found itself exchanging rifles and Lewis guns for searchlights, to become the 43rd (5th DWR) AA Battalion Royal Engineers. Two years later (November 1938) the Regiment lost another of its Territorial battalions, when the 4th was transferred to the Royal Artillery with the title 58th Anti-Tank Regiment (4th DWR) RA. The plan had been that the TA would provide thirteen divisions (one armoured, three motorised and nine infantry) but by March 1939 it was clear that this force would be too small for the war that now seemed inevitable. All existing Territorial units were therefore duplicated so as to provide a total of 26 divisions. As a result the 6th and 7th Battalions each raised a second battalion and the 4th Battalion, 58th Anti-Tank Regiment RA, formed the 2nd/58th, which later became the 68th Anti-Tank Regiment RA.

Shortly afterwards it was announced that from July all men aged 20 would be conscripted for six months training with the regular army, followed by three and a half years with the TA. These conscripts, the first ever in peacetime, were given the ancient name of militiamen.

*********************

In October 1930 the 1st Battalion, under the command of Lieutenant Colonel W C Wilson DSO,OBE,MC, moved to Aldershot, to join the 2nd Brigade of the 1st Division. There it took part in brigade and divisional exercises, ceremonial and sport. Although the Battalion had numerous successes in rugby competitions while stationed at Devonport, including the winning of the Southern Command Cup in 1928, 1929 and 1930 it had not been able to progress beyond the semi-final stage in the Army Cup, the

1 DWR winning team in the Infantry Transport competition at the Aldershot Show 1931 and 1932

pre-eminent event in the military sporting calendar. The move to Aldershot brought about a change in fortune. In March 1931 the Battalion beat 1st Training Battalion RE to win the cup. The successful XV, captained by Lieutenant H G P Miles, included no less than seven players who had been awarded army caps. This was the first occasion the 1st Battalion had won the cup. The Regiment's previous successes had been when the 2nd Battalion won the cup in 1907, the year in which the Army Rugby Cup was instituted, and again in 1914.

The great crowd-pulling event in the Aldershot of the 1930s was the spectacular Aldershot Tattoo in Rushmoor Arena, where troops in period costumes (and with appropriate weapons) fought battles of the past, and massed bands in full dress entertained audiences of thousands. Another annual event was the Aldershot Horse Show which included competitions for the best turned-out infantry transport sections. The 1931 Show saw the Battalion winning the Infantry Transport Cup and coming equal second in the Farnborough Challenge Cup for the best all-round infantry transport section in the Aldershot Command. The following year the Battalion won both the Infantry Transport Cup and the Farnborough Challenge Cup.

In January 1934 Lieutenant General Sir Herbert Belfield KCB,KCMG,KBE,DSO, the Colonel of the Regiment, was forced to resign owing to ill health. He was succeeded by

Brigadier General P A Turner CMG. Three months later General Belfield died. He had been the much respected Colonel for twenty-five years. During his tenure the following regimental institutions were established under his guidance:

    The Regimental Chapel in York Minster (1923)
    The Regimental Journal, the 'Iron Duke' (1925)
    The Regimental Museum (1921) and Archives (1929)
    The Old Comrades Association (1st and 2nd Battalions) (1926)

Alliances were also established with the North Saskatchewan Regiment, later renamed the Yorkton Regiment, of Canada (1922) and 33rd Battalion Australian Infantry (1929).

The following year the Battalion, under command of Lieutenant Colonel G S W Rusbridger, embarked for a tour of duty in Malta. Apart from the opportunities this offered for joint exercises with the navy and some ceremonial duties, the routine was not particularly demanding. In November 1935, Henry Valerian George Wellesley, Earl of Mornington,[h] the son of the 5th Duke of Wellington, was commissioned into the Regiment as a Second Lieutenant from Sandhurst and joined at Malta. At the end of 1937 the Battalion, under the command of Lieutenant Colonel W M Ozanne MC, returned to England, taking with it five Maltese soldiers, the first to serve in a British infantry regiment. In a farewell editorial the Times of Malta commended the officers and men of the Regiment for the manner in which they had entered into the life of the island. It also commented: *"The excellent record of the men during the stay is a model one; of this they may well be proud"*. On arrival in England the Battalion was stationed at Bordon in the 3rd Brigade of the 1st Division.

                              \*\*\*\*\*\*\*\*\*\*\*\*\*\*\*\*\*\*\*\*

By now the effect of the 1934 rearmament programme began to reach the infantry. Likewise the effect of Mr Hore-Belisha's rejuvenation of the Army Council made itself felt. In February 1936 it was announced that thirteen infantry regiments would convert their regular battalions to machine gun battalions, armed with the Vickers medium machine gun as their principal weapon. Those not so converted, which included the Duke of Wellington's Regiment, would lose their machine gun companies and become rifle battalions, deploying just four rifle companies. Their only automatic weapons would be Lewis light machine guns. In future each infantry brigade would consist of three rifle battalions and one machine gun battalion.

In 1938 mechanisation reached the infantry, when its horse transport was replaced by 3-ton lorries and 15cwt trucks. At the same time, the CO and the other mounted officers lost their government chargers.[i] Also in 1938 there was a welcome change in the army's light automatic weapon, when the Lewis gun of First World War vintage was superseded by the Bren gun.[j] A much more reliable, and lighter, weapon than the antique, stoppage-prone Lewis, this was to remain in service until 1968. Other weapons

---

(h) He succeeded to the title of 6th Duke of Wellington in 1941. He was killed in action at Salerno in 1943.
(i) The Regiment's most notable charger was that of the commanding officer of the 2nd Battalion. Named The Camel it came to the Battalion in 1912, served throughout the war, being wounded four times, and was discharged in 1922.
(j) The name was derived from the town of Brno in Czechoslovakia where the weapon was developed and the arms factory at Enfield where it was manufactured for the army.

introduced at this time were the 2in and 3in mortars and the .55in Boyes anti-tank rifle.

Something also had to be done to make the profession more attractive. In 1936 all subalterns with thirteen year's service had been given their captaincy. Two years later the Secretary of State for War introduced time promotion, eight years to captain and seventeen to major. Some improvements were also made to the pay, marriage allowance and terms of service of soldiers, and a programme of barrack building was begun.

In April 1939 the new battle dress was introduced which the army was to wear on the parade ground and in the field for the next twenty-odd years. Of khaki serge, it was inspired by ski wear, and consisted of a short 'blouse' (open necked with tie for officers but buttoned-up for other ranks), rather baggy trousers and short ankle puttees, later replaced by webbing gaiters. The first headdress (for infantry) was a very unmilitary deerstalker style of floppy canvas hat, but by 1939 the serge side hat or field service cap had been adopted, though on active service this was replaced by the steel helmet. Battle dress was never popular. The brief blouse gave no protection to the vulnerable lumbar regions, while on occasion the buttons securing it to the trousers were prone to burst asunder. The side hats could not ward off either pelting rain or blazing sun, and were apt to fall off at the double.

For more than a century the soldier had drilled and marched in fours. Now, in 1939, this was changed back to the ancient threes, the men forming up in three ranks, and the familiar command "Form fours!" (from two ranks) was gone for ever. In early 1939 the home-based infantry battalions received their versatile little mechanical workhorse, the Bren carrier. These were lightly armoured, open-topped vehicles with tracked running gear adopted from the light tank, and as the name implied, were primarily armed with the Bren LMG. Each battalion now deployed its carrier platoon in Headquarters Company, with ten Bren carriers. Until the arrival of the American jeep, these vehicles performed all sorts of tasks, ferrying up ammunition, evacuating wounded and even acting as the successor to the commanding officer's charger as a means of mobility.

As Europe moved towards its second great conflict the infantry had, just in time, been organised and equipped to face the challenges ahead.

CHAPTER 18

# The Second World War

*1940 Dunkirk, St Valery en Caux*
*1942 Sittang*
*1943 Djebel Bou Aoukaz*
*1944 Anzio, Monte Ceco, Fontenay Le Pesnil, Chindits*

In January 1933 Adolf Hitler had become Chancellor of Germany. In defiance of the Treaty of Versailles he almost immediately started to re-arm the country. Then, in quick succession, he re-occupied the Rhineland (1936), annexed Austria (March 1938) and took possession of the Sudeten area of Czechoslovakia (October 1938). The latter event led to the Munich agreement and Neville Chamberlain's claim that this promised *"peace in our time"*. In March 1939 Hitler annexed the rump of the Czechoslovak state. Between June and August Britain, France and Russia conducted negotiations in an endeavour to establish a peace front to block further Nazi expansion. The negotiations became deadlocked and then, on 23 August, Germany and Russia suddenly concluded a non-aggression pact. The following day Britain and Poland signed a pact of mutual asssistance. At the same time Poland called up its reservists. On 1 September Germany attacked Poland and on 3 September Britain and France declared war on Germany.

The location of the various battalions of the Regiment during the first few months of the war was as follows:–

| | |
|---|---|
| 1st Battalion: | Embarked for France with the British Expeditionary Force on 24 September 1939 |
| 2nd Battalion: | Moved from Multan to Delhi on 6 October 1939 |
| 1/4th Battalion: | (58th Anti-Tank Regiment RA): 49 (West Riding) Division. Halifax. |
| 2/4th Battalion: | (68th Anti-Tank Regiment RA). Halifax |
| 5th Battalion: | (43rd Anti-Aircraft Battalion RE). Huddersfield |
| 1/6th Battalion: | 147 Brigade. 49 (West Riding) Division. Malton. November 1939 |
| 1/7th Battalion: | 147 Brigade. 49 (West Riding) Division. Malton. November 1939 |

1 DWR, 1940. An Austin 7, with the quartermaster at the wheel

2/6th Battalion:   137 Brigade. 46 Division. Keighley
2/7th Battalion:   137 Brigade. 46 Division. Huddersfield

******************

At the outbreak of war the 1st Battalion mobilised at Bordon and on 24 September 1939 crossed to France under command of Lieutenant Colonel E C Beard MC [a] as part of the 3rd Brigade of the 1st Infantry Division (Major General H R L G Alexander). The two other battalions in the 3rd Brigade were the 2nd Battalion Sherwood Foresters and the 1st Battalion King's Shropshire Light Infantry. The composition of the brigade remained the same throughout the war.

From September until May ensued that strange period of inactivity described by Churchill as the twilight war. More colloquially it was known as the phoney war. The Dukes with their brigade were moved up to the Franco-Belgian frontier near Cobrieux and here, like the rest of the BEF, they set about digging defences as an extension of the Maginot Line, in which the French had invested so much confidence. Typically of the phoney war period it was forbidden to cut the crops to gain fields of fire. Further advance into Belgium itself was ruled out, because of that country's neutrality. Towards

---

[a] Lieutenant Colonel Beard had succeeded Lieutenant Colonel Ozanne, who had been appointed to command a brigade in August 1939. In January 1940 Beard was himself promoted and Lieutenant Colonel S B Kington then assumed command.

the end of November General Lord Gort, C-in-C of the BEF, agreed with his French opposite number, General Gamelin, that the British should occupy part of the Maginot Line itself, and the 3rd Infantry Brigade was moved to Metz and from there to the actual front. Here the Dukes became the first British battalion to occupy a front-line position, but in fact, apart from patrol activity and the occasional appearance of a German reconnaissance plane or Stuka dive-bomber, there was little to indicate the near presence of the enemy. Instead, the Battalion again had to labour with entrenching tools to make the position defensive and habitable, for it was found that the French had done nothing. However, patrolling was maintained and during November a listening patrol under Lieutenant H A R Bucknall crossed into enemy territory – the first soldiers of the BEF to do so. On 7 December the Battalion withdrew to a camp near Kedange.

Since the situation along the whole front was so quiet it was deemed safe for the King to visit his troops in person, and on 9 December he, accompanied by Lord Gort and the Duke of Gloucester, inspected the Battalion. It was, wrote an officer, *"an unusual parade...."*

> *"On the previous day the Battalion had arrived in new billets entirely caked in dried yellow mud. Tin hats, eyebrows, equipment, leggings and boots were of one 'uniform' drab colour. Greatcoats stood up on their own without human support. By dint of hard work.... and some unorthodox devices, such as walking on to the parade ground with a sandbag (empty) over each boot, the Battalion managed to achieve quite a respectable turnout."*

The remainder of the winter and early spring passed with little activity apart from interminable digging of defences. Meanwhile, war or no, the Battalion strove to maintain some semblance of peacetime drill and panache. At Battalion Headquarters in a stationmaster's house at Bachy, guard-mounting was performed every day with the drums present under the drum-major.

A few weeks later the phoney war was over. On 10 May three German army groups invaded Belgium, Holland and Luxembourg, having outflanked the Maginot Line. At this date the Dukes were still in billets at Bachy. In the early hours of the 10th, the Adjutant, Captain David Strangeways, was awakened by a private of the orderly room staff with *"David, Sir, David"*. However, this was not undue familiarity: DAVID was the codeword for Gort's Plan D, the advance into Belgium. This was to be on a two-corps front across the Belgian plain to the River Dyle where a front would be established with the French. The order for the advance found the Battalion fully prepared. The drill for the move had been rehearsed many times. In the event the real thing proceeded more swiftly and smoothly than any rehearsal had done. Within ten hours the Battalion was ready and only waiting to be informed of the start time. During the afternoon and night there was some intermittent bombing by German aircraft, but no material damage was done.

1 DWR in France, 1940

The advance through Belgium was unopposed, except by the cheering populace in Brussels who welcomed the "Tommies", as they still knew them, with gifts of fruit, wine and flowers. But as the advance continued, progress was slowed by civilian refugees on foot, in cars, horse drawn carts and wheel-barrows, which suggested that all was not well up front. The Dyle line, about 18 miles south east of Brussels, was reached on 12 May and yet again the Dukes dug themselves in, convinced that this time it was for the real thing. The following day the supporting artillery of 29th/97th Battery, 19th Field Regiment RA, came into action. On the evening of the 14th the enemy retaliated with fairly heavy 77mm and 105mm artillery fire, but in their slit trenches the Dukes escaped with only one casualty. On their right flank, however, the Sherwood Foresters fought a stiff battle and suffered so heavily that the Dukes' D Company (Captain J T Rivett-Carnac) was temporarily attached as reinforcement.

The Battalion was certain that its turn would shortly come with a determined enemy attack. But not so. On 16 May Colonel Kington received orders that the whole Dyle line was to be evacuated, and on the following morning the Battalion was withdrawn without having fired a shot. This rearward move was necessary because both flanks had become exposed, that on the right by the French being over-run by the German panzer groups with their Blitzkrieg tactics, sweeping round that flank between the Aisne and the Oise, and heading for Paris. On the left Holland had capitulated and the Belgians were in full retreat.

So, after only five days on the line of the Dyle, the Battalion found itself withdrawing back through Brussels to an area five miles to the west of that city. However, after only a few hours the Battalion was ordered to continue its withdrawal that night (18th) as the British flanks had again been exposed. After a difficult and tiring march due to pitch darkness, unknown country and inaccurate maps, the Battalion arrived at its allotted area only to find that orders were waiting, instructing it that the withdrawal would be continued almost at once. After a halt of only three hours, the Battalion was on the march again, until it reached its area on the River Dendre. Here, on 19 May, it took up a defensive position and dug in. The respite was welcome as the troops had been continuously on the move since leaving the Dyle. The morale of the men was as high as ever, but they were not destined to fight on the Dendre.

Gort now planned a withdrawal to the line of the River Escaut, some 35 miles west of Brussels, where he hoped to make a stand. Having covered this distance (by bus and on foot) by 23 May, with surprisingly little interference by the German pursuit, the Dukes again dug in. This was at Pont-à-Chin, where there was a bridge over the river. Colonel Kington impressed on the sapper unit detailed to blow the bridge that his rearguard and other elements of the 3rd Brigade were still to come in, but such was the state of nervousness among some officers that the bridge was blown prematurely, resulting in the abandonment of a section of the Dukes' carriers, whose crews had to swim for it.

It had now become clear that the whole existence of the BEF was threatened, and its communication with Britain in danger of being broken. Gort was resigned to a final withdrawal. If his army was not to be annihilated, he had to save what he could by a run for the coast at Dunkirk, and evacuation. Evacuation through Dunkirk started on 27 May. Any chance of saving the situation vanished when the Belgians capitulated at midnight 27/28 May.

The next stage of the Battalion's withdrawal was to a point just east of Lille, where it remained for three days. On the afternoon of the 27 May, during a day of increased dive bomber activity, the Battalion received orders that it was to prepare for a long and arduous march that would begin that night. It was to march through Lille and from there along the railway line to Armentières, where it was to turn north and proceed through Poperinghe to Hondschoote, near Dunkirk. Everything but essential equipment and weapons was to be left. Even B Echelon was abandoned, so that from now until the end the Battalion was to be entirely dependent on its own resources for rations and cooking. The railway line was found without difficulty and one of the hardest parts of the retirement began. It is difficult to conceive of more energy sapping experience than marching along a railway in daytime, let alone at night. Tension on the march was increased by the volume of enemy activity which seemed to surround the Battalion on all sides. Arriving south of Armentières after covering twenty-five miles in less than eight hours, officers and men had only a couple of hours rest before they were on the march again.

Orders were received for the Battalion to make direct for the beaches at Dunkirk, but on the way it was diverted to the village of Les Moeres, about five miles south of the beaches, to take up defensive positions to cover the final phase of the withdrawal. On arrival at Les Moeres all ranks were exhausted, having covered 50 miles practically without a halt and without food. A request to Brigade HQ for rations was met with the reply that the Battalion must now feed itself and live off the country. As there was much untended livestock and plenty of vegetables in the fields, this posed no great problem.

The Battalion had the task of defending some 5,000 yards of a canal and its bridges: a length of front which would normally be allotted to a brigade. The Battalion was also now much reduced in strength and, as a result, A and B companies were amalgamated under command of Captain T St G Carroll. Defensive positions were established on the north side of the canal, with large gaps between them. A/B Company was on the right and C Company (Captain W A Waller) on the left. D Company was in reserve. To the right of the Dukes was a Guards brigade and on the left a TA battalion from another division. The whole area was flat and intersected by canals and dykes, while frontal fields of fire were obstructed by abandoned vehicles, guns and civilian carts on the opposite bank of the canal. The abandoned military equipment was, however, a source of ammunition for 29th/97th Field Battery RA and of Bren guns for the Battalion, who acquired three times the normal scale.

Although the noise of bombing could be heard from the Dunkirk direction, the Dukes were not affected until the afternoon of 30 May when the Germans hurled a storm of artillery, mortar and machine-gun fire on the position. With the splendid support of the 29th/97th Field Battery [b], the Battalion fought off repeated infantry attacks for hours. Early in the morning of the 31st the battalion on the left was withdrawn and a flank guard was formed under Major Temple of 2nd Foresters. Enemy activity increased and casualties mounted. Captain P E Skirrow was killed when a shell demolished C Company's HQ. Later the same day Captain Waller was severely wounded. Command of C Company was then assumed by Captain J Harrison, who had been in charge of the brigade anti-tank guns. A/B Company was pulled back about half a mile to a smaller canal and on the following day (1 June) C Company was also pulled back. Major Temple was killed and command of the flank guard, which now consisted of seven platoons from several different regiments, was taken over by Major A H G Wathen. Still the German attacks continued unabated and the men of the Battalion began to wonder when the order would come for them to retire and if, when it did, it would be feasible to carry it out. Meanwhile casualties mounted. Fifty eight other ranks had been killed, with numerous others wounded. But the Dukes line held. By now wireless communication had broken down, and with no orders forthcoming it seemed that the Battalion would be left to fight it out to the bitter end. However, at dusk the 3rd Brigade intelligence officer appeared in a light tank, bringing orders that the Battalion was to withdraw to the beaches at dusk. Breaking off contact, it accordingly retired, surprisingly without pursuit, and arrived on the beaches at Bray-Dunes in the small hours of 2 June.

---

[b] After returning to England the Battery and the Dukes presented an identical silver salver to each other to commemorate their close association.

# THE SECOND WORLD WAR

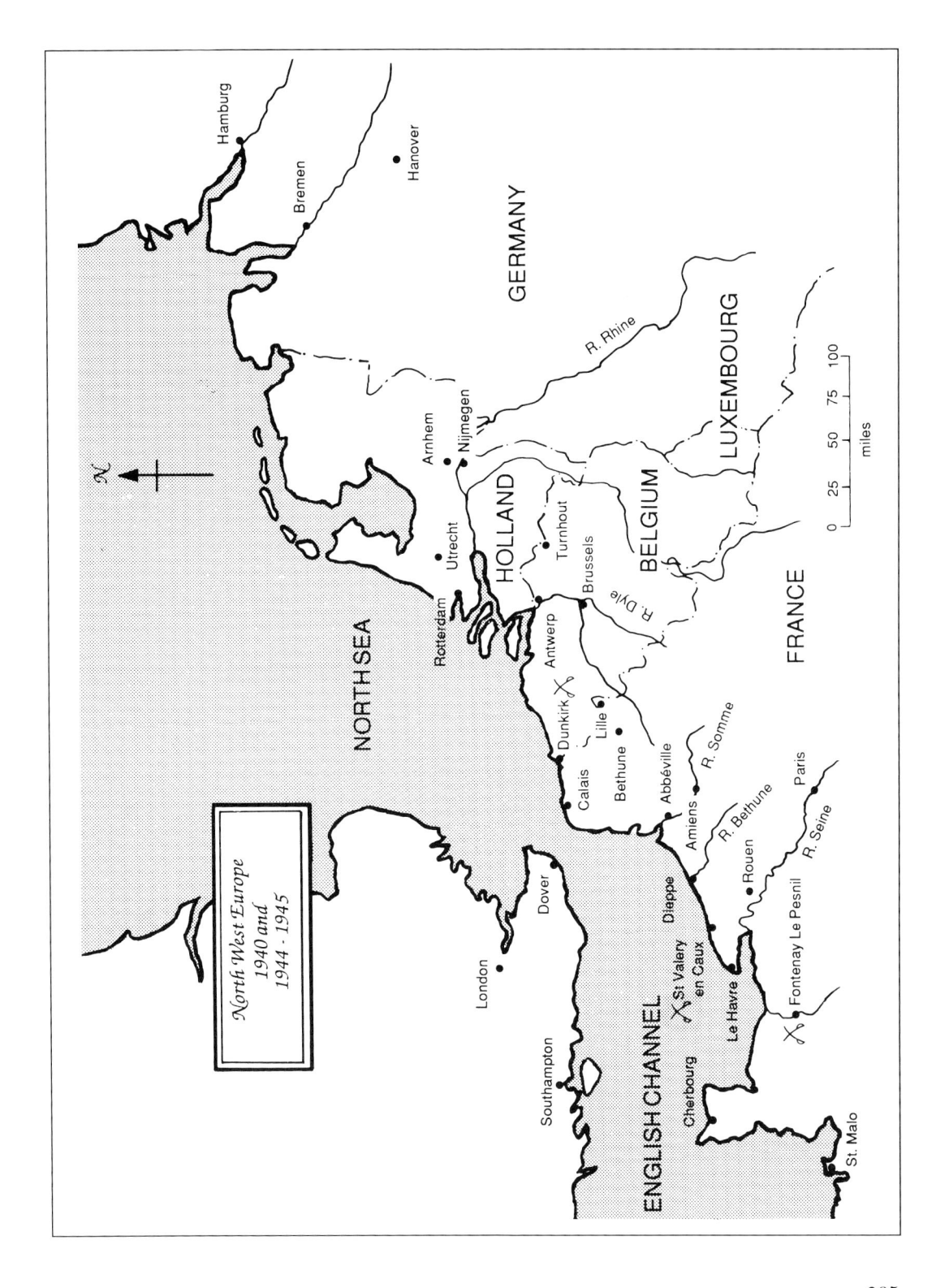

*North West Europe 1940 and 1944 - 1945*

The Battalion had been told that boats would be awaiting to ferry it out to the allotted ship. No boats were found and instead the Battalion was compelled to trudge in darkness some eight miles through the dunes to the mole at Dunkirk. Here it was informed that there was to be no further service that night, so back to the beach the men trudged again to scoop holes in the sand and attempt some sleep. Sunday 2 June dawned bright and sunny and the dive bombers resumed their raids. Throughout that day most of the Battalion managed to keep together, men burrowing into the sand in efforts to find cover from the incessant bombing and shelling, while they saw others being formed up and marched to the mole for embarkation. When darkness fell the Dukes in their turn struggled along the Mole to scramble into waiting craft.

In the confusion and shelling, however, some men of the Battalion had become separated from the main body, and one of them was Captain D I Strangeways. Resolving to use his own initiative, he collected a party of twenty-two men from Battalion HQ and signallers, and after spotting a Thames sailing barge just offshore, led his men to swim out and board her. Although obviously abandoned, the craft was found to be perfectly seaworthy, with food and water in the galley. "Skipper" Strangeways organised his party into two watches, and after some problems in working out which halyard did what, sail was hoisted and with Strangeways at the wheel the 'Iron Duke', as it was now named, set off for England. Navigation was by means of a school atlas and Strangeways' own compass. Halfway across there was a scare as a flight of bombers roared over, but fortunately they decided to ignore the innocent looking vessel. In the afternoon a RN patrol boat appeared and gave a true course for Dover.

The Battle of France had cost the Battalion two officers killed and 70 other ranks killed, besides many more wounded, the total of which is not recorded. After its return Colonel C J Pickering, Colonel of the Regiment, received the following tribute from Brigadier T N F Wilson, Commander 3rd Infantry Brigade:

*"HQ 3rd Infantry Brigade*
*13 June 1940*

*Dear Colonel Pickering,*
*I am very proud to have had the privilege of having under my command such a magnificent battalion as the 1st Battalion of your Regiment. During the recent operations their fighting efficiency and stubborn determination were in keeping with the highest traditions of the past....... They never once gave any ground unless ordered to do so, and on more than one occasion inflicted severe losses on the enemy. The steadiness of all ranks, under heavy enemy fire, sometimes in very exposed positions, was exemplary. I would particulary mention the defence of the final bridgehead in front of Dunkirk. The Battalion was ordered to hold a very extended and exposed position. For the last 48 hours they were subjected to constant and heavy enemy pressure. No reserves were available.*

> *It was essential for the safety of the force as a whole that this position should be maintained intact...... the Battalion succeeded in this difficult task as a result of first-class leadership and the courage and determination of all ranks. They then carried out a successful withdrawal when still in close contact and still under pressure........ I am afraid this is but an inadequate tribute to a fine performance."*

***************

Although the BEF had been successfully brought back from Dunkirk the fighting, in which two battalions of the Dukes were to become heavily involved, still continued in France. At the end of March 1940 the 46th Division was informed that it had been temporarily allocated for pioneer duties in connection with transportation services and the building of camps in France. One of the brigades in the Division was the 137th. The three battalions in the Brigade were the 2/5th West Yorks and the 2/6th and 2/7th Battalions of The Duke of Wellington's Regiment. It was intended that the period of this duty would be no more than three months and the battalions were ordered to take their band instruments and mess equipment with them.

The Division crossed to France at the end of April and was stationed near St.Nazaire on the west coast where the troops were employed road making, laying railway lines, erecting huts, unloading ships and working on ammunition and petrol dumps. On 17 May, a week after the Germans had invaded Holland and Belgium, the GOC 46 Division offered Lord Gort the use of his division in a defensive role, to help stem the German advance. The following evening, the Division entrained for a secret destination. which turned out to be Béthune. Progress was very slow due to the movement of refugees and troops but by the afternoon of 20 May the four trains transporting the Brigade were approaching Abbéville, about 50 miles SW of Béthune. The 2/6th and 2/7th were in the last two trains when, a mile short of Abbéville, both were brought to a halt. Abbéville, it appeared, was now occupied by the Germans. The two trains were then attacked from the air and the troops hastily detrained. The other two trains had disappeared ahead.

The Dukes' battalions, some 1,400 strong, were now in a sorry plight – out on their own without maps and with no knowledge of the locality. Attempts to make contact with any other British formations proved fruitless. As a first step the two battalions moved to higher ground where a more secure defensive position could be established. The following day (21 May) the two commanding officers, (Lieutenant Colonel E H Llewellyn MC, 2/6th and Lieutenant Colonel G Taylor, 2/7th), decided to withdraw towards Dieppe, about 50 miles to the west. The 2/7th would take the coastal side of the railway line and the 2/6th the inland side.

The nature of the country over which the 2/6th marched was so difficult that it was very hard to maintain contact, even within platoons. It was also very hot. Food was very difficult to obtain as the refugees had been through in large numbers and had cleared the countryside like a swarm of locusts, and the water was undrinkable. However, despite these difficulties most of the Battalion had reached either Dieppe or Rouen by 23 May. On 26 May the Battalion was once again united at Rouen. There it formed part of Beauman Force, which consisted of all British regiments which had not been caught in the Dunkirk pocket. On 29 May the Battalion's mechanised transport, which had moved separately from St.Nazaire, rejoined. During this period the Dukes worked strenuously on improving the Rouen defences.

On 30 May the 2/6th was moved to Bruz, near Rennes, some 160 miles to the west. It remained there for the next eight days during which the opportunity was taken for the men to fire their Bren guns and anti-tank rifles and to re-equip the Battalion. On 6 June, three days after the completion of the evacuation at Dunkirk, the Commanding Officer was informed that the Battalion was to form part of C Brigade, together with 2/4th King's Own Yorkshire Light Infantry, of Beauman Force. Next morning it left by train for an unknown destination. At 2pm the following day it arrived near Rouen to be informed that it was to take up positions between two bridges over the Seine, the intervening country comprising a front of about 12 miles. Initially the positions were on the east bank but because of German advance to the north and south the Dukes were obliged to withdraw to the west bank. By noon on 9 June the enemy activity had greatly increased, with accurate mortar and machine gun fire and low level bombing on the Dukes' positions. It now became essential to narrow the Battalion's frontage and this was achieved by withdrawing to a position at Venables with good observation and good fields of fire. The front was now less than two miles. Fighting continued throughout the 10th but enemy flank attacks increasingly jeopardised the position. That evening the Battalion successfully broke off contact and was withdrawn to Bernay. There, on 12 June, it was visited by a senior medical officer who decided that it was unfit for battle for at least three days. It was ordered into rest billets where it remained for several days until the feeling grew that it had been abandoned. The Battalion therefore started to march towards Cherbourg, some 100 miles distant. On its way it learnt that France had, on 16 June, sought an armistice from the Germans. Fortunately the Battalion met a RASC column which then transported it to St.Malo. A ship was leaving the harbour, but returned to pick up the Battalion, which arrived at Southampton the following day (18 June). The Battalion had suffered approximately 85 casualties, of whom 3 officers and 18 other ranks were killed.

The 2/7th, having managed to unload a couple of vehicles from their train, sent out a party to try and find water and food. In the process they made contact with a French railway engineer whom they informed of the plight of a French hospital train, filled with wounded, which was broken down near their position. The Battalion spent the rest of 22 May helping the French extricate the train. The engineer, delighted with the success of the operation, offered to take the Battalion to Dieppe in a train made up of cattle trucks. Early in the morning of 23 May the Battalion arrived at Dieppe. Like the 2/6th, it now became part of Beauman Force. The Battalion was one of several allotted the task of holding a defensive position along the line of the River Béthune where it made great efforts strengthening the defences.

On 9 June the Battalion was informed that it was to become part of 51st Division, that the Division would withdraw through it, and that once this had been completed, the bridge over the River Béthune at Dieppe was to be blown. This having been completed, the Battalion was brigaded with 4th Seaforth and 2nd Black Watch. By 11 June a new defensive position had been established in the area near Veules-les-Roses. There was a general state of confusion which was further aggravated by a heavy air raid. By now it was clear that the Division was surrounded and plans were made to evacuate it through St Valery-en-Caux. By late afternoon some 40 German tanks were attacking the position of the 2/7th who were without artillery or machine guns, apart from two 20mm anti-tank guns. These each fired one round but when the tanks replied that was the end of the 20mm guns. When night fell the Battalion withdrew to St.Valery and early the following morning (12 June) evacuation to the ships waiting off shore was successfully carried out, though not without many men of the Battalion being wounded. Most of them spent the next five years as prisoners of war. Among them was Lieutenant Colonel G Taylor who had been captured when going to supervise the withdrawal of the last of his companies. The Battalion's casualties were three officers and 62 other ranks killed, 13 other ranks wounded and 97 prisoners-of war.

The 2/7th Battalion gained the battle honour **St.Valery-en-Caux** for the Regiment.

The actions of the two Territorial battalions sent to France only partly trained and partly equipped, and then engaged in fighting a highly professional enemy armed with tanks and other equipment of the most modern design, were deserving of the highest praise.

However neither battalion was to see overseas service again. In mid 1942 137 Infantry Brigade was converted to an armoured brigade, the battalions becoming armoured regiments. In September 1943 they were placed in suspended animation when 137 Armoured Brigade was re-formed as 2nd Armoured Delivery Regiment.

*******************

During October/November 1942 General Montgomery and his 8th Army had defeated Rommel at El Alamein. By 5 November he had pushed Rommel back one hundred miles. On the night 7/8 November an Anglo-American army landed in French Morocco and Algeria. The objective of the invasion was to link up with the 8th Army and thus clear the North African shores of the enemy so that the Mediterranean could be opened up to allied shipping. The initial landing was made by the Americans who were followed by the British 1st Army. Casablanca, Oran and Algiers were soon captured. The next stage was to push on to Tunis some 450 miles from Algiers. However the strength of the enemy and the appalling weather brought the advance to a halt about 30 miles from Tunis.

By February 1943, when movement again became possible, the 1st Army consisted of two Corps. 46 Division, which was in V Corps, included 58th Anti-Tank Regiment RA

(4th DWR). Among other reinforcements sent to join 1st Army at that time were the 1st and 4th Divisions. One of the units that arrived with the 4th Division was the former 8th Battalion of the Regiment. Raised in July 1940 it was, a year later, converted into a tank unit, becoming 145 Regiment RAC (8th DWR). The Regiment was in 21 Tank Brigade, but shortly after arrival in the theatre it was transferred to 25 Tank Brigade and informed that it was to be employed in support of 24 Guards Brigade (1st Division) in the forthcoming operations. It was equipped with Churchill tanks.

With the 1st Division was the 1st Battalion of the Dukes, 38 officers and 800 men strong, and now under command of Lieutenant Colonel C D Armstrong DSO,MC (East Surreys) (c). The Battalion, which since Dunkirk had been employed on coastal defence duties and carrying out intensive training in the UK, embarked at Avonmouth on 26 February and disembarked at Bone (120 miles west of Tunis) on 11 March. By this date the 8th Army had driven the Axis forces out of Libya, forcing Rommel to retreat towards Tunisia. The next few weeks were spent in preparation for the major offensive to capture Tunis, the Dukes being occupied with constant patrolling. On 5 April a platoon-strength patrol surprised a German post and killed twenty-five, for which exploit its leader, Lieutenant L B Denman, was awarded the MC, the first immediate award to the 1st Division in the North African campaign. But, contrary to orders, Colonel Armstrong had insisted on accompanying the patrol, and when it encountered heavy machine-gun fire on the withdrawal he was severely wounded. Evacuated two days later, he was succeeded in command by Lieutenant Colonel B W Webb-Carter.

By 18 April the whole of the 1st Division's artillery, some 650 field and medium guns, were assembling in the Medjez-el-Bab plain, preparatory to the advance on Tunis, thirty miles to the north-east.

The 1st Division occupied a five-mile line to the north of the plain, just beyond which rose a long whale-backed feature known to the troops as Banana Ridge. This was really in no-man's land: beyond it in commanding positions were the German's first line defences. To enable the offensive to be launched it was essential that this ridge should be occupied. The 1st Dukes was assigned the task. Moving up stealthily, during the night 19/20 April, the Battalion took over from a platoon of Grenadiers and deployed along the ridge with no opposition. In order not to alert the enemy with undue noise, they were forbidden to dig in, but had to lie in the open among what natural cover they could find, while behind them the massive concentration of artillery was taking place. However just after dusk the peace was shattered as the Germans awoke to the threat. Lieutenant Colonel Webb-Carter:

> *"The enemy came in strength, some of his forces attacking straight up the ridge, some working round the flanks and in to the plain behind...... while fires blazed up as some of our guns and ammunition dumps were set alight before they could be got away.*
> *Meanwhile on the ridge itself our troops were hard pressed.*

---

(c) Lieutenant Colonel A H G Wathen had commanded the Battalion from March 1942 to January 1943.

*D Company (Captain P R Faulks) on the right had the enemy on three sides of them; A Company (Captain T F Huskisson) on the left found one of their platoons completely isolated, while B Company ( Captain A P R Smith) in the centre were being subjected to fierce machine gun and mortar fire..... As dawn approached, C Company (Captain A G Peel )were ordered forward from their reserve position to make their way to join B Company who had by then suffered a number of casualties. It proved an exciting journey across the plain, where German tanks had joined the infantry and several clashes took place before the ridge was eventually reached.... When day broke, we were better able to take stock of our surroundings. Enemy tanks and infantry still swarmed over the plain; bodies of the enemy still occupied several strong points on the ridge; but the Dukes held firmly to their position in the face of the worst that tanks and mortars and machine guns could do."*

By midday on the 21st, following a dawn counter attack by the tanks of 145 Regiment RAC (8th DWR) under command of Lieutenant Colonel A C Jackson, the tide of battle had swept beyond Banana Ridge. Unable to dislodge its staunch defenders, assaulted by the British 25-pdrs and 5.5in gun-howitzers, the Germans lost heart and turned in full retreat, leaving behind scores of dead and wounded, and several who gave themselves up to the Dukes. *"It was, for most of us, our first real taste of battle, but we had the satisfaction of knowing that a grand job of work had been done. Not only had we administered a severe defeat on some of Hitler's crack troops – mainly Hermann Goering Grenadiers – but we had undoubtedly averted what might have been a major disaster".* (Webb-Carter) The 1st Loyals (North Lancashire) were also heavily engaged, putting in a costly flank attack on the left of the ridge, in which they lost their commanding officer. Thus today The Duke of Wellington's and The Queen's Lancashire Regiment are the only two to share the battle honour **Banana Ridge**. In gaining it the Dukes lost 17 killed, 35 wounded and 30 missing, presumed prisoners.

The tenacity of the Banana Ridge battalions enabled the British 1st Army to continue the advance on Tunis. The plan was that an assault against the German positions would start on 23 April with the object of securing the high ground overlooking the Tunis plain. The attack would be made by the 4th Division on the right and 1st Division on the left. The 3rd Brigade was in reserve but for the initial phase the Dukes were put under command of 2nd Infantry Brigade, tasked to capture a feature running from Pt 174 to the north west. This having been achieved by the North Staffs and Loyals, the 1st Battalion was ordered to relieve them. However, it was discovered that Pt 174 itself had not been occupied so when the Dukes, heavily dive bombed, reached the lower slopes it was found that the crest had been occupied by the Germans. The Dukes clung to the reverse slope of the feature, but any attempt to get over the crest was met by withering mortar and machine gun fire. By dusk the Battalion was very weak and stretched but despite Webb-Carter's urgent pleas to Brigade for

*North Africa 1943*

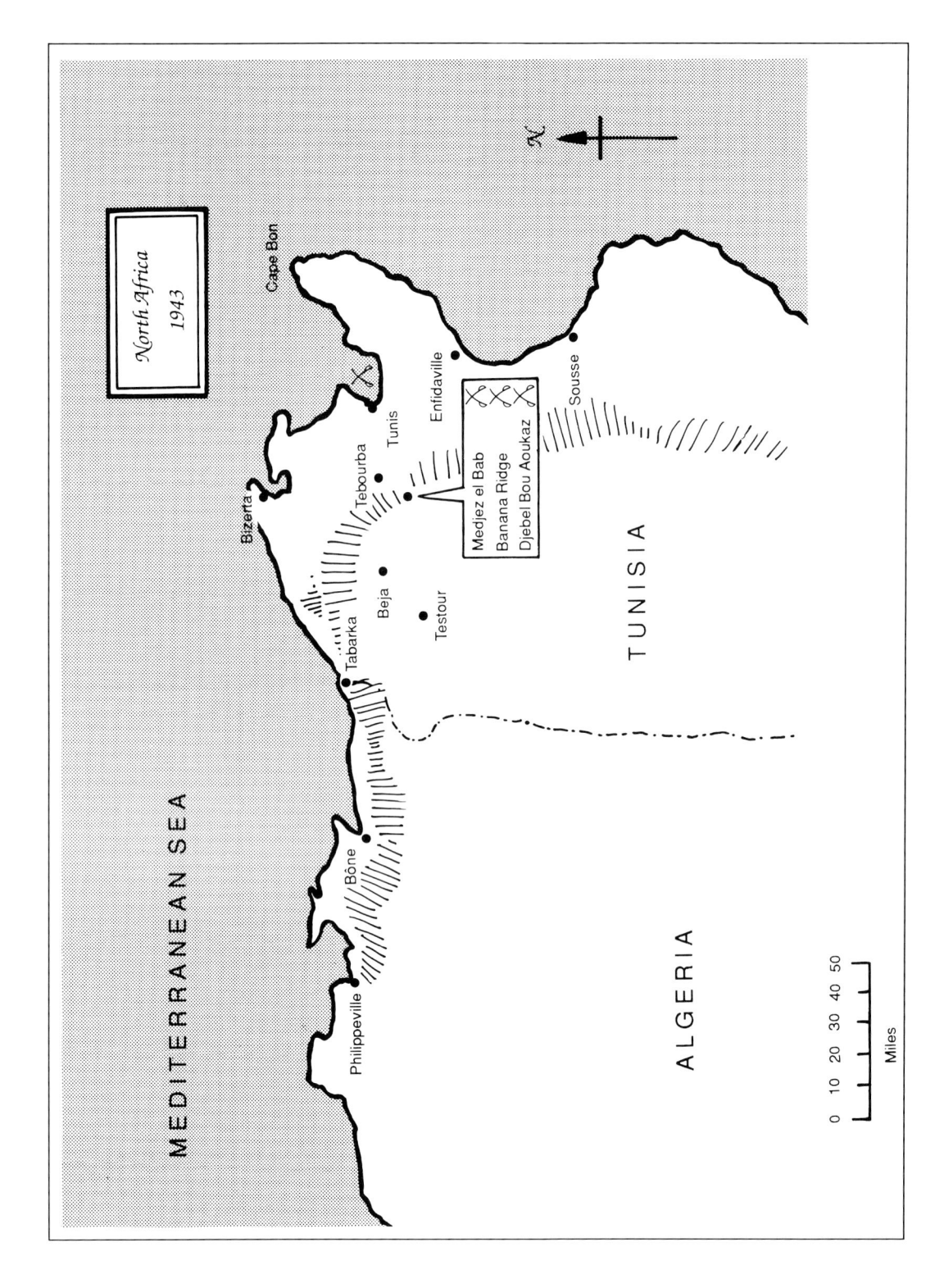

reinforcements, none arrived. The enemy now began to infiltrate the position and, communications with Brigade being broken, the Dukes evacuated at midnight, just before a very large German force occupied the position.

During the next ten days the Battalion was in reserve and reorganising. During that time the 24th Guards Brigade and 25 Tank Brigade were engaged in a long and arduous attack, the final objective of which was the Djebel Bou Aoukaz feature, which dominated the Medjaz el Bab - Tunis road; the axis of the armoured thrust to Tunis. The Guards fought magnificently and almost achieved complete success. The 5th Grenadiers captured Pt 171, the feature immediately before the Bou, and some of the Scots Guards, after suffering heavy casualties, actually reached the Bou. However they were too weak to hold it and were dislodged by a strong German counter-attack.

The 3rd Brigade was now given the task of capturing the Bou. The plan was that the Dukes would attack on the left, from the 5th Grenadiers position on Pt 171 and 1 KSLI on the right, from a position held by the Gordons. Reconnaisances were carried out on 3 and 4 May. Colonel Webb-Carter had intended that the Battalion should form up for the attack in a wadi behind Pt 171. However he was fortunate to be on Pt 171 and see a German mortar bombardment which made it clear that the wadi was a death trap. It was not possible to move up in daylight, but a position was found which the troops could occupy by night. But this meant that they had then to remain concealed and motionless until 5 o'clock in the evening of 5 May, when the attack on the Bou was to start. This they did in an outstanding display of discipline.

The Commanding Officer's plan was for an attack with two companies forward and two in support, directed on four features of the Bou, one of which appeared on the map as Dr Brahim, and was thus dubbed the Doctor. There was to be a preliminary bombardment by all the Divisional guns.

> *"At 1645 hours the barrage started – there was an immense whistling over our heads and we could see our shells beginning to burst on the lower slopes of "Doctor".... At 1650 hours we looked back at the little wadi where most of the Battalion lay and saw C Company (Captain S R Turnbull) rise out of the ground and, well extended, begin their advance... At 1700 hours dead (zero hour) C Company had reached the line of the olive grove where B Company (Captain A P R Smith) was waiting. Both Companies – B on the left and C on the right – now advanced, definitely committed to attack, and behind them A (Major P P Benson) and D (Captain A H Jacobsen) had left the precarious haven of the little wadi and were advancing steadily.... And then with a sudden and appalling crash down came the German defensive fire.... the noise was bewildering, the smoke was now eddying in quite thick clouds, but in between its whirls could be seen the pathetically thin lines of Yorkshiremen pushing stoically on. As one looked – sick with anxiety – one could distinguish some of the Lilliputian figures falling and*

> *stretcher bearers running forward to carry out their task...*
>
> *As the companies began to ascend the rocky slopes of the Bou the defenders started to bring rifle and machine gun fire to bear on the intrepid infantrymen picking their way upwards. Lieut. Denman was killed, and soon after Lieut. Millard, leading his platoon in an attack on a machine gun nest, fell – killed instantly by a bullet in the throat. Companies had gone into the attack only two weak platoons strong, and now casualties who could be ill spared began to occur right and left. Major Benson – shot in the arm – had to be evacuated, and it fell to Captain Jacobsen (D Company) to collect the fragments of A, C and D into one composite body to assault Pt 226".* (Webb-Carter)

By nightfall on the 5th the Dukes and the KSLI had achieved control of the Bou, except for the actual peak at Pt 226. At midnight the KSLI on the right flank suffered a heavy counter-attack, which it fought off with many casualties. Then at 3am on the 6th the British guns opened up with a heavy barrage preliminary to the advance of the 4th British and 4th Indian Divisions, now secure from the neutralised Bou.

At dawn the fighting on the KSLI front died down as the Germans switched their attention to the Dukes who were subjected to ferocious machine gun, sniper and mortar fire. Doggedly fighting back with rifles, Brens and their own mortars, they clung to their positions. Leading a gallant attack on a machine gun nest, CSM R J Shilleto was killed. During the lull before midnight the carrier platoon had performed wonders in grinding up to company positions with water and ammunition – thus demonstrating that the routes were practicable for tracked vehicles. Colonel Webb-Carter therefore requested Brigade HQ to send up some armour to deal with the strong mortar emplacements. But not even a single Churchill appeared. Instead, a weak company of the York and Lancasters was sent up from its reserve position – little more than a morale booster. For the next eight hours the Dukes endured more mortaring and shelling, but at noon on the 6th the fire slackened and Webb-Carter received reports that, led by tanks of the 7th Armoured Division, the infantry of the 1st Army was pushing up the road to Tunis. The Dukes – literally bloody but unbowed – were masters of the Bou and the fall of the Axis in North Africa was now inevitable. Lieutenant Colonel Webb-Carter was awarded the DSO for his bravery during the battle.

The fierce contest for the **Djebel Bou Aoukaz** feature cost the Battalion 114 casualties, including 31 killed. It also earned that battle honour, shared only with the King's Shropshire Light Infantry. 145 Regiment RAC (8th DWR) had three officers and 28 other ranks killed during the battle for the Bou.

On 12 May 1943 units of the 7th Armoured Division entered Tunis and General Alexander signalled to Churchill: *"It is my duty to report that the Tunisian campaign is over. All enemy resistance has ceased. We are masters of the North African shores".* This was indeed the end of the two year struggle to oust Rommel and the Axis from North Africa, and although the Dukes were involved only in the final phase, they had played a significant role.

Members of 1 DWR relaxing on Pantellaria, 1943

But although the Axis had been defeated, there was still another job for the Battalion. Midway between the coasts of Tunisia and Sicily lay the little island of Pantellaria, the last outpost of Musssolini's empire, reported to be strongly defended. It had to be taken out. The 1st Division with the Dukes' 3rd Brigade was detailed for the combined air, sea and land operation which went in on 11 June. After a devastating air and naval bombardment, the Battalion raced ashore in its landing craft, expecting determined resistance. But, demoralised by the navy and RAF, the Italians had no stomach for further fighting, and the Battalion was met only by droves of surrendering soldiers with white flags. For the invaders it was a bloodless victory. The capture of Pantellaria was a prelude to the seizure of Sicily, essential for the allied invasion of Italy.

On 3 September the allies landed in Italy. Within a fortnight the 8th Army had occupied southern Italy as far north as Bari. Meanwhile, Mussolini having fallen from power in late July, Italy capitulated on 8 September. The next day the 5th US Army, consisting of an American and a British Corps, landed at Salerno, 30 miles south east of Naples. Among the British troops was the 46th Division, which included 58th Anti-Tank Regiment RA (4th DWR), commanded by Lieutenat Colonel W S F Tetlow, and No 2 Commando. It was with the latter unit that the 6th Duke of Wellington was killed. The Germans, under Marshal Kesselring, unperturbed by the loss of their Italian allies,

1 DWR in Italy, 1944. Major General Penney, GOC 1 Division,
with Lieutenant Colonel B W Webb-Carter DSO, inspects the Bren carriers

resisted strongly. Poor planning by the allies did not help. As a result it was not until 1 October that Naples fell.

The allied plan was now to advance through Kesselring's Gustav Line to capture Rome. A joint British-American force would aid the attack by landing at Anzio, 60 miles in the rear of it, and 40 miles from Rome.

The 1st Battalion was committed to the Italian campaign in December 1943, when it landed at Taranto. On 17 January 1944, still commanded by Colonel Webb-Carter, it was routed by trucks to the west coast port of Castellamare, there to embark in LCIs and LSTs [d] as a unit of the British 1st and US 3rd Divisions tasked to spearhead the Anzio operation.

The landing on 22nd January took the Germans completely by surprise, as was intended, and a bridgehead was easily established. Then followed several days of inaction, due to lack of initiative in the higher command, despite the fact that the original beach-head, which included a perimeter roughly seven miles from Anzio, had been made good by noon on the 23rd. However, in the circumstances the dilatoriness of the American commander was fortunate as any advance towards the Alban Hills would almost certainly have led to the defeat of the force, as the enemy had reacted rapidly.

---

(d) LCI - Landing Craft Infantry. LST - Landing Ship Tank.

*Italy
1944*

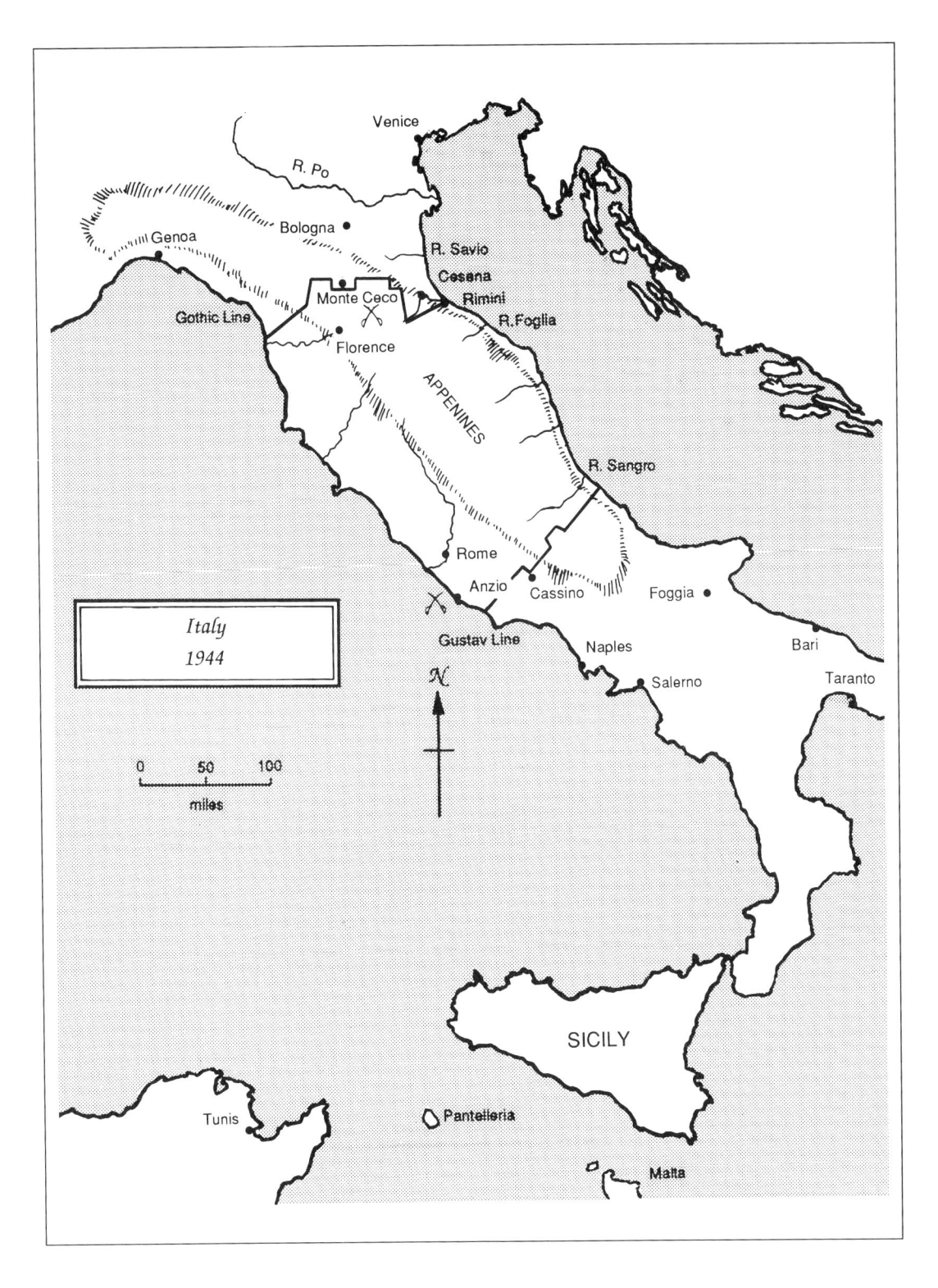

Rushing up his 14th Army, Kesselring effectively hemmed in the allied force in its perimeter, and only after four months of bitter fighting was a breakout possible.

After being the last to land, on the 23rd, the Dukes with their old comrades of the 3rd Brigade – 1st KSLI and 2nd Foresters – were pushed forward to a position on the perimeter. Apart from shelling, there was no enemy resistance. It was not until the 30th that their battles began with an attack on the enemy strongpoint of Campoleone Station on the main line to Rome. The attack went in at 1400 hours in the face of furious shelling, but no infantry opposition. By next morning the Brigade had consolidated a position just short of the Campoleone railway. Despite the shellfire there were surprisingly few casualties. The push forward to Campoleone Station had established a salient in the perimeter, approximately 4 miles deep and 1 mile wide, protruding from the main beach-head, and at its apex the Dukes and their Brigade were dug in. This was the farthest forward that any of the landing force reached before the final break-out.

It was now ten days after the initial landing and the element of surprise was lost. In that time the Germans had concentrated a force of some four divisions, one of which was armoured. By 4 February the position in the salient was critical. The German armour had swept round both flanks, virtually isolating the 3rd Brigade, while their infantry and guns were hammering away along the front. To save the Brigade from extermination a withdrawal was ordered, for which the London Scottish and 46th Royal Tanks managed to clear an escape route in the rear. The KSLI and Foresters succeeded in retiring with few losses, but the Dukes, temporarily commanded by Major M M Davie, hard-pressed by tanks, bombarded by artillery fire and fearsome Nebelwerfers (multi-barrelled mortars), suffered rough handling. By late afternoon D Company had been completely overrun with decimating casualties, the survivors captured. Soon after, the other companies and Battalion HQ ran straight into a group of tanks and *"all hell was let loose"* (Major Davie). Pinned down with no cover, they too lost heavily. Only the coming of darkness allowed the remainder to continue the withdrawal, by which time no more than 300-odd were left. Eleven officers and approximately 250 other ranks were reported missing.

Five days after the Battalion had fought its way out of the trap at Campoleone, during which it had had no time to recover and little time to refit, the Battalion was informed that it was to come under command of the Guards Brigade. The orders were to take over from a combined battalion of Grenadier and Scots Guards who were precariously holding a position overlooking a disused railway line, called the Railway Bed. It was raining hard. By first light on 10 February the Battalion was established along the embankment of the Railway Bed. That evening it reverted to the command of 3 Brigade. In the early hours of the 11th the Germans launched an attack in some strength. It was now C Company's turn to suffer virtual extinction. A Company (Major T F Huskisson), assisted by a troop of tanks launched a successful counter attack, but at the moment of victory Major P P Benson, who had taken over command of the Company when Major Huskisson was wounded, was killed. In the thick of it at Banana Ridge, wounded at Bou Aoukaz and an inspiring leader at the attack on Campoleone, the death of Major Benson was a sad loss. Major P R Faulks was also wounded so that A and the remnants of C Company were commanded by subalterns. That evening the Battalion was withdrawn from its isolated position at the Railway Bed which it had held against overwhelming odds for the past thirty six hours. On 15 February it retired to the B Echelon to reorganise, refit and rest.

On the night of 24 February the depleted Dukes were ordered to relieve the 1st Irish Guards in a confusing area of ridges and gullies called the Wadis.

> *"We had gone through Campoleone, and the almost miraculous extrication of the Battalion from there after being surrounded. We had fought the battle of the Railway Bed. We were punch drunk or, in the new phraseology 'bomb happy'. Every company commander, three second-in-commands, the adjutant, the signal officer and the mortar officer were casualties. John Streatfeild, the IO, and Jim Sills kept Battalion HQ going for me. A large draft of reinforcements, good lads, but quite untried had arrived but were not assimilated. The weather was terrible..To this cheering background I heard we were to relieve the Irish Guards".* (Webb-Carter)

The Wadis were cut up by long deep, heavily overgrown, gullies in which the distance from the enemy was frequently no more than 20 - 30 yards. They had been the scene of some of the heaviest close-combat fighting in the beach-head. This first tour of the Dukes was to be the worst of all. The weather was bad and the Germans numerous. For the next nine days companies, platoons, even sections, grimly fought off enemy attacks, under atrocious conditions of rain, sleet and snow. It was also very difficult to get rations to the companies. On 1 March D Company put in an attack on one of the wadis, only to be overwhelmed with practically total casualties.

Having again been withdrawn to a reserve area on the 5th, the Battalion could muster only two companies as fighting units, but while in reserve these were reinforced by 250 officers and men from the Royal Fusiliers and East Yorkshires. On 29 March the Battalion, now organised in three companies, again went into the Wadis where it spent the next ten days, during which there was a steady drain of casualties, mainly due to mortar fire. From 20 to 30 April the Battalion was in the Wadis for the third time, but by now the situation had become comparatively quiet: the German onslaught on Anzio had slackened.

On 11 May the great offensive on the main southern front began. It was now the time for the beach-head forces to carry out the original objectives of the landing which was to get astride the arterial roads and railways and thus cut the enemy's communications. On 23 May they finally broke out of the Anzio perimeter. On the 28th the main and beach-head forces linked up, but the opportunity to destroy the retreating Germans totally was thrown away. General Mark Clark, an Anglophobe, ignored General Alexander's orders, and headed for Rome and the honour of being first into the city instead.

In their last Anzio battle, on 23 May, the Dukes lost twelve killed with 74 wounded and missing, including five officers. Thus the battle honour **Anzio** cost the Regiment 39 officers and 921 other ranks – nearly 11 per cent of the 1st Division's total casualties.

On 5 June General Mark Clark's US forces entered evacuated Rome. On the following day Colonel Webb-Carter received two signals: first, he was awarded a Bar to his DSO; second, the 1st Dukes were to have the honour of representing the 1st Division in the ceremonial entry into Rome on 8 June. Later the Dukes were told that the Battalion was to represent the whole of the British army in Italy and not merely the 1st Division. Spruced up with hastily acquired supplies of khaki blanco, the Battalion was transported to Rome. The only music available was an assembly of pipes and drums of the Scottish and Irish battalions, to whose skirl the Battalion marched past in perfect order. When Webb-Carter stepped up to the saluting base to meet General Mark Clark he remarked. *"You have a good outfit there, Colonel"*.

By this date news had filtered through of the successful launching of the Second Front in France with Operation Overlord. This was a great morale-booster as the allied armies in Italy began their advance north towards the next objective, the forcing of the Gothic Line. A formidable system of natural and man-made defences, the line extended some 200 miles from the Gulf of Genoa on the west, to the Adriatic Sea, and was dominated by the barrier of the Apennine mountains. The Dukes with their 3rd Brigade formed an element of XIII British Corps, on the centre axis of the Allied advance. Although steadily withdrawing to their Gothic defences, the Germans put up stiff resistance everywhere and by the time the Dukes crossed the Arno river at the end of August they had suffered 76 casualties. While holding the line of the Arno they were reinforced by some twenty or thirty Italian partisans - the first and last time the Dukes were to see them. On 6 September the Battalion learnt with regret that its Commanding Officer, Colonel B W Webb-Carter, who had proved himself a leader of outstanding courage, stamina and skill, was to leave. His sartorial elegance, even under the most adverse conditions, was renowned throughout the 1st Division and the 5th Army. His place was taken by Colonel F P St. M Shiel (South Wales Borderers). By September the advance had reached the Apennines. An unusually wet autumn had reduced the narrow roads and tracks into quagmires, or raging torrents, so that tanks and even jeeps were bogged down. For transport of ammunition and supplies to company and platoon positions the Battalion now had to rely on mules, though frequently these, too, became "bellied".

On 2 October, during a rapid advance by 3 Brigade, the 2nd Foresters managed to get a platoon on to Monte Ceco, an ugly feature of 760 metres, which dominated the country for miles around, but shortly after dark on the evening of the 3rd they were pushed off it again. On the night 4/5 October a company of 1st KSLI made another attempt on Monte Ceco, but, having met determined opposition and suffered heavy casualties, it was ordered to retire. Since the occupation of Monte Ceco was essential before further progress could be made, the Dukes were ordered to attack the feature on the night of 6/7 October.

From information provided by patrols the Commanding Officer decided to attack Monte Ceco from the south and west. However, a gallant attempt by two companies during the night was met with a hail of fire and the positions reached proved to be untenable in daylight. As a result it was decided to re-launch the attack from the west. This went in on the afternoon of the 8th. It was pouring with rain and the mud was knee deep in places. Enemy reaction to the attack was prompt and heavy fire from spandaus and mortars from features further north pounded down on Monte Ceco. But by late afternoon the two leading companies were firmly established on the crest of the mountain. Two determined counter-attacks by the enemy were repulsed with heavy losses. Unfortunately, just at the moment when Colonel Shiel could feel justifiably proud of the success of the operation, he was mortally wounded. During the final phase of the operation Private R Burton won the first Regimental Victoria Cross of the war for his outstanding bravery in eliminating three spandau machine gun posts. Casualties during the action, which brought the Regiment the battle honour **Monte Ceco**, were 72, of which two officers and 12 other ranks were killed.

After the death of Colonel Shiel, Lieutenant Colonel B McCall, Royal Fusiliers, took command of the Battalion, which despite reinforcements could muster only three companies of less than 100 all ranks each. For the next four months the Dukes were constantly in action, attacking strongpoints, holding threatened sectors and patrolling. In December rain was succeded by heavy snow, with drifts up to seven feet deep, and this did nothing to ease the difficulties of supply, the manning of positions, or the discomfort of daily existence. Some alleviation was provided by the issue of waterproof trousers and hooded smocks, but even these could not keep men warm in exposed slit trenches. By 29 December the Battalion was holding a position on Monte Cerere in the mountains south of Bologna. There was little enemy activity except shelling, and day and night patrolling. On the night of the 29th a patrol under Lieutenants H T Johnston and D Morgan set out to reconnoitre a forward area, and were not seen again. These were the Battalion's last casualties of the campaign.

For some time rumours had been circulating that the 1st Division was to be withdrawn from Italy for operations elsewhere. When the move was confirmed on 27 January 1944 the posting was not to a main theatre of war but to Palestine. Since the fall of Rome the Battalion's battle casualties had amounted to twelve officers and 227 other ranks – nearly ten per cent of the total losses of the 1st Division – a division which suffered more heavily than any other in Italy during the same period. The Battalion was withdrawn by train to Taranto and arrived at Haifa on 22 February, its distinguished services in the Second World War completed.

*************

While the 1st Battalion was fighting its way up central Italy, following the fall of Rome, 145 Regiment RAC(8th DWR) was similarly engaged with 8th Army on the eastern coast. However it did not arrive in Italy from Tunisia until 3 May 1944. Its time

*Italy, 1944. A captured German "Panther" tank manned by 145 Regiment RAC (8 DWR)*

in Tunisia was spent training. During a grenade throwing practice a live bomb fell into a practice bay. Major A G Kempster, being unable to scoop it out, threw himself on it and thereby saved the lives of the other two occupants of the bay. For this act he was posthumously awarded the George Cross – the highest award for gallantry when not in contact with the enemy.

On arrival in Italy the Regiment, now commanded by Lieutenant Colonel E V Strickland, went first to Foggia where it was reorganised into two squadrons of Churchill and two of Sherman tanks. Then followed a series of moves, the first of which was in June when the Regiment moved to just south of Cassino to undertake training with 2nd Canadian Brigade. Then, in July, it was moved to a new concentration area near Florence where it came under command of 2nd New Zealand Division.

Field Marshal Alexander's plan was to hold the enemy in the west and, by a secret concentration of the 8th Army on the Adriatic coast, where the narrow maritime plain broadened into the Po valley, to turn the left flank of the enemy's defences. In August therefore 145 Regiment was moved to join the 8th Army concentration on the Perugia plain. During the climb over the mountains the Regiment's transporters frequently stalled so that the tanks had to be offloaded in order to tow the transporters – a cause of much caustic wit. The Regiment was once again with 2 Canadian Brigade. Also with 8th Army was 58th Anti-Tank Regiment RA (4th DWR).

The 8th Army's advance up the coast involved the crossing of a series of rivers, the first of which was the Metauro. This was followed by the crossing of the River Foglia on 1 September. In mid September the fighting at the crossing of the River Ausa was particularly bitter as every attempt was made to get the enemy in the Po valley on the run before the winter set in. From 23 September until 16 October the 1st Canadian Division, including 145 Regiment, was withdrawn to Riccione for rest. On the 17 October the Division was again in action, following up the enemy who had now been pushed from the Gothic Line. By 23 October the River Savio had been crossed. On 31 October the Regiment reverted to command of 21st Tank Brigade, thus ending its close relationship with 1st Canadian Infantry Division.

On 30 November, at Cesena, 145 Regiment RAC (8th DWR) together with 142 Regiment RAC, was informed that due to increasing manpower shortages, the two regiments were to be disbanded. This took place at Spoleto on 17 January 1945.

46th Division, of which 58th Anti-Tank Regiment (4th DWR) formed an element, was not withdrawn from the line until December 1944. It was then moved to Greece. However, the Regiment remained in Italy until the European war ended in May 1945.

\*\*\*\*\*\*\*\*\*\*\*\*\*

In September 1939 the 2nd Battalion, under the command of Lieutenant Colonel F H Fraser DSO,MC, was located at Multan in the southern Punjab, with detachments at the pleasant hill-station of Dalhousie in the foothills of the Himalayas. In October it was posted to the viceregal capital of New Delhi. The Dukes had not yet been issued with any mechanical transport, Bren carriers (or Bren guns), radios or mortars. With one company in the escort lines on the viceregal estate and another in the Red Fort in Old Delhi on internal security duty, the scope for any form of collective training was limited. In December 1940 Lieutenant Colonel H B Owen took over command, Lieutenant Colonel Fraser having left to command a brigade in Singapore. On 2 November 1941 the Battalion moved to Peshawar. Here it was more concentrated, but such were the requirements of service on the North West Frontier that training for modern war was impossible.

Japan entered the war in December 1941. Its onslaught against the British possessions in the Far East had carried all before it with a ferocity and speed for which the weak and ill-prepared British and Indian formations were no match. Hong Kong fell on 25 December 1941 and on 9 February 1942 the Japanese landed on Singapore Island. Meanwhile on 20 January they launched an attack against Moulmein in southern Burma.

At the end of January the Dukes were ordered to join a composite force of approximately two brigades, hastily assembled to strengthen the garrison in Burma. At last the Battalion was issued with Bren guns, 3in mortars, radios and the .55in Boyes anti-tank rifle. But like the rest of the British troops in the Far Eastern theatre, they had had no training in jungle warfare at which their enemy was to prove so adept. Embarking at Madras on 9 February, the Battalion spent the time on the voyage

2nd Battalion The Duke of Wellington's Regiment
Officers – Delhi March 1940

Back: 2Lt D N Simonds, Lt A C S Savory, 2Lt J E V Butterfield, 2Lt D C Roberts, 2Lt W D M Coningham, 2Lt J N Baxter, Lt H V Barrington, 2Lt J A A Christison, Lt G Foster, 2Lt A D Firth, 2Lt A B M Kavanagh, 2Lt J A Williams
Front: Capt J Robinson, Capt P P de La H Moran, Maj C K T Faithfull, Maj H B Owen, Lt Col F H Frazer DSO MC, Capt R de la H Moran, Maj C R T Cumberlege, Lt (QM) J Coulter, Capt R H Burton

instructing the men in their new weapons. It arrived at Rangoon on the 14th. The following day Singapore capitulated to the Japanese forces. The Battalion's strength was thirty officers and some 730 NCOs and men – none of whom had yet seen active service in the war.

Four days after landing the Battalion was sent to Pegu to help form a firm base there. However, no sooner had it reached its destination than orders were received for D Company (Captain W D M Coningham) to proceed to the Sittang River in order to guard the railway bridge, over which all requirements for the troops east of the river had to pass. At that time only one division was opposing the Japanese. This was the 17th Indian Division which had, by early February, fallen back to a defensive line at Kyaikto. By 20 February, out-numbered and threatened on his flanks, the Divisional Commander (Major General Sir John Smythe VC) was planning to withdraw to a more suitable position on the west bank of the Sittang. That same day Lieutenant Colonel Owen was ordered to move the Battalion immediately to Kyaikto to join 46 Indian Infantry Brigade, (3/7 Ghurka Rifles and 5/17 Dogras). Travelling by train the Battalion arrived at Kyaikto in the early hours of 21 February and promptly set about digging trenches.

On the afternoon of the 22nd the Battalion was ordered to move to a harbour area prior to a general withdrawal to the Sittang River the following day. During the short march this entailed it was strafed by planes of the RAF and five men were killed – its first casualties of the campaign. That evening B Company (Captain D N Simonds) was detached to reinforce a battalion of the Burma Rifles. It was intended that it would rejoin the Battalion before the withdrawal began, but this started earlier than planned with the result that the Battalion left before B Company could rejoin. The Japanese, following up the Division, adopted their usual practice of infiltrating through the jungle to block the withdrawal route. The distance to be marched was about 18 miles along a dusty road, flanked on either side by thick jungle, so that visibility sometimes only extended for a few yards. Because of the detaching of B and D companies the Battalion strength was no more than 15 officers and 260 other ranks. After 9 miles the Dukes fought their first battle against the Japanese when they encounterd a strongly held road block. A fierce battle raged for the next hour which involved all three battalions of 46 Brigade. A Company (Captain E Mason) was given the task of clearing the enemy from a position near the tail of the column, which they did with dash and courage, but the density of the jungle resulted in many men failing to regain contact with the column. C Company (Major J Robinson), by now the only company available, was then given the task of protecting the rear of the Brigade as the withdrawal got under way once more.

Because of the dense jungle, troops had almost to link arms in order to maintain contact. Even so, before long the Battalion had been split into three – the main body under Major Robinson, a small party with the Commanding Officer and the remnants of A Company under Captain Mason. The latter arrived at a spot near the Sittang bridge only to run into contact with the main body of the Japanese. After a short action Mason and his party were taken prisoners. It was late in the evening before the Battalion's main body, 139 all ranks, reached Mokpalin village, two miles short of the river. There it spent a miserable night trying to dig in with bayonets (there were no entrenching tools), without food or water. To add to the discomfort the night was bitterly cold and there were no blankets or greatcoats.

Throughout the night of the 22nd and during the 23rd desperate efforts had been made to get the transport over the bridge, on which planks had been hurriedly laid between the railway lines to make the semblance of a roadway. A terrible decision now faced General Smythe as the Japanese pressed their attacks on the bridge. If the bridge was blown, two thirds of his Division would be cut off. If it was captured by the Japanese, the way would be open for them to march on Rangoon. Early in the morning of 24 February the bridge was blown.

At day break enemy activity increased. As the day wore on the situation became more and more confused. By mid morning it had become so grave that the troops were ordered to make for the river and construct bamboo rafts with which to cross it. Owing to the current and the 1,000 yard width of the river the men had to abandon their arms, equipment and much of their clothing. Many non swimmers were drowned. B Company (Captain Simmonds), after an exhausting march, found a ferry some 10 miles north of the bridge and on arrival on the west bank made its way to Waw. Lieutenant Colonel Owen and his small party had swum across the river on the evening of the 23rd. During the night dacoits entered the village where he and his batman were sleeping and murdered him. In the short engagement on the previous day he had shown his coolness and courage as a commander in the field. Small and dapper, with an eyeglass always firmly fixed in his right eye, he was held in high regard by all ranks.

During the afternoon the swimmers with the main body of the Dukes started to make a life line from pier to pier of the bridge. As enough rope could not be found, Major Robinson, Corporal Fox and Lance Corporal Roebuck swam, under constant rifle fire, to the west bank to bring extra lengths. Through their efforts many men, including several hundred Indian and Gurkha soldiers, successfully reached the west bank. Major Robinson was later awarded the MC and the two NCOs the MM for their gallantry. One who escaped was Sergeant Bill Crowther:

> "On the morning of the 23 February 1942 I found myself behind a machine gun and Bandsman Les Williams feeding the belt through. While our ammunition lasted I suppose we were enjoying ourselves... When our ammunition ran out I started to dismantle the gun, throwing the breech block into the river. I said "Follow it, Les". To which he replied: "Not me. I've to take my chances with the Japs. I can't swim..." So I shook hands with him, wished him the best and dived in. I spent my childhood days swimming, so the Sittang held no terrors for me. Mind you there were still snipers and aircraft. How long I spent in that river I do not know – helping chaps to anything that floated". (e)

---

(e) After the war Bill Crowther went to live near Stafford. On a bitterly cold winter's night in 1972 he was helping a friend, who owned a transport café, to organise the parking of the lorries. The driver of the last lorry to park was ex-bandsman Les Williams.

Most of those who survived the crossing arrived at the opposite bank wearing little more than shorts and were without boots or headgear. One NCO was, much to his disgust, placed in arrest by an officer of a base unit withdrawing from Rangoon, for his slovenly attire. With battle casualties and men drowned in the crossing, the Dukes lost more than 100 officers and men. The Battalion was awarded the battle honour **Sittang** for its actions.

Withdrawn to Pegu to re-clothe, re-equip, rearm and re-form the Battalion was, for a short time, amalgamated with 1 KOYLI who had also suffered severe casualties. On 6 March the two battalions separated and the Dukes, now commanded by Major C K T. Faithfull, were organised into Headquarters Company and 1 and 2 Companies. Mustering 420 men they were placed under command of 16th Indian Infantry Brigade, 46 Brigade having been disbanded. The carrier platoon was detached to Headquarters 17 Division.

London and Delhi were shocked at the speed of the retreat and when on 27 February the GOC, Lieutenant General T Hutton, decided to evacuate Rangoon, General Wavell, the Commander-in-Chief, flew to Burma and rescinded the order. He then arranged for General Sir Harold Alexander to replace Hutton. At about the same time Major General Smythe was replaced by Major General D T Cowan. Wavell also instructed Alexander to do everything possible to hold Rangoon. A determined counter attack at Pegu, on 5 and 6 March, by 7 Armoured Brigade, 48 Indian Infantry Brigade and 63rd Indian Infantry Brigade, which had only recently disembarked at Rangoon, proved abortive and convinced Alexander that Rangoon must be evacuated. This took place on 7 March.

Meanwhile, the Japanese 33 Division was taking a wide sweep to the north of Rangoon with the intention of entering the city from the north west. To protect its southern flank the division established a series of blocks on the main road to the north of Taukkyan. The first to encounter these blocks was Captain J A A Christison with three carriers of the Battalion's Reconnaisance Platoon. He dismounted to inspect the block but on withdrawing to report the situation, he and four soldiers were killed and two of the carriers destroyed (f). Two determined attacks by 1st Gloucester Regiment failed to clear the road. A third assault on 8 March found that the Japanese had withdrawn. If the commander of the Japanese division had not so diligently obeyed his orders to get to Rangoon as fast as possible and had instead stayed to fight General Alexander's army at Taukkyan, the Burma campaign might have ended there.

Early on 8 March the Dukes withdrew through Taukkyan and took the road north to Prome. By marching and the use of road and rail transport the Dukes arrived just south of Prome on 26 March. There had been much digging of defence positions but no contact with the enemy.

On the 13th, Lieutenant General William Slim was appointed by Alexander to command the 1st Burma Corps (Burcorps). His first task was to set up a long-stop to the Japanese advance in the Irrawaddy valley. The American General Stilwell's Chinese

---

(f) Captain Christison was the only son of Lieutenant General Sir Phillip Christison, a former commanding officer of the 2nd Battalion.

*Burma 1942*

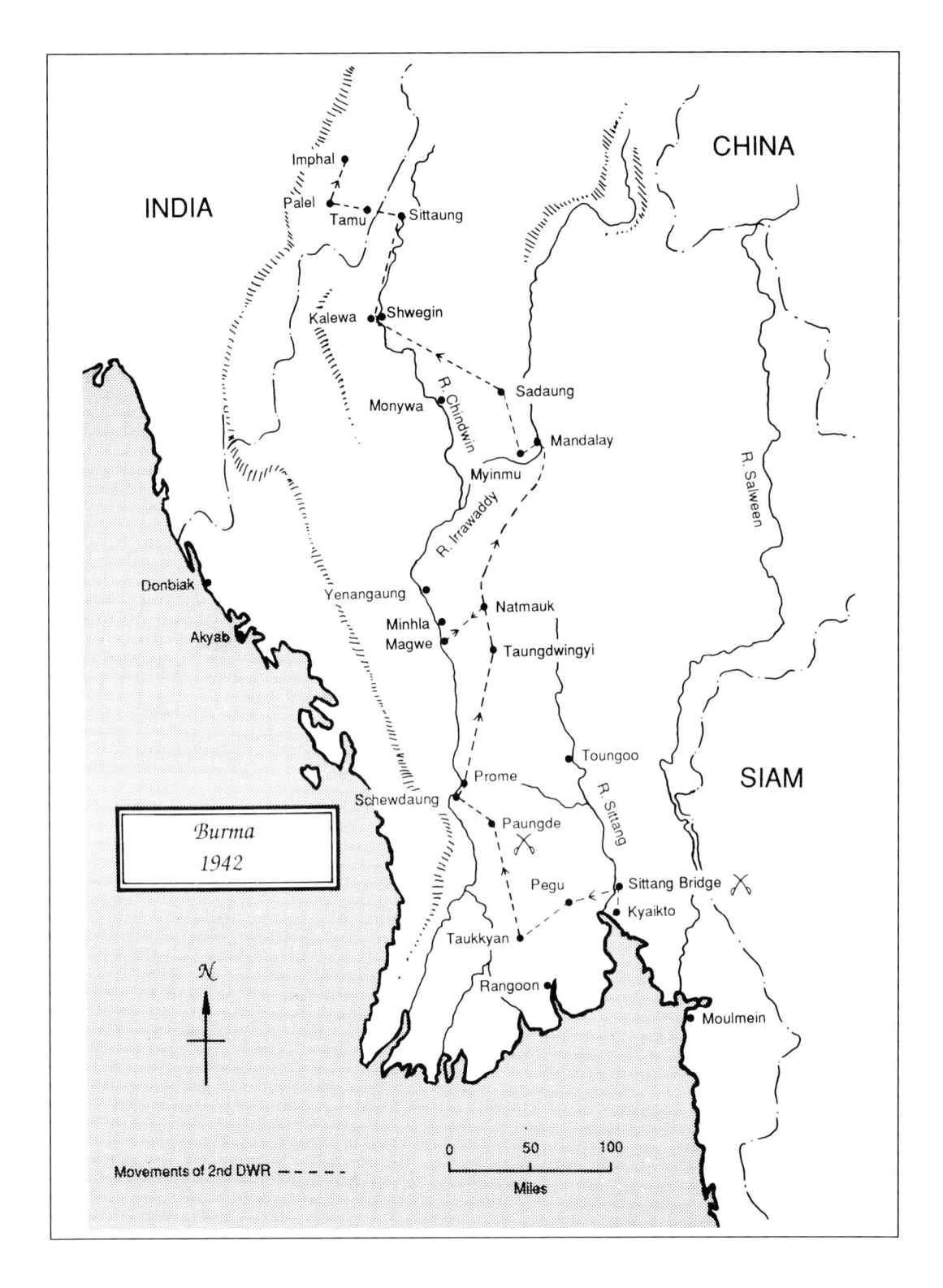

Movements of 2nd DWR -----

Army would cover the left flank at Toungoo and thereby release 1st Burma Division to join 17th Division in the Irrawaddy valley. On 28 March mounting pressure on the Chinese at Toungoo led Alexander to direct Slim to launch an attack southwards from Prome with 7th Armoured Brigade and the 17th Division. The ensuing battle initially took place in the area of Paungde where No 1 Company (Captain W D M Conningham) advanced against stong opposition. However, after having inflicted heavy losses on the Japanese, it was forced to withdraw, being outnumbered and outflanked. During this action Captain Conningham was killed. As the force withdrew towards Shwedaung numerous road blocks had to be cleared. On 30 March the main road block was met and attacked by the 1st Cameronians and 1st Gloucesters with the Dukes in reserve. Almost immediately No 2 Company (Major J Robinson) was drawn into the attack in support of the Gloucesters. Again heavy losses were inflicted on the Japanese, but in the process the Company had 30 casualties. Later, during the withdrawal, an air attack inflicted further 15 casualties. Among those killed was Major Robinson. Constantly in the thick of things ever since the crossing of the Sittang he had proved himself to be an inspiring leader. By this stage the Japanese had complete air superiority. This meant that not only were they able to bomb and strafe the troops of Burcorps unmolested, but it also led to a severe lack of information about the enemy's movements.

For its actions over the period 28-30 March the Battalion was awarded the battle honour **Paungde**. During the operations since the Sittang the Battalion had suffered five officers killed and one wounded, 31 other ranks killed and 86 wounded. On 1 April Major Faithfull was evacuated to hospital and command of the Battalion was assumed by Lieutenant Colonel S M C Theyre (Wiltshire Regiment).

On 3 April Slim issued orders for Burcorps to withdraw from the area of Prome to occupy a defensive position stretching from Minhla on the Irrawaddy to Taungdwingy, which was occupied by Chinese forces. On 4 April the withdrawal started with the Dukes, no more than 220 strong, acting as rearguard to 17 Division. Apart from the fact that April is one of the hottest months in Burma, the area was one of the most arid in the country. So, after a dispiriting defeat, the Division now had to face the miseries of retirement through heat and dust, without water, and under constant attack from the air. For the British troops there was no mail from home to bring comfort and home itself was an increasingly remote prospect.

For 1st Burma Division, now holding the oil fields at Yenangaung, matters were even more serious. Between 11 and 19 April it fought one of the bitterest actions of the retreat. Eventually, blocked front and rear by the Japanese, it had to fight itself free, losing in the process all its artillery and transport.

Since there was now little hope of stemming a further Japanese advance before the arrival of the monsoon, Alexander's only option was to extricate what he could of Burcorps by a withdrawal to the security of the Indian frontier. On 15 April 16 Brigade withdrew from Taungdwingy and started on the long march to the River Chindwin. On arrival at Natmauk the Battalion was detailed to create a diversion along the road to Magwe before continuing its withdrawal. By the 29th it was near Mandalay. The next day it marched 21 miles south west to Myinmu with the object of protecting Monywa. The following night there was a return march of 25 miles to Sadaung, in great heat and with little water.

On 3 May the Dukes arrived at Shwegin, on the banks of the Chindwin, where all wheeled transport was abandoned and destroyed. 16 Brigade was ferried across to Kalewa and there held the line of the river while the rest of the Burma army passed through. The main body of the army then had to trudge 90 miles up the Kabaw valley to Tamu. The Dukes, by now reduced to 180 all ranks, together with 48 Brigade, were the last to leave Kalewa. On the night of 11 May they embarked in two paddle steamers of the Irrawaddy Flotilla Company, arriving at Sittaung two days later.

Between the Chindwin and the haven of the Indian frontier at Imphal lay a daunting barrier of hot and waterless dense bamboo jungle, mountain ridges and deep ravines traversed only by single-file, precipitous tracks. The monsoon rains came on 12 May and within a week the downpour had become torrential. As the Dukes trudged grimly on, scaling one ridge to find another and yet another, malaria and dysentry took their toll. From Tamu, reached on 17 May, the Battalion made for Lokchao where transport was expected to carry it over the Indian frontier to Imphal. But the rains had halted all motor traffic and the weary column faced yet another ridge and twenty miles to the hard road at Palel and, the most welcome sight for many weeks, a column of RIASC lorries. On 22 May the 2nd Dukes, or what remained of them, arrived in Imphal. On the same day Lieutenant Colonel Theyre was evacuated to hospital and Major Faithfull, who had rejoined three weeks earlier, assumed command.

General Slim had this to say of those final days of the 900 mile withdrawal that had cost Burcorps some 13,500 casualties in killed, wounded and missing:

> *"Ploughing their way up slopes, over a track deep in slippery mud, soaked to the skin, rotten with fever, ill-fed and shivering as the air grew cooler, the troops went on, hour after hour, day after day. Their only rest at night was to lie on the sodden ground under the dripping trees, with-out even a blanket to cover them....*
> *On the last day of the nine-hundred-mile retreat I stood on a bank beside the road and watched the rearguard march into India. All of them, British, Indian and Gurkha, were gaunt and ragged as scarecrows. Yet, as they trudged behind their surviving officers in groups pitifuly small, they still carried their arms and kept their ranks, they were still recognizable as fighting units. They might look like scarecrows, but they looked like soldiers too".*

Unfortunately, many of those responsible for receiving the survivors at Imphal behaved as though a contemptuous sense of superiority was the right reaction. For the lack of preparedness in the reception arrangements there was some excuse, because everything was in short supply. For the lack of consideration shown to the men who had endured a retreat of 900 miles in burning heat, often short of water and food, and pressed by a relentless and superior enemy, there can be no excuse. Lieutenant General N Irwin, the commander 4 Corps, who was responsible for the reception area, spoke harshly and critically. Slim said to him, *"I never thought an officer whose command I was about to join could be so rude to me"*. Irwin replied, *"I can't be rude. I'm senior"*.

It was Slim, however, who was to go on to greater things and with his 14th Army recapture Burma from the Japanese.

*************

After a short stay in Imphal the 2nd Dukes left for Ranchi, in Bihar, where they were re-formed as a mechanised support battalion, one of several highly mobile, heavily armed, assault units. Each company now had an unprecedented number of 27 Bren guns. The Battalion then embarked on an intensive training programme to prepare itself for its new role.

In September 1942 the 14th Indian Division had started to advance down the Arakan coast towards Akyab Island. The original plan was to include a seaborne landing on Akyab by two brigades, but by mid November other commitments and lack of resources led to the cancellation of this part of the plan. 14 Division was then committed to a frontal assault against the Japanese. Good progress was made but by January 1943 the advance was halted near Donbiak. The campaign was directed by Lieutenant General Irwin, now Commander Eastern Army, who began to feed reinforcements to 14 Division to such an extent that it was soon trying to control the operations of nine brigades. Among the reinforcements were two troops of tanks of 146 Regiment RAC. This had been raised as the 9th Battalion of the Dukes in 1940 and, like the 8th Battalion, had been converted to an armoured regiment in 1942. The six tanks arrived in the Arakan on 30 January. They were in action on the 31st when three of the tanks were destroyed. Once again the futility of employing tanks in penny packets was revealed. The Japanese went on the attack and by May 14th Division was back where it had started. General Irwin now intimated to Slim, who had become involved in the later stages of the Arakan campaign, that he, Slim, was to be relieved of his command of 15 Corps. However, at about the same time Irwin himself was relieved of his command so he sent Slim a signal which said: *"You are not sacked, I am"*. In October 1944 Slim was appointed to command the Eastern Army, later to become 14 Army.

In July 1942 Major Orde Wingate, a highly unconventional officer, had put forward to Wavell, the C-in-C India, his scheme for Long Range Penetration Groups (LRPG) to operate behind Japanese lines in Burma and create havoc. This was eventually approved and given high priority for manpower and equipment. The badge of the force was the Burmese mythological lion, the 'Chinthe', which quickly became Chindit. Promoted brigadier, Wingate marched his first Chindit brigade into Burma in February 1943 and for the next three months carried out raids and harrassed behind the enemy lines. Of the 3,000 men who had left Imphal about 2,200 returned, most of them unfit for future LRPG duties. However some important lessons were learnt, especially about what could be achieved with air supply. But the most immediate positive result was psychological, particularly following the Arakan debacle. The need for the expansion of the Chindit force had been demonstrated and, learning of this, Lieutenant Colonel Faithfull persuaded GHQ in Delhi to have the 2nd Battalion included in the newly raised 3rd Indian Division (Special Force).

In late 1943 the Battalion accordingly joined 23 Infantry Brigade (Special Force) then assembling in the Central Provinces near Jhansi. The other units in the Brigade were 4th Battalion Border Regiment, 1st Battalion Essex Regiment and 60th Field Regiment RA (in an infantry role). Each of the battalions was divided into two columns identified by their old regimental numbers. Thus the Dukes' columns were 33 and 76. Each column comprised some 400 officers and men, 70 mules, 12 chargers and 12 bullocks. The large number of pack animals was required for carrying the column's equipment which included medium machine guns, 3in mortars, radios, charging engines, fuel, engineer stores, explosives and medical stores. Replenishment was to be by air drops and for this purpose a RAF liaison officer, special radio equipment and operators were attached to each column.

For six months the troops of 3rd Indian Division underwent a rigorous programme of training. Wingate demanded that every man should be capable of marching 90 miles through virgin jungle carrying a 60lb pack, beside 50 rounds of rifle ammunition, two Bren gun magazines and grenades. *"No jungle was to be described as impenetrable before it had been penetrated"*.

The Dukes practised skills unknown in the recent retreat e.g. navigating through thick jungle avoiding roads and tracks, clearing drop sites for the air supply, constructing air strips, crossing rivers with mules and individual cooking. Three weeks of every month between September 1943 and March 1944 were spent in this way, by which time the Battalion had become a fully-operational Chindit unit. In March 1944 Lieutenant Colonel Faithfull was posted to command the 1st Wiltshires in the Arakan and was succeeded by Lieutenant Colonel E W Stevens MBE.

In December 1943 Lieutenant General Sir Philip Christison's 15 Corps embarked on a limited offensive in the Arakan with the aim of capturing Akyab, whose airfields were a constant menace to Calcutta. Steady progress had been made when on 4 February 1944 the Japanese launched an attack. However 15 Corps stood firm and was maintained by air. By the end of the month the Japanese, who had hoped to draw Slim's reserves down to the Arakan in preparation for their main offensive further north against Imphal and Kohima, had been defeated.

The offensive was launched in March. Initially the Japanese met with success and were able to isolate both Imphal and Kohima. Among the reinforcements ordered forward from India to the area of Dimapur were HQ 33 Corps[g], 2 Division and 23 Infantry Brigade (Special Force), which had been on the point of flying into Burma to join the rest of 3 Division already landed and in action.

---

(g) In 1943 a new Indian Corps had been raised in Wellington, south India, by Lieutenant General Sir Philip Christison. It was he who gave it the number 33.

# THE SECOND WORLD WAR

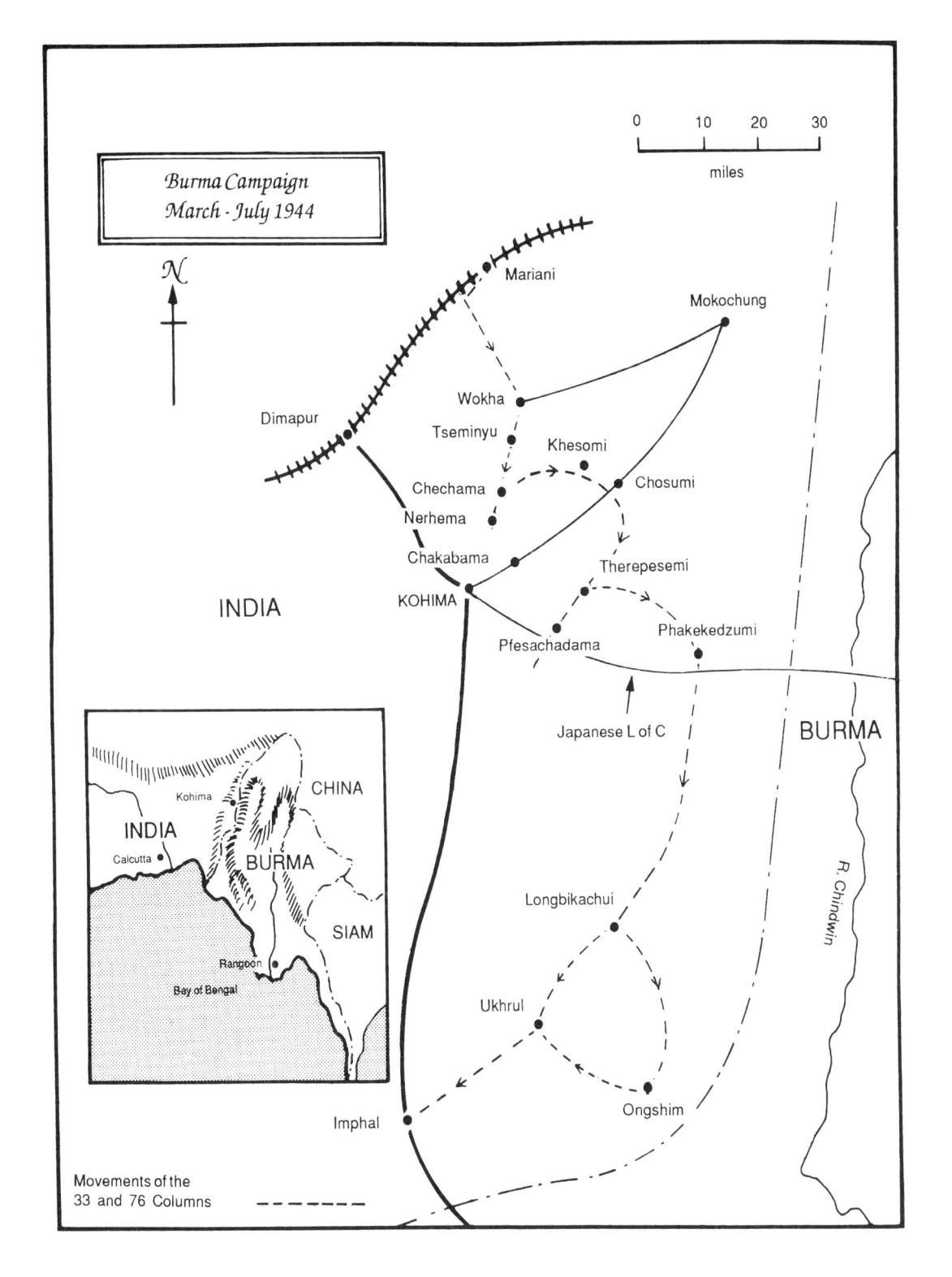

*Burma Campaign
March - July 1944*

The task allotted to 33 Corps was to advance southwards along the axis of the Dimapur-Imphal road, initially to relieve the embattled troops who were staunchly defending Kohima, and next the four divisions surrounded at Imphal. 23 Brigade was to assist these operations by harassing the Japanese lines of communication running through the Naga Hills, to the east of the road. Its plan was for the columns to advance from the railhead at Mariani on a broad front with 1 Essex on the right, then 2 DWR and 4 Border and, on the left, 60 Field Regiment RA.

On 10 April Lieutenant Colonel Stevens led 76 Column out of Mariani and into the Naga hills, followed a week later by 33 Column (Major S R Hoyle). Even at this early stage the difficulties the columns were to encounter became apparent when they had to climb a hill rising 2,300 feet in 3 miles. Such isolated parties of the enemy as were met were driven back towards Kohima. However, one party was surprised at Tseminyu where six of the enemy were killed and one captured. Four men of 76 Column were wounded. In the meantime 33 Column had managed to improve the track from Woka to Mokochung, where Brigade headquarters was located, so that it was passable for jeeps.

*76 Column moves into the jungle, 1944*

33 Column was next ordered to occupy Chechama. On arrival there Major Hoyle discovered that approximately 100 Japanese were at Nerhema, guarding a large grain store. That night he was able to identify all the main Japanese positions. The next morning he launched an attack which, supported by Hurricane fighter bombers, led to the defeat of the Japanese and the occupation of Chechama.

The Dukes were now given two new tasks. First, to clear the Mokochung track from Chosumi to Chakabama, where there were reported to be some 1,000 Japanese, and then to harass the Japanese lines of communication in the area of Pfesachadama. Conditions had now worsened considerably. The villages were more isolated and impoverished and the tracks narrow, steep and difficult for men to use, let alone loaded mules. The terrain was more formidable and the monsoon had broken and drenching rain fell for days at a time. The evacuation of wounded meant a 60 mile carry by litter to the nearest dressing station.

76 Column was ordered to move from Chechama to Khesomi which, in the difficult

conditions, took a week. On arrival at Khesomi 33 Column passed through to Chosumi where it took over from 4 Border the tasks of dealing with the Japanese entrenched there and at Chakabama. 76 Column now prepared to harass the Japanese lines of communication. Leaving behind all its administrative element, mules and heavy weapons, it moved to establish a firm base for patrols on high ground overlooking Pfesachadama, some twenty miles to the east of Kohima. On 29 May a patrol was sent to observe the Japanese line of communication, now less than a mile away.

As 76 Column made its presence felt, the Japanese took swift action. A group of about 60, guided by a disloyal Burman, attacked the base at dawn the next day. During this most bitter fighting, the Japanese attacked repeatedly with the bayonet, screaming and yelling. All these attacks were driven back with losses. At times they succeeded in over-running a post, but an immediate counter-attack restored the situation. Colonel Stevens now realised that the Japanese attackers were a holding force, trying to pin him down, pending the arrival of a stronger force during the night. So stealthily, carrying the wounded, 76 Column slipped away – literally slipped, as the hillside was very steep. The remainder of the night was spent in a valley several thousand feet below in pouring rain and without cover. The next day they rested. As soon as it was pitch dark, led by a Naga headman, they moved to Therepesemi. Here a new base was established and patrolling continued.

Chindits receiving supplies, 1944

76 Column's casualties were three soldiers killed and one officer and 14 soldiers wounded. The Japanese had 17 killed.

Meanwhile the strong Japanese position at Chosumi was still holding out, but a series of encircling attacks by 33 Column forced them to withdraw from both Chosumi and milestone 28.

Following these actions 33 and 76 Columns, after a long march, concentrated at Phakekedzumi where the seriously wounded and sick were left. Operations had now been going on for three months and the strain was telling as malaria, dysentery, heatstroke and jaundice took their toll. Although the siege of Kohima had been raised, the work of the Dukes was not yet done. Despite their defeat, lack of supplies and medical facilities, the Japanese refused to give in. So on 17 June 33 Column marched south, followed by 76 Column a day later. By 30 June, after several successful engagements with the enemy, the columns reached Longbikachui. There they reorganised with 33 Column taking all the unfit men. The 76 Column was ordered forward to operate against the Japanese communications in the Ukhrul area which involved yet more hard marching.

On 12 July orders were received that all organised enemy resistance was at an end and on the 20th the Dukes and their 23rd Brigade were withdrawn through Ukhrul to Imphal, where about 50 per cent of the force had to be admitted to hospital. On the 22nd the remainder were transported to Dimapur. Before leaving Dimapur for Bangalore in southern India, Colonel Stevens received a copy of General Slim's Special Order of the Day:

> *"On the successful conclusion of this phase of operations in the Imphal area, I wish to convey to you and all ranks of 23 Brigade my high appreciation of the great contribution which you have made to the defeat of the Japanese. 23 Brigade was given a task which was a real test of its skill and determination and toughness, but never during the one-thousand mile moves of your columns over some of the most difficult country in the world was any difficulty, whether provided by nature or by the enemy too great for its commanders and men to overcome. 23 Brigade should be proud of the part it has played in the destruction of the Japanese forces. You have more than sustained the reputation of the Special Force."*

For its services during 1944 the Regiment was awarded the battle honour **Chindits 1944.**

\*\*\*\*\*\*\*\*\*\*\*\*

On 6 June 1944 the long-awaited and long-prepared-for Second Front opened when the British 2nd Army, with the US 1st Army on its right, landed at dawn on the Normandy coast. Among the follow-up formations was 49 (West Riding) Division.

Shortly after embodiment in September 1939 the 1/6th and 1/7th Battalions of the Regiment were moved to Malton. Both were in 147 Infantry Brigade of 49 (West Riding) Division TA. In April 1940, following the German invasion of Norway, 49 Division was sent there to support the Norwegian army. Two of its brigades were landed but because of the rapid German advances it was decided not to land 147 Brigade; so after ten days in crowded transports it returned to England. With the Norwegian ports in German hands Iceland became of great strategic importance and an expedition had to be sent to occupy and fortify it without delay. 147 Brigade was selected for this task and 1/6th and 1/7th Battalions left Glasgow for Reykjavik on 13 May. Later they were joined by the rest of 49 Division. The respective commanding officers of the two Dukes Battalions were, at this time, Lieutenant Colonel J H C Lawlor and Lieutenant Colonel J W N Haugh. The Battalions returned to England in April 1942. From mid-1943 the Division was training for the role of an assault division for the coming landing on the French coast. However in January 1944 its role was changed to that of a follow up division. In place of an assault against the beaches the Division had now to prepare for a break-out battle.

On 9 June the 1/6th and 1/7th Battalions embarked in HMS Cheshire and arrived off the Normandy coast on 11 June. By the evening of that day they were concentrated five miles inland. The 1/6th, now under the command of Lieutenant Colonel R K Exham, was the first to see action. On 16 June it received orders to carry out an attack the next day on Parc de Boislonde, a thick wood located on a ridge overlooking Fontenay le Pesnil. The attack, supported by a squadron of tanks and the fire of four field regiments, was successful but the enemy's defensive fire had taken a heavy toll. The following morning the Germans launched a counter attack and the 1/6th was forced back. Casualties were again heavy. In the two days of fierce fighting 16 officers and some 220 men were killed or wounded.

As a result of the heavy casualties and loss of equipment the Battalion was withdrawn to brigade reserve. Located in a pleasant chateau, remote from the noise of battle, the Battalion set about absorbing reinforcements and refurbishing itself. However, almost immediately it was spotted by a German reconnaissance plane and shortly afterwards was heavily shelled. After half-an-hour the shelling stopped by which time the Battalion had had 20 further casualties. In the afternoon of that same day (20 June) the Battalion was ordered to parade for an address by the brigade commander. As it started to assemble it was again shelled and more casualties were incurred. When the parade was eventually held the Battalion was told that Colonel Exham was leaving to command another battalion – a strange decision in view of the buffeting the Battalion's morale had received. His successor was Lieutenant Colonel A J D Turner MC (Suffolks) who did not join until 25 June, on which day 49 Division was to carry out an attack in the area of Fontenay. The objectives given to 147 Brigade were, first, the village of Fontenay Le Pesnil, and then another village beyond it, called Rauray. 1/6th objective was to fill a gap on the flank of 147 Brigade's advance but as the attack proceeded the Battalion came under increasingly heavy mortar fire and once again suffered heavy casualties. It achieved its objective but was now, in the opinion of the commanding officer, in need of time for a thorough reorganisation and rest. He therefore wrote a lengthy report to that effect. When this reached General Montgomery, he reacted swiftly by first dismissing the commanding officer and then, on 8 August, ordering that the 1/6th be disbanded and be used to find drafts for 1/7th. The Battalion arrived back in England on 17 August 1944. In the short period it had been in Normandy it had 19 officers and 350 men either killed or wounded.

On 17 June 1/7th Battalion (Lieutenant Colonel J H O Wilsey), which had been in reserve, moved forward into the battle area preparatory to an attack on Fontenay Le Pesnil. The country in which the troops were operating was thick bocage; copses, woods, small fields, tall hedges and sunken roads with eight foot banks all of which restricted both visibility and fields of fire. It was hardly suitable country for the Battalion's 330 folding bicycles, so the commanding officer ordered them to be temporarily put in a wood. There they were run over and squashed by a squadron of tanks – much to the relief of the Battalion. On the following day the Battalion was in action in the area of Le Parc de Boislande from which the 1/6th had earlier been forced to withdraw. On 22 June it was relieved for a few days before taking part in 49 Division's attack on Fontenay Le Pesnil. Throughout the 25 and 26 June the Battalion was heavily engaged against strong German defences, which included elements of two Panzer divisions. The final assault started on the afternoon of 26 June when the German positions were attacked by the tanks of the Sherwood Rangers supported by the 1/7th and the whole of the divisional artillery. By the evening all objectives had been captured. The battle had cost the Battalion some 120 men killed and wounded. It earned the Battalion the battle honour **Fontenay-Le-Pesnil.** On 19 July it was withdrawn from the area for its first rest since landing.

At the end of July the allies broke out of the Normandy beach-head and by the end of August the River Seine had been reached, which the 1/7th crossed on 3 September. It now became important to liberate Le Havre and repair the dock area in time to help the winter build-up of the allied armies. The task was given to 1 British Corps (49th and 51st Divisions). The attack on Le Havre began on 10 September. The 1/7th, which was at that time 30 officers and 864 other ranks strong, took part in the very successful operation. Le Havre fell on 12 September by which time the rest of 21 Army Group was 200 miles to the east. However 1 Corps quickly rejoined and by 23 September the 1/7th had moved through Brussels and was on the southern bank of the Leopold canal, about 18 miles east of Antwerp. The task now was to clear the Belgian/Dutch frontier area northwards to the river Maas. By 30 October this had been achieved and the 1/7th had advanced to Roosendaal in south Holland.

With the failure of the allied airborne operations against Arnhem all hope of entering the heart of Germany before the winter had faded. On 1 November 1944 the 1/7th was transferred to 1st Canadian Army and to a position in the salient across the Rhine, north of Nijmegen. Early in December a German parachute battalion made a determined attempt to capture the great Nijmegen bridge, but stout resistance from the 1/7th eventually wore down the attackers, forcing them to withdraw. Over 50 Germans were killed within the Battalion area and over 100 were taken prisoner. Two days before Christmas the Battalion moved back to billets in Nijmegen. Early in the New Year the Battalion lost its much respected Commanding Officer when Lieutenant Colonel Wilsey was appointed to command a brigade. He was succeeded by Lieutenant Colonel C D Hamilton DSO (j), who had previously commanded 11th Battalion Durham Light Infantry until it had been broken up to provide reinforcements.

In April 1945 the 1/7th took part in the break-out from the Nijmegen salient prior to 1st Canadian Army starting its drive to the North Sea to cut off the German 15th

---

(j) He became Sir Denis Hamilton, at one time Editor in Chief of Times Newspapers.

A warning on the road to Arnhem, 1944

1/7th DWR advance towards Ede, west of Arnhem, on tanks of 5th Canadian Division, 1944

Army in North Holland. On 12 April 49 Division captured Arnhem and then drove off towards Rotterdam. By 7 May it was at Utrecht, disarming three German divisions, the day before the war in Europe ended.

*****************

In October 1944 the 5th Battalion (43rd (5 DWR) AA Battalion RE) [k], which had been employed on searchlight duties in the UK since the outbreak of the war, was converted to infantry for garrison duties abroad. Its new title was 43rd Garrison Regiment RA (5 DWR) and under command of Lieutenant Colonel F A Carline it moved to La Panne in Belgium in December. La Panne was about five miles west of Dunkirk which was held by 11,000 German troops under command of Admiral Frisius. Their perimeter was approximately 45 miles but they were well provided with artillery and Admiral Frisius was a determined commander. The encircling allied troops were mostly composed of Czech formations. While at La Panne, the 5th continued with its training when not employed guarding ammunition dumps, stores and vital communications.

On 11 February 1945 the Regiment, now renamed 600th Regiment (5 DWR) RA, took over a sector of the western perimeter, coming under command of Czech Independent Armoured Brigade. On 15 April the Regiment and a company from a Czech motor battalion took part in an attack to try and regain ground from which some French troops had been driven. However, the strength of the Germans had been underestimated and, unsupported by tanks, the attacking force was unable to prevail against heavy enemy artillery, Spandau and mortar fire. The Regiment's casualties were 17 killed and 63 wounded.

The general surrender of the German armies in the West took place on 8 May, but it was not until 10 May that Admiral Frisius capitulated.

**************

At the end of the war, in August 1945, the location of the battalions of the Regiment was as follows:

1st Battalion: Near Gaza, in Palestine, commanded by Lieutenant Colonel C W B Orr OBE. The British Government was uncomfortably aware that, while the Jews living in Palestine and the many more seeking entry from Europe had both a political claim and a cause for sympathy, the claims of the Arabs were equally strong. The Jewish settlers had a military organisation in being, the Haganah, which had begun to exert pressure by acts of sabotage and civil disobedience. It stopped short of murder; but there was no such restraint among the Stern Gang and the Irgun Zvai L'eumi.

In June and July the Battalion had been in Syria and Lebanon where the inhabitants were in a state of revolt against French rule. The Dukes' main task was to provide escorts

---

(j) The title was changed to 43rd Searchlight Regiment RA in December 1944.

for the safe evacuation of French troops and civilians from Damascus and the surrounding countryside to Beirut in Lebanon. The worst mission they faced was the disarming of a native battalion which had murdered their French officers.

From December 1945 to April 1946 the Battalion was in Egypt before returning once again to Palestine where it joined the rest of 1st Division and 6th Airborne Division for further internal security duties in connection with illegal immigration. Stationed at Peninsular Barracks at the main port of Haifa, it was comparatively easy for the Dukes to deploy quickly to the town or to the neighbouring coast-line where illegal immigrants were most likely to put ashore and escape over the beaches into the welcoming hands of a Jewish reception committee. On the night 16/17 June, 1946 the Haganah mounted a massive show of strength, destroying or damaging eight bridges around Palestine's frontiers. Again, on 17 June, there was a strong raid on the Kishon railway workshops in Haifa, followed on the next day by twelve Irgun gunmen entering the Officers' Club in Tel Aviv and kidnapping four officers. It was against this background that the Battalion had to operate. In the next month, General Bernard Montgomery, CIGS, visiting Palestine, advocated a new "get tough" policy to break the illegal organisations. Thus was launched Operation Agatha in which the Battalion took a major part. The aim of this operation was to seek out and capture all VIJs (Very Important Jews). The Battalion's area of responsibility was part of Haifa town. Despite the numbers arrested (2,659 men and 59 women on the first day alone) and the capture of a major Jewish arsenal at Meshek Yagur, the operation was a failure in that the "right" important Jews were not captured. On 22 July the Irgun retaliated when the King David Hotel in Jerusalem, which housed GHQ and the offices of the Palestine government, was blown up with the loss of ninety-one lives.

In December 1946, under command of Lieutenant Colonel C R T Cumberlege, the Battalion was flown to Khartoum following an outbreak of civil disturbance, which turned out to be of no account. So, when in February 1947 Lieutenant Colonel B W Webb-Carter DSO, OBE, succeeded Lieutenant Colonel Cumberlege, for the first time since 1939 the Battalion began to revert to a normal peacetime existence. At the end of the year the Battalion returned to the UK.

2nd Battalion: At Dehra Dun, in India, commanded by Lieutenant Colonel J H Dalrymple. It remained there until December 1945 when it moved to Meerut. In May 1946 Lieutenant Colonel F R Armitage assumed command. The following May the Battalion moved to Delhi and on 3 June 1947 the Viceroy, Earl Mountbatten, announced plans for the partition of India and Pakistan. The transfer of power was not accomplished without anti-British rioting and looting in major cities. This soon developed into communal riots between Hindus and Muslims. British battalions had to be called in to help the police. Partition into two independent states from 15 August 1947 brought to an end British efforts to control the growing communal violence and savagery. One of the final duties of the Battalion, before leaving India, was to provide a guard of honour when the Viceroy left Viceroy House for the last time. On 19 September, under command of Lieutenant Colonel C R T Cumberlege, it embarked for the UK.

1/4th Battalion (58th Anti-Tank Regiment RA): At Santa Sevra, north of Rome, before moving to Austria as part of the Army of Occupation. It was disbanded in 1946.

2/4th Battalion. (68th Anti-Tank Regiment RA): One battery of the Regiment was sent to Malaya in 1941 and its members made prisoners when Singapore fell in February 1942. The Regiment went to France in July 1944 as part of 59 Division. In the subsequent fighting it had three officers and 56 other ranks killed. In August 1944 the Division was disbanded.

5th Battalion. (600th Regiment (5 DWR) RA: At Dunkirk. Before disbandment it undertook guard duties at Headquarters 21 Army Group .

1/6th Battalion: At Colchester acting as an infantry primary training centre. It was disbanded in October 1946.

2/6th Battalion: By 1945 the battalion had been absorbed into an Armoured Delivery Regiment, but some squadrons continued to wear the Regimental badges.

1/7th Battalion: In Germany where it remained until disbanded in late 1946

2/7th Battalion: Was placed in suspended animation in September 1943.

8th Battalion. (146 Regiment RAC): Disbanded in Italy in January 1945.

9th Battalion: One squadron took part in the Arakan operations from January to March 1945. At the end of the war the Regiment was at Ahmednagar in India. From December 1945 to November 1946 one squadron was in Sumatra on peace keeping duties. The Regiment was disbanded early in 1947.

CHAPTER 19

# Rationalisation, Reductions and Reorganisations: 1945 - 1970

*"With the end of the Far East war, the emergence of the super-powers and the political decision to withdraw from the Empire, the future organisation of the Regular Army was subjected to the most fundamental reassessment since the time of Cardwell's reforms, its primary function 'conventional' within the framework of the new North Atlantic Treaty Organisation. There followed a period of rationalisation (a new euphemism for 'reduction') which created as many anomalies as it solved, and as much dust and heat as the celebrated General Order 41 of 1881. That the marching and counter-marching of the period to 1970 was necessary is no longer a matter for argument; that it was conducted with much misgiving reflects the historic divide between political expediency and military imperatives".* [a]

In 1939 the infantry establishment of the regular army had consisted of five regiments of Foot Guards and 64 regiments of the line (128 battalions) to which had been added, during the war, The Parachute Regiment and the Special Air Service Regiment. By 1970 rationalisation had slimmed this establishment to five regiments of Foot Guards and 33 regiments of infantry (48 battalions) including the Brigade of Gurkhas, which had been added in 1948.

The first change came in 1946 when the Foot Guards and the infantry of the line were grouped on a regional or category basis and lettered consecutively from A to P. This unimaginative arrangement, which ran counter to any territorial structure, was amended in 1948 when eleven regional brigades were formed together with a Guards brigade, a Light Infantry brigade and a Green Jacket brigade. As a result the Dukes became a member of the Yorkshire and Northumberland Brigade, together with The Royal Northumberland Fusiliers, the West Yorkshire Regiment, the East Yorkshire Regiment, the Green Howards and the York and Lancaster Regiment.

In the meantime the India Independence Act of 1947 had brought to an end two centuries of British rule and with it a need to reassess the army's overseas commitments. It was decided to reduce all infantry regiments, except the three senior Regiments of Foot Guards and The Parachute Regiment, to single battalions. The method of

---

(a) Quoted from "A companion to the British Army" by David Ascoli (Harrap Ltd) 1983.

reduction was to be carried out by suspended animation, disbandment or amalgamation. In January 1948, at a meeting of senior officers of the Regiment under the chairmanship of General Sir Philip Christison, who had succeeded Colonel Pickering as Colonel of the Regiment in 1947, it was agreed that the Regiment's two regular battalions should amalgamate. The formal amalgamation took place at Strensall on 17 June 1948 when General Christison handed over the 2nd Battalion's two stands of colours to the 1st Battalion.

Scarcely had the army learned to live with the problems of rationalisation when the politicians let loose an awkward, if inevitable, dog of peace. Although the Labour Government, which came into power in 1945, had been keen to disengage from military comitments overseas, it soon became clear, following the demobilisation of the wartime soldiers, that some form of conscription would be necessary if Britain was to fulfil her responsibilities in the unsettled post-war period. In July 1947 a National Service Act was passed to become effective on January 1949. This imposed an obligation on men conscripted for initially one, and from 1950 two years with the Colours, followed by a further three and a half years with the Territorial Army.

And now in 1957 the Government decided to suspend conscription and to phase out National Service by 1 January 1960. The effect of ending National Service was to create a crisis of manpower in the army. Even the modest establishment of 20 cavalry regiments and 64 single battalion infantry regiments could not be sustained by voluntary enlistment. In the autumn of 1957 a committee was set up to consider the best method of reducing the infantry by 17 battalions. For the basis of reorganisation the group/brigade system of 1946/48 was selected, and by 1958 fifteen pairs of battalions were chosen for amalgamation within 14 brigades, each of which consisted of three or four battalions. In the Yorkshire and Northumberland Brigade this resulted in the amalgamation of the East and West Yorkshire Regiments to form The Prince of Wales's Own Regiment of Yorkshire. The Brigade also lost the Royal Northumberland Fusiliers to the newly formed Fusilier Brigade and consequently was re-named the Yorkshire Brigade. At the same time a Brigade Depot was established at Strensall and all existing regimental depots were closed. The only other change, as far as the Regiment was concerned, was that it had to adopt the Yorkshire Brigade cap badge of a white rose surmounted by a crown. At the same time the Regiment substituted the 'elephant' collar badge with the crest of the Duke of Wellington, previously worn as a cap badge.

In 1962 a committee was set up to implement the Army Council's decision *"that the infantry shall be organised into large regiments"*, a process that had already started with the conversion of the East Anglian Brigade into the East Anglian Regiment. Had the Army Council pressed ahead with its plan, twelve large regiments of three or four battalions would have emerged. Instead it only encouraged *"a move voluntarily towards the large regiment"*. The Yorkshire Brigade did not accept the invitation.

For years there had been rumours about the creation of a single "Corps of Infantry", analogous to the Royal Artillery, in which soldiers would owe allegiance primarily to the corps and be liable to be posted to any unit within the corps as circumstance dictated.

However there was such violent opposition to such an attempt to tamper with the infantry regimental system, the core of the fighting spirit of the infantry, that the idea was abandoned in favour of smaller groupings. In July 1967 the Ministry of Defence announced the formation of six divisions. The Dukes were allotted to the King's Division, formed from the Lancastrian, Yorkshire and North Irish Brigades. The other regiments in the Division were the King's Own Royal Border Regiment, the King's Regiment, The Prince of Wales's Own Regiment of Yorkshire, the Green Howards, the Royal Irish Rangers and the Queen's Lancashire Regiment.[b] All the regiments, except the Dukes and the Green Howards, had, by this time, undergone some form of amalgamation and lost their original identities. With the demise of the brigade system distinctive regimental cap and collar badges were once more taken into wear. On 14 November 1969 the 1st Battalion, then in Hong Kong, held a "re-badging" ceremony at which the Yorkshire Brigade badges were replaced by those so long familiar to members of the Regiment.

*******************

Between the wars the Depot at Halifax fulfilled the normal functions of an infantry depot – recruiting and training recruits for the regular battalions, assisting Territorial units, organising reunions and regimental gatherings plus numerous other activities connected with the domestic affairs of the Dukes. Shortly after the outbreak of war in 1939 the Depot was converted into an Infantry Training Centre under command of Lieutenant Colonel A E H Sayers. By the end of 1939 it had expanded into an establishment some 2,000 strong.

In August 1941 a reorganisation of the system of training recruits took place. Under the new system the Infantry Training Centres of the Dukes and the Durham Light Infantry combined to form 4 Infantry Training Centre at Brancepeth Castle, County Durham. During the life of 4 I T C a small party, under Major S E Baker MBE,TD, remained at the barracks at Halifax to safeguard Regimental interests against the day when the Dukes would return to their old home. This occurred in November 1946 when 33 Primary Training Centre (DWR) was established in the barracks under the command of Lieutenant Colonel J H Dalrymple. However it only had a short existence and was disbanded in April 1948 following the move of the 1st Battalion to Strensall to take up the duties of Group Basic Training Battalion for the Yorkshire and Northumberland Brigade. The first intake of recruits was received on 4 March 1948 and at fortnightly intervals thereafter. The period of training was ten weeks. The Depot at Halifax was again reduced to a skeleton staff.

In October 1950 orders were received for the 1st Battalion to be 'reactivated' and to reorganise on a full infantry battalion establishment. In March 1951 the Battalion moved to Chiseldon. One result of this change was that recruit training was once again to be undertaken at the Depot, though the first intake did not start to train at Halifax until November 1951. At about the same time the barracks was renamed "Wellesley Barracks".

---

(b) The York and Lancaster Regiment was disbanded in 1968.

On Waterloo Day 1945 the Corporation of Halifax had granted the Duke of Wellington's Regiment *"the privilege, honour and distinction of marching through the streets of Halifax on all ceremonial occasions with bayonets fixed, colours flying and bands playing"*. In 1952 the Regiment was able to exercise this privilege when a ceremonial parade was held to mark the 250th anniversary of the raising of the Regiment. That same year the County Borough of Huddersfield decided to grant the Regiment its Freedom and a parade took place there on 13 September 1952 to mark *"the conferment of an honour by a proud corporation on a gallant Regiment with an illustrious record"*. Seven years later, on 20 June 1959, the Regiment was also granted the Freedom of the Borough of Spenborough.

In August 1959, as a result of a decision to close all regimental depots, the Yorkshire Brigade Depot was established at Strensall, as part of HQ Yorkshire Brigade, with responsibility for training all recruits. So the Depot at Halifax was closed on 6 August. However, because building work was still in progress at Strensall, the Regiment's recruits were sent to the depot of the Prince of Wales's Own Regiment of Yorkshire, at Beverley, which was to be phased out later. The arrangement did not prove satisfactory and from November 1959 the Dukes' recruits were trained at Strensall.

The closure of the barracks at Halifax was a sad blow for the Regiment. All that now remained was a small Regimental Headquarters staff, consisting of two retired officers and four civilians. The first Regimental Secretary was Major J H Davis who was assisted by Lieutenant Colonel D J Stewart (late York and Lancaster). Among the civilians, and described as a typist, was ex-RSM S E Code MBE, who in his real role of General Secretary of the Regimental Association had been a great support to a succession of Depot commanders and was a vital and much respected link between past and present members of the Regiment.

Of most immediate concern to the Regiment was the future of the Regimental museum. Happily the Borough of Halifax offered to display it in a section of its Bankfield Museum and this offer was accepted by Major General K G Exham who, in 1958, had succeeded General Christison as the Colonel of the Regiment. The Museum was formally declared open at its new location on 23 April 1960 (St George's Day).

The year 1963 saw the Regiment's final farewell to its ninety-year old Wellesley Barracks when the premises, covering fifteen acres, were sold to Halifax Corporation for £33,000 – a remarkable bargain. The formal handover ceremony took place on 21 September. A guard of honour was provided by the 1st Battalion, and on the sounding of Retreat the Regimental flag was hauled down from the Keep for the last time. Regimental Headquarters was now housed in the small single storey building which had once contained the museum. In 1964 the name of the barracks was changed to Wellesley Park.

**********

In 1947 the Territorial Army was reconstituted to form a reserve of nine divisions. However it was decided that, with one or two exceptions, regular infantry regiments would have only one territorial battalion. For the Dukes the 7th Battalion was selected. With its headquarters at Milnsbridge and commanded by Lieutenant Colonel S R Hoyle

MC, recruiting began on 1 May 1947. The former 4th, 5th and 6th Battalions became respectively: 382 Anti-Tank Regiment RA (DWR) TA; 578 (Mobile) Heavy Anti-Aircraft Regiment (5 DWR) TA and 673 Light Anti-Aircraft Regiment RA (DWR) TA. In 1951 382 Anti-Tank Regiment became a field regiment.

On 1 May 1955 the TA Anti-Aircraft Command was disbanded. The result was a radical reorganisation of the Territorial Army. For the former Dukes battalions this meant that 382 Field Regiment RA (DWR) became 382 Medium Regiment RA (DWR) TA (Lieutenant Colonel J F Crossley MBE,TD). It comprised P (4 DWR), Q (5 DWR) and R (6 DWR) Medium Batteries RA. Although wearing the RA cap badge the members of the Regiment were permitted to retain the elephant as collar badges and the officers, warrant officers and non commissioned officers their red lanyards. Two years later the War Office approved the 5th Battalion again becoming infantry when it joined with the 7th Battalion to become the 5/7th Battalion DWR TA under the command of Lieutenant Colonel J Davidson.

The next change occurred in 1961 when further War Office plans for the reorganisation of the Territorial Army resulted in the amalgamation of 382 Medium Regiment with 5/7th DWR to form The West Riding Battalion The Duke of Wellington's Regiment. However it also had only a short existence.

In 1964 a new Labour Government came to power, committed to introduce radical reorganisation and retrenchment in the armed forces. First, the three service ministries for Navy, Army and Air Force were scaled down and merged into a single Ministry of Defence. Then in 1966-67 the Territorial Army suffered the axe. On 1 April 1967 this loyal part-time reserve was redesignated a "Territorial and Army Volunteer Reserve" – an augmented title on paper but a drastic reduction in fact. Many units were disbanded, others amalgamated, and the total strength was reduced from 120,000 all ranks to just 50,000. The new force was split into three categories: T & AVR I, II and III. The first two would be available to reinforce the regular army, I at any time, II only when all other reserves had been called up. T&AVR III would be employed only for home defence.

The result of these changes, as far as the Dukes were concerned, was the disbandment of the West Riding Battalion. From it emerged two distinct units, namely C Company (DWR), 1st Battalion Yorkshire Volunteers, a unit of T & AVR II based on Halifax, and The West Riding Territorials DWR (T & AVR III) with battalion headquarters in Huddersfield. The latter was another short lived unit. It was disbanded in 1969 apart from a cadre of eight all ranks, under the command of Major K M McDonald TD.

Following a General Election in 1970 the new Conservative Government reversed many of the decisions of the previous government. One of its first acts was to expand the T & AVR by 10,000 men. As a result the cadre of the West Riding Territorials was reformed as C Company (DWR) 3rd Battalion Yorkshire Volunteers, with headquarters at Huddersfield.

# CHAPTER 20

# The Korean War

*1953 The Hook*

The 1st Battalion's duties as a training centre ended in October 1950 when it was re-activated as a first-line combatant unit under command of Lieutenant Colonel J H Dalrymple, to join the 61st Lorried Infantry Brigade of the 6th Armoured Division. It moved to Chiseldon in Wiltshire and, in between intensive training, spent a month at Bisley administering the ARA and NRA camps. In 1950 the Battalion had sent a team to the ARA meeting for the first time since the end of the war. The team was not placed in any of the competitions, but Major F R St P Bunbury won the Army 100 Cup. But in 1951 Major Bunbury's team was far more successful. Having swept the board at the Salisbury Plain small arms meeting, the team went on to Bisley. Apart from seven members qualifying for the Army 100, the team came 3rd in the inter-unit competition (the KRRC Cup), was placed 2nd and 3rd in two other rifle events, and won the LMG pairs for young soldiers.

At the end of World War II Germany had been divided into four zones of occupation by the allies (Britain, France, USA and USSR). The British Army of the Rhine (BAOR) formed the military element in the British zone. As a result of the war all the European countries were in dire stress economically. So, in 1947, the USA offered aid to Europe – the Marshall Plan. But the Soviet Union, preferring a disrupted Europe where communism might flourish more easily, replied by initiating the cold war. This led the nations of western Europe to decide that closer unity between them was essential in order to stand up to the Soviet threat. In March 1948 a Western Union (Benelux countries, Britain and France) was formed, initially for economic purposes. The Soviet reaction was to blockade Berlin, which created even greater tension and considerable alarm. In September 1948, therefore, it was decided to form a Western Union Defence Organisation which would prepare plans for combined action in case of attack. Meanwhile, America and Canada realised that they also needed to become involved and in April 1949 the North Atlantic Treaty was signed, joining twelve countries together in a defensive alliance, the North Atlantic Treaty Organisation (NATO), one element of which was BAOR. In April 1951 General Eisenhower assumed

An officer of the Light Company 76th Regiment, c 1854

A soldier of the 76th Regiment, c 1856

Seringapatam, 1791
The grenadiers of the 76th Regiment at the first attack on Seringapatam on 15 May 1791
*(By permission of the Director, National Army Museum)*

Deig, 13 November 1804
The 76th lead the storm on the fortress

Uniforms of the 76th Regiment, 1856-1867

The battle of Paardeberg, 18-27 February 1900.
General Piet Cronje's laager
*(By permission of the Director, National Army Museum)*

Anzio, 1944. The 1st Battalion in the "wadis"

Korea, 1953. The Hook at night
*(By permission of the Officers of the Royal Engineers)*

Soldiers of the Dukes in the 1970s

operational control of the military forces of this defensive alliance. This was the situation in western Europe when, in December 1951, 6th Armoured Division joined BAOR, the 1st Battalion being stationed at Minden. Its weapons were mostly unchanged from 1939: the venerable .303 Lee-Enfield rifle (the SMLE), the Bren gun, the long-serving Vickers medium machine gun and a platoon of 3in mortars. It did, however, have a platoon of 17-pounder anti-tank guns. Normal attire was still the serge blouse and trousers of battle dress. Full Dress had gone [a], but from 1950 onwards Number 1 dress had been issued to the band, drums and NCOs. The Battalion's stay in Minden was short, for there was also tension on the other side of the globe. But there had been time to take part in the Rhine Army small arms competition in which it all but swept the board in the individual championships, Corporal J S Bailes becoming the champion shot of the Rhine Army.

On 25 June 1950 the North Korean army had launched a surprise attack across the 38th parallel against the unprepared and weak forces of South Korea. At the end of World War II Korea had been arbitrarily divided at the 38th parallel, with the USSR occupying the northern part of the country, and the USA occupying the south. In 1947 the United Nations had attempted to unify the country. However, as the USSR would not agree to the inclusion of north Korea, the Republic of Korea, with its capital at Seoul, was set up in the south in 1948, leading to frequent clashes along the border of the 38th parallel. The forces of the communist government of North Korea were well-trained and adequately equipped with Soviet-supplied armour and guns, while the South Korean army was little more than a constabulary force, which the Americans had left with no tanks, no medium guns and little transport. By 26 June the invaders had captured Seoul and were pressing on towards the southern coast and the main port of Pusan.

The United Nations Security Council now stepped in, authorising General MacArthur to send American forces from Japan. Three under-strength divisions were hurriedly shipped to Pusan and rushed to Taejon. But this did not stem the enemy's relentless pressure, and by early August the Americans and South Koreans had retreated to form a small perimeter around Pusan. At this juncture Britain became involved with the dispatch of the 27th Infantry Brigade from Hong Kong. At first comprising only the 1st Middlesex and 1st Argyll and Sutherland Highlanders, these were shortly joined by the 3rd Royal Australian Regiment, and became the 27th Commonwealth Brigade.

Following a successful seaborne attack on Inchon, MacArthur was back in Seoul by the end of September. Instructed by the United Nations *"to secure stability throughout Korea"* he moved across the 38th parallel and drove the North Korean army back to the Yalu river on the frontier of China. This provoked China to enter the war in November 1950 and the United Nations' forces were now faced by Mao Tse Tung's Peoples' Liberation Army. There followed a see-saw of advance and withdrawal by both sides until by August 1951 the front had been stabilised along the 38th parallel and a period of stalemate set in. Another British Brigade, the 29th, had been sent out in November

---

(a) The officers also lost their service dress, swords and mess kit. However, all three were re-introduced at various times in later years, as was Full Dress for the band and drums.

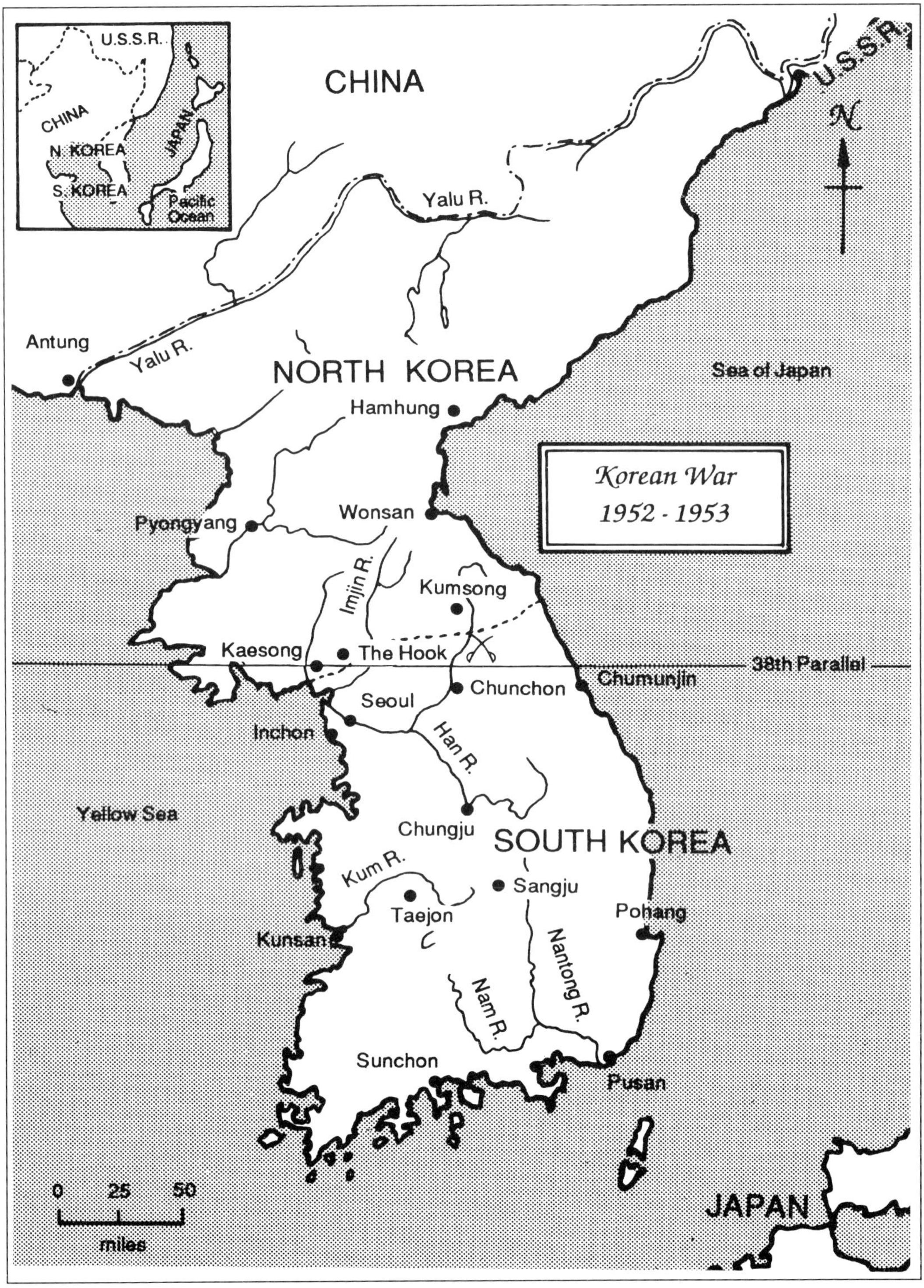
Korean War
1952 - 1953
U.S.S.R.
CHINA
N. KOREA
S. KOREA
JAPAN
Pacific Ocean
CHINA
U.S.S.R.
N
Yalu R.
Antung
Yalu R.
NORTH KOREA
Sea of Japan
Hamhung
Wonsan
Pyongyang
Imjin R.
Kumsong
Kaesong
The Hook
38th Parallel
Chumunjin
Chunchon
Seoul
Inchon
Han R.
Yellow Sea
Chungju
SOUTH KOREA
Kum R.
Sangju
Taejon
Pohang
Kunsan
Nantong R.
Nam R.
Sunchon
Pusan
0 25 50
miles
JAPAN

1950. In August 1951 the 27th and 29th British Brigades were combined with the 25th Canadian Infantry Brigade and supporting arms to form the 1st Commonwealth Division. (Major General M M A R West DSO)

Early in 1952 the Commanding Officer, Lieutenant Colonel F R St P Bunbury, DSO, received notification that the 1st Battalion was earmarked for a tour in Korea and it was posted back to Yorkshire from Germany. While in Yorkshire the Battalion took part in a parade at Huddersfield, on 13 September, when the Regiment was presented with the Freedom of the Borough. A large percentage of men was almost time-expired and ineligible for Korea, and although many were replaced, the Battalion was by no means up to strength. When it embarked at Liverpool on 22 September 1952 on the old trooper HMT Devonshire the Battalion was only 600 strong, with a high proportion of National Service conscripts.

After a voyage which included a typhoon in the South China Sea and an outbreak of food poisoning, the Dukes landed at Pusan on 30 October. There followed another uncomfortable journey of some 150 miles by Korean Railways to a

Lieutenant Colonel F R St P Bunbury DSO with Major General M A R R West CB, DSO, GOC Commonwealth Division

staging camp just north of Seoul, where the Battalion, as a unit of the 29th Brigade (Brigadier D A Kendrew DSO), took over from the 1st Battalion the Welch Regiment [b], who had been in action for almost a year and were now posted home. After a fortnight spent drawing and sorting kit and equipment, the Battalion moved up to the line to occupy a position at Yong Dong, a hill overlooking the Samichon valley, just across the 38th parallel. It had been found that the only sure way of stopping the Chinese was to select features of tactical importance and to hold these at all costs. The Hook was one such feature. Yong Dong was also counted among the hills dubbed *"vital ground"*. However, capturing the Hook would have been a necessary preliminary to an assault on Yong Dong. It was thus an excellent training ground for a fresh unit.

After a month on the Dong the Dukes were considered ready for more active duty. On 1 December the Battalion was ordered to relieve the Durham Light Infantry in a sector of the line a few miles further north, known as Naechon. An abrupt change in

---

(b) The other units in the brigade were 1st Battalion The King's Regiment, 1st Battalion The Black Watch, 20th Field Regiment Royal Artillery and supporting arms.

the weather coincided with the move. Winter envelops Korea with freezing cold winds and at night the temperature falls well below zero. However, the troops were provided with good winter clothing, including heavy woollen socks, long white pants, crotcheted string vests and heavy fleece trousers for inner protection, over which went gaberdine trousers, a thick flannel shirt and a heavy pullover. A combat jacket topped by a hooded parka completed the uniform. In the line men lived in slit trenches, bunkers and dug-outs, the latter known as "hoochies", for which various types of space heaters were contrived, varying from the efficient, but smelly, to the highly explosive. Rats, attracted by the warmth, were a constant problem.

Because the British positions were wired in and surrounded by minefields, the Chinese correctly appreciated that night attacks were the best way of capturing them. So, to try to anticipate this and get some warning of an attack, a screen of patrols was thrown forward. Depending on the nature of their tasks they were variously described as "fighting", "reconnaissance" or "standing" patrols. During December a Dukes fighting patrol, led by Second-Lieutenant D J Holland, clashed with a party of Chinese in no-man's-land and caused them some casualties. As a result Lieutenant Colonel Bunbury decided to send out a further patrol in order to try and capture a prisoner. The ten man patrol, commanded by Second Lieutenant D Borwell, filed out into no-man's-land on Christmas Eve. An ambush was laid by cutting a telephone cable, but by the time two Chinese soldiers came to repair it, the snatch party (Lieutenant Borwell, Corporal A McKenzie and Corporal T Dickie) was so stiff from the cold that it could not move quickly enough to capture them. In January patrols reported that the Chinese were preparing to strengthen a new position and a later patrol confirmed that a tunnel was being constructed. It was decided to raid and blow up the tunnel in daylight, at a time when the rising sun would make observation difficult for the Chinese. Lieutenant R M Harms was nominated patrol commander with Second-Lieutenant I Orr in charge of the assault party. The raid took place on 24 January 1953 and was entirely successful. Both officers were awarded the MC. This success was a great boost to the morale of the Battalion.

In the meantime, in October 1952, a decision had been taken to adjust responsibilities in the front line. The Commonwealth Division sidestepped to the left, giving up three thousand yards on its right to a Korean division, which meant that it now took over responsibility for the Hook, which was then held by the 7th US Marines. The Black Watch was ordered to relieve them. However the day before this was due to happen the Chinese bombarded the Hook. The effect of their artillery fire was devastating and the subsequent attack by the Chinese troops was only driven off after determined strikes from the airforce. When therefore the Black Watch started to take over it found the defences had been ruined and that all but two of the front line bunkers had been destroyed. So the commanding officer of the Black Watch, Lieutenant Colonel David Rose, took a leaf out of the Chinese book and dug and tunnelled a new series of bunkers whose entrances faced away from the Chinese fire. The Black Watch finally took over the position on 14 November. Four days later the Chinese attacked again. In the ensuing

Reverse slope bunkers and a communication trench, Naechon position, winter 1952.

battle the Duke's machine guns were in action and fired 50,000 rounds. The attack was beaten off but the Black Watch had twelve men killed, 73 wounded and 20 missing. After the battle they were relieved by a Canadian unit.

At the end of January 1953 the Commonwealth Division was withdrawn from the line for the first time since its formation eighteen months earlier. However there was little rest as General West's brigades and battalions embarked on a hectic round of field training and tactical exercises. In April the Division returned to the front line and the Black Watch again took over the Hook position.

The adequate defence of the Hook feature required one rifle company to be deployed on each of four hills – Pt.121 on the left, the Hook proper, the Sausage, and Pt.146 on the right. This meant that there was no reserve to give depth to the position with the result that one company from the reserve battalion was loaned to the Hook battalion. As the Dukes were then the reserve battalion one of its companies, given the title of 'V' company (or more commonly, the "Black Dukes"), was attached to the Black Watch and deployed on Pt.146.

On the evening of 7 May, following a heavy bombardment during the day, the Chinese launched an attack against the positions of the Black Watch. By daybreak they had been driven back and it became clear that it had been no more than a reconnaissance in force prior to a major attack. Brigadier Kendrew decided therefore it was time to relieve the Black Watch. On the night of 12/13 May the Dukes took over from them. The dispositions of the companies were : Pt.121, D Company (Major E J P Emett); The Hook, B Company (Major A D Firth); Sausage, C Company (Major A B M Kavanagh) and Pt.146, V Company (Black Watch). A Company (Major R E Austin) was in reserve. Major Emett's company was on the extreme left of the Commonwealth Division. To the left of his company was a Turkish battalion.

For the next four days and nights the Dukes were busy familiarising themselves with the plans for artillery defensive fire (DF), the layout of the minefields, and counter-attack tasks, as well as strengthening the bunkers and laying additional barbed wire. The respite ended on the night 17/18 May when a considerable amount of enemy movement took place on the spurs running up to the Hook position. The OC B Company ordered a sweep to be made by a strong patrol. This resulted in a clash with a Chinese patrol of some strength. The Dukes' patrol disengaged and the enemy was then driven off by artillery fire. Early on the morning of the 18th a Chinese deserter surrendered to C Company and gave the information that a full scale attack on the Hook was imminent and that this time the Chinese intended coming to stay. The attack would be made by five assault companies followed by three more, who would take over and hold the captured positions. The Chinese would not only outnumber the Dukes by something like five to one but the proposed method of approach up the re-entrants would give them relative immunity from the existing planned artillery fire. The deserter believed the attack would take place two months after 12 March 1953.

Apart from the occasional bombardment the Dukes had a quiet day on 19 May, but during the night the scale of the Chinese barrage increased and within an hour and a half 1,000 shells and mortar bombs fell on the Hook. The next night the Chinese launched a series of strong probes, supported by heavy artillery fire, with over 4,000 shells landing in and around the defences. As no enemy penetrated the positions it looked likely that the probes were planned as a rehearsal, to discover the DF plan, and to reconnoitre the defences in detail. Brigadier Kendrew now decided to redeploy his brigade by dividing the Hook position into two, and bringing another battalion into the line. As all three of his battalions were now deployed, the 1st Battalion Royal Fusiliers, from 28 Brigade, was placed under his operational command. One result of these moves was that the Black Watch now deployed two companies on Pt.146 with another immediately in rear.

The most cogent question now was where the Chinese would concentrate their attack and when. With this information available, Colonel Bunbury could get the gunners to concentrate their fire on the forming-up places as soon as the full-scale attack appeared to be certain. So patrols were sent to investigate the Chinese positions on 23 and 24 May. Both were successful in locating some of the caves in which the Chinese would assemble troops prior to an attack. In the meantime, the immediate approaches to the Hook were to be heavily wired on all sides, a task given to Second Lieutenant J Stacpoole and his Assault Pioneers. By the morning of 26 May the wiring programme was well advanced. That same day it was decided that B Company on the

Hook, who for ten days had had very little sleep, would swop places with D company on Pt.121. The following day The King's replaced the Black Watch on Pt.146, who took the King's place on the Yong Dong feature.

As the enemy attack now seemed imminent the CO ordered a listening patrol of Captain C Glen and Corporal D Taylor into no-mans-land on the evening of 26 May, to give advance warning. At 10.15am on 28 May the Chinese artillery carried out destructive shoots on the Hook position. By late afternoon many of the bunkers had been rendered useless. Colonel Bunbury now ordered two platoons of A Company up to the Hook as a reserve for use in counter-attack. As this disposed of his reserve, a company of the King's moved into the position vacated by A Company. Colonel Bunbury also ordered Major L F Kershaw to take over the job of patrol master from Major Austin, who had been out on the Hook for five nights in succession, supervising and co-ordinating the patrols.

At 7.53pm, still in broad daylight, the enemy suddenly brought down a tremendous concentration of artillery fire on the Hook, and to a lesser degree, on B Company (Pt. 121) and C Company (Sausage). The guns destroyed or neutralised all the automatic weapons along the front of the forward platoons on the Hook. Within a few minutes of the opening of the bombardment by the Chinese there was hand to hand fighting in the bunkers and trenches. Eventually the men were forced back into the shelter tunnels which were defended until the entrances were destroyed with explosives. Among those who had to withdraw to a tunnel, with ten men of Second Lieutenant E Kirk's platoon, was Major Kershaw, who had gone forward to maintain contact with Captain Glen and Corporal Taylor. The Chinese followed close behind them and a savage fight took place until the enemy blew in both front and rear entrances to the tunnel. Sealed into a tomb the ten men remained alive in the depths. *"It was Hell in a four-and-a-half foot hole"*, said one of them later. Major Kershaw, though badly wounded, kept up their morale. It was not until dawn broke on the 29 May and rescue parties broke into the tunnel that he lapsed into unconsciousness. Meanwhile the Chinese had gained a foothold on the Hook and Major Emett asked for everything the gunners could give. Bunbury hesitated as Glen and Taylor were still in no-mans-land. A signal was sent, telling them that they had five minutes to get out of the danger zone but they did not receive it, as their radio

The entrance to a tunnel in the Hook forward platoon location after the Chinese attack on 29/30 May 1953

was out of action. They, meantime, were headed for Pt.146. En route they encountered mines, one of which killed Captain Glen and wounded Corporal Taylor, who managed to reach Pt.146 shortly after daybreak.

At 8.45pm the Chinese launched a second attack on the Hook. Heavy fighting took place and a platoon from B Company, on Pt.121, under command of Lieutenant D S Gilbert-Smith, was sent to reinforce the Hook. His platoon was replaced by one from the King's. At 10.00pm, as they deployed, the enemy attacked Pt.121 with two fresh companies, but caught in heavy artillery, tank and machine gun fire, they suffered appalling casualties and the attack crumbled. The Chinese next switched their attention to Pt.146. However the troops involved were caught in the open and were all but wiped out by artillery fire.

The final attack on the Hook started at half-past midnight on 29 May. This time they attempted a lateral approach. As 90 men moved in front of Pt.121 they were caught not only in an artillery and mortar concentration, but by the machine guns of B Company. The attack never stood a chance. How many Chinese remained alive when the attack was called off is not known, but in the morning thirty bodies were counted on the wire.

Meantime the Dukes had set about recovering the ground they had lost on the top of the Hook. The task was given to the platoons commanded by Lieutenant D S Gilbert-Smith and Second Lieutenant M J Campbell-Lamerton. The initial plan proved unworkable as the whole of the top of the hill had literally changed shape, with rubble and tangled wire preventing any forward movement. The only way to make progress was up the line of the original trenches, a slow and laborious business. It was not until 3.30am that the Hook was finally back in the Dukes' hands.

At dawn on 29 May the full extent of the devastation on the Hook was revealed. Ten thousand Chinese shells had ploughed six foot furrows in the terrain and trenches, eight foot six inches deep, had been smashed in so that they were now scarcely more than knee high. Shredded sandbags and tangled bundles of barbed wire littered the area. Among the debris the grisly remains of Chinese soldiers testified to the effect of the counter artillery fire. After Brigadier Kendrew had visited the scene he said, *"My God those Dukes, they were marvellous. In the whole of the last war I never saw anything like that bombardment. But they held the Hook, as I knew they would"*. However because of the Battalion's heavy casualties and the possibility of a further attack he ordered that the Dukes were to be immediately relieved by the 1st Battalion Royal Fusiliers. The Battalion also received a congratulatory message from General Maxwell Taylor, Commanding General 8th Army, *" ...The courage and agressiveness displayed in repulsing a numerically superior enemy reflect great credit upon the first battalion of The Duke of Wellington (sic) Regiment. I wish to commend all participating personnel for their outstanding performance of duty"*.

The Chinese casualties were estimated at 250 dead and 800 wounded. The British losses amounted to 149 of which the Dukes had three officers and seventeen other ranks killed and two officers and 84 other ranks wounded. 20 other ranks were listed as missing. In addition the Battalion had had 50 casualties from artillery and mortar fire between 10 and 28 May.

*The Hook from Ronson. Photograph taken after the ceasefire, July 1953*

The high Chinese casualties were largely due to the magnificent support given by the Divisional artillery and the heavy guns of 1 US Corps artillery. Between them they fired 38,000 rounds. The Dukes had also received invaluable support from 1st Royal Tank Regiment and 1 King's.

The action brought honours and immediate awards: Lieutenant Colonel F R St P Bunbury received a bar to his DSO; Major L H F Kershaw was awarded the DSO, Captain E J P Emmett the MC, and there were four MMs to other ranks. The Regiment was also granted the battle honour **The Hook 1953.** The Battalion was again in the line some weeks after the battle of the Hook.

At 2200 hours on 27 July 1953 the Korean War came to an end with the formal declaration of a truce. Both sides withdrew to create a demilitarised zone, the Dukes occupying a camp south of the Imjin river. The three-year struggle had cost the Commonwealth and American forces some 400,000 casualties, while the North Koreans and Chinese were estimated to have lost one-and-a-half million. But these sacrifices achieved little. The country was still divided.

On 8 November, having been relieved by the 1st North Staffords, the Dukes were railed down to Pusan for a posting to Gibraltar. Before embarkation on 13 November they paraded at the United Nations Memorial Cemetery to pay last respects to their comrades lying there. The Battalion arrived at Gibraltar on 10 December.

On 10 May 1954 the Queen and the Duke of Edinburgh paid a state visit to Gibraltar, celebrating the 250th anniversary of Britain's capture of the Rock.

Gibraltar 1954. The Queen invests Lieutenant Colonel F R St P Bunbury with the bar to his DSO

Gibraltar 1954. 1 DWR march past the Queen carrying the Colours of the 2nd Battalion

A detachment of the Dukes with the Queen's Colour as part of the Combined Services Royal Guard of Honour, paraded at the gangway of the Royal Yacht, while other detachments lined the streets for the procession to the Governor's residence, where yet more Dukes found the guard. The military climax of the visit was a review, when 1,500 sailors and soldiers marched passed the Queen, the Dukes parading with the four Colours of the 2nd Battalion.

On the following day an Investiture was held aboard the Royal Yacht, when Lieutenant Colonel F R St P Bunbury was decorated with a bar to his DSO and ten other members of the Dukes received the decorations they had been awarded for their services during the Korean war. Shortly afterwards Colonel Bunbury was posted to the War Office and was succeeded by Lieutenant Colonel R de la H Moran OBE. Meanwhile General Franco had shown his displeasure at the visit by the Queen by closing the frontier between Spain and Gibraltar. Thereafter the Battalion was confined to the Rock. Although a welcome relief from Korea, the tour in Gibraltar was often onerous, due to the many ceremonial and guard duties that had to be undertaken. Before leaving, in September 1955, the Battalion provided a gymnasium as a youth centre for the Spanish civil war refugee community living in a "shanty town" on a strip of land towards La Linea.

CHAPTER 21

# The End of the Empire
# 1956 - 1970

By the end of the Second World War the British army, numbering some three million men, was spread over a large part of the globe – from the United Kingdom to Japan and from the Baltic to the Caribbean. However, with rapid demobilisation reducing these numbers, and despite the introduction of National Service in 1947, the two decades following the end of the war found the army being stretched to the limit by a series of counter-insurgency actions, deriving, directly or indirectly, from Britain's gradual withdrawal from her former colonial empire. At one time or another additional troops (usually infantry battalions) had to be deployed in Palestine, Malaya, Kenya, Cyprus, Suez, Muscat and Oman, Jordan, Iraq, North Borneo, Yemen and Aden. To help cope with these emergencies no fewer than eight 2nd battalions were resurrected and the period of National Service increased from eighteen months to two years. In addition, in 1950, a strategic reserve had been established with the re-forming of 3rd Infantry Division.

Thus, on returning from the Rock, the 1st Battalion was posted to Chiseldon Camp, near Swindon, as part of the 3rd Infantry Brigade in the Strategic Reserve. While stationed there it was presented with new Colours on 25 May 1956 by the 7th Duke of Wellington. For the first time all ranks wore the recently re-introduced blue Number 1 Dress.

That same year President Nasser of Egypt nationalised the Suez Canal. Britain brought strong diplomatic pressure on Egypt to continue to accept international control, and when that had no effect, military pressure. Planning for military action continued during the autumn months, jointly with France. In August the 3rd Infantry Brigade was ordered to the Middle East. The Battalion was supposed to go to Libya but, not being allowed to land, it was re-directed to Malta to form part of the follow-up force. After the Suez operation was called off, the Battalion was sent to Cyprus at short notice, arriving at Famagusta on 13 November.

Since 1955 Cyprus, a Crown Colony, had been suffering terrorist activities by the EOKA movement, led by General Grivas, which was campaigning not only for the end of British domination but also for the subjugation of the Turkish population and complete union, or Enosis, with Greece. There were murders, bombings, ambushes, mining of

*340*

**Cyprus
1956 - 1957
1967 and 1975**

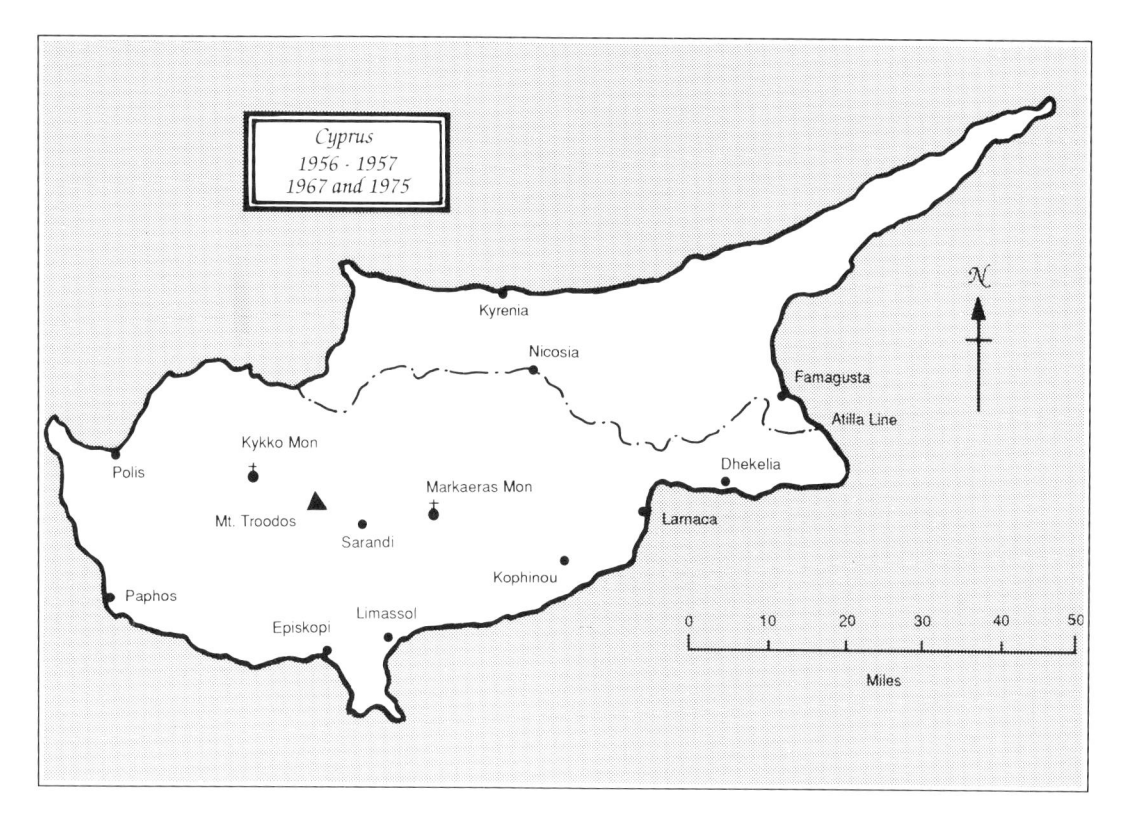

roads, but rarely any face to face action. Combating these activities involved constant patrolling and manning of check points, but the main task was the cordoning and searching of villages for EOKA terrorists and arms and ammunition. At its peak 26 major units were engaged in this way.

After a few relatively routine operations in the Famagusta area, including the first of many cordons and searches, the Battalion was deployed, at very short notice, in the Troodos mountains on Operation Golden Rain. During this operation ambush groups were established on all tracks during the night, with orders to shoot at anything that moved. Second Lieutenant C Laurence, returning from a listening patrol, was accidentally shot and killed by one of the ambush parties. At the end of the operation the Battalion moved directly into Kernia Camp, near Nicosia. During December there was a number of other searches, including a major one in Nicosia when a large part of the town was cordoned off.

Between 18 and 22 January 1957 Operation Black Mac in the Troodos area resulted in the discovery of a hide containing three terrorists, each with a price of £5,000 on his head, and a quantity of arms, ammunition and explosives. An even more successful operation, code named Whiskey Mac, which started at the end of February, took place in the area of the Markhaeras Monastery. Information had been received that Afxentiou, one of the more notorious of the EOKA leaders, had for long periods lived in a hide near the monastery. The arrest of a man who knew the location of the hide led to a decision to try and snatch Afxentiou. Major D M Harris, who commanded the company in the area where the hide was said to be located, drew up a plan which involved sending in two snatch parties at dawn on 3 March. One of the snatch parties, commanded by Captain J M Newton, discovered the hide and, on being summoned to do so, four men crawled out slowly, offering no resistance. From them it was learnt that Afxentiou was still inside the hide. His response to a call to come out was a burst of fire which killed Corporal P Brown: it was clear Afxentiou intended to sell his life dearly. Eventually, some six hours later, after the hide had been set on fire, he was killed.

After only ten days back in Nicosia the Battalion was again in the area of Mount Troodos, this time on Operation Lucky Mac, the aim of which was to capture Grivas. Based on the Kykko Monastery, the Battalion spent eleven weeks in and around the village of Milikouri, carrying out searches and laying ambushes, mostly in persistent rain, but all to no avail.

In September 1957 the Battalion was posted to Northern Ireland where Lieutenant Colonel P P de la H Moran succeeded his brother in command. The Dukes were based in Palace Barracks, Belfast, with one company detached at Londonderry.

Early in 1958 Lieutenant Colonel Moran instigated new courses – based on the principles of outward bound training – the Regiment being the first in the army to do so. Later these courses were formalised as an Adventure Training School, under the direction of Captain D S Gilbert Smith MC. Activities included rock climbing, initiative tests, swimming and patrolling. A club was established where the members could practise their hobbies, including the building of canoes and dinghies. In the spring of 1959 fifteen members of the Battalion rowed their canoes from Orlock Point to Portpatrick in Scotland, a marathon effort lasting nine hours. In 1958 a team was once again sent to the ARA meeting at Bisley, coming 9th in the KRRC Cup (the unit championship). In the following year it came 4th.

While the Battalion was in Northern Ireland it was decided that the standard calibre of rifle ammunition for NATO forces would be 7.62mm. As the Royal Small Arms Factory could produce nothing suitable of that calibre, Britain turned to Belgium which had already a 7.62mm self loading rifle in production. This was accordingly adopted, and so, after serving for more than sixty years, the Lee-Enfield was phased out.

In October 1959 the Battalion moved to England to join 19 Infantry Brigade Group of the new UK strategic reserve, under command of Lieutenant Colonel A D Firth MBE,MC. After six months at Warley Barracks, Brentwood, it moved to Meeanee Barracks, Colchester.

In July 1960 the Governor of Kenya, concerned at events elsewhere in Africa, requested to be reinforced with an additional British infantry battalion. As a result the Dukes, the Spearhead battalion of the strategic reserve, were given 48 hours notice to move by air to Kenya. The Battalion, 650 strong, was air-lifted by RAF Transport Command to Nairobi, flying via Cyprus, Turkey and Aden, in deference to Arab sensibilities. For the next four months the Battalion was based on the accommodation of 5th Battalion The King's African Rifles, near Nakuru, 100 miles north of Nairobi, at an altitude of 6,000 feet. However, it spent the larger part of its time on valuable training for its role, in widely dispersed company camps. As a result all ranks saw and became accustomed to a great deal of the territories in which internal security operations might occur. At the same time they met some of the population of Kenya, both on European farms and in more tribal settings. Throughout there were unique opportunities for relaxation and to see wildlife. A team climbed Mount Kenya, other parties walked to the top of Mount Kilamanjaro. Some Kenya rugby clubs were defeated before the season ended in September. Finally, the Battalion managed to dominate the East Africa Command Rifle meeting before flying home on 24 November 1960. Although the original threat did not lead to an actual operation on this occasion, the Dukes were the first unit to prove the success of the components and procedures of the new strategic reserve concept, as well as the extent of the high quality specialised training involved.

In June 1961 a similar but more serious crisis arose. Elements of 24 Infantry Brigade were flown from Kenya to Kuwait, threatened by Iraq. A strong battalion group from UK was again required to re-establish the reserve in Kenya. The Dukes were selected and flew to Kenya with HQ 19 Infantry Brigade on 1 July, but less one company composed almost entirely of National Servicemen due for release. Accommodation was in Muthaiga camp, Nairobi, temporarily vacated by 1st Battalion The King's Regiment, by then in Kuwait. The programme was very much the same as in 1960. Companies were even more widely dispersed, deploying to Eldoret in the north west and almost as far as Lamu on the coast. If anything, training was even more intensive. With National Service drawing to an end the opportunity was taken to form an all regular company. Halfway through the tour units of 24 Brigade started to trickle back from Kuwait and 1 King's reclaimed its camp. The Dukes were moved to Gil Gil. In November HMT Nevasa, carrying 32 Medium Regiment from Hong Kong to UK, called at Mombasa to pick up the Battalion which disembarked at Southampton on 1 December 1961. It was the last voyage of the Nevasa as a troopship as trooping by air had now become the norm.

In July 1962 the Battalion, now commanded by Lieutenant Colonel A B M Kavanagh MC, staged at Barnard Castle Co Durham, prior to a move, in October, to Bourlon Barracks at Catterick Camp.

On 31 December 1962 National Service came to an end and while at Barnard Castle the Battalion bade a ceremonial farewell to the last of its National Servicemen before they returned to civilian life. The regular army, now once again on an all-volunteer basis, was relieved to be free of the time and manpower consuming problems of training its transient soldiers. On the other hand many saw them go with regret. Besides bringing with them their craft skills and usually a higher level of education, they had made admirable soldiers who had performed well under active service conditions and behaved well when in barracks. With the cessation of National Service recruiting adequate numbers of volunteers became a problem, one result of which was that pay and conditions of service improved considerably.

In the meantime, in August 1962, B Company, under command of Major D E Isles, had been detached for a tour in the Central American enclave of British Honduras.[a] Being responsible for the defence of the colony, the government decided that a garrison would be maintained there to counter any incursions by Guatemala, which had long laid claim to the territory. There was also strong encouragement for a British military presence from Washington, for the USA was nervous about possible trouble in its Central American "backyard". The ten-month tour of B Company was unaccompanied, which enabled the adoption of a most professional approach to peace time soldiering, and full advantage was taken of the unique training opportunities. Compensation for the hard and rigorous training existed in the good facilities for sport of all kinds and opportunities for sea bathing and deep sea fishing.

By now B Company had learned that it was to be known as "Burma" Company. A Special Battalion Order of 14 November, 1962 announced that companies would be re-designated after battle honours, thus:

>    HQ Company    – Hook Company
>    A  Company    – Alma Company
>    B  Company    – Burma Company
>    C  Company    – Corunna Company [b]

When the time came to relieve Burma Company it was decided that this would be the subject of an exercise. Accordingly, on 15 May the Commanding Officer, Battalion HQ and Alma Company (Major R M Harms MC) arrived by air, ostensibly as reinforcements to help counter an incursion into the territory of British Honduras. After completion of the exercise Burma Company was flown back to the UK.

Alma Company did not rejoin the Battalion until March 1964 by which time it had moved to Osnabrück in Germany to become a mechanised infantry battalion in 12 Infantry Brigade Group. This involved intensive training in the driving and maintenance of the Humber Armoured Personnel Carrier, or APC. Officially designated FV 1611, it was a lightly armoured 4x4 vehicle carrying a section of eight men and although described as FV (Fighting Vehicle), it had no armament other than the infantrymen's weapons. In fact, it was no more than a "battle taxi" for hopefully timely transport of infantry through fire-swept zones to positions where they could dismount to fight on their feet. The vehicles were acutely uncomfortable. Because of this and their shape and notorious unreliability, they were commonly nicknamed "Pigs". However, before the BAOR tour ended, they were replaced by the FV 432, a tracked vehicle built by GKN Sankey, with a six- cylinder Rolls-Royce engine giving a speed of about 30 mph. Being tracked, it had of course a much superior cross-country performance, so that mechanised infantrymen could keep up with the armour. In addition to the new APCs other new weapons had now to be mastered. The Bren LMG was replaced by the General Purpose Machine Gun, or GPMG, ("Gimpy" to the soldiers) and the 3" mortar

---

(a) The colony was renamed Belize in 1973 and granted independence in 1981.
(b) Later D Company and Support Company were formed and became respectively Dettingen Company and Somme Company.

by the 81mm weapon. The Battalion also had the 120mm MOBAT (Mobile Battalion Anti-Tank), the 84mm Carl Gustav platoon anti-tank weapon and was one of only three battalions that then had the Vigilant anti-tank wire guided missile for troop trials.

In their mechanised role the Dukes were training for a real threat; with the Cold War at its height there was no knowing what might happen, and Battalion, Brigade and FTXs (Formation Training Exercises) kept them fully stretched on the Soltau training area and the Sennelager live-firing ranges. On 1 May 1965 Lieutenant Colonel A B M Kavanagh MC handed over command of the 1st Battalion to Lieutenant Colonel D E Isles.

One of the more memorable events of 1965 was the 150th anniversary of the Battle of Waterloo, which saw representatives of the thirty-eight "Waterloo Regiments", cavalry and infantry, attending several ceremonial parades and functions. On Waterloo Day itself (18 June) a Memorial Service was held at Hougoumont Farm, scene of the desperate fighting on Wellington's right flank. All thirty-eight colour parties, together with representative detachments, marched into the orchard behind the farmyard, to the strains of the Dukes' own march "The Wellesley", and then formed a hollow square with the Colonels of the regiments in the centre. On that June afternoon of 1815 the Hougoumont outpost had been a dreadful scene of carnage, the dead and wounded British and French soldiers lying in the congested area, the farmhouse in flames. Now, 150 years later, the orchard was ablaze with the splendid spectacle of some sixty standards, guidons and colours fluttering above scarlet and blue uniforms.

The culmination of the year's training was exercise Bar Frost when 12 Brigade went to Norway in September for a two week NATO exercise against troops of the US Marines and Norwegian army. Paradoxically, despite the intensive training in a mechanised role, the Battalion was employed as ordinary infantry with much marching and climbing in foul weather conditions. There was no snow, except on the mountain tops, but it rained for most of the exercise and it was bitterly cold at night.

In September 1965 the Colonel of the Regiment, Major General K G Exham, CB,DSO, was succeeded by General Sir Robert Bray, KCB,CBE,DSO, then serving as Commander-in-Chief Allied Forces Northern Europe.

The 1966 training year, which was particularly intensive, included fourteen days in Denmark, exercising with the Danish Life Regiment. The training cycle ended in October back in Germany, with a fortnight's Formation Tactical Exercise over an area of some 80 square miles. The fast moving manoeuvres by fully mechanised "friends" and "enemy" involved crossings of the River Weser, during which the FV 432s performed admirably. The year ended with an excellent report following the Annual Administrative Inspection. During the tour in Germany the Battalion had many sporting successes, including twice winning the Army Rugby Cup. The Dukes also embarked on cross-country ski-ing, winning the 20 km patrol race and having Lieutenant M P C Bray and Corporal Hirst selected for the 1972 Olympic biathlon team.

In May 1967 the Dukes exchanged the north German plain for a six months' tour in Cyprus, exactly ten years since their previous tour. Although by a tripartite agreement between Turkey, Greece and Britain in 1960, the island had become an independent

Cyprus 1967. A United Nations observation at Stavrokono post manned by 1 DWR

republic with dual rule by Greek and Turkish Cypriots, this did not bring communal peace and the two factions continued to snarl at each other, with periodic outbreaks of violence. In an attempt to establish some semblance of law and order, the United Nations set up the United Nations Force in Cyprus (UNFICYP) in 1964. The British contingent consisted of one infantry battalion, an armoured car squadron, and detachments of the Royal Corps of Transport and other supporting arms. With Battalion HQ in Polemidhia Camp, near Limassol, the four rifle companies were deployed at Polis, Paphos, Limassol and Kophinou within the Limassol Zone for which the British were responsible.

The main task was to try and keep the peace between the constantly warring factions of Greek and Turkish Cypriots who were primarily concerned with squabbling among themselves rather than confronting UN soldiers. This meant the manning of many static observation posts overlooking fortified Greek and Turkish positions and also constant patrolling to obtain intelligence. Companies and platoons, though not attacked, often found themselves in the hazardous situation of sitting in the crossfire between Greeks and Turks, before they could persuade them to accept a ceasefire. Particularly violent and dangerous situations which the Dukes had to handle were at Ayios Theodoros and at Limassol. On both occasions many rounds from small arms and heavy calibre weapons were fired by both sides, between which stood the *cordon sanitaire* rushed into

THE END OF THE EMPIRE

place by the Dukes.

In October 1967 the Dukes were relieved in Cyprus by the 1st Royal Green Jackets, and returned to Osnabrück. Before the Battalion left the island the commander of the British contingent sent it a farewell message: *"..you have enhanced the Regiment's reputation and gained the respect of many Greek and Turkish Cypriots in the Limassol Zone as well as the United Nations force as a whole"*. In November Lieutenant Colonel D E Isles was succeeded in command by Lieutenant Colonel D W Shuttleworth.

Towards the end of the tour in Cyprus there had been rumours of a posting to Hong Kong and these proved true. First, however, the Battalion was to leave Germany for a home posting to Gordon Barracks, Gillingham, Kent, for six months to allow reorganisation, training and embarkation leave. And so early in 1968 the Dukes handed over its barracks in Osnabrück to the 1st Devon and Dorset. In his letter of farewell the Oberbürgermeister expressed genuine sorrow in saying good-bye. *"...as in the course of the many years they have spent in our midst, the members of your Regiment have become so much a part of our community that we have come to look upon them as fellow citizens."*

The six months stay in England was a hectic period and it was a relief when the airlift to Hong Kong started in June 1968, The Battalion took over Stanley Fort on Hong Kong Island, one of the most attractive barrack locations then left to British troops stationed overseas. The primary role of the Battalion was internal security in support of

Hong Kong 1968. Men of 1 DWR on patrol while on border duty

*347*

*Hong Kong 1969. Members of 1 DWR deploy during an exercise from a RAF Whirlwind helicopter*

the Hong Kong Police, with particular responsibility for Hong Kong Island. Another related task for the Battalion was the manning of posts on the sensitive border with China. As a result of attacks the army had taken over the security of the posts and responsibility for patrolling the border area. Patrolling was also carried out on the many offshore islands. A major problem for the colony was the flood of illegal immigrants trying to escape from China by land and sea.

The Battalion's tour of two and a half years in Hong Kong passed off quietly. It included a period of active training, from individual to battalion level, involving a considerable use of helicopters. There were ceremonial guards, amphibious exercises with the Royal Navy, company training at the Jungle Warfare School in Malaysia, a large exercise in New Zealand and a platoon detached in Korea as part of the United Nations Honour Guard. And, of course, intensive sporting activity.

During the tour the Battalion absorbed about one third of the officers and soldiers of the 1st Battalion The York and Lancaster Regiment, which had been disbanded following an army reorganisation in 1967, which also established the King's Division. One result of this was that the Dukes' old and familiar cap badge replaced that of the Yorkshire Brigade.

On 12 April 1969 new Honorary Colours were taken into use to replace the sixty-three year old colours which by then were in a poor state of repair. The ceremony was held on the parade ground of Stanley Fort, with all ranks immaculate in their tropical Number 3 Dress, or "whites". On the saluting dais were the Governor of the colony, Sir David Trench, and the Colonel of the Regiment, General Sir Robert Bray. Before the old colours were marched off, General Bray removed the ancient original spearheads and affixed them in the pikes of the new colours.

In May 1970 Lieutenant Colonel Shuttleworth departed to take up a staff appointment. His successor was Lieutenant Colonel C R Huxtable MBE. The Hong Kong tour of the Battalion was completed in November 1970, with a home posting to Catterick, where it took over Somme Barracks. Soon after returning from block leave, the Battalion was plunged into intensive practice of ceremonial drill and spit-and-polish for a spell of public duties in London, relieving the Foot Guards from the mounting of the Queen's Guard at Buckingham Palace, the St. James's Palace Guard, the Tower of London Guard and the Bank of England Picquet. The Dukes returned to Catterick in March, to arduous tactical training, culminating in an amphibious exercise in the Mull of Kintyre.

By now the long retreat from the former Empire had finally come to an end, leaving only a handful of battalions scattered about the globe. This had led to further reductions in the strength of the army and in 1968 the Government had announced *"Britain's defence forces, apart from those needed to meet certain residual obligations to dependent territories ...should... be concentrated in Europe"*. The new policy confined the army to BAOR and a Strategic Reserve in the UK. There seemed no longer any likelihood of the urgent operational tasks which so often had provided a spur to recruitment and a sense of purpose in the ranks. Then, out of the blue, emerged a new unforeseen role. In October 1968 there had been a major civil rights demonstration in Londonderry in Northern Ireland. In August 1969 an infantry battalion was sent there to aid the hard pressed Royal Ulster Constabulary. By October ten battalions were policing Ulster.

CHAPTER 22

# Keeping the Peace and Training for War 1970 - 1992

The army did not only have to come to terms with its new role. There were other social changes which, in some respects, were even more significant. No longer did the army recruit young men with a minimum of education and little knowledge of the world. Improved educational standards, the influence of television and holidays abroad, had widened the soldiers' knowledge of the world considerably and had brought with it a reluctance to accept that things had to be done in a certain way simply because they had always been done that way. This had consequences in the approach to discipline.

From the early 1960s soldiers started to marry younger with the result that when the Battalion moved from station to station it was accompanied by 200 or more wives and at least as many children. Married quarters were often not available for all of them and separations ensued. For the majority who did accompany the Battalion there were also separations due to major exercises, training overseas, such as in Canada and Kenya, and operational tours of up to six months in Northern Ireland, Belize and Cyprus. By the 1980s many wives had a job or career which they were unwilling to give up and this, together with the growing popularity of house ownership, created new tensions as military duties conflicted with domestic priorities.

Sustaining the good morale of the families was of no less importance than that of the soldiers and in this task a succession of Unit Families Officers and their staffs did much valuable work.

Changes in weapon technology and the greater range of weapons meant that it was no longer possible to train effectively without access to considerably larger training areas. These were overseas, which led to yet more troop movements and more disruption.

The need to recruit soldiers led, in 1970, to the introduction of the "military salary". Previously soldiers had been paid a relatively low salary, supplemented by free board and lodgings and by marriage allowance. The new scheme was aimed to equate with equivalent civilian trades. At first it worked well, but it took a major pay rise in 1978 to restore full comparability. The consequent great increase in manpower costs led to considerable pressure to reduce numbers. As a result everyone had to work harder and move faster.

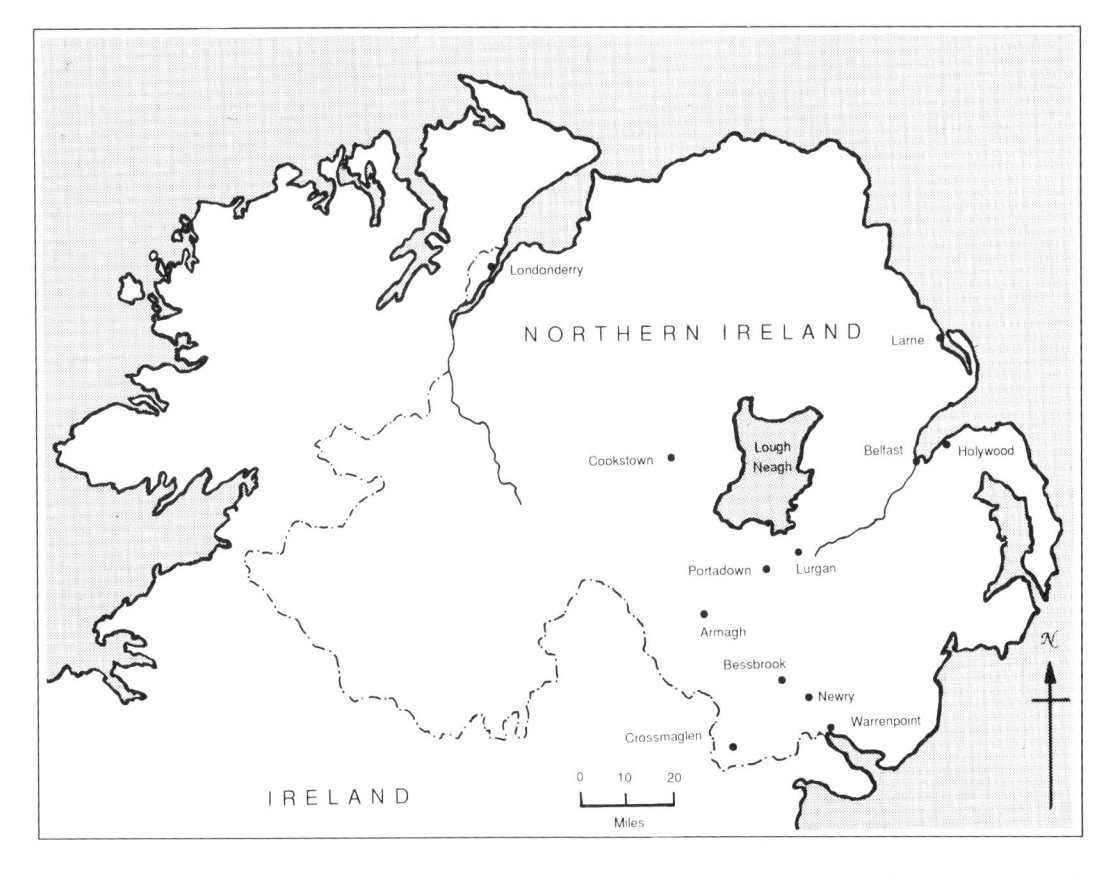

*[Map of Northern Ireland showing Londonderry, Larne, Cookstown, Lough Neagh, Belfast, Holywood, Portadown, Lurgan, Armagh, Bessbrook, Newry, Warrenpoint, Crossmaglen, and the border with Ireland.]*

The effect of all these changes was to produce a highly professional army equipped with a wide range of sophisticated weapons. But the constant movement and the many tasks the army had to undertake led it to be overstretched.

It is against this background that the movements of the 1st Battalion in the period between 1970 and 1992 have to be seen.

In June 1971 the 1st Battalion, under the command of Lieutenant Colonel C R Huxtable, left Catterick for its first tour in Northern Ireland, following the outbreak of the demonstrations in Londonderry in late 1968. In the meantime the Irish Republican Army (IRA) had been exploiting the grievances of the Catholic population in a campaign against law and order with acts of terrorism. The Battalion was deployed into company bases in the north and east of Belfast, and the first weeks of the four-month tour were comparatively peaceful. This enabled the companies to become familiar with the New Lodge Road, Unity Flats and other areas in which they were to operate. The routine of patrols, searches, quick reaction forces and cordons for marches and bomb clearance operations was soon established.

With daily and nightly patrols on foot or in vehicles, platoons were constantly exposed not only to ambush and sniping, but to abuse, bottles, bricks and firebombs from the local populace (many of them children), who regarded the soldiers as a legitimate enemy rather than a force striving to maintain a semblance of peace. The IRA took every advantage of the curious situation in which, as one soldier lamented, they had thrown away the rule book while the security forces were bound by the law of the land. A patrol might spot a known terrorist on the street, but unless he were actually engaged in violence or there was hard evidence to secure his arrest, the patrol could only ignore him.

In August 1971 the Government introduced internment of suspects without trial which involved the Battalion and the Civil Police in a considerable operation of rounding up and processing detainees. The internments sparked off a daily eruption of rioting in the Catholic areas of the city, with missile-hurling mobs backed up by snipers with more lethal weapons. During the period from June to September the Battalion's vehicles – Land-Rovers, Bedfords and 'Pig' APCs – covered more than 190,220 miles on patrol, escort and riot control.

In October 1971 the Battalion moved back to Catterick. The spell in Ulster had brought half-a-dozen casualties, from missiles and bullets, but none of them fatal. In February 1972 the 1st Battalion took part with 24 Air Mobile Brigade in an amphibious exercise, Sun Pirate, in the Caribbean where a landing supported by naval gunfire was followed by "anti-guerilla" operations in the British Virgin Islands. In April the Battalion was once more posted to Northern Ireland for a four-month "roulement" (rota) tour (as opposed to resident battalions who had longer tours and were accompanied by the families). The Battalion arrived in Ulster just after direct rule had been imposed from Westminster and the Secretary of State, William Whitelaw, had initiated his "hearts and minds" policy by setting free scores of interned IRA suspects.

Since the Battalion's previous tour in the Province there had been a split between the official IRA and the more radical provisional IRA, the "Provos", who were armed with sophisticated weapons, Armalite high-velocity rifles, Thompson sub-machine guns, M1 carbines, rocket launchers, and a variety of electronically-controlled explosive devices, besides seemingly unlimited supplies of ammunition and explosives. This was the situation faced by the Dukes, who were deployed in the notorious area of South Armagh with one company detached in Belfast. Soon after taking over patrolling in the Ballymurphy area of Belfast on 6 June, Private G Lee of Alma Company was killed by a sniper – the Battalion's first fatal casualty in Northern Ireland. On another occasion, in Ballymurphy, two privates were wounded by a single bullet through the visor of their Pig. Later in the same area Lieutenant A D Meek was wounded in an attack on his Pig while escorting a journalist. On patrol in Crossmaglen in South Armagh a Pig of Somme Company was blown up by a land mine, killing Lance Corporal T Graham and Private J Lee and wounding Lance Corporal R Bradley so severely that his leg had to be amputated. There were several other casualties from brickbats and bullets during the ceaseless tasks of patrols, searches and vehicle checks. An attempted hijacking of two lorries by five armed IRA men on the Belfast-Dublin road was successfully frustrated, though the terrorists escaped. During the tour the Company's detachments searched 7,384 cars, 384 lorries "and 1 invalid chair and a bicycle". They trudged well over 1,000 miles on foot patrol and completed 100 hours flying time on helicopter sorties.

The Battalion returned to Catterick at the end of July (1972). In November Lieutenant Colonel C R Huxtable relinquished command, being succeeded by Lieutenant Colonel P A Mitchell. March 1973 found the Dukes yet again in Northern Ireland, this time on an accompanied tour of eighteen months. Based at Ballykelly in the Londonderry district, with companies and platoons dispersed in out-stations, it was heavily engaged in the now familiar tasks of foot and mobile patrols, check points, riot control, searching for arms and explosives and "lifting" of IRA suspects. Despite all the efforts the scale of terrorism and outrage continued unabated. For the period from January to December 1973 the statistics for the Province were as depressing as ever: 3,818 incidents of IRA shootings, 968 bombings, landmines and booby-traps; 66 soldiers killed, 299 wounded; 85 civilians assassinated. Known terrorist casualties amounted to no more than 45 killed. The Dukes lost two of their number to IRA action: Second Lieutenant Fawley was killed by a booby trap in a follow-up operation near Lough Neagh and Corporal Ryan was shot by a sniper in the Brandywell area of Londonderry. Another fifteen men were wounded, though none of them fatally.

In mid-November the Battalion was relieved by the 1st Worcestershire and Sherwood Foresters, to be posted to Aldershot where it was quartered in Mons Barracks.

Earlier in the year, on 5 March 1974, the following announcement was published in the London Gazette:

> *Brigadier His Grace The Duke of Wellington MVO,OBE,MC,BA(late Household Cavalry) is appointed Colonel-in-Chief of The Duke of Wellington's Regiment, January 23, 1974.*

This was the first appointment of a Colonel-in-Chief for the Regiment.

In 1975 there was a change of Colonel: on 7 July General Sir Robert Bray retired, to be succeeded by Major General D E Isles, OBE, who had become the first infantryman to hold the appointment of Director General of Weapons (Army) – which traditionally, since the early 19th century, had been a Royal Artillery prerogative.

In April of the same year the Battalion, commanded by Lieutenant Colonel J B K Greenway MBE, was sent to Cyprus on a six months unaccompanied tour. The previous year a group of pro-Enosis officers had staged a coup as a result of which Turkey had invaded the northern part of the island. Cyprus was effectively partitioned and the UN established the Attila Line between the Greek affiliated south and the Turkish occupied north. As a consequence many Greek and Turkish Cypriots found themselves in the wrong part of the island. Initially the Dukes were based at Episkopi but were then moved to Dhekelia. Throughout the tour Alma and Corunna Companies operated as part of the UN force, under command of 1st Royal Tank Regiment, and were awarded the United Nations medal. They took part in Operation Mayflower which involved moving 8,000 Turkish Cypriots from the Paphos and Polis districts to the north of the island. The whole operation went off free of incidents.

Soon after returning to Aldershot, in December 1975, the Battalion was given the

# THE HISTORY OF THE DUKE OF WELLINGTON'S REGIMENT

Minden, 1978. 1 DWR on parade as a mechanised infantry battalion

role of a Spearhead battalion, prepared to move at 48 hours' notice to any troublespot. The troublespot proved to be (yet again) Northern Ireland. The Battalion flew out on 7 January 1976 for a nine week spell of the all-too-familiar duties. On this tour the companies were deployed as reserves under sundry commands in South Armagh and elsewhere, calls for their services being so frequent and various that they dubbed themselves "Rent-a-Duke". Despite the fact that the "Provos" were as murderous as ever, inflicting 176 fatal casualties on the security forces and civilian population, the Dukes escaped with no losses and were able to return unscathed to Aldershot in April.

Having been serving as mostly foot-bound internal security infantry in Cyprus and Ulster, in the summer of 1976 the 1st Battalion left Aldershot for Minden, Germany (BAOR). Now a unit of 11th Armoured Brigade, 1st (British) Corps, the Battalion once more reverted to a mechanised role, mounted in its tracked FV 432 APCs. This entailed intensive training and retraining. In mid 1977, under command of Lieutenant Colonel M R N Bray, it was flown to Northern Ireland for another roulement tour. The area of operations was Londonderry and its environs with the old routine of patrolling, searches and check points. Having returned from their Ulster tour to resume their Rhine Army duties at Minden in November 1977, the Dukes underwent some restructuring as a result of the Government Defence Review. This involved the abolition of Somme (Support) Company which was replaced by a fourth rifle company with the title "Dettingen" Company. The Reconnaissance Platoon with its Ferrets also disappeared. Their tasks were taken over by units of the Royal Armoured Corps, while the Drums, as Defence Platoon, became a rifle platoon in Dettingen Company. (a)

Since 1971, when Britain had to give up military training rights in the Libyan desert, the only area available for large-scale battle group exercises for the Rhine Army has been based at Suffield in Canada. Known as BATUS (British Army Training Unit Suffield), the vast expanse of rolling Alberta prairie is ideal for realistic mechanised operations with tanks, APCs and guns (which are permanently maintained at Suffield). After assembly and preliminary "getting-to-know-you" training in Germany the individual battle groups are flown out to Canada to take over vehicles and guns and take part in a four-week intensive programme, culminating in live-firing exercises. During the summer of 1978 Battalion HQ ran one of these battle group training periods with no fewer than fourteen regiments represented in the group. Two Dukes' companies went to Suffield as part of other battle groups. Although BATUS meant unremitting arduous weeks of active service conditions, it was welcomed as a change from the restricted FTXs and other exercises in Germany.

In September 1979 came orders to prepare for yet another tour in Ulster. For the regiments in BAOR these recurrent spells of IS duty in Northern Ireland meant severe interruption of their primary tasks as front line NATO troops. Even a four-month roulement tour involved dismounted training or re-training for patrol work, check-point and search procedures, and much else. Further, a roulement tour was unaccompanied, while all the APCs had to be left behind, thus necessitating a sizeable rear party

---

(a) The experiment was short lived. Less than two years later the Battalion reverted to its previous organisation.

remaining in Germany to look after families and maintain the vehicles.

On 22 October 1979 the 1st Battalion, commanded by Lieutenant Colonel W R Mundell, was once more airlifted to Belfast's Aldergrove airport, to be deployed in the hazardous Tactical Area of Operations – the streets of Belfast itself. Companies were based in Springfield Road, Ballymurphy, Lower Falls and Turf Lodge. Five days later the Battalion suffered its first casualty, at the hands of the Ballymurphy Gun Team. An echelon vehicle was ambushed outside Battalion Headquarters at Springfield Road and a young soldier of the KOSB, from whom the Battalion was taking over, was seriously wounded. His life was saved by Lance Corporal Tate DWR, injured in the same incident, who applied instant first aid while under gun fire. He was awarded the Queen's Gallantry Medal for his bravery. Later Privates Peel and Bacon were guarding two seriously wounded soldiers and a policeman in the intensive care ward of the Royal Victoria Hospital when an IRA murder squad, disguised as doctors, burst in and uncovered its concealed weapons. Prompt action by Private Peel caused them to panic and flee, firing a haphazard burst as they did so. He returned the fire but was hit in the arm, leading to a month's stay in hospital.

In the unhealthy Springfield Road area patrols continued day and night, some-times attracting no more than "aggro" with bricks and bottles from school children thrown against the sides of the armoured Pigs. However, there was always the knowledge that a more serious incident could occur. In December WO2 David Bellamy APTC, attached to 1 DWR was shot and killed in the back of a police landrover, together with a RUC constable. Increasingly aggressive patrolling aimed at dominating the area led to arrests and the finding of weapons, but still the IRA bombing campaign continued. Towards the end of the tour Private Pryce of Somme Company fell in a hail of bullets as he was patrolling on foot down the Whiterock Road.

In February 1980 the Battalion resumed its mechanised role in Minden. Once more, after a block leave, there was hectic retraining of APC drivers and the regaining of the Battalion's mechanised skills at Sennelager and Soltau. All of this culminated in a massive Corps exercise (Crusader) in which the Dukes, as part of 4 Division, first dug in and defended the inner German border and then changed

Catterick, 1981. The Colonel-in-Chief presents new Colours

sides to join the West German and American force to attack the British 1st and 2nd Divisions. It was a fitting climax to the Battalion's tour in BAOR, which ended in November 1980.

On return to the UK it was again posted to Somme Lines, Catterick. In February 1981 the Dukes had a second spell of public duties in London. The drill and ceremonial involved was an excellent preparation for the presentation of new Colours by the Colonel-in-Chief, Brigadier The Duke of Wellington, which took place at Catterick on 4 April. On 17 July the Queen opened the new Humber Bridge, the guard of honour being provided by Corunna Company.

In December 1981 the Battalion once again flew out to Aldergrove Airport, on a four month unaccompanied tour, to take over from the 1st Battalion Devonshire and Dorset Regiment in South Armagh. During this tour the operations were marked by the continual use of helicopters to deploy patrols and to re-supply bases. Somme Company, with the more experienced soldiers, became the patrol company and the Reconnaissance Platoon became the Close Observation Platoon. Patrols, overt and covert observation points, searches and road blocks became the routine. Several IRA operations were frustrated and some significant finds made, including a 1,000 pound land mine at Camlough. The tour ended at the end of April 1982 when the RAF flew the Battalion in Chinook helicopters from South Armagh to the playing fields at Catterick. On 30 April Lieutenant Colonel W R Mundell was succeeded by Lieutenant Colonel C R Cumberlege.

In 1982 Major General Isles relinquished his seven-year tenure of the Colonelcy. On 22 October he handed over to Major General C R Huxtable CB, CBE. The year 1982 was a busy one for the Dukes. In mid-June the Battalion flew out to Canada for realistic battle training in exercise Pond Jump West. Based at Camp Wainwright in Alberta, it spent six-weeks practising all its skills as a first-line infantry unit. Unlike the BATUS Tour in 1971, this was purely a battalion exercise with no other-arms units under command.

No sooner did the Battalion return to Catterick in September than it was again airborne, this time to Germany to take part in the BAOR Exercise Keystone. Back in Catterick at the end of October, the Battalion found itself once more a Spearhead unit, to be prepared for a troublespot move at 48 hour's notice. But no call came. Instead, the new year of 1983 found it embarked for another tour of garrison duties in Gibraltar.

The Gibraltar tour saw the Battalion busily employed with guards at the Convent, the Ceremonies of the Keys, operational training and the successive despatch of rifle companies for three-week exercises in Portugal. The Battalion also embarked on a major community project. From the mid 1970s onwards the Gibraltar Museum Committee had sought to restore the Northern Defences, which comprise a unique system of fortifications dating back to the inhabitation of Gibraltar by the Moors in the early 8th century. Colonel Cumberlege decided to set the Dukes onto this task, which involved the clearance of a large site of trees, illegal constructions such as chicken coops, and vast quantities of rubbish. The task was started in mid 1983 and not withstanding numerous difficulties such as a strike by the local Public Works

Gibraltar 1983. The ceremony of the Keys

Belize, 1985, crossing a river

Department, a lack of suitable tools and the great difficulty of getting the rubbish off the site, the Mayor of Gibraltar was able to throw the switch that illuminated the newly exposed defences just one year after the initial planning had started.

In recognition of its contribution to community relations the Battalion was awarded the Wilkinson "Sword of Peace for the Army" for the year 1984. The Wilkinson Sword Company annually presents one Sword of Peace to each of the three services, to the units judged to have made the most valuable contributions towards establishing good and friendly relations with the inhabitants of any community at home or overseas.

In January 1985 the Battalion returned home, to be stationed at Bulford, Wiltshire, as a unit of the 1st Infantry Brigade. It was now commanded by Lieutenant Colonel E J W Walker. The Battalion hardly had time to settle into Bulford before it was required to fly out to Belize on a six month unaccompanied tour. The opportunity to carry out jungle training proved invaluable and all ranks benefited from the experience. The return to Bulford was followed by another period of training as a unit of the United Kingdom Mobile Force (UKMF), with specialist cadres for Mortar, GPMG, Milan and the Close Reconnaissance Platoon, the latter mounted in the Fox armoured car or CVR (W) – Combat Vehicle Reconnaissance (Wheeled). A 4x4 vehicle armed with the Rarden 30mm cannon and capable of 65mph on the road, this was a marked improvement on the old Ferret Scout car it had replaced. While the mortarmen, machine gunners and anti-tank Milan platoon had long been familiar with their weapons, the Fox with its armament was a novel acquisition, which meant intensive training for its crew of driver, gunner/radio operator and commander/loader. As with tank crews, all had to be capable of taking over each others duties in the event of casualties.

From snow-bound Bulford in February 1986, a battle group of the Dukes flew out to Kenya for a two month training exercise involving jungle/forest training and live firing, plus such adventure-training activities as mountaineering on Mount Kenya, and some enjoyable R & R relaxation in the Indian Ocean resort of Malindi. Back in Bulford, in May 1986 a display team with band and drums went north to cement associations with native Yorkshire. The tour of the freedom towns culminated with the opening of the refurbished Regimental museum at Halifax on 17 May. Later in the year the Battalion took part in a large-scale NATO exercise (Bold Guard), which involved the deployment of a brigade from the UK, across the North Sea, to Schleswig-Holstein. Once arrived there the Battalion carried out training with 173 Panzer Grenadier Battalion.

In January 1987 Lieutenant Colonel A D Roberts MBE succeeded Lieutenant Colonel E J W Walker in command and took the Battalion to Ulster for yet another tour. This was an accompanied two-year tour, with the Battalion being based in the familiar Palace Barracks, Holywood, with a company on rotation permanently deployed to Bessbrook Mill or West Belfast and countless extra call-outs to meet emergencies in all areas of eastern Ulster.

Though the level of terrorism was unabated, with the IRA's almost daily bombings, shootings, sectarian murders and more, the Dukes were fortunate in not suffering a single fatal casualty. During this tour the Battalion received the 5.56mm rifle,

Northern Ireland. Lieutenant Colonel W R Mundell and Brigadier The Duke of Wellington, the Colonel-in-Chief.

designated SA 80, to replace the 7.62mm SLR, the Sterling 9mm sub-machine gun and GMPG in the rifle sections. With the Battalion at this time were one WO and seven NCOs, who had served in all eight of the tours the Battalion had undertaken in Northern Ireland since 1971.

In February 1989 the Battalion began to pack for the move to Clive Barracks at Tern Hill in Shropshire, where it was to take over from the 2nd Parachute Regiment. In the small hours of 20 February 1989 three members of an IRA active service unit were disturbed by vigilant sentries when trying to enter the barracks. The terrorists were, however, able to place three bombs near one of the barrack blocks which, when they exploded, destroyed the building. Fortunately the occupants, which included thirty NCOs and men of the Dukes' advance party, were just able to evacuate the building before the bombs exploded. As a result there were no casualties. After such an unwelcome introduction to Shropshire, the Battalion embarked on the intensive training

Northern Ireland. Anti-riot duties

needed for its new role as Home Defence Unit. This was followed, in September, by a two month move to the Wainwright training area in Canada, where skills and procedures at all levels were fully tested. Just before departure to Canada, Lieutenant Colonel A D Meek took over from Lieutenant Colonel Roberts in command of the Battalion.

The next scheduled event was the despatch of a rifle company group (240 men) to the Falklands and South Georgia from March to July 1990. However, preparations were interrupted by the national ambulance strike from December 1989 to March 1990. The Battalion was called upon to lend assistance of soldiers as ambulance drivers and medical orderlies. Furthermore, Tern Hill became the logistic base for mounting this assistance to the whole of the Western District. By the end of the strike 152 men of the Battalion (including the whole of the band) had been involved.

During the Falklands tour Alma and Burma Companies were combined into Waterloo Company under Major S C Newton, while Major P R S Bailey commanded the troops on South Georgia. The challenges ranged from demanding training , the climate and terrain, to avoidance of boredom. The remainder of the Battalion at Tern Hill was given the task of planning and conducting the UKLF Milan concentration in June and July at Otterburn. Twenty four platoons (from both regular and TA units) came for two weeks each and for the Battalion it meant six weeks in Northumberland.

In October 1990 Brigadier W R Mundell OBE succeeded General Sir Charles Huxtable as Colonel of the Regiment.  The Battalion was on Spearhead duties between September and October and between November 1990 and March 1991 it was tasked with assisting the outload of stores from UK bases to the Gulf, yet another mundane job

South Georgia 1990. A patrol of 1 DWR at Hodges Mountain hut

meaning long hours of tedious work. Then in January 1991 the band went to the Gulf as medical orderlies as part of the Gurkha Ambulance Squadron.

On 4 May 1991 the Mayor of Skipton, on behalf of the Town Council, conferred on the Regiment the Honorary Citizenship of Skipton. This distinction bears the same rights and privileges associated with the grant of a "Freedom".

In July 1991 the Battalion moved to Bulford to join the Allied Command Europe Mobile Force (Land) or AMF(L). Not only was it the only British infantry unit in a truly multi-national force but it also necessitated being trained in arctic warfare. The Dukes' first experience of the Force was in September when they deployed to Denmark for exercise Action Express, which included forces from Germany, Italy, Belgium, Holland, Luxemburg, the USA and Denmark. Finally there was Norway and the first full winter training for arctic warfare. Based near Bergen, the Battalion had two months in which to become proficient at this physically demanding role. Not only did everyone have to become expert at survival, but also capable on cross country skis with a 60 pound rucksack on the back. The finale of the training was the participation in a major NATO exercise with Brigade North of the Norwegian Army, the UK/NL Landing Force and a US Marine Amphibious group. At the end of March 1992 the Battalion returned to Bulford. In April Lieutenant Colonel D M Santa-Olalla MC succeeded Lieutenant Colonel Meek in command of the Battalion.

Meanwhile world events had been changing at great speed: between 1985 and 1989 the communist empire in eastern Europe had disintegrated and a new spirit of co-

Norway 1992. Members of 1 DWR with BV 206 (Snowcat) vehicle during winter warfare training

operation prevailed between the West and the CIS (as the USSR had now become). This led the governments of the western allies to review the need to maintain their armed forces at a level they considered necessary in the days of the cold war and thus to reap, in some part, the financial benefits of the so-called *peace dividend*.

In Britain this led to a tri-service study ('Options for Change'), with the aim of reducing the strength of the armed forces. At first, it was proposed to reduce the army from a strength of 155,000 to some 125,000, involving the loss, either by disbandment or amalgamation, of fourteen battalions of infantry. In the event, it was announced in July 1991 that seventeen battalions (three more than expected) were to be cut and that the army would have a strength of 116,000, leaving only thirty eight battalions in the Order of Battle. The Dukes, being one of the few regiments that had not been affected by previous reorganisation and reductions, viewed the future with acute apprehension. But, in the event, the Regiment, with its distinguished and unique title, retained its entity. Further welcome news was received in September 1992, when it was announced that the 3rd/4th Battalion Yorkshire Volunteers would re-form as the 3rd Battalion The Duke of Wellington's Regiment (West Riding) (Yorkshire Volunteers), with its headquarters at Sheffield. Now with both a regular and a territorial battalion, and with the Regimental area extended into part of South Yorkshire, the Dukes had every reason to look forward with confidence to the next phase of their long history.

CHAPTER 23

# Epilogue

*In the process of establishing a high "ésprit de corps" it is very easy for regiments to come to believe that they are, in some way, special. Whatever the individual merit of such a claim, all regiments have one thing in common – they are members of that truly unique British contribution to military organisation: the regimental system. Only those who have experienced it fully understand its strengths. As for the Dukes, General Sir Charles Huxtable put it succinctly when he wrote, after vacating the colonelcy in 1990:*

> "We are not a smart, social regiment. We do not seek to be ever in the headlines. We do not pretend to have some special expertise. Indeed perhaps what makes us special is that we do not seek to be any of those things.
> 
> We are ordinary straight forward folk who stick together. We have in the Dukes some of the best soldiers in the world. I would back the Dukes' soldier – the good, honest straight forward, hard working Yorkshireman – against any soldiers in the world. From these first class soldiers we have consistently obtained outstanding senior NCOs and Warrant Officers and hence have always had a very powerful Sergeants' Mess. Finally we have officers who are not afraid to get their boots muddy and who understand the soldiers they lead. If you put these assets together in an organisation that works hard and plays hard; which gets on with its job, and if you ensure there is a proper understanding and communication between the various groups and add those very loyal and supportive families, you end up with a first class professional Regiment. A Regiment which will do any job it is given anywhere in the world and will stick at it until it is successful. You get a feeling of mutual support and respect, you get a group of people with strong bonds of friendship, of history, of enjoyment, of endeavour and achievement. In short, you get The Duke of Wellington's Regiment".

# APPENDIX 1

# The Colours

*The following is an account of the succession of Colours of the two regular battalions of the Regiment. It does not include details of the Colours of the Militia, Territorial Army and Volunteer battalions.*

By the time the British army was formed after the restoration of the monarchy in 1661, the display of standards and ensigns was already an established practice, carried over from the Civil War. Every company had its own standard or ensign and as there were from ten to twelve companies in each regiment, this meant ten or twelve colours. The standards throughout a regiment were all different, but had a similar theme, which was usually some private badge of the colonel or part of his coat of arms, multiplied according to the seniority of the company.

Colours continued in this way until about the time of William III (ie the end of the 17th century) when, owing to changes in infantry tactics, the number of colours in each regiment was gradually reduced to two or three. Another change occurred when the Union with Scotland took place in 1707, which resulted in the white cross of St.Andrew on a blue ground being incorporated with the red cross of St.George on the second or lieutenant colonel's colour, and the inclusion of a small union flag in the upper corner of the first, or colonel's, colour.

The excess of individuality displayed by colonels did not commend itself to King George II. Accordingly a Royal Warrant was issued in 1743 with the intent of emphasising a regiment's allegiance to the Crown. To this end it was laid down that the First Colour of every regiment was to be the King's and to consist of a Great Union throughout. The Second Colour was to be the colour of the facings of the regiment with a Union in the upper canton. For those regiments (such as the 33rd) which had red or white facings the Second Colour was to be a red St.George's cross in a white field. In 1747 there was a second Royal Warrant, which included the instruction that in future the number of the regiment would be displayed on the colours. Hitherto, although each regiment had a number, it had not been displayed on any part of the regimental equipment, regiments having previously been identified by the name of the colonel. Perhaps because the army was engaged in the war of the Austrian Succession, the Warrant was largely ignored. On 1 July 1751 the King issued his third Royal Warrant which stated in unequivocal terms that in future *"No Colonel to put his Arms, Crest, Device or Livery on any part of the Appointments of the Regiment under his Command."* From these three Warrants stems much of the unique character of the British army.

In subsequent years various warrants were issued regarding the design and size of colours. Although now much smaller, being 3' 9" x 3' as compared to the 6' 6" x 6' of earlier years, the basic design differs relatively little from that laid down by King George II.

***************

## SUCCESSION OF COLOURS OF THE 33RD REGIMENT AND 1ST BATTALION

Nothing exists of any stand of colours of the 33rd pre-dating the regulations of 1747. The earliest reference to the colours of the Regiment is an account of the storming of Valenza in 1705, which was published in the *London Post* on 1 June. After referring to the failure of the initial assault the paper recorded *"Duncanson's (33rd) Regiment then advanced most bravely with Colours flying"* and drove the defenders back into the castle. The next stand of colours of which there is evidence was presented about 1739.

Stand 1      Probably presented in 1739. Retired in 1745.
                  The evidence for the existence of these Colours appears in return of accoutrements of the 33rd prepared in 1754. They were probably presented by Lieutenant General Johnson when he became Colonel of the Regiment in 1739.

Stand 2      Presented 1745. Retired 1749.
                  Like Stand 1 these Colours were shown in the return prepared in 1754 which formed part of the evidence in a dispute between the widow of General Johnson and his successor, Lord Charles Hay. An order issued in Flanders in March 1745 directed: "All regiments that have worn-out or torn Colours to bespeak new ones and charge them to their Colonels".
                  These Colours were no doubt provided in compliance with that order.

Stand 3      Presented in 1749. Retired in 1761.
                  In 1907 the 7th Duke of Richmond and Gordon had a catalogue prepared of the contents of the museum at Gordon Castle. Listed among the contents was the remnant of a Regimental Colour of the 33rd Regiment which, it is stated, came into the possession of the 3rd Duke of Richmond during his tenure of command of the 33rd Foot, 1756-1758. However, since new colours were presented in 1761 it is more likely that it came into the possession of the family through his younger brother, Lord G H Lennox, who commanded the 33rd from 1758-1762. There is now no trace of the Colour.

Stand 4      Presented in 1761. Retired about 1771. In the Regimental Chapel, Halifax Parish Church.

APPENDIX 1 THE COLOURS

This is the earliest surviving stand of Colours of the 33rd Regiment. The Inspection Report for 1770 records that new Colours were presented in 1761. They are in relatively good condition because they were extensively restored in 1882. They were given to the Regiment in 1948 by Lord Wharton, a descendant of Lieutenant General John Johnson.

Stand 5   Probably presented in 1771. Retired in 1787.

These Colours were carried throughout the American War of Independence. It is said that Lord Cornwallis, the Colonel of the 33rd, smuggled them back to England after he had been given parole following the defeat at Yorktown. When the Regiment returned from North America in 1787 it was stationed at Taunton where these Colours were laid up in St. Mary Magdalene Church. There they remained until about 1864. There is no record of their existence after that.

Stand 6   Presented 1787. Retired 1801.

The Inspection Return for 1787 records that the Regiment had new Colours presented in that year. In 1801 the Union with Ireland resulted in a change in the Union Flag and this stand of Colours was therefore replaced by a new stand incorporating this change. They were reported still to be with the Regiment, then in India, in 1808, but what happened to them later is not known.

Stand 7   Presented 1801. Retired 1813.

In 1799 the Regiment had taken part in the capture of Seringapatam which, in 1813, was authorised as a battle honour. The practice of awarding battle honours and emblazoning them on the colours had only started at the beginning of the century. "Seringapatam" was the first battle honour to be emblazoned on the Colours of the 33rd.

Stand 8   Presented 1813. Retired 1832. In the Regimental Chapel, Halifax Parish Church.

In 1813 the 33rd returned to England and the opportunity was taken not only to replace the Colours made in India but also to have the newly authorised battle honour emblazoned on them. Robert Horne was paid £32 on 28 July 1813 for the new Colours. They were carried at the battles of Bergen-op-Zoom, Quatre Bras and Waterloo. In 1822 the 33rd proceeded to the West Indies and remained there until 1833 when the Colours were reported as *"being very old and scarcely to be distinguished as Colours"*.

Stand 9   Presented 1832. Retired 1854. In a container below the altar in the Regimental Chapel, York Minster.

In 1832 new colours were presented at Weedon by General Sir Charles Wale, Colonel of the Regiment. The centre of all the colours previous to this stand had been the Regimental number in Roman figures, surrounded by a wreath. In this stand the number was in Arabic figures encircled by the words "First Yorkshire West Riding", the title since 1782. It was the only

367

stand to bear this title and the only stand to have the number in Arabic figures. The Colours were carried at the Duke of Wellington's funeral in 1852. They were retired in 1854 and handed over to the Commanding Officer, Lieutenant Colonel F R Blake. After his death his widow presented them to the Royal United Services Institution which in turn gave them to the Regiment in 1926.

Stand 10   Presented 1854. Retired 1879. In the Regimental Chapel, Halifax Parish Church

On 18 June 1815 a General Order was published which read: *"Her Majesty the Queen has been graciously pleased to command that the 33rd Regiment of Foot shall henceforth bear the name of the 33rd (or Duke of Wellington's) Regiment, which honourable distinction will be inscribed on the Colours of the Regiment"*. On 28 February 1854, while stationed in Dublin, a new stand of colours, incorporating the change of title, was presented by the Colonel of the Regiment, General Henry D'Oyley. On the following day the Regiment embarked for the Crimea. The Colours were carried throughout the war. By this time more accurate rifle fire had made colours an easy target so that at the battle of the Alma the 33rd had five officers and ten sergeants either killed or wounded while with the Colours. The battle is generally regarded as the last occasion when colours were carried in a European pitched battle. The Colours were also carried during the Abyssinia campaign and the storming of the fortress at Magdala was the last time the 33rd carried its Colours in action.

Stand 11   Presented 1879. Retired 1925. In a container below the altar in the Regimental Chapel, York Minster.

New Colours were presented to the Regiment at Kamptee, India, by Major General Mark Walker. It was the last stand of Colours to bear the number XXXIII in their centres. They were also distinguished by the large number of battle honours carried on the Regimental Colour. Arising out of the amalgamation of the 33rd and 76th in 1881 to form the Duke of Wellington's (West Riding Regiment) the battle honours of the 76th Regiment had been added to it, while between 1882 and 1889 six further honours were authorised. To those were also added the three honours gained for the Boer War. By the time of the First World War the Colour had eighteen honours emblazoned on it. The colours of other regiments were becoming similarly cramped. As a result it was decided, following the end of the war, that regiments could select ten of the honours awarded to them for emblazoning on the King's Colour. However these honours were never added to this stand as the Colour was considered too old to bear the additions.

Stand 12   Presented 1925. Retired 1956. In the Regimental Chapel, Halifax Parish Church.

## APPENDIX 1. THE COLOURS

A new stand was presented to the 1st Battalion at Gosport on 30 July 1925 by Lieutenant General Sir Herbert Belfield, Colonel of the Regiment. The centre of the King's Colour had the words "West Riding" surrounded by "The Duke of Wellington's Regiment" and ten First World War battle honours emblazoned on the horizontal cross of the Union flag. The Regimental Colour had the 1st Battalion badge in the centre and the 2nd battalion badge on the lower cross of the Union. The centre was surrounded by a wreath. Nineteen battle honours were emblazoned on it.

Stand 13   Presented 1956. Retired 1981. In the warrant officers and sergeants mess of the 1st Battalion.
On 25 May 1956, when the 1st Battalion was stationed at Chiseldon Camp, Wiltshire, new Colours were presented by the 7th Duke of Wellington. The Queen's Colour included the ten Second World War honours and the two Korea battle honours were added to the Regimental Colour. The other difference between this stand and Stand 12 was a St Edwards crown surmounting the centre circle rather than the Imperial crown. Prior to 1976 it was required the colours should be laid up in a church in perpetuity, after they had been retired. Under the more relaxed rules after that date it was decided that this stand would be laid up in the warrant officers and sergeants mess of the 1st Battalion.

Stand 14   Presented 1981. This stand was presented at Catterick on 4 April 1981 by the Colonel-in-Chief, Brigadier the Duke of Wellington. The only difference between this and the previous stand is that the scroll bearing the Regimental motto is placed below the regimental badge in the centre of the Colour rather than above it.

### THE SUCCESSION OF COLOURS OF THE 76th REGIMENT AND 2ND BATTALION

The 76th's facings were red and its Regimental Colour was, therefore, similar to that of the 33rd ie. a red St George's cross in a white field.

Stand 1    Presented 1787. Retired 1801. Fragments in the Regimental Chapel, York Minster.
The 76th Regiment was raised in 1787 and in common with most regiments at that time the only distinguishing marks on the Colours were the regimental number in Roman figures in the centre of each, surrounded by a wreath of roses and thistles.

Stand 2    Presented 1801. Retired 1808.
As a result of the Union with Ireland in 1801 an Order in Council was issued stipulating, among other things, that the shamrock would be

introduced into the Union wreath wherever that ornament or badge occurred. As a result new colours were issued to the Regiment. The Regiment was at that time stationed in India, but it is not known where the Colours were presented. The Colours were carried in the war against the Mahrattas in 1803 and 1804. The 76th returned to England in 1806. That same year, as recommended by the East India Company, King George III approved the word "Hindoostan" to be borne on the Regiment's colours. Subsequently the King also approved a recommendation by the Commander-in-Chief India that the Regiment should be permitted to place the "Elephant" on its colours. When new Colours were presented in 1808 this stand was handed over to Major John Covell, then commanding the Regiment. The Colours were described as "reduced to their poles". It is not known what happened to them.

Stand 3   Presented 1808. Retired 1830. Only the spearheads now remain.

On 27 January 1808, while stationed in Jersey, the 76th was presented with new colours by Lieutenant General Sir George Don. Normally colours were provided at the expense of the colonel of the regiment. However this stand was given to the Regiment by the East India Company "... *in testimony of it's meritorious services*". Because of this and because the Colours bore the honorary distinctions of Allyghur, Delhi, Agra and Leswaree, they are regarded as the Regiment's first stand of Honorary Colours, even though they were the only Colours carried by the Regiment for the next 22 years. The Colours were consecrated by the Dean of Jersey *"in the usual way"*, the first recorded occasion of the consecration of a stand of colours of the Regiment. A fuller description of this stand is given in the Honorary Colours section (see page 371).

Stand 4   Presented 1830. Retired 1863. In a container under the altar in the Regimental Chapel, York Minster.

In 1828 Lieutenant Colonel Maberley MP, the Commanding Officer of the 76th, applied for a new stand of Colours. These were received in 1829. They were of the regulation pattern with the single battle honour "Peninsular" placed below the centre wreath, the latter surrounding the Regimental number which was in Arabic figures. Above the wreath was the "Elephant" (without either mahout or howdah) with the word "Hindoostan" displayed above it like a battle honour, despite the fact that the original grant stipulated that the Elephant would be circumscribed by Hindoostan. The stand was probably brought into use at Templemore in Ireland in 1830, but there is no record of a presentation ceremony.

Stand 5   Presented 1863. Retired 1888. In the Regimental Chapel, Halifax Parish Church.

This stand was presented at Aldershot on 29 April 1863 by General Sir J L Pennefather KCB, commanding Aldershot Division. It was considerably different from the previous stand. In accordance with a warrant issued in 1844 the Queen's Colour was quite plain apart from the regimental number in roman figures, with a crown above it. The Regimental colour had the "Elephant" below the wreath, with the word "Hindoostan" beneath it on a scroll similar to that for the battle honours Peninsular and Nive. This juxtaposition was due to a crown being placed above the wreath. Both Colours were considerably smaller in size than those of the previous stand. It was the last numbered stand to be carried by the 76th.

Stand 6   Presented 1888. Destroyed by fire in 1901.
On 2 May 1888, while the Regiment (now 2nd Battalion The Duke of Wellington's Regiment) was stationed in Bermuda, a new stand was presented by Lieutenant General T C Gallway, the Governor and Commander-in-Chief of Bermuda. The Regimental Colour carried the battle honours of the 1st Battalion plus four battle honours previously only carried on the Honorary Colours. (Allyghur, Delhi 1803, Leswaree and Deig). Approval for these honours to be added to the Regimental Colour had been given in 1886. Agra had not been approved, presumably because the 76th, although present, had not taken an active part in the battle. However it was still carried on the Honorary Colours. The Colours were destroyed by fire at Rangoon on 20 December 1901 while the battalion was attending a musketry camp. All that was recovered was the lion off the pole of the Queen's Colour.

Stand 7   Presented 1906. Retained by the 1st Battalion until unfit for further use, when they were placed in the officers mess of the 1st Battalion.
New Colours to replace those destroyed by fire were received just prior to the Battalion's return from India in 1905. Presentation was therefore deferred until the Battalion arrived back in England. At Lichfield, on 20 October 1906, the 4th Duke of Wellington presented the new regulation stand and a new stand of Honorary Colours. The Regimental Colour carried the badges of both the 33rd and 76th. The latter is shown as an elephant (without mahout or howdah) with the word Hindoostan above it. In 1927 the King approved of the badge being altered back to its original design. The 1st Battalion had the newly approved badge placed on its Regimental Colour but, for some reason it was not placed on the Regimental Colour of this stand. On the amalgamation of the 1st and 2nd Battalions in 1948 this stand was carried on rare occasions, but in effect retired.

## THE HONORARY COLOURS

Stand 1   Presented 1808. Retired 1830. Only the spearheads now remain.,
Following the capture of Allyghur and Delhi in September 1803 the

Governor General of India issued a special General Order of which the following is an extract:

*"In testimony of the peculiar honour acquired by the Army under the personal command of His Excellency General Lake, the Governor General in Council is pleased to order that honorary colours, with a device properly suited to commemorate the reduction of the fortress of Allyghur on the 4th and the victory obtained at Delhi on September 11, be presented to the Corps of cavalry and infantry (European and Native) respectively employed on these occasions. The honorary colours granted by these orders to His Majesty's 27th Regiment of Dragoons, and to the 76th of Foot, are to be used by these corps while they shall continue in India, or until His Majesty's most gracious pleasure be signified through His Excellency the Commander-in-Chief."*

New colours, paid for by the East India Company and with the spearheads suitably inscribed to record the gift, were presented to the Regiment in Jersey on 27 January 1808. The Colours, which were basically of the normal pattern then in use, incorporated " *...a device properly suited to commemorate the reduction of the fortress of Allyghur and the victory at Delhi"*. They also bore the names and dates of the victories at Agra and Leswaree. At a time when the emblazoning of battle honours on a regiment's colours was still a rarity the Colours were therefore particularly distinguished. In addition they bore the "Elephant" circumscribed by the word "Hindoostan" in their centres.

At the annual inspection in 1827 the Colours were described as *"very old and very ragged"*.

**Stand 2** Presented 1830. Retired 1888. Queen's Colour destroyed by fire in 1901. Regimental Colour in the Regimental Chapel, York Minster.

When, in 1829, Lieutenant Colonel Maberley applied for a new stand of colours to replace those presented by the East India Company in 1808 he was expecting the replacements to be identical. Instead he received a stand *"similar to those usually borne in the Army (upon which are omitted those names so honourably recording former services)."* He therefore wrote to the East India Company *"petitioning for a renewal of the mark of approbation before conferred upon us."* Having been advised that the King had no objection, the Company replied that it would give it great satisfaction to present the 76th Regiment with a new set of Colours. In a subsequent letter the Company requested Lieutenant Colonel Maberley to present the Colours to the Regiment in the name of the East India Company. This he did at Templemore on 3 July 1830 and it is from that date that the Regiment was the possessor of four colours. When the Colours were retired in 1888 they were mounted and framed, the Queen's Colour being placed in the officers mess and the Regimental Colour in the warrant officers and sergeants mess.

**Stand 3** Presented in 1888. Destroyed by fire in 1901.

By 1886 the Colours presented in 1830 were 56 years old and had become unservicable. The commanding officer therefore wrote to the Secretary of

State for India (the successor of the East India Company ) asking that the colours might be repaired. The request was granted and the colours were despatched to London where it was found that the embroidery was too worn to be used again. Application was then made for a new stand to be presented. The request was approved and the colours were taken into use early in 1888, while the Battalion was stationed in Bermuda. There is no record of any formal presentation or consecration ceremony as is the case with the normal regulation colours. On 29 December 1901 the officers mess bungalow at Rangoon was destroyed by fire while the Battalion was away at a musketry camp. The wooden building burnt to the ground in less than an hour and the whole of the regimental plate, many valuable pictures and books and both stands of Colours perished.

Stand 4   Presented 1906. Retired 1969. In the Regimental Museum, Halifax.

Following the destruction of the Colours application was again made to the Secretary of State for India for the Colours to be replaced. This was agreed and the new Colours reached the Battalion, then in India, in 1903. However as the Battalion was due to return to England it was decided to postpone the formal presentation. On 20 October 1906, at Lichfield, the 4th Duke of Wellington presented new Regulation and new Honorary Colours to the Battalion. Both stands of Colours were consecrated. This is the only occasion when it is known for the Honorary Colours to have been consecrated. By 1932 it was becoming clear that by the time the Colours were due to be replaced there was unlikely to be an India Office to defray the cost. An Honorary Colours Fund was therefore opened to which many past and serving officers, warrant officers, non-commissioned officers and soldiers contributed.

Stand 5   Presented 1969.

On 12 April 1969, at Hong Kong, a new stand of Honorary Colours was taken into use, the cost of which had been met from the Honorary Colours Fund. The Colours are in all respects the same as those presented to the Regiment in 1808 by the East India Company except for the addition of the 76th battle honours earned since that date. During the parade the Colonel of the Regiment, General Sir Robert Bray affixed the original spear heads to the new Colours. They are inscribed:

76 Regt

THESE COLOURS WERE PRESENTED TO THE
REGT BY THE CHAIRMAN & COURT OF DIRECTORS
OF THE HONOURABLE THE EAST INDIA COMPANY
IN TESTIMONY OF IT'S MERITORIOUS SERVICES
AND DISTINGUISHED BRAVERY IN THE DIFFERENT
ACTIONS RECORDED UPON THEM

APPENDIX 2

# The Succession of Colonels of the Regiment

From the inception of the regular army in 1660, the colonelcy of a regiment was valued and esteemed for its prestige, close association with the Court, and as a source of income. This was so because not only did the colonel receive pay of his rank, but he was also allowed to draw the pay of a captain of a company. More important still, the income was added to by the way in which a regiment was maintained. This consisted of an annual payment to the colonel, made up of two elements: "subsistence", which went to the men, and "off reckonings", which were intended to cover the cost of clothing, equipment, rations etc. It was mainly from these off reckonings that a profit could be made. Occasionally there might be a loss and in order to minimise such a possibility (or to increase the 'profit') malpractices were not unknown. Bad food, poor quality clothing and false muster rolls were a few such dubious practices. On the other hand some colonels spent considerable sums of their own money to dress and equip their regiments in handsome style.

Because of the prestige of the appointment, regiments often changed hands for large sums. Older regiments were particularly attractive as after each war the younger regiments were the first to be disbanded. When colonelcies were not purchased the appointment was usually granted to officers who had earned the distinction. However, colonelcies were also granted for political reasons as senior officers were often MPs or had political influence through their family connections. Officers who were colonels of the 33rd Regiment and who were also MPs at some time, were Field Marshal George Wade (Hindon and then Bath), Major General Lord Charles Hay (Haddington), Field Marshal Sir John Griffin Griffin (Andover), General Charles Marquis Cornwallis (Eye), Field Marshal The Duke of Wellington (Rye), and General Lord Charles Henry Somerset (Scarborough).

Where large sums of money had been involved it was not surprising that the colonels concerned thought in terms of 'owning' their regiments, an attitude encouraged by the fact that a regiment took its name from its colonel, the name changing each time there was a change in the colonelcy. Many colonels further reinforced the 'ownership' of their regiment by having their family crest or part of their coat of arms emblazoned on the colours and accoutrements of the regiment. If money had become the only criteria for a colonelcy then all kinds of dangers would have arisen. The power of the Crown would have been diminished particularly in its inability to reward officers of merit and loyal service, efficiency would have suffered and resistance to change, because of vested interests, would have grown. All this was apparent to King George I when he ascended the throne in 1714. He was determined to put an end to the practice of purchase, but finding this difficult to do decided to regulate what he could not stop. Thus not only was it decreed that the King's permission was required before a regiment could be sold, but also the price which could be asked was laid down. Gradually the number of colonelcies which were the subject of purchase was reduced, Steps were also taken, in 1751, to forbid the use of armorial bearings on colours and accoutrements. In future a regiment was to be known by its number rather than by the name of its colonel. The system of 'off reckonings' which had so much potential for abuse did not cease until 1851, when the colonel's responsibility for clothing his regiment was ended. It was not until 1881 that the appointment of a colonel became a purely honorary one.

Until the beginning of the 20th century a colonel usually retained his appointment until his death. Now the tenure of the appointment is initially for five years which may be extended to a maximum of ten years or reaching the age of 65 (whichever is the earlier).

Although some of the colonels retired from the active list on reaching the rank of lieutenant colonel, they nevertheless attained the rank of lieutenant general or, in some cases, general. This was a reflection of the then system by which promotion beyond lieutenant colonel was determined by seniority in that rank. This meant that anyone who became a lieutenant colonel would inevitably become a general if he lived long enough. In the list that follows the final rank attained by each colonel has been shown and not the rank he may have held while he was Colonel of the Regiment.

*******************

## SUCCESSION OF COLONELS.
### 33rd REGIMENT. 1702 - 1881

**Colonel George Hastings, 8th Earl of Huntingdon. 14 March 1702-2 March 1703**
In March 1702 Queen Anne authorised the raising of fifteen new regiments of foot and marines. Colonel the Earl of Huntingdon raised one of them which later, when regiments were known by their number rather than by the name of their Colonel, became the 33rd Foot. Huntingdon's Regiment was the first of the newly raised regiments to proceed overseas, arriving in Holland at the end of June 1702. In February 1703 it was reported that Huntingdon had decided to vacate the colonelcy " *in order to travel*", but a more likely reason is that he was suffering from ill health. He died of malignant fever on 22 February 1704, at the early age of 28, thus ending in the words of

one writer *"a career which promised so much advantage to his country, exultation to his friends and celebrity to himself"*.

**Colonel Henry Leigh 3 March 1703 - 11 February 1705**
Colonel Leigh was, for a short time, Colonel of the 33rd, but nothing else is known about him.

**Colonel Robert Duncanson. 12 February 1705 - 9 June 1705**
In 1689 the Earl of Argyll raised a regiment of foot to which Duncanson, then a major, was appointed in order to train it. Early in 1692 King William III had decided to "extirpate that sept of thieves" of MacIan of Glencoe and it was Major Duncanson who sent the order on 13 February 1692 to Captain Campbell, then lodging with the Macdonalds, " to fall upon the rebels, the Macdonalds of Glencoe, and to put all under 70 to the sword." When the 33rd was raised in 1702 Duncanson became the Regiment's first lieutenant colonel. At the outbreak of the War of the Spanish Succession he accompanied the Regiment to Flanders and there took part in Marlborough's campaigns of 1702 and 1703. In March 1704 the Regiment arrived in Portugal. In 1705 an attack was made on the fortress at Valencia d'Alcantara. The allies' force consisted of 700 Portuguese, two Dutch regiments and the 33rd. At a critical point *"Colonel Duncanson advanced with some courage and conduct, restored all things, and bravely pushed with colours flying into the breach"*, where he received wounds from which he died one month later.

**Field Marshal George Wade. 9 June 1705 - 19 March 1717**
George Wade was appointed an ensign 10th Foot (Royal Lincolns) in 1690 and served in Flanders during the early years of the war of the Spanish Succession (1702-1713). In 1704 he went to Portugal on the staff of the commander of the English forces, Lord Galway. He commanded a brigade, which included the 33rd, at Almanza in 1707 where Wade's brigade bore the brunt of the fighting and incurred heavy losses. In 1714 he was appointed major general of the forces in Ireland where the 33rd had been sent after the peace of 1713. He was appointed Colonel of the 3rd Dragoon Guards in 1717, General of Horse in 1739 and a Privy Councillor in 1742. In 1743 he was Field Marshal and C-in-C British forces in Flanders. He became Commander-in-Chief England in 1745, when he commanded the forces against Prince Charles Edward. He died in 1748 and his monument is in Westminster Abbey. However his most famous monument is the roads of Scotland which he was responsible for building when he was Commander-in-Chief Scotland (1724-1740). *"Had you seen these roads before they were made, you would lift up your hands and bless General Wade."*

**Lieutenant-General Henry Hawley. 19 March 1717- July 1730**
Henry Hawley was born in 1679 and by 1706 was a captain in Queen Anne of Denmark's Regiment (The 4th Queen's own Hussars). During the War of the Spanish Succession he served in Spain and was present at the Battle of Almanza. In 1712 he assumed command of his regiment. In 1717 he became Colonel of the 33rd and two years later led the Regiment in the descent on Vigo, a reprisal raid for the Spanish support of the Young Pretender. Hawley who was essentially an officer of Dragoons, was appointed

Colonel of the 13th Hussars in 1730 and of the 1st Royal Dragoons in 1740. In 1745 he commanded the cavalry at Culloden before becoming Commander-in-Chief Scotland, where his well known harshness made him unpopular. He held strong views on most matters and did not hesitate to express them. Thus in 1725, while still Colonel of the 33rd, he wrote; *"I am entirely against officers having wives till they are in a post to be able to keep them following them about. There never was a subaltern good for anything after he was married and very few Captains."*

**Lieutenant-General Robert Dalzell. 9 July 1730 - 7 November 1739.**
In 1682 Robert Dalzell was appointed ensign in the 21st Foot (Royal Scots Fusiliers), later transferring to the 28th Foot (The Gloucestershire Regiment). He served with that regiment in Flanders and was present at the Battle of Ramillies in 1706. In that year the 28th, now commanded by Dalzell, went to Spain where it was cut up at Almanza along with 14 other regiments, including the 33rd. Dalzell, who had been promoted major general in 1727, was appointed Colonel of the 33rd in 1730 in the middle of the long period of peace which had begun in 1719 and which ended in 1739 with the war of Jenkin's Ear, the curtain raiser to the war of the Austrian Succession. In that same year Dalzell was appointed Colonel of the 38th Foot (The South Staffordshire Regiment). Dalzell was a soldier of great experience who, it is stated *"made 18 campaigns under the greatest commanders in Europe"*. He died in 1758, aged 96, and was buried in St. Martins-in-the-Fields.

**Lieutenant-General John Johnson. 7 November 1739 - 19 November 1753.**
John Johnson at the age of 16 was commissioned a cornet in the 2nd Dragoon Guards, then on active service in Spain. In 1708 he was appointed captain in the 5th Foot (Royal Northumberland Fusiliers). In 1728 he was appointed a captain in the Coldstream Guards with the rank of lieutenant colonel in the army. Johnson was appointed Colonel of the 33rd in 1739. With it he saw much active service during the war of the Austrian Succession (1742-1748) and the '45 rebellion, including at Dettingen, Fontenoy and Lauffeld. At this period the Regiment's nickname was "Johnson's Jolly Dogs". It was not until 1751 that the regiments were designated by their number rather than by the name of their Colonel.

**Major-General Lord Charles Hay. 20 November - 1 May 1760.**
Gazetted an ensign in the 3rd Foot Guards in 1722, Lord Charles later served in the 33rd Regiment in the rank of captain for two years before transferring to the 9th Dragoons. In 1741 he became a lieutenant colonel in the 1st Foot Guards. At the battle of Fontenoy (1745) he taunted the French by accusing them of running away at Dettingen before inviting them to fire first. In 1754 the 33rd was in Scotland helping to build roads, of which there is a reminder in an inscribed stone at the Well of Lecht. In 1757 Lord Charles was promoted major general and went to North America. There he vented his anger of the dilatoriness of Lord Loudon by exclaiming *"the general was keeping the courage of his Majesty's troops at bay and expending the nation's wealth in making sham sieges and planting cabbages when he should be fighting"*. He was sent home for trial by court martial but the decision of the Court was never made public as he died before it could be announced.

**Field Marshal John Griffin Griffin, 4th Lord Howard de Walden.**
**4 May 1760 - 20 March 1766.**
John Griffin Whitewell entered the 3rd Foot Guards in 1739 and spent all the 20 years of his regimental service with them. In 1749 the Countess of Portsmouth died leaving him her estate at Audley End, near Saffron Walden, on condition that he assumed the surname of Griffin. At the start of the Seven Years war he took part in the raid on Cherbourg in 1758 (as did the 33rd) and the subsequent retreat from St.Cas, where the Guards and the grenadier companies acted as rearguard and were almost massacred in the hurried scramble for the boats. In 1760 Major General Sir John Griffin Griffin as he now was, was appointed Colonel of the 33rd. In the same year the 33rd was sent to Germany as was their Colonel, who commanded a brigade before being seriously wounded. He was MP for Andover from 1749 until 1784 when he went to the House of Lords as Baron Howard de Walden, having successfully established his claim to that title. He was made Field Marshal in 1796 and died the following year.

**General Charles Cornwallis, 1st Marquis Cornwallis KG.**
**21 March 1766 - 5 October 1805.**
Lord Charles Brome, the eldest son of Earl Cornwallis, started his military career in the 1st Foot Guards and by 1761, age 23, was commanding the 12th Foot (Suffolk Regiment) on active service in Germany. In 1766 he was appointed Colonel of the 33rd Regiment and soon made his mark. By 1772 the 33rd was reported to be *"one of the finest regiments in His Majesty's service"*, a reputation the Regiment was to sustain throughout Cornwallis' long period as Colonel. Such was the high standard set that the Regiment was known as the "Pattern". In 1782 it was proposed that regiments should be allied to counties. Cornwallis pressed for the 33rd to be associated with the West Riding as *"the 33rd had always recruited in the West Riding and has the general goodwill of the people of that part of the Country"*. Cornwallis is best remembered as the general who surrendered to Washington at Yorktown in 1781, for which, however, he was not held to blame. On the contrary, one commentator at the time said of him *"deservedly the favourite of every person of every rank under his command"*. He was Governor and C-in-C of India from 1785 to 1793. In 1795 he was appointed Master General of the Ordnance, with a seat in the Cabinet and from 1798 to 1801 he was Viceroy and C-in-C, Ireland. In 1805 he again went to India as Governor and C-in-C, where he died shortly after his arrival. There is a statue of him in St.Paul's Cathedral. Cornwallis was Colonel of the 33rd for 39 years.

**Field Marshal Sir Arthur Wellesley, 1st Duke of Wellington KG,GCB,GCH.**
**30 January 1806 - 31 December 1812.**
The Hon Arthur Wesley (as the name was then spelt) was born in 1769, the 3rd son of the Earl of Mornington. Between 1786, when he was first commissioned, and 1793 when he transferred to the 33rd as a major, he served in six regiments, including for a short period in the 76th. Five months after joining the 33rd he assumed command. In 1794 he took the Regiment to the Netherlands to join the army of the Duke of York. In 1796 the 33rd went to India where it took part in the capture of Seringapatam (1799). The Commander-in-Chief (General Harris) described the Regiment, under Wellesley, as *"a*

*model regiment beyond all praise."* Arthur Wellesley's period in command ceased in 1802 and he wrote to his successor *"I have commanded them now for nearly ten years, during nine of which I have scarcely been away from them and I have always found them to be the quietest and best behaved body of men in the army"*. In 1806 he succeeded the Marquis of Cornwallis as Colonel of the Regiment. Four years later he was offered the more lucrative Colonelcy of a two battalion regiment, but declined as *"I have no wish to be removed from the 33rd of which I was Major, and Lieutenant Colonel and then Colonel"*. However in 1812 he was offered the colonelcy of the Royal Horse Guards and that was an honour he could not decline. Field Marshal The Duke of Wellington died in 1852. One year later on the 38th anniversary of the Battle of Waterloo the title of the Regiment was changed to: The 33rd (or Duke of Wellington's) Regiment.

**General Sir John Coape Sherbrooke GCB. 1 January 1813 - 21 February 1830**
John Sherbrooke was appointed an ensign in the 4th Foot in 1780 and by 1783 was a captain in the 33rd. He became a major on the same day that Arthur Wellesley assumed command. He accompanied the 33rd to India in 1796 and played a prominent part in the defeat of Tipoo Sultan at Seringapatam. In 1807 he was in service in Egypt and one year later was in command of the British troops in Sicily. In 1809 he was appointed Colonel of the 68th Foot (The Durham Light Infantry). That same year he joined Arthur Wellesley in Portugal as his second in command. In 1811 he was appointed Lieutenant Governor of Nova Scotia, where he had served with the 33rd when he had first joined the Regiment. Two years later he became Colonel of the 33rd. In 1816 he was appointed Captain General and Governor of Canada. The town of Sherbrooke in Quebec Province is named after him. He died in 1830.

**General Lord Charles Henry Somerset. 20 February 1830 - 22 February 1831.**
Lord Charles Somerset was the second son of Henry, fifth Duke of Beaufort. One of his younger brothers was Fitzroy Somerset, later Lord Raglan, who achieved notoriety in the Crimea. Lord Charles Somerset was commissioned into the 1st Dragoon Guards in 1785. With the outbreak of war against France, Lord Charles enlisted men for the 103rd Foot of which regiment he became Colonel in 1795. A year later that Regiment was disbanded and he was given command of the 3rd Battalion of the 4th Foot. From 1804-1806 he was joint Paymaster to the Forces under Pitt and again, under Portland, 1807-1813. In the latter year he was appointed Governor of the Cape of Good Hope. For one reason or another Lord Charles's period as Governor was not a happy one, chiefly due to his insistence on running the colony as if it was a private estate. His period as Governor ended in 1825. He was Colonel of the 1st West Indian Regiment from 1804 until he was appointed Colonel of the 33rd in 1830.

**General Sir Charles Wale KCB. 25 February 1831 - 19 March 1845.**
Charles Wale was commissioned into the 88th Foot with whom he saw service in the West Indies. Later he served in the 97th Foot in the defence of Gibraltar before transferring to the 12th Foot. After a period on half pay he became a captain (in 1799) in the 20th Foot. One year later he was a major in the 85th Foot and before the year was out, lieutenant colonel in the 67th (The Hampshire Regiment) with whom he served in

Jamaica. In 1805 he accompanied the regiment to India, but returned to England and exchanged into the 66th Foot (The Berkshire Regiment). Wale's numerous changes of regiment were not untypical of the times and were usually due to purchasing a promotion or a desire not to proceed on some particular service. In 1809 he was again in the West Indies, this time as a brigadier, and again saw active service. From 1812 to 1815 he was Governor of Martinique. In 1831 he was appointed Colonel of the 33rd Regiment and a year later presented new Colours to the Regiment while it was stationed at Weedon.

**Lieutenant General Sir Henry Sheey Keating KCB. 4 April 1845 - 12 September 1847**
Henry Keating was commissioned into the 33rd Regiment in 1793 and soon saw active service, being a member of the force which included the grenadier and light companies of the 33rd, which was sent to the West Indies in 1794. Keating was twice wounded and after being captured spent the next 18 months on a prisoner of war hulk at Rochelle. In 1800 he transferred to the 56th Foot (Essex Regiment). In 1809 he commanded a force, which included the grenadier and light companies of the 33rd, which captured the Ile de Bourbon (now Réunion). In 1837 he was appointed Colonel of the 90th Foot (Cameronians) and in 1841 Colonel of the 54th Foot (Dorset Regiment). Four years later he was appointed Colonel of the 33rd. Keating was the first Catholic to be promoted to the rank of general after the higher military ranks had been opened to officers of that faith in 1817.

**General Henry D'Oyley. 28 September 1847 - 26 September 1855**
Henry D'Oyley was commissioned as an ensign in the Grenadier Guards in 1797 with whom he served throughout his regimental career. He was with his regiment in Flanders in 1799, where he was taken prisoner. Subsequently he served in the Corunna and Walcheren campaigns in 1808 and 1809. He was wounded at the battle of Waterloo. Following the death of the Duke of Wellington he was instrumental in obtaining permission for the Duke's name to be incorporated into the title of the Regiment, a decision that was notified on 18 June 1853. The following year, a week before the Regiment embarked for the Crimea, General D'Oyley presented a new stand of colours to the Regiment which, for the first time, incorporated the name of the Duke.

**Field Marshal Sir Charles Yorke GCB. 27 September 1855 - 31 March 1863**
Charles Yorke was a son of Colonel John Yorke who commanded the 33rd from 1781 to 1793. In 1807 he was commissioned into the 35th Foot (The Royal Sussex), but one year later exchanged into the 52nd (Oxford and Buckinghamshire Light Infantry) with whom he served throughout the Peninsular War. He was also present at the battle of Waterloo. In 1851 he served in the Kaffir War in the rank of major general. He was appointed Military Secretary in 1854. In 1855 he was appointed Colonel of the 33rd, a position he held until 1863 when he was made Colonel of the Rifle Brigade. From 1875, until his death in 1880, he was Constable of the Tower of London.

**General William Nelson Hutchinson. 1 April 1863 - 29 June 1895.**
William Hutchinson was commissioned as an ensign into the 46th Foot (DCLI) in 1820. In 1824 he transferred to the 76th Foot with whom he remained for eight years. In 1832

he again transferred, this time to the 20th Foot (The Lancashire Fusiliers) which regiment he subsequently commanded before being appointed a captain and lieutenant colonel in the Grenadier Guards. He was a man of varied interests. He patented an invention relating to the steering of steam engines and wrote a book on dog handling. In his Will he referred to the efforts he had made to forward the cause of navigable ballooning. He was appointed Colonel of the 33rd Regiment in 1863 and continued in the appointment jointly with General Darlby George of the 76th when the two Regiments were amalgamated in 1881 to form The Duke of Wellington's Regiment. After General George was appointed Colonel of another regiment in 1886, General Hutchinson remained Colonel of The Duke of Wellington's Regiment until his death, at age 92, in 1895. He was Colonel for a period of 32 years.

## SUCCESSION OF COLONELS
## 76th REGIMENT. 1787 - 1881

**General Sir Thomas Musgrave Bt. 12 October 1787 - 31 December 1812.**
Thomas Musgrave entered the army in 1754 as an ensign in the 3rd Foot (The Buffs). After service in the 64th Foot as a captain he transferred to the 40th Foot as a major in 1775. A year later he became the lieutenant colonel and greatly distinguished himself in an action at Germantown, near Philadelphia, in October 1777. He then went to the West Indies as Quarter Master General but he left when he fell ill. He returned to America in the rank of brigadier general and became the last British commander of New York. In October 1787 he raised the 76th Regiment, the recruits for which came chiefly from the Musgrave family estates. He accompanied the Regiment to India and commanded the infantry in General Medows' campaign against Tipu Sultan in 1790. On return to England he was promoted to lieutenant general and appointed Lieutenant Governor of Tilbury Fort. He became a general in 1802. In 1807 he produced the Standing Orders for the 76th Regiment. He died on 31st December 1812 and was buried in the churchyard of St.George's, Hanover Square.

**General Sir George Prevost Bt. 2 January 1813 - 16 February 1814.**
George Prevost, after service in the 25th Foot (KOSB), joined the 60th (Royal Americans) in the rank of major in 1790. Shortly afterwards he was sent to the West Indies with his regiment. He became lieutenant colonel in 1794 and commanded the troops in St.Vincent. In May 1798 he was appointed military governor of St.Lucia, becoming civil governor three years later. In 1808 he became Lieutenant Governor and Commander-in-Chief Nova Scotia and three years later Governor of Lower Canada. In 1812 the USA declared war against Britain. Prevost's conduct of the military operations was less than successful and led to the humiliations at Suckett Harbour and Plattsburg (at which the 76th was present). In 1815 he was summoned to England to meet charges arising from his defeat at Plattsburg. He obtained permission to be tried by court martial; but the consequent anxiety ruined his health and he died on 5 January 1816.

He was Colonel of the 76th for only one year before being appointed Colonel of the 16th Foot.

**General Christopher Chowne. 17 February 1814 - 18 July 1834.**

Christopher Tilson, as his name was then, was appointed an ensign in the 23rd (Royal Welch Fusiliers) in 1778 and served in that regiment for five years before becoming a captain in an independent company of foot. In 1794 he was appointed major in the 99th Foot and within the same year, commanding officer. The regiment was disbanded in 1798. In June 1799 he joined the 44th Regiment (Essex) and assumed command in 1802. He was promoted major general in 1808 and was in command of Portuguese troops during Wellington's Peninsular campaign. In 1812 he changed his surname to Chowne, though for what reason it is not known. Promoted lieutenant general in 1813 he was appointed Colonel of the 76th in the following year, an appointment he held for 20 years until his death in July 1843.

**General Sir Peregrine Maitland GCB. 19 July 1834 - 1 January 1843.**

Peregrine Maitland was appointed an ensign in the 1st Foot Guards in 1792. He served with his regiment in Flanders (1794), Corunna (1808) and Walcheren (1809). He commanded the 1st Brigade of Guards at the battle of the Nivelle and at the passage of the Nive in 1813 (at which the 76th was also present). He became a major general in 1814 and commanded the 1st Brigade of Guards at Quatre Bras and Waterloo. From 1818 to 1828 he was Lieutenant Governor of Upper Canada and then Lieutenant Governor of Nova Scotia until 1834. His next appointment was Commander-in-Chief of the Madras Army, but he resigned in 1838 because of his dislike of the East India Company's failure to enforce its order exempting native Christians from compulsory attendance at native religious festivals. He was Governor and Commander-in-Chief at the Cape of Good Hope from 1844 to 1847. Before becoming Colonel of the 76th in 1834, he had been Colonel of the 1st West Indian Regiment. In 1843 he was appointed Colonel of the 17th Foot (Leicesters).

**Lieutenant General George Middlemore CB. 2 January 1843 - 30 May 1843.**

George Middlemore received a commission in the 86th Foot (2nd Royal Irish Rifles) in 1793 and saw service with the Regiment at the Cape, Madras, Ceylon, Bombay and Egypt. In 1804 he obtained his majority in the 48th Foot (Northamptons) and served with it in the Peninsula. He greatly distinguished himself at the battle of Talavera in 1809. Wellington said of him: *"He is an excellent officer, and if his conduct then did not, I may say, demand promotion, his good conduct and attention to duty would warrant it."* He became a major general in 1830 and for five years commanded the troops in the West Indies. In 1836 he was made Governor of the Island of St.Helena. He was only Colonel of the 76th for a few months before becoming Colonel of his old regiment, the 48th Foot.

**Lieutenant General Sir Robert Arbuthnot KCB. 31 May 1843 - 6 May 1853.**

Robert Arbuthnot entered the army as a cornet in the 23rd Light Dragoons in 1797. He served with his regiment at the capture of the Cape of Good Hope in 1806 and in South America as aide-de-camp to General (afterwards Lord) Beresford with whom he was made a prisoner of war. On return from South America he became a captain in the 20th

Light Dragoons and resumed his position on Beresford's staff throughout the greater part of the Peninsular war. Few officers have taken part in so many general actions. He was present at no less than fourteen during the campaigns in Spain and Portugal. He was an officer of conspicuous gallantry and particularly distinguished himself at Albuera. He attained the rank of major general in 1830 and in 1838 was appointed to command the troops in Ceylon, after which he commanded a division in Bengal. He was appointed Colonel of the 76th in 1843, a position he held until his death in May 1853.

**General William Jervois KH. 10 May 1853 - 5 November 1862.**
William Jervois was appointed an ensign in the 89th Foot (Royal Irish Fusiliers) in 1804. On becoming a captain in 1808 he transferred to the 53rd (KSLI). In 1810 he was appointed to the staff of Lord Blayney for a diversionary attack in Andalusia in southern Spain. The force consisted of 1,400 men, including 500 French deserters, between them speaking five different languages. In the ensuing campaign Jervois was wounded in the attack on the fortress at Feungirola. In 1813 he joined the staff of Sir Gordon Drummond in Canada and was present at many actions fought against the Americans, including the storming of Fort Niagara and the attack on Buffalo. In 1823 he went on half pay. He became Colonel of the 76th in 1853 and held the appointment until his death in 1862.

**Lieutenant General Joseph Clarke. 6 November 1862 - 27 February 1871.**
Joseph Clarke was appointed ensign in the 76th in 1810 and remained with it for the next forty-seven years. In this respect he was markedly different from his predecessors, none of whom had served in the Regiment before assuming the appointment of Colonel. He would have seen active service in Spain (Nive) and North America (Plattsburg), but after 1814 he enjoyed forty-three years of peaceful soldiering in Canada, Ireland, the West Indies, Corfu and Malta. He assumed command of the 76th in 1839 when the Regiment was stationed in the West Indies and continued in command until 1857 - a period of eighteen years. In that year he went on half pay but, as was the custom, he continued to be promoted, becoming a lieutenant general in October 1864. He died in February 1871.

**Lieutenant General Matthew Smith CB. 28 February 1871 - 27 April 1875.**
Matthew Smith was appointed an ensign in the 9th Foot (Norfolks) in 1819. He served on the staff during the 1st Afghan War (1839-42). In 1846 he exchanged as major into the 29th Foot (Worcesters) and served with it in the war against the Sikhs in 1848-49. After the battle of Chilianwala, in which he was wounded, he was appointed to command the 24th Foot and led the Regiment at the battle of Gujrat. However the appointment was not approved by the Horse Guards and a year later he was transferred back to the 29th. In 1854 he assumed command; but one year later exchanged into the 81st (Loyals) who were then stationed in Lahore. When the Indian Mutiny broke out in 1857 the 81st were the only British troops in Lahore and Smith played an important part in the disarming of the mutinous Indian troops garrisoned there. He went on half pay in 1863 and became a lieutenant general in 1872.

**General Frederick Darley George CB. 28 April 1875 - 12 March 1886.**
Frederick George was gazetted a cornet in the 11th Light Dragoons in 1825. Eight years later he joined the 22nd Foot (Cheshires) as a captain. He served in Sir Charles Napier's campaign in Scinde in 1842-43 and was present at the battles of Meanee and Hyderabad, where he commanded the regiment. In 1844 the regiment was sent south to Poona and from there embarked on a small war against the state of Kolhapar in which George took part He was DAAG Windward and Leeward Islands in the West Indies, in the rank of lieutenant colonel, from 1853-1858. In the latter year he went on half pay. He became a general in 1877. When the 76th Regiment was linked with the 33rd in 1881 he continued as Colonel jointly with General Hutchinson, Colonel of the 33rd, until he became Colonel of his old Regiment, the 22nd, in 1886.

## SUCCESSION OF COLONELS
## THE DUKE OF WELLINGTON'S REGIMENT (WEST RIDING).
## 1881 - 1992

**General George Erskine. 30 June 1895 - 7 October 1897.**
George Erskine was appointed ensign in the 33rd Foot in 1832 and subsequently served with the Regiment in the Crimea War. He became a lieutenant colonel in 1854 and commanded a depot battalion until going on half pay two years later. In 1857 he was appointed lieutenant colonel of the Military Train before first becoming Deputy Inspector of Volunteers (1860) and then Inspector General. In 1868 he became Inspector of Army Clothing. From 1873 to 1878 he was Brigadier General, Chatham. He was promoted lieutenant general in 1877 and three years later was placed on the retired list. In 1888 he became Colonel of the Argyll and Sutherland Highlanders, an appointment he held until assuming the Colonelcy of The Duke of Wellington's Regiment in 1895. Despite a not undistinguished career, General Erskine received no honours, a fact commented upon in the Army and Navy Gazette following his death in 1897. Under the heading 'Plain General George Erskine' the obituary recorded: *"Not even a CB! And yet he was a veteran of fame and service, a most valiant captain, a sturdy soldier of ancient type."* The writer expressed the hope that in the future *"heed would be given to the claims of patient merit."*

**General Sir Hugh Rowlands VC,KCB. 8 October 1897 - 1 August 1909.**
Hugh Rowlands was appointed an ensign in the 41st (Welch) Regiment. At the outbreak of the Crimea War in 1854 he was a captain. The 41st, together with the 33rd, formed the vanguard of the troops sent to Constantinople in that year. He was present at the battles of Alma and Inkerman. It was at Inkerman that he was awarded the VC for saving the life of Colonel Hayley of the 47th Regiment(Lancashire). His name was gazetted in the first list of recipients of the new decoration. In 1866 he succeeded in command of his regiment which was followed, from 1875-1878, by command of the 34th(Cumberland). Subsequently he saw service in South Africa where he commanded

the troops in an action against the Kaffirs. His appointments included command of Madras District and Scottish District. He retired in 1896 and a year later was appointed Colonel of The Duke of Wellington's Regiment.

**Lieutenant General Sir Herbert Belfield KCB,KCMG,KBE,DSO.**
**2 August 1909 - 23 January 1934.**

Herbert Belfield, was commissioned into the 101st Foot (Royal Munster Fusiliers). His first experience of active service was in 1895 when he was selected to be Chief Staff Officer of the Ashanti Expedition. There was no fighting, but his good work secured him his brevet as lieutenant colonel. In July 1897 he was appointed to command the 2nd Battalion The Duke of Wellington's Regiment, then stationed in Natal. During the Boer War he was AAG on the Headquarters staff. In 1902 he became Inspector General of the Imperial Yeomanry in South Africa. On returning to England he was appointed to command 4 Brigade at Aldershot, having first spent a year as AAG 4 Corps. In 1907 he became GOC 4 Division and held that appointment until he retired in 1912. He was recalled in 1914 and appointed Director of Prisoners of War, a post he held for the duration. He ceased to be Colonel of the Regiment in January 1934 and died four months later on 19 April. His ashes are interred in the Regimental Chapel, York Minster, beneath a tablet which records that he was responsible for the establishment of the Chapel as a Regimental shrine.

**Brigadier General P A Turner CMG. 24 January 1934 - 30 October 1938.**

Percy Alexander Turner was commissioned as 2nd lieutenant in the 3rd (Militia) Battalion of the Regiment. Two years later he joined the 2nd Battalion with whom he served in Nova Scotia, the West Indies and South Africa. In South Africa he was in a party of three officers and fifty-one non-commissioned officers and men who saw service in Matabeleland in 1893-94. During the second rising, known as the Rhodesia Campaign, he served on the staff of the force commander. On the outbreak of the Great War he was sent to France as Commandant of the Military Base Depot at Le Havre. In December 1914 he was promoted lieutenant colonel and assumed command of the 2nd Battalion. In the battle of Hill 60 he was wounded in both legs. Recovered from his wounds he was appointed to command 195 Brigade Home Forces and, later, 224 Mixed Brigade. He retired in 1920. Soon after he began to produce 'Regimental Notes', the forerunner of the 'Iron Duke' and it was chiefly due to his initiative that the Regimental journal started in 1925.

**Colonel C J Pickering CMG,DSO. 31 October 1938 - 1 November 1947.**

Charles Pickering joined the Regiment from the 3rd (Militia) Battalion KOYLI in 1900 and, after completing a course at Hythe, was posted to the 2nd Battalion which was then in Rangoon. He attended a course at the London School of Economics in 1911 and was then appointed brigade major 148 Brigade and, early in 1915, went out with it to France. Later that year he assumed command of 1/4th Battalion DWR. Shortly afterwards he was severely wounded. Then followed six months in hospital after which he was appointed AAG 67 division. In 1918 he became AAG Aldershot Command. In 1920 he was at the Staff College from where he was sent to Ireland as AAG on the staff of the Commander-in-Chief. In 1925 he assumed command of the 2nd Battalion, then stationed in Cairo, and took it to Singapore and India. On vacating command in 1929 he became AA and QMG at Aldershot and held the appointment until he retired in 1933. He was Colonel of the Regiment from 1938 until reaching the age limit in 1947.

**General Sir Philip Christison Bt. GBE,CB,DSO,MC.**
**1 November 1947 - 1 November 1957.**

Philip Christison was commissioned into the Queen's Own Cameron Highlanders in 1914 and served on the Western Front during World War I. He was wounded at the battle of Loos in 1915. He was awarded the MC in 1916 and a bar to the medal in 1917. By the end of the war he was commanding the 7th Battalion of the Cameron Highlanders. He was appointed brevet lieutenant colonel in 1933. He commanded the 2nd Battalion of The Duke of Wellington's Regiment from 1937 to 1938 before being promoted to command 4th (Quetta) Indian Infantry Brigade. His promotion, thereafter, was rapid and by 1942 he was a lieutenant general. In that year he raised 33 Indian Corps. Subsequently he commanded 15 Indian Corps in the Arakan. At the end of the war he was in Singapore where he accepted the surrender of the Japanese 7th Army Area. 15 Corps was then sent to the Dutch East Indies and Christison became Commander Allied Forces Netherlands East Indies. On return to the UK he was successively General Officer Commanding Northern and Scottish Commands. He retired in 1949.

**Major General K G Exham CB,DSO. 1 November 1957 - 30 September 1965**

Kenneth Exham's father and brother (Major General R K Exham) both served in the Regiment. He was commissioned in 1924 and joined the 2nd Battalion with which he served in Egypt, Singapore and India. After a short period in England between 1929 and 1931 he went to Malaya where he became the first adjutant of the newly raised Malaya Regiment. He then attended a Russian language course and qualified as a Russian interpreter. In November 1939 he was Brigade Major 4th Infantry Brigade in France. When Russia was invaded by Germany in 1941 he was appointed head of the army section of the British Military Mission, Moscow. He returned to England in 1943 and within a space of one year was successively the commanding officer of 1/7th DWR, 9 Worcesters and 1/6th DWR. In 1944 he was appointed to command 6 RWF with whom he gained a DSO. In 1947 he commanded 149 Infantry Brigade TA. Following an appointment at the War Office he attended the Imperial Defence College after which he became Chief of Staff Western Command. His last appointment, before retiring in 1959, was GOC Nigeria District.

**General Sir Robert Bray GBE,KCB,DSO. 30 September 1965 - 7 July 1975**

Bobby Bray was the son of Brigadier General R N Bray who commanded the 2nd Battalion from 1918 to 1921. He was commissioned in 1928 and after two years with the 1st Battalion was posted to the 2nd Battalion in India. He was adjutant from 1935 - 1937. During the war he served in Norway, the Middle East and North West Europe. He took part in the Normandy landing at which time he was serving with the Parachute Regiment. In November 1944 he was appointed to command the 2nd Battalion the

Gloucestershire Regiment. He was awarded the DSO in 1944 and a bar in 1945. After attending the Imperial Defence College he was made BGS HQ BAOR and from 1953 - 1954 commanded a brigade in Korea. On return to the UK he was Director Land/Air Warfare for three years. In 1957 he became GOC 56 (London) Division TA. Two years later he went to Aden as Commander Land Forces Arabian Peninsular. On his return home in 1961 he became GOC-in-C Southern Command. His next appointment was Commander-in-Chief Allied Forces Northern Europe. In 1967 he went to SHAPE as Deputy Supreme Commander. He retired in 1971.

**Major General D E Isles CB,OBE,DL. 7 July 1975 - 22 October 1982.**
Donald Isles was commissioned into the Regiment in 1943 and joined the 1st Battalion in Italy in 1944. He served with the Battalion in Palestine, Egypt, Syria and the Sudan. On return to the UK he became adjutant of 33 PTC (DWR). In 1948 he was appointed GSO III 49 Armoured Division (TA). From 1950 to 1953 he attended the Technical Staff and Guided Weapons Courses at the Royal Military College of Science where, in 1959, after a period of regimental soldiering, he returned as a member of the directing staff. In 1961 he attended the Joint Services Staff College. He was AMA at Paris, from 1963 to 1965 when he assumed command of the 1st Battalion in BAOR. In 1967 he took the Battalion to Cyprus as part of the United Nations Force. On vacating command in 1967 he was appointed AMS and, on promotion, as Colonel GS at the MOD(Army) and then at the Royal Armament Research and Development Establishment. He next served as Assistant Defence Attaché at Washington, before retiring in 1978 from his final appointment as Director General Weapons (Army).

**General Sir Charles Huxtable KCB,CBE. 22 October 1982 - 22 October 1990.**
Charles Huxtable was commissioned into the Regiment in 1952 and served with the 1st Battalion in Korea. After two years at the Depot he returned to the Battalion as signals officer and served in Malta, Cyprus, Northern Ireland (where he became adjutant in 1958) and Kenya. A tour as an instructor at the Signals Wing of the School of Infantry was followed by attendance at the Staff College in 1962/63. He was then GSO II 2 Division before returning to the Battalion as a company commander. In 1968 he was selected to attend the Joint Services Staff College. He then joined the directing staff at the Staff College. Having commanded the Battalion from 1970 to 1972 he was next posted to be Colonel GS in the Ministry of Defence. In 1976 he was appointed to command the Dhofar Brigade in Oman followed by a further tour in the Ministry of Defence as a Deputy Military Secretary. From 1980 to 1982 he was Commander Land Forces Northern Ireland after which he became Director of Army Staff Duties. From 1983 to 1986 he was Commander Training and Arms Directors, which was followed by his appointment as Quarter Master General. His last appointment before retirement was Commander-in-Chief UK Land Forces. He was Colonel Commandant of the Ulster Defence Regiment from 1991 and on its amalgamation with the Royal Irish Rangers in 1992, to form the Royal Irish Regiment, was appointed the Colonel of the new regiment.

**Brigadier W R Mundell OBE. 22 October 1990 -**

Dick Mundell was commissioned into the Regiment in 1958 and joined the 1st Battalion in Northern Ireland. He then served with the Battalion in the UK, Kenya, British Honduras and Germany before being appointed an instructor in the signals wing of the School of Infantry. He then became GSO III HQ 48 Gurkha Infantry Brigade in Hong Kong. After a tour of duty with the 1st Battalion, which included the first two operational tours in Northern Ireland, he was posted to the Junior Division of the Staff College as a GSO II instructor. In 1977 he was appointed MA to the Commander-in-Chief BAOR. He commanded the 1st Battalion from 1979 to 1982 during which it was twice deployed to Northern Ireland. He was commander 6 Armoured Brigade (later 6 Airmobile Brigade) in Germany from 1983-1984. He then became Commandant of the School of Infantry. After a tour as Deputy Commander North East District he was appointed Brigadier Infantry BAOR. In 1990 he was appointed Honorary Colonel of the 3rd Battalion Yorkshire Volunteers (West Yorkshire). The following year he again assumed the appointment of Deputy Commander North East District. He retired in 1992.

# APPENDIX 3

# Succession of Lieutenant Colonels

*The following lists give the succession of lieutenant colonels of the two regular battalions of the Regiment.*

The lists have been compiled from Army Lists, Digests of Service and other Regimental records. The succession in the 33rd Regiment between Duncanson vacating the appointment in 1705 and Howard assuming the appointment in 1715 is far from clear. Between these dates the 33rd was cut to pieces at Almanza (1707), had to surrender at Brigheura (1710) and was disbanded for a short period in 1714. In the late 18th and during most of the 19th centuries a second lieutenant colonel was appointed during periods of active service, when the de facto commanding officer was often required to command a higher formation. The names of second lieutenant colonels, where appointed, are not included in the lists. Details of officers appointed to temporary command of the 1st and 2nd Battalions as a result of casualties during both world wars have been included where known.

****************

**33rd Regiment: 1702 to 1881**

| | | | |
|---|---|---|---|
| R Duncanson | March 1702 | J Yorke | April 1781 |
| P Honeywood | February 1705 | The Hon A Wellesley | September 1793 |
| E Stanhope | December 1707 | A Gore | October 1802 |
| O D'Harcourt | January 1708 | W G K Elphinstone CB | September 1813 |
| T Howard | March 1715 | S Moffatt | May 1821 |
| J Archer | March 1717 | C Knight | September 1830 |
| R C Cobbe | October 1721 | J M Harty | July 1841 |
| Hugh, Viscount Primrose | December 1738 | R Westmore | June 1842 |
| R Sampson | June 1741 | G Whannell | April 1843 |
| H Clements | September 1744 | F R Blake | October 1848 |
| G Mure | May 1745 | J D Johnstone CB | March 1855 |
| Sir James Lockhart-Ross | February 1749 | J E Collings CB | January 1959 |
| Charles 3rd Duke of Richmond | June 1756 | A S Cooper CB | October 1868 |
| | | T B Fanshawe | September 1873 |
| Lord George Lennox | May 1758 | E F Chadwick | March 1878 |
| H Oakes | April 1762 | J D Johnstone | May 1879 |
| J Webster | April 1774 | F J Castle | October 1879 |

389

## 1st Battalion The Duke of Wellington's (West Riding Regiment): 1881-1920

| | | | |
|---|---|---|---|
| W Bally | March 1884 | P T Rivett-Carnac | November 1900 |
| F J Tidmarsh | October 1887 | H D Thorold | November 1904 |
| D C de Wend | November 1889 | C V Humphries | November 1908 |
| C Conor | October 1892 | W M Watson | March 1912 |
| G E Lloyd CB,DSO | November 1896 | R E Maffett | February 1916 |

## 1st Battalion The Duke of Wellington's Regiment (West Riding): 1920-1947

| | | | |
|---|---|---|---|
| R K Healing | February 1920 | B W Webb-Carter DSO | April 1943 |
| N G Burnand DSO | February 1924 | F P St M Shiel DSO | |
| F H B Wellesley | June 1926 | (South Wales Borderers) | September 1944 |
| W C Wilson DSO,OBE,MC | June 1930 | B McCall | October 1944 |
| G S W Rusbridger | June 1932 | (Royal Fusiliers) | |
| W M Ozanne MC | June 1936 | C W B Orr OBE | April 1945 |
| E C Beard MC | August 1939 | C R T Cumberlege | October 1946 |
| S B Kington | February 1940 | B W Webb-Carter | |
| A H G Wathen | March 1942 | DSO,OBE | February 1947 |
| C D Armstrong DSO,MC (East Surreys) | January 1943 | | |

## 1st and 2nd Battalions amalgamated as 1st Battalion: 1948-1992

| | | | |
|---|---|---|---|
| C R T Cumberlege | July 1948 | C R Huxtable OBE | May 1970 |
| J H Dalrymple OBE | February 1950 | P A Mitchell OBE | November 1972 |
| F R St P Bunbury DSO | December 1951 | J B K Greenway MBE | March 1975 |
| R de la H Moran OBE | May 1954 | M R N Bray | May 1977 |
| P P de la H Moran | September 1957 | W R Mundell OBE | August 1979 |
| A D Firth OBE,MC | February 1960 | C R Cumberlege | April 1982 |
| A B M Kavanagh OBE,MC | February 1962 | E J W Walker OBE | October 1984 |
| | | A D Roberts MBE | January 1987 |
| D E Isles OBE | May 1965 | A D Meek | September 1989 |
| D W Shuttleworth | November 1967 | D M Santa-Ollala MC | April 1992 |

\* \* \* \* \* \* \* \* \* \* \* \* \* \* \*

## 76th Regiment: 1787-1881

| | | | |
|---|---|---|---|
| G Harris | October 1787 | G H Dansey | January 1839 |
| Hon W Monson | December 1797 | J Clarke | September 1839 |
| M Symes | August 1808 | R C Lloyd | July 1857 |
| M Shawe | February 1809 | H Smythe CB | July 1859 |
| J Wardlaw | May 1810 | H C Brewster | December 1863 |
| W L Maberly | September 1827 | J Hackett | February 1872 |
| H Gillman | March 1832 | G R Hopkins | August 1876 |
| J Clarke | June 1833 | C R Richardson | October 1876 |
| J F Love KH | September 1834 | C T Caldicott | November 1877 |
| E Studd | March 1835 | J H Tripp | November 1879 |
| A F Macintosh KH | August 1838 | J M Allardice | February 1880 |

APPENDIX 3. SUCCESSION OF LIEUTENANT COLONELS

**2nd Battalion The Duke of Wellington's (West Riding Regiment):1881-1920**

| | | | |
|---|---|---|---|
| T T Hodge | February 1885 | E G Harrison CB,DSO | October 1914 |
| E G Fenn | October 1886 | W E M Tyndall DSO | December 1914 |
| E Nesbitt | March 1890 | P A Turner | April 1915 |
| C W Gore | March 1894 | R N Bray CMG,DSO | June 1915 |
| H E Belfield | July 1897 | A G Horsfall DSO | November 1916R |
| S J Trench | December 1899 | J A Hennicker MC | October 1917 |
| F M H Marshall | December 1903 | P L E Walker | January 1918 |
| K E Lean | January 1907 | (17th Hussars) | |
| F A Hayden | February 1908 | W G Officer | March 1918 |
| J A C Gibbs | March 1912 | F Pawlettt DSO,MC | |
| K McLeod | August 1914 | (Canadian Army) | April 1918 |
| H K Umfreville | September 1914 | R N Bray CMG,DSO | December 1918 |

**2nd Battalion The Duke of Wellingtons Regiment (West Riding): 1920-1947**

| | | | |
|---|---|---|---|
| C L Smith VC, MC (Duke of Cornwall's LI) | September 1921 | S M G Theyre (Wiltshires) | April 1942 |
| C J Pickering CMG,DSO | March 1925 | C K T Faithfull | May 1942 |
| J C Burnett DSO | March 1929 | E W Stevens OBE | March 1944 |
| M M Cox MC | March 1933 | J H Dalrymple OBE | October 1944 |
| A F P Christison MC (Camerons) | February 1937 | E R Armitage OBE | June 1946 |
| | | G T Chadwick OBE (KOYLI) | March 1947 |
| F H Fraser DSO,MC | February 1938 | | |
| H B Owen | December 1940 | C R T Cumberlege | September 1947 |
| C K T Faithfull | February 1942 | | |

The 2nd Battalion was amalgamated with the 1st Battalion on 17 June 1948

\* \* \* \* \* \* \* \* \* \* \* \* \* \* \* \*

**Officers Commanding the Regimental Depot: 1873-1959**

| | | | |
|---|---|---|---|
| Colonel J E Collings CB | 1873 | Major W T McGuire-Bate | 1925 |
| Colonel E Blewitt | 1878 | Major M N Cox MC | 1928 |
| Colonel F Freer | 1881 | Major M R Whittaker | 1931 |
| Colonel F J Castle | 1885 | Major R O'D Carey | 1934 |
| Colonel T T Simpson | 1886 | Major V C Green | 1937 |
| Colonel E G Fenn | 1891 | Major A E H Sayers | 1939 |
| Colonel A G Spencer | 1896 | Lieutenant Colonel D Paton | 1941 |
| Colonel H B LeMottee | 1898 | During the Second World War the | |
| Colonel R W H Harris CB | 1901 | Regimental Depot was closed | |
| Major E R Houghton | 1905 | Lieutenant Colonel J H Dalrymple OBE | 1947 |
| Major J A C Gibbs | 1907 | | |
| Major K A Macleod | 1910 | Major R E Austin | 1948 |
| Major E M K Parson | 1913 | Major W Skelsey | 1950 |
| Brevet Colonel H D Thorold | 1914 | Major J H Davis | 1952 |
| Lieutenant Colonel E M K Parson | 1915 | Major A C S Savory MBE | 1954 |
| Brevet Colonel M V Le P Trench | 1919 | Major D C Roberts | 1956 |
| Major J C Burnett DSO | 1922 | Major R H Ince | 1958 |

**Regimental Secretaries 1959-1992**

| | |
|---|---|
| Major (Ret'd) J H Davis | 1959 |
| Major (Ret'd) G C Tedd | 1976 |
| Lieutenant Colonel (Ret'd) W Robins OBE | 1984 |

APPENDIX 4

# The Victoria Cross

The Victoria Cross was instituted by Royal Warrant on 29 June 1856. The Warrant begins:

> *"Whereas we take into our Royal consideration that there exists no means of adequately rewarding the individual gallant services either of officers of the lower grades in our naval and military service, or of warrant and petty officers, seamen and marines in our navy, and non-commissioned officers and soldiers in the army, it is ordained that the cross shall only be awarded to those officers or men who served us in the presence of the enemy, and shall have then performed some signal act of valour or devotion to their country."*

The idea originated with the Prince Consort and he is said to have designed the medal. The cross carries with it an annuity of £10. In 1902 King Edward VII sanctioned for the cross to be given to representatives of soldiers who would have been entitled to it had they survived.

The decoration consists of a bronze Maltese cross which, until 1942, was made from the metal of Russian guns captured at Sebastapol. It is worn with a red ribbon by recipients in the army, and with a blue ribbon by those in the navy.

************

**Abyssinia Campaign, 1867/68**
　　3691 Drummer Michael MAGNER - 33rd Regiment.
　　949 Private James BERGIN - 33rd Regiment.

For their conspicuous gallantry, in the assault of Magdala, on the 13th April, 1868. Lieutenant General Lord Napier reports that while the head of the column of attack was checked by the obstacles at the gate, a small stream of officers and men of the 33rd Regiment and an officer of Engineers, breaking away from the main approach to Magdala, and climbing up a cliff, reached the defences and forced their way over the wall, and through the strong and thorny fence, thus turning the defenders of the gateway. The first two men to enter, and the first in Magdala, were Drummer Magner and Private Bergin of the 33rd Regiment. (London Gazette, 28 July, 1868.)

Drummer Michael Magner

Private James Bergin. He later transferred to the 78 Highlanders (2nd Battalion Seaforths)

### The Boer War, 1900-02

2522 Sergeant James FIRTH, 1st Battalion. The Duke of Wellington's (West Riding Regiment)

During the action at Plewton's Farm, near Arundel, Cape Colony, on the 24th February, 1900, Lance Corporal Blackman having been wounded and lying exposed to a hot fire at a range of from 400-500 yards, Sergeant Firth picked him up and carried him to cover. Later in the day, when the enemy had advanced to within a short distance of the firing line, Second Lieutenant Wilson being dangerously wounded and in a most exposed position, Sergeant Firth carried him over the crest of the ridge, which was being held by the troops, to shelter and was himself shot through the nose and eye whilst doing so.

( London Gazette, 11 June, 1901)

Sergeant James Firth

# APPENDIX 4. THE VICTORIA CROSS

**The First World War, 1914-18**

2nd Lieutenant Henry KELLY, 10th Battalion. The Duke of Wellington's (West Riding Regiment)

For most conspicuous bravery in attack at Le Sars on 4th October, 1916.

He twice rallied his company under the heaviest fire, and finally led the only three available men into the enemy trench, and there remained bombing until two of them had become casualties and enemy reinforcements had arrived. He then carried his Company Sergeant-Major, who had been wounded, back to our trenches, a distance of 70 yards, and subsequently three other soldiers. He set a fine example of gallantry and endurance.

(London Gazette, 25 November, 1916)

Second Lieutenant Henry Kelly MC and bar

15805 Private Arnold LOOSEMORE 8th Battalion. The Duke of Wellington's (West Riding Regiment)

For most conspicuous bravery and initiative during the attack on a strongly held enemy position south of Langemarck, Flanders, on 11 August, 1917.

His platoon having been checked by heavy machine-gun fire, he crawled through partially-cut wire, dragging his Lewis gun with him, and single handed dealt with a strong part of the enemy killing about twenty of them, and thus covering the consolidation of the position taken up by his platoon. Immediately afterwards his Lewis gun was blown up by a bomb, and three of the enemy rushed for him, but he shot them all with his revolver.

Later, he shot several enemy snipers, exposing himself to heavy fire each time. On returning to the original post he also brought back a wounded comrade under heavy fire at the risk of his life. He displayed throughout an utter disregard of danger.
(London Gazette, 14 September, 1917)

Sergeant Arnold Loosemore DCM

**24066 Private Arthur POULTER 1/4th Battalion. The Duke of Wellington's (West Riding Regiment) (TF)**

For most conspicuous bravery when acting as a stretcher-bearer, at Erquinghem-Lys, on 10th April, 1918.

On ten occasions Private Poulter carried badly wounded men on his back to a safe locality, through a particularly heavy artillery and machine-gun barrage. Again, after a withdrawal over the river had been ordered, Private Poulter returned in full view of the enemy, who were advancing, and carried back another man who had been left behind wounded. He bandaged-up over forty men under fire, and his conduct throughout the whole day was a magnificent example to all ranks. This very gallant soldier was subsequently seriously wounded when attempting another rescue in the face of the enemy.

(London Gazette, 28 June, 1918)

*Private Arthur Poulter*

**34506 Private Henry TANDEY, D.C.M., M.M. 5th Battalion. The Duke of Wellington's (West Riding Regiment). (T.F.)**

For most conspicuous bravery and initiative during the capture of the village and the crossings at Marcoing and the subsequent counter-attack on 28th September, 1918. When, during the advance on Marcoing, his platoon was held up by machine-gun fire, he at once crawled forward, located the machine-gun, and with a Lewis gun team, knocked it out. On arrival at the crossing he restored the plank bridge under a hail of bullets, thus enabling the first crossing to be made at this vital spot.

Later in the evening, during an attack, he with eight comrades, was surrounded by an overwhelming number

*Private Henry Tandy DCM MM*

of Germans, and though the position was apparently hopeless, he led a bayonet charge through them, fighting so fiercely that 37 of the enemy were driven into the hands of the remainder of his company. Although twice wounded, he refused to leave until the fight was won.

(London Gazette, 14 December 1918)

2nd Lieutenant James Palmer HUFFAM, 5th Battalion. The Duke of Wellington's (West Riding Regiment) (TF)

For conspicuous bravery and devotion to duty on 31st August, 1918. With three men he rushed an enemy machine-gun post, and put it out of action. His post was then heavily attacked and he withdrew fighting, carrying a wounded comrade. Again on the night of 31st August 1918 at St.Servin's Farm accompanied by two men only, he rushed an enemy machine-gun post, capturing eight prisoners and enabling the advance to continue. Throughout the whole of the fighting from 29th August to 1st September, 1918 he showed the utmost gallantry.

(London Gazette, 26 December, 1918)

Second Lieutenant James Huffam

**The Second World War, 1939-45**

5891907 Private Richard BURTON 1st Battalion. The Duke of Wellington's Regiment (West Riding)

In Italy on 8th October, 1944, two companies of the Duke of Wellington's Regiment moved forward to take a strongly-held feature 760 metres high. The capture of this feature was vital at this stage of the operation, as it dominated all the ground on the main axis of advance.

The assaulting troops made good progress to within twenty yards of the crest, when they came under withering fire from Spandaus on the crest. The leading platoon was held up and the Platoon Commander was wounded. The Company Commander took another platoon, of which Private Burton was a runner, through to assault the crest, from which four Spandaus at least were firing. Private Burton rushed forward and engaging the first Spandau's position with his Tommy-gun, killed the crew of three.

When the assault was again held up by murderous fire from two more machine guns. Private Burton, again showing complete disregard for his own safety, dashed forward toward the first machine-gun, using his Tommy-gun until his ammunition was exhausted. He then picked up a Bren gun and firing from the hip, succeeded in killing or wounding the crews of the two machine-guns. Thanks to his outstanding courage the Company was then able to consolidate on the forward slope of the feature.

The enemy immediately counter attacked fiercely, but Private Burton, in spite of most of his comrades being either dead or wounded, once again dashed forward on his own initiative and directed such accurate fire with his Bren gun on the enemy that they retired, leaving the feature firmly in our hands.

The enemy counter-attacked again on the adjoining platoon position, and Private Burton, who had placed himself on the flank, brought such accurate firing to bear that the counter-attack also failed to dislodge the Company from its position.

Private Burton's magnificent gallantry and total disregard of his own safety during many hours of fierce fighting in mud and continuous rain were an inspiration to all his comrades.

(London Gazette, 4 January, 1945

*Private Richard Burton*

4624899 Corporal (Acting Sergeant) Hanson Victor TURNER
(Joined The Duke of Wellington's Regiment in 1940, earned posthumous award of the Victoria Cross while serving with the 1st Battalion The West Yorkshire Regiment).

In Burma, at Ningthoukong, soon after midnight on the night of 6th/7th June, 1944, an attack was made by a strong force of Japanese with medium and light machine-guns. In the first instance the attack largely fell on the S.W. corner of the position which was held by a weak platoon of about 20 men of which Sergeant Turner was one of the section commanders. By creeping up under cover of a nullah the enemy were able to use grenades with deadly effect against this portion of the perimeter.

Three out of the four light machine-guns in the platoon were destroyed and the platoon was forced to give ground. Sergeant Turner with coolness and fine leadership at once reorganised his party and withdrew 40 yards. The enemy made determined and repeated attempts to dislodge them and concentrated all fire they could produce in an effort to reduce the position and so extend the penetration. Sustained fire was kept up on Sergeant Turner and his dwindling party by the enemy for a period of two hours. The enemy, however, achieved no further success in this sector. Sergeant Turner with a doggedness and spirit of endurance of the highest order repelled all their attacks, and it was due entirely to his leadership that the position was ultimately held throughout the night.

When it was clear that the enemy were attempting to outflank the position, Sergeant Turner determined to take the initiative in driving the enemy off and killing them. The men left under his command were the minimum essential to maintain the position he had built up with such effect. No party for a counter-attack could therefore be mustered and speed was essential if the enemy were to be frustrated. He at once, boldly and fearlessly, went forward from his position alone armed with all the hand grenades he could carry, and went into the attack against the enemy single handed. He used his weapons with devastating effect and when his supply was exhausted he went back for more and returned to the offensive again. During all this time the enemy were keeping up intense small arms and grenade fire.

Sergeant Turner in all made five journeys to obtain further supplies of grenades and it was on this sixth occasion still single handed, while throwing a grenade among a party of the enemy, that he was killed.

His conduct on that night will ever be remembered by the Regiment. His superb leadership and undaunted will to win in the early stages of the attack were undoubtedly instrumental in preventing the enemy plan from succeeding. The number of enemy found dead the next morning was ample evidence of the deadly effect his grenade throwing had had. He displayed outstanding valour and had not the slightest thought of his own safety. He died on the battlefield in a spirit of supreme self sacrifice.

(London Gazette, 17 August, 1944)

Corporal (acting Sergeant) Hanson Turner

\*\*\*\*\*\*\*\*\*\*\*\*\*\*

## THE GEORGE CROSS

The George Cross was instituted in September 1940. The cross is intended primarily for civilians - men and women - and the award to members of the fighting services is confined to actions for which purely military honours are not normally granted. It may be awarded posthumously. It is awarded only for "acts of the greatest heroism or of the most conspicuous courage in circumstances of extreme danger". The decoration is a plain silver cross with a circular medallion in the centre bearing a representation of St George and the Dragon surrounded by the words 'For gallantry'. The ribbon is dark blue.

### The Second World War, 1939-1945

Captain Robert Llewellyn JEPHSON-JONES RAOC

He was commissioned into The Duke of Wellington's Regiment in 1925 and served in both the 1st and 2nd Battalions. Shortly before the outbreak of war he transferred to the RAOC. He was awarded the GC together with Lieutenant Eastman RAOC for bomb disposal work during enemy air attacks on Malta in 1940.

On various dates, Captain Jones and Lieutenant Eastman RAOC, worked under dangerous and trying conditions and performed acts of considerable gallantry in dealing with a large number of various un-exploded bombs, some of which were in a very highly dangerous state and of the German delay action type.

On one occasion these two officers showed particular gallantry in dealing with a 1,000 lb German bomb. They made two attempts to explode the bomb but it failed to detonate. At the third attempt and when the bomb was in a most dangerous state, they succeeded in detonating it. On a second occasion these officers, assisted by a Master Rigger, succeeded in removing a 440 lb high explosive Italian un-exploded bomb, which had been under water for a week, from a 20 foot deep well inside a house. The bomb which was fused at both ends was also in a dangerous state and had to be raised to the ground floor by means of a gin, tackle, sling and rope. This operation was doubly dangerous as there was a possibility of the sling slipping while the bomb was being hauled up and further because the bomb was two and half feet long, the mouth of the well only three feet one inch wide, for safety the bomb had to be kept horizontal if possible and pulled up thus. Lieutenant Eastman, assisted by the Master Rigger, guided the bomb from the floor of the well, while Captain Jones went to the top to guide it through the opening. They succeeded in getting the bomb out although there was only six inches clearance as it came through the mouth of the well.

(London Gazette, 24 December 1940)

Major Andre Gilbert KEMPSTER 8th Battalion The Duke of Wellington's Regiment. (145 Regiment Royal Armoured Corps)

On August 21, 1943, near Phillipeville, Major Kempster was carrying out grenade throwing practice with two others in the same pit. A grenade which was thrown by Major Kempster rolled back into the pit. He tried to scoop it up and failed. By this time detonation was due. Without hesitation Major Kempster threw himself on the grenade just before it exploded and received fatal injuries. By his self-sacrifice Major Kempster undoubtedly saved the lives of the two other occupants of the pit. Major Kempster's act meant certain death, and he must have known this at the time. His was a supreme act of gallantry.

(London Gazette, 9 November 1943)

## THE ALBERT MEDAL

The Albert Medal was instituted in 1866 for saving life at sea. In 1877 it was extended for saving life on land. Only 235 were ever awarded for saving life on land before it was substituted by the George Cross in 1971. Two members of the Regiment were awarded the medal:

Second Lieutenant Arthur HALSTEAD, MC 10th Battalion The Duke of Wellington's (West Riding Regiment), was awarded the medal in gold for saving a soldier's life during instruction in the throwing of live bombs. As a result he was fatally wounded.

(London Gazette. 1 January 1918)

Lieutenant Fred KELLY, 6th Battalion The Duke of Wellington's (West Riding Regiment) was awarded the medal in bronze for saving a soldier's life during rifle grenade practice. (London Gazette. 26 April 1918)

## OFFICERS WHO SERVED IN THE REGIMENT SUBSEQUENT TO BEING AWARDED THE VC

Colonel A R Dunn: Exchanged into the 33rd from the 100th Foot in 1864. He commanded the Regiment in the Abyssinia campaign until he was killed in a shooting accident in January 1868. He was awarded the VC in 1857 for his bravery during the charge of the Light Brigade at Balaclava, when he was serving with 11th Hussars.

General Sir Hugh Rowlands: Colonel of The Duke of Wellington's Regiment from 1897 to 1909. Commissioned into the 41st Foot (The Welch Regiment) he gained the VC for saving the life of the commanding officer of the 47th Foot during the battle of Inkerman. His name appeared in the first list of recipients of the new decoration, in February 1857.

Colonel C L Smith: Commissioned into the Duke of Cornwall's Light Infantry. Commanded the 2nd Battalion The Duke of Wellington's Regiment from 1921 to 1925. Awarded the VC in 1904, while serving with the Somali Mounted Infantry, for his gallant attempts to save the life of an officer of the RAMC.

APPENDIX 5

# Militia, Volunteers, Territorial and Cadet Forces

The system of gathering volunteers to defend the nation long preceded Britain's permanent standing army. Even in Saxon times it was understood that lords and peasants must arm at their country's call. The first recorded attempt to formalise the practice was in 1181 when the Statues of the Assize of Arms required that knights, tenants and their followers should be armed to a standard within their means and that henceforth they would be part of the forces of the Crown rather than the retainers of powerful lords. The volunteer forces of today have their origins in this early organisation but have come through many changes along the way.

This early movement developed during the 16th and 17th centuries into a statutory home defence or constitutional force known as the militia which was only embodied in times of war. The infantry of the militia was organised into battalions on a county basis and from 1756 under a scheme put through Parliament by Pitt each county was required to provide a set quota of men, if necessary using a ballot system if sufficient volunteers were not forthcoming. This system was under the command of the Lord Lieutenant of each county. Volunteers for the force were paid a bounty to serve. Those selected by ballot from among the able bodied men of the county, minus a wide range of exceptions, had the option of paying a substitute to serve in their place. From early in the 19th century, officers and men from the militia were encouraged to volunteer for service with a line regiment and were paid a bounty to do so, thus providing a considerable number of partially trained recruits for the regular force. In addition to the militia some local auxiliary volunteer units existed in the 18th century to defend their locality in the event of invasion, or to assist the magistrates in the event of riot. From 1803, with the threat of war, this force was considerably expanded, but after Waterloo these units and the militia went into decline.

By 1847, with the regular army spread thinly round the globe, doubts were expressed about the country's ability to defend itself in the event of war in Europe, and the Duke of Wellington made an impassioned plea for the establishment of an adequate home force. Nothing was done, however, until after the Crimea War when France, Britain's ally in that conflict, again began to adopt an aggressive stance. Fears of invasion swept through Britain and in May 1859 the Secretary of State for War, Major

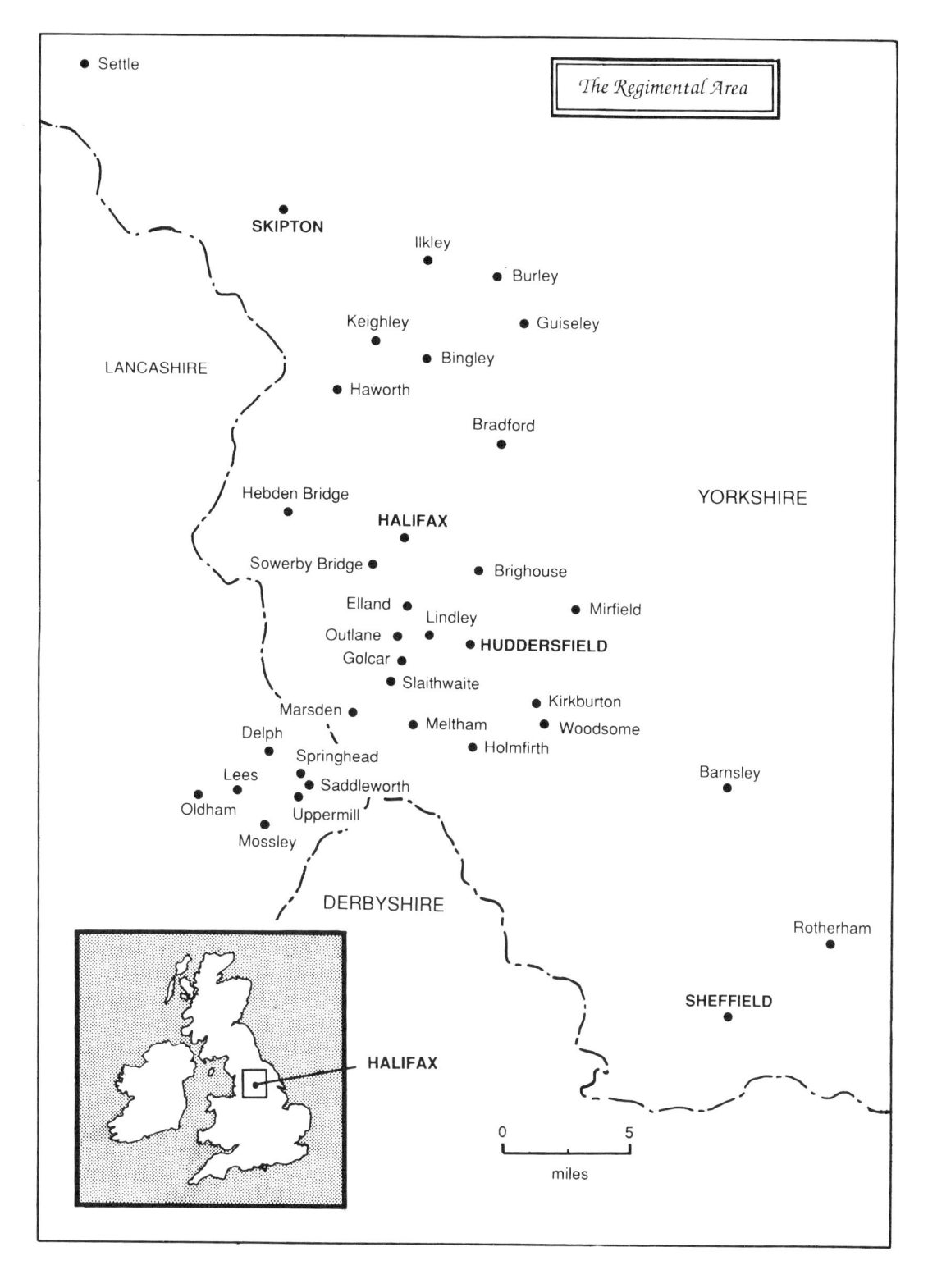

APPENDIX 5. MILITIA, VOLUNTEERS AND TERRITORIAL FORCES

*The Regimental Area*

General Jonathan Peel, authorised the raising of a volunteer force under the Yeomanry and Volunteer Act of 1804. Old units were brought back to full strength and many new volunteer corps were raised in the industrial areas. It is estimated that by 1 October 1860 over 100,000 volunteers were under arms. By May 1861 the strength was 170,000. In the West Riding the rapid expansion of the volunteer force was under the control of the Lord Lieutenant, The Earl Fitzwilliam, and units of the Yorkshire West Riding Rifle Volunteers were established in Halifax, Huddersfield, North Craven, Skipton, Burley, Guiseley, Holmfirth, Saddleworth, Keighley, Mirfield, Howarth, Meltham and many other places. Initially each small local corps was raised independently and its constitution and uniforms regulated by a committee or the commanding officer. It was intended that the force be trained as light infantry or riflemen to act as skirmishers on the flanks and lines of communications of any hostile army, hence the uniforms of the new corps were green or, in some cases grey, rather than the traditional scarlet of the infantry of the line. Within a short time some of the small corps in the West Riding were grouped together to form administrative battalions or battalion sized groups under new titles, producing nine Corps of Yorkshire Rifle Volunteers with headquarters at York, Sheffield, Bradford, Halifax, Wakefield, Skipton, Huddersfield, Leeds and Doncaster.

Under this consolidation of independent corps in 1860 the 4th Yorkshire West Riding Rifle Volunteer Corps had its headquarters in Halifax with four companies there and others in Sowerby, Brighouse, Hebden Bridge and Upper Shibden Hall. The 5th Administrative Battalion of the same corps had its headquarters and five companies in Huddersfield with other companies or sub units in Saddleworth, Delph, Lydgate, Slaithwaite, Marsden, Golcar, Woodsome, Kirkburton, Mirfield, Meltham, Outlane and Lindley. The 2nd Administrative Battalion had its headquarters in Skipton with companies or sub units in Settle, Burley, Guiseley, Ingleton, Keighley, Haworth and Bingley. In 1880 the 2nd and 5th Administrative Battalions were renumbered as the 9th and 6th Yorkshire West Riding Rifle Volunteer Corps respectively. Despite orders to the contrary both the Halifax and Huddersfield Battalions had colours made and presented.

In 1881 the 33rd and 76th Regiments were linked to become the 1st and 2nd Battalions of the Duke of Wellington's (West Riding Regiment) with a territorial recruiting area within the West Riding known as No. 33 Regimental District and a District Headquarters and Depot in Halifax. The three Yorkshire West Riding volunteer battalions whose headquarters were at Halifax (4th), Huddersfield (6th) and Skipton (9th) became, in 1883, the 1st, 2nd and 3rd Volunteer Battalions of The Duke of Wellington's (West Riding Regiment). The green or grey uniforms of the rifle volunteer battalions were replaced by scarlet tunics except that gold lace was not permitted and they were required to wear a letter "V" on the shoulder straps denoting volunteer. As part of the reorganisation the 6th Regiment of West Yorkshire Militia, originally formed in 1759 as Sir George Savile's Regiment of Militia, was split into two battalions which became the 3rd and 4th Militia Battalions of the new Regiment. The 4th Militia Battalion was absorbed into the 3rd in 1890.

## APPENDIX 5. MILITIA, VOLUNTEERS AND TERRITORIAL FORCES

1st Volunteer Battalion in the Isle of Man, 1899

Although primarily intended for home defence, the 3rd Militia Battalion and active service companies of volunteers from the three volunteer battalions were to serve in the Boer War alongside their regular counterparts and helped to earn the battle honour **South Africa 1900-1902** awarded to the regiment.

Reorganisation in the regular army initiated by the Secretary of State for War, Richard Haldane, was followed in 1908 by sweeping changes to form a new Territorial Force (TF) with an establishment of 314,000. The Territorial Force included fourteen infantry divisions, each of twelve battalions in three brigades with supporting artillery and other services. One of these divisions was the West Riding Division TF, consisting of the 1st West Riding Brigade with four battalions of the West Yorkshire Regiment TF, the 2nd West Riding Brigade with four battalions of the Duke of Wellington's (West Riding Regiment) TF and the 3rd West Riding Brigade with two battalions of the York and Lancaster Regiment TF and two battalions of the King's Own Yorkshire Light Infantry TF. New terms of service required the territorials to attend an annual camp of 14 days, attend evening training parades at their local drill hall, and to fire an annual musketry course. Territorial Force Associations were established in each county/area to administer the new arrangements. The 1st Volunteer Battalion The Duke of Wellington's Regiment in Halifax was redesignated the 4th TF Battalion. The 2nd Volunteer Battalion in Huddersfield was divided to form two TF battalions, the 5th and

5 DWR, Maxim machine gun team 1906

7th, the 5th with headquarters in Huddersfield and companies in Huddersfield, Holmfirth, Mirfield and Kirkburton, and the 7th with headquarters and one company in Milnsbridge and further companies in Slaithwaite, Marsden, Uppermill, Mossley and Lees. The 3rd Volunteer Battalion in Skipton became the 6th TF Battalion. The territorials were now dressed in the home service pattern khaki serge uniform with boots and long puttees of the regular army pattern, but wore a brass letter "T" on their shoulder strap. The basic weapon was still the .303in rifle but each territorial battalion was to receive two Maxim machine guns mounted on horse drawn limbers.

On the outbreak of war in 1914 the Territorial Force was mobilised and although the conditions of enlistment required home service only, the vast majority of officers and men quickly volunteered for service overseas. The force was expanded and each of the four original battalions of the Regiment formed second battalions which were numbered 2/4th, 2/5th, 2/6th, 2/7th. These battalions were eventually to form 186th Infantry Brigade as part of the 62nd West Riding Division. The West Riding Division was sent to France in April 1915 and shortly afterwards was retitled to become the 49th (West Riding) Division with the three brigades retitled No 146, 147 and 148 Infantry Brigades, the four battalions of the Regiment forming 147 Infantry Brigade. The division and the brigade were to remain in France or Flanders until the end of the war during which time they saw much action. The 62 (West Riding) Division arrived in France in January 1917 and saw action at Arras, Ypres and Cambrai and took part in the final major battles of the war.

The 3/4th, 3/5th, 3/6th and 3/7th TF Battalions of the Regiment were formed in April 1915 and were used at home as training and drafting units until the end of the war. The 3rd Militia Battalion, which was redesignated as the 3rd Special Reserve Battalion in 1908, carried out a similar role. This battalion was disembodied in May 1919 and has not been reactivated since.

The Territorial Force was reconstituted in 1920 as the Territorial Army (TA) and the 4th, 5th, 6th and 7th Battalions were re-formed in their areas of Halifax, Huddersfield Skipton and Milnsbridge.

In the mid 1930s, with the threat of war again apparent. many units of the Territorial Army were given new roles. In December 1936 the 5th Battalion became 43rd (5th DWR) Anti-Aircraft Battalion Royal Engineers TA and equipped with searchlights. The Battalion mobilised in 1939 and in August 1940, when the Royal Artillery took over the responsibility for searchlights, it became 43rd Searchlight Regiment Royal Artillery (5DWR). Further role and title changes followed in October 1944 when it became 43 Garrison Regiment Royal Artillery and, later in February 1945, 600 Regiment Royal Artillery (5DWR). During this period the Battalion was operating in the infantry role in France following the landings in Normandy in June 1944. At the end of the war the Battalion moved to Germany before returning to UK at the end of 1945.

In November 1938 the 4th Battalion became 58 Anti-Tank Regiment Royal Artillery (1/4th DWR). In April 1939 a second regiment was formed with the title 68 Anti-Tank Regiment Royal Artillery (2/4th DWR). Batteries of these two regiments saw

Self propelled guns of 382 Field Regiment (4 DWR) 1951-1952

considerable action during the war with service in France 1940, North Africa 1943, Italy (Salerno), 1943-45, Palestine 1944, Greece 1945, Malaya and Singapore 1941-42, Normandy and North West Europe 1944. 68 Anti-Tank Regiment (2/4 DWR) was disbanded in August 1944 to reinforce other units.

The 6th and 7th Battalions both raised second battalions in April 1939, the original battalions becoming the 1/6th and 1/7th and the new battalions 2/6th and 2/7th. All were mobilised in the infantry role in 1939, the 1/6th and 1/7th again as part of 147 Infantry Brigade of 49 Division. When in April 1940 the move of the Brigade to Norway was aborted due to the rapid advance of the Germans it was diverted to Iceland where it remained until April 1942. Both battalions landed in Normandy shortly after D Day and saw extensive action. After losing 19 officers and 350 men killed and wounded in a very short time the 1/6th was withdrawn from the theatre in August 1944. The 1/7th fought its way through France, Belgium and Holland before moving to Germany as the war ended. The 2/6th and 2/7th went to the St.Nazaire area of France in April 1940 mainly for labouring duties but with the collapse of France they were caught up in heavy fighting before the bulk of both battalions managed to escape, the 2/6th through St.Malo and the 2/7th from a beach near St.Valery. Both were later converted to Royal Armoured Corps, 114 and 115 Regiments RAC (DWR), but neither was to see action again.

APPENDIX 5. MILITIA, VOLUNTEERS AND TERRITORIAL FORCES

673 Light Anti-aircraft Regiment (6 DWR), 1949

Following the end of the Second World War, the Territorial Army was reconstituted in January 1947. The 4th Battalion continued in Halifax in its artillery role as 382 (4 DWR) Regiment RA (TA), initially as an anti-tank and finally a medium regiment, until becoming in April 1961 a rifle company of The West Riding Battalion. In April 1967, on formation of the Yorkshire Volunteers, this company became C (DWR) Company of the 1st Battalion and in January 1988 D (DWR) Company of the 3rd Battalion.

The 5th Battalion continued in Huddersfield and was reconstituted in January 1947 as 578 Heavy Anti-Aircraft Regiment RA (TA), and from May 1955 as Q (5 DWR) Battery 382 Medium Regiment RA (TA). In May 1957 the battery was converted to infantry and amalgamated with the 7th Battalion to become 5/7th Battalion The Duke of Wellington's Regiment TA. The 5/7th became part of The West Riding Battalion in March 1961 with its headquarters at Huddersfield and companies or detachments in Huddersfield, Mirfield, Halifax, Keighley, Skipton, Holmfirth and Mossley. The reduction of the Territorial Army in 1967 to one battalion in the whole of Yorkshire resulted in the formation of the Yorkshire Volunteers and the cadreisation of the West Riding Battalion. The cadre was expanded to company strength in April 1971 to become C (DWR) Company 3rd Battalion Yorkshire Volunteers. The headquarters of the Battalion was established in Huddersfield at the same time.

The 6th Battalion was reconstituted in Skipton in January 1947 but later the same year was redesignated 322 and shortly afterwards 673 Heavy Anti-Aircraft Regiment RA

*409*

(TA). 673 Regiment became a Light Anti-Aircraft Regiment in January 1949 and in May 1955 became R (6 DWR) Battery 382 Medium Regiment RA (TA). The Battery became a rifle company of The West Riding Battalion in April 1961.

The 7th Battalion was reconstituted in Milnsbridge in January 1947 with companies or detachments in Milnsbridge, Slaithwaite, Mossley, Springhead, Uppermill, Sowerby Bridge, Elland and Halifax. The Battalion amalgamated with Q (5 DWR) Battery 382 Medium Regiment RA (TA) in May 1957 to form 5/7th Battalion The Duke of Wellington's Regiment (Wst Riding). Following the formation of the Yorkshire Volunteers in 1967 the Dukes element was reduced to a single company. However, when the Volunteers were increased to three, and then four battalions, a second company was linked with the Dukes. Following the reductions in the armed services under "Options for Change" the 3rd and 4th Battalions were merged, on 1 April 1992, to form 3rd/4th (West and South Yorkshire) Battalion. Six months later there was a further change when it was announced that that the Yorkshire Volunteers would be disbanded and would be reformed as territorial battalions of the three regular Yorkshire regiments. The new title selected for the 3rd/4th Battalion was 3rd Battalion The Duke of Wellington's Regiment (West Riding) (Yorkshire Volunteers). With its headquarters at Sheffield and companies or detachments in Keighley, Halifax, Huddersfield, Barnsley and Rotherham it gave the Regiment an enhanced representation in the part of South Yorshire, formerly allocated to the York and Lancaster Regiment, which had been added to its regimental area some months earlier.

*******************

A number of Volunteer Corps raised in 1859 unofficially founded cadet companies as a means of recruiting. These companies were later recognised by the War Office and in 1863 all Volunteer Corps were authorised to form cadet corps. The Huddersfield Volunteers were one of the first units in the country to establish a cadet corps and in August 1862 paraded a detachment of thirty cadets, dressed in scarlet jackets and grey trousers at a review of Volunteers in Doncaster. In 1864 at a similar review by the Lord Lieutenant, Earl Fitzwilliam, 86 cadets from Huddersfield were on parade.

The Army Cadet Force (ACF), the Combined Cadet Force (CCF) and the University Officer Training Corps (UOTC), (now administered by the Territorial Force Association in each area) originate from the earlier cadet movement. A major expansion of the cadet force took place in 1942 after which many cadet units worked in support of the Home Guard. The Regiment currently (1992) has ACF detachments in Huddersfield, Halifax, Keighley, Skipton, Mirfield, Heckmondwike and Thongsbridge. These detachments, along with two Royal Artillery detachments, form D Company Yorkshire (N & W) Army Cadet Force which has its headquarters at Huddersfield. The Army detachments of the CCF contingents at Giggleswick School and Leeds Grammar School are also badged to the Regiment.

# VOLUNTEER AND TERRITORIAL UNITS IN THE DWR AREA OF THE WEST RIDING
## 1859 - 1993

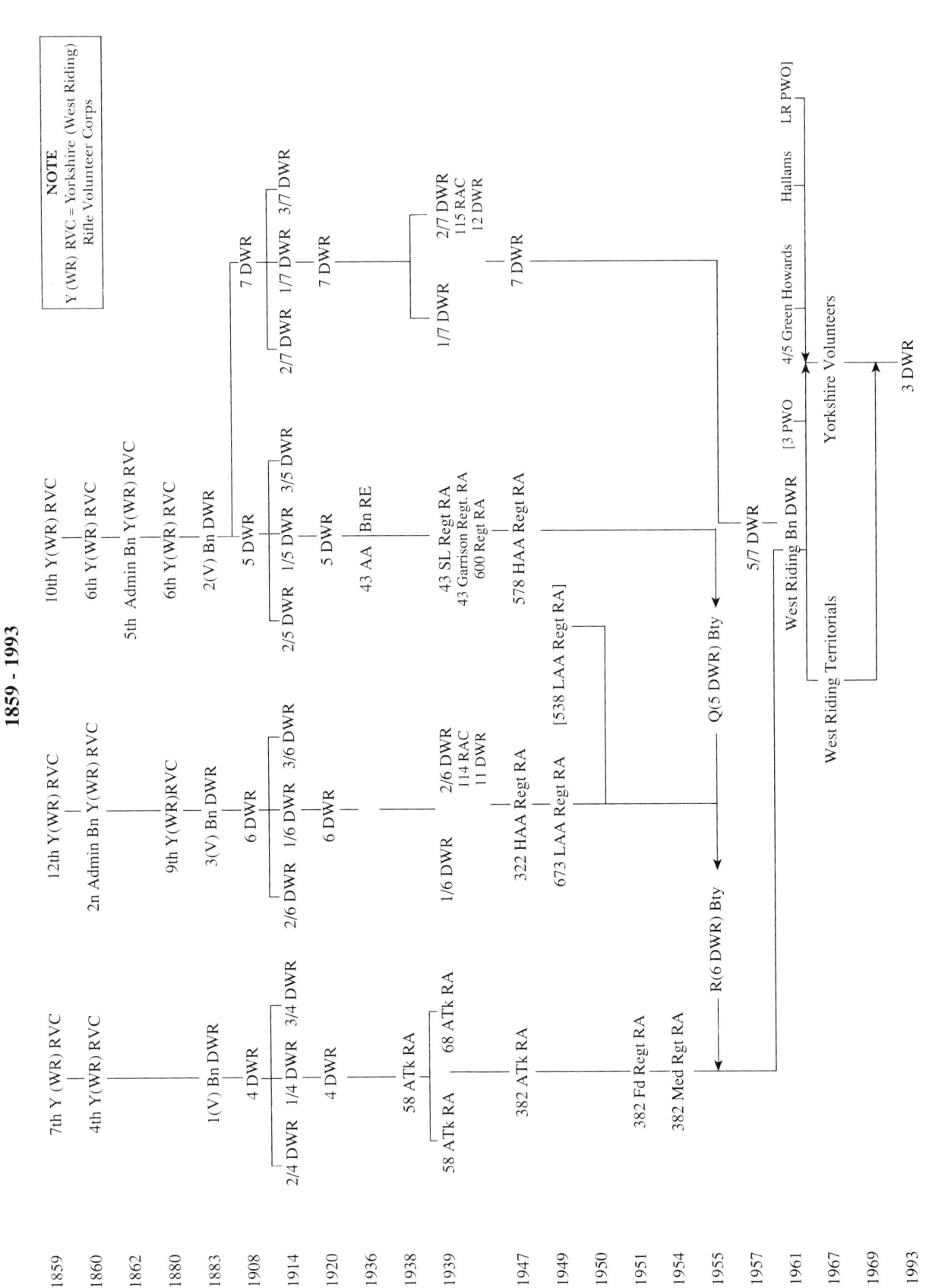

**NOTE**
Y (WR) RVC = Yorkshire (West Riding) Rifle Volunteer Corps

|  | | | | | |
|---|---|---|---|---|---|
| 1859 | 7th Y (WR) RVC | | 10th Y(WR) RVC | | 12th Y(WR) RVC |
| 1860 | 4th Y(WR) RVC | | 6th Y(WR) RVC | | |
| 1862 | | | 5th Admin Bn Y(WR) RVC | | 2n Admin Bn Y(WR) RVC |
| 1880 | | | 6th Y(WR) RVC | | 9th Y(WR)RVC |
| 1883 | 1(V) Bn DWR | | 2(V) Bn DWR | | 3(V) Bn DWR |
| 1908 | 4 DWR | | 5 DWR | 7 DWR | 6 DWR |
| 1914 | 2/4 DWR  1/4 DWR  3/4 DWR | | 2/5 DWR  1/5 DWR  3/5 DWR | 2/7 DWR  1/7 DWR  3/7 DWR | 2/6 DWR  1/6 DWR  3/6 DWR |
| 1920 | 4 DWR | | 5 DWR | 7 DWR | 6 DWR |
| 1936 | | | 43 AA  Bn RE | | |
| 1938 | 58 ATk RA | | | 1/7 DWR | |
| 1939 | 58 ATk RA  68 ATk RA | | 43 SL Regt RA<br>43 Garrison Regt. RA<br>600 Regt RA | 2/7 DWR<br>115 RAC<br>12 DWR | 2/6 DWR<br>114 RAC<br>11 DWR  1/6 DWR |
| 1947 | 382 ATk RA | | 578 HAA Regt RA | 7 DWR | 322 HAA Regt RA |
| 1949 | | | | | 673 LAA Regt RA  [538 LAA Regt RA] |
| 1950 | | | | | |
| 1951 | 382 Fd Regt RA | | | | |
| 1954 | 382 Med Rgt RA | | | | |
| 1955 | R(6 DWR) Bty | | Q(5 DWR) Bty | | |
| 1957 | | | 5/7 DWR | | |
| 1961 | | | West Riding Bn DWR | [3 PWO] | |
| 1967 | | | West Riding Territorials | 4/5 Green Howards  Hallams | LR PWO] |
| 1969 | | | Yorkshire Volunteers | | |
| 1993 | | | 3 DWR | | |

APPENDIX 6

# Music of the Regiment

**The Regimental Band**

Military bands started to come into existence during the second half of the 18th century. By 1780 most regiments had managed to form small wind ensembles of no more than six to eight musicians, as much for prestige as for the entertainment of their officers and guests. Such *"Bands of Musick"* were quite unauthorised, the musicians being drawn from the ranks and the cost of instruments and musical scores funded entirely by the officers.

The first reference to the band of the 33rd Regiment occurs in the Inspection Report for 1769, but there is no record of its strength or instrumentation. In the Inspection Report of March 1774, at Plymouth, it is stated that the Regiment had nine musicians. The next reference appears in the letters of Major William Dansey. After the surrender of Yorktown in 1781, Dansey wrote from James Island to the Commanding Officer, Lieutenant Colonel Yorke (then in England) informing him that as some of the potential musicians were training with the Buffs (who had been the first line regiment to establish a band, in 1754), *"...we shall have a tolerable band of musick"*. A year later however, he was complaining that some of the bandsmen had refused to extend their service. *"My dear Colonel, Could you enlist two clarinets and what other Musick you think proper, especially a Horn or two. I never wish to be without a band as long as I have a penny to spare, and the whole of us here are of that opinion"*. In 1798, when the Regiment was in Calcutta, William Hickey recorded in his memoirs, *"At Rees retreat I frequently met Colonel Sherbrooke, who used to send the band of his Regiment, and a very capital one it was, over to play for us during dinner."*

The first mention of a band in the 76th Regiment occurs in the book *War and Sport in India 1802-1806*, written by Lieutenant John Pester who recorded that on 3 September 1803, the day before the storming of the fortress at Ally Ghur, at sunset he *"went to the 76th to hear their band"*. In the Standing Orders of the Regiment, issued in 1807, the following paragraph appears: *"Drummers"*:

> *The Drum Major and the Master of the Band rank as Sergeants in the Regiment . . . The drummers and band are particularly under the charge of the Drum Major who is responsible for their conduct, dress*

## APPENDIX 6. MUSIC OF THE REGIMENT

*and soldier-like appearance; but he will not interfere with the Master of the Band, who must take charge of the band and instruct them in musick, practising at least two hours a day."*

This division of responsibility, with the drum major attending to discipline and turnout and the bandmaster solely to musical instruction, continued down the years.

It was not until 1803 that bands were officially recognised when regulations for the first time permitted one private soldier in each company to be trained as a musician and a sergeant to act as bandmaster. In 1822 the number of musicians was fixed at ten, not including boys. In the following year the authorised number was increased to a sergeant and fourteen musicians. By 1837 official opinion had changed so far from earlier indifference as to express the view *"a band was essential to the credit and appearance of a regiment"*. However no grants were made by the government and the band remained entirely dependent on the officers for all its funding. In 1812 the 33rd's Colonel, the future Duke of Wellington, presented a complete set of instruments and in 1816 his successor, Sir John Sherbrooke, donated £50 to the band fund. During this period it was customary for regiments to hire civilian musicians as music masters. They were usually German or Italian as only foreigners were then supposed to be any good at military music.

Until the late 1850s the state of military music in the army could only be described as disorganised. Each regimental band was a law unto itself, relying solely on its master for his own personal preferences as regards instrumentation, repertoire and performance. As civilians, the music masters were not subject to military discipline, and did not accompany their bands on active service. During the Crimea War, when at a grand review of British forces on the Queen's birthday, the massed bands created cacophony. The Duke of Cambridge was so appalled that when he became Commander-in-Chief he instituted a government-sponsored "Military Music Class" in which harmony was to be established by the formalised training of army bandsmen and bandmasters. This became the Royal Military School of Music. The first entry of 85 students from 40-odd regiments assembled in February 1857. Among them were two members of the 33rd, Sergeant W. Coulton and Boy W. Walsh.

The days of the hired civilian music master were over. Potential bandmasters (enlisted men) had to qualify on a twelve-month course at the school, having previously attended a "pupils" course. On appointment to a band they were ranked as staff sergeants: it was only in 1881 that the rank of WO1 was introduced. A unique entry in the 76th's "Digest" for December 1871 shows "1 Trained Bandmaster". This must have been M. Gray, for another entry in 1895 states that Bandmaster A. Gray was struck off strength on retiring after 25 years service. A photograph of the 2nd Battalion's band at Tipperary in 1884 shows 36 performers, including a string double bass. By the late 19th century most regimental bands had formed string ensembles to provide orchestral music for balls and mess functions.

Though not combatant soldiers, most bandsmen accompanied their regiments on

# THE REGIMENTAL QUICK MARCH

*The Wellesley*

## APPENDIX 6. MUSIC OF THE REGIMENT

active service. In addition to enlivening the troops with music on the march, they acted as stretcher-bearers. After the second world war bandsmen acquired a secondary role, being trained as medical orderlies.

Until after the second world war the establishment for regimental bands in the infantry remained fairly constant at about 36 musicians. While the Corps of Drums' instruments - drums, bugles, fifes - were provided entirely out of public funds, the expense of band instruments, and music, was met by a small annual grant under Allowance Regulations, supplemented by officers' contributions to the band fund. After the war successive cuts in defence expenditure saw reductions in the establishment: by 1982 it had fallen to one WO1 as bandmaster and 21 bandsmen.

**Regimental Marches**

Ever since the creation of Britain's standing army in 1661, regiments had marched, or ridden, past a saluting base to some melody of their own choice. Many were arrangements of traditional folk tunes; some were borrowed from operatic airs, others were composed by bandmasters themselves. Until 1881 regiments were allowed complete freedom in their choice of marches, but in that year the War Office ordered that all scores should be submitted to the Royal Military School of Music, Kneller Hall, for official approval and subsequent publication by the authorised firm of Boosey & Hawkes. Not until 1883 were all the infantry quick marches finally authorised. Since then the titles have been recorded in successive issues of the official manual *Instructions for Bands*.

The Regimental Quick March of The Duke of Wellington's Regiment is The Wellesley and is unique to the Regiment. But the origins of the melody are obscure. Some say that it was discovered among the papers of the 1st Duke after his death in 1852, while another legend ascribes it to an arrangement of a set of Danish quadrilles acquired at some unknown date. Whatever the true origins, the tune was officially approved with the rest in 1883. In 1948 after the amalgamation of the 1st and 2nd Battalions, Bandmaster D. Seed added an introductory fanfare for bugles, this having been the Regimental bugle call of the 2nd Battalion. Although this Seed version was unofficial, it was preferred by the Regiment for all occasions except when the band joined with others on a massed bands parade, when the authorised version had to be performed. However, in 1988 Lieutenant Colonel A D Roberts, commanding the 1st Battalion, approached the Army Band Office, requesting authorisation of the Seed arrangement, which was duly given. When bugles are not available the introductory fanfare is performed on cornets.

As in other regiments, several additional, unofficial airs were adopted by the Dukes, to be played on strictly Regimental functions. Thus after the 1948 amalgamation of the 1st and 2nd Battalions the Colonel of the Regiment, General Sir Philip Christison, approved the following to be played on certain occasions: Ilkla Moor, I'm Ninety-Five, and Scotland the Brave, in that order.

Ilkla Moor, long popular in both Battalions, was arranged as march for band and bugles by Bandmaster D Seed in 1948. I'm Ninety-Five, an inspiring quickstep, an old unofficial march of the 33rd, has been used by a number of regiments. In 1881 it became the official march of the 95th, The Rifle Brigade. Scotland the Brave, was the unofficial march of the 76th and was played on parade before The Wellesley.

The following marches are played during the ceremony of Trooping the Colour:

| Officers and warrant officers: | Take post: | Destiny (33rd slow march) |
|---|---|---|
| The troop: | Slow march: | Destiny |
| | | Logie of Buchan |
| | | (76th slow march) |
| | Quick march: | The British Grenadiers |
| | Slow march: | Grenadiers March |
| March past: | Slow march: | Mallendorf |
| | Quick march: | I'm Ninety Five |
| | | Scotland the Brave |
| | | The Wellesley |

Other marches played by the Regiment are:

Cock o' the North. It was a favourite tune of Lieutenant Colonel Lloyd, who was killed in action in the Boer War. After his death it was decided that the music should always be included in the ceremony of Beating of Retreat.

Rule Britannia. Played after the four Regimental marches on guest nights in the officers mess. The custom originated in the 33rd. It was not played in the 76th.

**The corps of drums**

Long before the creation of Britain's standing army in 1661 foot soldiers had been marching to the *spirit-stirring drum* and the squeal of the *ear-piercing fife*, as Shakespeare had it. In Marlborough's day each regiment had two drummers per company, so the then twelve companies boasted twenty-four drummers in all. In addition there was an extra drummer for the colonel, making 25. When a regiment was formed in square the drummers joined the colonel and the colours in the centre of it. If the colonel wished to issue a command he instructed the drum major, who then gave the order for the 25 drummers to beat it out. When the regiment advanced in line the sound of the drumming gave the men the encouragement and strength required to face and overcome the fears and horrors of the battlefield. The drummers also had other duties, apart from the conveying of commands, including parleying with the enemy, recruiting by beat of drum and carrying out sentences of corporal punishment. The drummer held a distinctive place in the military hierarchy and for that reason was paid more than a private soldier.

The fife, which went into disuse in Cromwellian times, was at first only re-introduced

APPENDIX 6. MUSIC OF THE REGIMENT

to royal regiments such as the Guards. The regiments of foot again began to have fifes in 1747. In 1748 the 33rd Regiment was permitted four fifes instead of four drummers.

In the days when trumpet and bugle were the chief means of relaying routine and executive orders in barracks and in the field, all regiments were required to use the identical calls first laid down in the official manual of 1798. When several regiments were manoeuvring together or quartered in close proximity, within earshot of each others trumpeters and buglers, confusion could arise as for whom a particular call was intended.

To remove doubts around 1838 exclusive regimental calls were introduced, to be sounded before all others. The short, four-or-five-bar calls are still extant, having been published, together with other routine and executive calls, in the successive issues of the manual *Trumpet and Bugle Calls for the Army*.

From the earliest days the drum has remained close to the heart of a regiment and like the colours it carries the battle honours of the regiment emblazoned upon it.

## BUGLE CALLS

### THE DUKE OF WELLINGTON'S REGIMENT (West Riding)

APPENDIX 7

# Three previous Regiments numbered 76

There have been four regiments numbered 76. Although prior to 1751 regiments were not known by their numbers, an order of precedence had long been established. A regiment's position in that order of precedence was important since at the conclusion of each war retrenchment followed and it was the youngest (or highest numbered) regiments which were the first to be disbanded. Thus, there had already been three regiments numbered 76 before the raising of the 76th Regiment in 1787 which was destined to become the 2nd Battalion The Duke of Wellington's Regiment. There is no common factor connecting any of the regiments to each other, beyond the number 76.

**LORD HARCOURT'S REGIMENT: 1745 - 1746.**

In 1742 war broke out between England and France over the question of the succession to the throne of Austria. In 1745, while the main part of the English army was engaged in the fighting in Flanders, Bonnie Prince Charlie landed in Scotland and quickly gathered an army of Highlanders. Having fought a successful action at Prestonpans, near Edinburgh, on 30 September; he turned south and marched into England. As a result of this threat 13 new regiments of Foot were raised. One of them was raised by Lord Harcourt at Thame, near Oxford. It was known as Harcourt's Regiment, (taking its name from its Colonel, as was then the custom), and ranked 76th in the order of precedence. By 13 November the Regiment was reported "half compleat" and a short while afterwards two of its companies were sent to relieve the Guards at Windsor. At the end of the year Harcourt's was sent to do duty in Suffolk and at Landguard Fort, Harwich. In June 1746, following the defeat of Bonnie Prince Charlie at Culloden on 16 April, Harcourt's Regiment was returned to Thame for disbandment - *"the men to be given a bounty of only six days pay as to give more might have deterred them from re-enlisting in old regiments for which a bounty of two guineas was payable."*

**76th REGIMENT: 1756 - 1763.**

In May 1756 war again broke out between the English and French following the capture of Minorca by the French. Augmentation of the infantry soon became necessary and an order was therefore issued in August for 15 regiments, all stationed in England, to each raise a second battalion. In November a new regiment was raised in Ireland by Colonel Lord George Forbes. As the highest numbered regiment then existing was the 60th, the new regiment was numbered 61. In 1758, the following order was issued in connection with the second battalions raised two years previously:

> *" His Majesty is pleased to Regiment the 15 Battalions of Foot which were raised in 1756 and to direct that they take rank from the time of their Raising in the same manner as if they had been immediately formed into Regiments".*

The effect of the order was to make all 15 regiments senior to the 61st with the result that they assumed the numbers between 61 and 75. Since there could not be two regiments both with the same number 61, Lord Forbes' regiment was redesignated the 76th. Next it came the turn of the 76th Regiment to raise a second battalion. In October 1758 a warrant was issued for a £9,500 advance for a *"2nd Battalion to Lord George Forbes Regiment ordered from Ireland to the coast of Africa"*. In the following year the 2nd Battalion was redesignated the 86th. (It was disbanded in 1763).

In January Lord George Forbes was succeeded as Colonel by Lieutenant General William Rufane. At about the same time the 76th was once again recruited to two battalions. Both battalions served in the siege of Belle Isle (1761), at the taking of Martinique (1762), and were disbanded in 1763 following the signing of the peace treaty at Versailles.

## 76th REGIMENT OF (HIGHLAND) FOOT: 1777 - 1784.

After the end of the Seven Years War in 1763 all regiments junior to the 70th Foot had been disbanded. When the disturbance in America began in 1775 there was once again a need for new regiments, but low pay and the prospect of fighting in what amounted to a civil war did nothing to induce men to enlist. All that changed when France entered the war in 1778 and many new regiments were raised, including several in Scotland. In December 1777 letters of service were granted to Alexander, 1st Lord MacDonald of Slate, empowering him to raise a new regiment, the 76th of (Highland) Foot - often referred to as the 76th (MacDonald) Highlanders. By March 1778 it was 1,086 strong. It spent a year training at Fort George and was then warned for service in America. After a fruitless journey to Jersey to meet what proved to be a non existent French threat, the regiment arrived in America in August 1779 where it was deployed in and around New York. In the absence of Lieutenant Colonel John Macdonnel, who had been taken prisoner before he could assume command, the Regiment was commanded by Major Lord Berridale.

In February 1781 the Regiment was sent south, to Virginia. In May it joined up with the force commanded by Lord Cornwallis and soon distinguished itself in a brush with enemy troops commanded by the Marquis de Lafayette. In the meantime Lord Berridale had handed over command to Major Francis Needham as he had to return to Scotland upon inheriting the title of Earl of Caithness. In October 1781 the 76th was among the regiments forced to surrender at Yorktown. It also had to surrender its colours, which are depicted in a portrait of George Washington in the Metropolitan Museum.

The 76th returned to Scotland after peace was signed in 1783 and was disbanded at Stirling Castle in March 1784.

APPENDIX 8

# Rugby in the Regiment

The rugby playing tradition in the Regiment almost certainly dates from the time when the 33rd and 76th Regiments of Foot were linked together under the Cardwell reforms of 1872. As a part of that process a common depot was established at Halifax in the West Riding of Yorkshire in 1877 and from then on there was a steady recruitment of young men who had played rugby.

The 2nd Battalion was the initiator of serious rugby in the Dukes for, when stationed in South Africa from 1893 to 1896, the XV succeeded in winning the two open challenge cups - the Murray and the York and Lancaster for three years in succession. After a short time in Burma the Battalion was posted to India where, in 1903 and 1905, it won the Calcutta Cup, the premier rugby trophy in that country. In 1907 the Army Rugby Challenge Cup competition was played for the first time and was won by the 2nd Battalion. Meanwhile in India, between 1906 and 1914, the 1st Battalion won all three of the Presidencies' Open Rugby Challenge Cups – those of Calcutta, Madras and Bombay. In all, the 1st Battalion won the Calcutta Cup nine times, the Madras Cup seven and the Bombay on six occasions. In 1914 the 2nd Battalion won the Army Cup for the second time.

In 1923 the 1st Battalion arrived home from Turkey and in this year Second Lieutenant C K T Faithful joined the Battalion. He was an English International and under his leadership the XV began to take shape. He was joined in 1925 by W F Browne who had captained the Sandhurst XV. He led the Irish pack and was capped twelve times for that country.

In 1927 and 1928 the 1st Battalion met the King's Own in the semi-final of the Army Cup. On both occasions the Battalion lost, but, in 1931, under the captaincy of H G P Miles, the Dukes at last won the Cup again. The XV contained seven Army Caps including Corporal George Townend playing at fly-half, even though his ten Army Caps and his England trial were all gained as a forward. The next season saw the Dukes knocked out at an early stage, but in 1933 the Cup was again won. In 1934, although having a very good XV, it was beaten in the semi- final round. From 1935 to 1937 the Battalion was stationed in Malta. In 1938 both F J Reynolds and C F Grieve toured South Africa with the British Lions, however even the possession of these two internationals, and Lieutenant J Harrison, as members of the 1938 Army XV, in addition to Captain C L Troop (England), the 1939 semi-final against the Welch Regiment was lost. During

**1st BATTALION THE DUKE OF WELLINGTON'S REGIMENT (West Riding)**
Winners Army Rugby Cup 1930-31

*Back:* Pte E Humpish, Cpl A Goodwin, Lt. C K T Faithfull, Pte G Annesley, Pte J Stork, Pte E Bentley, Pte L Eyre
2/Lt W H Summers, 2/Lt B W Reynolds, Lt J H Dalrymple  Lt H G P Miles, Cpl G Townend, 2?lt C L Troop, L/Cpl F Dowas
*Front:* L/Cpl M Reid    L/Cpl J Robinson

1st Round v 2nd Scots Gds 75-0.  2nd Round v 2nd King's Regt. 46-0.  3rd Round v 2nd Bord Regt. 3-0;
4th Round v 1st Cheshire Regt. 21-0;  Semi Final v 2nd Cameron Hrs. 36-0;  Final v Training Battn. R.E. 21-0.
TOTAL POINTS – For 202;  Against 0.

this time the 2nd Battalion was stationed in India where it won the Calcutta and All India Championship in 1937, having been runners up in 1930, 1933 and 1934.

After the end of the second world war all battalions of the Regiment were soon again playing rugby. The 1st Battalion, captained by Major T F Huskisson, a pre-war English international, had a particularly good season in the Middle East in 1945/46. However, it was not until the late 1940s that the 1st Battalion, by then stationed at Strensall, had a well-balanced XV of youth and the not-so-young. Second Lieutenants Hardy and Shuttleworth were just starting their rugby careers and Private Turnbull - the first of the Dukes' great players from the Rugby League, who was to be followed in later years by Saville, Scroby, Field, Curry and Renilson, had also just joined. In 1949 D W Shuttleworth won the first of his twenty-two Army Caps, while in 1952 Hardy and Shuttleworth played together for England in the Calcutta Cup match. This was an army first - the half-backs in an international coming from the same regiment. With D S Gilbert-Smith being capped for Scotland the XV now boasted three internationals.

# APPENDIX 8. RUGBY IN THE REGIMENT

Competition in the Army Cup was now very fierce as the larger corps, notably the Royal Signals, were taking an interest and the combination of their larger establishments with a fair measure of judicious internal posting ensured some titanic struggles for the Battalion. However, the latter part of the 1950s provided three good seasons in Northern Ireland; under the captaincy of D W Shuttleworth, the Ulster Junior and Senior Leagues were won and the Dukes were also runners-up in the Ulster Cup and, more significantly, the Army Cup was won in 1958 for the first time since the war. As a tribute Ulster put out a full Province side for the Regiment's farewell match at Ravenhill which was won by the Dukes. A powerful player towards the end of this period was Captain Michael Campbell-Lamerton who later, in 1961, gained the first of his twenty-three caps for Scotland as well as touring South Africa with the British Lions.

The team foundations, so well laid in Ireland, ensured a brilliant series of successes between 1964 and 1968 when the Army Cup was won for four years running, under the captaincy first of W R Mundell and then of I P Reid, a holder of ten Army Caps won in these years. It was at this time that a group of soldiers from Fiji, headed by Waqabaca, joined and played for the Battalion. In 1969 the Battalion moved to Hong Kong where it beat the New Zealand Regiment twice to win the FARELF Cup and having eight Regimental players in the colony side for the Asian Cup Competitions. Returning to England in 1972 the Army Cup was won again and Sergeant Dickens achieved a Regimental record by winning his fifth Army Cup winner's medal.

From that day the Dukes have remained a major force in army rugby. The successful squad of the 1960s was eventually replaced by several good young officers and soldiers who ensured that whenever the Battalion was in the country, and not on an operational tour in Ulster, the XV was the team that had to be beaten in the Army Cup. Army Cup wins were recorded in 1975, 1978, 1979 and 1981, with runners-up medals in 1976, 1977, 1983 and 1989. Seventeen Dukes were awarded Army Caps in this period and Captain Harvey, a combined services player, also captained the Army XV. While the core of the XV has been largely based in the officers' mess, many soldiers have represented the Battalion. Two in particular are worthy of special note: RSM Robinson (later Major and Quartermaster) joined the Battalion in the early 1960s as a promising young centre. He played continually for the Battalion for over twenty years, gained three Army Caps and coached both the Battalion and Army XV. CSM Williams, with seventeen Army Caps, was perhaps the most feared and respected wing forward in the Army for over ten years.

The Dukes having won the Army Cup fourteen times - more than any other regiment - and being runners-up seven times, it can be said that the Duke of Wellington's and rugby are synonymous to all in the British Army.

## ARMY CUP: WINNERS

| | |
|---|---|
| 1907 | 2nd Bn v Training Bn RE - 5pts to nil |
| 1914 | 2nd Bn v 1st Bn Gloucestershire Regt - 6pts to 3 |
| 1931 | 1st Bn v Training Bn RE - 21pts to nil |
| 1933 | 1st Bn v 2nd Bn Leicestershire Regt - 19pts to 8 |
| 1958 | 1st Bn v 1st (BR) Corps Troops Coln RASC - 23pts to 5 |
| 1965 | 1st Bn v 1st Bn Welsh Guards - 11pts to 6 |
| 1966 | 1st Bn v 63rd Para Squadron RCT - 9pts to 3 |
| 1967 | 1st Bn v 7th Regt RHA - 14pts to 3 |
| 1968 | 1st Bn v 1st Bn Welsh Guards - 20pts to 3 |
| 1972 | 1st Bn v 1st Bn Royal Regt of Wales - 15pts to 8 |
| 1975 | 1st Bn v 3rd BAPD RAOC - 12pts to 6 |
| 1978 | 1st Bn v 8th Signal Regt Royal Signals - 13pts to 12 |
| 1979 | 1st Bn v 1st Bn Royal Regt of Wales - 12pts to 7 |
| 1981 | 1st Bn v 7th Regt RHA - 20pts to nil |

## ARMY CUP: RUNNERS UP

The 1st Battalion was beaten in the final in:
- 1960 by 1st Bn KOSB - 9pts to nil
- 1961 by 1st Bn KOSB - 6pts to 3
- 1962 by 1st Bn Welsh Guards - 9pts to 6
- 1976 by 1st Bn Royal Regt of Wales - 10pts to 4
- 1977 by 1st Bn Royal Regt of Wales - 22pts to 9
- 1983 by 21st Engineer Regt RE - 8pts to 4
- 1989 by 7th Signal Regt Royal Signals - 20pts to 7

## ARMY CAPS

List of Duke's who have represented the Army against the Royal Navy. Royal Air Force or French Army

| NAME | YEAR FIRST CAPPED | NUMBER OF CAPS |
|---|---|---|
| GW Oliphant | 1914 | 1 |
| WF Browne | 1924 | 16 |
| CKT Faithful | 1924 | 10 |
| E Dowas | 1927 | 2 |
| G Townend | 1928 | 10 |
| BW Reynolds | 1931 | 3 |
| CL Troop | 1931 | 7 |

# APPENDIX 8. RUGBY IN THE REGIMENT

| NAME | YEAR FIRST CAPPED | NUMBER OF CAPS |
|---|---|---|
| GW Annesley | 1931 | 1 |
| E Bentley | 1931 | 1 |
| HGP Miles | 1931 | 1 |
| FJ Reynolds | 1937 | 3 |
| CF Grieve | 1938 | 2 |
| J Harrison | 1938 | 3 |
| DW Shuttleworth | 1949 | 22 |
| DE Isles | 1950 | 2 |
| EMP Hardy | 1950 | 11 |
| PJ Taylor | 1951 | 3 |
| DS Gilbert-Smith | 1952 | 12 |
| B Saville | 1958 | 1 |
| SR Arnold | 1959 | 2 |
| J Scroby | 1959 | 2 |
| P J Davies | 1959 | 4 |
| MJ Campbell-Lamerton | 1960 | 13 |
| C Renilson | 1961 | 2 |
| IP Reid | 1962 | 10 |
| T Waqabaca | 1963 | 4 |
| CJG Edwards | 1964 | 9 |
| CJW Gilbert | 1966 | 7 |
| AR Redwood-Davies | 1971 | 1 |
| PJ Bird | 1972 | 1 |
| M Cuss | 1973 | 4 |
| JM Thorn | 1973 | 2 |
| NJ Newell | 1974 | 1 |
| P Robinson | 1975 | 3 |
| TC Sinclair | 1975 | 4 |
| P Elwell | 1976 | 1 |
| GOW Williams | 1967 | 17 |
| WAN Atkinson | 1977 | 4 |
| CF Grieve | 1977 | 1 |
| GD Shuttleworth | 1981 | 1 |
| A Kay | 1983 | 2 |
| CA Harvey | 1983 | 9 |
| HA Kelly | 1986 | 4 |
| G Knight | 1989 | 3 |
| AJ Wheatley | 1989 | 2 |
| RA Preston | 1990 | 2 |
| MB Taylor | 1990 | 4 |
| CM Buss | 1991 | 2 |
| SC Pinder | 1992 | 2 |

## INTERNATIONAL HONOURS

### ENGLAND

| | | | |
|---|---|---|---|
| WC Wilson | 1907 | 2 | |
| CKT Faithfull | 1924 | 3 | |
| CL Troop | 1933 | 2 | |
| T F Huskisson | 1937 | 8 | |
| FJ Reynolds | 1937 | 3 | |
| EMP Hardy | 1951 | 3 | |
| DW Shuttleworth | 1951 | 2 | President of the Rugby Football Union 1985/86 |

### IRELAND

| | | |
|---|---|---|
| WF Browne | 1925 | 12 |

### SCOTLAND

| | | |
|---|---|---|
| CF Grieve | 1935 | 1 |
| DS Gilbert-Smith | 1952 | 1 |
| MJ Campbell-Lamerton | 1961 | 23 |

### BRITISH LIONS

South Africa-1938
CF Grieve
FJ Reynolds

South Africa-1962
MJ Campbell-Lamerton

New Zealand and Australia-1966
MJ Campbell-Lamerton (Captain)

APPENDIX 9

# The Regiment's Chapels, Museum, Journal and Alliances

**The Chapels.**
The Regimental Chapel in York Minster was dedicated on 12 May 1923 as a memorial to over 8,000 men of The Duke of Wellington's Regiment (West Riding) who died in the First World War 1914-1919 and to other past members of the Regiment. Originally dedicated as All Saints Chapel by Archbishop Bowet of York in 1413 this chapel, like others, was dismantled at the time of the Reformation around 1550 and remained unused until restored for the Regiment in 1923. Memorials to those killed in the Crimea, Abyssinia and South Africa were moved into the chapel from other areas of the Minster. Roll of Honour books listing those killed in both world wars and Korea are also in the chapel. The framed remains of colours on display in the chapel are the first stand presented to the 76th in 1787 and the Honorary Colours presented to the 76th in 1830. Other colours of the Regiment, originally laid up in the chapel but now unfit for display, are lodged in a container behind the altar.

An annual Regimental Service is held in the Minster, normally on the nearest Saturday to All Saints Day.

A Regimental Chapel in Halifax Parish Church was dedicated on 22 September 1951 as a memorial to the 1,200 officers and men of the Regiment who died in the Second World War. A Roll of Honour Book lists the names of those killed during the war. Later the names of those killed in the Korean war were added. The colours in the chapel include the remains of those carried at Waterloo and the Crimea and the stand presented to the 33rd in 1761. Also located in the Church are the memorials to eleven members of the 3rd (Militia) Battalion who lost their lives in the Boer war, the 1,371 members of the 1/4th and 2/4th Battalions who died in the First World War and the 748 members of the 9th (Service) Battalion who died during that war.

**The Regimental Collect**

*" O Lord of Hosts who did thrice bid the leader of Thine ancient people*
*to be strong and of good courage, and didst promise him good success,*

*grant that The Duke of Wellington's Regiment may ever prosper in obedience to Thy law and in Thee alone do valiantly, so that we may tread down the enemies of our souls, for Jesus Christ our Saviour's sake."*

**The Regimental Museum.**
The Museum was first established at the Depot, Halifax, in 1921. Since then it has, for one reason or another been moved six times. Since 1960 it has been established at Bankfield, one of the museums of the Calderdale Metropolitan Borough Council. It was comprehensively refurbished in 1984/86 to take advantage of more modern display techniques. In 1991 it was formally registered by the Museums and Galleries Commission as complying with the standards laid down in the commission's guidelines for museums in the United Kingdom.

Associated with the Museum are the Regimental Archives. These were established at the Depot in 1929 when a filing cupboard was sufficient for their contents. By 1992 a separate room was required to accommodate all the records, books, maps, photographs, official war diaries and personal papers then held by the Regiment.

**The Regimental Journal.**
Early Regimental magazines or notes were produced on a battalion basis. In 1886 the 1st Battalion, then serving in India, published a monthly paper, *The Duke of Wellington's Journal*. It is not recorded when publication ceased, but it was probably when the Battalion left India in 1888. In 1897 the 1st Battalion started publication of a quarterly magazine called *The Havercake Lad*. Publication stopped when the Battalion was ordered to South Africa. It was started up again in 1905 but finally lapsed in 1907. In 1921 Brigadier General P A Turner produced *Regimental Notes* with news of all battalions. In 1924 it was decided to replace the notes by a regimental magazine and the first issue of *The Iron Duke* was published in May 1925. It has been produced without interruption ever since, though now reduced to three issues a year as opposed to the four a year up to 1967.

**Alliances and affiliations.**

**Canada:** From 1919-1936 the Regiment had an alliance with the North Saskatchewan Regiment (later renamed the Yorktown Regiment). Lieutenant Colonel F Paulett DSO MC of the Saskatchewan Regiment had commanded the 2nd Battalion of the Dukes during the latter months of the First World war. The alliance ceased when the Yorktown Regiment was disbanded in 1936.

In May 1953 the Regiment formed an alliance with Les Voltigeurs de Quebec, a reserve, French speaking unit of the Canadian Army. The Regiment was formed in 1862.
**Australia:** In 1929 the Regiment formed an alliance with the 33rd Battalion (The New England Regiment). However, very soon afterwards the battalion was placed in suspended animation. It was reformed in 1933 and the alliance continued until the 33rd Battalion was disbanded after the end of the 2nd World War.

## APPENDIX 9. THE REGIMENT'S CHAPELS, MUSEUM, JOURNAL AND ALLIANCES

**Pakistan:** Since 1966 the Regiment has been allied with the 10th Battalion the Baloch Regiment. The battalion which has undergone many changes of title was formed in 1844 as the Balooch Battalion. From 1867 to 1868 it took part in the Abyssinia campaign alongside the 33rd Regiment.

**Royal Navy**

**HMS Iron Duke:** In 1923 the 1st Battalion was among the reinforcements sent to Chanak in Turkey. Also sent there was the 25,000 ton battleship, HMS Iron Duke. An affiliation between the ship and the Dukes was established, which lasted until the ship was decommissioned in 1945.

**HMS Cleopatra:** A cruiser of 5,700 tons whose pennant number was 33. In 1947 the ship was affiliated with the Regiment. The affiliation was of short duration as the ship was decommissioned soon afterwards.

**HMS York:** In 1985 an affiliation was formed with HMS York, a stretched type 42 destroyer. This affiliation will cease in 1993 when HMS Iron Duke, a frigate of the 'Duke' class is due to be commissioned and when an affiliation with the Regiment will be formed.

APPENDIX 10

# The Old Comrades

At a meeting in the Union Jack Club, London, on 4 October 1912, attended by the Colonel of the Regiment, Lieutenant General H E Belfield, representatives of both regular battalions, the Depot and past and serving members of the Regiment, it was decided to form an Old Comrades Association. This was to foster esprit-de-corps, bring together old comrades and serving members of the Regiment, and to establish a dinner club. It was also agreed that the means of providing aid to ex-members of the Regiment in need should be investigated. The annual subscription was set at 6d ($2^1/_2$ pence) and it was stipulated that the cost of the annual dinner should not exceed 2s 6d (25 pence) per head, exclusive of liquor. This organisation was formalised in 1926 under the title The Old Comrades Association (33rd and 76th Regiment and 1st and 2nd Battalions The Duke of Wellington's Regiment (West Riding) in a Trust Deed.

Following the end of the First World War most of the Territorial and Service battalions formed Old Comrades Associations of their own. At the end of the Second World War an attempt was made to merge the funds of the various associations. However, as this did not meet with the approval of the Charity Commissioners it was decided, instead, to form a new Regimental Association to embrace all who had served in the Regiment, or their dependants, irrespective of in which battalion they had served. The Association came into being in November 1945 and thereafter became the principal old comrades association within the Regiment. All subscription and legacies, unless otherwise directed, are credited to the benevolent funds of the Association, including those received through the Day's Pay Scheme under which serving soldiers are encouraged to contribute a day's pay per year. Applications for assistance are processed by a committee at Regimental Headquarters, who act on behalf of the Trustees of the Association. Other funds for which the Trustees are responsible are:

> The Mitchell Trust Fund; For the assistance of those disabled in the First World War and secondly those resident in Halifax.
> The McGuire Bate Trust Fund; to assist officers serving or who have served in the Regiment or their widows.
> The War Memorial Fund; for the renovation and furnishing of the two Regimental chapels and for assistance in the education of children of members or ex-members of the Regiment.

# APPENDIX 10. THE OLD COMRADES

Branches of the Regimental Association, which usually meet once a month, are located in most of the major towns in the West Riding of Yorkshire as well as in York, Sheffield and London. Annual dinners are held in the West Riding and in London. No better example of the atmosphere at such reunions can have been written than that given by J B Priestley in his book *English Journey*. In October 1933 he was present at the 10th Battalion re-union dinner in Bradford, attended by 270 former members of the Battalion:

*The re-union battalion dinner which had brought me here when I ought to have been continuing my journey elsewhere, was held at a tavern on Saturday night. The battalion was the 10th Duke of Wellington's, of the 23rd Division, which did good work in France and then in the later stage of war did equally good work on the Italian Front.*

*I was with this battalion when it was first formed when I was a private just turned twenty: but I left it as a casualty in the summer of 1916 and never saw it again, being afterwards transferred to another regiment. The very secretary who wrote asking me to attend this dinner was unknown to me, having joined the battalion after I had left it. So I did not expect to see many there who had belonged to the old original lot, because I knew only too well that a large number of them, some my friends, had been killed. But the thought of meeting again the few I would remember, the men who had shared with me those training camps in 1914 and the first half of 1915 and those trenches in the autumn and winter of 1915 and the spring of 1916, was very exciting. There were bound to be a few there from my old platoon. Number eight. It was a platoon with a character of its own.*

*When the battalion was swaggering along, you could not get Eight Platoon to sing: it marched in grim, disapproving silence. But there came a famous occasion when the rest of the battalion, exhausted and blindly limping along, had not a note left in it: gone now were the boasts about returning to Tipperary, the loud enquiries about the Lady Friend: the battalion whacked and dumb. It was then a strange sound was heard coming from the stumbling ranks of B Company, a sound never caught before: not very melodious perhaps nor light-hearted, but miraculous: Number Eight Platoon was singing. Well, that was my old platoon, and I was eagerly looking forward to seeing a few old remaining members of it.*

*Never have I seen a tavern stairs or a tavern upstairs so crowded, so tremendously alive with roaring masculinity, as I did that night. Most of the faces were strange to me, but here and there, miraculously, was a face that was not only instantly familiar but that at once succeeded in recalling a whole vanished epoch, as if I had spent long years with its owner in some earlier incarnation. We sat down jammed together, in a dining room that can never have held more people in all its existence. It was not full, it was bursting. We could hardly lift the roast beef and apple tart to our mouths. Under the coloured-paper decorations, we sweated like bulls. The ale went down sizzling. But we were happy, no doubt about that. We roared at one another across the narrowest of tables.*

*The toast in memory of the dead, which we drank at the end of the dinner, would have been very moving, only unfortunately when we were all standing up, raising our glasses and silent, there came from a very tinny piano in the far corner of the room what sounded to me like a polka very badly played. I tried to think, solemnly, tenderly, about my dead comrades, but this atrocious polka was terribly in the way. I sat down, bewildered. "Damn fool played it all wrong", growled the major, our chairman in my ear. "Should have been much slower. Regimental march y'know". That little episode was just like my life; and I suppose that is why I am at heart a comic writer. You stand up to toast your dead comrades: the moment is solemn and grand; and then the pianist must turn the regimental march into something idiotically frivolous, and ruins the occasion.*

*I had arranged to meet, in a little ante-room, the survivors of my original platoon, and as soon as I decently could, I escaped from the press of warriors in the big room, to revisit my own past. There were about eight of us present, and we ordered in some drinks and settled down to remember aloud. I had not seen any of these fellows for seventeen years. I knew them all, of course, and they seemed little older. The difference was that before they had all been soldiers, whereas now their respective status in civilian life set its mark upon them, and now one was a clerk, another a tram-conductor, another a mill-hand, and so forth.*

*As a figure after figure, comic and tragic, came looming up through the fog of years, as place after place we had been in caught the light again, our talk became more and more eager and louder, until we shouted and laughed in triumph, as one always does when Time seems to be suffering a temporary defeat. Frensham, Aldershot, Folkestone, Maidstone, Bully Grenay. Neuve Chapelle, Souchez - how they returned to us! Once again the water was rising around our gum boots. We remembered the fantastic places; that trench which ran in front of a grave yard, where the machine gun bullets used to ricochet off the tombstones: that first sight of Vimy Ridge in the snow, like a mountain of despair. We recalled to one another the strange coincidences and dark premonitions: poor melancholy B, who muttered, "I'll be lying out there tonight", and was a dead man that very night; grim Sergeant W, who said to the draft. "This is where you can expect to get your head blown off", and had his own head shattered by a rifle-grenade within three hours. And little Paddy O, who had always seemed such a wisp of a chap, with everything about him drooping, who looked the same as ever, ready to drop at any moment though he never dropped and the Central Powers must have spent hundreds of thousands of marks trying to kill him, little Paddy, I say, came close to me, finished his beer and asked me, stammeringly as ever, if I remembered sending him from the front line for some water for the platoon on a summer morning in 1916. "Nay" he stammered, "I wasn't gone for more then t-ten minutes, and when I c-come back, where you'd been, Jack lad, there was n-nobbut a bloody big hole and I n-never set eyes on you again till to-night". And it was true. I had sent him away on a ten minutes errand: immediately afterwards a giant mortar had exploded in the very entrance to the little dug-out where I was dividing up the platoon rations; I had been rushed away, and was gone before he returned; and it had taken us more than seventeen years to find one another again.*

# BIBLIOGRAPHY

**Histories of The Duke of Wellington's Regiment (West Riding).**

| | |
|---|---|
| Lee. A | *History of the 33rd Foot.* (Jarrold and Sons 1922.) |
| Hayden. F | *Historical records of the 76th (Hindoostan) Regiment 1787- 1881.* (The Johnsons Head 1908.) |
| Bruce.B. | *History of The Duke of Wellington's Regiment (1st and 2nd Battalions) 1881-1923.* (The Medici Society 1927.) |
| Barclay. C | *History of The Duke of Wellington's Regiment 1919-1952.* (William Clowes and Son. 1953.) |
| Lunt. J. | *The Duke of Wellington's Regiment (West Riding).* (Leo Cooper 1971) |
| Moore.N | *Records of the 3rd Battalion The Duke of Wellington's Regiment (West Riding) 1760-1910.* (Gale and Polden 1910.) |
| Bales. P | *History of the 1/4th Battalion The Duke of Wellington's Regiment (West Riding). 1914-1919.* (Edward Mortimer 1920.) |
| Pattison. F | *Recollections of Waterloo.* (The author. 1871) |
| Wilcox. W | *Chindit column 76.* (Longman's Green. 1945) |
| Barker.A | *Fortune Favours the Brave. The Hook, Korea, 1953* (Leo Cooper 1974.) |
| Anonymous | *History of the 76th (Hindoostan) Regiment* (Published by the Regiment. Secunderabad 1875)) |

*The Iron Duke,* journal of The Duke of Wellington's Regiment (1925-1992)
All quotations from the letters, diaries and reports of members of the Regiment are from articles published in the journal or in earlier Regimental histories.
Manuscripts: Digests of services of the 33rd and 76th Regiments. Histories of the 8th, 9th and 10th Battalions during the First World War

**Other sources.**

| | |
|---|---|
| Aldington. R | *Wellington* (William Heinemann 1946) |
| Ascoli. D. | *A companion to the British Army 1660-1983* (Harrap.1983.) |
| Atteridge A | *History of the 17th (Northern) Division.* (Robert Maclehose. 1929) |
| Baker. A. | *Battle Honours of the British and Commonwealth armies.* (Ian Allan 1986.) |
| Barthorp. M | *The armies of Britain 1485-1980.* (National Army Museum. 1980.) |
| Barthorp. M | *Heroes of the Crimea. Battles of Inkerman and Balaclava* (Blandford. 1991.) |
| Berry. R | *History of volunteer infantry 1794-1874* (Simkin, Marshall, Hamilton, Kent. 1903) |
| Beevor. A | *Inside the British Army.* (Chatto and Windus. 1990) |
| Blackmore. H | *British military firearms 1650- 1850.* (Jenkins. 1961) |
| Bush. E | *Gallipoli.* ( George Allen and Unwin. 1978) |
| Callahan R. | *Burma 1942-1945.* (Davis Poynter. 1978.) |
| Cole. D and Priestley. E | *British Military History 1660-1936.* (Sifton Praed. 1936.) |

| | |
|---|---|
| D'Este. C | *Fatal Decision. Anzio and the battle for Rome.* (Harper Collins. 1991) |
| Dalton. C | *English army lists and commission registers 1661-1714* |
| Devenish J (ed) | *War and Sport in India 1802-1806.* |
| Dictionary of National Biography. | |
| Farmer. G | *The rise and development of military music.* (William Reeves. 1912) |
| Forrest D. | *Tiger of Mysore. The life and death of Tipu Sultan.* (Chatto and Windus. 1970) |
| Fortescue. J | *History of the British Army* (13 volumes). (Macmillan. 1910-1929.) |
| Gatliff. J. | *Stations Gentlemen* (Faber and Faber 1938) |
| Gowing. T | *Voice from the ranks.* (Folio Society. 1954) |
| Graves. R | *Proceed Sergeant Lamb.* (Methuen. 1941 |
| Guedella. P | *The Duke.* (The Reprint Society. 1931) |
| Hay. G | *The constitutional force.* |
| Hayter. T (ed) | *An 18th century Secretary at War. The papers of William, Viscount Barrington.* (Army Records Society. 1988) |
| Haythornwaite.P | *Wellington's military machine.* (Spellmount. 1989) |
| Hibbert. C | *The destruction of Lord Raglan.* (Longmans. 1961) |
| Houlding. J | *Fit for service. Training in the British Army 1715-1795.* (OUP. 1981) |
| Jackson. B | *Notes and reminiscences of a Staff Officer relating to Waterloo and St Helena.* (John Murray. 1903) |
| Longford. E | *Wellington. The years of the sword.* (World Books. 1971). |
| Lunt. J. | *'A hell of a licking'. The retreat from Burma, 1941-42* (Collins. 1986) |
| Luttrell. N | *A brief historical relation of State affairs from September 1768 - April 1714.* (Oxford 1857) |
| Macksey. P | *The war for America. 1775-1783.* (Longmans. 1964) |
| McLaren. J | *The History of Army Rugby* (Army RFU. 1986) |
| Magnus. P | *Kitchener. Portrait of an Imperialist.* (John Murray. 1958.) |
| Milne. S | *Standards and Colours in the Army. 1661-1881.* (Goodall & Suddick. 1893) |
| Norman. C. | *Battle Honours of the British Army* (John Murray. 1911.) |
| Pakenham. T | *The Boer War.* (Weidenfeld and Nicholson. 1979) |
| Palmer. A | *Dictionary of twentieth-century history 1900 -1991.* (Penguin. 1992) |
| Pickup. K | *West Yorkshire Rifle Volunteers 1859- 1887.* (The Author. 1978) |
| Podmore. A | *Yorkshire Volunteers 1859-1986* (The Regiment 1986) and other unpublished material |
| Powell. G. | *The History of the Green Howards* (Arms and Armour. 1992) |
| Priestley. J. | *English Journey* (Heinemann. 1949) |
| Robinson. E | *History of the Devonshire Regiment. 1685-1815.* (The Regiment. 1988) |
| Ross. C (ed) | *Correspondence of Charles, First Marquis Cornwallis 1859* |
| Savory. R | *His Britannic Majesty's Army in Germany during the Seven Years War.* (OUP.1966) |

| | | |
|---|---|---|
| Selby. J | *The Road to Yorktown* (Book Club Associates. 1976) | |
| Shipp. J | *Memoirs of the Extraordinary military career of John Shipp late Lieutenant in HM's 87th Regiment.* (1829) | |
| Slim. W | *Defeat into Victory.* (Cassell.1961) | |

Society for Army Historical Research. Journal:

| | | |
|---|---|---|
| | Atkinson. C | *Marlborough's sieges*    Vol. 13 |
| | | *More light on Almanza* Vol. 25 |
| | | *Brihuega. 1710*    Vol. 21 |
| | | *A Royal Dragoon in the Spanish Succession war.* Ed. Special publication No. 5 |
| | | *Gleanings from the PRO on Jenkins ear, Austrian succession and the '45.* Vol. 22 |
| | Burne. A | *Cornwallis at Yorktown* Vol. I7 |
| | Cleare. G | *County names for regiments 1782*    Vol. 36 |
| | Fyers. E | *Operations in Pennsylvania 1777* Vol. 8 |
| | Leslie. N | *The succession of Colonels of the British Army. From 1660 to the present day* Special publication. No. 11(1974) |
| | Pimlott. J | *Raising four regiments for India1787- 88.* Vol. 52 |

| | |
|---|---|
| Spencer.E(ed) | *Memoirs of William Hickey. Vol 1V* (Hurst & Blackett. 1948) |
| Stanhope. P | *Notes of conversations with the Duke of Wellington 1831- 1851.* (OUP.1888) |
| Trevelyan. G | *England of Queen Anne.* (Longmans, Green. 1959) |
| Walton. C | *History of the British Standing Army.* (Harrison and Sons. 1894.) |
| Wellesley. M | *The man Wellington through the eyes of those who knew him* (Constable. 1937) |
| Wellington, Ist Duke of. | Wellington papers, Southampton University |
| Wellington, 2nd Duke of(ed) | *Supplementary despatches, correspondence and memoranda of Arthur, Duke of Wellington* (John Murray 1858-1872) |
| Woodham-Smith C | *The Reason Why.* (Constable 1953) |
| Wryall E | *History of the 62nd (West Riding) Division. 1914-1919* (John Lane) |
| Young. P and Lawford. Js | *History of the British Army.* (Arthur Barker. 1970) |

# INDEX

*With a few exceptions, ranks shown are those ultimately attained and not necessarily current at the date of reference.*

Abbéville 287
Abercromby, Gen, Sir J, 108
Abercromby, Gen, R 83, 84, 93, 94, 95, 109
Abyssinia Campaign (1867-1868) 182-191
    Annesley Bay 184, 185
    Dildi 188, 191
    Magdaia 184, 185, 188, 190, 191, 368, 393
    Senafe 185, 186
    formations
        1st Bde 189
        2nd Bde 188, 189
    killed and wounded 189, 190
Ackworth, Col, L R
Aden 205, 340, 342
Adventure training 342
Affiliations with the Royal Navy
    HMS Cleopatra 428
    HMS Iron Duke 265, 428
    HMS York 428
3rd Afghan war (1919) 263-265
    Spin Baldak 264
    11 Brigade 264
    57 Brigade 264
    killed and wounded 264
Afghanistan, Emir of 263
Afxentiou, see *Cyprus 1956-1957*
Agra, see *1st & 2nd Mahratta wars*
Ahemednagar 322
Airey, Maj Gen R 160
Aisne, river 236, 246, 282
Akyab island 311
Albert medal, 401
Aldershot 191, 267, 275, 276, 353, 356, 370
Alexander, F-M Earl of 268, 270, 273, 280, 293, 299, 302, 307, 308
Alcantara,
    see *war of Spanish succession*
Algeria 289
Alison, Gen, Sir A 204
Allardice, Lt Col, J M D 203, 390
Alliances with other regiments
    Australia 277, 428
    Canada 277, 428
    Pakistan 428
Allied Command Europe Mobile Force (Land) (AMF(L)) 363
Ally Ghur –
    see *1st and 2nd Mahratta wars*
Alma – see *Crimean war*
Almanza –
    See *war of Spanish succession*
Amalgamations
    33rd & 76th Regiments 201-203
    1st & 2nd Battalions 99, 324, 371, 390, 415
    3rd & 4th (Militia) Battalions 204
    5th & 7th Battalions 327, 410

3rd & 4th Battalions Yorkshire Volunteers 410
American war of Independence (1775-1783) 58-72
    Brandywine 63
    Brooklyn Heights 60
    Camden 66, 67
    Charleston 59, 65, 73
    Fort Washington 61
    Freehold 64
    Germantown 63, 79, 381
    Guilford Court House 68, 69
    Verplanks 65
    White Plains 61
    Yorktown 59, 70, 72, 73, 367, 378, 412
    formations
        3rd Bde
        4th Bde 63, 66
        Lt Col J Webster's Bde 66
        Lt Col J Yorke's Bde 70
    killed and wounded 59, 60, 61, 63, 67, 69, 72
2nd American war (1812-1814)
    Plattsburg 134, 381, 383
    Maj Gen Robinson's Bde 134
Ancram, Gen, Earl of, 42, 56
Annesley Bay –
    see *Abyssinia campaign*
Antwerp 129, 131, 139, 142, 318
Anzio, see *2nd World war*
Arakan 311, 322
Arbuthnot, Lt Gen, Sir R 198, 382
Archer, Lt Col, J 26, 389
Archives, see *Museum*
Arikera, see *3rd Mysore war*
Armitage, Col, F R 321, 391
Armstrong, Lt Col, C D 290, 390
Army reforms
    County names 74, 75
    Cardwell 193, 194, 195, 201, 323
    Childers 201
    Duke of Cambridge 201
    Haldane 229
    Localisation scheme 194, 200, 201
    "Geddes axe" 262
    Hore-Belisha 272, 273, 277
    "Options for change" 363, 410
Arnhem 318, 320
Arno river 300
Arras, see *1st World war*
Astorga 127
Atatürk, K, 265
Atkins, Pte, Thomas 153
Atkinson C T 18, 24
Attila line, see *Cyprus 1974*
Aubers Ridge 240
Austin, Maj, R E 334, 335, 391
Austria 232, 259, 260, 279

Austrian succession, war of (1742-1748) 25-38
    Dettingen 28, 29, 30, 31, 33, 34, 377
    Fontenoy 34, 35, 36, 37, 38, 39, 377
    Lauffeld 38, 377
    Rocoux 37
    killed and wounded 31, 36, 38

Bailes, Cpl, J S 329
Bailey, Maj, P R S 361
Baird, Gen, Sir D 102, 103, 126, 127
Baker, Maj, S E 325
Balaclava, see *Crimean war*
Bally, Lt Col, W 205, 390
Baluchistan 264
Banana Ridge, see *2nd World war*
Band and Drums, see *Appendix 6*
Bangalore, see *3rd Mysore war*
Bankfield Museum, See *Museum*
Barton, Ensign, B J (later Col) 184
Barton, Lt Col, B J, 236, 237, 239, 240
Battle honours 24, 32, 48, 88, 103, 111, 126, 128, 133, 152, 178, 182, 191, 204, 218, 223, 240, 246, 260, 265, 289, 291, 294, 300, 301, 307, 309, 316, 318, 337, 344, 369, 367, 370, 371, 372, 405, 417
Bayonne 133
Beard, Lt Col, E C 280, 390
Belfast, see *Northern Ireland*
Belfield, Lt Gen, Sir H 211, 231, 265, 276, 277, 369, 385, 391, 430
Belize 344, 350
Bellamy, WO II, D 356
Benjamin, Ensign, H 52
Benson, Maj, P P 289, 293 294, 298, 299
Bergen-op-Zoom 367
    See also *Holland (1813-1814)*
Bergin, Pte, J VC 190, 191, 393
Best, Lt Col, T A D 249
Béthune 236, 287
Béthune river 236, 288, 289
Bhurtpore –
    see *1st & 2nd Mahratta wars*
Bisley 328, 342
"Black week" see *Boer war*
Blake, Lt Col, F R 155, 156, 157, 160, 168, 368, 389
Blandford 41
Blewitt, Col, E 391
Bligh, Lt Gen, T 37, 43, 44
Bloemfontein 216, 217, 218, 223, 224, 225
Blücher, Marshal (Prussian) 143, 147, 151

436

Boer war (1899-1902) 214-228
    "Black Week" 216
    "Kitchener's Kopje" 222
    Ladysmith 216
    Paardeberg 218, 223
    Kimberley, relief of 216, 217, 218
    Mafeking relief of 225
    Rhenoster Kop 225, 226, 227
    formations
        Cavalry Div 216
        6 Div 216, 217, 218, 219, 220, 224
        7 Div 223
        9 Div 217, 218, 219, 223
        13 Bde 216, 218, 219, 220, 222
        18 Bde 219
        killed and wounded 218, 223, 225, 227, 228
Bokstel, see *Netherlands campaign, 1793-1795*
Bombay 83, 98, 181, 182, 193, 382
Borwell, 2nd/Ltd, D I 332
Boswell, J 53n
Bourlon Wood 149, 250
Boutflower, Lt Col, E C 264
Boyes, Capt, W 113
Bradford, Brig, R B 249
Bradley, L/Cpl, R 352
Brandywine, see *American war of Independence*
Bray, Brig Gen, R N 242, 244, 262, 267, 391
Bray, Gen, Sir R 386, 345, 349, 353, 373
Bray, Brig, M R N 345, 355, 390
Breda 93, 140
Brewster, Lt Col H C 390
Brihuega – see *war of Spanish succession*
British Army of the Rhine (BAOR) 328, 357
British Expeditionary Force (BEF) 233, 279
British Honduras, see *Belize*
British South Africa Company 209
Brooklyn Heights, see *American war of Independence*
Brown, Gen, Sir G 1160, 164, 174
Brown, Cpl, P 342
Brown, Capt, W F 421, 424, 426
Browning, Capt, J S 247
Brunswick, Hereditary Prince of
Brussels 33, 36, 233, 283,318
Bucknall, Lt, H A R 281
Buller, Brig. Gen, 160
Bunbury, Brig, F R St P 328, 331, 332, 334, 335, 336, 337, 339, 390
Bunbury, Capt, H W 154, 155

Bulford 359, 361
Burnand, Lt Col, N G 265, 390
Burnett, Lt Col J C 267, 391
Bülow, Gen, (Prussian) 139
Burton, Pte R *VC* 301, 397
Byng, F-M, 1st Viscount 248, 249, 250, 251

Cambrai, see *1st World war*
Campaigning conditions
    extreme cold 51, 95, 127, 172, 188, 258, 260, 345
    extreme heat 64, 81, 118, 236, 265, 268, 272, 308, 311, 315
    rain, floods and mud 15, 64, 69, 81, 84, 133, 147, 181, 188, 191, 237, 247, 299, 301, 309, 345
    shortages of food 69, 83, 172, 191, 311
    shortages of drinking water 221, 272, 308, 311
    sickness and disease 51, 71, 81, 82, 83, 89, 97, 153, 155, 163, 172, 182, 315
Campbell, Gen, Sir J 35
Campoleone, see *2nd World war*
Calcutta 80, 88, 95, 110, 123, 179, 230, 312 412
Caldicott, Lt Col, C T 195
Calthorpe, Col, S G 169
Cambridge, Duke of 160, 164, 167, 201, 205
Camden, see *American war of Independence*
Campbell, Lt Col, J, 108
Campbell-Lamerton, Col, M J 336, 423, 425, 426
Campoleone, 298
Canada 131, 133, 200, 357, 383
Cape Colony 216, 223, 22, 228, 394
Cape Town 96, 207, 216, 228
Caporetto 259
Cardigan, Earl of 160, 164, 168, 170
Cardwell, Mr E, see *Army reforms*
Carey, Maj, R O'D 391
Carline, Lt Col, F A 320
Carolinas – North and South 65-70
Carrol, Maj, T St G 284
Castle, Col, F J 193, 205, 389, 391
Cavery, river, see *3rd & 4th Mysore wars*
Cawnpore 89, 110, 115, 118, 119, 181
Chadwick, Lt Col, E F 192, 193, 389
Chadwick, Lt Col, G T
Chaman 264, 265
Chamberlain, Neville 275, 279
Chambly 134
Champlain, lake 134

Chanak 265, 267
Chapels
    Halifax Parish Church 366, 368, 370, 427
    York Minster 260, 277, 367, 369, 372, 385, 427
Charleroi 143, 144
Charleston, see *American war of Independence*
Chatham 78
Chatham, Gen, 2nd Earl of 128, 131
Cherbourg 41, 42, 43, 288
Chesapeake Bay 63, 71
Chindits, see *2nd World war*
Chindwin river 309, 310
Childers, Mr H, see *Army reforms*
Chiseldon 328, 340, 369
Chosumi 314, 315
Chowne, Gen, C 382
Churchill, Sir Winston 257, 280, 293
Christison, Gen, Sir A F P 274 386, 324, 326, 391, 415
Christison, Capt, J A A 307, 312
Ciudad Rodrigo
Civil power – aid to
    in 18th century 27
    India 321
    Leith 265
    Liverpool 267
    Palestine 321
    Wick 199
    see also *Northern Ireland*
Clark, Gen, M (American) 299, 300
Clarke, Lt Col, J 197, 198, 200, 390
Clarke, Lt Gen, Joseph 383
Clements, Lt Col, H 33, 36, 389
Clinton, Gen, Sir H 59, 60, 64, 65, 70, 71, 72, 143
Cobbe, Lt Col, R C 27, 389
Code, RSM, S E 326
Colchester 54, 191, 322, 342
Collins, Capt, D, 44, 51, 52
Collins, Ensign, W, see *Dansey, Lt Col, W*
Collings, Brig, J E 181, 184, 191, 389, 391
Colonels
    allowances 10, 374
    role 3, 4, 40, 45
    succession of, see *Appendix 2*
Colours: succession of, *Appendix 1*
Connigham, Capt, W D M 305, 308
Conor, Lt Col, C 206, 340
Constantinople 160, 257
Cooke, Maj Gen, 139, 142
Cooper, Lt Col A S 185, 191, 389
Cornwallis, Gen, 1st Marquis 367, 374, 378
    appointed colonel 33rd 55

*437*

in America 59-71
   at New York 60
   in Carolinas 65-70
   Yorktown 70-71
reputation 72
West Riding title for 33rd 74, 75
high state of training of 33rd 56, 57, 75
Gov Gen, India 77, 107
In 3rd Mysore ware 81-88
Corunna, see *Peninsular war*
Cowan, Maj Gen D T 307
Cox, Lt Col, M N 268, 391
Crimean war (1854-1856) 159-178
   Alma 165, 173, 176, 344, 368
   Balaclava 163, 169, 170, 171, 172, 177, 182
   Inkerman 169, 171, 172, 173
   Sevastapol 159, 163, 168 169, 170 ,171, 174, 175, 176, 177
   Scutari 160, 167, 172, 176
   formations
      Light Div 160, 165, 167, 169, 171, 174, 175, 176
      1st Div 160, 167
      2nd Div 165, 171
      Cavalry Div 168
      1st Bde 160, 171, 176
      2nd Bde 160, 165
      Guards Bde 167, 171
      Light Bde 164, 170, 171
      Heavy Bde 170
   killed and wounded 165, 167, 168, 172, 172, 176, 177
   sickness casualties 172, 176, 177
Cronje, Piet (Boer) 216, 217, 218, 219, 220, 222, 223
Crossley, Lt Col, J F 327
Crowther, Sgt, W 306
Cumberland, Gen, Duke of 28, 33, 34, 36, 37, 38, 39
Cumberlege, Lt Col, C R T 321, 322, 390, 391
Cumberlege, Lt Col, C R 357, 390
Cutts, Lt Gen, Lord 13
Cyprus (1956-57)
   Afxentiou 341, 342
   ENOSIS 340
   EOKA 340, 341
   Grivas, Gen 340, 342
   Kykko Monastery 342
   Markaeras Monastery 341
   Nicosia 341
Cyprus (1967)
   Limassol Zone 346
   Polemidhia Camp 346
   UNFICYP 346
Cyprus (1974)
   Attila Line 353
   Episkkopi 353

Dalzell, Lt Gen, R 27, 377
Dalton, C 17, 20n, 27
Dalrymple, Lt Col, J H 28, 31, 33, 321, 325, 327, 390, 391
Damascus 321
Dand 270, 271, 272
Dansey, Lt Col, G H 197, 390
Dansey, Lt Col, W 50, 52, 54, 56, 57, 59, 60, 64, 73, 412
Dardanelles 258, 265
Daulhat, Maj, P 41, 43, 45, 47, 48
Davidson, Lt Col, J 327
Davie, Lt Col, M M 298
Davis, Major, J H 326, 391, 392
Deesa 181, 182
de Gex, Brig, F J 223
Deig, see *1st and 2nd Mahratta wars*
Delhi, see *1st and 2nd Mahratta wars*
Dempsey, Pte, J 162, 163
de Minas, Gen, (Dutch) 20
D'Erlon, Count, (French) 148
D'Harcourt, Lt Col, D 22, 389
Dendre river 283
Denman, Lt, L B 290
Depot, Halifax 194, 202, 325
Dettingen, see *War of Austrian succession*
Devonport 266
de Wend, Lt Col, D C 205, 390
de Wet, Gen, (Boer) 217, 218, 222, 223, 225
Dickie, Cpl, T 332
Dieppe 287, 288, 289
Dildi, see *Abyssinia campaign*
Dimapur 312, 314, 316
Disbandments and reductions, "No standing army" 1, 26
   after war of Spanish succession 1, 24
   after war of Austrian succession 41
   after war of American Independence 76
   after 1st World war: "Geddes Axe" 262
   after 2nd World war: 1946/48, 323, 324; 1957, 327
   "Options for change" 363
Discipline
   Bad behaviour 165, 132, 188
   Good behaviour 38, 105, 106, 118, 139, 343
Djebel Bou Aoukaz, see *2nd World war*
Don, Lt Gen, Sir G 122, 126, 370
D'Oyley, Gen, H 156, 157, 159, 368, 380
Dress, see *Uniforms*
Duncanson, Col, R 4, 15, 16, 366, 376, 389

Dunkirk, see *2nd World war*
Dunlop, Lt Col, 102
Dunn, Col, A R *VC* 182, 184, 185, 401
Dunn, Bdsm, T 190
Dyle river 281, 282, 283

Edwards, 2nd/Lt, R E 258
Egypt 257, 258, 265, 267, 321, 379, 387
Eindhoven 93
Elliot, Lt Col, W 105
Elphinstone, Major Gen, W G K 139, 140, 143, 144, 145, 151, 152, 153, 389
Emett, Maj, E J P 334, 337
ENOSIS, see *Cyprus 1956-1957*
EOKA, see *Cyprus 1956-1957*
Episkkopi, see *Cyprus 1974*
Erskine, Gen, G 211, 384
Everitt, Lt 243
Exham, Capt, F S 226
Exham, Maj Gen, K G 326, 345, 386
Exham, Maj Gen R K 271, 317, 386

Faithfull, Lt Col, C K T 307, 308, 309, 391, 421, 426
Falklands 361
Famagusta 340,341
Fanshawe, Lt Col, T B 175, 176, 193, 389
Faulks, Maj, P R 291, 299
Fawley, 2nd/Lt 353
Fenn, Lt Col, E G 207, 391
Firth, Brig, A D 334, 342, 390
Firth, Sgt, J, *VC* 223, 394
Flank companies 57, 91, 103, 108, 109, 120, 121, 127, 182
   grenadier company 8, 16, 105, 112, 145, 153, 182
   light company 63, 134, 135, 181
Flushing 128, 129
Foch, Marshal (French) 251
Foggia 302
Fontenay-le-Pesnil
   see *2nd World war*
Fontenoy
   see *War of Austrian succession*
Forbes, Lord George, see *Appendix 7*
Fort Washington, see *American war of Independence*
Fortescue, Hon J W 5, 9, 15, 16, 18, 30, 31, 33, 34, 36, 44, 61, 66, 69, 72, 95, 99, 103, 115, 118, 119, 122, 125, 136, 142, 145, 188
Fox, Cpl, 306
France 408
Fraser, Lt, N 210
Fraser, Maj Gen 119, 120

Fraser, Brig, F H 274, 303, 391
Freedoms conferred on the Regiment by
    Halifax 326
    Huddersfield 326, 331
    Spenborough 326
    Skipton (honorary citizenship) 362
Freehold, see *American war of Independence*
Freer, Col, F 205, 391
French, F-M, 1st Earl of Ypres 217, 233, 238, 241

Gallipoli 243, 257, 258
Galway, Earl of 16, 17, 18, 20, 21, 376
Gates, Gen, H (American) 65, 67
Gatliffe, Lieut, J 75n
Geldermalsen, see *Netherlands campaign*
George, Gen, F D 203, 381, 384
Germaine, Lord G, see *Sackville*
Germantown, see *American war of Independence*
Gibbs, Lt Col, J A C 216, 233, 235, 391
Gibbs, Maj Gen, S 138
Gibraltar 26, 39, 265, 337, 339, 357, 358, 379
Gilbert-Smith, Maj, D S 336, 342, 422, 425, 426
Gillman, Lt Col, H 390
Glen, Capt, C 335, 336
"Glorious reinforcement" see *Seven Years war*
Gloucester 2, 7, 11, 56
Goodlad, Capt, W 103, 105
Gordon, Capt, E 198, 199
Gore, Brig, A 138, 140, 142, 145, 389
Gore, Lt, A 105, 106,
Gore, Lt Col, C W 207, 391
Gore, Maj, J 55, 73
Gore, Captain Sir Ralph (Earl of Ross) 38
Gort, F-M, 6th Viscount 281, 283, 287
Gosport 265, 266
Gothic Line 303
Gough, Lt Col, T B 176, 177
Gough, Brig. Gen, H 231, 251
Graham, Maj. Gen, T 138, 142
Graham, L/Cpl, T 352
Grammont, Comte de (French) 29, 30, 31
Granby, Lt Gen, Marquis of 44, 47
Green, Maj, V C 391
Greene, Gen, N (American) 68, 69
Greenway, Brig, J B K 353, 390
Grenadier company, see *Flank companies*

Grieve, Maj, C F 421, 425, 426
Griffin-Griffin, Lord Howard de Walden, F-M 45, 49, 50, 55, 374, 378
Grivas, Gen, see *Cyprus 1956-1957*
Grosvenor, Lt Gen, T 129
Guilford Court House, see *American war of Independence*
Gulf war (1991) 361
Gustav Line 296

Hackett, Lt Col, J 390
Haganah, see *Palestine 1945-1946*
Haifa 301, 321
Haig, F-M, 1st Earl 241, 244, 245, 246, 247, 248, 249, 251, 254
*Halifax Courier and Guardian* 195
Halkett, Maj Gen, Sir C 143, 151
Halstead, 2nd Lt, A, 401
Hamilton, Lt Col, C D 318
Hamilton, Gen, Sir Ian 257, 258
Hamilton, Lt Gen, Sir J 81
Harcourt, Gen, 1st Earl, see *Appendix 7*
Hardy, Col, E M P 422, 425, 426
Harms, Col, R M 332, 344
Harris, Gen, 1st Lord 88, 97, 98, 99, 103, 105, 378
Harris, Maj, D M 342
Harris, Col, R W H 391
Harrison, Lt Col, E G 236, 237, 238, 241, 391
Harrison, Capt, J 284
Harty, Lt Col, J M 154, 155, 389
Haugh, Lt Col, J W N 317
Havercake Lads, see *Recruiting*
Hawley, Lt Gen, H 26, 27, 376
Hay, Maj Gen, Lord Charles 34, 39, 40, 45, 366, 374, 377
Hayden, Lt Col, F A 228, 231, 241, 391
Healing, L Col, R K 265, 390
Helles, Cape 257
Hemingway, Pte, G 145
Henniker, Lt Col, Sir R J A 247, 391
Hickey, W 95
Hill 60, see *1st World war*
Hindenburg Line 245, 248, 249, 250, 254, 255
Hindoostan 110, 114, 115, 119, 121, 124, 126, 370, 371, 372
Hitler, Adolf 275, 279, 291
Hodge, Lt Col, T T 206, 207, 391
Holland (1813-1814)
    Merxem 139
    Bergen-op-Zoom 142
    casualties 142
Holland, 2nd/Lt, D J 332
Holkar, Jaswant Rao 118, 119, 121, 122

Honeywood, Gen, Sir P 5, 17, 22, 389
Honourable East India Company (HEIC) 77, 79, 80, 81, 82, 88, 102, 109, 110, 114, 123, 124, 126, 179, 181, 196, 197, 206, 370, 372, 373, 382
Hong Kong 303, 325, 329, 343, 347, 348, 349
Hopkins, Lt Col, G R 390
Hook, the, see *Korean war*
Horsfall, Lt Col, A G 244, 246, 247, 391
Houghton, Maj, E R 222, 391
Hougoumont, see *Waterloo campaign*
Houlding, J A 75n
Howard, Lt. Col, Thomas 26
Howe, Gen, Sir W 56, 59, 60, 61, 62, 63, 64
Hoyle, Lt Col, S R 314, 326
Huddersfield 326, 327, 410
Hudson river 60, 65
Huffam, Maj, J P *VC* 254, 397
Hull 138, 152
Humphries, Lt Col, C V 230, 390
Huntingdon, 8th Earl of 2, 3, 4, 8, 9, 11, 12, 15, 375
Huskisson, Maj, T F 291, 298, 422, 426
Hutchinson, Gen, W N 182, 203, 380, 384
Hutton, Lt Gen, T 307
Huxtable, Gen, Sir C 349, 350, 353, 357, 361, 364, 387, 390
Huy, see *war of Spanish succession*
Hyder Ali 76, 102, 103
Hyderabad, Nizam of, see *3rd & 4th Mysore wars*
Hyderabad 107, 384

Iceland 316, 408
Imjin river 337
Imphal 309, 311, 312, 314
Ince, Lt Col, C W G 240
Ince, Maj, R H 391
Indian Mutiny (1857-1858) 179-182
Ingoldsby, Brig. 33
Inkerman, see *Crimean war*
Inspection reports 55, 56, 74, 143, 153, 196, 206, 367, 412
Ireland (Eire) 27, 74, 179
    Cork 59, 91
    Curragh camp 231, 265
    Dublin 57, 74, 179, 231, 232, 262, 265, 267
    Fermoy 179, 193
Irrawaddy river 307, 308
Irwin, Lt Gen, N 311
Isle of Wight 26, 42, 44

*439*

Isles, Maj Gen, D E  344, 345, 347, 353, 357, 387, 390, 425

Jackson, Lt Col, A C 291
Jacobsen, Capt, A H 293
Jaipur 118
Jameson, Dr, L S 209, 214
Jaswant Singh, Rajah 121, 123
Jephson-Jones, Col, R *GC* 400
Jersey 372
Jervois, Gen, W 383
Joffre, Marshal (French) 236, 245
Johnson, Lt Gen, J 27, 28, 36, 39, 366, 367, 377
Johnston, Lt Col, H J 257, 258
Johnston, Lt, H T, 301
Johnstone, Lt Col, J D 170, 173, 176, 177, 178, 181, 389
Johnstone, Lt Col, J D 193, 389
Journals, Regimental, see *Appendix 9*

Kalewa 309
Kamptee 192, 268, 368
Karachi 184, 262
Kassel 47, 49, 51
Kavanagh, Lt Col, A B M 334, 343, 345, 390
Keating, Lt Gen, Sir H S 109, 156, 380
Keighley 410
Kelley, Lt, F, 401
Kelly, Lt Col, R 174
Kelly, 2nd/Lt, H, *VC* 244, 395
Kelly-Kenny, Gen, Sir T 219, 222
Kempster, Maj, A G *GC* 302, 400
Kendrew, Maj Gen, D 331, 332, 334, 336
Kennedy, Capt, J.M. 131, 134
Kenya 340, 342, 343
Kershaw, Maj, L F 335, 337
Kesselring, F-M (German) 295, 296, 298
Khesomi 31, 315
Khyber Pass 263, 264
Kimberley, see *Boer war*
King George I 25, 375
King George II 28-33, 365
King George III 73, 370
King William III 112, 365
Kington, Lt Col, S B 280, 282, 390
Kitchener, F-M, 1st Earl of 216, 218, 219, 220, 222, 223, 227, 228, 240
Kloster Kamp, see *Seven Years war*
Knight, Lt Col, C 151, 154, 389
Knox, Maj. Gen, C E 216
Knox, Capt, J 103
Korean War (1950-1953)
    The Hook 331-337
    Pusan 329, 331, 337
    1st Commonwealth Div 331-337, 344
    25th Canadian Bde 331
    27th Commonwealth Bde 329, 331
    29th Bde 329, 331
    killed and wounded 333, 336
Krüger, P, President of Transvaal 207, 214
Kuwait 343
Kyaikto 305
Kykko monastery, see *Cyprus (1956-1957)*

Lafayette, Marquis de (French) 70, 71, 73
La Haye Sainte, see *Waterloo campaign*
Lahore 205, 230, 232, 262
Lake, 1st Viscount 113, 114, 115, 117-125, 372
Lamb, Sgt, R 57, 69
Lauffeld, see *War of Austrian succession*
Lawlor, Lt Col, J H C 317
Lean, Lt Col, K E 230, 391
Lebanon 321
Le Cateau 235
Lee, Pte, G 352
Lee, Pte, J 352
Le Havre 41, 233, 318, 385
Leigh, Col, H 15, 376
Leith, Maj. Gen, J 127
LeMottee, Col, H B 391
Lennox, Gen, Lord G H 41, 45, 48, 49, 366, 389
Les Moeres 284
Leswaree, see *1st & 2nd Mahratta wars*
Lethbridge, Lt Col, F W 259
Libya 290, 340
Lichfield 371,373
Liège, see *war of Spanish succession*
Lieutenant Colonels, succession of, see *Appendix 3*
Light company, see *Flank companies*
Ligny, see *Waterloo campaign*
Ligonier, Brig, Sir J 37, 38
Limassol, see *Cyprus 1967*
Lister, Pte, H 254
Llewellyn, Lt Col, E H 287
Lloyd, Lt Col, G E 206, 216, 222, 226, 227, 390
Lloyd, Lt Col, R C 390
Lloyd-George, D 251, 262, 265
Localisation scheme, see *Army reforms*
Lockart-Ross, Lt Col, Sir J 38, 389
Loe Agra, see *North West Frontier of India (1935)*
Loosemore, Sgt, A *VC* 247, 395
Loudoun, Lt. Gen, the Earl of 45

Love, Lt Col, J F 390
Lucan, Earl of 160, 164, 168, 169, 172
Ludendorff, Gen (German) 251, 253
Luttrell, N 17, 18, 22
Lys, see *1st World war*

Maas river 318 *(see also Meuse)*
Maberly, Lt Col, W L 179, 196, 197, 370, 372, 390
MacGrigor, Capt, C 99, 103,
Macintosh, Lt Col, A F 390
Macdonald, Lord. See *Appendix 7*
Macleod, Maj, W 112, 113, 115
MacRae, Lt Col, K 121
MacArthur, Gen, D (American) 329
McCall, Lt Col, B 301, 390
McDonald, Maj, K M 327
McGrath, C/sgt, J 181, 182
McGuire, Pte, P 170
McGuire-Bate, Maj, W T 391
McLeod, Lt Col, K R 235, 391
McKenzie, Cpl, A 332
Madras 76, 180, 84, 97, 109, 303, 382
Maffett, Lt Col, R E 262, 264, 390
Maginot Line 280, 281
Magner, Dmr, M *VC* 190, 191, 393
Magdala, see *Abyssinia campaign*
1st & 2nd Mahratta wars (1803-1806) 110-125
    Agra 115, 118, 119, 120, 121, 370, 371, 372, 412
    Ally Ghur 111, 112, 113, 114, 118
    Bhurtpore 119, 121, 123, 125
    Deig 119, 120, 121, 371
    Delhi 113, 114, 115, 118, 370, 371, 372
    Leswaree 117, 370, 371, 372
    Sassnee 110
    killed and wounded 109, 114, 115, 117, 118, 120, 121, 122, 123
Maitland, Gen, Sir P 198, 382
Major, Cpl, G E S 221n
Malaya 322, 340, 386
Mallavelly, see *4th Mysore war*
Malta 160, 200, 277, 340, 383
Marchant, Lt Col, B St J 225
Mariani 314
Markhaeras monastery, see *Cyprus 1956-1957*
Marne, see *1st World war*
Marsh, Lt H 174
Marshall, Lt Col, F M H 230, 391
Marlborough, 1st Duke of 7-11, 28
Mashonaland, see *Rhodesia 1893, 1895*
Mason, Capt, E 305
Matabeleland, see *Rhodesia 1893, 1896*
Maxwell, Col. Hamilton 82, 86

440

Mauritius 108, 179
Medjez-el-Bab 290
Medows, Gen Sir W 81, 86, 87, 381
Meek, Col, A D 352, 361, 362, 390
Mentschikov, Prince (Russian) 165, 168
Merxem, see *Holland*
Messines 246
Meuse, river 12, 14
Middlemore, Lt Gen, G 382
Miles, CSM, E 244
Militia
   3rd (Militia) Battalion 194, 216, 228, 385, 404, 405, 407
   4th (Militia) Battalion 404, 407
   6th West Yorkshire Militia 194, 195, 232, 404, 407
   appendix 5
Millard, Lt, 294
Minden 44, 329, 355, 356
Mitchell, Col, P A 353, 390
Modder river 216, 217, 218, 219, 222
Moffat, Lt Col, S 153, 154, 389
Moira, Maj Gen Lord
   see *Lord Rawdon*
Mons, see *1st World war*
Monson, Lt Col, Hon W 88, 111, 112, 117, 119, 120, 122, 123, 124, 125, 390
Mont St, Jean, see *Waterloo campaign*
Monte Ceco, see *2nd World war*
Monte Cerere, 301
Montgomery, F-M, 1st Viscount 317, 321
Moore, Lt Gen, Sir J 126, 127, 128
Moran, Brig, P P de la H 342, 390
Moran, Lt Col, R de la H 339, 390
Morgan, Lt, D, 301
Morice, Lt Col C 139, 140
Mornington, Earl of – 6th Duke of Wellington 277, 295
Mornington, Lady 80, 90
Mornington, Lord – Marquis Wellesley 94, 97, 98, 110, 118, 119
Mountbatten, Earl 321
Mounted infantry 208, 209, 216, 223
Muller, Lt Col 140
Multan 274, 279, 303
Mundy, Lt Col G V 174, 177
Mundell, Brig, W R 356, 357, 361, 387, 390, 423
Mure, Lt Col, G 36, 38, 389
Museum & Archives, see *Appendix 9*
Musgrave, Gen, Sir T 63, 78, 79, 80, 81, 82, 131, 381
Music, see *Appendix 6*
Mussolini, B 295
Muttlebury, Lt Col, 140, 151
Muttra 120

3rd Mysore war (1789-1792) 81-88
   Arikera 84
   Bangalore 82, 83, 84, 99
   Seringapatam 82-88
   2nd Bde 82
   killed and wounded 83, 84, 87, 88
4th Mysore war (1799) 98-103
   Mallavelly 99
   Sultanpettah tope 100
   Seringapatam 101-103, 367, 378, 379
   killed and wounded 99, 103

Naga Hills 314
Nairobi 343
Napier, Lt Gen, Sir R 184, 185, 188, 191, 393
Napoleon Bonaparte 126, 127, 128, 131, 132, 133, 138, 142, 143, 144, 147, 148, 150, 151,152
Napoleon III 159
National service 324, 343
Nesbitt, Lt Col, E 207, 391
Netherlands campaign (1794-1795) 91-95
   Bokstel 93
   Geldermalsen 94
   2nd Bde 93
   3rd Bde 93
   sickness casualties 94, 95
Neuve Chapelle 251
Newton, Maj, J M 342
Newton, Maj, S C 361
Ney, Marshal (French) 144
Nicosia, see *Cyprus 1956-1957*
Nightingale, Florence 172
Nijmegen 12, 318
Nive, see *Peninsular war*
Nivelle, Gen (French) 245, 246
Nivelle, see *Peninsular war*
Noailles, Marshal (French) 28,29,30
Norcott, Maj Gen, Sir A 95
Norford, Capt H 120
North Atlantic Treaty Organisation (NATO) 328, 342
North West Frontier of India (1935) 205, 206
   Loe Agra 268, 269, 270
   Mohmand 270-273
   Nowshera Bde 268, 269, 272
   killed and wounded 270, 271, 272
Northern Ireland
   Ballymurphy 352, 356
   Belfast 342, 351, 352, 356, 359
   IRA 351, 352, 353, 357, 360, 361
   Holywood 359
   Londonderry 342, 349, 351, 353, 355
   "Provos" 352, 355

   South Armagh 352, 355
   killed and wounded 352, 353, 356
Norway 316, 345, 362, 386, 408
Nowshera 205, 268, 269, 272

Oakes, Lt Col H 54, 56, 57, 389
Oath of Loyalty 62
Old Comrades, see *Appendix 10*
Officer, Lt Col, W G 391
O'Kelly, Lt Col, H K 235
Orange, Prince of 142, 144, 145
Orr, Lt Col, C W B 320, 390
Orr, 2nd/Lt, I, 332
Osnabrück 344, 347
Ostend 92, 246
Owen, Lt Col, H B 303, 305, 391
Ozanne, Maj Gen, W M 277, 280, 390

Paardeberg, see *Boer War*
Palestine (1945-1946) 320
   Haganah 321
   Irgun Zvai L'eumi 320
   Stern Gang 320
   1st Div 321
   6th Airborne Div, 321
Pantellaria 295
Parkinson, Lt Gen, E 140, 143, 144n
Parole 21, 72, 73
Parson, Lt Col, E M K 391
Paschendaele, see *First World War*
Paton, Lt Col, D 391
Pattison, Lt, H 145, 148
Paungde, see *2nd World War*
Pawlett, Lt Col, F 391
Pay and allowances 3, 5, 78, 124, 137, 153, 213, 277, 343, 350
Peel, Pte 356
Peel, Capt, A G 291
Pegu 307
Pelissier, Gen (French) 176
Peninsula war (1808-1814) 126-128, 132, 133
   Corunna 26, 127, 128, 344, 380, 382
   Nive 133, 371, 382, 383
   Nivelle 132, 382
   Maj Gen Leith's Bde 127
   Maj Gen Lord Aylmer's Bde 132, 133
   killed and wounded 127, 128, 132, 133
Penney, Maj Gen, 296
Perron, Capt, A G 291
Perron, Gen (French) 110, 111, 113
Peshawar 205, 264, 268, 270, 271, 303
Pester, Lt, J 122, 412
Pétain, Marshal (French) 246, 251
Peterborough, Gen, Earl of 17, 18

*441*

Philadelphia 62
Piave, see *1st World war*
Pickering, Col, C J 267, 286, 324, 385, 391
"Pilcher's Pets" 230
Pitt, William 89
Plattsburg, see *2nd American war*
Plymouth 412
Pogson, Sgt, E 237
Polemidhia camp, see *Cyprus 1967*
Pont-à-Chin, 283
Poulter, Pte, A *VC* 395
Pretoria 225, 227, 228
Prevost, Gen Sir G 131, 133, 134, 135, 381
Price, Maj, O 269
Primrose, Lt Col, Viscount H 28, 389
Prize agents 121, 190
Prome 307
Public duties, London 348, 357
Pusan, see *Korean war*

Queen Anne 2, 25
Queen Victoria 170, 173

RAF 269, 270
    Helicopters 348, 357
    Hurricane fighter bombers 314
Raglan, F-M, Lord 160, 163, 165, 168, 170, 172, 176, 379
Rangoon 216, 230, 305, 306, 307, 371
Rawdon, Lord (later 1st Marquis Hastings) 66, 67, 92, 93
Rebellion of 1745
    Brig Bligh's Bde 37
Recruiting
    County connection 74, 75
    In England 5, 6, 75, 78, 198
    In Ireland 131, 179
    "Havercake Lads" 95
    In West Riding 95
Regiments:
Cavalry:
Life Guards 147
1st Royals (Royal Dragoons) 15, 47
1 DG (1st King's Dragoon Guards) 5, 379
2 DG (2nd Dragoon Guards) 17, 27, 377
3 DG (3rd Dragoon Guards, Carbiniers) 5, 26, 31, 184, 191, 376
11th Light Dragoons (11th Hussars) 182, 384
12th Light Dragoons (12th Royal Lancers) 90
15th Light Dragoons (15th King's Hussars) 45, 139
16th Light Dragoons (16th Queen's Lancers) 153
19th Light Dragoons 84
20th Light Dragoons (20th Hussars) 382
23rd Light Dragoons 382
29th Light Dragoons 117

Royal Armoured Corps:
1st Royal Tank Regiment 353
46th Royal Tank Regiment 298
145 Regiment RAC (8 DWR) 290, 291, 294, 301, 302, 303, 322
146 Regiment RAC (9 DWR) 311, 312, 322
Royal Artillery:
19 Field Regiment RA 282
20 Field Regiment RA 331
43 Searchlight Regiment RA (5 DWR) 275, 407
43 Garrison Regiment RA (5 DWR) 320, 407
58 Anti-Tank Regiment RA (1/4th DWR) 275, 279, 289, 295, 302, 322, 407
60 Field Regiment RA 314
68 Anti-Tank Regiment RA (2/4th DWR)
382 (4 DWR) Anti-Tank Regiment RA 327, 410
382 (4 DWR) Medium Regiment RA 327, 410
578 Heavy Anti-Aircraft Regiment RA 327, 410
600 Regiment RA (5 DWR) 320, 322, 407
673 Light Anti-Aircraft Regiment RA (DWR) 327, 410
Infantry:
1st Foot Guards (Grenadiers) 33, 34, 39, 55, 140, 167, 293, 380, 382
2nd Foot Guards (Coldstream) 20, 39, 69, 162, 167
3rd Foot Guards (Scots) 45, 167, 378
Irish Guards 299
Royal Scots (1st) 140, 141, 211
Queen's (Royal West Surrey) (2nd) 15, 17, 128
The Buffs (East Kent) (3rd) 79, 216, 218, 223, 229, 381, 412
King's Own (4th) 181, 184, 188, 189, 191, 245, 325, 329, 343, 379, 421
Royal Northumberland Fusiliers (5th) 45, 323, 324, 377
Royal Warwickshire (6th) 16, 17, 18, 20, 22, 24, 250
Royal Fusiliers (7th) 160, 165-168, 171, 175, 176, 177, 299, 334, 336
King's Liverpool (8th) 11, 13, 37, 92
Royal Norfolk (9th) 15, 17, 20, 57, 383
Lincolnshire (10th) 16, 376
Devonshire (11th) 15, 30, 45, 49, 52
Suffolk (12th) 33, 55, 93, 100, 102, 104, 108, 378, 379
Somerset LI (13th) 13, 33
West Yorkshire (14th) 287, 323, 324
East Yorkshire (15th) 299, 323, 324
Leicestershire (17th) 13, 15, 16, 17, 20, 65, 70
Royal Irish (18th) 7, 13, 18
Green Howards (19th) 26, 33, 37, 160, 168, 211, 323, 325
Lancashire Fusiliers (20th) 45, 47, 49, 245, 379, 381
Royal Scots Fusiliers (21st) 31, 37, 377
Cheshire (22nd) 120, 121, 122, 137, 154, 384
Royal Welch Fusiliers (23rd) 31, 41, 45, 49, 65, 66, 69, 70, 72, 160, 165, 166, 168, 171, 175, 177, 382
South Wales Borderers (24th) 206, 300
King's Own Scottish Borderers (25th) 33, 37, 49, 139, 233, 238, 381
Cameronians (26th & 90th) 184, 309, 386
Royal Inniskilling Fusiliers (27th & 108th) 186
Gloucestershire (28th & 61st) 27, 216, 218, 223, 307, 309, 377
Worcestershire (29th & 36th) 83, 86, 89, 383
East Lancashire (30th & 59th) 126, 127, 144, 147, 151
East Surrey (31st & 70th) 290
Duke of Cornwall's LI (32nd & 46th) 37, 63, 267n, 380
Border (34th & 55th) 139, 142, 174, 175, 176, 312, 314, 384
Royal Sussex (35th & 107th) 380
Royal Hampshire (37th & 67th) 63, 255, 379
South Staffordshire (38th & 80th) 27, 73, 105, 206, 377
Dorsetshire (39th & 54th) 380
South Lancashire (40th & 82nd) 63, 79, 82
Welch (41st & 69th) 80, 81, 90, 101, 108, 139, 141, 142, 144, 145, 147, 151, 160, 223, 289, 331, 384
Black Watch (42nd & 73rd) 33, 60, 93, 95, 102, 103, 144, 145, 147, 151, 208, 331-334
Oxfordshire & Buckinghamshire LI (43rd & 52nd) 37, 70, 83, 88,

442

151, 216, 218
Essex (44th & 56th) 92, 93, 145, 216, 223, 312, 380, 382
Sherwood Foresters (45th & 95th) 184, 188, 282, 284, 298
Loyal North Lancashire (47th & 81st) 291, 383, 384
Northamptonshire (48th & 58th) 90, 382
Royal Berkshire (49th & 66th) 73, 211
Royal West Kent (50th & 97th) 211, 233, 238
King's Own Yorkshire LI (51st & 105th) 45, 48, 49, 50, 52, 126, 206, 225, 233, 238, 239, 288, 307, 385
King's Shropshire LI (53rd & 85th) 132, 294, 298, 379, 383
Middlesex (57th & 77th) 78, 160, 174, 329, 380
King's Royal Rifle Corps (60th) 381
Wiltshire (62nd & 99th) 225, 312, 382
Manchester (63rd & 96th) 241
North Staffordshire (64th & 98th) 63, 65, 131, 291, 337, 381
York and Lancaster (65th & 84th) 122, 128, 132, 154, 209, 323, 325, 348
Durham LI (68th & 106th) 41, 318, 325, 379
Highland LI (71st & 74th) 78, 79, 83, 102
Seaforth Highlanders (72nd & 78th) 95, 129, 135, 139, 250, 289
Queen's Own Cameron Highlanders (79th) 74
Royal Irish Rifles (83rd & 86th) 108, 122, 160, 382
Royal Irish Fusiliers (87th & 89th) 88, 383
Connaught Rangers (88th & 94th) 160, 379
Argyll and Sutherland Highlanders (91st & 93rd) 141, 144, 170, 329, 384
Prince of Wales Leinster (100th & 109th) 82
Royal Munster Fusliers (101st & 104th) 120, 211, 225, 385
Rifle Brigade 139, 156, 175, 176, 380
Royal Engineers
43rd (5 DWR) Anti-Aircraft Battalion RE 275, 320, 407
Regiments numbered 76, see *Appendix 7*
Reviews – see *inspections*
Reynolds, Maj, F J 421, 425, 426
Rhenoster kop, see *Boer war*
Rhodesia

Matabeleland 207, 209, 385
Mashonaland 209, 210
killed and wounded 210
Richardson, Lt Col, C R 390
Richmond, F-M, 3rd Duke of 41, 366, 389
Rivett-Carnac, Maj, J T 282
Rivett-Carnac, Lt Col, P T 207, 210, 227, 282, 390
Roberts, Lt Col, A D 359, 361, 390, 415
Roberts, Maj, D C 391
Roberts, F-M, 1st Earl 216, 217, 218, 222, 223, 224, 225, 227
Robertson, Capt Lt J 89
Robins, Lt Col, W 390
Robinson, Maj, J 305, 306, 308
Rocoux, see *war of Austrian succession*
Roebuck, Cpl, 306
Rome 301
Rommel, Marshal, E (German) 289, 290, 293
Roosendaal 93, 318
Rose, Lt Col, D 332
Ross, Gen, A 82, 88
Ross, Maj Gen R 136
Rottenburg, Lt Gen, Sir F 134
Rouen 288
Rowlands, Gen, Sir H 211, 231, 401
Royal Navy, see *Affiliations*
Rugby, see *Appendix 8*
Army Cup 275, 276, 345, 421, 422, 423, 424
Army caps 425
International honours 426
Ruremonde, see *war of Spanish succession*
Rusbridger, Lt Col, G S W 277, 390
Russell, Mr W, of *The Times* 178
Ryan, Cpl 353

Sackville, Lt Gen, Sir G (later Lord Germaine) 42, 44, 59, 65, 66
St. Arnaud, Marshal (French) 162, 163, 165, 169
St. Cast, see *Seven Years war*
St. Ledger, Maj Gen, J 96
St. Malo, see *Seven Years war*, 288
St. Nazaire 287, 288, 408
St. Valery-en-Caux, see *Second World war*
San Sebastian 132
Salamanca 127
Salisbury Plain 55, 266, 328
Sampson, Lt Col, R 28, 389
Santa-Ollala, Lt Col, D M 362, 390
Saragossa, see *war of Spanish succession*
Saratoga 64, 65

Sassnee, see *1st and 2nd Mahratta wars*
Savory, Lt Gen, Sir R A 48
Savory, Maj, A C S 391
Saxe, Marshal (French) 33, 35, 37
Sayers, Lt Col, A E H 325, 391
Scheldt
Scindia, Maharaja of
Scotland
Edinburgh 39, 198, 265
Glasgow 198, 316
Leith 265
Wick 198
Seed, BM, D 415
Seine river 288, 318
Senafe, see *Abyssinia campaign*
Seoul 329
Seringapatam, see *2rd & 4th Mysore wars*
Service at sea 64, 65, 89
Sevastapol, see *Crimean War*
Seven Years War (1756-1763) 40-53
Kloster Kamp 49, 50
St. Cast 43
St. Malo 43
Warburg 47, 49
Wilhelmsthal 52
Vellinghausen 52
3rd Bde 41
Maj Gen Grifin's Bde (later Brudenell's) 45, 49
killed and wounded 44, 48, 49
Shaw, Capt R 82, 86
Shawe, Lt Col, M 128, 131, 390
Shee, Maj J 98, 99, 103, 105
Sheffield 267, 363
Sherbrooke, Gen, Sir J 74, 91, 93, 98, 102, 104, 105, 178, 379, 413
Shiel, Lt Col, F P St. M 300, 301, 390
Shilleto, CSM, R J 294
Shuttleworth, Brig, D W 347, 349, 390, 422, 425, 426
Shwegin 309
Sicily 295, 379
Sills, Maj, H J T, 299
Simmonds, Maj, D N 305, 306
Simpson, Gen J 176, 177
Simpson, Col, T T 121, 391
Singapore 267, 303, 305, 322, 386
Sittang river, see *2nd World War*
Skirrow, Capt, 284
Slim, F-M, 1st Viscount 307, 308, 309, 311
Smith, Capt, A P R 293
Smith, Lt Col, C L *VC* 267, 401, 391
Smith, Lt Gen, M 383
Smith-Dorrien, Gen 220, 235
Smythe, Lt Col, H 390
Smythe, Maj Gen, J 305, 306, 307
Somerset, Gen, Lord C H 154, 374, 378

*443*

Somme, see *1st World War*
South Georgia 361
Spanish succession, War of
  (1702-1713) 12-24
    Alcantara 16, 17
    Almanza 18, 20, 22, 377, 389
    Brihuega 23, 389
    Huy 15, 16
    Liège 14, 16
    Ruremonde 14, 16
    Saragossa 22
    Valencia de Alcantara 17, 18, 375
    Venloo 12, 16
    Brig F Hamilton's Bde 12, 14, 15
    Brig G Wade's Bde 16, 17
    casualties 13, 14, 17, 20, 22, 23, 24
Spearhead battalion 342, 355, 361
Spence, C/Sgt, G 167, 168
Spencer, Col, A G 391
Spin Baldak, see *3rd Afghan war*
Stacpoole, Fr, Alberic 334
Stahremberg, F-M
Stanhope, Lt Col, E 389
Stanhope, Lt Gen, J 22
Stanley, Mr H M of *The New York Herald* 184
Stevens, Lt Col, E W 312, 314, 315, 316, 391
Stewart, Lt Col D J 326
Stilwell, Gen (American), 307
Strangeways, Canon, D I 286
Straslund 138
Streatfeild, Maj, J L, 299
Strensall 324, 325, 326
Strickland, Lt Col, E V 302
Stopford, Gen, Sir F 257, 258
Stuart, Lt Gen J 98, 101
Studd, Lt Col, E 390
Sultanpettah tope, see *4th Mysore war*
Sumatra 322
Suvla, see *1st World war*
Swat river 268, 269
Symes, Lt Col, M 88, 126, 128, 390
Syria 387

Tamu 310
Tandy, Pte, H *VC* 254, 255, 396
Tate, L/Cpl 356
Taukkyan 307
Taunton 26, 74, 367
Taylor, Sgt, A E 237
Taylor, Cpl, D 335, 336
Taylor, Lt Col, G 287, 289
Taylor, Gen, M (American) 336
Tedd, Maj, G C 392
Templeton, Lt, C 122, 123
Tern Hill 361
Territorial Army/Force, see

*Appendix 5*
Tetlow, Lt Col, W S F 295
Thain, Lt, W 140, 144
Thiepval 244, 245
Theodore, King of Abyssinia 184
Theodore's drum 190
Therepesemi 315
Theyre, Lt Col, S M G 309, 391
Thorold, Lt Col, H D 390, 391
Tidmarsh, Lt Col, H D 390
Tidworth 265
Tipu, Sultan of Mysore, see 3rd & 4th Mysore wars
Titles of the Regiment
  33rd (or 1st Yorkshire West Riding) Regiment 74, 75
  33rd (or Duke of Wellington's) Regiment 157
  The Halifax Regiment (Duke of Wellington's) 202
  The Duke of Wellington's (West Riding Regiment) 203
  The Duke of Wellington's Regiment (West Riding) 203, 262
Todleben, Col (Russian) 169
Training: recruits 6
  Halifax – Depot 325, 326
  4 ITC 325
  33 PTC 325
  Strensall 324, 326
Training: overseas
  Belize 359
  Canada 355, 357, 361
  Caribbean 352
  Denmark 345, 363
  Germany 355
  Kenya 350, 359
  Libya 355
  New Zealand 348
  Norway 361
Transport, animal
  bullocks 82, 98, 111
  horses 267
  elephants 82, 188
  mules 185, 188, 274
Trench, Lt Col, M V le P 220, 224, 228, 391
Trench, Lt Col, S J 391
Trichinopoly, see *3rd Mysore War*
Tripp, Lt Col, J H 390
Troop, Gp Capt, C L 424, 426
Troopship
  HMT Devonshire 331
  HMT Nevasa 343
Tunis 290
Turnbull, Capt, S R 293
Turner, Lt Col, R J O 317
Turner, Brig, P A 238, 277, 385, 391
Turner, Sgt, V *VC* 398
Tyndall, Lt Col, W E M 238, 391

Uniforms
  badges 324, 327, 348, 365, 370, 371
  battle dress 278, 329
  caps 266, 278, 324, 348
  chevrons 137
  coats 9, 40, 162
  cocked hats 9, 40
  No. 1 Dress 329, 340
  No. 3 Dress 348
  epaulettes 137
  facings 8, 9, 40, 79, 157, 202, 229, 266, 369
  khaki 185, 211, 266
  sam browne belt 212, 213
  shakos 136, 162
  topi 185, 266
  trousers 9
  webbing equipment 211, 212
Ulster – see *Northern Ireland*
Ukhrul 316
Umfreville, Lt Col, H K 235, 391

Victoria Cross, see *Appendix 4*
Valencia de Alcantara, see *war of Spanish succession*
Vanbrugh, Sir John 5
Varna 162, 172
Vehicles
  APCs 344, 352, 355, 356
  Carriers 278, 283, 296, 303, 307,
  CVR (W) 359
  Ferrets 355, 359
  FV 1611 344
  FV 432 344, 345, 355
Vellinghausen, see *Seven Years war*
Venables 288
Venloo, see war of *Spanish succession*
Verdun 242, 244, 245
Verplanks, see *American war of Independence*
Vigo 26, 127
Viljoen, Gen, Ben (Boer) 225, 226
Virginia 68, 70, 73
Volunteers see *Appendix 5*
Wade, F-M, G 16, 21, 22, 24, 25, 26, 33, 39, 374, 376
Wadis, see *Anzio*
Walcheren campaign (1809) 128-131, 380, 382
  3rd Division 128
  sickness casualties 129, 131
Wale, Gen, Sir C 154, 367, 379
Waller, Col, W A 284
Wallis, Capt, A B 165, 166
Walker, Brig, E J W 359, 390
Walker, Lt Col, P L E 391
Warburg, see *Seven Years war*
Wardlaw, Lt Col, J 131, 134, 196, 390

Waterloo campaign (1815)
　　Quatre Bras 144, 145, 152, 367, 382
　　Waterloo 147, 367, 380, 382
　　Guards Bde 140, 145, 152
　　5th Bde 143, 144, 147, 151
　　killed and wounded 145, 147, 152
Wathen, Lt Col, A H G 284, 290, 390
Watson, Lt Col, W M 230, 390
Wavell, F-M, 1st Earl 307, 311
Weapons
　　anti-tank
　　　　Boyes 278, 288, 303
　　　　MILAN 359, 361
　　　　120 MOBAT 344, 345
　　　　Vigilant 345
　　bayonets 8, 13, 79, 83, 114
　　"Brown Bess" 7, 8, 9, 13, 26, 27, 136
　　grenades 8, 13
　　halberds 9, 79
　　machine guns
　　　　Bren 278, 288, 303, 311, 329, 344
　　　　GPMG 344, 360
　　　　Lewis 245, 266, 269, 277
　　　　Maxim 212, 221
　　　　Vickers 221, 266, 277, 329
　　mortars 121, 189, 250
　　　　2" 277
　　　　3" 277, 329, 344
　　　　81mm 344
　　　　RARDEN 30mm cannon 359
　　muskets 7, 8, 9, 13, 26
　　rifles
　　　　Minié 162, 171, 176
　　　　Snider 185, 189, 190, 195
　　　　Martini-Henry 195, 212
　　　　Lee-Enfield 179, 212, 257, 266, 329, 342
　　　　7.62mm SLR 342, 360
　　　　SA 80, 359
　　swords 9
Webb-Carter, Brig, B W 290, 291, 293, 296, 321, 324, 390
Webster, Lt Col, J 56, 57, 66, 67, 69, 389
Weedon 154, 367, 380
Well of Lecht 39, 377
Wellesley Barracks 325
Wellesley, Lt Col, F H V 266, 390
Wellesley, Col, A, see Wellington, 1st Duke
Wellington, FM, 1st Duke of 368, 374, 378, 379
　　service prior to joining 33rd 79, 90
　　in Netherlands campaign (1794-95) 92-95
　　in Calcutta 96

Manila expedition 96, 97
4th Mysore war (1799) 97-103
Governor of Seringapatam 104
Peninsula war 126, 132
Concern for the 33rd 98
33rd "above all praise" 105
farewell message on vacating command 106
appointed Colonel of 33rd 107
farewell message on vacating colonelcy 109
name given to 33rd 157
Wellington, 4th Duke of 230, 371, 373
Wellington, 6th Duke of, see Mornington, Earl of
Wellington, 7th Duke of 340, 369
Wellington, 8th Duke of, Colonel-in-Chief 353, 357, 369
Wesley, see Wellington, 1st Duke
West, Maj Gen, M M A R 331, 332
West Indies 90, 95, 381, 382, 383, 385
　　Barbados 95
　　Demarara 197
　　Guadeloupe 91, 95
　　Jamaica 153
　　St. Lucia 91, 95, 197, 381
Westmore, Lt Col, R 155, 389
Whannell, Lt Col, G 155, 389
White Plains, see war of American Independence
Whittaker, Maj, M R 391
Wilhelmsthal, see Seven Years War
Wilkinson Sword of Peace 359
Williams, Bdsm, 306
Wilsey, Brig, J H O 317, 318
Wilson, Lt Col, W C 275, 390, 426
Wilson, Brig, T N F 286
Willemstad 37, 139
Williamsburg 70, 71
Windsor 75, 138
Wingate, Maj Gen, O 311, 312
Worrell, Pte, R 176
1st World war (1914-1918) 232-261
　　Arras 245, 247, 251, 260
　　Cambrai 248, 249, 254, 260
　　Hill 60 238, 239, 240, 260, 385
　　Lys 251, 260
　　Marne 253, 260
　　Mons 233, 236, 255, 256, 260
　　Passchendaele 246, 247, 248, 250, 251
　　Piave 259, 260
　　Somme 242, 243, 245, 251, 253, 260
　　Suvla 257, 260
　　Ypres 236, 237, 238, 240, 241, 246, 247, 252, 260
　　killed and wounded 235, 237, 238, 239, 240, 242, 243, 244,

245, 246, 247, 249, 251, 252, 254, 255, 258, 260
formations
　　British Expeditionary Force 233
　　3rd Army 248, 251
　　5th Army 251
　　2nd Corps 233
Divisions
　　3rd 233
　　4th 242, 245, 247, 253
　　5th 233
　　10th 244
　　11th (Northern) 244, 257
　　17th 240
　　23rd 240, 243, 260
　　40th 250
　　49th (West Riding) 238, 242, 255, 407
　　62nd (West Riding) 240, 249, 250, 251, 252, 255, 256, 260, 407
　　1st West Riding 240
　　2nd West Riding 240
Brigades
　　12th 242, 245, 247, 250
　　13th 240
　　15th 239, 240
　　32nd 244, 257, 258
　　33rd 257
　　34th 257
　　68th 259
　　69th 243, 259
　　70th 259
　　146th 248, 407
　　147th 240, 247, 251, 255, 407
　　148th 243, 407
　　185th 249, 250
　　186th 240, 249, 250, 251, 252, 255, 256
　　187th 249
Battalions of DWR. Chapter 16 and Appendix 5
　　1st
　　2nd
　　3rd
　　1/4th, 2/4th, 3/4th
　　1/5th, 2/5th, 3/5th
　　1/6th. 2/6th, 3/6th
　　1/7th. 2/7th. 3/7th
　　8th
　　9th
　　10th
　　11th
　　12th
　　13th
2nd World war (1939-1945) 279-320
　　Anzio 296, 299
　　Banana Ridge 290, 291, 298
　　Chindits 311, 312, 316
　　Djebel Bou Aoukaz 293, 294, 298
　　Dunkirk 283, 284, 286, 288,

*445*

    290, 320
    Fontenay le Pesnil 317, 318
    Monte Ceco 300, 301
    Paungde 309
    St. Valery en Caux 289
    Sittang 305, 307, 309, 310
    killed and wounded 284, 286, 288, 289, 294, 300, 301, 305, 307, 309, 314, 315, 318, 320, 322
  Formations
    British Expeditionary Force (BEF) 279, 280, 281, 283, 287
    21 Army Group 318, 322
    1st Army 289, 290, 294
    1st Canadian Army 318
    8th Army 289, 290, 295, 302, 303
    14th Army 311
    1st Corps 318
    1st (Burma) Corps 307, 309
    4th (Indian) Corps 311
    13th Corps 300
    15th (Indian) Corps 311, 312
    33rd (Indian) Corps 312, 314
  Divisions
    1st 280, 290, 291, 295, 296, 299, 300, 301, 321
    1st (Burma) 309
    1st (Canadian) 303
    2nd 312
    2nd (New Zealand) 302
    3rd (Indian) (Special Force) 312
    4th 290, 291
    4th (Indian)
    7th (Armoured) 294, 309
    14th (Indian) 311
    17th (Indian) 305, 309
    46th 280, 287, 289, 295
    49th (West Riding) 279, 316, 317, 318, 320, 408
    51st (Highland) 289, 319
  Brigades
    2nd 291
    2nd (Canadian) 302
    3rd 280, 281, 283, 286, 291, 292, 295, 300
    7th (Armoured) 307, 309
    16th (Indian) 307, 309, 310
    21st (Tank) 290, 303
    23rd (Special Force) 312, 314, 316
    24th (Guards) 290, 293, 298
    25th (Tank) 290, 293
    46th (Indian) 305
    48th (Indian) 307
    63rd (Indian) 307
    137th 280, 287, 289
    147th 279, 316, 317, 408
    Beauman Force 288
  Battalions of DWR. Chapter 18 and Appendix 5

    1st
    2nd
    1/4th, 2/4th
    5th
    1/6th, 2/6th
    1/7th, 2/7th
    8th
    9th
Wylie, Lt Col, A K 216
Wynberg 207
Wynter, Ensign, W A 182, 185, 190
Wynyard, Maj Gen, G 73, 74

Yalu river 329
York 206
York, F-M, Duke of 92, 93, 94, 378
Yorke, F-M, Sir C 380
Yorke, Col, J 70, 73, 90, 412, 389
Yorkshire Brigade 326
Yorkshire & Northumberland Brigade 323, 324, 325
Yorkshire Volunteers, See *Appendix 5*
Yorktown, see *American war of Independence*
Ypres, see *1st World war*

Zierenberg 49
Zula 185